History of Crime and Criminal Justice Series

Social Control in Europe
Volume 2, 1800–2000

Edited by

Clive Emsley, Eric Johnson,

and

Pieter Spierenburg

The Ohio State University Press
Columbus

Library of Congress Cataloging-in-Publication Data

Social control in Europe.
    p. cm. — (History of crime and criminal justice series)
    Includes bibliographical references and index.
    ISBN 0-8142-0971-8 (set: alk. paper) — ISBN 0-8142-9048-5 (CD-ROM)
    1. Social control — Europe — History. I. Roodenburg, Herman. II. Series.

    HN373.S563 2004
    303.3'3'094 — dc22
                                    2004005763

Volume 2 ISBN: 0-8142-0969-6
Volumes 1 and 2 are available as a two-volume set: 0-8142-0971-8

Cover design by Dan O'Dair.
Type set in Adobe Garamond.
Printed by Thomson-Shore, Inc.

The paper used in this publication meets the minimum requirements of the
American National Standard for Information Sciences—Permanence of Paper
for Printed Library Materials. ANSI Z39.48-1992.

9 8 7 6 5 4 3 2 1

CONTENTS

Acknowledgments   vii

Social Control and History: An Introduction
PIETER SPIERENBURG   1

Part One: Communities and Entrepreneurs

1. Social Control and Forms of Working-Class Sociability in
   French Industrial Towns between the Mid-Nineteenth and the
   Mid-Twentieth Centuries
   JEAN-PAUL BURDY   25

2. Control at the Workplace:
   Paternalism Reinvented in Victorian Britain
   HAIA SHPAYER-MAKOV   70

3. Social Change, Popular Movements, and
   Social Control in Scandinavia, 1864–1914
   ULF DRUGGE   93

4. Social Control in Belgium: The Catholic Factor
   JAN ART   112

5. Priceless Children? Penitentiary Congresses Debating Childhood:
   A Quest for Social Order in Europe, 1846–1895
   CHRIS G. T. M. LEONARDS   125

6. Caring or Controlling? The East End of London
   in the 1880s and 1890s
   ROSEMARY O'DAY   149

7. Community and Social Control:
   An Enquiry into the Dutch Experience
   VINCENT SLEEBE   167

Part Two: Policing and the State: Liberal vs. Totalitarian Regimes

8. Control and Legitimacy: The Police in
Comparative Perspective Since circa 1800
CLIVE EMSLEY   193

9. Policing the Poor in England and France, 1850–1900
PAUL LAWRENCE   210

10. The Police, Gender, and Social Control:
German Servants in Dutch Towns, 1918–1940
LEO LUCASSEN   226

11. Some Thoughts on Social Control in "Totalitarian" Society:
The Case of Nazi Germany
ERIC A. JOHNSON   245

12. Social Control in Fascist Italy: The Role of the Police
JONATHAN DUNNAGE   261

13. Violence, Surveillance, and Denunciation: Social Cleavage in the
Spanish Civil War and Francoism, 1936–1950
ANGELA CENARRO   281

14. Vichy France: Police Forces and Policemen, 1940–1944
JEAN-MARC BERLIÈRE   301

15. Political Justice in the Netherlands: The Instrumentalization of the
Judicial System during the German Occupation, 1940–1945
GERALDIEN VON FRIJTAG DRABBE KÜNZEL   318

16. Policing Amsterdam during the German Occupation:
How Radical Was the Break?
GUUS MEERSHOEK   330

17. Control and Consent in Eastern Europe's Workers' States, 1945–1989:
Some Reflections on Totalitarianism, Social
Organization, and Social Control
MARK PITTAWAY   343

18. Deviance, Control, and Democracy: France, 1950–2000
SEBASTIAN ROCHÉ   368

Bibliography   395
Index   441

Acknowledgments

T his volume results from a project for which Herman Diederiks had taken the initiative shortly before his death. In the course of that project, the contributions were discussed in three successive meetings: in Amsterdam (1997), Leuven, Belgium (1998), and Loures, Portugal (2000). The project was supported by the N. W. Posthumus Institute, with funds obtained from the Netherlands Organization for Scientific Research (NWO). The editors greatly appreciate the support given by these institutions. We are also grateful to Steven Hughes for organizing the meeting in Leuven and to Leonor Sá, Silvia Sardeira, and Valerie Humphreys for organizing the one in Loures.

Social Control and History: An Introduction

PIETER SPIERENBURG

W hat is social control? If anything, it is a classic concept, which many scholars use as a matter of course. Few, however, care about providing an explicit
statement of what they understand it to be. This classic notion is subjected to
close scrutiny in the present collection. It examines formal and informal types
of control over the last two centuries of European history, thus providing an integral perspective on the efforts at control by various agencies and the responses
to them. Yet, each contributor deals with more than just institutions or impersonal mechanisms. The authors focus on real people, some more powerful, some
less, in Europe's past and present.

Although, over the last few decades, much work has been done on a variety
of separate institutions that sought to change or influence people's behavior, these
institutions have never been examined in their totality. For example, the history
of crime and justice and that of religious teaching have coexisted as largely uncon-
nected subdisciplines. We know much about the state machinery of control (courts,
police, prisons), but less about its relationship to popular sanctions and attitudes.
Separate studies exist of such subjects as charity, labor, and communal life, but
there is no overall analysis of how these settings operated as informal structures
of control, through uplifting the habits of the poor, for example, or through patron-
izing the workforce. Finally, the literature on twentieth-century dictatorial
regimes is immense, but little has been published yet on ordinary law enforcement under these regimes. This collection brings these various elements
together in a comparative manner.

Social Control: The Concept's Origins

Although a classic concept, none of the classical European sociologists included
social control in their scholarly vocabulary. It is absent from the work of

1

Durkheim and Weber. The concept's origins are unequivocally American; it appears to have become popular in Europe only after the Second World War. Popularity was instant in the United States from May 1901 when a thirty-four-year-old professor named Ross first introduced the idea in a book. The date of its appearance makes social control a decidedly twentieth-century notion, which needs fresh scrutiny at the start of the twenty-first century. Such an exercise could begin with the person of its intellectual father. Although historians—but less so sociologists—routinely cite Ross as the author who introduced the idea of social control, very rarely do they take account of the intellectual and political context in which he did so.

Edward Alsworth Ross (1866–1951) was a farmer's son from Virden, Illinois.[1] An orphan at age nine, he was raised in the home of a local justice of the peace. His foster parents cared enough for him to send him to college in Iowa. As a graduate student, Ross spent two years in Germany, studying philosophy in Berlin, but there is no record of his meeting any of that country's young generation of social scientists. Back in America he turned to economics, which he taught at several universities and from the mid-1890s at Stanford. There, he gradually redirected his attention to sociology. The switch of disciplines was one reason for a conflict with the university's cofounder and governor, Jane Stanford, widow of Leland Stanford, who finally fired him in 1900. Ross developed the concept of social control more or less simultaneously with becoming a sociologist. From 1896 onward he published a series of articles as a preview (so the idea actually dates from just before the twentieth century). By the time he collected the articles in a book, the concept of social control had already gained notoriety. Ross applied for a chair at the University of Wisconsin, which at the time housed the largest sociology department in the Unites States, but the state legislature withdrew the post's funding. He finally became a professor at Wisconsin in 1906.

Social Control reads as an erudite essay on human society, with an emphasis on the problem of social order. The book discusses a wide range of societies, from ancient Greece and various non-Western nations to the United States in the author's own days. The bibliography includes such classic figures as Herbert Spencer, Emile Durkheim, and Ferdinand Tönnies. Intriguingly, Ross concludes that social control will be all the more necessary as we move from "community" to "society," adding in a footnote that he developed this thought before becoming acquainted with Tönnies' book but that the ideas are similar.[2] Essentially, however, Ross is concerned with classifying and labeling institutions and practices, much like Max Weber a few years after him. The crucial passage, summarizing the overall thesis, is tucked away in a discussion two-thirds of the way through the text. Ross first admits that society is a kind of fiction: There is nothing to it but people affecting one another in various ways. "The thesis of this book is that from the interactions of individuals and generations there emerges a kind of collective mind evincing itself in living ideals, conventions, dogmas, institutions, and religious sentiments which are more or less happily adapted to the task of safeguarding the collective welfare from the ravages of egoism."[3] This is a remarkably modern statement, to the extent that it acknowledges that society is an abstract, not an actor who can "do" things and that processes of change are blind, not set in motion consciously by powerful individuals or groups. It is also an outdated statement, to the extent that it minimizes the role of conflict in social relations and unabashedly expresses personal contentment.

Order, then, is equated with peaceful social relations and a degree of collective harmony. It is the opposite of an aggressive assertion of self-interest. It is equally the opposite of a ruling class's exploitation of subordinate groups, which Ross calls class control, not social control. Ross admits that order has not always prevailed historically, but he seems to consider episodes of disorder as the exceptions. The book's first page addresses the problem of order with a metaphor: The flow of traffic at a crowded city junction is orderly when persons and vehicles move in different directions but do not collide with each other. Similarly, all members of society have different interests, but they share conventions for avoiding collisions most of the time. Why is this so since, after all, it would be more logical to assume a state of disorder? Surely, people are not born with a set of commandments etched upon their souls or with inherited cooperative instincts. At that point, social control enters the picture. Ross first identifies its sociopsychological foundations, each operating in different situations: sympathy, sociability, sense of justice, and resentment (which another person may show if we injure him). The means of social control are rather variegated, the primary ones being public opinion and the law, in that order. In other words, people act more or less peacefully because they value others' judgments and because the state coerces them toward it. Although the latter comes second, Ross nevertheless concludes that the law "however minor its part at a given moment in the actual coercion of citizens, is still the cornerstone of the edifice of order."[4] The entire selection of the various means of social control is unsystematic; it further includes religious beliefs and sanctions (among which are notions of brotherhood), education, custom, and a host of minor sources, one of which is a sense of honor.[5] Throughout the book, finally, Ross mixes analysis with considerations of policy and recipes for ameliorating institutions. When discussing criminal justice, for example, he advocates a "scientific penology" that graduates punishments according to both the harmfulness of the offense to society and its attractiveness to the criminal.[6]

Although *Social Control* must be judged first of all on its own merits, any evaluation of the book should take the author's later work and his political beliefs into account. Ross's personal ideology was far from consistent over time. During the 1890s he advocated "state socialism" and supported Populist causes. After 1900 he turned to a more moderate advocacy of federal intervention and mediation in labor conflicts. At the same time, he called for restrictions on immigration, particularly of Asians. Despite this, he traveled to China for six months in 1910, to acquaint himself with Chinese culture. When the First World War broke out, he championed international arbitration by disinterested third parties as a solution, but when Wilson called for war in April 1917, Ross and other intellectuals with pacifist leanings rallied behind their president. Ross visited Russia in the crucial years 1917–1918, but in the 1920s he became a great admirer of Taylor and Ford. His Russian contacts were good enough to persuade the Soviets to release his fellow sociologist Pitirim Sorokin, whom he got a job in the Unites States. During the depression Ross again advocated federal intervention, supporting the "other" Roosevelt's New Deal. As late as 1935, a committee investigating communism on campuses summoned Ross to its meeting. Generally, then, he appears as a man of contrasts. He supported women's rights, but he was convinced of the racial superiority of Anglo-Saxons. He advocated a strong government, but he cosponsored a speech on the Madison campus by the anarchist Emma Goldman, which almost got him fired again.

A bullet fired at his predecessor made Theodore Roosevelt president in the same year that *Social Control* appeared. He became Ross's most influential political friend. They shared the conviction that large corporations, the latter-day "sinners," should be kept in check for the public benefit. Roosevelt initiated antitrust measures, and his "square deal policy" sought compromises between employers and workers without favoring either party. Advocating government as compromise, Ross considered the square deal a form of social control forced upon workers and employers. His *Sin and Society* (1907), a mixture of sociological observations and political statements, diagnosed a basic condition of the world he lived in: The interdependence that characterized modern society meant that all members of the social body were at each other's mercy to a greater extent than ever before.[7] This situation created the opportunity for new forms of wrongdoing, the quintessential sinners being the large corporations. Unlike traditional small businessmen, the managers of corporations had no moral scruples and hardly felt restrained by public sentiment. So they had to be kept in check by state intervention, seen as a form of beneficial social control.[8] The preface to *Sin and Society* was a personal letter signed by Roosevelt. The president called *Social Control* an impressive work, adding he had read everything published by Ross since.

The presidential attack on corporate capitalism was short-lived. William Howard Taft, Roosevelt's successor, wooed the business community by instituting a committee on monopolies that proclaimed the inevitability of corporations in 1912. Ross expressed his intense disappointment with this "dirty deal." The outcome was predetermined, he noted, since there were no social scientists on the committee. Taft had ignored "scholars and social workers who have given twenty years or more of their lives to the disinterested and impartial study of the problem of industrial peace."[9] This statement provides the final key to Ross's scholarly and political concerns. No doubt, he had wished to be on that committee himself. He viewed the sociological mission as providing practical insights into social problems and giving policy makers expert advice. A major goal was to promote the majority's welfare and security without endangering social tranquility. In this project, social control was a crucial factor, but note that it included state control.

Ross's Legacy

It would take a lifetime to work through the vast number of books and articles on social control published in the twentieth century, and especially after the Second World War, when sociology had become a well-established discipline. This section, then, is certainly not a discussion of social control theory or of the way the concept has been handled within various schools of social science. It merely samples a few collective volumes, sociological and historical, in order to show the wide range of applications to which the concept has been put.[10] This is evident from even a cursory look. Take one of the earliest textbooks on the subject by Roucek and "associates," first published in 1947. Meant as reading for introductory courses in sociology and social psychology, it takes a broad view of agencies of social control. The book opens with the principal "institutions" involved (state, law, and government; religion; marriage, home, and family; education) and continues with elements of social control in areas such as the economy, art, literature, and the mass media. The preface to the second edition of 1956 proudly announces a new chapter on television, "this ever-more-important means of public communication and control." Had it been the 1990s, the new chapter, no doubt, would have dealt with the Internet. The introduction defines social control as "those processes, planned or unplanned, by which individuals are taught, persuaded, or compelled to conform to the usages and life-values of groups."[11] Essentially, it comes down to "attempts to influence others," or everything that is not self-control. Thus, despite the broad view taken, the insight that the formation of self-control also is a social process is lacking.

A volume entitled *Social Control and Social Change* exemplifies the move away from a static perspective in the social sciences, which became manifest by the late 1960s. Sociologists, social psychologists, and even biologists contributed to this collection. A chapter on the biological basis of social behavior, for example, offers sections on "the physiological and genetic bases of social control." In the chapter on changing concepts of masculinity and femininity, the emphasis is on culture rather than biology. Its central concept is the sex role, as one type of "social role," which men and women acquire through learning. The word "gender" was not yet fashionable! Chapters on play and games (involving "ludic controls"), the American radical Right, and the growth of populations indicate that, for this team of authors, social control is virtually everything. The concept gets no formal definition, but chapter 1 delineates the field on the basis of a few practical problems: "that of producing constructive social change without the use of destructive methods, . . . that of inducing individuals to take up desirable kinds of social behavior within the framework of what is presumably a well-organized society, . . . that of the undesirable effects of social control" (in particular its "misuse" for exploiting others or enforcing rules that run counter to human biology).[12] In line with the broad approach, the preface states "many people understand control to mean only restriction of action rather than the positive interstimulation that is the chief subject of this book."[13]

Historians turned to social control a little later. In *Social Control in Nineteenth-Century Britain* (1977), A. P. Donajgrodzki, the editor, claims that this is "the first collection of historical essays making use of the concept."[14] To date, it is probably the best-known historical work with social control in its title. In this collection, the emphasis clearly lies on nonstate control. The contributions deal with, among other things, charity organizations, educational policy, metropolitan fairs, and the Salvation Army. To justify this emphasis, the editor cites a passage from Ross's work, without paying any further attention to it. According to Donajgrodzki, his contributors share the belief "that social order is maintained not only, or even mainly, by legal systems, police forces and prisons, but is expressed through a wide range of social institutions, from religion to family life, and including, for example, leisure and recreation, education, charity and philanthropy, social work and poor relief."[15] In this case, too, we miss a formal definition; Donajgrodzki is content with the observation that the institutions his book deals with "contributed to social order."[16]

We find the emphasis exactly reversed in the collection *Social Control and the State* (1983), edited by Stanley Cohen and Andrew Scull. Although not apparently from its title, this volume contains historical perspectives, some of them going back to the eighteenth century. They focus on either crime and prisons or insanity and its treatment, the latter equally with reference to the state and the social order. The introduction, entitled "social control in history and sociology," firmly links our concept with state agencies (the very first words are "the interrelationships between the modern state and its apparatus of social control"). Another revealing sentence accuses authors who use the word "reform" of cherishing a naive, value-laden view of a continuous movement "from barbarism to enlightenment, from ignorance to expertly guided intervention."[17] For Cohen and Scull, it seems, social control is mainly a negative category, which refers to checking deviant people and labeling deviance; it is the opposite of "benevolent intentions."

This perspective necessarily leads to a disproportionate emphasis on control from above.[18] In contrast to Donajgrodzki, Cohen and Scull, even though they appear to dislike it, do believe that social order is maintained primarily by legal systems, police forces, asylums, and prisons.

In a study published two years later, Stanley Cohen put his emphasis on the control of crime and delinquency, in particular the interventionist strategies of state-sponsored professionals. He comments on (then) recent developments in a cynical tone. The cynicism extends to the notion of social control itself, which he calls a Mickey Mouse concept, but not after he has provided us with a formal definition, again in the very first sentence. Social control refers to "the organized ways in which society responds to behaviour and people it regards as deviant, problematic, worrying, threatening, troublesome or undesirable in some way or another."[19] The problem with this definition, of course, is that it represents society as an actor. Who actually does the responding? Aren't the deviants and undesirables part of the very society that supposedly deals with them? Don't they interact with others? Or are we to assume that "society" in reality means the state and its agents and institutions? Then, what about social control in stateless societies? Clearly, the various pathways and trajectories taken by the concept of social control have led us to another dead end here.

Are we to conclude, then, that Ross's legacy is totally confusing and worthless? In 1901, social control already referred to many things, and it has become more of a container concept ever since. Moreover, whereas some authors consider it primarily a by-product of all kinds of institutions and social interaction, others connect it squarely with the mighty apparatus of the state. Nevertheless, social control has been a successful concept, providing scholars with a convenient term whose connotations they understand. Let me underline again that Ross himself clearly meant it to cover both the formal institutions of the state and all kinds of nongovernmental arenas, some of them at the "bottom" of society. Thus, Ross allowed for top-down as well as bottom-up perspectives on social control. In this, we can still follow him today, but we need an updated and sharper focus. We cannot simply adopt all of Ross's premises a hundred years later. Casting our net back to the sixteenth century for a moment, we must reject the prima facie equation of order with peaceful social relations and the idea that social control functions most smoothly in democratic societies. In fact, early modern communities tolerated a relative amount of interpersonal violence, if they thought it justified, and twentieth-century totalitarian regimes, known for their organized violence, still had to reckon with public opinion and accept a measure of compromise. Finally, Ross's notion that social control is often based on a degree of consensus and ideals of harmony can be adopted and used to analyze communities and voluntary associations in the past.

Social Control As Conflict Settlement

The misleading notion of society as an actor is absent from the work of criminologists such as Donald Black (1984) and Alan Horwitz (1990). They do identify the controllers—as persons and groups who act upon other persons and groups. They acknowledge, moreover, that social control involves both formal control emanating from the state and a host of informal reactions and interventions at nongovernmental levels of society, including, for example, the power of gossip. Notably, Horwitz emphasizes that social control does not require the existence of consensus regarding the definitions of appropriate behavior.[20] A recent book by Mark Cooney builds upon this work. Although it deals primarily with violence, it is relevant for our task of updating the concept of social control.

Cooney, too, acknowledges that the state, where it exists, forms merely a part of society and that top-down and bottom-up perspectives are equally important. His aim is to outline a formal theory of conflict. In particular, he addresses the question "when do conflicts erupt into violence and when do they end peacefully, through mediation, reconciliation or by still other means?" Admittedly, social control involves more than just regulating, repressing, or preventing the strife between two parties. The policing of men's and women's morals, for example, even in the absence of discord, falls outside Cooney's framework. Yet, for a large part, social control has to do with regulating conflicts in one way or another. So-called third parties are the central feature in Cooney's theory. These may encourage the contestants to fight or to facilitate physical aggression, but alternatively they may mitigate the contestants' violence, stop it, or even prevent it from happening. As third parties Cooney considers "all those who have knowledge of a conflict, actual or potential."[21] They include not only the principals' friends or enemies, bystanders, and possible mediators but also the police who can arrest one or both contestants (or decide not to intervene) and the judge who may punish them. Thus, "private" persons are included in the same category along with state agents. Whether social control proceeds top-down or bottom-up, the controllers are viewed consistently as a third party in a conflict.

Whether third parties are official law enforcers or self-appointed mediators, the status difference with the contestants is of crucial importance. According to Cooney, the judgment of third parties is most readily accepted if their social status is moderately superior to that of the principals. Thus, a too hegemonic state agency finds itself no less at a disadvantage than a mediator from the contestants' peer group. Besides status, other factors affect the degree of effectiveness of informal as well as state-based third-party settlement. An analysis of the strengths and weaknesses of both comes down to a series of "yes-buts." One advantage of state control, for example, lies in its broader jurisdiction. Informal control often operates in a local setting only, so outside it people must resolve conflicts in a different way. On the contrary, some stateless societies boast well-developed systems of informal settlement. However, they have no way of handling the minority of "intractably violent people"—those who constitute a persistent threat to their neighbors and won't listen to any palaver. Obviously, state agents are better equipped to deal with such persons. The state may use coercion in settling disputes between ordinary people not especially bent on fighting or even force two parties to comply with its ruling if they both find it totally unacceptable. However, whereas state coercion is backed by greater force, it can alienate people and breed resentment or even protest and resistance. Informal settlement, by contrast, has greater acceptance potential, but it depends on cooperation and consensus. The moral authority of one's community, to be sure, often ensures compliance. "Disputants may well find it harder to disobey the consensus of informal tribunals than the mandates of judges and police officers."[22]

Up to now, this is a formal analysis, with few historical-processual dimensions. The only element implying change is the proposition that reliance on the state to settle conflict may cause systems of informal settlement to wither away. Paradoxically, this statement alerts us to the historical situations in which it does not apply. Historians easily imagine the growth of state supervision supplanting or suppressing ecclesiastical discipline, community sanctions, and other forms of informal or semiformal control. However, this volume shows that, if informal means of conflict settlement decline before an advancing state, new informal controls often take their place. For example, the nineteenth century not only witnessed the establishment of the police but also industrialization, which brought industrial paternalism with it in some cases and, in others, a set of informal controls at the workplace. Simultaneously, community sanctions and ecclesiastical discipline remained alive in many regions of Europe. On the other hand, some modern inner-city neighborhoods witness both an ephemeral presence of state institutions and a decline of the moral authority of community elders. Thus, it is not always a question of either–or.

Having completed his survey, Cooney concludes that we lack a clearcut answer to the question whether state or informal settlement is more effective. Therefore, "from the point of view of reducing violence, the optimal social system would combine the moderate status superiority of informal settlement with the extensive jurisdiction of the state."[23] This is policy advice not unlike that offered by Edward Ross, with its implementation left undiscussed. A more adequate knowledge of the historical development of social control and conflict settlement in various sectors of society could help implement such proposals. One obvious amendment to Cooney's scheme is the observation that in early modern communal settings with little state intervention, the community refrained from acting as a third party in certain situations. In particular, members would view some cases of violence as a form of redress by one principal upon another. Conversely, communities might act and pass judgment over single individuals thought to show improper behavior, sexually or otherwise. These amendments notwithstanding, Cooney's analysis has been helpful in furthering our discussion. Notably, his concept of third parties has made us alert to the fact that social control, when also based upon community consensus, always concerns interaction between a number of people, each of whom may have his own particular interest at stake.

To conclude, social control involves a variegated set of practices and beliefs. Sometimes it has the character of conflict settlement, at other times it can be viewed more adequately as the enforcement of norms or the regulation of behavior. Always it concerns people or groups acting upon other people or groups. There are at least two parties involved, but often a third party plays a crucial role. Settlement or regulation can be obtained through care and relief, through arbitration, or through containment and punishment of behavior judged unacceptable. The set of norms and values involved in all these processes is subject to change over time. Social control, then, essentially constitutes a sensitizing concept: It draws attention to the relationships between various mechanisms inducing people to act in a way that is desirable according to a certain standard or ideal. In all societies social control constitutes a major key to understanding violence, conflict, and problems related to the formation and acceptance of social norms. As the present collection and its companion volume show, this crucial function of social control is operative regardless of the period one examines or a country's political system. It works in the early modern period as well as in recent times and in both democratic and authoritarian societies.

The Historiographical Background

An integrated study of social control—in modern Europe no less than during the ancien régime that preceded it—could hardly have been accomplished without the existence of several traditions of research, even though the concept of social control itself played only a minor role in each of them. Foremost among these traditions is the historical study of crime and criminal justice. The second, the history of church discipline, although concentrating on the Reformation period, has alerted us to the role the churches played in regulating the social and moral order also in the nineteenth and early-twentieth centuries. The third, the study of popular culture, equally extends from the early modern into the modern period. The last two, finally, the social history of industrialization and the analysis of totalitarianism, form a significant background to a number of contributions in this volume in particular. These five traditions are briefly indicated, taking European history from about 1500 onward into view.

The history of crime and criminal justice was first developed as a field of research in the middle of the 1970s. Historians discovered the value of court records as a major source to uncover the social world of the people who transgressed the law as well as to understand the development of judicial practices and official responses to deviant behavior. This resulted in an interdisciplinary effort in which historians were joined by sociologists, lawyers, and a few anthropologists. Their investigations covered a broad period from the later Middle Ages until World War I. Less work has been done for the twentieth century though. Beginning in France, England, and the Netherlands, the study of court records later spread to countries and regions like Scandinavia, Germany, and Italy. Understandably, this research covered the crime as well as the control side of deviance. To the extent that it dealt with the latter, major themes include: the criminal law in its social context;[24] the origins and development of the police;[25] the impact of state justice on local communities;[26] punishment as a cultural and political factor;[27] the life of marginal groups and attitudes toward them;[28] and banditry.[29] The result was an increased understanding of the methods used, over time, to deal with criminal and illegal behavior as well as new insights into the sociocultural environment of lawbreakers.

It followed from the nature of its subject that the history of crime and criminal justice concentrated on the institutions of formal control: courts, police, and other state agencies. This was especially so until the beginning of the 1990s. Since then, however, a shift of focus has become visible. For one thing, crime historians began to take lower courts, like the French *prévôtés* or German village courts, into consideration.[30] In rural areas as well as urban environments, such courts dealt for a large part with petty conflicts among neighbors. The studies making use of their records, therefore, focused on the character of communal relations, with gender, honor, and neighborliness as central issues. Similar studies have been published analyzing neighborhood and gender conflicts handled by police courts of the nineteenth and early twentieth centuries.[31] A second recent trend concerns the history of violence, both quantitative and qualitative. We are now well informed about the long-term trend in the number of homicides, from the fifteenth century to the present day, in countries such as England, the Netherlands, and Sweden.[32] On the qualitative side, studies of the sociocultural context of violence have alerted us to its Janus-faced nature, as a producer of both disorder and order, in past communities.[33] These recent trends in the historiography of crime and justice make it easier to link up with the second and third traditions identified here.

The history of moral regulation by church bodies began as a largely independent field of study. The "classic" form of discipline was exercised by consistories or presbyteries in Protestant parts of Germany, the Dutch Republic, and among Huguenot communities in France. Investigators making use of consistory records focused on such issues as the process of confessionalization, social relations among church members, and the "civilizing" efforts of the church elite.[34] Parallel studies into Catholic moral regulation, notably in southern Europe, primarily concerned the Inquisition. These studies have contributed to our knowledge of popular culture and the elite offensive against such popular practices as love magic or unorthodox devotion.[35] A question relating to both Protestant and Catholic Europe concerned the differentiation, analytically as well as in the minds of contemporaries, between crime and sin.[36] Especially in the latter case, the opportunity offered itself for linking up with the history of criminal justice. In England, moreover, a strong link between crime history and the history of ecclesiastical discipline already existed because of the peculiar institution of the Church courts, dealing with matters related to marriage and the family.[37] Because of its state backing, this institution came close to formal control, which also applied to the Inquisition. Although church discipline was on the wane already by the eighteenth century, it revived in some regions, the northern provinces of the Netherlands for example, in the following century. Apart from this, the ideological and institutional hold of church leaders, as well as common priests and pastors over their flock, remained an important source of informal social control well into the twentieth century.

In the wake of ecclesiastical discipline, poor relief agencies have functioned as agents of social control. During the early modern period, charity was often, but not always, a church matter. Poor relief functioned as a control mechanism to the extent that the people applying for assistance had to adjust their behavior to the norms and rules of those distributing relief. In the nineteenth and twentieth centuries, charity was transformed into welfare, distributed by the state as a rule. However, social control remained an important feature of the relations between welfare agencies and their recipients. This was true of official welfare as well as the semiofficial initiatives by philanthropists.

The third research tradition, dealing with popular culture and elite attitudes, has obvious connections with the previous two, if only because judicial and consistorial records reveal a lot about the life of common people. Overviews of the history of popular culture date from the late 1970s.[38] Although the sixteenth and seventeenth centuries constituted the heyday of Europe's traditional popular culture, much work has been done also on the workers' culture of the nineteenth and early-twentieth centuries. Local communities—rural villages and, increasingly, urban neighborhoods—were a central focus of this research. The popular culture embedded in these settings involved a shared world view and much feasting and merrymaking, but also the supervision of behavior. Charivari is only the most obvious mechanism of informal social control operating within local communities.[39] In fact, control was an aspect of virtually all communal relationships. We may think of gossip, informal supervision, dispute settlement by community elders, and the negotiation of honor. Urban neighborhoods, moreover, sometimes knew formalized associations, which among other things regulated the common life of the inhabitants. Complementarily to communal agencies, guilds and fraternities exercised similar functions.[40]

Here we have the clearest example of a bottom-up perspective on social control. Unorganized communities as well as neighborhood associations, guilds, and fraternities, although exercising control functions, worked according to consensual concepts such as brotherhood, friendship, and harmony, rather than hierarchy and authority, which were the key concepts of formal control. Although the eighteenth-century withdrawal of the elites from popular culture meant that local communities lost a number of functions to overarching organizations, community life remained vigorous nevertheless. A couple of studies focusing on the modern period have shown that neighborhood ties continued to be strong and coherent until at least the early-twentieth century.[41] In this case, too, neighborly life involved both shared pleasures and mutual scrutiny. A warning must be added here: a focus on social control at the community level cannot simply be equated with a bottom-up perspective, and neither should everything connected with the law and criminal justice be viewed as top-down social control. The notion of legal pluralism may help us to understand this. Scholars using that term emphasize the wide spectrum in the settling of disputes, from processes of negotiation to processes of adjudication. They view both the courts and a broad range of semiformal and informal institutions as suppliers of services, to which people may or may not choose to turn when they are in conflict.

The fourth and fifth types of research concern more specific subjects, but they fall squarely within the period discussed in this volume. The social history of industrialization has dealt with various themes. One of them revolves around industrial paternalism and the control of workers. In the modern period, industrial employers often embarked upon "civilization offensives" aimed at the moral behavior of their dependents. Simultaneously, the leadership of labor movements had their own disciplinary agenda, focusing on a change of habits from drinking in bars to regulated leisure and reading. Although regulating the behavior of members was not the principal or original function of economic institutions, they have exercised social control from an early date. This was true of the guilds and journeymen's associations of the ancien régime no less than the industrial establishments of a more recent period. The historiography of totalitarian regimes, finally, comprises numerous studies, but the focus on social control is relatively novel.[42] That focus has the additional advantage of remedying a neglect of the first tradition discussed. As explained above, the historiography of crime and justice has hardly extended to the twentieth century. Therefore, this book's series of articles on social control, including policing and justice, in countries under Nazi or Fascist, or Communist, rule fills a serious gap. The authors all show a remarkable similarity in that none believe that the traditional notion of totalitarianism as developed by Hannah Arendt fits with reality. This conclusion forms the basis for a more general comparison of social control in twentieth-century liberal and authoritarian regimes.

Different as they are, these two research traditions complement each other nicely to the extent that they concern nonstate and state institutions, respectively. Thus, they reproduce the contrast between informal and formal social control, a distinction prominent in our discussion up to now. Although we may have to distinguish an intermediate category of semiformal social control for the early modern period, for the nineteenth and twentieth centuries the above dichotomy appears sufficient. We should of course realize that absolute dichotomies, without overlaps or cross ties, never exist in history. Given that, the first part of this volume focuses largely on informal control, whereas the second part is concerned primarily with the apparatus of the state.

Phases in the History of Social Control

It is important to realize that the period dealt with in this volume only represents the last two phases of what can be described as the long-term history of social control in Europe. As a rough chronology, five phases may be distinguished. Between about 1200 and about 1500, a system of criminal justice developed in Europe under the aegis of princes and urban patriciates. Originally, courts were merely complementary to community-based institutions for resolving conflicts. For example, the higher courts punished thieves whom the community could not handle. Urban courts largely dealt with outsiders to the locality. The sixteenth and seventeenth centuries must be considered a separate phase, because the three main forms of control—state justice, church discipline, and community supervision—all operated together. The late-sixteenth and the seventeenth centuries constituted the high point for church discipline. Thus, semiformal and informal means of control loomed large in the lives of villagers and townspeople. The state's penal system, however, was attuned to social control at a general level, that of maintaining public peace and order. Although the eighteenth century saw much continuity with the preceding phase, the decline of church discipline still makes this period a separate phase in the history of social control. In addition, the eighteenth century witnessed an increasing social gulf between the elites and the popular classes.

Since the end of the ancien régime, according to the conventional view, the impact of penal law on the lives of the population became greater.[43] The fourth phase, roughly from 1800 to 1950, covers the period when an industrial economy emerged as well as the European system of nation-states. In the wake of these developments, a new system of formal social control became firmly established. However, informal types of control did not suddenly vanish. As this volume shows, the activities of economic and moral entrepreneurs, among others, ensured a degree of informal supervision of behavior. Village and neighborhood controls declined in some places but remained vigorous in others. Even Reformed church discipline was revived or had stayed alive in certain parts of Europe.[44] It should be added that, with the shift from the small world of the guilds to the larger one of industrial paternalism, social control at the workplace lost a good deal of its bottom-up, consensus-based character. Finally, both formal and informal types of control continued to be permeated by patriarchal views of social order.[45]

During the fifth and last phase, from about 1950 until today, formal control clearly predominated. Under the impact of the emergence of the welfare state, the principal overall development of this period, informal controls receded rapidly. State agencies, however, soon proved unable to exercise effective supervision in all social arenas. For one thing, they now face problems of control because of globalization. In particular, international criminal groups are organized more efficiently than the institutions of cross-state police cooperation set up to confront them. In this matter, informal controls are marginal, and it seems unlikely that in the future their role can become significant to any degree. This may be different in the case of the second arena in which problems of supervision have become apparent in recent decades: inner cities with a heterogeneous population. The disappearance of informal controls has been noted and deplored since the 1980s, by administrators at the national level and leaders of local communities. In every major European city, they are faced with an increasingly complex, multicultural variety of groups who share the urban space, giving rise to specific problems. Administrators have responded with a renewed interest in control, also, and especially by means other than the official state apparatus backed by criminal law. The development of future policies in this area might be served by a better understanding of longitudinal processes of shifting forms of social control, as discussed in this book.

General Themes and the Contributions

Although, obviously, there is no single master theory capable of accommodating all of this volume's findings, a few general themes recur. Some contributors, for example, refer to the concept of social discipline, first developed by German historians. This concept, however, has been used most often with reference to the early modern period. As an alternative, the notion of civilization offensives may be useful. The campaigns that historians have studied under that rubric were especially characteristic of the phase 1800–1950. "Civilization offensive" refers to the more or less conscious efforts by powerful groups to change the norms and conduct of others in the direction of the former's standards of civilized behavior. The term leaves open the extent to which they are successful, if at all. Political elites, church people, philanthropists, and moral entrepreneurs are among the groups who have launched civilization offensives in the past. The concerted campaign, in the late-nineteenth and early-twentieth centuries, to improve the housing conditions of the poor constitutes an example. Through it, the campaigners hoped, the moral standards of the targeted group, regarding cleanliness and sexuality would be uplifted as well. Civilization offensives are top-down phenomena almost by definition. Standards of conduct, however, may also become more "civilized" without such offensives, through pressure from below or from one's peers. That is the case, for example, when elite groups raise their own standards because they feel that imitation of their conduct by others makes them less distinctive or when a religious community wishes to demonstrate its purity in the eyes of the rest of the population.

Another important theme is that of the negotiation concerning imposed rules. It is firmly acknowledged in this book that the regulation of behavior is always a two-way process. Previous scholars have often viewed disciplinary efforts (reforms of popular festivals by religious leaders, for example, or policemen's activities as domestic missionaries) as a top-down phenomenon: The "superiors" had specific ideas about a godly life, the obedient worker, or the law-abiding citizen, with which they impregnated the "inferiors." Viewed from this angle, the principal research question concerns the degree of rule enforcement's success: How far did the inferiors live by the rules the superiors held up to them? However, as this collection demonstrates, people seldom act as passive recipients of social control. Sometimes they resist; more often, they negotiate and bend the rules of the game. Such a top-bottom interaction is equally characteristic for preindustrial local communities as for twentieth-century authoritarian states. To conclude, considerable negotiation has always existed between the people and the state as well as between ordinary churchgoers and ecclesiastical institutions, workers, and employers, and so on. Consequently, informal social control has been equally, or perhaps more, forceful than formal social control in all societies over the past five centuries, independent of whether they were monarchical, democratic, authoritarian, or totalitarian.

The contributions to this volume are grouped into two parts. The first bears the title "Communities and Entrepreneurs," the latter term referring to both economic and moral entrepreneurs. These two types come together in the opening essay by Jean-Paul Burdy. He discusses the disciplinary efforts of the Catholic Church as well as the rise of industrial patronage in France, but he equally deals with networks in working-class neighborhoods and the competing initiatives from Catholic and Socialist organizations. Thus, his essay effectively combines the perspectives from above and from below. The subject of discipline and the world of work is elaborated further in the contributions by Haia Shpayer-Makov and Ulf Drugge, dealing with England and Scandinavia, respectively. In each case, the efforts of entrepreneurs to create a kind of self-sufficient industrial community form a major theme. Discipline, it seems, worked more effectively when combined with the provision of benefits. In a different way, this principle also operated in the Belgian situation, discussed by Jan Art. Liberal and Catholic organizations maintained the allegiance of their followers through the distribution of jobs, charity, and other social services. In addition, Art demonstrates the continuity, from the ancien régime, of religious social control, exemplified by the contemporary adage that one priest is worth ten *gendarmes*.

The principle that discipline works most effectively when combined with the provision of benefits was equally manifest in the relations between philanthropists and their beneficiaries. For the experts, many of them philanthropists, at the international penitentiary congresses discussed by Chris Leonards, the well-being of children came first. In connection with the benefit principle, the issue of negotiation, too, becomes prominent again. This emerges clearly from Rosemary O'Day's case study of a London housing project. Although charity was the starting point, the philanthropists, who had set up the building project and continued to act as its patrons, also tried to influence their clients' behavior. For their part, however, the tenants were able to manipulate their controllers to some extent. The latter were forced to accept, for example, that the tenants occasionally enjoyed an alcoholic drink, as long as they refrained from making a living from crime or prostitution. Thus, the relationships between working-class clients and middle-class patrons loosely parallel those between early modern local communities and representatives of overarching institutions. The final contribution of the first part, by Vincent Sleebe, explicitly addresses communal relationships. His study of the Netherlands shows that communal relationships were pervasive even in the modern period, although their importance declined as the preindustrial world slowly passed away.

Although the first part has its main chronological base in the nineteenth century, several contributions trace their subject matter well into the twentieth. Conversely, most contributions of the second part, titled "Policing and the State," exclusively discuss twentieth-century events. This section compares social control under authoritarian regimes with its counterpart in liberal democracies. Again, the principal focus is on the day-to-day relations between the people and state agencies, rather than on such formal institutions of control like prisons. This emerges clearly from Clive Emsley's introductory essay, comparing the police—including their relations with the public—under various regimes. Paul Lawrence examines the attitudes of the English and French police to the poor, concluding that the severity of repression depended on the person and the offense. For example, contrary to the opinions of contemporary social commentators and the intentions of legislators, the police treated gamblers and prostitutes with much greater understanding than tramps. This image of a compromising and differentiating social control is reinforced by Leo Lucassen's case study of police supervision of foreign immigrants, many of them female domestic servants, in Dutch towns in the 1920s.

The principal question giving unity to the contributions on the authoritarian regimes of the first half of the twentieth century is "How radical was the break?" The authors concerned are all critical of Hannah Arendt's notion of totalitarianism as a system that daily intruded into the lives of every citizen. As it turns out, the repression from totalitarian regimes was selective, primarily aimed at certain target groups. Having reached this conclusion earlier in a book on Nazi society focusing on Gestapo and court records, Eric Johnson here supplies new evidence, based on extensive survey research, to bolster his argument. In particular, he compares the first-hand experiences of Jews and non-Jews from several German cities and demonstrates that although both groups of people frequently violated the laws of the Third Reich (in mostly minor ways, such as listening to outlawed foreign radio broadcasts, telling anti-Nazi jokes, criticizing Hitler in discussions with friends, etc.) only Jews were usually punished for such behavior. Most "ordinary Germans," on the other hand, were not Jewish, and the Gestapo generally seems to have had very little interest in trying to punish them.

Johnson's fellow contributors largely corroborate his German findings and place them in a comparative European perspective. Thus, Jonathan Dunnage argues that the police in Fascist Italy, its institutional structure largely left unchanged, continued their surveillance of the Left, whom they had distrusted equally before Mussolini's takeover. Likewise, in Franco's Spain, repression essentially meant targeting people who had actively supported the "vanquished" (the groups defeated in the Civil War). As Angela Cenarro shows, denunciations played a significant role in this effort. For the years of World War II, the thesis of a "nonradical break" can be tested in occupied countries and satellite states. In Vichy France, as Jean-Marc Berlière shows, there was a kind of break indeed, to the extent that its rulers immediately felt the need to purge the police of leftists and alleged freemasons. However, successive governments were uncertain how to proceed in this, and a more or less loyal police force was not created until the regime's final months. The example of the Netherlands is instructive as well. As Geraldien von Frytag Drabbe Künzel argues, the politicization of the agencies of justice came about only in a gradual fashion. The occupiers instituted a dual system, in which the Dutch courts and police were supplemented by German courts and the Gestapo. The brunt of repression fell upon resistance groups and persons evading transport to Germany for forced labor. In a complementary essay on policing in occupied Amsterdam, Guus Meershoek concludes that, although a few totalitarian elements can be observed, on the whole Arendt's model does not apply.

Thus, even the "ultimate example of social control" involved a measure of accommodation and negotiation, and the break was less radical than previous scholars assumed. The totalitarian model did not imply a complete contrast with previous practices and certainly not an all-encompassing supervision of the entire population. The notion of an all-encompassing supervision should be qualified even for the Communist dictatorships established in eastern Europe after World War II. In a wide ranging essay, Mark Pittaway argues that concepts such as "totalitarianism," "total dictatorship," or "thoroughly dominated societies" do not adequately describe the reality of these eastern European countries. On the other hand, the leaders and regimes of the twenties and thirties, the military occupations of the forties, and the party dictatorships of the fifties through the eighties do contrast markedly with the experience of the liberal democratic states of the last third of the twentieth century. In practically all of the latter, problems of control have intensified and become more complex during recent decades—a development highlighted by increasing homicide rates no less than petty crime. Politicians are hoping to restore the kind of communal supervision prevalent in the distant past. However, as Sebastian Roché argues in a provocative essay that concludes this volume, various recent trends constitute a formidable impediment to such policies. Paradoxically, the extension of state-sponsored institutions has led to a weakening even of formal controls.

As the essays of this volume show, the study of historical social control forms an important contribution to assessing the possibilities and impossibilities in our present predicament.

Notes

I am grateful to Clive Emsley and Astrid Ikelaar for their comments on a draft version. Some ideas developed by Herman Roodenburg, while he was working with me on various introductory texts, also resound in this introduction.

1. Unless otherwise mentioned, the biographical data on Ross are taken from McMahon, *Social Control and Public Intellect.*

2. Ross, *Social Control,* 432. This 1939 edition, the only one available to me, is an unaltered reprint of the 1901 original.

3. Ibid., 293.

4. Ibid., 125.

5. On honor: Ibid., 239–40.

6. Ibid., 110.

7. Ross, *Sin and Society,* 4.

8. We find this idea already in Ross, *Social Control,* 87–88: In "the century we are just entering on" the state should be strengthened in order to counter powerful private interests.

9. Ross, quoted in McMahon, *Social Control and Public Intellect,* 97.

10. The sample refers to works devoted exclusively to social control. Of course, major

sociological theorists such as Talcott Parsons amply discussed the subject in their general works.

11. Roucek et al., *Social Control*, 3 (this 1970 edition is a reprint of the 1956 edition).

12. Scott and Scott, eds., *Social Control and Social Change*, 1.

13. Ibid., x.

14. Donajgrodzki, ed., *Social Control in Nineteenth-Century Britain*, 9.

15. Ibid.

16. Ibid., 16.

17. Cohen and Scull, eds., *Social Control and the State*, 2.

18. Yet, Mayer's contribution to the volume (17–38) criticizes such a top-down view, without mentioning the editors.

19. Cohen, *Visions of Social Control*, 1.

20. Horwitz, *The Logic of Social Control*, 9. Black wrote the foreword to Horwitz's book.

21. Cooney, *Warriors and Peacemakers*, 6.

22. Ibid., 63.

23. Cooney, *Warriors and Peacemakers*, 66.

24. Hay et al., *Albion's Fatal Tree;* Faber, Strafrechtspleging en criminaliteit; Beattie, *Crime and the Courts;* Diederiks, *In een land van justitie;* Huussen, *Veroordeeld in Friesland.*

25. Bayley, "The Police and Political Development in Europe"; Storch, "The Plague of the Blue Locusts"; Storch, "The Policeman As Domestic Missionary"; Emsley, *Policing and Its Context;* Emsley, *Gendarmes and the State.*

26. Castan, *Honnêteté et relations sociales;* Castan, *Justice et répression;* Kent, *The English Village Constable;* Schulte, *Das Dorf im Verhör;* Roeck, *Als wollt die Welt schier brechen.*

27. Spierenburg, *The Spectacle of Suffering;* Zysberg, *Les galériens;* Gatrell, *The Hanging Tree;* Evans, *Rituals of Retribution.*

28. Hufton, *The Poor of Eighteenth-Century France;* Küther, *Menschen auf der Strasse;* Beier, *Masterless Men;* Spierenburg, *The Prison Experience;* Geremek, *Het Kaïnsteken.*

29. Cobb, *The Police and the People;* Danker, *Räuberbanden im alten Reich;* Blok, *De Bokkerijders;* Egmond, *Underworlds.*

30. See, among others, Frank, *Dörfliche Gesellschaft;* Gowing, *Domestic Dangers.*

31. See, for example, D'Cruze, *Crimes of Outrage.*

32. See especially Johnson and Monkkonen, eds., *The Civilization of Crime.*

33. One example is Spierenburg, ed., *Men and Violence.*

34. Van Deursen, *Bavianen en slijkgeuzen;* Estèbe and Vogler, "La genèse d'une société protestante; Monter, "The Consistory of Geneva"; Schmidt, *Konfessionalisierung.*

35. Bennassar et al., *L'Inquisition;* Haliczer, ed., *Inquisition and Society;* Monter, *Frontiers of Heresy.* For an overview of all Inquisitorial activities in three countries, see Bethencourt, *L'Inquisition.*

36. Compare Schilling, "History of Crime"; and Schilling, ed., *Kirchenzucht und Sozialdisziplinierung.*

37. See especially Houlbrooke, *Church Courts;* and Ingram, *Church Courts.*

38. Burke, *Popular Culture;* Muchembled, *Culture populaire;* Yeo and Yeo, eds., *Popular Culture.*

39. Le Goff and Schmitt, eds., *Le charivari;* Rooijakkers and Romme, eds., *Charivari.*

40. See, among others, Garrioch, *Neighbourhood and Community;* Brennan, *Public Drinking;* Roodenburg, "Freundschaft." Ongoing research by Aries van Meeteren into seventeenth-century Leiden will increase our understanding of the mechanisms of control at the neighborhood level.

41. In particular: Burdy, *Le soleil noir.* See also his contribution to this volume.

42. Aspects of social control are discussed in Gellately, *The Gestapo;* Gellately, *Backing Hitler;* and Johnson, *Nazi Terror.* The article by Jan T. Gross "Social Control under Totalitarianism," 59–77 is rather superficial and focuses only on Poland at the beginning of Soviet hegemony.

43. A recent assessment of the growth of state control in the German world is Härter, "Soziale Disziplinierung."

44. For the Netherlands: Sleebe, *In termen van fatsoen;* for Davos: Schmidt and Brodbeck, "Davos zwischen Sünde und Verbrechen."

45. See Miller, *Transformations of Patriarchy.*

Part One

COMMUNITIES AND ENTREPRENEURS

Social Control and Forms of Working-Class Sociability in French Industrial Towns between the Mid-Nineteenth and the Mid-Twentieth Centuries

JEAN-PAUL BURDY

TRANSLATED BY HELEN ARNOLD

The idea here is to analyze the forces and forms used for containment and social control in French urban settings, from the early period of industrialization (the 1830–1840s) to the interwar period (1920–1940), with emphasis on the creation of working-class or popular neighborhoods, followed by suburbs, as subdivisions of urban space. But it is also to spell out the evolution and limits of social control. First, we should not underestimate the efforts made by the Catholic Church to adjust to an increasingly secular society and to the Republican and sometimes secularist state—whence the generally binary pattern of containment found in urban social life (section I). At the same time, the developing industrial firms attempted to gain control over the nascent working class through patronage and paternalistic initiatives (section II). But the informal social life and networks found in working-class districts also contained a great many elements of social organization and self-discipline, elusively patterned, the longevity and efficiency of which are variable (section III). Finally, with the assimilation of working-class neighborhoods by the city, the development of working-class suburbs, and the birth of the new post–World War I political landscape, the earlier agencies of social organization and containment changed, especially in the socialist or communist-dominated "red suburbs," which remained missionary country for the Church (section IV).

In the working-class neighborhoods of European industrial towns between the mid-nineteenth and the mid-twentieth centuries, social control may be schematically defined as the interaction between two elements: formal, "official" agents, whose objective was either to construct, fortify, or challenge the existing order (political and religious institutions as well as companies come to mind, and later on, political parties and labor unions), and informal modes of functioning depending on the degree to which individuals, families, and groups were integrated in webs involving immigrant groups or social life defined by neighborhood or professional proximity, and in relationships sufficiently structured on a class basis as to influence the private life of individuals. In all of these cases we may postulate the existence of pressure exerted on the individual through surveillance and discipline by the group or a portion of the group, along with external control in the case of societal action on individuals or large portions of the group.

Cities are complex economic, social, and cultural entities, the locus par excellence of circulation and exchanges. They are a good place for analysts to approach forms of social control and their evolution, especially in working-class neighborhoods, since it is in these particular urban areas that one can gain the most intimate understanding of working-class identities.[1] Most of the examples discussed are French. Industrialization did not proceed at the same pace and along the same lines in France as the first industrial revolution in England. Instead of being rapid, it extended over a relatively long span of time and space.[2] Rather than being concentrated in the large, highly urbanized centers, it trickled through the countryside, whence the lesser flagrancy of those "social pathologies" of which social investigators of the time were so fond. It is clear, however, that French towns and cities did experience some symptomatic pathologies during a few decades of sometimes exponential growth. In addition to the natural growth of their populations, there was an influx of migrants from the countryside, followed by migrations from afar. Towns, with their traditional limits and enclosures, were at the breaking point; overcrowding, already a patent feature of housing under the ancien régime, was sometimes spectacular. With an inadequate water supply, no sewerage system, and overall poor hygiene, the risk of epidemics and so forth was multiplied. Drinking, rising crime rates, and urban violence fed the anxieties of the ruling classes. As publicist Saint-Marc Girardin, speaking of the 1831 revolt of the Lyon silk weavers (the *canuts*), put it in his famous saying: "the barbarians are inside the city," and "the working classes [have become] the dangerous classes." There was great fear, then, that the institutions— be they governmental, religious, or social, traditional or recent (including schools, hospitals and charitable institutions, occupational associations, and recreational clubs)—would prove incapable of coping with such a dark situation.

The reality turned out to be more varied: the Church (part I) and the factories (part II) developed new forms of *encadrement*.[3] The existing social networks and forms of working-class sociability provided another series of patterns of containment and self-discipline (part III). The extension of suburbs around the big cities, from the turn of the twentieth century, was attended by new episodes of ideological and religious mobilization (part IV). A historical approach to social control cannot elude an examination of the dynamics of processes that generate innumerable potential disruptions of our frames of analysis.

I. The French Church in Industrial Cities: The Limits of Disenchantment, Nineteenth through Early-Twentieth Centuries

From the French Revolution on, relations between the state and churches have tended to be structured by the specifically French theme of secularism. Nonetheless, any approach to social control must necessarily deal with the Catholic Church—by far the predominant religion. With its robust hierarchical structure, it constantly attempted to adjust, so as to combat de-Christianization in general and the secularization of urban life in particular. In 1905 the separation between church and state was legally instated after decades of guerrilla warfare between secularist republicans (many of whom were Protestant) and the Catholic Church, one translation of which was a social scene divided into citizens' groups of two diametrically opposed persuasions. The secularization and hence the laicization of the urban French social scene followed more circuitous, less linear, and more belated paths than it would seem.[4]

Industrial Cities: "Spiritual Wastelands"?

The French Revolution did indeed accelerate a process begun under the ancien régime, in that it brought French society across a first threshold of laicization.[5] The nineteenth-century Catholic Church was totally opposed to the Revolution and the Republic and rejected the "social atheism" born of the eighteenth-century Enlightenment, viewed as taking shape in the rapidly expanding urban areas, the utmost "disenchanted world."[6] At the time, the great industrial cities, and especially their new working-class districts and faubourgs, were viewed as seats of irreligiousness and therefore of social disorder, as opposed to the rural world, purportedly sustaining more respectful attitudes. This elicited alarmed outcries, such as the call issued by the bishop of Béziers in the Languedoc area when a working-class faubourg resisted the Bonapartist coup d'état in December 1851, demanding "a church, a presbytery and a priest in the midst of these new barbarians."[7] Clearly, from the Church's viewpoint, the swelling of the industrial towns had momentarily created real "spiritual wastelands," such as the new *arrondissements* in Paris and the new *communes* of the Seine *département*. Some church officials referred to these as "that China that surrounds Paris" (Monseigneur de Ségur, in 1860) or again "the tribes from unexplored lands" and "African territories" in the suburbs (Monseigneur Richard in 1900). As early as the mid-nineteenth century, urban France, like its colonies, became "missionary country."

It was in fact hard, on the whole, to enforce the discipline of religion, and the urban areas were undeniably being de-Christianized. The usual criteria are well known: fewer participants in the Easter week celebrations, growing numbers of purely civil marriages with no subsequent church ceremony,[8] loss of religion among men whereas the women continued to uphold the faith, and so forth. The number of priests increased, but their numbers in the urban dioceses declined considerably throughout the century,[9] and complaints were repeatedly voiced about the lack of vocation and the aging of the priesthood. Church personnel varied considerably in size, however: there were more practicing Catholics and more clergymen in the small or medium-sized towns, in the parishes of villages swallowed up by towns, and in some bourgeois parishes in the city centers, which were well endowed and had any number of clerical and paraclerical personnel (including sextons, beadles, vergers, organists, choristers, etc.), whereas churchgoers as well as clergymen were fewer, on the whole, in the industrial working-class districts and the faubourgs of the big cities.

Slowly but surely, then, the French Catholic Church definitely tended to lose its spiritual influence and social control over working-class families, with local and regional differences in timing. The diversity of urban life led most people to move away from what they considered a reactionary institution too close to the bosses, whereas the minority of practicing Catholics withdrew into seclusion and cared little about the indifference of the majority. Urbanization, difficult living conditions, and the beginnings of socialism tended to foment unbelieving and militant secularism among working people, particularly so since many priests took unacceptable stances. Their conditionally paternalistic attitudes (very often only regular churchgoers could receive assistance from the Church) and close ties to employers (especially to the mining company owners) were important factors.

That the Church faded out of the worker's horizon was not entirely due to the upcoming republican, Masonic, and socialist currents. It was also the product of the weaknesses and deficits of the institution itself and its clergymen, which were partly responsible for the development of anticlericalism, which took on radical forms in the revolutionary crises of 1848 and 1871.

Regional and Local Variables

While there was a definite trend toward de-Christianization in the industrial towns and cities, considerable regional differences in situation and behavior are visible over the long term, sometimes even between neighboring cities. First, one must recall that while some rural areas were still strongly permeated with Christianity, some parts of rural France were already partially de-Christianized, and the hub cities already seemed to be islands of irreligion. The example of western France comes to mind here, with its "blue" (Republican) cities in the midst of the coun-terrevolutionary "white" rural Vendée area where the Chouans, in arms, fought the Republic and its "hellish columns," during the Revolution, "for God and the King."[10] Often, cities reflected the attitude of the surrounding countryside, from which much of their recent population originated, so that industrial cities were not necessarily extremely irreligious. Religious practices structured by numerous Church-related institutions continued to prevail in Lyon for instance, the second largest city in France, which had been Catholic since Roman times and was tra-ditionally a center of trade and industry (printing, silk mills, chemicals, and met-allurgy). This was even more so in nearby Saint-Etienne, a multi-industrial city (housing textile, coal, weapons, and steel) peopled by migrations from the rural Massif Central and purveyor of people with religious vocations for some time to come.[11] For decades, the religious leanings of different groups in Saint-Etienne's Soleil neighborhood could be identified by the migrants' place of origin. The vast majority were Catholic with, in their midst, a group of Protestants established in a few districts of the Haute-Loire *département* since the Reformation in the six-teenth century. Pastors and a coherent series of Protestant charitable organizations— either directly religious, such as Thursday Schools (religious instruction for children), or more social, such as Workers' Circles and the Blue Cross temperance league— provided leadership for the Protestant community.

Religion left its mark on groups of rural migrants to the cities in varying degrees, then. Migrants to Paris from devoutly Catholic Brittany retained their ties to the Church for a long time: the *Oeuvre des Fidèles bretons* (Charity of the Breton Faithful) dates back to before 1830, and in 1863 two Jesuits founded the *Oeuvre des Bretons de Paris* (Charity of the Bretons of Paris), whose parish was to become Notre-Dame-de-la-Gare in the Montparnasse neighborhood, Paris's Breton neighborhood. Similarly, sermons were delivered in Breton at the church of Saint-Denis, a suburb north of Paris, until the post–World War I years. Conversely, some groups from other regions took no interest in religion: for instance, peo-ple from the southern part of the Massif Central where radical republicanism already prevailed, some of whom were to become prominent Republicans.[12] The contrast between men and women was much more clear-cut in the cities than in the countryside and cut across all social lines. De-Christianization was slowed down by women's abiding faith, to which the clergy clung. With lead-ership in short supply, and much later on, with the decline in vocations, women (from the upper classes in the nineteenth century) became invaluable volunteer organizers of diocese and parish charitable works, including catechism, youth clubs, schools, libraries, vestries, sewing rooms, and so forth. This gender factor is present in other aspects of social control and self-discipline.

For the nineteenth century, then, one can no longer refer to a universal urban context such that cities would represent the locus in which all inhabitants share the same values and where forms of control, with their strengths as well as their weaknesses, are uniformly established. Cities took in, integrated, or rejected groups from rural areas whose ties with religion varied upon arrival. Their settlement in the urban world was usually mediated by time-worn networks through which they preserved, adapted, or rejected their previous religious practices (or the lack thereof). The outcome was a contrasting constellation of working-class districts, depending on the geographic origins and the work done by their inhabitants. Some tended to turn their back to religious practices, whereas others maintained Sunday churchgoing and holiday processions. In the long run however, people's relations to religion tended to become individualized, and most gradually floated away from the Church. But the Church did not remain passive.

Building Churches and Charities: The Ongoing Effort of the Church to Adjust to Industrial Society

The Catholic Church, which won most of its prerogatives back through the Napoleonic Concordate of 1801 and retained them until they were challenged by the rather secularist Third Republic, took a resolutely adaptive and reconquering stance. This is quite obvious during the period between the conservative Restoration (1815) and the end of the Second Empire (1870), with the reconstitution of the urban brotherhoods and the resumption of local religious festivities and pilgrimages, and the creation of thousands of new parishes, often in the new urban faubourgs. Many religious orders devoted to teaching, for men and even more for women, were organized throughout this industrial period, and these enabled the Church to maintain its hold on education, particularly up to the Third Republic (1870–1940).

From the 1830s to the early years of the Third Republic, large numbers of churches were built in new parishes. It is known that churches (like temples and mosques) are major markers of religion within the social space, and some anticlerical critics of the time stigmatized the "obsession with stones" of those church-building priests. The Second Empire (1852–1870) was marked by the great urbanization projects of Paris's prefect Haussmann, but it was also a period of intense construction of major religious buildings, still visible in our contemporary urban landscapes. These neo-Romanesque, neo-Gothic, and Romanesque-Byzantine edifices rose from the ground in significant numbers in the wake of the upheaval produced by the avenue-piercing (the demolishing of houses and other structures to allow construction of the great Parisian avenues and boulevards) of Baron Haussmann and his successors of the Moral Order period, in the fast growing districts inside cities and in their immediate periphery.[13] This is true of the Sacré-Coeur of Montmartre, in Paris, the Fourvière basilica in Lyon, and Notre-Dame-de-la-Garde in Marseilles.

The mission of re-Christianizing the cities, even more than the rural areas, was an ongoing theme in nineteenth-century France. The effort to develop the presence of the Church in the spiritual, social, and real-estate life of industrial cities and their new neighborhoods should not be underestimated, then. This was accomplished with the support of company owners in particular: Given the organic ties between the parish clergy and the owners of the large mines and steel works, the housing developments built in Saint-Etienne's mining and metallurgical faubourgs were mainly structured around the church, thanks to the efforts of both the mining companies and the clergy.[14] In their determination to regain ground, the parishes also developed charitable works and youth clubs, and later, after 1871, there were the workers' societies inspired by the social Catholicism of Albert de Mun and La Tour du Pin.[15] In Grenoble, an Alpine garrison town but also a center of the glove-making and electrical and metallurgical industries, social Catholicism inspired employers to set up associations such as cauldron maker Emile Romanet's Saint-Bruno Catholic Society in the Berriat neighborhood (1904) with its aid workshops, lectures, and so forth.[16] The introduction of these new parish activities (schools, youth clubs, sports, music clubs, and so on) points to the need, at the time, to counter the growing de-Christianization of urban society as well as to the Church's determination to adjust to the new situation, in a society that was to take secularization much farther still.

Over and beyond its spiritual action, then, the Church retained some major social functions, including that of aiding the people, inherited from Medieval charitable religious institutions. The number of charitable religious institutions in the cities progressed to the point that the need was felt to compile a register of them: in 1897, a directory of Parisian charitable and provident societies included over 4,000 charities; a handbook of charities, published in Lyon (the "capital of charity") in 1893 and revised and completed in 1926, reported 683 charities.[17] The Church never ceased its concern with the poor, an apprehensive concern, sometimes intent on preserving its monopoly of charity. In Lyon, again, the list of charities aimed at workers and paupers includes Frédéric Ozanam's Conférences de Saint-Vincent-de-Paul (1833), father Chevrier's Prado in the working-class faubourg of La Guillotière (1864), Camille Rambaud and Paul du Bourg's Cité de l'Enfant-Jésus, aimed at aiding elderly working-class households, and so forth. These urban organizations, which recruited their members from the bourgeois and aristocratic elites, distributed tickets for bread, meat, clothing, and shoes. At the end of the century, they set up placement services for the unemployed and vacation camps for children. In immediate pre–World War I France, there were close to 1,700 Saint-Vincent-de-Paul *conférences* (groups) with 27,850 active members. Urban society did tend to receive less direct leadership from priests, statistically speaking, but at the same time, the number of charities of religious inspiration was constantly on the rise in urban settings.[18]

Marianne versus Marie: Rivalry between the Republic and the Church, and the Bipolarization of Social Spaces, 1880–1914

The institutional and political consolidation of the Republic from the 1880s on modified the terms of the Church's role. As Max Weber put it, French society was then organized along "legal-rational" lines, with a laicization of collective norms and secularization of individual behavior that seriously jeopardized the system by which the Church maintained its hold on society.

During this period of militant laicism, the respective positions of the Church and the secular—if not to say anticlerical—Republic were played out essentially on a symbolic level, especially in urban areas. Maurice Agulhon has extensively studied the combat between those two female figures, Marianne and Marie.[19] The former embodies and symbolizes the Republic (very male, in point of fact) whereas the importance of the latter for the Catholic Church is exemplified by the popularity of Marie worship in the nineteenth century. This produced an outburst of busts and statues of Marianne in public places. The guerrilla warfare lasted half a century. It gave the radical-socialist city government of Saint-Etienne the possibility of slipping a bust of Marianne (denounced by the clerical party as "the Red virgin") from an angle of a working-class square named Côte-Chaude to the center of the square, directly in front of the Church entrance, and also, it enabled a neighboring town council to inscribe a syncretic "Let the children come to me," a traditional Catholic formula, on a bust of Marianne placed over the door of an asylum.[20]

Both applied the same logic to the coverage of urban space, with Republican strategies employing educational rituals, ceremonies, festivities, and parades that necessarily competed with those staged by the Church. Secular processions mirrored the religious processions: in 1883, a procession singing the Marseillaise, that national, revolutionary hymn, carried a bust of Marianne like the Blessed Sacrament around the city of Reims, in Champagne, in whose cathedral French kings were crowned until the Revolution. Here we have a symbolic struggle aimed at challenging the Catholic Church's time-honored monopoly on religion and at providing the Republic with secularized rites that contribute to the ideological control of the population.[21] More modestly but equally symbolically, the tide of militant secularism of the 1880–1900 period occasionally resulted in the systematic renaming of streets. It took such day-to-day decisions, which sometimes produced serious political clashes, to eliminate religion from everyday life and ways of thinking.

The new urban Republican monuments rivaled with the churches, formerly the only imposing buildings in urban neighborhoods until they were dwarfed by the factories and mines. The new Republican regime tended to construct buildings that imposed the authority of the state and of the local administration—préfectures, sous-préfectures, town halls, and so on—within the urban context. Republican allegories and pagan mythology flourished in the interior decoration of their ceilings and reception rooms. The same was true of the statues, which did much to fill urban space with the symbols of a new ideal. The state turned Paris into a great republican, secular, and patriotic museum, a monumental geographical symbol of urban laicization.

The Bipolarization of Urban Schools and Citizens' Groups

The role of the Republic and the Church in French society may be measured by the organization of the educational system and the evolution of the controversy over education since 1850.[22] For it is a fact that schools, like welfare, were initially the main Church strongholds in French society, not only because of the large network of private schools (more and more congregations devoted to teaching were setting up schools, including many for girls) but also because of the Church's position within public schools as well, up to the end of the nineteenth century.[23] We will not enter into the details of the legislation and controversy over schools but will simply mention some landmarks in the history of the secularization of urban life and in the consolidation of the Republican ideology within society at large. The 1881–1882 Jules Ferry school legislation (making elementary school compulsory, nondenominational, and free of charge) was followed by the construction of many nondenominational schools, some of which asserted their laicism in engravings on their façade. Crucifixes were not allowed in the newly built schools and were removed from the walls of the older ones during subsequent rehabilitation. Henceforth, the Republic's new schools (set up with some difficulty in the western towns), just as visible as the new town halls, formed an architectural and political counterpoint to the dense network of Church-run schools. This legislative apparatus, accompanied by much construction and training work, legitimated the state-as-educator and its Republican state ethic.[24]

One indication of the determination of Catholics to adjust to the new social constellations and to reconquer the ground lost in the parishes is the way they organized community groups around parishes and Catholic schools. Bipolarization of local community groups developed in the last decade of the nineteenth century and lasted for over a half-century. The territorial basis of this organization was the administrative subdivision of urban space—usually the neighborhood, basically.

During the first half of the nineteenth century, brotherhoods, *pénitents du Midi* (penitents from the South), Norman charities, Béthune charities, and other groups, as well as trade corporations, gradually disappeared. Sometimes, however, two corporation processions—one religious, the other secular—coexisted for a few years. This was often the case for the miners' Sainte-Barbe festivities. Thereafter, between the end of the nineteenth century and the early post–World War II years, social life in urban neighborhoods took on a binary structure, reflecting an ideological struggle, generally bipolar. A third term—Protestantism—was occasionally present, but with some rare exceptions it tended to rally the secular pole.[25] This was the case in Saint-Etienne, in the Soleil district; whereas the chapel was the only sign of Protestant religious activity, a Protestant brotherhood was organized at the end of the nineteenth century. It was a sort of community center (symbolically lodged in an extremely ill-reputed former dance hall and café!), housing after-school youth clubs, a workers' circle, a library, an alcohol-free refreshment room, and so forth. The Protestants, being a religious minority with recollections of the wars of religion, the Huguenot exile, and the Catholic foundations of the French monarchy, soon chose to support the Republic and its policy of laicism.[26] The Catholics aimed at organizing youth in their after-school activities as well as in schools. A truly popular social life arose then within the youth clubs, which expanded enormously between 1890 and 1910, the idea being to keep working-class youth from deserting the Church. Many parishes also created organizations for adults: there were clubs for heads of household, women's leagues, discussion groups, and groups for running charities and, starting in 1884, forerunners of the Christian trade unions. With this will to "reconquer from the bottom up," a new kind of priest developed: an "organizer of charitable works, whose work site was the world." Here we have a shift from a sacerdotal, ecclesiastic function to a community function.

Employers were for the most part faithful supporters of the Church (and vice versa) in these moves to provide religious leadership for the working-class population and to structure its time and space outside the workplace. One good example of this is the feast of the miners' patron saint, Sainte-Barbe day, celebrated on December 4 and a holiday in the mines. Until the Second World War the Church played on religious feeling about the worship of Sainte-Barbe (her bust could be found in the bottom of every mine pit) to combat de-Christianization. There was a procession in hierarchical order (the banners, the management and engineers, followed by the office workers, and last, the miners) preceded by a solemn high mass, also organized hierarchically. The miners' representatives, in turn, followed by trade unionists, attempted to laicize Sainte-Barbe and to cloak the fourth of December festivities in corporation and family attire. The working-class movement made pointed allusions to this collusion, aimed initially at French workers and later at immigrants when they tended to flock in, sometimes brought in by the companies. In Saint-Etienne, for instance, as well as in northern France, the Polish miners who arrived just before World War I and even more so after the war came with Catholic priests and nuns who maintained a sort of guardianship over their flock for decades. During the interwar period the coal-mining and metallurgical companies of Saint-Etienne subsidized this exceptionally large group of clerical personnel, which rejoiced the right-wing press while the French working class disapproved, at the least: "during the religious feasts, the Polish had their own festivities, and even a special mass just for them every week . . . , with their own processions, their own chaplains."[27]

The Republicans reacted by creating their own networks, including one called the *Fédération gymnique et sportive des Patronages de France* (Gymnastic and Sports Federation of French Youth Clubs), characterized by a closely knit fabric of secular associations to offset the Catholic parishes. The parallelism between these organizational structures (the Church with its youth clubs on the one hand, the school with its secular associations on the other) is remarkably clear-cut, both in the membership of these after-school sports, musical, cultural, and other associations and in the way they were organized. Their goals and practices are astonishingly similar: the idea was to act on the body and the soul (or the mind) of the population and to "occupy the ground" in every sense of the expression. The result was rivalry for occupancy of and thoroughfare in the urban territory, with annual festivities, sporting competitions, bands, banners, regularly scheduled or occasional parades, decoration of streets, the assertive presence of symbols, and so on. As they often marched down the same streets on the same day, the rival associations had to be careful not to end up at the same place at the same time. It was not until the interwar period that the secularist, often definitely left-wing camp, got the upper hand, although the population at large was certainly increasingly indifferent to these disputes, with the exception of militant circles.

The Great Separation: 1901–1905

The "second level of separation" peaked with two basic texts. The July 1, 1901, bill on associations provided the means for examining the situation of religious congregations of teachers, which had proliferated since 1880; a bill dated July 7, 1904, forbid them to teach. Whereas there were 13,000 metropolitan congregational schools in 1880, there were only twenty-seven left by 1912. Since the control over urban youth was an ongoing stake, many institutions took on a secular status to continue to exist. At this point the Church made every attempt to set up free schools run by the dioceses and managed by teachers trained in religious teaching schools, which rivaled unsuccessfully with the Republican teaching schools that trained the nondenominational elementary school teachers, those "black hussars of the Republic" (in Charles Péguy's phrase).

The Act of Separation between church and state, abolishing the 1801 Concordate, was passed by the Chamber of Deputies in July 1905 and by the Senate on December 9, 1905.[28] For the first time a secular state was instated.

No churches were closed in its wake, and freedom of worship was not curtailed. There was no will to eradicate the different religions in France, nor to prohibit or restrict freedom of worship. The objective was political and ideological and aimed at limiting the networks by which the Church kept a hold on the social body—first and foremost, schooling. Religion was not by any means eradicated from society through coercion and unilateral propaganda, although some radical municipalities did deliberately emphasize the changeover by engraving the motto of the Republic ("French Republic: Liberty, Equality, Fraternity") on the façades of the churches they now owned.

This new legislation, in step with the structural trend toward de-Christianization of society at large, undeniably caused the presence of religion to regress, both symbolically and socially, on the land and in real estate, in the everyday life of a great many French cities over a moderately long period of time. Here as elsewhere we are clearly seeing a "French exception." For over a century French society was marked by the combat between the Catholic Church and a secular—if not to say laical—trend epitomized by the first decades of the Third Republic. The issue was whether Catholicism, by far the dominant religion for centuries, would maintain its ages-long hold on spiritual and social leadership. The outcome is a contrasted picture, but one in which France definitely differs from other European countries, at least until after World War II. Indeed, religion was pushed out of public life and relegated to private life to a large extent, secularism was institutionalized, and both de-Christianization and secularization were quite visible.

All of this necessarily reinforced the role of the state and of other organizational structures in social (and especially urban) life. Up to World War I, employers played a most prominent role in organizing and disciplining the working-class population, although the extent of their control changed over time and was more or less effective for different groups.

II. Controlling Working-Class Manpower: Patronage and Industrial Paternalism in the Early-Nineteenth to Early-Twentieth Centuries

Large portions of the broad range of French company owners empirically implemented and occasionally thought out ways to protect and organize their workers outside the workshops or the pits, sometimes as early as the eighteenth century.[29] Two distinct phases may be seen, with industrial paternalism unobtrusively replacing traditional patronage.[30] Company towns and regulated working-class housing projects (predominantly rural rather than urban), those extreme forms of employer control brought to light by the all-embracing analyses of Michel Foucault and his followers in the 1970s, were few and far between in France. Paternalistic policies took on varied forms and objectives in the cities and concentrated mainly on stabilizing and training the labor force.

From Patronage to Industrial Paternalism

Industrial towns are spaces of social life that developed around a manufacturing plant, a factory, or a mine. They were a manifestation of the reign of new industrial discipline, as the plants, followed by the larger factories, attempted to organize time rationally and to settle down and discipline workers. One dimension of social control is industrial paternalism: it is the descendent of the ancien régime patronage but took on new forms corresponding to the first industrial revolution. Traditional patronage, defined as employers' paternal, protective attitude toward their workers, mostly applied in small enterprises of the craft shop or pre- and protoindustrial urban workshop type. Social relations between masters, journeymen, and apprentices were still distinctly marked by the traditional apprenticeship and trade guild statuses. Patronage also characterized the social relations between ironmasters, who were landowners, and their rural work force. This is the framework in which charity, generally in nonmonetary forms, took care of ailing, aged, or temporarily unemployed dependents from the eighteenth century to the 1880 crisis years (during which many small traditional production units disappeared). These completely informal charitable works were a way of closely controlling workers in and out of the workplace.

Alongside these domestic types of relationships within small workshops, there were the brotherhoods and urban, working-class friendly societies of the ancien régime, which reappeared at the beginning of the First Empire: in 1803 for the glove makers of Grenoble; in 1804 for the Lyon hatters; under the Restoration for the masters and workers in *passementerie* (trimmings) works (the silk ribbon weavers) and velvet works of Saint-Etienne. For quite a while the brotherhoods were the only authorized associations, along with the friendly societies, at first tolerated and later authorized under the Second Republic (1848–1851). These forerunners of the trade unions were organized on a neighborhood basis and persisted throughout the century. Membership fees were relatively high and provided traditional mutual aid in case of sickness, unemployment, old age, or disability and for burial. Despite the fact that guilds had been banned by the French Revolution in 1791 under the Le Chapelier Act, they constituted an element of corporatist social self-discipline in the cities of the first industrial revolution and as such compensated for the lack of protective legislation.

The ribbon-making industrials of Saint-Etienne, however, did not invest in specific company charities but preferred personal philanthropic works aimed at the poor (who were not necessarily workers or former workers in their plants), or public action. In this particular city, manufacturers formed a closely knit social group, well structured by systematic intermarriages. They had sufficient control over the town halls of the industrial area to be able to affect society at large through aid and policies combating pauperism and financing of religious and hospital charities. Although the ribbon makers professed and proclaimed their paternalism, their financial commitment was actually extremely modest. For textile mill owners in the first half of the nineteenth century, this was above all a conservative way of exercising power and maintaining control over the working-class population—first, by running urban political life, and second, by lavishing sanctimonious discourse, but perhaps above all, by putting the Catholic Church to work at organizing the spiritual and moral leadership of the women who composed the major part of the labor force in the workshops. The archives, photos, and individual narratives all indicate the pervading presence of the religious dimension of paternalism in these textile shops, where hiring often depended on a recommendation by the parish priest or the teaching nuns. Practically every workshop had its statue of the Virgin Mary or a small chapel, and there are references to daily prayers before starting work, reciting the rosary out loud, and singing hymns during the month of Marie (May), processions in workshop chapels, and so on.[31] In Alsace, prior to the German occupation (1871–1918), many Catholic, Lutheran, and Jewish textile works owners practiced old-style philanthropic paternalism, with the distribution of aid to needy new mothers, guaranteed support of mutual aid societies through honorary membership, and asylums for the destitute elderly, for example.

Protective action was relatively frequent in these early industrial manufacturing plants and generally rural rather than urban, regardless of the industry and of the religious or ideological leanings of the owner. They varied in extent but were usually modest even if they did tend to gain control over individuals and the group. Coverage of medical expenses seems to have been the most popular practice, with home visits of doctors, and free care by nuns who were often employed by the company and were usually "little sisters" of the Saint Vincent de Paul order (whose dedication was almost unanimously appreciated, as witnessed by workers' autobiographical accounts). For the most part, workers in these companies received various forms of traditional religious and municipal aid, marginally completed by occasional assistance from their employer.

Participation in the company-organized relief funds—some twenty-odd in the 1830s—was compulsory for miners. The funds were financed essentially by deductions from wages and by fines, but miners lost the benefit of their contributions when they changed pits, as they constantly did. In 1845 the *Compagnie des Mines de la Loire* (the Loire Valley Mining Company) was formed by the merging of six companies: the Great Company was the first major capitalist merger in France, spurred by the Saint-Simonians (followers of Saint Simon), industrialists, and proclaimed social reformers, who were the main champions of relief funds and retirement funds between approximately 1840 and 1860.[32] Along with the rationalization of the work process, the Great Company intended to develop a social policy along innovative ethical lines combining "concern with and control of the worker's fate." It founded three hospitals, free pharmacies, *asiles* (havens, that is, nursery schools), schools, and sewing rooms. The moralizing intention was inseparable from a hygienist project: "The Company has neglected nothing . . . , its intention, by showing workers and their children an example of comfort and cleanliness, is to stimulate a taste for these within families, since those of the Loire valley offer a most sorry sight, in this respect." These projects caused a general outcry from the local notabilities, those traditional employers who feared they would lose their authority over the work force. According to them, true philanthropy had to be modest: "the Company has emphatically pointed to those works of humanity and protection that would rightfully be expected of it. It should be humbled in its praise of its own doings. True charity acts less ostentatiously."[33]

The steel mills followed the example of the mines. Company relief funds seem to have been very widespread from the 1820s on. The intention was to prevent or at least to discourage fee-paying workers from changing jobs, since any worker who left lost all rights to receive assistance. At the De Dietrich plant in Alsace, a rural ironworks later to become a metallurgical and mechanical engineering plant in Mulhouse run by an extremely pious Lutheran family from the pre-Revolution days (there continued to be Bible readings and sermons for workers until the mid-nineteenth century), contribution to the medical assurance and retirement funds was compulsory for permanent workers as of 1827. In the middle of the century, most of the major steel works had set up medical aid funds, while some provided free care and distributed aid to the ailing and to widows. Until a very late date, however, France was a country of small businesses employing a handful of workers, and these provisions did not affect the small craft shops, in which most of the manpower was to be found.

Company Towns and Working-Class Housing Projects: An Infrequent Pattern in France

From the mid-nineteenth century on, a number of large companies began to develop actual institutionalized social policies that tended to take care of workers "from the cradle to the grave" and to set up real "family policing" by regulating work, housing, and conduct in and outside of the factory. Throughout the Second Empire, social economics recommended that employers develop institutions of this sort, depicted as necessary tools for effectively controlling the growing labor force, which was sometimes beginning to organize the preludes to trade unionism. These practices (including medical services, dispensaries, schools, etc.), rapidly spreading through the larger-sized factories, were noticed by the publicists whose writings made them seem to be the prevailing model, which they were not, quantitatively speaking. The first to formally establish this type of aid were mostly the large capitalist companies run by the Saint-Simonians,[34] for which controlling the work force was both a means and a goal, as was the case, for instance, for the large railroad companies (Paris-Orléans, Paris-Lyon-Méditerranée, Nord) in the 1840s.[35] In every instance the goal of stabilizing and controlling the work force was explicit.

Nineteenth-century France counted many company towns centered around a single company, often in an isolated rural area, albeit their size varied considerably. Le Creusot, in the Saône-et-Loire *département* (in Burgundy), run for over a century (from the 1830s to the 1960s) under the iron rule of four generations of the Schneider dynasty, is archetypal: The owners first built barracks (collective housing), then tracts of individual or attached houses, and last, a housing project on public land. The children studied in Schneider schools, became apprentices in the factory, belonged to all sorts of sports and musical clubs, and if possible went to work for the company. Like Jules Chagot and his heirs in the neighboring mining basin of Blanzy-Monceau-les-Mines, who set up no less than thirty-nine company institutions to control their workers between 1834 and 1900, the Schneider family set up relief and contingency funds and free medical care, and founded a central pharmacy (which later became a hospital), clinics, and a retirement home for elderly workers; each of these was named after a member of the dynasty. The stained glass windows of one of the churches represented the founders dressed in Medieval attire. During the grandiose ceremonies celebrating the anniversaries of the owners' birthdays, the entire city was mobilized.[36]

The rules governing the company's factories listed the company's "generous gifts" (a widely used term to designate social institutions) and stressed the elevating and sometimes even the disciplinary dimensions connected with them for beneficiaries in their outside life. In 1900, the Schneider factory regulations reminded workers that "relief will be suspended for any worker found in a cabaret or suffering from venereal disease. Ailments resulting from drinking or brawls will be regarded as resulting from loose behavior and as such will receive no aid" (article 20). "Since these benefits are granted by Schneider and Co. entirely free of charge, they retain the character of 'generous gifts'" (article 6). The owners were intent on keeping control of the entire company town, well beyond the gates of the factory. Being the only employers in the area, it is true that they had almost complete power to do so.[37]

In the textile industry, the most frequently mentioned examples of generous gifts come from Alsace (the "Mulhouse model") or from northern France. Nonetheless, the example of the Blin-et-Blin weaving mills in Normandy (founded by Jewish owners who left Prussian-occupied Alsace after 1871) shows how social insurance and assistance institutions were created from the late 1880s on with a specific paternalistic optic tending to reduce the tutelary authority previously exerted over the work force.[38] While there is nothing unusual about the institutions themselves, the breadth of their application indicates a more specific logic. The relief associations were nondenominational, since several faiths coexisted within the working-class population (there were nonbelievers, Catholics, Protestants, and Jews of Alsatian descent who followed the owners into exile in 1871). They were extremely open, including women workers and workers' wives, and were not restricted to weavers. There was a "firm intention to emancipate workers from the employer's control." Workers who only did a short stint in the Blin factory could join the mutual societies and continued to receive benefits after leaving the company, provided they continued to pay their dues. Management of the mutual funds, although substantially supported by the owners, was soon handed over to worker members. The same was true of the retirement fund, financed by the company and managed jointly by the employers and the workers, with the latter in the majority.

These options are apparently atypical, but they do foreshadow later legislation creating national funds and medical agencies that were both secular and not run by employers, thus thwarting earlier attempts by traditional patronage and modern paternalism to control the labor force. We clearly have here the beginning of a transitional phase tending toward the welfare state. Concerns remained unchanged, however. In Saint-Etienne's Soleil and Marais neighborhoods, where a tremendous housing shortage prevailed after the working class flooded in during World War I, a few companies such as the PLM (Paris-Lyon-Marseille) railroad company, Casino, a chain of department stores, and the Société Métallurgique du Marais built small HBMs (*Habitations à Bon Marché*), modern low-cost housing.[39] In all three instances, access to the housing was conditioned both by status (work in the company, family size) and by "the candidate's morality." One had to have "a good record" and "good morals" to benefit from this housing.[40] Later, the HBM companies that ran the social housing projects were rather finicky as to the quality of future inhabitants of their apartments. Definite continuity may be seen, in this respect, between the employers' requirements and the content of the welfare state legislation.

Employer Assistance and Social Control Policies

Scholars find it increasingly difficult to operate a distinction between the economics and the political and ideological factors determining paternalistic policies, as we did some years ago. The different dimensions are closely intertwined. The primary objective of company policies in France was to solve the recurrent problem of training manpower, linked to each new phase of industrialization. There was a need to take a group of people, often of rural extraction, and to attract and settle, control and train them to produce, and perhaps even reproduce, an industrial labor force working in companies established far from the cities, or in industries made repulsive by the extremely rough working conditions, the constant risk of work accidents, and the wear on the body.

Employer policies applied to the workshops and pits, then, but to the surrounding urban environment as well; they provided housing for some of the workers near their workplace and company ownership of buildings such as clinics, schools, churches, and playgrounds.

In the 1970s, many sociologists and some historians inspired by Michel Foucault's analyses and often influenced by ideological preconceptions (social and mental life being gradually pervaded by the capitalist order), as well as their reliance on normative discourse and regulations as sources, tended to concentrate on those elements that are stable, controlled, and increasingly controlled, whence their focus on mining companies' housing projects for workers, with their character-istically all-encompassing regulationism.[41] In fact, such examples were only rel-evant for a minority of workers, particularly those in the mining and iron and steel industry areas of northern and eastern France, or for young women work-ing in the live-in textile factories of the southeast, under the supervision of nuns acting as both forewomen and chaperones.[42] With few exceptions they did not apply to the large cities (Paris or Lyon), nor to cities with several types of indus-trial plants (Saint-Etienne), any more than to the characteristically French ver-sion of industrialization prevailing in innumerable small towns and country towns. Publicists, monographs, and company reports all stress the beneficial effects of these social policies in settling the labor force: reduced turn-over of the skilled and unskilled personnel, tied to the company by the length of their employment, their participation in the control mechanisms set up by the factory (housing, schools), as well as in the employer's conceptions and ceremonies (company festivities). These should not be allowed to overshadow the numbers of restless workers always on the move, of whom there were always more than one would imagine. The historians of the 1980s–1990s have therefore seriously qualified the assertions of the 1970s historiography, placing prisons, the army, the factory, and the work-ing-class neighborhood in the same register.

The employers' ideological justifications were extremely varied, and there is hardly any sense in looking for any shared ideological or religious reasoning, includ-ing for their social welfare action. By and large, employers—ranging from the Protestant owners of textile mills or mechanical engineering plants in the east; or the conservative, Jansenist, or socially inclined Catholic owners of textile mills and chemical plants in the north or southeast; to the Jewish textile mill owners of the east or the west—were all faced with the need to organize their labor force, and all resorted to the same tactics. A socialist employer such as Jean-Baptiste André Godin who made cast-iron stoves in his cooperative (*familistère*) in the town of Guise (in the Aisne *département*) fit into this vast panorama of pioneering social policies as well.[43] He built a model housing project to lodge his workers near the foundry shops, with a nursery, schools, a clinic, a library, and so forth. As a convinced Fouriérist, he wished to provide his workers with the equivalence of wealth and involved them in the management of relief funds and other social and cultural institutions. At the same time, he made sure that the standards set up by the familistère were respected by the beneficiaries, barring which their membership was terminated. Alongside these strong personalities and staunch dynasties, modern capitalist firms such as the mining companies and the railroads were also developing large-scale social welfare policies. Here again, this is true irrespective of their ideological or religious leanings, which might be anything from technology oriented, predominantly secularist rationalism to strict Catholicism. In every case the explicit objective of these social policies was to defuse the latent social discontent. They were a means of combating socialism and abolishing the social question—the obsession of the "bourgeois century"—and a relatively effective means, both within the workplaces and in the outside world.

But the trees of social policies and normative discourse of all varieties (patronages, paternalism, housing project regulations) should not be allowed to hide the forest. Even if aid policies were more widespread among employers than is commonly believed and extended far beyond the large companies in rural areas, these practices remained limited in extent in comparison with the numbers of people affected by industrialization, especially in the cities. Furthermore, whereas their instigators often alleged the goals of moral and social control, it is important to relativize the actual facts (justifications sometimes seem artificial in comparison with the small scope of actual practices) and their effectiveness (they never succeeded in preventing worker mobility). "Strategists advocated, pell-mell, one-family homes, private property and cleanliness, enhanced family intimacy, determination to achieve stability, public parks and gardens, the elimination of community life and of drinking places . . . . Many interpretations . . . have been grounded in these normative disquisitions, and are overly wont to believe in the efficacy of the preachings of administrators of health, morality and education."[44] It is important, then, to compare discourse with practices, for which abundant, convincing literature is available.

III. Solidarity and Sociability: Forms of Cultural Identity and Social Self-Discipline in Working-Class Neighborhoods, Mid-Nineteenth Century to 1920s

By definition, institutional analysis is indispensable for the study of modes of social control, construed as the implementation of standards, explicit or implicit, secular or religious, enabling institutions to suffuse social life with a modicum of coherence and to affect its functioning—for bolstering or constructing religious or ideological control, or implementing government policies, for example. Nonetheless, institutional analysis is insufficient. It cannot grasp the role of the intricate interweaving of informal networks, of the many different forms of solidarity and sociability, in structuring the various ways in which groups impose self-discipline on their members in urban society. This is true despite the obvious fact that unlike institutions, governmental or other, social control is not the main function here. It is at this level that analysis of the working-class neighborhood is relevant.

Working-class neighborhoods are the stopping places of migratory networks. They are peopled by groups integrated in networks based on geographic origin and membership in a trade. Although integration is always difficult, it is facilitated by various forms of sociability and solidarity structured by gender. Paradoxically, the opposition between neighborhood and city is a factor in structuring social identity. One cannot postulate any general, ongoing stability, however, and credit the resulting social self-discipline based on networks and sociability with excessive efficiency: cities remain essentially in flux.

Working-Class Neighborhoods As Stopping Places of Migratory Networks

Life styles and ways of living are basic elements, along with work, in defining working-class identity, and therefore working-class culture. The impression of belonging to a neighborhood, to a place where people reside and work, stems from its often quite homogeneous social and occupational composition. This founds attachment to the neighborhood as a social space, and to forms of cultural identity that translate as active sociability and solidarity and greatly facilitate a sort of social self-discipline in which the group keeps an eye on its members.

Industrial cities of the time were the hubs of geographic migration networks: the rapid influx of population was essentially due to large-scale migrations, with individuals constantly coming and going. The neighborhood was the place where these migrants arrived. The image of the immigrant arriving all alone with his bundle of belongings in an industrial town where he knows no one is more of a cliché than a historical reality. Migrations, whether they were from the French countryside or from foreign countries, followed well-defined, often long-standing channels, based on networks in which trade-based traditions, kinship, and friendship were intermeshed. This explains why people stayed together *entre pays* (among people from the same area) in the neighborhoods where they first arrived, although these never were totally homogeneous. Paris's rue de Lappe was definitely Auvergnat territory, and in the houses around some courtyards the inhabitants all came from the same village: the streets around the Montparnasse railroad station were Breton; the Marais was full of Jewish immigrants from eastern Europe, with a distinct difference between the rue des Francs-Bourgeois—the "faubourg Saint-Germain" (affluent residential area) of the Jewish neighborhood—and the filthy, overcrowded rue des Rosiers. But these were merely pockets of provincial or ethnic concentrations, whereas there actually were Auvergnats, Bretons, and Jews throughout the city.[45]

These channels, along with the relative concentration of people of the same origins in the same areas and workplaces, tended to sustain the old lifestyles and ways of living, with cultural attitudes harking back to the regions and communities from which they originated. This sometimes deferred integration, particularly since most migrants (and later, immigrants) viewed their stay in the working-class neighborhood as temporary and planned to return sooner or later to their village of origin: the city was seen as a stopping-off place, for the purpose of working. The memoirs of Martin Nadaud, a worker from the Limoges region (who became a prominent Republican in the 1880s), show the extreme isolation experienced by the peasant workers from the Limoges area in the collective bedrooms and furnished rooms they inhabited when they came to do seasonal work as masons in Paris's construction works under the July Monarchy.[46] Half a century later, the Bretons living in Saint-Denis, north of Paris, were not very integrated either: they colonized some streets (and were not to be seen elsewhere) and remained immersed in their community, one mainstay of which was the continued use of their language.[47] Social self-discipline was enforced by cohabitation (often meaning overcrowded housing), the control exerted by the elderly over young people, numerous kinship ties, epistolary relations with the family, the surveillance of savings, put aside for purchasing land and property "at home," and so forth.

Thanks to these migratory currents, some parts of the urban landscape—often streets or pockets, sometimes entire neighborhoods—were quite homogeneous. This was the case in Saint-Etienne, a rapidly growing city whose industries were coal mining, metallurgy (arms, cycles, tools, and mechanical engineering), and textiles (ribbon making and passementerie). Newcomers came from the nearby poor, mountainous areas and took a long time to adjust to city life. The countryside was very present everywhere except in the very center of the city until a late date. There were the "whites," those peasants who came down from the mountains to work as miners during the winter months, miners in smocks and clogs returning to the fields for the heavy summer farm work—haying and harvesting. Families from the same village grouped together in a same neighborhood. There was the enduring presence of religious practices, under the surveillance of the Catholic priests and Protestant pastors, who often acted as go-betweens for employment in industry and distributed the "certificates of good morals" demanded by industrials before hiring new workers. The Lyon canuts, or silk weavers, picked grapes in the Beaujolais tens of kilometers north of Lyon. In Brittany, the Breton-speaking metallurgists of the Brest naval dockyard went to work in the nearby countryside during the summer. In Limoges, porcelain makers retained close ties with their home towns in the Limousin region. Popular rural traditions—fairs (*ducasses*), bazaars, rummage sales, carnivals, and so forth—were particularly resilient in the cities of northern France. These are typically Flemish traditions; not a surprising fact, since numerous Belgian workers were to be found in the Lille-Roubaix-Tourcoing conurbation throughout the nine-teenth century.[48] At first, while people remained closely tied to the countryside and did not really accept the idea that they were settling permanently in the indus-trial town and in a working-class job, it seems that both institutional norms (such as those enforced by the churches) and informal ones carried over from home towns (enforced by kinship and neighbors), certainly stricter than those imposed by the city, were operational. Any deviation from the socially imposed norm was noticed and the news was passed along, through various channels, to the place of origin.

Solidarity, Sociability, Intimacy

The move from country to city represented a break, and in some cases a true cultural shock, which was the case for girls who were sent to serve as maids in bourgeois families and later married into the working class. Often the city was felt to be a strange place, and a hostile one, obviously maladjusted to the influx of migrants and the subsequent proliferation of slums, working-class barracks and precarious forms of residence and housing, sometimes foreshadowing the shantytowns to come. Cities were hard on migrants, who had left behind a rural, farming society, a village community in which sociability and solidarity were nec-essary elements. Urban industrial work, with its rhythms, exerted new constraints on bodies and minds. The processes of breaking with the old world and of deac-culturation produced what historians clearly identify as "city arrival pathologies": increased criminality, extensive illegitimate sex life and prostitution, abandoned children, drinking, and some physical degeneration. These are clichés found in novels as well as in investigations by the bourgeois of the times and by the author-ities, for whom "working classes" meant "dangerous classes," but they were also very powerful social realities.[49]

During that period, recent arrivals, who often came with a group of seasonal workers, were still close to the peasant world, and their contact with the city was almost marginal. But once they chose to settle in the city definitively, they became full-fledged workers belonging to the city and the neighborhood. This is illus-trated by the constant tension between permanently settled workers and tem-porary migrants. The latter were often of the same geographic and social origins, and in the case of unskilled workers, they were employed at the same industrial jobs, by and large. But seasonal workers were always viewed as out-siders, competitors for jobs, by workers whose settlement may well have been recent. Integration was only conceivable for people who had migrated once and for all, who went down to the city to work in a factory or mine with no prospect of returning to the village, except somewhat mythically, in some far distant future.

The admixture of a farming or rural past, the changes represented by arrival in the city and work and lifestyles in the working-class neighborhood, produced an assertive social identity, sometimes remembered by participants as the independent neighborhood culture. Group cohesiveness was above all a necessity, owing to the harsh living and working conditions, especially in the mines, where accidents were everyday fare, amplified at regular intervals by terrible catastrophes. The same was true of collective self-discipline: it was the price paid for protecting the group and allowing it to reproduce itself over time. This cohesion was not devoid of violence in everyday life, owing to the presence of *gros bras* (strong guys), those heavy wine drinkers who spent their time in the countless cabarets to be found around mines and ironworks. "Disturbance of the daytime or night-time peace," "drinking in a public place," "drunken brawls" were the ordinary fare of police dockets for decades.

At the same time, it is important to point out that seasonal workers were often present within working-class families, either as subtenants of already overcrowded lodgings or as heads of household, and quite often as widowed mothers (one out of three landlords was a widowed woman). While subletting was rare in Paris and the other large cities, where furnished rooms (popular hotels) were preferred, it was the rule for miners and glass blowers, and was extremely widespread in Germanic countries. Whether among the miners of the Soleil neighborhood in Saint-Etienne (one out of ten to twenty households between 1870 and 1914), Manchester's textile workers, or the *Schlafgänger* steel workers of the Ruhr, subtenants embodied the very negation of the moral control that was demanded of the laboring classes.[50]

Some other forms of housing did in fact contribute to direct social control. This was the case for people lodged by their employers (workers in shops, restaurants, and department stores). These live-in jobs, mostly filled by the young and unwed (and probably by more women than men), were transitional. Quantitatively, they may have represented a substantial fraction of closely guarded residents, but lodging personnel was only conceivable for small urban businesses or isolated semirural companies (the live-in factories of the southeast). Morality may not have been less endangered there than in working-class subrentals, especially where young women were concerned.[51]

Sententious bourgeois preaching, focused on "that delicate matter," constantly stigmatized subletting, viewed as contributing to the breakdown of the family. Special emphasis was placed on the numerical superiority of men in those neighborhoods, making women much sought prey. This meant two things: They refused to understand the main arguments in favor of such apartment sharing (cheaper lodgings for the subtenant and much needed income for the woman who sublet), and they believed in behavior, on the part of the "dangerous classes," which was more a figment than a fact. For one thing, studies have shown that landlords very often sublet to relatives or to people from their home region or their confession (Protestant seasonal workers were lodged by Protestants), and this

conditioned relations within the shared housing. Secondly, an in-depth historical anthropological approach has shown how strategies tended to define separate spaces to preserve intimacy for parents and children, and girls and boys, within
the cramped living space (in Saint-Etienne, there was usually one large room rather
than two small ones).

This is a far cry from the alleged unrestrained, lascivious overcrowding of the
nineteenth-century investigations. In narratives, one constantly encounters,
incidentally, a detail touching on the furnishings or arrangement of the room,
strategies for "marking" and sharing the small space, the usual one being the use
of heavy drapes. A midwife testifies on conditions early in the century: "I remember a woman who had a very large room, there were two wardrobes, one on each
side, and in the middle there was a curtain. On one side, there was the bedroom
with two beds, the rest was part kitchen and part for the children." In addition
to curtains, witnesses mention folding screens, and sometimes simply "the wardrobe
door left open at night."[52] Washing was another problem, especially in mining
families, where a wooden tub in the middle of the only room was the only facility. Here again, we hear the same story over and over: "When we washed up,
since there were five of us, we went outside. We never, ever, washed in front of
each other. That was a thing my mother would never have tolerated. Everybody
did it that way, there was much more decency than there is today" says one miner's
daughter (also the wife of a miner), who worked as a *clapeuse* (coal sorter) before
World War I.[53]

Social Homogeneity, Collective Identity, and Social Cohesion

Neighborhoods are not simply pieces of a city's patchwork. Working-class
neighborhoods may be divided into different types according to the history, size,
and functions of different industrial cities. Their social and occupational composition was more or less homogeneous depending on whether the city was a
metropolis with a wide variety of functions and activities (Paris, Lyon, Lille, Marseilles),
a middle-sized city with a number of industries (Saint-Etienne, Nantes,
Limoges), an industrial town depending on a single dominant activity or company or on a relatively undiversified secondary sector (the textile industry in Roubaix,
ironworks in le Creusot), and so forth. Nonetheless, in most cases the social and
cultural identity of working-class neighborhoods was the outcome of quite strong
social homogeneity resulting from the dominant presence, over a long period of
time, of a majority of workers in one or two trades. This legitimated the feeling
of belonging to the neighborhood and therefore tended to define social relations,
as well as kinship and occupational networks.

In Saint-Etienne, a rapidly growing manufacturing center in the nineteenth century, this was the case in the Valbenoîte neighborhood, occupied first by workers

from the passementerie and weapons factories, then by those in the dyeing industry. Passementerie and silk ribbon weaving works were built on the hills to avoid the fumes of the metallurgical plants and the dust from the mines. In buildings whose high ceilings could house the high-warp looms (like those on Croix-Rousse Hill in Lyon), the weaving works gradually evolved an environment of their own, each with a specific pace, social and trade expressions, clubs, patron saint festivities, and so forth. For over a century the Soleil neighborhood was inhabited by miners and steelworkers, and some actual occupational dynasties can be documented within what is a partially settled and partly constantly changing population. Even more than the steelworks, it was definitely the mine, the great devourer of men, that imposed its requirements and the neighborhood identity on urban Saint-Etienne.[54]

When one dominant manufacturing or industrial activity with its specific working conditions and know-how structured the neighborhood, a hierarchy developed among different groups, affecting both the urban landscape and the working class. Systems of representation encompass and piece together specific technical competencies, social and cultural values, and lifestyles. This was the case for the trimmers of Saint-Etienne in their neighborhood, the canuts of Saint-Georges and Croix-Rousse in Lyon, or again, the glove makers of Grenoble. However diversified, working-class culture, both formal and informal, is defined to a large extent by work, which is at the heart of nineteenth-century city life. As the century unfolded and the migratory forms characteristic of the early industrialization period declined, this central role was gradually reinforced. With the waning of trade guilds and seasonal migrations, housing tended to become more permanent and work more regular. "Back home" solidarities tended to be replaced by stronger occupational and class ties. Little by little, this century-long trend produced the working class.

Although the substance of this working class was constantly being reconstructed, there definitely was some stability, particularly illustrated clearly by the well-documented existence of inherited professions. In some neighborhoods, and some French cities, people were miners and sons of miners, steelworkers for generations on end, or trimmings makers and daughters of trimmings makers. This socioprofessional stability, it should be stressed, was obviously a factor in structuring social control, sometimes enforced by one generation on the next on the basis of membership in a trade, and thence on the basis of lifestyle, ways of working and living, and of behaving individually and in groups. The potential for social self-discipline and the ways of enforcing it were clearly greater in groups structured by their trade: ownership of one's dwelling, for instance, made possible by a highly skilled job, was a sign of rank in the social hierarchy. The relative stability of these home owners was reflected in their integration into organized sociability networks. Conversely, those who remained at the bottom of the occupational scale were much more residentially mobile, often bordering on complete insecurity.

In these working-class neighborhoods dress and demeanor were definite social appurtenances. In Saint-Etienne, you could distinguish a miner from a metal-worker or a passementerie worker by details of their attire or by the way they knotted their scarves around their neck. On the Paris boulevards, one could tell a bourgeoise or a *demi-mondaine* (a woman of dubious reputation) from a loose-haired working-class woman, a clerk wearing a fedora from a cap-wearing arti-san or worker. Workday dress was distinctive and therefore drew other people's attention to the wearer. In popular Saint-Etienne a few women (usually widows and daughters of miners) were employed in the coal mines, mostly at sorting coal. These *clapeuses,* as they were called in the local terminology, were often pitied and looked down upon somewhat as working "at the men's place" and doing "rough work." They were noticeable, and noticed, because they left their job and returned home in coal-dust-covered clothing. This was a far cry from the clean trades such as passementerie work and from the delicate materials, and silk in particular, assigned to women. Here we have a relatively negative collective judgment by workers.[55] This is one form of social self-discipline, by which a person wearing eccentric clothing by the standards of the neighborhood or the occupational group is imme-diately identified, and it is true despite the fact that city-dwelling workers were very clothes-conscious and invested more in "Sunday best" than in everyday cloth-ing. This is true of workers in Lyon during the Second Empire as well as of mil-itant workers at the early trade union conferences.

Tenacious Forms of Neighborhood Culture

The neighborhood was perceived as having a life of its own. Autobiographical narratives attest to this spontaneously, through references to its identity and feel-ings of belonging, expressed in innumerable everyday details. This was enhanced by the fact that the limits of each neighborhood were often easily iden-tified by its patterns and pace, as each industrial activity demanded a specific workaday circulation and definite timetables. The fact that people lived near their workplaces (partly because there was little public transportation) and many moth-ers worked at home contributed to surveillance and relations between neighbors. Social and occupational proximity thus produced tenacious forms of sociabil-ity, a true neighborhood culture with its norms, its codes, and its models to be transmitted. The street and the district were familiar and afforded protection of sorts: proximity is reassuring.

Kinship networks were one of the structuring elements for forms of self-dis-cipline and control. Let us take a few examples. To find a job, the kinship net-work was invaluable: a recommendation from a relative was consistently used to gain employer acceptance, since the presence of a relative whose qualities and defects they had already assessed was viewed by employers as a guarantee of good conduct. This reliance on relatives had repercussions on the learning of a trade, with its codes and rituals. When a father or an uncle, a mother or a sister "got you into" a shop, training was usually done under their responsibility, if not under their direct supervision. Fathers watched over and initiated their sons, as mothers watched over their daughters. The individual's integration in the kinship network was also one major factor in social mobility. The "utilizable family" (the relatives one saw, to whom one could turn for help) played a pivotal role in determining people's trajectories, their access to a trade, to property, to shopkeeping, and so on.

The connections between family and kinship networks and work itself were also most conducive to informal social life, which intersected with all the other forms of sociability. Family ties did not by any means exclude ties to the outside world: to the contrary, they encouraged them. When one had relatives in a neighborhood, each of them acted as go-between in contacts with the other residents. Kinship bridged the distance between individual and community. This explains why "familiarity" is a key word in the autobiographical narratives collected by studies in oral history, telling of the time—always gone—when one was "among one's own kind." Neighborhood familiarity was predicated on social homogeneousness and relatively similar standards of living. Aside from the immediate neighbors, "we knew each other, necessarily," and this produced forms of social life in which several generations often mingled. To take some details of the networks, the places, and the practices illustrating this sociability, there were: exchanges of services, goods, gossip, and insults on the threshold of the house or in the courtyard of the apartment house, along with dense, all-important exchanges within the family, which actually almost always extended beyond the neighborhood. It is noteworthy, too, that this sociability and these cultural practices were located in clearly allotted and designated places for each sex. For instance, the water hydrants and wash houses were for women, and the cabarets and gardening allotments were for men.[56] It is in these different locations that the essential definitions of social roles and of gender roles in particular are assimilated: this is where norms, along with their voluntary or involuntary transgression, are learned.

Familiarity has its limits. Over and beyond the memories of a convivial atmosphere constantly referred to in interviews, the neighborhood is also an agency of diffuse, all-pervading social control. Chatting often centered on malicious gossip. In these accounts the drawbacks of neighbors are often put on a par with the difficulty in protecting one's own intimacy and that of one's family in cramped housing with thin walls. *Monsieur et Madame Pipelet* (Mr. and Mrs. Gossipmonger), the concierge couple in their lodge, were well-known figures in nineteenth-century Paris apartment houses. They spied on tenants for both landlord and police. They took advantage of their mail-distributing function to ferret into the secrets of the addressees and propagated rumors and gossip in the house.[57] When there were no concierges, in the working-class districts, their function was fulfilled, so to speak, by the constant presence of watchful eyes, a sort of "looking after one another" sometimes very close to pure and simple surveillance. This was particularly true for relations between boys and girls, or between men and women. Given the crowded living conditions, the streets were wont to be children's main if not exclusive playgrounds. But girls started helping their mothers with housework at an early age and did not go out as much as boys. They could not escape their mother's watchful eyes, or those of the neighbors, and did not play at the same games as boys. Girls did not "hang around in the streets" as much. This pitiless neighborhood surveillance aimed at identifying any abnormal situation. One woman worker from Saint-Etienne tells about the interwar period: "People were neighborly, they were serviceable, there's no doubt about it. But there was a good side and a bad side to that, there's no doubt about that either. We hardly had any private life. If you didn't see something, your neighbor did . . . . It was sort of like a small town . . . . You know everyone, and when you put a foot out there's always someone who says, 'Hey, there's so-and-so going by'!"[58] Small talk was instrumental in structuring the group and its space, but it was also a form of social constraint, a low-keyed form but one that was transmitted for decades, thanks to people's lasting presence in the same neighborhoods, and to women's memory, much more detailed than that of men where personal relations are concerned.

Laundering, done at the wash house, was one of working women's main activities up to the interwar period. Wash houses were both places where highly specialized work was done, and the hub of women's social life. Washerwomen washed their family's laundry, whereas laundresses were professional washers. Aside from the *buandier*, the launderer-owner of the place, there were only women in the wash house, whose walls resonated with the noisy work, the hubbub of conversations, shouting and singing. The news and comments exchanged reflected the level of collective surveillance in the neighborhood: "We were always informed about everything. . . . All the news my mother knew, she had learned at the wash house. . . . Since there was one right next door . . . we knew all the news. That was one of the places where everyone in the area went, it was very, very important," said one metalworker in Saint-Etienne. He was corroborated by a woman worker: "it was Radio-Laundry! Everything was public news . . .; the women knew everything, they didn't know anything."[59] Men workers themselves talked a lot about women's chattering in the wash house, giving the impression that they vaguely perceived it as vain and somewhat threatening. Much information was transmitted by the wash house, backing many judgments, often severe, of individual and collective behavior.

A discussion of men's social life may focus on the garden allotment just as well as on the cabaret or the café. Initially, garden allotments were often set up by employers or churches. Statistically speaking, they became a massive fact in the late-nineteenth century. The ideological, social, and political reasons behind the creation of those gardens are well known: the produce grown supplemented wages. But above all, their propagators viewed them as the natural and ideal locus of the social order, a prophylactic means and an educational model. The regulations governing their use made it possible to maintain strict control of tenants' attitudes. But it is important to go beyond the statutes and normative discourse, to look at the actual practices and customs. Did the gardens really "awaken the atavistic longing to own and work the land," and by the same token, "keep the worker out of the cabaret"? Historical and anthropological studies on working-class neighborhoods abundantly show that the gardens, where only men were to be found, for the most part—women were simply tolerated in them to tend to flowers or to some crops—were also given over to social life and to drinking: "The garden was also a place where you got plastered," one Saint-Etienne worker confides.[60] Leeks were probably not as good an antidote to the cabaret as their employer or clergyman proponents had hoped. Any analysis of social control must necessarily compare discourse and realities.

Transgressions of the more or less institutionalized norms are indirect reflections of the existence of formal and informal social control. For instance, until the mid-nineteenth century, *charivaris* (shivarees) were performed to inform a person that the group had an eye on his conduct. In one working-class neighborhood, for example, coal miners organized a charivari in 1841 against a widowed ribbon weaver who intended to remarry. Or again, in the Soleil neighborhood of Saint-Etienne, at the laundresses' day feast: "So, they dressed me up as a man; I put on some dirty work clothes to go fetch some wine; we had some good parties, with sausage, a nice piece of cheese, a good glass of wine . . . A bunch of us women went out, we came back with two or three liters of wine each, and we sang," tells a laundress born in 1895. Here, we have all the carnival-type components of the topsy-turvy—for one day a year, on the third Thursday in Lent—including laundresses disguised as men (with work clothes), "getting plastered" with *canons de pinard* (bottles of red wine), and transgressing norms, actually a far cry from the very official festivities organized up to the First World War by radical-socialist town halls for the Queen of the Laundresses.[61]

Neighborhoods and Acculturation to City Life

If we push some social practices and working-class discourse on proximity and sociability to the extreme, we find the claim that the neighborhood was a truly independent area within the city, achieved through a constant determination, not necessarily crowned by success, to take over the various spaces of the district, in a battle against the city and the employers, and through the assertion of a spatially circumscribed social identity. This is obvious in the large cities but may also be seen in the company towns, those completely fabricated company-built urban spaces. Le Creusot, a town created in Burgundy in the 1840s by the Schneider factory-owning dynasty, exemplifies this trend in France. Historical anthropology studies show the constant attempts to circumvent the close control exerted over the town by the employer through the company-built public facilities (town hall, clinics, schools, retirement homes, water supply, etc.) covering the entire social fabric. The scenes were the backyards, the few cabarets authorized by the zoning regulations, and the rural fringes of the city. But the workers never became really familiar with the city, for lack of shops, cafés, spaces uncontrolled by the "ironmaster" in which to socialize and feel free.

Often the working-class neighborhood was in fact defined in opposition to the city, construed as the central area and its bourgeois neighborhoods. In the nineteenth century the police and the criminal justice system were partially responsible for this demarcation, just as social as it was spatial. This differentiation corresponded to the gregarious actions and claims of youth groups, those apaches or hoodlums claiming allegiance to their neighborhoods when they traveled in bands to outlying dances or to the city center, as well as fights with rival gangs and occasionally with the police. Early twentieth-century Paris had its *Costauds de Belleville,* the *Bande des Amandiers,* and so forth.[62] Their exploits were widely popularized by popular newspapers and their illustrated supplements, such as *Le Petit Journal* and *Le Petit Parisien.* Concern was voiced, just as morbid curiosity had been expressed in earlier days for the criminal immoderation of Lacénaire and Troppmann. The ruffians made society tremble, as the anarchists had made it tremble not so long ago. As long as the hoodlums fought each other or beat up some chance passerby on a street corner in the Belleville or Charonne district, there was no serious problem: "The barbarians are fighting among themselves." But when they descended from time to time into the heart of the capital, then the matter became intolerable. The old fears of the 1830s were revived, with workers compared to "barbarians camping in the faubourgs": the inhabitants of Belleville during the 1871 Commune harked back to the canuts from the Croix-Rousse section of Lyon in 1831. Here again, as in Saint-Etienne's Soleil neighborhood, we have an intertwining of the reality of everyday violence with the myths of the dangers lurking in working-class areas, with both sides asserting that the working-class neighborhood had a social identity opposed to the city. France is not unique in this respect: the same gap, real or socially constructed, may be found in the Borgo San Paolo faubourg of Turin and in many English cities.[63]

The impression of belonging to a neighborhood, a combination of the feeling of community and the sense of territoriality, is often asserted against the city. This does not mean there is a "neighborhood culture," however, a territorialization in the sense of a physical and cultural separation, viewed by Edward P. Thompson as the essence of working-class consciousness.[64] We may get the idea that working-class neighborhoods became static once individuals and groups had settled there, but it is important to remember how many people were on the move and only temporarily present in a neighborhood. Furthermore, although some variable portion of the population definitely was stable, this should not conceal the potential of both individuals and families to develop tensions, ambitions, and projects, for which the city offered many means of expression. Here, social control—both institutional and even more, informal—encountered obvious limits.

From the late-nineteenth century on, working-class districts (especially the outlying ones) were increasingly tied to the city through the development of normalizing and unifying community facilities (schools and clinics) and of mass transportation facilities, conducive to exchanges. The city brought lighting, as it put in the gas mains, and it brought water, through pipelines that were always undersized for local needs. Electrical streetcars linked neighborhoods to the city center, enabling people to travel back and forth to work in larger numbers if not necessarily more rapidly. Mapping of everyday work-related circulation yields indications of how occupation, gender, and age conditioned the way people used the city. For example, while working-class children kept very much to their neighborhood, adolescents—especially boys—were more open to city life. Their trade schools or evening courses were often "in town." This, plus the group jaunts to the center, provided opportunities for prolonged, direct physical contact, without any adult mediation, with the city center. Women were either "from the district" (when they were housewives with no wage-earning activity outside their home) or "from the city" where they worked (laundresses and seamstresses went into town for deliveries to their customers; other women were employed in offices and shops) or went shopping. Men's relations with the city were increasingly diversified depending on their trade. In Saint-Etienne, for instance, arms makers and passementiers traditionally had professional relations tying them to the city centers (the major manufacturers had their warehouses there), whereas miners, many of whom were immigrants, increasingly tended to retreat to the pit districts in the faubourgs. Metalworkers, by contrast, circulated frequently between the big companies on the outskirts, the factories near the center, and the many small workshops scattered around the city. Working-class groups were heterogeneous: differences in their stability or mobility within the city seem to have accentuated social and cultural distances at the dawn of the twentieth century, and this experience itself produced increasingly diversified references on which to construct values and identities.

IV. Changes in Social Structure in the City and Its Suburbs? The First Half of the Twentieth Century

The originality of cities stems from their dense, socially heterogeneous population. Cities offer new opportunities, especially large cities with diversified functions. This explains why social behavior and cultural attitudes may have been relatively stable or extremely mobile in urban areas during the latter half of the nineteenth century. From the twentieth century onward, the efficiency of social control was inversely proportional to the extent of opportunities for mobility within the social and economic space represented by the city.

The evolution of the social geography of nineteenth-century Paris is tied to those periods of great industrial transformation beginning in the 1830s, followed by the 1850s and the 1880s.[65] The capital's working-class neighborhoods were scattered, and their composition varied. There continued to be working-class districts and mixed districts in the city center, even after Haussmann executed his great urban renovation projects. In every French—and no doubt, European—industrial city, the midtown was composed of bourgeois areas and shop-lined streets juxtaposed but also had right next to the new main arteries narrow streets with courtyards, run-down buildings, roof-top maids' rooms and garrets, and blocks of workshops. In both Paris and Lyon, the working-class districts were in the heart of town or close to it: in Lyon, Town Hall Square is at the bottom of the hill on which the Croix-Rousse canut district was located. The same is true of the Crêt-de-Roch passementier district and the miners' district of le Clapier in Saint-Etienne, only a few minutes walk from the city center. Vicinity does not necessarily mean familiarity, however: in itself, it cannot bring individuals to mingle, nor can it cancel social distances.

It would be artificial to completely oppose the working-class neighborhood and the city center, then. The great urban renovation projects begun before Haussmann's time and pursued beyond it caused a slow but sure migration of working people from the city center to the outlying communes annexed in 1860. What used to be villages or small towns became working-class *arrondissements* and districts, cut off from each other, with poor connections to the center and no public facilities. But the small, traditional manufacturers, artisans, and shopkeepers so characteristic of industrial Paris throughout its history largely remained in the old, central neighborhoods. This distortion necessarily produced back-and-forth migrations on foot, long before mass transportation was developed for suburban commuters. So there were working-class districts (such as Montmartre and Belleville) with a predominantly residential vocation, and crafts work and manufacturing districts (including the Saint-Antoine and Saint-Marcel Faubourgs, La Chapelle, Grenelle, and Ivry) with their combination of housing and workplaces. This may almost be described as the regionalization of Paris's working class, producing a variety of conditions, behavior, and traditions depending on location, industrial specialization, and the specific human environment, despite the profound social identity and manifestations of class consciousness.[66] The social fabric of popular, working-class districts was diversified, then, as were social relations and the forms of sociability to be found in them.

Whereas some households were remarkably stable as to their residence, if not always their trade, other working people were extremely mobile, not only because they fled their landlords (depicted by the grotesque name and face of Mister Vulture) and his concierges (Monsieur et Madame Pipelet) but also as a means and sign of social mobility. Cities are open places, theaters on which to play one's rise or fall, with constantly changing boundaries of luck and misfortune. Mobility was differentiated: the most skilled workers of Parisian industry (the mechanical engineers, the ironworkers, and the bronzesmiths), for whom the job market was wide open, extending throughout Paris, were most mobile. The most stable working people were often the poorest, least skilled people: the day laborers, sugar refiners, and leather workers. The city offered a great variety of work opportunities, including the resource represented by the many part-time jobs, enabling women to continue to earn some wages, or to resume work.

Residence in the more contrasted environment of the city center definitely exposed anyone who was not too attached to a very restricted circle to a greater variety of incentives, as well as images and information about city life and its promises. This produced different patterns of formal control and social self-discipline: The juxtaposition within the same area of various groups, of families following different paths and harboring contrasting ambitions and chances of achieving them, modified the behavior of each and all, accentuating the differences and sharpening perceptions of them. Large cities were conducive to upward and downward mobility, structured around the presence of more or less extensive, stable hard-core groups. To a large extent, length and permanency of residence in the working-class neighborhood conditioned the existence of places where mutuality and ties forged by proximity intermingled with kinship relations.

City Lights

In his autobiographical writings, Georges Navel, son of a metalworker from Pont-à-Mousson in Lorraine who retreated to Lyon at the onset of World War I, tells how fascinated he was as an adolescent when he traveled across the city by tramway. "I remember," he says, "how delighted I was by the street lights, the shops all lit up, my first contact with the big city. . . . We were suddenly less poor and had more freedom. My father was no longer dependent on the big factory."[67] This was true of the large cities, where workers who had migrated there in a more or less distant past were most wont to take advantage not only of the economic potential but also of the potential for seeing and enjoying. The right to the city has been put into practice and occasionally formulated as a demand by working people for a long time. Arlette Farge and Daniel Roche have illustrated this for eighteenth-century Paris: cities are "places for living."[68] For ever so long, working people have aspired to and actually practiced the right to use public space freely, to circulate unrestrictedly, to stop anywhere, and to reside and work everywhere, with constant attempts by the police to limit and regulate these practices. This was true not only for the small urban trades, fruit and vegetable vendors, street hawkers, and traveling show people, but for a great many working people. Cities are public places.

"Free time," institutionalized by the Front Populaire in 1936, was not totally new to working people. Workers were given time off out of necessity in the nineteenth century, when the number of working days was cut down by the extremely seasonal and fluctuating character of industrial production, but this nonetheless allowed them to enjoy some leisure time activities. Some of these were linked with the geographic origins of city-dwelling workers who often retained ties to the countryside. The canuts of Lyon went to their "chateaux," those frail cabins built on tiny garden plots on the Croix-Rousse plateau, or to the banks of the Saône and the Rhone, just as workers from Saint-Etienne went up to the farmhouse inns on Mount Pilat, just behind the city, and as Parisians were already boarding the pleasure trains that took them to the banks of the Marne and the Seine, and later as far as Normandy. But often the scene of leisure time activities was more directly the city and its fringes. When minister Thiers had a new belt of fortifications built in Paris in 1840, the area around the "fortifs" on which no building was permitted (the "zone") became frontier country for ragmen, bohemians, apaches, and their likes, but also for Parisian workers who flocked to the guinguettes and dance halls, where the tax-free wine was cheaper than in town.[69]

The city is "a theater with a thousand galleries."[70] In the vicinity of working-class housing and districts there were the boulevards, with their comings and goings, their parades and events, the theaters, shows, and shops, cafés with their outdoor terraces, cabarets, dance halls, and brothels. Here one became acculturated to and domesticated urban life, in all its forms and places, but at the same time, one could break with the social control exerted by the group and the occupational community. Cities meant shows and pleasure. Dances represented a transgression for the girls who attended them, both because they were the best place to meet the opposite sex and because they elicited physical and sexual involvement. Going dancing, even in groups, meant leaving the neighborhood, escaping from the family circle and the neighbors for a while, and going out on the town. The operas, light operas, and melodramas performed in Paris's theaters were attended by working people, and the same was true of the marionette theaters such as the Guignol in Lyon.

Thus, at least up to the First World War, large cities represented a combination of stability and mobility, desires to remain in the traditional neighborhoods and moves to exploit the many opportunities offered by urban life or to comply with the necessities of one's work. This substantiates the idea that cultural behavior, specific ways of being and doing, thinking, expressing, and acting were not the same for people in Paris and Lyon, Saint-Etienne and Limoges, le Creusot and Longwy. Georges Duveau had already noticed this in 1946 when he said of workers in Paris and Lyon: "That worker, however oppressed by his work, breathes a relatively liberatory intellectual atmosphere. . . . Men who are pervaded by life in the great city . . . are to some extent heirs to all of the dreams accumulated by the city over the centuries. Paris cradles the worker making a billfold in a small shop in the Saint-Denis faubourg and the metalworker in Cail in the same enveloping rhythm." He contrasted this "urban worker type with an independent personality" (who definitely corresponds to the *Sublime Worker*, the emblematic figure of the Parisian worker as depicted by Denis Poulot in 1869) with "the worker from a company town," found among the metalworkers of the Schneider factory in the Creusot, the spinners in semirural Normandy factories, and the clock makers at the Japy factory in Franche-Comté.[71]

The Suburbs of Paris, Initially an Unstructured Space

During the first twenty-five years of the twentieth century, the trends foreshadowed in the latter decades of the previous century took more definite form in France's main industrial city. In the other great cities, working people who left the city center generally did not go beyond the faubourgs, even if these tended to be farther than ever from the city. In Paris it was in the suburbs that the new industrialization was taking place and the population expanding rapidly. For a long time suburbs had no public facilities, and communications remained faulty. New forms of social confinement were developed, along with new social relations between those areas where working people worked and resided, and the city. These were reinforced by some highly territorialized political practices of the workers' movement.

The decision to reside in the suburbs was usually made under constraint. Suburbs began to exist as such at the end of the nineteenth century as the city lost much of its industry to its outskirts.[72] Suburbs represented a break with the city center, but also with the old working-class districts. For workers from those districts, to become a suburbanite meant being uprooted, in a sense: It involved breaking the neighborly relations that governed attitudes and movements within the mother city. Their main demand up to 1914 was to live inside the city, or in its nearby faubourgs. They consistently refused to be pushed out into the periphery, to places that were not a part of the city. Departure to the suburbs only became a deliberate choice, with people accepting housing there, after the First World War, with the legislative encouragement of housing developments for low-priced private homes. Even still, only a minority of city-dwelling workers could make that choice, whereas for the others—the working class had been considerably transformed by an influx of immigrants, who at times represented far over half of the suburban population between the two world wars—the suburbs mostly represented a new form of confinement.

Like the old working-class neighborhoods, the suburbs were defined geographically, socially, and culturally and had "a range of political and cultural attitudes with an identity of their own."[73] One could still find ethnic and trade-linked groups and networks in the suburbs during the interwar years, but they were submerged in suburban reality, synonymous with the very failure of the city. With their lack of public facilities, distance from the center, and inadequate transportation and often muddled admixture of land still given over to farming, mixed in with small workshops or large factories and sprawling housing developments, suburbs introduced new forms of social and cultural segregation. Whereas autobiographical narratives by working people throughout Europe reminisce abundantly about social life in the working-class districts, life in the suburbs was often made of a gradual breakdown of neighborly solidarity into narrow, privatized fragments in which the shriveled remains of social proximity no longer had the same positive, integrating connotations as in the urban districts.

One must take care not to paint too black a picture, however. The poetical writings of Blaise Cendrars and photographer Robert Doisneau's pictures of the suburbs in the 1940s and 1950s unquestionably depict the warmth of life in suburbia in a way that likens it to the inner city districts.[74] Similarly, whether or not networks built around interests, kinship, proximity, and trades disappeared or failed to develop is a moot question. When housing projects for private homes began to spread in the 1920s and 1930s, they were partially occupied by Parisian workers, who lived side by side there with employees, small shopkeepers, and people with modest independent means. As of the 1928 Sarraut Act requiring the management of facilities and maintenance work in these projects by a management committee, new control structures began to be set up to make sure the regulations were respected, for example, and soon thereafter, to demand action by the local administration to provide public facilities including publicly distributed water and gas and sewerage, as well as schools and transportation. This kind of residence-linked action was new and no doubt harked back to the old attitudes partaking of collective action and management strategies.[75] The need for water, with its implications in terms of petitions to town halls, mostly by women, and vigilance to avoid wasting of water during shortages (by children in particular) is quite comparable to what one might find in the industrial city districts a century earlier.

The "Red Suburb," a Politically Structured Space

Whereas the urban working-class neighborhoods seemed to be more integrated in the city, and the spatial and social reality of the suburbs asserted itself massively, this new space tended to be structured by some forms of political and cultural expression emanating from the workers' movement, which established norms that represented a new form of social control, in a certain sense. Indeed, strikingly enough, the impression of a neighborhood or suburb identity often expressed in working people's accounts coincided with the rise of left-wing political movements in these neighborhoods, some of which were to be "red" districts or suburbs for half a century. This shows how territorially defined some of the political practices of the working-class movement actually were. Its various offshoots, including parties, trade unions, associations of all sorts, secular friendly societies, and so forth, mostly developed their activities on a local scale, in the working-class districts or suburban *communes*. This was true for the socialists in the cities of the Nord-Pas-de-Calais region, and even more so, and more effectively so, for the communists in the industrial suburbs close to Paris.[76] It is true that the latter had easier access to the neighborhood than to factories, workshops, or mines. Militants offered a definition of working-class people's identity that was both social and political and was structured by a dense network of associations and affiliations.

In the recently industrialized suburban environment, militant (political and trade union) activities along with citizens groups (secular friendly societies, sports and music clubs, etc.) provided opportunities to reassert feelings of individual and collective membership in a community. Socialist events in northern France and communist ones in the Paris suburbs thus stressed and reinforced frontiers, the internal limits of the proletarian territory. The main components of the workers' movement tended to reinforce or recreate a degree of social and political confinement in the urban environment of the "red suburbs" that was a compelling reality until the 1970s. To some extent this new social and political pattern may be viewed as an outcome of the above-mentioned period of binary ideological structuring. For despite the relatively few studies on the question and even fewer on a comparison with communist influence, it does seem clear that the Catholic Church pursued its activity during the same period and extended the efforts previously made in the urban working-class neighborhoods to establish its influence in the suburbs.

Catholic Action in the Suburbs

The 1920–1955 period has been called the "golden years of French Catholicism."[77] At that time the Church of France took advantage of the Separation Act, which it had fiercely combated, as well as of the less conflictual atmosphere produced by cohabitation in the World War I trenches, to reinforce its system for gaining ascendancy, and it seemed to be about to win back some of the influence it had prior to anticlerical, laical Republican days. True, confrontational laicism had been replaced by compromising laicism, which would go to the point of a friendly cooperation policy in the mid-1930s. What repercussions did this have on city life? Parishes, whether the old ones or those created in the suburban districts that came straight out of the urban designers' projects (all of which included the construction of a church or a chapel just like any other public facility), remained the most powerful integrative agency, thanks to the great many newly ordained priests (1,000 to 1,200 a year, with a peak in 1947). The parish is where children were sent to catechism, increasingly taught by women. It was a place to socialize: their youth clubs, familiarly known as *patros,* were increasingly popular, as was the Catholic scout movement, whose competitors were the secular youth movements with close ties to the left-wing parties. With the rediscovery of processions by adults, the Catholics repossessed themselves of the streets. As the fight over schooling subsided, "free schools," meaning denominational schools, came into their own once again. There continued to be a wide range of parish activities, ranging from clubs, vacation residences, and family associations (the *Mouvement Populaire des Familles*) to sections of the Catholic CFTC trade union, up to the 1950–1960 period. These helped to keep the number of practicing Catholics relatively high in some places.

During this period, some employers continued to implement strategies for disciplining the work force indirectly, outside the factories, through all sorts of support to religious charities, inspired by some offshoots of social Catholicism, and sometimes more prosaically by instrumentalizing religion to fight the rise of socialism. Marius Berliet, the owner of the Lyon automobile and lorry factory of the same name, contributed to the construction of a number of churches in the new urban districts and the communes on the outskirts of east Lyon, such as Parilly (near the Vénissieux workshops): his factory donated cement and other building materials. The same is true in 1935 for the Saint-Jacques parish in the new low-rent district of Lyon called "United States" (designed by Tony Garnier), in the aftermath of a campaign launched by the archbishop in 1935 for the creation of a parish church to replace the hangar that had served as place of worship until then. When the Society of Free Schools issued bonds, Berliet bought some out of "Christian generosity, a sense of moral obligation and . . . the theme of social fear." In 1936 the Rhodiaceta chemical factories manufacturing artificial fibers built a chapel in the town of Péage-de-Roussillon, for the explicit purpose of countering the "red strike cultivators" among whom many Spanish workers were to be found. The chapel was intended "to become an asylum for workers subjected to dangerous influences," in the words of Monseigneur Caillot, archbishop of Grenoble.[78]

The great novelty of the interwar period was the popularity of Specialized Catholic Action in a soil already sown early in the century by such Catholic social movements as *le Sillon* (the Furrough). This new organization was informed by a determination to instill new dynamism into the apparatuses of the clergy. Its intention was to create a new, specialized evangelism adapted to each milieu as opposed to having a territorial basis only. *Action catholique ouvrière* (ACO, Working

People's Catholic Action) succeeded in getting a foothold in some companies and in swelling the still feeble ranks of Christian trade unionism. The *Jeunesse ouvrière chrétienne* (JOC, Young Christian Workers) was created in Clichy, a suburb of Paris, in October 1926. The city had just voted in a communist mayor, and Abbé Guérin, vicar of the parish, proclaimed his intention of "making working people lean towards Christianity rather than towards socialism," thanks to the JOC. The JOC succeeded in winning the battle for young workers in popular districts, an area that had been partially deserted for lack of combatants. These movements were characterized by the intensity of the activism within them, sometimes comparable to the then outstanding militancy found in the Communist Party. There were several meetings each month, any number of militant public interventions (selling their periodical on the streets, with the risk of having to fight off vendors of both the communist paper, *l'Humanité,* and the extreme-right press), and field investigations aimed at defining action and interventions, in accordance with the rule "see, judge, act."[79]

"Marxist City, Missionary Country": Evangelizing the Suburbs

For two centuries the religious factor was consistently influential in French political and cultural life, as we well know. Logically, then, parish organizations and the groups set up by the Church in French cities were more or less dynamic. For the Church, the suburbs of the Paris region were originally practically unknown territories, especially after the First World War. The socialist and communist left experienced some difficulty in winning elections in the rapidly spreading suburbs, but when they did their victory was generally lasting. The Church considered the "red belt" as a secular space, by default. Sometimes churches were lacking there just as much as other public facilities, and there were no more priests than there were municipal employees or bus drivers.

It would be a mistake to believe that the suburbs were abandoned, left to the problems of workers and employees bogged down in their unserviced housing projects and to the town governments slowly but surely filling in the map of the red suburbs. "Marxist City, Missionary Country" is the title of a book published in 1957 by Madeleine Delbrêl, a lay Catholic missionary who had worked in a southeastern suburb of Paris between 1933 and 1964 and who describes the enduring Catholic intervention in the heart of the red suburbs. The scene is Ivry, "the city with three hundred factories," won by a Guesdist as early as 1896, then by the Communist party in 1925. Maurice Thorez, general secretary of the French Communist Party, first sent to Parliament in 1932, represented Ivry there for several decades.[80] The experience related by Madeleine Delbrêl, like that of the other new-style missionaries, corroborates other testimony about the Paris suburbs as well as some outlying faubourgs of Lyon and Marseilles.[81] One salient remark: "the fascination by a city containing all the ingredients for working-class detachment, which these missionaries were determined to demonstrate was not a fatality, and the progression of which could be stopped by new pastoral methods."[82] For while parish facilities did exist, in terms of buildings, the balance of power in terms of social forces was obviously extremely unfavorable to the Church. The number of churchgoers shows the extent to which the working class was de-Christianized, and often assertively anticlerical. Although it held out its hand, religion remained the opium of the people, and Christian missions and municipal anticlericalism (especially strong in Ivry) were opposed and complementary for decades, although direct confrontation tended to be replaced (generally from 1935 to 1936 on) by parallel if not joint action on social matters and occasionally in politics. At some points "the hopes of Liberation nourished hopes of a new Pentecost reconciling working people, at last, with a rejuvenated Church."[83] The Vatican's condemnation of the worker-priests was a serious blow to the action of suburban missionaries.

The worker-priest movement is quite exemplary of the suburban situation. It stemmed from consideration of the difficulty of reconquering the working class, more apt to believe Stalin than the social doctrine of the Church. This had been the case for nearly a century. The main reference was a book written by father Henri Godin, *La France, pays de mission?* (1943), calling for a more offensive attitude than that taken by Catholic Action. The Church's special ties to Vichy did not suffice to reconquer the ground lost. The worker-priests, authorized by cardinal Suhard within the Mission de France, were then to attempt to be "like a fish in water," to immerse themselves in the working masses, getting hired in the big factories or on the construction sites, in the working-class neighborhoods. Father Loew worked on the docks in Marseilles, Abbé Depierre was a metalworker in Montreuil. This continued until they were taken out of the water by the Pope's reiterated interdiction: once in 1954–1955, and again in 1959.[84]

Contrasts in the City: Constraints and Freedoms

Culture, like all informal and formalized practices, is inscribed in dialectic relations. It is the outcome of a complex synthesis between history and modernity, between the normative model it represents, potentially, and the cultural input and collective experience of the ethnic, social, professional, religious, and political groups of which it is a conglomerate. This requires delicacy to give any simple interpretation of the resulting social forms and of the modes of discipline and social control, be they implemented through religious institutions, employer-run institutions, the organization of solidarity and sociability networks, or others.

Cities form a universe that is both simple and complex, permanent and fleeting, individualized and collective. Over and beyond the structure, then, it is important to try to perceive the range of rules and aspirations, dilemmas and possibilities that both produce and make possible individual and collective choices. Viewed in this way, the differential appropriation of codes and representations by various groups and individuals is just as important as how these codes and representations are distributed. Analysis of urban culture involves thorough assessment of the evolution of ways of being, doing, working, and inhabiting the city, all inscribed in its history and landscapes as well as in its functional, social, and cultural divisions. Comparison of evolving modes of social control throughout Europe would certainly uncover some variables tied to each country's specific political and religious history. However, the broad lines of the French pattern would most probably be found in neighboring countries as well.[85] Cities produce differences, and therefore elements of freedom, just as much as they produce constraints; they generate as much autonomy as control.

Notes

1. My main references here are: Duby, *La ville de l'âge industriel;* Ariès and Duby, eds., *Histoire de la vie privée;* Perrot, "Anthropologie culturelle"; Lequin, ed., *Ouvriers dans la ville;* Burdy, *Le Soleil noir;* Magri, "Villes, quartiers."

2. For literature on the French industrial revolution, see Hau et al., *"Industrialisation et sociétés . . . Bibliographie."*

3. The French *encadrement* is semantically very rich and may be rendered as a combination of organizing, control, containment, leadership, and disciplining. These terms have been used here interchangeably, depending on the context (translator's note).

4. In the nineteenth century, over 90 percent of French people were Catholic. The remaining 10 percent were Calvinist Protestants (mainly in the southeast and southwest) and Lutherans (in Alsace), or Jews (in the southeast, Alsace, and above all, in Paris): Zeldin, *Religion et anticléricalisme.* I borrow, in a revised form, from Burdy, "La ville désenchantée? . . ."

5. In the words of Jean Baubérot, a French specialist in the historical sociology of secularism.

6. The expression is currently used by Marcel Gauchet, a French specialist in the evolution of democracy in the last century.

7. Lagree in Lebrun, ed., *Histoire des catholiques:* 343–44.

8. French Republican law recognizes civil marriage before a municipal official only. This may be followed by a religious wedding ceremony at a church, viewed as a purely private affair.

9. In 1802 there were 375 priests, or one priest for 1,600 Parisians; in 1860, 661 priests, or 1 : 2,956; in 1906, 866 priests, or 1 : 4,445. See Daniel, *L'équipement paroissial d'un diocèse urbain.*

10. Martin, *Blancs et Bleus;* and idem, *La Vendée de la mémoire.*

11. Lequin, *500 Années Lumière.*

12. Perfectly illustrated by the *mémoires* of a mason worker who became a senator: Nadeau, *Léonard, maçon de la Creuse.*

13. The "moral order" designates the period during which the monarchist, conservative coalition was in power, after the bloody crushing of the Paris Commune in 1871, until a truly Republican government was set up between 1875 and 1877.

14. See Burdy, *Le Soleil noir;* and Colson et al., *Un quartier industriel.*

15. Durand, ed., *Cent ans de catholicisme social; Christianisme et monde ouvrier;* Von Bueltzingsloewen and Pelletier, eds., *La charité en pratique.*

16. Chorel, "Emile Romanet, un catholique social dans l'industrie grenobloise au début du siècle," 232–45.

17. From Dumons and Pelissier, "Laïcat bourgeois," 19–20 and 292–305.

18. In fact, these religious organizations were often vectors of the new Republican social legislation: Catholic jurists were more or less directly involved in drawing up French social law. These confessional charitable and philanthropic institutions, with their time-honored know-how actually acted as mediators between the state, local communities, and the assisted members of the community.

19. Agulhon, *Marianne au combat;* idem, *Marianne au pouvoir;* idem, *Les métamorphoses de Marianne;* Agulhon and Bonte, *Marianne.*

20. In Villars (Loire), a *commune* bordering Saint-Etienne.

21. Ozouf, *La fête révolutionnaire;* Ihl, *La fête républicaine.*

22. See Ozouf, *L'Ecole, l'Eglise et la République;* and Zeldin, "Orgueil et intelligence," on the respective roles of the two systems.

23. Dubesset and Zancarini, "Scolarisation et encadrement des filles: deux modèles concurrents," pt. 1 of *Parcours de femmes.*

24. This study excludes cities in the Alsace-Moselle region, occupied by Germany between 1870 and 1918. They escaped the secularist legislation of the Third Republic and came under both local law and German law. To be precise, they were ruled by the 1801 Concordate, with denominational elementary schools and the organization of religious teachings (or of substitute "morality" courses) within schools and on school time, delivered by specially appointed teachers.

25. For Saint-Etienne, for instance, see Burdy, *Le Soleil noir,* chap. 8.

26. Encrevé and Richard, *Les protestants.*

27. Burdy, *Le Soleil noir,* 188–92.

28. Act of separation, article I: "The Republic ensures freedom of belief. It guarantees the right to worship freely . . ." Article II: "The Republic does not recognize, pay wages for, or subsidize any religion. Consequently, as of the 1st of January of the year following the promulgation of the present Act, every expenditure relative to the exercise of religion will be eliminated from the budgets of the national government, the *départements,* and the *communes.*"

29. This discussion is confined to organization outside the workplace and does not address on-site organization.

30. For a discussion of paternalism and of the welfare state: Hatzfeld, *Du paupérisme à la sécurité sociale;* Debouzy, ed., *Paternalismes d'hier et d'aujourd'hui;* Gueslin, "Le paternalisme revisité . . ."; Rosanvallon, *L'Etat en France,* pt. 3; and Ewald, *L'Etat-Providence.*

31. Burdy, *Le Soleil noir,* 146–47; Dubesset and Zancarini, *Parcours de femmes,* 64–65.

32. Guillaume, *La Compagnie des Mines de la Loire,* for all quotations in this paragraph.

33. *La ville de Saint-Etienne aux grands pouvoirs de l'Etat.*

34. A group of manufacturers and social reformers inspired by the doctrine of social reformer Saint-Simon (1760–1825), who founded many of the major French industrial plants, railroad companies, and banks.

35. Ribeill, "Gestion et organisation du travail"; Chevandier, *Cheminots en usine.*

36. Devillers and Huet, *Le Creusot;* Frey, *Le Creusot;* Cheysson, *Le Creusot* (Cheysson headed the Creusot factory from 1871 to 1874); Turgan, *Le Creusot* (Turgan wrote dozens of articles on French factories of *Second Empire*).

37. Melucci, "Action patronale, pouvoir, organisation." The 1900 regulations are published in *Patrons et ouvriers au XIXe siècle.*

38. Daumas, *L'amour du drap.*

39. This was the first, turn-of-the-century form of controlled rental housing for the needy, later to become HLM (*Habitations à Loyer Modéré,* or low-rent housing).

40. Burdy, *Le Soleil noir,* 86–87.

41. This ideological analysis is epitomized by Murard and Zylberman, *Le petit travailleur infatigable.*

42. Vanoli, "Les ouvrières enfermées."

43. Godin, *Solutions sociales;* idem, *Le Familistère de Guise ou les équivalents de la richesse;* idem, *Le Familistère Godin à Guise;* idem, *Godin et le Familistère de Guise à l'épreuve de l'histoire.* This experience, often cited in the 1970s, was the only one of its kind in France.

44. Pinol, *Le monde des villes au XIXe.* For questioning of the normative approach, see Faure, "Comment se logeait le peuple parisien."

45. Raison-Jourde, *La colonie auvergnate.*

46. Nadeau, *Léonard.*

47. Brunet, *Saint-Denis la ville rouge.*

48. Merriman, *Limoges la ville rouge;* "Sociabilité et mémoire collective."

49. Corbin, *Les filles de noce;* Dewerpe, *Le monde du travail en France;* Charle, *Histoire sociale de la France au XIXe siècle.*

50. Niethammer and Bruggemeier, "Urbanisation et expérience ouvrière de l'habitat."

51. Corbin, *Les filles.*

52. Burdy, *Le Soleil noir,* 92–93.

53. Ibid.

54. On the importance of kinship networks: Burdy, "Des usages et des images"; Vant, *Imagerie et urbanisation.*

55. Burdy, *Le Soleil noir,* 36–37. While male miners were given washrooms in the early 1800s, the mining company did not put in showers and changing rooms for women until after the 1936 strikes.

56. For women's place in urban spaces and the division of roles, see Burdy, Dubesset, Zancarini, "Rôles, travaux et métiers de femmes"; Perrot, ed., *Travaux de femmes dans la France du XIXe*; idem, *Métiers de femmes*; idem, *Une histoire des femmes est-elle possible?*

57. It was Süe, *Les mystères de Paris,* who introduced the couple of porter-concierges named Pipelet (Gossipmonger). Whence the coining of *pipelette,* designating an overly talkative person who says more than he should. See *Le Parisien chez lui au XIXe siècle.*

58. Burdy, *Le Soleil noir,* 113–14.

59. Ibid., 161–62.

60. Ibid., 170.

61. Ibid., 157 and 163–64.

62. Jacquemet, *Belleville au XIXe siècle.*

63. Gribaudi, "Identité individuelle et sociabilité"; Jalla, "Le quartier comme territoire et représentation"; Schwartz, *Le monde privé des ouvriers.*

64. In *The Making of the English Working Class.*

65. Gaillard, *Paris, la Ville.*

66. Gaillard, *Paris,* 214. Also, Faure, *Les racines de la mobilité populaire.*

67. Navel, *Passages;* and idem, *Travaux.*

68. Farge, *Vivre dans la rue;* Roche, *Le peuple de Paris.*

69. Faure, "Classe malpropre, classe dangereuse?"

70. In Michelle Perrot's words.

71. Poulot, *Le Sublime.*

72. This discussion is confined to the popular, working-class suburbs, the largest, population-wise. See Fourcaut, ed., *Un siècle de banlieue parisienne;* Faure, ed., *Les premiers banlieusards.*

73. Magri and Topalov, eds., *Villes ouvrières.*

74. Cendrars and Doisneau, *La banlieue de Paris.*

75. Magri, "Le mouvement des locataires."

76. Fourcaut, *Bobigny, banlieue rouge;* idem, *Banlieue rouge, 1920–1960;* idem, *La banlieue en morceaux;* Girault, ed., *Sur l'implantation du PCF;* Hastings, *Halluin-la-Rouge.*

77. Cholvy and Hilaire, *Histoire religieuse de la France contemporaine.*

78. Liswski and Guery in Durand, ed., *Cent ans.*

79. Burdy, *Le Soleil noir,* 230–32.

80. Fouilloux, *Les communistes et les chrétiens.*

81. Delbrêl, *Ville marxiste, terre de mission.* And Catholic priests' accounts: Lhande, *Le Christ dans la banlieue;* Delestre, *Trente-cinq ans de mission au Petit-Colombes;* Daniel, *Aux frontières de l'Eglise;* Gray, *Quand s'ouvrent les clôtures.*

82. There were also small Protestant communities, active locally: Poulat, *Naissance* . . . , 136.

83. Fouilloux, *Les communistes et les chrétiens,* 173.

84. Poulat, *Naissance des prêtres-ouvriers.*

85. See, for instance, chaps. 8 and 9 in Hohenberg and Hollen Lees, *La formation de l'Europe urbaine.*

CHAPTER 2

Control at the Workplace: Paternalism Reinvented in Victorian Britain

Haia Shpayer-Makov

Scholars often observe that the concept of social control is problematic and lacks any uniform definition.[1] In effect, any form of domination could be subsumed under this expression. Still, it is generally accepted that social control entails a relationship of power and involves attempts by superordinates to channel subordinates into "orderly behaviour regardless of what they [think] or [feel]."[2] The term thus implies the manipulation of conduct toward a desired end and will be used in this paper in this sense.

One of the important areas in which social control is intrinsic is work. To be sure, there have always been work formats devoid of relations of domination, such as self-employment or cooperatives, but whenever work organizations consisted of both employers and employees, control was an inevitable part of the system. Since work forms a significant part of our lives, is the basis of physical and economic survival, and is a key element in defining social status and class in most of the world, an investigation of the operation of control in the world of work is essential to an understanding of human relationships both in the present and in the past.

This article examines dominance and subordination in labor relations in Britain during the nineteenth century. More specifically, it focuses on the re-emergence of paternalist systems of employment in an economy increasingly pervaded by laissez-faire concepts, illuminating the persistence of notions of control associated with the preindustrial world and their adaptation to a modern bureaucratic setting. Attention is centered on a new form of paternalism created in several large-scale work organizations using novel managerial techniques and on the manual workers employed in these organizations. The assumptions made by the new paternalist employers about what motivated employees to submit to control, the motives of the employers in devising paternalist policies, and the practices they adopted to induce their workers to conform are examined. Furthermore, in order to appreciate the impact of paternalist policies in a period of the disintegration of traditional labor relations and the rise of new concepts regarding the rights of labor, the relationship between control policies and their effects is explored. The article assesses the reaction of labor to paternalist strategies of employment at a time when the majority of workers were no longer subject to such control systems. Thus, the perspectives of both the controllers and the controlled are provided. In conclusion, an attempt is made to shed light on the motivation for and the reality of control in work organizations where the issue of control was viewed as central.

Labor Relations in Victorian Britain

Deep-seated transformations in British society and the British economy during the Victorian period impacted strongly on the world of work. Old occupations disappeared, and new ones emerged. The organization of work was restructured, and new systems of economic compensation were established. The shift from domestic industry to the factory and from rural areas to the cities, the separation of ownership from management, the growing size of workplaces, and the rise of bureaucracies entailed changes in every aspect of work. Inter alia, these changes prompted the wholesale re-evaluation of authority relations. Traditional forms of control were eroded, and employers sought new ways of organizing, monitoring, and gaining the cooperation of their labor force.[3] The need to supervise quality of work, labor productivity, and work time more effectively became acute. Efficiency became the catchword of both employers and leaders of opinion. In an age of growing mass production, employers felt threatened by the autonomy exercised by artisans and craftsmen and aimed at limiting their judgment and independence. New techniques of power were meant to accustom the worker to the demands and rhythm of industrial production and administrative work. Considerable effort was invested by interested parties in legitimizing the new forms of control.

Employers were by no means a monolithic group, and work environments were not uniform. Employers used a variety of employment policies depending on type of organization, size and technology, product or position in the labor market. Nonetheless, a dominant pattern emerges when examining labor relations in Victorian Britain.

Historians have observed that British employers in the nineteenth century, unlike their counterparts in the United States, Germany, and Japan, tended not to invest much energy in planning and pursuing long-term systematic policies regarding their labor force. Most employers of the period externalized activity related to the workforce. They relied on outside training; fluctuations in demand and supply dictated recruitment and laying off; top supervisory positions were filled essentially by external recruitment; and pay and conditions of work were determined by market forces and the cost of living in the area.[4] This was so largely because of the elastic supply of labor in the period, which created little inducement to form internal markets.[5] Although there were occasional periods of labor scarcity, on the whole the nineteenth century was marked by the availability of labor, allowing employers to hire and fire at will or to rely on subcontractors.

Most employers, then, perceived employment relations as based on the right of both sides to act freely with no obligations involved. Still, the paternalist impulse implying mutual obligations and the anticipation of long-term relations between employers and employees—albeit within a strict hierarchical setting— had not disappeared from the world of work with the introduction of capitalist modes of production into the rural and industrial economy. Paternalism survived in country areas and, more importantly, infiltrated into towns and urban settings where it was transformed to accommodate new needs and interests. For some employers it was simply a case of continuing a tradition to which they were accustomed.[6] Yet even employers in the newly emergent industries and public services adopted a paternalist mind-set, either forging novel policies or resorting to the old rural style.[7] Historical accounts in the past tended to play down the persistence of paternalist notions of employment in the nineteenth century and emphasized the predominance of labor relations based on an external market mechanism. Recently, however, scholars such as David Roberts and Patrick Joyce have pointed to the vitality of paternalism in various social and economic domains, for example, the cotton factories of Lancashire.[8] Both maintain, though, that by the end of the nineteenth century paternalism had withered away and ceased to be a social force. Arguably, however, the paternalist approach to labor relations actually became more widespread at the turn of the century, albeit in a rearticulated format.[9] The development of bureaucratic work organizations seems to have reinvigorated paternal forms of management.

Evolving in the highly stratified rural social structure of preindustrial society, paternalism had always been essentially a system of control, manifested in various social relations ranging from the family to religion, schools, asylums, hospitals, and very definitely the world of work.[10] Employer paternalism was based on a long-term reciprocal relationship between employer and employee in which the employer undertook to provide his workers with a measure of material welfare in return for deference and acquiescence to work norms. It "involved the transfer of non-cash benefits and, in some cases, cash benefits outside the formal wage bargain."[11] That such gifts were given to those who were in no position but to receive confirmed their "lowlier status."[12] Also central to the system was the extension of control to after-work hours. In order to legitimize this approach, employers entrenched the view that social relations in the workplace were akin to family relations. The employer encouraged the perception of himself as a father who, obligated to care for and educate his family, could impose constraints and discipline if necessary and intervene in their private lives.[13]

The paternalist system could take many forms. In preindustrial communities governed by the landowning classes, paternalist relations were marked by personal, face-to-face contact between employer and employee. The authority of employers stemmed from their position of power in the community and in the local employment market alongside the discretionary provision of gifts and benefits that underscored the dependency of employees. This system was carried over into some of the small and medium-size industrial firms that dominated the labor market during the nineteenth century. While most of these firms adopted a supply and demand policy, hiring and firing on the spot and motivating labor principally through the pay envelope, some established a more elaborate system of compensation and personal relationships with the workforce that extended beyond the workplace. No defined model existed, and employers integrated a variety of paternalist practices according to need, inclination, and type of organization. The attention bestowed by the owners of firms on their workers ranged from a friendly greeting to an invitation to celebrate the birth of a son or the birthday of a family member and could go as far as setting up company towns or villages for the firm's workers, including the provision of a church, a school, a store, or a dance hall.[14]

Whether paternalist or not, control at the workplace increasingly relied on intermediaries—foremen and managers—employees of the firm themselves who bridged the divide between the owner and his workers. The growing scale of industry, coupled with the mounting complexity of mass production on the one hand and worker resistance on the other, rendered this new control element more indispensable. Most firms lacked the resources to create complex management structures, relying instead on the authority of a single employer and his helpers, or on subcontractors.[15] However, large enterprises and the rapidly expanding state administration, both local and national, could not function without a more structured mode of control and a widening of the chain of command. These needs gave rise to the introduction of bureaucratic control over the work process.

Bureaucratic control has been defined by Richard Edwards, in his seminal work *Contested Terrain*, as "the institutionalization of hierarchical power."[16] According to Edwards, "the 'rule of law'—the firm's law—replaces 'rule by supervisor command' in the direction of work, the procedures for evaluating workers' performance, and the exercise of the firm's sanctions and rewards; supervisors and workers alike become subject to the dictates of 'company policy.' Work becomes highly stratified; each job is given its distinct title and description; and impersonal rules govern promotion." Historians usually associate the rise of institutions operated along these lines with the end of the nineteenth century. A closer examination of the world of work earlier in the century, however, reveals that although in

Britain bureaucratic forms of control were not widely used (compared to continental powers), the period saw an upsurge of such organizational methods.

While most bureaucratic employers opted for a contractual relationship with their workforce based principally on the cash nexus, a minority fused this system of control with the paternalist premise that the provision of benefits in excess of pay would help enforce labor subordination. This minority was far from insignificant. It included the Metropolitan Police of London, established in 1829, and the other large police forces that were set up in the country during the following three decades, which developed as ground-breaking bureaucratic organizations. The prison services and the general post office, reorganized around the same time, followed the same pattern, as did various other state administrative bodies. Railway companies, too, emerging in the mid-1830s, adopted this style of labor management, although they varied greatly in work conditions. The size of the labor force in these work organizations amounted to hundreds of thousands.[17] The lingering presence of paternalist precepts and their integration with modern perceptions of labor management in industry and state administration will be illustrated below principally by two new occupations and work organizations—the railways and the police—and by an older employer, the postal service, representing the civil service as a whole. In all three, the great majority of employees were ordinary wage workers.

Some historians claim that without the element of personal contact between employer and employee, work organizations governed by rule-based procedures cannot be considered paternalist. Bob Morris, for instance, argues that "in the pure form of employer paternalism, the transfer of benefits was firmly identified with the personality or family of the owner-manager capitalist."[18] Significantly, however, the rule-based system of domination in these organizations was imbued with metaphors associated with family and with patriarchal relations of responsibility and economic dependency. The top managers, whether the commissioner of the Metropolitan Police, the chief constables of provincial police forces, the post masters, or the chairmen or directors of a railway company, periodically played the role of the traditional paternalist owner in the rituals sponsored by these institutions. Their language was couched in familial imagery, emphasizing their duty to protect the workers and expressing personal concern with their welfare.[19] This paternal role was accepted and emphasized by leaders of the community. During a police picnic in Coventry in 1888, the mayor explicitly referred to the chief of police as "a father to the police" and expressed his hope that the officers, in turn, "looked up to him with feelings of affection, combined with respect."[20] Moreover, bureaucratic standardization unfolded only gradually. Whereas in principle, depending on rank and task, a single set of employment rules and rewards was in place, in reality, standard procedures were only partially implemented during the nineteenth century, and the personal bias of supervisors often determined promotion and other bonuses.

Discretionary attitudes linking benefits to good conduct continued to be a means of gaining control. All this created the impression of favoritism and personal control. A paternalist approach, therefore, can be said to have been embedded in these organizations.

All techniques of employee control involve some assumptions about means and ends. Paternalism in the workplace seemed to involve more coherent planning than other systems. That is not to say that every paternalist employer carefully calculated his relations with his employees. Yet even the unstructured control and often erratic gift-giving by employers in the rural economy or in small industrial firms had certain ends in view. The strategy of domination in the paternalist bureaucracies was even more systematic. Central to its perception of paternalism was a consistent approach to all aspects of labor relations, which partly explains the recurrent combination of an internal labor market orientation with paternalism. Although arbitrary decisions may have abounded in institutions structured along bureaucratic, paternalist lines, the employment system was in no way random. Further, it did not simply react to market conditions but reflected the deeply held views of some employers regarding the monitoring of labor and enforcement of compliance. These calculations did not necessarily produce the intended results. In addition, each organization devised its own employment schemes. Moreover, policies evolved dynamically and changed over time. Still, the system-based approach elicits certain generalizations about the social perceptions of the controllers and the measures they used to implement their views.

Bureaucracy and Paternalism

The bureaucratic paternalists were a disparate sector but nevertheless shared three interrelated goals. The first one was common to all employers—to ensure that employees followed orders and obeyed work regulations, a goal that became more pressing with the advent of industrial capitalism. Organizations such as the railways invested considerable capital in technologies and infrastructure and depended on the maximization of productivity for quick and high returns on such investment. As the century wore on, the profit motive became ever more dominant as capitalist notions became widespread and as competition to British industry mounted in the world markets, resulting in greater pressure on workers to perform better. The drive toward greater efficiency was not, however, limited to organizations dependent on profits for survival. State-run institutions subsidized by public funds, such as the police, the post office, and the prisons, too, were governed by the ethos of productivity and effective performance. Limited public expenditure was the widely supported policy throughout the century, putting pressure on all public administrators to keep costs to a minimum.[21] Punctuality and rigid time schedules were enforced in all work organizations, with or without a profit motive. In the case of railway work, nonadherence to a time schedule could result in accidents and loss of life.[22] Assuming the worker would not naturally conform to the firm's rules and regulations, employers devised various methods of control that would compel the workers to be obedient. The worker was expected to abandon any previous right of decision making or personal inclination and rely on the top manager to make the rules and on the supervisors to enforce them.

In their desire to induce compliance and maximize the effectiveness of worker performance, the bureaucratic paternalists were no different from employers who did not adopt a paternalist system. What distinguished the paternalists from the rest, however, was the second goal—a civilizing mission to educate and mold the behavior and mental world of the workers to suit the employers' purposes. Obedience to rules was not sufficient; authority should be seen as legitimate and worker subordination as natural.[23] Moreover, the new dictates of work demanded that workers be motivated to do their utmost in fulfilling their tasks.[24] The aim was to get workers to internalize the firm's norms and identify with its goals. Closely correlated was a desire to instill middle-class notions of work, respectability, and morality in the workers. The worker was to be the subject of reeducation and behavioral control, which would make him a compliant and cooperative laborer.[25] As in traditional paternalism, supervision was to be imposed both during and after work, in contrast to most industrial workplaces where, once outside the factory gates or work boundaries, the worker was free to do as he pleased.

The third shared aim was a stable workforce and low turnover. Admittedly, not many firms could "operate for long without the positive commitment of at least a section of their workforce," but for some this requirement was more crucial.[26] The entire employment strategy of bureaucratic paternalists was, in fact, shaped by the perception that the loss of capable employees was detrimental to the efficient running of the organization and that the movement of labor elsewhere should be forestalled.[27]

Indeed, turnover was costly. The police, the post office, and the railway companies provided internal training for new workers followed by informal instruction on the job under experienced employees. The Metropolitan Police authorities estimated that it took over two years for a constable to learn his duties and that before a policeman was worth his pay, his cost to the police was £500, a large investment at the time (the late 1880s).[28] Sorters in the post office started as learners and remained learners for two to three years before they obtained an established appointment.[29] Obviously, employers wanted to secure a return on their investment. In addition, there was the cost of labor replacement in the form of recruitment and selection expenses and the reduced productivity of other employees during the integration of new workers. Moreover, internal training often imparted skills that could not be acquired elsewhere. The departure of workers with firm-specific skills was thus particularly damaging. The withdrawal of employees from their workplace also had a negative effect on the daily routine. Expected to provide continuous and coordinated service, the railway companies, police forces, post office, and the prison service depended on cumulative experience and a permanent presence. While the replacement of personnel could have positive implications when the dropouts were incompetent, disruptive, or unhealthy, generally the longer a worker stayed, the greater the asset he was to his employer.[30] The complex interplay of these objectives was the catalyst underlying the paternalist strategies.

The ability of the manager to translate policy directives into a work routine depended to a large extent on the authority relations at the workplace. Some employers believed that the recruitment of employees with a particular socioeconomic background would facilitate control in the workplace. For employers such as the army, railway companies, Metropolitan Police, and many other police forces, this favored employee pool consisted of rural workers, who were considered ideal because their qualities were thought to meet the vital objectives of good health, deference, malleability, and stability of employment.[31] The city was viewed as chaotic, alienating, and corrupting, and the city dweller as "stunted, narrow-chested, easily wearied; yet voluble, excitable, with little ballast, stamina or endurance—seeking stimulus in drink, in betting, in any unaccustomed conflicts at home or abroad."[32] The village, by contrast, was perceived as the source of physical and moral well-being, and the country worker as basically strong, obedient, enduring, and a "lump of raw material," which enabled employers to "mould him like wax, and make him do and learn just what is required."[33] Aiming at replicating paternalist rural social relations in the workplace, these employers went to great lengths to recruit laborers from country areas. Metropolitan Police Commissioner Edward Henry (1903–1918), intent on acquiring recruits untouched by city life, favored taking them "right from the plow."[34] This attitude to the rural worker reflected the preference of many employers for a labor force amenable to control, outweighing other considerations such as education or experience in urban life.

Still, even an ideal background was not a sufficient attribute to ensure compliance. Once recruited, even rural workers needed to be worked upon, disciplined, and supervised. To meet the objectives of bureaucratic paternalism, a distinct employment pattern was built up, a result of an assemblage of choices made by disparate employers over the years, combining aspects of the old aristocratic paternalism with modern middle-class notions of efficient management.

Although the spread of bureaucracies is associated with technical advances in industrial production and the need to coordinate activity in large enterprises, the direct supervisory role of bureaucracies was equally vital to labor management. In fact, bureaucracies had developed in military organizations as early as the seventeenth century as a means of tightening control over soldiers.[35]

Significantly, the proliferating bureaucracies of the nineteenth century incorporated military-style authority techniques in order to manage labor. Uniforms became the distinguishing mark of policemen, prison guards, postmen, and most railway workers. Drilling constituted the major part of the policeman's training and was an integral element in his daily routine. Even telegraph messengers "were at one time compelled to do exercises and to march together in military formations."[36] Military terms were used to describe command roles, such as the rank of a sergeant in the police. Most important, a rigid hierarchical structure was adopted as the organizing principle of the control system. Besides executing administrative tasks and coordinating between various units of operation that could be dispersed over a whole city (as in the case of police work) or even larger areas (as in railway work), the various supervisory ranks imposed decision, division, and specialization of tasks and mediated between top management and ordinary workers. In small-scale paternalist enterprises it was not exceptional for members of the owner's family to work alongside hired workers. In the new bureaucracies owners became removed figures ensconced in the distant central office, and power was delegated to supervisors who themselves were subject to hierarchical control.[37] With the development of large corporations, the owner was replaced by stockholders represented by boards of directors, as in the railway companies. In state-governed institutions, the employer was a nominated official.

The power strategy designed by paternalist employers was based on the assumption that the workers did not view their authority as legitimate or total and that discipline, therefore, needed to be enforced relentlessly. Whether in the police or prison service, in the post office or in railway employment, the worker was subject to a harsh disciplinary regime.[38] Managers punished workers for the slightest violation of the rules and did not hesitate to resort to dismissal in order to penalize some and deter the rest, although—with the gradual realization that expulsion conflicted with the aim of a stable workforce—other penalties, such as fines, reduction in pay, suspension, and demotion, were more commonly used. Various control mechanisms were also designed to inhibit undesirable behavior before rule-breaking occurred. To generate greater productivity in an environment marked by hard and often dangerous physical labor, work was carefully regulated and structured along a tight timetable, and punctuality was enforced through sanctions.[39]

Moreover, in an effort to reform the character of the workers and change their habits, their leisure time was subjected to intense supervision and regulation.[40] Some employers enforced attendance at church services and banned drinking after work hours.[41] All uniformed workers—policemen, postmen, prison guards, and railwaymen—were required to maintain a neat appearance off duty as well as on.[42] Pressure to lead a respectable life was unremitting. In 1857, under the instruction of the postmaster general, the chief medical officer of the post office conducted an investigation into "the domestic circumstances of the officers in the minor establishment" in London.[43] To this end, letter carriers, sorters, subsorters, stampers, messengers, porters, and laborers in some departments were required to fill out a form providing information about their families and about the condition of their dwellings. Furthermore, to help cultivate the organization's image, not only the worker but his family as well were obliged to exhibit exemplary moral behavior. Sometimes the worker's choice of a bride was subject to the approval of his superior, and wives' behavior was under scrutiny as well.[44] Unbecoming behavior by a wife could preclude a worker's benefits or even promotion.

Bureaucracies also utilized more "modern" surveillance techniques, monitoring the performance of workers by daily amassing and recording information that could then be used by management to assess manpower problems and exercise firmer control on employees.

Consonant with the paternalist attitude toward workers as children in need of guidance and protection, the police, prison authorities, and railway companies refused the workforce any formal organized representation even in the latter part of the nineteenth century when growing numbers of employers acquiesced to trade unionism.[45] No opening was allowed for independent judgment concerning conditions of employment. Apart from decisions concerning daily routines, which were placed in the hands of the middle ranks, power was concentrated at the top, where the prospect of a trade union at the workplace was viewed as a challenge and a threat to the absolute authority of management. Their expectation was that banning unions would have the effect of promoting industrial peace.

Positive Incentives

In the traditional world of production, "workers were for the most part non-accumulative, non-acquisitive and accustomed to work for subsistence rather than for an incentive based, 'rational' maximization of income."[46] However, most forms of labor control in the capitalist economy consisted of both positive and negative sanctions. Even manual workers showed a mounting reluctance to carry out their assigned tasks without incentives. As a corollary, employers, too, increasingly recognized that workers aspired to more than subsistence. Yet, while most employers focused on pay as the sole means of compensation, the bureaucratic paternalists constructed systems of incentives based on both monetary and nonmaterial rewards. In fact, central to the paternalist worldview, in whatever form, was an awareness that employers could not rely solely on coercive methods to exact compliance and that the provision of incentives was essential in inducing the voluntary consent of subordinates. Thus, at least in theory, the bureaucratic paternalists offered advantages usually denied to manual workers elsewhere. As large-scale bureaucratic enterprises, they could better afford to be providers of welfare and other benefits than smaller firms, since they were more likely to have the manpower and the financial resources for such an undertaking.

Employers obviously differed in how they were prepared to reward their workers. Wages in railway employment varied widely over a great number of grades, ranging from poorly paid porters to the privileged engine drivers whose wage exceeded that of skilled artisans.[47] In addition, some grades were granted premiums and bonuses, resulting in an increased annual income.[48] Police forces generally offered their workers low pay relative to skilled workers.[49] The initial wages of letter carriers, messengers, and sorters, too, were low, and years elapsed before their income reached the level of skilled workers.[50] As a result, even "the ordinary lad" found the starting pay in the post office less than attractive.[51] In all these occupations, the compensation for tolerating a relatively low monetary reward combined with harsh discipline was regular income and employment security. As Claud Hamilton, chairman of the Great Eastern Railway Company, explained: The lowness of pay of many railway workers was based on the assumption that "service is continuous and a man is never obliged to go about seeking employment."[52] Given that casual work was the major cause of poverty in Victorian Britain, this feature of bureaucratic paternalism indeed saved employees from the highly negative effects of precarious employment.

In addition to regular pay, the paternalist employers offered a degree of security against risks of income loss from illness or accident at a time when few employers provided their workers with welfare in times of need. These insurance benefits varied widely from employer to employer. The post office and the railway companies divided their labor force into permanent and temporary workers based on ease of replacement, with only the permanent staff entitled to monetary as well as nonwage benefits and security of employment.[53] The police, by contrast, extended benefits to all grades of employees. Moreover, the police generally took greater responsibility than railway companies in easing the burdens of the ordinary contingencies of life such as old age and disability. All policemen were provided with free medical care, sick leave, and sick pay.[54] If they became unfit for service in the execution of duty, they were entitled to receive a gratuity. Pensions in the Metropolitan Police were instituted as early as 1839 and were in principle awarded to officers with over fifteen years of service who, after strict medical examination, were found unfit for police service. The County Police Act of 1840 required that "where there was a police force there should also be a superannuation fund."[55] By 1870, almost all police forces in England and Wales had such a fund. Railway workers were not as privileged. The railway companies discriminated against manual labor in the provision of social protection. While clerks and stationmasters benefited from sick pay in case of disability through sickness, the manual grades usually had to rely on membership in a friendly society.[56] Only some of these were subsidized by the company. In case of injury on duty, some railway companies paid the full wage or part of it, depending on the company's good will.[57] Others offered gratuities or medical expenses. Railwaymen who were permanently disabled would in some cases be granted medical treatment and often a lump sum, though rarely a pension.[58] A small number of railway workers enjoyed some form of allowance in old age. Post office workers, as other civil servants, were offered medical care, and the "established" (permanent) staff was entitled to receive a noncontributory pension.

Another method of instilling motivation and commitment in workers was by granting nonmonetary rewards of various kinds. Policemen, for instance, received clothing, boots, and supplies of coal. Single officers in the Metropolitan Police were provided with police living quarters and married officers received a lodging allowance. House rent was sometimes granted by provincial forces as well. Railwaymen were likely to benefit by free or cheap fuel, clothing, and in some cases free travel, company housing, and educational facilities for themselves and their children.[59] Funeral expenses were also paid. Good conduct or exceptional performance was sometimes rewarded with special grants.[60] Postal workers received clothing, paid holidays, and from the 1890s, an allowance for boots. These kinds of work organizations also offered the prospect of internal mobility, that is, a better job with higher remuneration and more prestige, which was not widespread in British industry then. For those who were not as fortunate but behaved well, length of service entailed an incremental increase in wages.

In providing welfare benefits, some paternalist employers, such as the Quaker-run Cadburys, were motivated by genuine concern for the comfort of their workers and a desire to compensate them for a harsh work environment.[61] The rhetoric of all paternalist employers certainly aimed at creating this impression, but a more powerful impetus was the desire to gain total control over labor. Incentives were a managerial device to make it worthwhile for workers and lower-level managers to serve the firm's interests. Pensions were granted by the police in the belief that they "would induce men to join the service," "remain in the force," and be efficient.[62] The promise of equal opportunity to rise within the hierarchy served the same purpose. Negative sanctions were used as part of this control system. Fear of dismissal, and the potential loss of job security and the individual's cumulative contribution to the company's insurance or superannuation funds, was meant to serve as a deterrent to early departure or insubordination. Constables were likely to forfeit their pension when they were "guilty of any breach of the peace," when they refused "to render assistance to the police in the execution of their duty," or generally when they "misconducted themselves."[63] Similarly, constables had "no claim whatever upon the superannuation fund" if they were discharged from the service even for "a very trifling offence."[64] As a way of inducing conformity to rules, the secretary of state ordered in 1845 that the highest rate of pension should be paid only to policemen with exemplary behavior, while a lesser amount would be given "to those men against whom there had been several reports."[65] The railway directors were guided by the same thinking. As a witness to the Royal Commission on Superannuation in the Civil Service (1903) commented, the railway companies provided "continuous employment to a man for a lifetime so long as he does his duty well and behaves properly."[66] If the worker resigned, he could lose part or even all his contributions to the company's friendly society.[67] In the case of dismissal, he forfeited all his contributions.[68]

The discretionary nature of social benefits thus enabled managers to exert direct control over labor by discriminating between employees whom they considered deserving and those not favored. Striking railwaymen, for instance, were forced to leave company lodgings, while workers who did not join their workmates in a strike were given gratuities.[69] Medical assistance, too, served as a control mechanism: company doctors had as their primary aim getting ill or disabled workers back to work quickly.

Moreover, the paternalist welfare systems were designed to provide protection at the least cost. Many of the promises remained on paper or were not implemented systematically. Despite the semblance of unified standards and impartiality, welfare provision, especially before the 1870s, was discretionary and selective, often dependent on the whim and personal bias of the superior officer, chief constable, or foreman.[70] A case in point was railway employment, where although occupational injuries and accidents were rife, workers had no legal claim to compensation and depended on the company's benevolence.[71] Even in the police, where every employee was meant to receive a pension and contributed weekly toward this end, only a small proportion of the recruits were actually granted paid retirement before the Police Pension Act of 1890 made it compulsory for police authorities to do so.[72] Further, the social insurance structure and special awards were partly or even wholly financed by the workers themselves. Policemen were forced to contribute between 2 and 5 percent of their pay to the superannuation fund. This fund and the police sick fund were also supported by stoppages of the men's pay during sickness and fines imposed on the men for misconduct.[73] Similarly, in the early years, fines for disciplinary offenses were used by railway companies to pay monetary compensation to workers who were permanently incapacitated.[74] In some lines, workers were forced to subscribe to the employer's provident or insurance societies, in which they had hardly any voice. Often, companies used these funds to pay workers the allowances to which they were entitled from the firm.[75] Some payments were actually conditional on membership in the company's societies.

New Methods toward the End of the Century

Only in the last two or three decades of the nineteenth century, under internal and external labor pressure and the further entrenchment of bureaucratic methods in workplaces, did the provision of welfare gradually become less discretionary.[76] High employee turnover in organizations that were dependent on workforce continuity and the activity of working people in national politics made it clear that workers expected better terms of employment.[77] This realization coincided with the economic depression of 1873–1896, which elicited widespread labor unrest. In response, paternalist employers sought newer methods to control workers, widening the scope of incentives designed to placate and retain labor while simultaneously maintaining or even tightening their authority in the workplace.[78] Sensing the growing strength of labor in the workplace and in the country at large, they pursued policies aimed at greater manipulative control but not easily identifiable as such. Falling prices in the world market during the depression and the rise in labor costs prompted the railway companies to try to maintain profits by increasing workloads while cutting down wages, housing subsidies, free coal, and other bonuses. They also resorted to a flexible policy of labor supply, laying off labor periodically and thereby eroding the security of employment typical of railway work.[79]

As a result of these "changing methods of work and styles of management," the reciprocities underlying the paternal bargain were undermined.[80] Nonetheless, the railway companies still needed to compensate the rest of the workers sufficiently so that they would stay on and conform. While backing down on some of the paternalist arrangements, they were prepared, toward the end of the century, to extend financial support to new ventures that benefited railway employees.[81] The police forces and post office, which were largely untouched by market fluctuations but contended with periodic shortages of labor as a result of continual growth, became even more willing to increase spending on social insurance and other incentives for their permanent employees.

Company-sponsored welfare was expanded, although a large proportion of the funding of these projects still came from the workers' earnings themselves.[82] Orphanages and convalescent homes were established, and workers were encouraged to invest and take part in the administration of self-help provident societies and saving schemes.[83] Additionally, large paternalist employers, including railway companies, devised various types of recreational activities for their workers.[84] They set up or subsidized sports and swimming clubs, football and cricket teams, orchestras, choirs, and performing groups.[85] The police, particularly in large urban centers, designated special venues at the workplace for games such as billiards, chess, cards, and dominoes, and invested in libraries and reading rooms stocked with books of a high moral standard.[86] They also organized family outings, dinners, and athletic competitions and instituted elaborate award ceremonies. These activities took place on the workers' own time, often under the supervision of foremen or superior officers.

The provision of after-work leisure epitomized the ideology of the new paternalists no less than the terms of employment during work. While conveying the impression of a benevolent policy aimed at creating a more rewarding work environment, work-related leisure was in reality designed to mold workers' free time. In paternalist thinking, the worker could not be trusted to be devoid of control even after hours. His leisure time, too, required supervision. However, in prescribing specific types of recreation, the new paternalists went further than the paternalists of preindustrial times. By controlling their employees' leisure activities, the new paternalists hoped to foster behavior commensurate with the firm's objectives—respectability, middle-class morality, enterprise, exertion, and self-improvement. Not only would supervised recreation help inculcate company values but it would also protect employees from "corrupting" influences outside work such as the pub and the music hall. "Whatever tends to elevate the moral tone of the young Constable is a decided gain to the public," declared a divisional superintendent of the Metropolitan Police.[87] Most important of all, the provision of recreation at the workplace was meant to serve as an inducement to join and stay in service.[88]

The social milieu of prize-giving ceremonies and sports events, dinners, and picnics evoked the image of an extended family. Top managers, often accompanied by members of their family, presided over or participated in many of these events.[89] Their presence contributed to the esprit de corps of the workers but also enhanced the authority structure. Maintaining a careful distance from the workers, it was often the chief executives or other senior officials who handed out the prizes, trophies, or awards to winners or to workers who proved worthy. They also delivered speeches praising the service while at the same time raising work norms.[90] More broadly, the presence of local dignitaries and, on some occasions, members of the aristocracy and even the royal family, helped perpetuate the immutable class structure.

The Response of the Workers

The paternalist system of welfare and leisure thus supported the requirements of management. Both private employers and state officials expected the system to produce the desired results. But intention should not be confused with effect. The salient question is: Did the workers in paternalist organizations respond to the system as expected, that is, did they become obedient, cooperative, and committed to their workplace? Obviously, reactions were not unified and changed with time and internal circumstances. Moreover, no clear-cut cause-and-effect relationship can be established between employment conditions and the workers' behavior and attitudes. Socioeconomic background, prior work experience, expectations, age, and the life cycle of workers were variables that mediated the effects of the work process. External circumstances, such as the supply and demand mechanism of the market, product prices, and technological innovations, also exercised considerable influence on the propensities and calculations of workers. Nonetheless, certain behavioral patterns are telling. Offering advantages rarely available in other occupations, the paternalist organizations were highly attractive as a source of employment. Yet, for most of the century these advantages failed to prevent the voluntary withdrawal of a large number of employees, especially in the police and railway service. Despite limited opportunities in the labor market, many employees in these large paternalist organizations refused to put up with the combination of meager wages, long hours, strenuous work, and harsh disciplinary practices, especially in light of uncertain welfare provision. Ample evidence from the period also points to the inability of the power structure to instill total discipline and commitment. Admittedly, policemen and railway and postal workers appear to have generally recognized the legitimacy of their supervisors' authority, but they were far from the model of deferential workers desired by management.

Significantly, whatever impact the paternalist system may have had on the conduct of the workers, they in turn imposed certain limitations on the employers' power to determine policy. Instances of open or tacit reluctance to comply with work demands, periodic agitation among policemen and postal and railway workers, and the unacceptable turnover rate in both the police and railway companies forced certain reappraisals on the part of management. This demonstrated that workers were not entirely powerless, even though their power did not derive from trade union negotiations but from the message they transmitted, often unintentionally. The message that labor stability, contentment, and better performance at work necessitated guaranteed benefits and a more sympathetic response to labor demands convinced paternalist employers not only to institute subtler means of control but also to ameliorate work conditions. While attempts at organized representation among policemen, postal workers, and railwaymen in the last third of the century, along with brief strike episodes, undoubtedly exerted direct pressure on employers to mitigate the worst excesses of the capitalist mode of production, indirect pressure in the form of withdrawal was a no less powerful influence.[91]

Not only did the decision makers try to conceal some of the coercive elements in the control system; their rhetoric, too, gradually changed. No longer did they dwell on the need to work for the benefit of the workplace. Increasingly, they presented themselves as representing the interests of the workers.[92] Their approach, though, was still paternalistic, reflecting a perception of management as powerful and experienced and workers as inexperienced and in need of guidance and protection. Emphasis was still laid on their role as providers and on the subservient position of the workers. On these grounds they rejected the right of workers to collective bargaining, claiming that they better knew what the workers needed and how to act on their behalf. Repeatedly, however, they now talked in terms of reconciling the values and desires of the workers with the needs of the employers, justifying management strategies in the name of harmonizing the interests of both sides.[93] In the face of expanding processes of democratization in society at large, employers were forced to modify their policies as well as their language.

With gradual attempts by employers to act upon this recognition in the latter part of the century, the rate of voluntary resignations declined. Having more to lose by departure, the workforce became progressively more stable and opted to press for the amelioration of work conditions inside the firm. A railway man now thought "very seriously" before he left the company, observed the chief accountant of the London and North-Western Railway Company at the beginning of the twentieth century.[94] The police, too, became a more permanent place of employment for a growing number of employees.[95] The goal of labor stabilization was largely achieved.

Yet workers became more demanding. The growing scope of benefits may have made the workers more dependent on their employers, but it also imbued in many a sense of power at being able to extract concessions. Expectations rose, as did the feeling by the workers that the gains they made were rights and not gifts. Moreover, the grudging improvements in working conditions were insufficient to compensate the workers for the many grievances they harbored, so that problems of discipline and work performance continued. Broad changes in the country had an effect as well, especially the accelerating rise of organized labor in the latter part of the century. The withdrawal of certain benefits from railway workers in the same period was another major influence. These developments evoked a more militant approach by the workers, who now put greater pressure on employers to allow unionization (as in the case of the police) or recognize existing unions (as in the case of the railway companies and post office). The provision of welfare benefits and work-related leisure may have helped enhance the authority structure for some employees, but not for all and not indefinitely.[96] Moreover, the workers did not fail to notice the control motivation behind the new initiatives. For instance, workers at the Great Eastern Railway Company charged that the superannuation fund set up in the 1890s was designed "to get an undue hold over the men, and thus coerce them, and have an influence over them which they [the company] would not possess if the fund was not established."[97] They also resented the thought that the fund "would be used to exert pressure on the servants to remain in the service."[98] However, even if the workers criticized various implications of the strategies used by the bureaucratic paternalists, they generally supported and participated in the welfare and recreational programs, while trying to steer them in a more acceptable direction. In sum, the employers' intention of molding a submissive type of worker and changing or reinforcing patterns of workers' behavior was not fully realized.

Clearly, power relations between the two sides were not equal. The employers controlled the means of livelihood of their employees and in times of acute conflict could seek help from the legal system, which generally upheld the priv-ileges of property holders and the powerful. Rank and file resistance took place within the confines of labor subordination and dependence on their employers. Workers, therefore, often chose to give vent to their discontent away from the observation of their superiors. Policemen, postal workers, and railwaymen who advocated the right to unionize had to meet in secret for fear of victimization.[99] Despite many instances of insubordination and militancy, it may be reasonably assumed that those who wanted to enjoy the benefits offered by the employers were generally deterred by the sanctions and complied with rules and regula-tions.[100] Some may have even identified with their employers' values and beliefs, as in the cotton factories in Lancashire depicted by Joyce, although congruence may have been the result of independent judgment and not of a deferential stance.[101] In any event, whatever the degree of insubordination or militancy at any one place, neither policemen nor railwaymen nor postmen altered the work process or the control structure in any fundamental way; nor could they prevent the many changes taking place in both industry and administration. They did, however, change the terms of their employment and improved their position at the work-place, particularly toward the end of the century. The employer's prerogative to determine the set of workers' rewards was not recognized.

Conclusion

This brief outline of the dominant interaction between bureaucratic paternal-ists and their lower-class subordinates obscures a rich variety of responses by both sides. It is evident, however, that the success of bureaucratic paternalism was ambigu-ous. On the one hand, the workforce became stable, to the benefit of the employ-ers, and employment was regular, to the benefit of the workers. On the other hand, however, hegemonic control over the workers was not attained. This stemmed from the effect of worker behavior, interests, and perceptions on the structure of employment and reward. In the process of negotiation and bargaining, which involved both explicit and implicit pressures, conflict, cooperation, and com-promise, neither side achieved total satisfaction but each secured some gains.

Traditionally, the transition in England from preindustrial to industrial soci-ety has been described as a shift from paternalism to liberalism, and from an organic society ruled by the ethos of the landed classes to an entrepreneurial one informed by individualistic middle-class thinking. Recent scholarship has aban-doned this dichotomous view. The landed elite in the eighteenth century had indeed absorbed economic notions associated with the middle classes, yet the country's employers and labor markets in the century that followed continued to be influenced by ideas and practices traditionally ascribed to rural society. The retention of paternalist notions in labor strategies is one example of such carry-overs in the nineteenth century, while also exemplifying the new patterns of thought and behavior that emerged with the contact between traditional perceptions and modern societal processes.

Symptomatic of the various types of paternalism that developed in the nineteenth century was a process of fusion of liberal tenets with landed concepts in the field of labor relations. The paternalism that characterized work organizations such as the police, postal service, and railway companies evolved in a context of growing rationalization, bureaucratization, and professionalization of state institutions and industrial production. Inherent in this new system of work were certain unresolved tensions. One such tension was between the goal of worker commitment and the size and impersonality of the organization. Another involved the employers' conceptualization of the worker who was viewed in true liberal terms as an economic agent reacting rationally to material incentives, while at the same time his freedom of choice was feared as a threat to the authority and interests of the employers. Moreover, he was portrayed at once as self-seeking yet in need of guidance and protection. As such he was caught up in a system of control marked by positive incentives side by side with harsh constraints. This system coalesced much earlier than is recognized by historians and in various forms continued to guide employers well into the twentieth century.

Notes

1. For criticism of the concept of social control see Stedman Jones, "Class Expression versus Social Control?" 162–70; and Wiener, "Review," 314–21.

2. Meier, "Perspectives on the Concept of Social Control," 42–44.

3. Melling, "Industrial Capitalism and the Welfare of the State," 226.

4. Gospel, *Markets, Firms, and the Management of Labour in Modern Britain,* 9, 11; Huberman, "Invisible Handshakes in Lancashire," 987.

5. Gospel, *Markets, Firms, and the Management of Labour in Modern Britain,* 29.

6. Bell and Newby, "The Sources of Variation in Agricultural Workers' Images of Society."

7. Norris, "Industrial Paternalist Capitalism and Local Labour Markets."

8. Roberts, *Paternalism in Early Victorian England;* Joyce, *Work, Society and Politics.*

9. Doyle, "The Invention of English," 90; Melling, "Welfare Capitalism and the Origins of Welfare States," 461–62. For the interwar period, see Jones, "Cotton Employers and Industrial Welfare between the Wars."

10. Fox, *History and Heritage,* 3.

11. Morris and Smyth, "Paternalism As an Employer Strategy," 196.

12. Newby, "The Deferential Dialect," 17. Also see Norris, "Industrial Paternalist Capitalism and Local Labour Markets," 472.

13. Newby, "Paternalism and Capitalism," 67.

14. Ibid.

15. E.g., Price, *Masters, Union and Men*, 29–30.

16. Edwards, *Contested Terrain*, 21.

17. The size of the postal workforce exceeded all other departments in the civil service put together. It expanded greatly during the latter part of the century, reaching about 113,500 men and women (over 24,000) in the early 1890s and 179,000 at the beginning of the twentieth century. Railway employment grew from a body of 60,000 to about 367,800 men between 1850 and 1884, reaching about half a million at the end of the century. The police forces in the British Isles numbered about 53,000 men by the mid-1880s.

18. Morris and Smyth, "Paternalism and Capitalism," 196. Also see *Roberts, Paternalism in Early Victorian England*, 270; Norris, "Industrial Paternalist Capitalism and Local Labour Markets," 473.

19. See, e.g., references to the chief constables in the superintendents' speeches at the Manchester police soiree and ball in 1872 and the police dinner at Salford in 1875, *Police Service Advertiser*, 23 February 1872, 5, and 5 February 1875, 3.

20. *Police Chronicle* (formerly the *Police Service Advertiser*), 18 August 1888, 5.

21. Parris, *Constitutional Bureaucracy*, 257.

22. "Departmental Committee of 1889 upon Metropolitan Police Superannuation," *Parliamentary Papers* (PP), 477.

23. Newby, "Paternalism and Capitalism," 65.

24. Kingsford, *Victorian Railwaymen*, 72.

25. See, e.g., Clinton, *Post Office Workers*, 77.

26. Lummis, *The Labour Aristocracy*, 18. Also see Huberman, "Invisible Handshakes in Lancashire."

27. See, e.g., Kingsford, *Victorian Railwaymen*, 148. The various royal commissions and select committees formed to investigate conditions of service in the organizations discussed in this article and in the civil service as a whole were guided by the assumption that a stable workforce was mandatory and that various means should be used to induce workers to stay in service. The army was similarly concerned with this problem (see "Committee Appointed by the Secretary of State for War," (PP), 86–161).

28. "Select Committee on Police Superannuation Funds," (PP), 1875, 589; "Departmental Committee of 1889 upon Metropolitan Police Superannuation," (PP), 431.

29. "Royal Commission on Superannuation in the Civil Service," (PP), 404.

30. Kingsford, *Victorian Railwaymen*, xv.

31. For the attractiveness of the rural worker for employers, see Shpayer-Makov, "The Appeal of Country Workers."

32. E.g., Masterman, "Realities at Home," 31. Also see Masterman, *The Condition of England,* 67.

33. Ibid., 7; *Police Review,* 21 August 1893, 399; Wynter, "The Police and the Thieves," 170.

34. Fosdick, *European Police Systems,* 201.

35. Dandeker, *Surveillance, Power and Modernity,* 66–67.

36. Clinton, *Post Office Workers,* 46.

37. For the complex hierarchy of command in the railway companies, see Kingsford, *Victorian Railwaymen,* 128–44; and in the post office, see Clinton, *Post Office Workers,* 45–59. For the simpler gradation of ranks within the police, see Moylan, *Scotland Yard and the Metropolitan Police,* 143–45.

38. For the strict disciplinary regime in the police, see Emsley, *The English Police,* 218–21; in the post office, see Clinton, *Post Office Workers,* 45–49; in the railway companies, see Kingsford, *Victorian Railwaymen,* 13–34.

39. For the harsh conditions of work in the post office, see Clinton, *Post Office Workers,* 49.

40. See, e.g., Chaloner, *The Social and Economic Development of Crewe,* 49, 197–202; Clinton, *Post Office Workers,* 77.

41. McKenna, *The Railway Workers,* 44–50; Steedman, *Policing the Victorian Community,* 119–20.

42. Emsley, *The English Police,* 9.

43. "Report on the Health of Officers in the Post Office," (PP), 625.

44. *Police Review,* 27 July 1900, 35.

45. Grint, *The Sociology of Work,* 74. For the trade unions that did emerge among railway workers, see Kingsford, *Victorian Railwaymen,* 82–85; among postal workers, see Clinton, *Post Office Workers,* 72–96. Unions in the postal service were formally recognized in 1906.

46. Dandeker, *Surveillance, Power and Modernity,* 178.

47. Kingsford, *Victorian Railwaymen,* xiv-xv.

48. Ibid., 104–5.

49. For wage rates in provincial forces in the latter half of the century, see Steedman, *Policing the Victorian Community,* 108–10; in London, see Shpayer-Makov, "The Making of a Police Labour Force," 116–17.

50. "Royal Commission on Superannuation in the Civil Service," (PP), 264. For wage rates in the post office, see also Clinton, *Post Office Workers,* 59–63. *Letter carriers* became *postmen* after 1883.

51. Ibid., 405.

52. Ibid., 288.

53. Ibid., 396; Kingsford, *Victorian Railwaymen,* 150–51.

54. For welfare provisions in the Metropolitan Police, see Shapyer-Makov, "The Making of a Police Labour Force," 112–13.

55. "Select Committee on Police Superannuation Funds," (PP), 1877, 103.

56. Kingsford, *Victorian Railwaymen,* 159–62.

57. Ibid., 152–54.

58. Ibid., 154–55.

59. Ibid., 110; McKenna, *The Railway Workers,* 50–55.

60. Kingsford, *Victorian Railwaymen,* 13–14, 107.

61. Child, "Quaker Employers and Industrial Relations," 294–96.

62. "Select Committee on Police Superannuation Funds," (PP), 376–77, 383, 498, 569, 581.

63. Ibid., 390, 403.

64. Ibid., 412.

65. Ibid., 573.

66. "Royal Commission on Superannuation in the Civil Service," (PP), 288.

67. Ibid., 163.

68. Kingsford, *Victorian Railwaymen,* 164–65.

69. Ibid., 78.

70. "Select Committee on Police Superannuation Funds," (PP), 1875, 375, 384; "Departmental Committee of 1889 upon Metropolitan Police Superannuation," (PP), 330; "Royal Commission on Superannuation in the Civil Service," (PP), 285.

71. Kingsford, *Victorian Railwaymen,* 152.

72. During the 1870s, only one in eight of those who entered police employment in England and Wales eventually obtained a pension ("Select Committee on Police Superannuation Funds," (PP), 1877, 134. Also see "Select Committee on Police Superannuation Funds," (PP), 1875, 388. For the post office, see "Royal Commission on Superannuation in the Civil Service," (PP), 262).

73. "Accounts Relative to the Metropolitan Police," (PP), 488.

74. Kingsford, *Victorian Railwaymen,* 154.

75. Ibid., 153.

76. For instance, in 1890, a Police Pension Act eliminated the discretionary element and made the receipt of a pension the right of all policemen.

77. For the extent of voluntary departure in the railway companies, see Kingsford, *Victorian Railwaymen,* 35–46; in the Metropolitan Police, see Shpayer-Makov, "The Making of a Police Labour Force," 109–11; in the provincial police force, see Steedman, *Policing the Victorian Community,* 92–96.

78. Melling, "Industrial Capitalism," 230.

79. For other responses by the railway companies to the squeeze on profits, see Price, *Labour in British Society,* 123–24.

80. Ibid., 125.

81. Fitzgerald, *British Labour Management and Industrial Welfare,* 33–36; Melling, "Welfare Capitalism and the Origins of Welfare States," 462–63.

82. See, e.g., "Royal Commission on Superannuation in the Civil Service," (PP), 282–83.

83. Findlay, *The Working and Management of an English Railway,* 31–33.

84. Fitzgerald, *British Labour Management and Industrial Welfare*, 35.

85. Redfern, "Crewe: Leisure in a Railway Town," 119–20; *Postman's Gazette,* 28 May 1892, 5.

86. *Police Review,* 25 May 1894, 244.

87. Extracts from "Reports by District and Divisional Superintendents," (PP), 366.

88. See, e.g., "Select Committee on Police Superannuation Funds," (PP), 1877, 147. That this was an important motivating factor in the army as well, see "Committee Appointed by the Secretary of State for War," (PP).

89. See, e.g., *Railway News,* 1 December 1888, 893; 8 December 1888, 948; 15 December 1888, 976–97; *Police Review,* 28 December 1900, 616; *Postman's Gazette,* 14 May 1892, 5; *Post,* 17 November, 1894, 351.

90. See, e.g., Redfern, "Crewe: Leisure in a Railway Town," 122; *Police Review,* 4 September 1893, 423; 19 May 1899, 232; *Postman's Gazette,* 3 March, 1894, 5; *Post,* 3 November 1894, 336.

91. For attempts at collective bargaining and strike action within the Metropolitan Police, see Reynolds and Judge, *The Night the Police Went On Strike,* 202–25; for industrial action in railway employment, see Kingsford, *Victorian Railwaymen,* 64–71; and in the post office, see Clinton, *Post Office Workers,* chaps. 4–8.

92. See, e.g., the evidence of Sir Edward Richard Henry, Chief Commissioner of the Metropolitan Police, in "Select Committee on the Police Forces," (PP), 709. Also see Findlay, *The Working and Management of an English Railway,* 28.

93. See, e.g., the evidence of Sir George Murray, Secretary to the Post Office, in "Royal Commission on Superannuation in the Civil Service," (PP), 399.

94. Ibid., 373.

95. Shpayer-Makov, "The Making of a Police Labour Force," 109.

96. Lummis, *The Labour Aristocracy,* 70.

97. "Royal Commission on Superannuation in the Civil Service," (PP), 283.

98. Ibid., 284.

99. Lummis, *The Labour Aristocracy,* 77. For instances of victimization in the post office, see Clinton, *Post Office Workers,* 84, 113–14, 121, 127, 132.

100. See quotation in McKenna, *The Railway Workers,* 56.

101. Joyce, *Work, Society and Politics.*

CHAPTER 3

Social Change, Popular Movements, and Social Control in Scandinavia, 1864–1914

ULF DRUGGE

Introduction

In 1862, the Norwegian sociologist and social anthropologist Eilert Sundt (1817–1875) visited England. His biographer, the American sociologist Martin S. Allwood, noted that the size and wealth of England impressed and depressed Sundt: "[S]ome people cannot admit that new and foreign things surprise them, but I admit that I was almost overwhelmed at the sight of the power and might of this country, yes, that I felt sick at heart at the thought of my poor Norway, whose entire glory in comparison collapsed to (forgive me the word)—wretchedness. I knew from before that England was a great and powerful country compared with Norway, but I had never been able to imagine the difference so great."[1]

After complaining about England's neglect of Norway as an independent nation because it "fused Norway and Sweden into one realm," Sundt apparently recovered somewhat from his feelings of inferiority: "[S]oon the oppressive feeling before this greatness and power was turned into anger at the pride and arrogance that were more and more evident, and from now on I was able to see somewhat better what was inside the surface, and in my anger (it was not right, but this is what happened) I more than once had occasion to rejoice at certain perversities and questionable things which disfigure this proud country."[2]

Then Sundt expressed his pride in being a Norwegian: "As conditions in our country are so burdensome and hard, so tight and precarious, so outright poor . . . it is most remarkable that, even so, things can be as they are. . . . That these few people who are spread out over our vast country have been able to stick together so well, that they have been able to create and maintain through the ages a civilized society, these peasants, these workers (there is no nation in Europe that so completely answers to the notion of a people of workers), who must fight so hard for their daily bread—this is indeed remarkable."[3]

Sundt noted the differences between the Scandinavian countries and England. However, Scandinavian countries, underdeveloped relative to England and in a west European perspective, developed during the nineteenth century into three welfare states.

This essay reflects on some specific historical aspects by focusing on social-control-related phenomena with an accent on the establishing stages of the most prominent Scandinavian popular movements.[4] First, key concepts are discussed. Second, the emergence of Swedish popular labor movements is analyzed with respect to Swedish historical conditions. Third, some topics from a case study of interested party activities and union efforts in a sawmill community situated in the most northern Swedish county (*län*), Norrbotten, are analyzed to illustrate the way these stages took form. Finally, the Swedish case will be compared to similar movements in Denmark and Norway.

Social Control and Some Related Concepts

In this essay the concept of social control is broadly applied. As the concept has already been discussed elsewhere in the book, some corresponding concepts will be introduced. Swedish historical analyses of popular labor movements have focused on the culture's promotion of orderly, steady workers.[5] The historian Ronny Ambjörnsson, for example, points to the desire to have orderly and steady workers as a significant project among sawmill owners in the first half of the twentieth century. Among certain key actors he found a tendency to move away from exterior means of controlling worker behavior and toward the kind of education that promoted self-control.[6]

Another historian, Björn Horgby, proposes the concept of a "workman's culture." He contrasts traits among workers that were significant with an orderly lifestyle with those that are more directed by personal desires. To Horgby, the concept of culture means "a collection of control mechanisms like plans, recipes, rules, instructions."[7] Furthermore, he states that "culture is created—and changeable—when people with their experiences are faced with new realities as it helps them to structure their actions both in mental and concrete terms."[8] Horgby also directs attention to the concepts of discipline and honor. Discipline, for example, could imply a two-sided social process initiated by both the elite and the masses. He regards honor as a "moral filter utilized by workers when they were encountering new realities and other cultures."[9] Examples related to a workman's concept of honor are easily found in early-twentieth-century labor unions. Unions repeatedly emphasized honesty. A worker who accepted and then appeared in a way subordinated to consequences of decisions made after a fair discussion was regarded as honorable. Moreover, a worker who strove to defend someone's rights before his self-interest was seen as honorable.

Patronage and paternalism have been applied to working conditions and working relationships between workers and their employers. Although traditionally referring to social relationships, these concepts have been referred to somewhat different historical conditions.[10] In Sweden, patronage has been mainly applied to relationships in the seventeenth century between a patron and his client in which their informally settled exchange may mean protection provided by the patron in exchange for service and loyalty.[11] Paternalism have in later centuries been applied in similar ways. In this essay, paternalism refers to a model of benevolent care and paternal considerations.

The Swedish Case: Historical Background

Until about 1870, Sweden was primarily a rural society with a sparse population that was relatively stable and firmly controlled. In 1850, about 90 percent of the Swedish population lived in rural areas,[12] and the land-owning peasants played a significant political role. In addition to being represented as one party in the Diet of the Four Estates, they were active in the local decision-making processes as jurors (*nämndemän*) in district courts and as members of Church courts and parish meetings. It has often been stated that the influence of local decision making, in combination with the relative equality among the various social classes, prevented Sweden from the kind of conflicts apparent between a dynastic upper class of landlords and the peasants that characterized the social situation in many other European countries.[13] The relatively high literacy rate in Scandinavian countries contributed to this political situation. Sweden as well as Denmark and Norway had fewer illiterate people per capita than the rest of the world.[14]

From a formal social control perspective, Sweden had a dual legal situation, at least until about the 1860s. The prevailing authorized legal systems were either linked to state laws or ecclesiastic law. Despite their different ideological foundations, these two legal systems existed with fairly similar demands on the population and included both formal and informal means to exert social control.[15]

The Swedish Evangelic Lutheran Church[16] depicted its ideas of social order in terms of a strictly hierarchical social system in accordance with The House Table.[17] These ideas influenced social life in such a way that religious discipline and master domination became distinct features within Swedish society. These ecclesiastical laws aimed to promote godliness, but most important, they upheld social order.[18] Various local arrangements had been established to support church control over private life matters. For instance, parish meetings and church councils were aimed at dealing with both strict church matters and with problems related to the family sphere.

The next period, which coincides with the beginning of the industrial era, started comparatively late in Sweden compared to western Europe. It included industrialization, secularization,[19] and urbanization,[20] processes that started almost simultaneously and changed social conditions in rural areas. Economic conditions that existed until this stage were characterized by far-reaching trade restrictions.[21] The beginning of the new industrial era resulted in a gradual decline of these restrictions as capital, goods, and labor were released from old restraints.

Due to the relatively low gross national product in the mid-nineteenth century,[22] with weak domestic demand for most products, and due to an inferior infrastructure in terms of transport, the easiest economic strategy for a country such as Sweden to improve its standard was to develop export industries. Moreover, such a strategy would certainly also lead to multiplier effects of various kinds. Thus, the development of a functioning infrastructure began, which in turn led to a steady expansion of the lumber and iron industries. As a result, there was rapid growth in mechanical and industrial enterprises.

While other countries went through a similar industrial expansion at the beginning of the 1870s, Sweden was able to keep this process going in a fairly steady way, which was comparatively unique in Europe. During the period that started in 1860 and ended at the beginning of World War I, only Germany showed a similar expansion.[23] One explanation was that Sweden started its expansion from a lower industrial level than many other western European countries. Furthermore, the wage level was far lower compared especially to England, while the education level was comparatively high. Primarily, however, Swedish industrialists derived advantages from their import of technical skill from abroad, which prepared them to mechanize and apply their production apparatus to meet the demand of lumber and iron products from abroad.[24]

Modern Sweden is often characterized as a well-organized society with respect to how popular movements become significant forces in society. Moreover, employers and employees formed associations or unions.[25] Industrialization meant popular movements with reform and social control ambitions. Free Church Societies[26] were started by the 1860s, and temperance societies appeared somewhat later. The first labor unions—at least in a more modern sense—began in the mid-1880s.[27] Initially, these movements were related and had at least one common goal uniting their efforts, namely to fight alcohol abuse.[28]

Swedish popular movements were not formed from state interests or from exterior interests, as was the case with many politically and religiously oriented movements in the rest of Europe, but they were formed by society at large. Moreover, they did not represent nationalistic forces, a phenomenon that often dominated the political scene in many other countries.[29] The bulk of their members were recruited among the lower class. Therefore, their social base was fairly similar. However, leaders of the temperance and Free Church movements were mostly recruited from the middle class.[30]

Temperance and Free Church Societies were undoubtedly influenced by activities abroad, while the Swedish labor movement seemed to have been a national movement. When the industrialization process proceeded, and when economic and social conditions worsened, popular movements were supported by more Swedes, and a number of workers apparently also found it necessary to form labor unions. However, it was hardly the industrialization process as such that increased the influence of labor unions in the Swedish society. Instead it was the power relations between employers and employees and certain work conditions that directed these collective efforts. These conditions were characterized by competition between employees and employers and between members within each of these groups. To fight for jobs was a significant factor behind the formation of unions.[31]

In fact, a number of workers' associations were established during the 1870s.[32] They were mostly related to certain categories of craftsmen influenced by middle-class attitudes with a trend to cultivate and educate and to deliver lectures on craftsmanship and general knowledge issues. Gradually, however, more social class oriented labor unions emerged, which were focused on working-class issues such as shaping strategies in order to act with unified efforts in their struggles in southern Swedish cities and towns.[33] In 1898, the labor unions formed a central union, *Landsorganisationen* (LO, The Swedish Confederation of Trade Unions).[34] Its relative strength was manifested in 1902 when about 20 percent of all Swedish workers outside the rural sector protested for universal suffrage by striking. This strike also marked the turn of the tide as their counterpart, *Svenska Arbetsgivareföreningen* (SAF, The Swedish Employers Confederation), was formed.[35]

However, after 1900 the majority of workers in unions were no longer skilled workers but were industrial semiskilled workers. Labor unions developed into a movement with mass appeal. In 1906, the number of Swedish workers in unions per capita was larger than in any other country.[36]

The Swedish Case: The Sawmill Labor Union Context

In its initial stage, the Swedish sawmill industry produced wood products and sawed lumber primarily in northern Sweden. This industry developed into the

largest lumber exporter in the world.[37] Two decades later, the pulp mill industry emerged in southern Sweden with few ownership connections to the sawmill
industry along the north Swedish coast.[38]

Most sawmills were located far away from population centers because the Swedish
lumber industry produced mainly for the export market. Furthermore, as industrial efforts of such a large scale were a fairly new element in Sweden, industrial
plants in general had very few old industrial centers in which to locate. Thus,
access to raw products and natural harbors became the two main factors that
influenced their locations. This was the case with the main Swedish sawmill district around the city of Sundsvall, where the number of sawmills within a fairly
small area was relatively large.[39]

In Sweden, sawmill owners and concerns were not influenced by traditions
with bonds back to preindustrial enterprises.[40] Most sawmills were owned by mer-
chant family businesses and were also, in a practical sense, directed by members
of these families. In other words, they were not directed by professional managers as was the case with the steel industry in the south. Furthermore, each of
these families concentrated on one sawmill, and its local bonds were striking.[41]
In fact, this has often been regarded as a major factor why relationships between
the employer and employee were relatively tense.[42]

Union activists were forced to consider what moves their employers would
make and were to a great extent also involved in internal union affairs about how
to unify employees into a strong entity capable of cooperating for common goals.
Klas Åmark believes that labor union activities should primarily be understood
as efforts to improve working conditions and to limit the competing elements
among the employees themselves due to the limited supply of job opportunities.[43] This interpretation seems to hold for union activities in sawmills, too. In
addition to daily working conditions, mobilization problems dominated the union's
agenda.

Initial Sawmill Organization Efforts in North Sweden

In this section, data from a case study of a sawmill situated in the county of Norrbotten
at the most northerly part of the Gulf of Bothnia, close to the Finnish border,
will illustrate some topics related to the process of forming unions. In about 1900,
a number of sawmills were already established in this area. The sawmill in Båtskärsnäs
was established in 1867 on a peninsula where just a handful of peasants had their
homesteads.[44] One of its founders, P. A. Svanberg, still ran it until 1901 when
his second oldest son, Gustaf Svanberg, took it over after being educated in England.
At this time the sawmill had about seven hundred workers. P. A. Svanberg was
a son of a land-owning peasant from a neighboring village. Due to his social back-

ground and with relatives who were sawmill owners, too, Svanberg was actually an insider in this area in more than one respect. Thus, he was certainly culturally competent enough to handle various locally bound problems.

Although the sawmill workers in Båtskärsnäs opposed a strong counterpart, that is, the Svanberg family, this factor did not restrain them from strike actions. This was true even though only a small number of workers joined labor unions. The majority of the workers in this part of Sweden were not union members. Among the five strikes that occurred in Båtskärsnäs between 1903 and 1907, nonunionists were the majority of strikers in four of them. During this period, strikes and other actions against the sawmill owners turned from loosely organized at the beginning of the 1900s into being fairly well organized at the end of the 1900s. All but two union activists in Båtskärsnäs—whose identities were in fact easy to distinguish after having checked the local debates recorded in union records—learned valuable lessons from union activities at sawmills in other north Swedish counties.

At the time when unions finally became forces to reckon with, sawmill owners showed open hostility toward all union efforts.[45] If an employer was informed about someone's union membership, this usually meant he was fired. In this respect, the Svanberg family was no exception. This forced union activism in secrecy. Interestingly, the first item on every union meeting agenda in Båtskärsnäs was to elect a door guard. The tactics employers used to counteract union activities by employees did not seem very coordinated in the 1900s. Some, like the Svanbergs, whose actions were fairly modest compared with many of the other sawmill employers, varied their messages from time to time. Others were persistently harsh and interfered with collective actions by unions.

Union meetings were formal, a mode that presumably originated from what union activists had experienced from meetings elsewhere. As a matter of fact, the meeting protocols were not completely new elements among the Swedish population in general. Some of the union activists had probably gained experience from local authority assemblies. Moreover, it seems reasonable to assume that these protocols helped activists to do the following: (1) Maintain coherence among members by widening their perspectives in order to include not only petty, individual problems but to consider also those that represented the workers as a collective. (2) Create a feeling of security among union members as well as prepare them to arrive at fair decisions of what strategies to choose in struggles with employers.

Union activists considered all workers as part of a larger entity even though the workers at sawmills represented a fairly heterogeneous group of people. This was also true as far as the employees at sawmills were concerned. Some of the employed were physically strong and experienced, while seasonal workers, who were far from settled in the community, possessed a relatively low social status. While the employers found the former relatively skillful, others were more or

less regarded as interchangeable. There are a number of examples of attempts by
the Svanberg family, for instance, to show partiality toward certain workers. This
gave rise to distressing internal conflicts among union members.

Union efforts were often countered with paternalistic steps staged by the sawmill
owners. In practice, these steps meant that the sawmill owners provided workers with housing facilities, health care, and so forth and that wages were sometimes paid for with food coupons. Consequently, the employees were either forced
to shop at company stores, or to convert coupons into money at a lesser value.
These arrangements kept the employees dependent on the company and had far-
reaching social control implications. Blacklisted employees were not allowed to
buy anything at these stores. Because housing was offered to employees, the threat
of eviction was repeatedly applied as a way to manipulate the Social Democratic
Party and labor union members to cease their activities. However, the coupon
system had another purpose, namely to prevent employees from abusing alcohol. Union activists were also forced to tackle this problem because it threatened the discipline among union members. Some of the most prominent
activists were involved with their local chapter of the temperance society.

Union activists looked on their organization as a kind of moral movement
that oversaw discipline problems and controlled behaviors at the workplace. However,
union activists did not support ideas that workers regarded labor unions as channels for discussing broader, political issues in ideological terms in the way many
of their Continental contemporaries apparently did, or for promoting an overall revolutionary movement.

Considering the early-twentieth-century labor disputes, union activists have
often been regarded as the aggressor. With the wisdom of hindsight, it is obvious that labor unions often played a moderating role with regard to nonunionists and to undisciplined union members. For nonunionists in key positions at
sawmills, it was far easier to deal with conflicts with their employers than for
union members. In principle, they just had to focus on their own interests. Union
members, on the other hand, were forced to focus their interests within the col-
lectives, and furthermore, representatives sanctioned their actions at the next level
of the union hierarchy. Simultaneously, representatives among the parties had
opportunities once more to evaluate the arguments presented and, moreover, to
reflect upon relative strength versus the arguments of their counterparts. These
considerations promoted new initiatives by both employees and employers in
order to bring about an end to labor dispute.

There is still one question to reflect on with respect to these power relationships: What roles did women play in this male-dominated power play? About a
hundred years ago, Swedish popular movement activities were almost completely
dominated by men. Except for leisure activities, women seemed to be completely
absent. However, labor union protocols are presumably misleading guides if one
is searching for aspects of life that concerned topics related to women, family

life, and reproduction, although a number of women were actually present in their communities. Some wives, single women, and children were also employed at sawmills. English historical research of communities representing the same patriarchal settings as characterized the Swedish sawmill communities indicate that wives played significant roles in the spheres of kinship, marriage, and work.[46]

The Swedish labor union party lost a general strike in 1909.[47] This meant that a large number of members left their locals, which in turn meant that locals lost almost all the influence they had previously gained.[48] Not until the end of the 1920s did they regain their influence.[49] In the 1930s, the labor unions began to play a significant moderating role in the Swedish labor market. Mutual understanding and desire for agreement informed their strategies.[50]

Sweden in a Scandinavian Context

Scandinavia has often been regarded as one single entity with few nuances. Without a doubt, there are obvious social, cultural, and political similarities in various respects if one compares Denmark and Norway with Sweden. For example, a common belief in Scandinavia is to organize interests and activities by way of forming popular movements; the Social Democratic and the Liberal parties in each of these countries developed a reform agenda within the framework of the political process; and finally, but not least, the languages in these three countries are fairly similar.

However, there are also some apparent differences to consider in the present context. Ron Eyerman and Andrew Jamison have analyzed what they call "new social movements" by comparing social conditional factors in various countries. They have also pointed to differences between Denmark and Sweden regarding the traditional roots of their current environmentalist movements. They have described these two traditions as follows:

> [T]here is a tradition in Denmark of alternative politics, primarily based in the countryside. That tradition was influential in the process of Danish industrialization through a network of cooperative dairies and people's high schools and it was revived in the resistance movement during the Second World War. It was largely because of such a tradition that the environmental movement was able to "mobilize" the population against nuclear energy, and it is an important reason why Danish environmentalism has merged into a broader movement of alternativism and rural collectivism. In Sweden, on the other hand, the environmental movement has been, almost from the beginning, much more

parliamentary in orientation. . . . Where Denmark has had a tradition of extraparliamentary "movements," those in Sweden have been all but integrated into parliamentary parties. It is this kind of difference that has also affected the ways in which social movements are conceptualized in the two countries. In Denmark a movement is located on the grassroots, while in Sweden the movement merges into the party, whether it be the social democratic "movement," the farmers' "movement," or for that matter the green "movement."[51]

Eyerman and Jamison state also that:

[I]n Sweden, the influence of the established political culture was extremely strong, and particular movement identity had difficulty in forming itself; . . . environmentalism was largely incorporated into the established institutions. By contrast, in Denmark and the Netherlands the cognitive praxis of the new environmental movement could continue to develop in its own space throughout the 1970s and even beyond.[52]

It is tempting to extend Eyerman and Jamison's analysis even further by way of expressing features that distinguish Sweden from Denmark with respect to public debate. By comparing historical aspects related to the popular movement and social control prerequisites, however, the aim below is to exhibit some of these differences between the Scandinavian countries that persist.

Denmark, 1864–1914[53]

Denmark's economy is based more on agriculture than Sweden's economy. The Danish linguist Flemming Lundgreen-Nielsen states that Danes are at heart still farmers.[54] Copenhagen's population compared to the rest of Denmark and its central intellectual and political position in the country are important factors to consider.[55] In addition, Copenhagen was important to the modernization process in general.

Before describing significant features of modernization, however, some background factors related to Danish history are worth considering. At the end of the 1840s, the royal autocracy ended, which meant that Denmark changed to a constitutional monarchy with the distribution of power similar to the two other Scandinavian countries.[56] The main issue in Denmark in the mid-nineteenth century, however, had to do with the duchies of Schleswig and Holstein. This issue led to an open conflict with Prussia. Two wars broke out in which Denmark—with little support from the other Scandinavian countries—was finally beaten by the united Prussian and Austrian armies in 1864, and the two duchies were lost.[57] This left the Danes feeling degraded and confused.

The Danish modernization process was above all an agricultural affair. In the mid-1860s, agricultural products mainly consisted of grain. The rural social structure included a fairly small number of influential landowners, a large number of small farmers, and a growing number of craftspeople and farm laborers. The situation in the countryside was characterized by social disruption.[58] In fact, it was fairly similar to the situation in southern Sweden. However, from the beginning of the 1870s through the 1890s, both the production and the social structure of the rural areas changed. The production of grain decreased due to the protectionist policies in potential markets like Germany and England, leading to a rapid increase in the export of refined agriculture products like bacon, eggs, and butter for the seemingly ever increasing English market.

The transformation of the farming sector was provided by popular movement efforts. Cooperatives started and were initially supported by the most powerful rural groups consisting of the landowners and successful farmers. However, the more that other segments of the population such as small farmers and tenants took part in this transformation process, the more they were engaged in cooperative societies, with social relational implications for the various social segments involved. Some types of self-regulated informal social controls took form. A fairly self-confident class of small producers emerged to become a vital social force within the democratic process of the country

The Grundtvigian movement, rooted in Denmark in the 1840s, and named after its initiator N. F. S. Grundtvig (1783–1872), influenced rural development and social reform. This movement challenged the National Danish Church's monopoly as the legitimate interpreter of how to view the society, of what is good or evil, and of blessing all politicians, a monopoly that broke down within a few decades.[59] Due to its positive attitude to life and its desire for a wider spiritual freedom in the churches and schools,[60] *Grundtvigianism* was a unique phenomenon within the Scandinavian context.[61] Due to its emancipation impulse, with its theological and religious broad-mindedness, and with its informal character, this movement should have been a fairly impossible phenomenon within the principally conservative context that existed in Sweden in the mid-nineteenth century. However, like most of the other revivalist movements in Denmark and Norway, which also included orthodox Lutheran variants in both these countries,[62] Grundtvigianism remained within the national Lutheran church. This was not the case with many of the Swedish Free Churches such as the most influential one, the Pentecostal movement.

The Danish industrial process started at about the same time as it did in Sweden—in the beginning of the 1870s. This process was not as rapid as in Sweden and was mainly located in and around Copenhagen, and to a far lesser degree in smaller cities such as Odense, Århus, and Ålborg. The Danish enterprises produced mainly for domestic markets in order to support both rural areas with equipment and cities with food products and building materials. With few exceptions, Danish factories were relatively small.

A large number of workers were living in Copenhagen and its suburbs where influences from abroad easily provided their leaders with ideological and organizational tools. Initially, mostly directed by publishers and other intellectuals, their messages addressed individual concerns to a greater degree than their Swedish equivalents. In fact, labor unions as well as political efforts related to working-class interests took form about one decade earlier than in Sweden and with clear Marxist elements. Rather soon, however, after setbacks in the mid-1870s,[63] these movements obtained a reformist character that resembled Swedish movements. While the Danish equivalent of the Swedish Confederation of Trade Unions, *De samvirkende Fagforbund,* was established in 1898, the first Social Democratic members of the Danish parliament *(Folketinget)* took office in 1884. In any respect, the close links between labor unions and the Social Democratic Parties have been a distinctive feature within all three Scandinavian countries. Later, the cooperative movement became a vital part of the labor movement.

Norway, 1864–1914[64]

The Norwegian Eidsvoll Constitution of 1814 was the end of Danish rule and the start of a royal union with Sweden. It was surprisingly radical in its details: the right to vote was more radically elaborated than elsewhere in Europe at that time. Norway had its own government, its own domestic administration, and its own parliament, the *Stortinget.* Furthermore, the scope of the king's authority became weaker in Norway than was the case in Sweden. Norway's role as a national unity was far more independent in its union with Sweden than it had been earlier with the Danish monarchy. Despite this, the Norwegian elite found it necessary to get rid of what they regarded as their surviving Danish social, mental, and cultural dependence.

Allwood describes the new Norwegian era as one in which "[f]reedom from Danish domination released a tremendous outburst of creative activity in the population of Norway."[65] Nationalism began to make its way into the national consciousness. By combining radical liberalism with national self-assertion, this new era became a force that could hardly be underrated in the long run although the governance of Norway was primarily a bureaucratic one ruled by an official class not counterbalanced by other forces as in Denmark. In 1884, however, Norway became the first parliamentary country in Scandinavia when the liberal political party, *Venstre,* directed by its popular leader, Johan Sverdrup (1816–1892), won the general election.[66] The participation in the general election in 1882 that preceded this event was as high as 72 percent. As a confirmation of the political radicalism in Norway, universal suffrage was introduced as early as 1898.

What strikes one when comparing Norway with both Denmark and Sweden during this time is its heterogeneous social, economic, and cultural character. For example, a farmer's situation in southeastern Norway was completely different from a farmer's situation along the west coast or in the north. This heterogeneity was a result of historical, cultural, and above all, geographical reasons. Similar to Sweden, Norway is long and narrow and sparsely populated. Norway's topography, however, with mostly thin strings of settled rural countrysides along the fiords, valleys, and the south, west, and north coasts, make it unique for a European country.

As with Denmark and Sweden, it seems necessary to start analyzing the period in Norway between 1864 and 1914 by examining its rural setting. Unlike Denmark and the southern parts of Sweden, the Norwegian countryside was not dominated by politically influential landowners. Many tenants who were leasing areas owned by the Church had the opportunity to buy property according to a law of 1821. This meant that freeholders owned almost all landed properties in rural areas, as was also the case in the northern part of Sweden. Therefore, there was no correspondence in Norway to the Danish peasant liberation process. While urbanization, combined with the extremely large emigration surges,[67] was common in the southern and middle parts of Norway, especially from 1884 to 1915, these tendencies were not seen in the north.

The urbanization and industrialization processes started later and not as rapidly as in Sweden. Furthermore, these processes were not concentrated only in urban areas as was the case in Denmark. It is true that the population of Oslo increased considerably during this period, and so did many of the other cities and towns, but there was also a parallel growth of new water-powered factories located a bit outside of cities and towns.

In general, Norwegian popular movements had more in common with Swedish movements than with Danish ones. However, activities related to such movements, mainly concentrated in southeast and central Norway, were initiated earlier in Norway than in Sweden.[68] Besides labor unions, the most significant popular movements in Norway consisted of Christian domestic missionary associations, temperance societies, and unlike the Swedish tradition, societies that were concerned with national identity issues.

Until the first years of the 1880s, labor unions were primarily local. Their members, who were primarily craftspeople and skilled workers as in Sweden, were often described as having fairly individual concerns that were too difficult to handle as collective actions.[69] Due to influences from abroad, however, both unions and political parties gradually turned to more national issues. The paternal social conditions that existed in older industries in Norway resembled those in Sweden.[70] However, there are some interesting features that distinguish Norway from Sweden in these respects. First, the Social Democratic Party was established earlier in Norway than in Sweden and dealt with union obligations, which lasted until the Norwegian Confederation of Labor Unions was formed in 1899. Second, while Swedish unions were almost totally demolished after having been defeated in the general strike and lockout in 1909, the Norwegian unions not only persisted but turned out to be considerably radicalized, as was the case with the Norwegian Social Democratic Party.[71] Third, the role of women in Norway as union members seems initially far more prominent than in Sweden. More men emigrated than women. This resulted in a population surplus of women in Oslo and in some other cities, where textile and match factories employed large numbers of female workers.

Some Concluding Remarks

The relatively homogeneous Swedish population and the population's high degree of involvement in local decision making at the end of the nineteenth century are important factors when considering Sweden from a social control perspective. Practical experiences at the local social level concerning decision-making processes, including discipline and meeting records, are essential factors that help to explain why the kind of formal character of the labor union meetings was salient. Furthermore, Sweden was sparsely populated, the urbanization process occurred relatively late, and the rapid industrialization process was linked less to old, crowded city centers in Sweden than in other parts of Europe. All these conditions meant that social class differences did not cause the kind of threats in terms of far reaching social conflicts and disorder that from time to time appeared elsewhere in Europe during this period. These conditions led to a social structure that was less permeated with social pressure than was the case in many other European countries.

The social, political, and cultural conditions in Denmark, Norway, and Sweden and the popular movements that grew out of these conditions are features that distinguish Sweden's popular movements from Denmark and Norway. The formal character of Swedish popular labor movements and the informal character of the Danish popular movements (grundtvigianism) resulted in general in different movements in Denmark at the grass roots level than in Sweden. The Danish popular movements were impossible in the Swedish conservative context and, to a somewhat lesser degree, the fairly provincial, more heterogeneous, and fairly open-minded Norwegian popular movements were also unsuited for Sweden. The question is whether these various elements from about a century ago were forgotten as historical relics, or whether these features still remain. The Danish priest and educator Poul Engberg argues that "harmony, social order, and lawfulness have always been the frame of reference that restrains the Swedish process of change."[72] Engberg concludes that this is the state of affairs because Swedes did not experience historical breakdowns, revolts, and catastrophes, or people such as Grundtvig, who realized that attempts to organize the real spirit of the community could result in major political risk.[73] If Engberg's statement is true, one should not be surprised to find Swedish popular movements of today to be organized in orderly, formal, centralized, and hierarchical ways, irrespective of what issues they are dealing with.

Consistent with Eyerman and Jamison the following conclusion can be made: To exert one's influence on the Swedish public means primarily to represent ideas or interests that have come to light within the scopes of established popular movements. To advocate for specific positions, one must be accepted by the political party system or the prominent formal organizations, or in other words, the establishment. If this is true—even though almost every Swede is a member of a number of organizations of different character, and though organizing abilities are and have been a manifest feature within the Swedish society—[74]the civil conversation tends to be fairly orderly in Sweden without displaying much spontaneity or civil disobedience. These features to a greater extent characterize the Danish public scene and could be at least partly explained by referring to historical conditions.

Notes

This essay uses data from The Research Archives, University of Umeå, Umeå, and The Archives of Popular Movements, Luleå. This research was partially supported by a grant from The Swedish Research Council.

1. Allwood, *Eilert Sundt,* 78–79.

2. Ibid., 79.

3. Ibid.

4. The concept of popular movements means here all kinds of collective actions that are more enduring than spontaneous, temporary mass operations. See for example Therborn, *Europa, det moderna,* 399–400.

5. See especially Ambjörnsson, *Den skötsamme arbetaren,* whose book title in English translation is "The Steady Worker." From documents, Ambjörnsson has studied workers and their leisure activities as they appeared in the first half of the twentieth century in a sawmill community just outside the city of Umeå, in the northern part of Sweden.

6. Ambjörnsson's analyses are consistent with ideas proposed by Elias, *The History of Manners,* vol. 1, although Elias's scope is, from various respects, far broader than

Ambjörnsson's. With respect to his data, Ambjörnsson has been criticized for having overestimated the role of steadiness among workers. See Franzén, "Egensinne och skötsamhet," 3–20.

7. Horgby, *Egensinne och skötsamhet,* 20 (author's trans. into English). Although the nature of this definition of the concept of culture is fairly narrow, it suits the purpose of the forthcoming analyses.

8. Ibid., 21 (author's trans. into English).

9. Ibid., 156 (author's trans. into English).

10. After Frédéric Le Play, and in a French history tradition, industrial relations like these are regarded as tantamount to *patronage.* In modern English usage, they are denoted as *paternalistic* ones. See Brooke, *Le Play,* 29. See also Noiriel, "Du 'patronage' au 'paternalisme,'" for applications of the concept of patronage.

11. See Droste, "Språk och livsform."

12. Carlsson, "Befolkningsutvecklingen från 1800-talets mitt," 28; and *Historisk statistik för Sverige,* 45.

13. See Therborn, "Hur det hela började," 34.

14. However, Swedes rarely knew how to write; it was almost exclusively attributed to individuals in authority positions. See Johansson, "The History of Literacy in Sweden."

15. In western Europe, Sweden was actually one of the last countries to introduce freedom of religion, initiated in 1860.

16. The Swedish Church has afterward often been called a state church but is formally viewed as a public church although until recently in close alliance with the state. The concept *unity church* is presumably the most adequate one for this period. See Martling, *Fädernas kyrka och folkets,* 21–22.

17. *The Lutheran Small Catechism,* in which *The House Table* was a part, was widespread among Swedish households in the nineteenth century.

18. Whether these influences were internalized among the Swedish population, or whether other secular influences replaced *The House Table* during the nineteenth century, is a question that has been debated among Swedish historians. See Harnesk, "Patriarkalism och lönearbete," 326–55; and Pleijel, "Patriarkalismens samhällsideologi," 221–34. For a survey of this debate, see Lindmark, *Uppfostran, undervisning, upplysning,* 151–222.

19. However, the Swedish secularization process had its main roots in rural areas. See ibid.

20. Here, it must be added that Sweden/ Finland was the least urbanized country in Europe at the end of the nineteenth century. In cities and towns, the number of inhabitants seldom exceeded 2000. See Therborn, "Hur det hela började," 27. While the population in Stockholm was about 93,000 in 1850, the third most populated city in Sweden, Norrköping, had only about 17,000 inhabitants. However, the number of people who lived in cities and towns increased from 10 percent to 21.5 percent between 1850 and 1900. *Historisk statistik för Sverige,* 45, 66, 61–65.

21. The aim of the guild system, for example, was primarily to regulate the supply of goods and services. See Åmark, *Facklig makt och fackligt medlemskap,* 22.

22. The Swedish gross national product per capita was rated far lower than countries in western Europe like Great Britain, Belgium, The Netherlands, and Denmark. See Therborn, "Hur det hela började," 26, and sources referred there.

23. Ibid., 28.

24. The Swedish lumber industrialists illustrate this. They were recruited from a fairly small group of mostly wholesale merchants, often with fairly wide international views. From their international experiences they understood how to stabilize an industrial expansion by addressing long-term considerations, that is, by establishing stock corporations and by buying, not always in the most honest of ways, large areas of forests to satisfy their need for raw materials.

25. Ibid., 39.

26. Those engaged in the free church movement were Protestants who belonged to Christian societies that were independent of the state. These societies primarily appeared in Sweden after religious freedom was proclaimed in 1860.

27. Lundkvist, "Folkrörelser och reformer, 1900–1920."

28. Lundkvist has found that regions with strong working-class movements also had strong elements from the other two principal movements. See ibid.; and Cornell, *Sundsvallsdistriktets sågverksarbetare, 1860–1890.*

29. Therborn, "Hur det hela började," 39.

30. Lundkvist, "Folkrörelser och reformer."

31. See Åmark, *Facklig makt,* 18–22, 39–40; and Ekdahl, *Arbete mot kapital,* 13–15.

32. The first Swedish strike of any national significance—spontaneous and with no unions involved–broke out in the Sundsvall area in 1879. About 5,000 sawmill workers walked out due to a 20 percent wage cut. The sawmill owners blamed the wage cut on a temporary recession. In order to end this strike, regional authorities called for military help. Finally, the workers lost, as many as 36 among them were detained, and a large number of the temporary hands became subject to police measures as they were regarded as *defenseless* according to the Vagrancy Act. Interestingly, members of Free Church Societies took an active part in this strike.

33. Åmark, *Facklig makt,* 61–62; Therborn, "Hur det hela började," 40; and Hirdman, *Vi bygger landet,* 62.

34. As was the case in Germany, Austria, and the Netherlands, worker parties and labor unions appeared almost simultaneously. See Therborn, "Hur det hela började," 41.

35. Until then, the most extensive labor market action was a lockout that occurred in 1905 and was initiated by employers. Among all the labor disputes in the year 1908, one-third were lockouts, or lockouts in combination with strikes, that started at the same time. Hirdman, *Vi bygger landet,* 84–86.

36. Kjellberg, *Facklig organisering i tolv länder,* 50, 52.

37. See Glete, *Ägande och industriell omvandling,* 160.

38. Ibid., 181, 199.

39. Ibid., 67–70, 142–45, 164.

40. Owners of preindustrial businesses had little influence on the Swedish industrialization process. Ibid., 79.

41. Ibid., 91, 106, 141, 168.

42. See Therborn, "Hur det hela började," 41; and Therborn, "Socialdemokraterna träder fram."

43. See Åmark, *Facklig makt,* 20.

44. Compared with every other county in north Sweden, and with reference to the various measures utilized to specify strike frequencies, strikes were comparatively frequent among industrial enterprises in the county of Norrbotten. Furthermore, when comparing strike frequencies among the four largest sawmills in the county, with respect to either the number of conflicts or the number of days on strike, the frequency of strikes in Båtskärsnäs was the highest. See *Arbetsstatistik E:1. Arbetsinställelser.*

45. Some of the sawmill owners were still hostile until the end of the 1910s.

46. See Lewis, "Introduction"; Gittins, "Marital Status, Work and Kinship"; Walby, *Patriarchy at Work;* Walby, "From Private to Public Patriarchy," 91–104; Dyhouse, *Feminism and the Family in England,* 3–4; Jackson, "Towards a Historical Sociology of Household," 153–72; and Collins, "Shifting the Center."

47. This strike was the greatest labor union mobilization ever in the world until the 1968 events in France. In fact, one-third of all Swedish workers outside the rural sector were on strike. See Therborn, "Hur det hela började," 45.

48. During the following two years, the number of members in labor unions dropped by half. See Åmark, *Facklig makt,* 20. See also Montgomery, *Industrialismens genombrott i Sverige,* 128.

49. Åmark, *Facklig makt,* 11.

50. The new Swedish labor market era has been called *saltsjöbadsandan* (the Spirit of Saltsjöbaden), a designation pointing to the moment in 1936 when representatives of labor unions and employers sat down in a corporate body to form the negotiation order for the future.

51. Eyerman and Jamison, *Social Movements,* 35

52. Ibid., 67.

53. This part is primarily based on Rerup, *Danmarks historie,* Bind 6. Concerning comparisons with Norway and Sweden, see Norborg and Sjöstedt, *Grannländernas historia.*

54. Lundgreen-Nielsen, ed., *På sporet af dansk identitet,* 12.

55. See for instance Bloch Ravn, "Oprör, spadseregange og lönstrejker i Köbenhavn för 1870"; and Wåhlin, "Opposition og statsmagt."

56. In Sweden this occurred in 1809 and in Norway in 1814.

57. In fact, there were only 400 volunteers recruited from Norway and Sweden.

58. Larsen, *Det levende ord,* 90.

59. Mörch, *Den ny Danmarkshistorie,* 256.

60. This was mainly achieved by Christen Kold (1816–1870) in a number of People's High Schools (*folkehöjskoler*) and led later to similar adult educational activities in the

other Scandinavian countries. See Bergstedt, *Den livsupplysande texten,* 280.

61. A description of fundamental features of the Grundtvigianism is in Engberg, *Grundtvig og det folkelige oprör,* Mörch, *Den ny danmarkshistorie,* 248–61; Larsen, *Det levende ord;* and Reich, *Frederik.*

62. In Denmark, one of these variants was the Inner-Mission *(Indre Mission)* founded in 1861 by the publisher Vilhelm Beck (1829–1901). One Norwegian equivalent was the neoorthodox/Pietist Society of Johnson's Christianian Inner-Mission *(Johnson Christiania Indremissionsforening)* founded in 1855 by a professor of Theology, Gisle Johnsson (1822–1894), who in 1868 also established the Norwegian Luther Foundation *(Den norske Lutherstiftelse).* See Flint, *Historical Role Analysis,* 34–59.

63. For a survey of union and political activities among Danish working-class people during the nineteenth century with a description of their initial problems, see Erichsen, *Om arbejderbevaegelsen,* 50–56.

64. This part is mainly based on a survey of the Norwegian history presented in *Norges historie,* Bind 11–12. Comparisons with Denmark and Sweden are based on Norborg and Sjöstedt, *Grannländernas historia.*

65. Allwood, *Eilert Sundt,* 9.

66. In fact, the Norwegian parliamentary government was established seventeen years before it took form in Denmark and thirty-three years before it was established in Sweden.

67. During the nineteenth century in Europe, only Ireland had a greater emigration rate per capita than Norway. See Flint, *Historical Role Analysis,* 10.

68. Vivid illustrations of union activities in the 1850s can be found in essays by Hvamstad, "Rikt foreiningsliv på Hadeland"; and Grankvist, "Tröndelags-bygderna."

69. For analyses of initial union efforts among carpenters in Bergen, see Ågotnes, *Frå handverkar til lönnsarbeidar?* 164–69.

70. See Furre, *Vårt hundreår,* 25, 63.

71. In 1918, the party proclaimed itself as revolutionary and became a member of the Third Communist International, a membership that lasted until 1923.

72. Author's trans. from the Danish.

73. Engberg, *Grundtvig,* 85–86.

74. See, for example, Therborn, *Europa, det moderna,* 401–3.

CHAPTER 4

Social Control in Belgium: The Catholic Factor

Jan Art

Introduction

During the ancien régime the churches constituted an essential link in the system of social control in almost every western European country. In certain regions the Catholic Church fulfilled this role until far into the twentieth century. This was, for example, the case in Belgium, especially in the Flemish part of the country.[1] Here, not only did the clergy succeed in attuning the legal code to its ethical standards (the law on contraception provides a good example) but it also managed to bring a large part of the population into public conformity at least with religious—and therefore not legally obligatory—codes of behavior. The aim of this essay is to suggest a few reasons for this phenomenon. Our point of departure is the belief that social control has a lot to do with power and enforcing codes of behavior. Therefore, my emphasis will focus on a description of the ways in which the Catholic Church succeeded in obtaining a position of power in Belgian society that allowed it to play a crucial role in the system of social control from the creation of the nation-state in 1830 until the 1960s.

A Tradition of Clerical Supremacy

In 1830 Belgium became independent, but the development of a strong central state was still in its infancy. Many factors contributed to this. The territory had been found on maps consecutively as the "Spanish," the "Catholic," and the "Austrian" Low Countries, then briefly as the *Départements Réunis,* and subsequently as part of the ephemeral "United Kingdom of the Netherlands." For the larger part of its history, Belgium was located on the periphery of the countries to which it belonged.

In addition to this it was the stepping stone between the Roman and the German cultural spheres. It was part of the "blue banana," of the relatively strongly urbanized, trade oriented and rich belt that crossed Western Europe from the south to the north, and of which the population had always been able to maintain a certain degree of autonomy against the centralizing and belligerent dynasties.[2]

Last, but by no means least, the territory was a stronghold of the Counter-Reformation in its battle with the heretic north, east, and west. The Roman Catholic Church had the monopoly *in religiosis* and the temporal powers could hold their ground only to the degree that they were legitimized by that Church—something with which Joseph II, as well as the French occupiers and the Protestant Willem I, had had to contend. This implied that in everyday life the population had to rely on the collaboration between the religious authorities and the local dignitaries for a number of basic services: education, social welfare, care of the sick and orphaned, to name only three. In rural regions, particularly, the clergy was the expressive leader of the local communities. There was no question of any religious disparity or plurality, which would have given the temporal power the opportunity to develop into an autonomous arbitrator, as was the case in the United Republic: the throne simply could not function without the altar. The Belgian constitution of 1830—on its adoption, the most liberal in Continental Europe—was not designed to alter this relationship in the short term. The Belgian state was a "night watchman state," only operating when local and private initiatives failed.[3]

National historiography has emphasized how this was a continuation of the ancestral tradition, but we may add that this arrangement was also convenient for free entrepreneurs and that it guaranteed the tax-paying voters a minimal tax pressure to ensure that the revenues were wisely spent. There was no question of a separation between church and state. The concordat, which stipulated that the state was responsible for the stipend of priests, remained valid. In addition, the initially precarious international situation of the early Belgian state militated against any tension between the worldly and the clerical authorities. According to the liberal Joseph Lebeau in 1841: "*L'union fait la force*" and "*un curé vaut bien dix gendarmes*" ("union yields strength," the motto of the Belgian dynasty, and "one priest is worth ten policemen").[4]

The Continuation of the Old Order, 1830–c.1850

Not only Catholic opinion but also the "king, government and clergy seemed to conspire to increase the Catholic presence . . . through the manipulation of appointments and elections."[5] For the king, "Catholicism stood for the principle of authority and the influence of the Church over society was a warrant for disciplined and obedient subjects." The basic assumption was that society could not do without religion and that, to be effective, churches needed greater independence from the state than eighteenth-century princes had been willing to grant. In short, according to Leopold I: "*La nation belge sera d'autant plus facile à gouverner qu'elle est religieuse*"[6] (the Belgian nation will be all the easier to govern while it is religious). The moderate faction of the Liberals also "held religion to be the central knot in the chain of tradition, 'the bond without which all the others are powerless to unite the members of the social body, ever ready to part.' ... The *centre gauche*, like Guizot in France, considered the Catholic Church as an indispensable ally in his discreet civilising mission" and was "quite willing to leave a large measure of influence to the Church in official institutions of moral relevance such as public education, welfare and the correctional system, provided that the State held the last word. . . . [In the 1840s, they] did not lift one finger against the interpenetration of Church and State in these sectors. Often they actively advanced it . . . [with the] classic example . . . : primary education. . . . Most doctrinaires, and at least some radicals were also not blind to the social issues of the Church of their day in expectation of a broader diffusion of *lumières*."[7]

The clergy took the opportunities for expansion offered by this *liberté comme en Belgique* (Belgian-style freedom) with both hands: new or reestablished orders and congregations shot up like mushrooms. These provided the manpower, in collaboration with the local authorities, for the establishment of a network of educational and welfare institutions.[8] The clergy played a crucial role in electoral conflicts and assured themselves of the kindly disposition of the parliamentary majority until around the middle of the nineteenth century. Moreover, where necessary, they succeeded in restoring and even expanding their grip on broad layers of the population. They were convinced that, in a parliamentary monarchy, whoever had the support of the people would come off best.

Pulpit and Confessional

Missionary work was the ancient and approved method used by the Catholic Church. This preaching movement achieved its greatest success from the 1830s to the 1870s and continued until the 1960s. Its role in maintaining the existing social order cannot be overestimated. The preachers, who visited a parish for about seven to ten days, and returned at least once every ten years, were usually members of orders and congregations that, owing to the Belgian freedom of association after 1830, were thriving again. They propagated an ultramontane variant of *le christianisme de la peur* (the Christianity of fear).[9] In other words they both threatened and comforted at the same time. They preached the legendary and frightening hellfire, but they also stressed that the gates through which one could escape hell were wide open. There was a reconfirmation of rules that could never be followed to the letter, and of the punishments that awaited transgressors now and in the hereafter. But, at the same time, the ways to find redemption were shown, via the sacraments offered by nonrigorous confessors, and by joining a pious society. Most of the preaching campaigns were followed by the foundation or reestablishment of a pious brotherhood, often specified in terms of sex, age, or civil status. At the same time, all social life that had not been approved by the clergy was systematically obstructed.[10]

The whole enterprise proved very successful; only some traditionally less religious parishes, principally located in the southern part of the country, showed some reluctance. The reasons for this success are easy to find. Because of the upheavals in the past decades, many communities had been thrown off balance and wanted to put matters in order; they wanted to get rid of the past. The confessional was often about very concrete matters: the problem of marrying next of kin and of the restitution of church goods bought during the French period was dealt with in the confessional box. The belief in God's punishments continued to be strongly held. At first the threat of war was very real; then, in the 1840s, there was famine in rural areas, and far into the nineteenth century all kinds of epidemics swept through the country. People who did not share the enthusiasm of the majority ran the risk of becoming the scapegoat of natural disasters. Fear of bringing down the community's wrath on oneself by deviant behavior played a significant role in these relatively small communities. The exhortations of the priests to accept one's fate and one's situation in life, and to secure oneself a place in heaven through an obedient way of life, were taken to heart to such a degree that one witness did not hesitate to ascribe Belgium's having been spared any serious upheaval in 1848 to the order confirming influence of the missionary movement.[11]

A comparison with Methodism and other revival movements, which arose around the same period in countries with a Protestant dominance, allows us to point out the specificity of the Catholic missionary movement.[12] John Wesley partly owed his success to the fact that he literally preached from outside the church and anticipated the wishes of a population confused by the beginnings of industrialization. Moreover, he encouraged personal conversion, individual responsibility, and therefore self-respect. By "dissenting" one distinguished oneself from the "others" and put oneself at a distance from the dominant elite that was strongly linked with the state church.

The aim of the Catholic missionary movement was first a restoration and reintegration, and this was supported by the traditional elite. The emphasis was on the restoration of the community. Whether one belonged to those who were saved could not be deduced from following a good life but could only be discovered in the hereafter—in the meantime one could only hope that confession would put one back on the right track. Having social ambitions was to be frowned upon; only those with a vocation for the priesthood were able to break loose from the obligations associated with the social class into which they had been born. Over a longer period we can point out the possible importance of abandoning the practice of so-called rigorous confession. Followers of the civilization theory have correctly drawn attention to the fact that the Reformation, as well as the Counter-Reformation, enhanced the notion of sin, and consequently also the population's self-control. Every believer had to account for his actions, the Puritan often by keeping a diary, the Catholic to his increasingly severe confessor.[13]

From this point of view the introduction, from the beginning of the nineteenth century, of the nonrigorist moral theology meant a breach of the trend. "After 1830, the Jesuits played a leading role, together with the Redemptorists, in converting the secular clergy to greater moral flexibility. Missions demonstrated what Liguori's adage 'lion in the pulpit, lamb in the confessional' could achieve. By midcentury, *souplesse* on the part of the confessor had become the norm, involving pragmatism about some offences (like dancing or theatre-going) and discretion about others (notably regarding sex in marriage). . . . In 1868, the papal nuncio considered 'the tremendous condescension' of confessors to be a general shortcoming of the Belgian clergy."[14] From then on frequent reception of the sacraments of confession and Holy Communion was propagated, a tendency that continued into the beginning of the twentieth century through papal decrees on frequent communion and early communion. In the period between the two World Wars, this led to the foundation of organizations such as the Societies of the Sacred Heart, the members of which were obliged to receive the sacraments at least once a month. Contemporary observers were well aware that this practice turned confession into a routine (or *Veralltäglichung*) that led to a decreasing awareness of sin, and this was an evil to which the Catholic Action reacted.[15]

The widespread notion of the past two centuries that Catholics have a lower concept of standards than Protestants might be explained by this important change in the perception of the Catholic sacraments.[16] However, the confession was one of the major channels through which the clergy could influence behavior before the Second Vatican Council.[17] We should have no illusions about people's behavior in private, but "sinning" in public, such as unmarried couples living together, was virtually impossible in small communities. Stressing the rules, while leaving open the possibility of absolution, and fighting public scandal gave rise to a very specific Catholic guilt management, and this can be very enlightening for the study of social control.

Primary Education

In 1842 a law on primary education was passed. The episcopate had every reason for rejoicing. Religion was now part of the curriculum, and the clergy could de facto supervise the teachers, who—in most cases—held a diploma from a Catholic normal school. One cannot underestimate the importance of the daily catechism education (because that was what religion came down to in the schools). Year after year, as a preparation for their first communion and confirmation, the pupils were expected to learn the answers to the catechism questions by heart. If and how they understood the catechism remains an open question, but it is clear that it offered them a vocabulary in which certain relations, self-images, tales of origin, and so forth were articulated and introduced into their daily lives. Original sin, hell and damnation, heaven and mercy, sin and forgiveness were parts of the stories by which young people situated themselves in the world. For a long time, these were the only stories at hand, because dissemination of literacy was very gradual and access to the written word was controlled by the Church. In short, through education the Church had a firm grip on what could be said and thought, and consequently on what was necessary for an individual to determine his or her attitude to and way of life. Loss of that control and the pluralization of discourses—which for many groups in Flanders happened only after the Second World War—is, perhaps, one of the causes of secularization, and one that, up until now, has been underestimated.

Summarizing, we may posit that between 1830 and about 1850 the Catholic Church succeeded in restoring and even expanding its ancient key position in the social control system within Belgium. This was also possible because, as a result of a lack in state initiative, the Church was able to acquire a quasi-monopoly in central social areas such as education and welfare, and it therefore possessed the real monopoly in religiosity.

Growing Polarization, Increasing Control, 1850–1950[18]

From the second half of the nineteenth century, the clerical hierarchy began to be challenged by several competitors. Until 1884 there were the laical Liberal governments; in the fin-de-siècle period, until after the First World War, there was the threat of a Socialist coup; and during the interwar years, there were divisions in the Catholic camp itself and nationalist, extreme right-wing movements. These competitors can be considered incarnations of the major political problems with which many young states are confronted.[19] The Liberals tried to develop a strong and autonomous laical state; the Socialists trumpeted the demands for better distributive justice and a voice in government; and between the two world wars, the Belgian state was confronted by problems of nation building. This phrasing of the period accentuates the political aspects of the modernizing process, and the clerical hierarchy perceived the problems of modernization in political terms. The clerical hierarchy was convinced that it could only fulfill its pastoral tasks if it could count on the collaboration of worldly powers. Its first priority was to maintain, or to bring back to power, a Catholic majority. As the right to vote was expanded (in 1848, 1893, 1918, and 1949) more, and larger, groups had to be controlled, and in the election battles the clergy was forced to use the same weapons as its opponents. In a nutshell this is the logic behind what was later called *verzuiling* (social compartmentalization): the development of an ever bigger and better organized form of Catholicism that gave its followers the opportunity to follow a Catholic way of life, and consequently also a Catholic way in the voting booth.

The foundations of this compartmentalization were laid in the period of the Liberal cabinets (1850–1884). As the regime tended to support clerical initiatives less and less, so the clergy was forced to call upon rich noblemen and citizens for the development of its infrastructure. The key association in this period was the society of St. Vincentius a Paulo, a charitable paternalistic organization in which rich taxpaying voters and militant Catholic laymen met for the purpose of helping the poor. (*Dieu comme but, les pauvres comme moyen*—God as the goal, the poor as the means). Almost every important community had such an association, or "conference," of like-minded people, and they soon began to occupy themselves with matters other than mere welfare initiatives. Support for the pope, youth care, the provision of books, education, and the press all came to be included in their area of activities; and often the members of the conference also met in the new Catholic electoral associations.[20] A succession of conflicts between the Liberal state government and the clerical hierarchy resulted in the clerical–anticlerical division coloring the whole of public life. Within a short period there were almost no apolitical societies left: either one was Catholic, behaved like a good Catholic, and was then supported by, for example, the followers of St Vincent, or one should beg from the Liberals. This polarization was especially apparent during the conflict over schools, which raged from 1879 to 1884, and when, even in the smallest village, parents were forced to choose between an "official" or "neutral" school, and a Catholic one.[21]

In 1884 the Catholic party won the battle for the taxpaying voter. The Liberal education legislation was slowly dismantled. However, the agricultural sector was moving through a deep crisis, and in 1886 bloody riots occurred in Wallonia between laborers and the police. Socialist leaders offered the authorities a choice: an extension of the franchise or a revolution. A revision of the franchise seemed inevitable, and it was brought to fruition in the beginning of the nineties. But the Catholic majority still managed to maintain itself, and this was due principally to the clergy's success in the field of social work. In the years preceding the first election under the new system (general multiple voting rights for men), the bishops urged parish priests to establish all kinds of social services: cooperatives, insurance funds, labor unions, in short, everything that could improve the material existence of the population, whether they were entitled to vote or not. Radical Liberals and Socialists had already established similar practices in the cities.[22] The Catholic government followed the principle of *liberté subsidiée* (subsidized liberty) by which the state restricted itself to creating social legislation and left it to the various social compartments to carry out.

This policy led to a unique Belgian situation: Services, which in most other countries were undertaken by the state, were carried out by private organizations with community funds. The underlying strategy is not difficult to understand. Catholic opinion was not favorable to a strong state, since it might turn against the Church if it fell into the hands of the wrong party. It was therefore considered much better to use state funds to expand further the Catholic network established in the period of the Liberal governments, thus securing the advances that had been made in certain fields, clawing back territory lost in others.[23] This strategy met with considerable success. Indeed, until 1999 the Catholic Party was almost always included in government, and at the time of writing a majority of the Flemish has attended a Catholic school, or has belonged to a Catholic union or health insurance scheme.

This evidence bears out Jacques Van Doorn's conclusion, put forward in 1956, that social compartmentalization implied a sharpening of social control. The gradual, but ultimately almost total, politicizing of social life has meant that the ordinary Belgian has had to make a "colored" choice in every aspect of life, and he has to profile himself as belonging to a certain faction. In the 1950s, during the second conflict over schools, a Catholic was even advised against using a certain brand of chocolate.[24] An aspect that has been less highlighted, but which has been just as real as the emancipating, safeguarding, and even modernizing qualities attributed to social compartmentalization, is that the latter made conformity to certain codes of behavior increasingly easy to enforce. Before 1850 the Church could only threaten with God's punishment: pestilence and cholera in this life, hell and damnation in the hereafter—the reality of the former increased the credibility of the latter. At the same time the Church appeared to be the only organization capable of mobilizing the staff required for dissemination of literacy and health care for the less fortunate, services that the state was willing to provide only in a very limited way. In the rural areas it was hard to find any nonreligious individuals or public sinners; and if there were some in the cities, it was a consequence of the failing clerical infrastructure rather than the result of a free choice by those involved. A century later the threat of God's punishment weighed less heavily, despite the fact that the clergy kept representing both world wars as expressions of God's wrath on people's misbehavior. At the same time, however, social services and, not least, the creation of jobs, remained good reasons for staying in the Catholic camp.

Social compartmentalization has ensured that in Flanders the major part of the nonprofit or social-profit segment within the tertiary sector remained in Catholic hands. This meant that access to large parts of the labor market was made dependent on conformity to certain standards of behavior. Until very recently in Catholic schools, divorce meant immediate resignation for teachers. Nor was this situation confined to the nonprofit sector. In the days of census suffrage, leaseholders ran the risk of losing their businesses if they did not vote for the right candidate. Preachers pleaded for the foundation of Catholic factories in their parish, in which Catholic bosses would employ Catholic workers. One might question the reasoning here once the workers had become members of labor unions, especially since the Belgian labor force became one of the most unionized in the world. A further consequence was that appointments in the civil service were also politically colored, even at the lowest level; and a "scientific" explanation has even been offered for this practice, namely that a bureaucracy should reflect the people's political opinion in the same way as legislation.

From this perspective the process of secularization, considered a growing public deviation from the Church's code of behavior, can be summarized in a very simple formula: The Church no longer has the means to enforce this conformity. And the same formula might be expressed as follows: Subjectively, the earlier conformity may not have been so much experienced as enforced, though objectively there was simply no alternative for large parts of the population.

This is not the place to relate fully the story of how the Church lost this power. However, to focus on the example of the creation of jobs: After the First World War the Catholic party could remain in power only by forming coalition governments. In practice this meant that the party was unable to keep the policy of compartmentalized job creation in its own hands, that there had to be room for others. In 2000, of the ten million inhabitants of Belgium, 900 thousand were employed by the government. The increasing importance of the tertiary sector in society brought this sector face to face with the logic of the market, so that the confessional characteristics of the compartmentalized organizations gradually disappeared. The autonomy of the compartmentalized segments was strengthened by a massive decline in the number of priests, with the declericalization of personnel as a consequence.[25]

A Few Comparisons

Does the chosen perspective help us to explain the differences between Flanders and Wallonia, and between Belgium and Holland? The Catholic element in Wallonia has never been as strong as it was in Flanders, and many Walloons have therefore lost their religion. While there may have been some reasons for this in the ancien régime, this phenomenon probably has most to do with the early industrialization of large parts of the Walloon region; it was the first region of Continental Europe to experience major industrialization. The Catholic elite and the Liberal employers could only offer a restricted, charitable, paternalistic response to the miserable conditions of the workers. When the Christian Democratic movement began to develop at the end of the nineteenth century, the terrain had already been occupied by the strong anticlerical socialist movement. It was the socialists who would subsequently succeed in translating support, first on a local and later on a national level, into political power.[26] In Flanders, which had remained a rural area for much longer, Christian Democracy arrived just in time to curb socialism. At the beginning of the twentieth century, when the mines in Limburg opened, the Church was ready to keep the loyalty of the miners.[27]

As long as the parties remained organized on a national level, the Socialist supremacy in the southern part of the country ensured that the Flemish Socialists did not become a minority. And, vice versa, the Flemish Catholics guaranteed the protection of the rights of their Walloon partners. From the 1960s, however, when the country and the parties were federalized, these counterweights disappeared and both parties became dominant in their respective areas. In this period Wallonia also witnessed the downfall of its traditional heavy industry, and this left the government as one of the most, if not the most, important employer. Flanders, on the other hand, was able to link up with the third industrial revolution. It became the economic center of gravity of the kingdom, with all the consequences in terms of an increase in welfare provision, differentiation, and a relative decrease of the social compartments' share in the labor market—in 2000, 25 percent of the population remained in state services. In the south the Church had never played such a strong controlling role as in the north, since politically speaking its presence was not as strong and the social compartmentalization strategy worked to the advantage of its opponent. The consequence of the economic recession in Wallonia was that the role of the dominant compartment as a provider of jobs remained; in 2000, 40 percent were in state services.

Compared to the Netherlands, Flemish public life remained very compartmentalized. Although secularization and autonomy found their way into the Flemish compartment organizations themselves, the outside labels for workers unions, health insurance, and even parties remained divided into Christian, Socialist, or Liberal.[28] This suggests that the social compartmentalization strategy has a different result, depending on whether it is applied in a country with a predominantly Protestant tradition, or in one with a significant Counter Reformation past.

Together with other authors[29] I am convinced that confessional differences help to explain differences in political culture. In Protestant countries the worldly powers found it easier to emancipate from religious power than in Catholic countries, and the civil service could more easily be accepted as an autonomous arbitrator in worldly matters. In addition, the Protestant tradition may have contributed to the relatively peaceful nature of the revolutions at the end of the eighteenth century. The installation of a modern regime did not necessarily imply a break with the past, and the polarization between old and religious, and new and secular, was never as sharp as in countries with a Catholic past. Moreover, the Protestant emphasis on freedom of conscience and self control advanced the formation of attitudes other than those inspired by the Catholic perspective, such as the theory that lies have no rights, the possibility of the forgiveness of sins, the principle of immanence, the *compelle intrare,* and so forth.[30]

If one looks at the Flemish–Dutch differences as outlined above, it is understandable that social compartmentalization was able to penetrate deeper into the Belgian state system. The irreconcilability between the two opposing parties lasted much longer. Dutch Catholicism attacked the compartmentalization strategy from a minority position. There, social compartmentalization tried to emancipate the Catholic part of the population and to integrate it in a social life dominated by Protestant culture. Once this goal had been reached, the compartmentalized organization lost its meaning, and all parties agreed to abandon it. Belgian Catholicism started out from a centuries' old monopoly position. The aim of social compartmentalization was to reestablish and maintain this ancient dominance and to arrive at a modern version of coexistence between throne and altar. In this way it fell back on an ancient clerical-pastoral theory, and the political cultural tradition that followed from it, in which the authority of the state always came second. These ancient roots help to explain why social compartmentalization organizations were able to maintain themselves in a secularized world, albeit under the flag of the intermediary field (in between civilians and the state), and why they often formed a front against the state.

All of this leads to an important, but nonhistorical question. Within Belgian political culture, church and state have always been considered complementary; the clerical standard was followed for a considerable period of time. But the weakening of clerical authority in Belgian public life, the fact that compartmentalization organizations continue to exist autonomously, and the fact that central government remains relatively weak, raises the problem—who, in the future, will perform the functions of social control that the Church used to fulfill?

Notes

1. A good English introduction to Belgian history is Witte et al., *Political History of Belgium,* although its bibliography was only published in the Dutch version (*Politieke geschiedenis van België,* 445–64). Boudart et al., eds., *Modern Belgium,* does not give references either. Kossmann's not so recent work (1978) *The Low Countries, 1780–1840* does include a selective bibliography, as does the more general Blom and Lamberts, *History of the Low Countries.* Recently, an important work on the political-religious history has been published: Viaene, *Belgium and the Holy See.* It includes most

of the Dutch literature on the period 1830–1860. Strikwerda, *A House Divided,* offers an interesting interpretation of the second half of the century. See also Els Witte, "The Battle for Monasteries, Cemeteries and Schools: Belgium." In *Culture Wars: Secular-Catholic Conflict in Nineteenth-Century Europe,* edited by Christopher Clark and Wolfram Kaiser, 102–28. New York: Cambridge University Press, 2003. The twentieth century is dealt with in great depth in the—often English—publications of religion sociologist Karel Dobbelaere (for his bibliography see Laermans et al., eds., *Secularization,* 321–38). For the Belgian case in an international context, see Mcleod, *Religion and the People.*

2. Lucassen and Davids, eds., *A Miracle Mirrored.*

3. Art, "Pourquoi la christianisation de la Flandre a-t-elle si bien réussi?" 511–20; Viaene, *Belgium and the Holy See,* 25–36.

4. Ibid., 130.

5. Ibid., 114.

6. Ibid., 150–51.

7. Ibid., 119, 121, 122, 130.

8. Art, "The Historiography of Male Members," KADOC—Studies on Religion, Culture, and Society. Leuven University Press: forthcoming (2004).

9. Delumeau, *La peur.*

10. Viaene, *Belgium and the Holy See,* 168–202.

11. Art, *Kerkelijke structuur,* 217. The situation in French-speaking Canada was rather similar. See Hardy, *Contrôle social.*

12. Mcleod, *Religion.*

13. Hahn and Willems, "Schuld und Bekenntnis," 309–30; Delumeau, *Le péché;* Delumeau, *L'aveu.*

14. Viaene, *Belgium and the Holy See,* 190; see also 198, 210.

15. Verbeke, "De biecht als sociale controle"; Art, "Het religieuze leven van de leken," 413–35; Gabriels, *De Bonden van het Heilig Hart;* Laermans, "Roman Catholicism and the 'Methodical Conduct of Life,'" 87–92.

16. Bird, "How Do Religions Affect Moralities?" 291–314; Carroll, *Guilt.*

17. Boutry, *Prêtres,* 377–451: "Au coeur de la vie religieuse: la confession."

18. What follows is a personal interpretation of one hundred years of Belgian history: the authors cited at the end of this article corroborate the facts I mention but do not always have the same view as I and often emphasize other aspects.

19. Almond and Powell, *Comparative Politics.*

20. De Maeyer and Wynants, eds., *De Vincentianen.*

21. Billiet, ed., *Tussen bescherming en verovering;* Lamberts, ed., *De kruistocht.*

22. Strikwerda, *A House Divided.*

23. Lamberts, ed., *Een kantelend tijdperk.*

24. Haagdorens, "De mobilisatie," 3–70; Tyssens, *De Schoolkwestie.*

25. See the publications of K. Dobbelaere in Laermans et al., eds., *Secularization,* 321–28.

26. Voye, *Sociologie du geste religieux;* Seiler, *Le déclin du cléricalisme.*

27. Vints, *Broekx.*

28. Art, "Religie en secularisering," 95–114.

29. That is, Martin, "Religion and Public Values," 313–31.

30. Bird, "How Do Religions Affect Moralities."

CHAPTER 5

Priceless Children? Penitentiary Congresses Debating Childhood: A Quest for Social Order in Europe, 1846–1895

CHRIS G. T. M. LEONARDS

In the late spring of 1848, Willem Hendrik Suringar, chairman of the Dutch Prison Society, was very uneasy and concerned about the upheaval in several European cities, notably in Mannheim and Paris, but even in Amsterdam where, as he put it, "released prisoners could play a pernicious role and could threaten and endanger the tranquility, possessions, health,—yes the very lives of many in municipality or town." Also in France, where there were allegedly between thirty and forty thousand released prisoners, it was most likely that large numbers of them were present at the outbreak of the Paris upheaval and "that they, assisted by wives, concubines and children, have formed a strong army that, *having nothing to lose,* had no thought of respect or fear whatsoever."[1]

It is striking that the Dutch chairman, at such an early date, in the strictly national setting of the annual meeting of the *Nederlands Genootschap tot Zedelijke Verbetering der Gevangenen* (Dutch Society for Moral Improvement of Prisoners), took this rather international view of the problem of delinquency. But at second glance, it is quite understandable that he was genuinely impressed by what he had heard and experienced at the conferences he had visited in recent years in Frankfurt am Main and Brussels where he had been received by fellow philanthropists to debate matters of prison organization and aftercare with renowned discussants like Édouard Ducpétiaux from Belgium, William Crawford from Britain, Karl Josef Anton Mittermaier from Germany, and Louis-Mathurin Moreau-Christophe from France.[2] Of course these forerunners in the field of philanthropy, social policy, penal theory, and practice were not unaware of what was going on in the streets, and they shared with him their fears, hopes, expectations, and intentions on the specter that seemed to be haunting Europe.[3]

To avoid—in Stanley Cohen's words—the use of social control as a Mickey Mouse concept, it should be made clear how it will be used in this contribution. It will surely not be used in such broad fashion as to cover "all social processes inducing some kind of conformity." Because crime control is our main focus here, we will try to stick to Cohen's not too narrow definition of social control implying "the organized ways in which society responds to behavior and people it regards as deviant, problematic, worrying, threatening, troublesome or undesirable in some way or another."[4] Nevertheless, it needs to be made quite clear that the boundaries between what is a strictly coercive kind of control and what is a more or less associative control are sometimes blurred or uncertain and also subjected to changes in the course of time.[5] What for instance in the first decades of the nineteenth century started as a strictly coercive endeavor—*prisons* for children— may, as *reformatories,* have become at the end of that same century of a totally different nature, in which associative aspects can be ascertained. In fact, I think, the very discussions at the penitentiary congresses that are under investigation here were all about finding out where the boundaries of social control were and where they actually should be. Whereas containment or banishment of crime remained the final goal of all actions, ideas on measures to be taken ranged from repressive to proactive, from "simple"" enforcement to "refined"" socialization. The problem of social order, in fact, in the sense of Durkheim's sociology, was the collective theme of discussions at the various congresses.

In this essay, I will focus on the ways in which care and aftercare for criminal children were conceptualized and put into practice in various parts of Europe. These new social technologies, whether they involved special residential care for juveniles or aftercare for released minors, originated at the so-called International Penitentiary Congresses that took place in major European cities in the second half of the nineteenth century and were then presented as innovative and original in separate European countries. In this field of endeavor, the first half of the century can be seen as the era of philanthropic tourism in which social and moral entrepreneurs visited each other and their loci of interest all over Europe.[6] In the second half of the century, they more and more gathered together at international congresses, which gradually became battlefields of governmental and nongovernmental agencies, of public and private enterprise, in the realm of social order and welfare—international markets for ideas and reported practices on aspects of social order. In the end these formal congresses not only acted as a center for information and debate for visitors but also grew in importance as authoritative institutions in their own right, strongly influencing national decision making.

I will follow discussions and decision making at the penitentiary congresses on the question of the treatment of juveniles leading to a shift of action from hard core criminal children ("dangerous children"), to the much broader and opaque category of endangered children ("children in danger"), to the discovery of the "innocent criminal child."[7] I will do so by first touching upon the history of Western ideas on childhood and children, then by describing the general scope of the congresses. Next, I will elaborate on some discussions on juveniles at the congresses in the 1850s and the 1870s through 1890s. After this, I will compare these supranational thoughts and resolutions with actual social policies and technologies at the national level. With the Dutch case—notably residential institutions for male juveniles—as an empirical point of reference, I will finally conclude by making some comparisons with national developments in other European countries.

The Debate on Childhood

In his essay "Authority and the Family," the late Christopher Lash argues that the democratization of the Enlightenment and civilization by his famous "forces of organized virtue" during the eighteenth and nineteenth centuries should be seen as part of the overall endeavor of the bourgeoisie to create uniformity as a condition for the development of industrial capitalism.[8] This rather functionalist, teleological approach turned out to be too monolithic and has been rightly amended in several respects. Nevertheless, it once in a while seems to pop up again, for instance to explain the debate on childhood that rose in European countries, especially during the second part of the nineteenth century and the first decades of the twentieth century. Hugh Cunningham, however, argues that besides this care for the future manpower needs of the state and the usual concern for children's souls, this period stands out in the European history of childhood because of a new reason for philanthropic concern with children: to "save them for the enjoyment of childhood."[9] From the 1830s on, first drawing on utilitarian views of the damage sometimes done to children's physical well-being but soon revived by sentimentalist and romantic ideas on the benefits of a good childhood, philanthropists started spending a large part of their efforts especially on children, in order to achieve their general humanitarian goals. These children supposedly represented the future, and their nature was still "plastic." A romantic view of childhood as properly dependent and protected, and as separate from adulthood, had become dominant and provided a motivating reference point for every philanthropist from the first half of the nineteenth century onward. Even criminal children seemed to be priceless! Of course not only privately organized agencies were involved, but—again in accordance with Cunningham's views—governmental influence in this field of juvenile action had slackened in most European countries after 1750, not to gain new momentum before the last quarter of the nineteenth century, especially with the general implementation of compulsory schooling.

The nineteenth-century debate on childhood had two especially major topics:

Children and their work were of first concern, but also the problem of vagrant, begging, and criminal children was very much at stake. In spite of the common bourgeois view that children were to be raised in the family, solutions for criminal children were usually based on old methods (e.g., residential institutions for orphans, such as prisons, reformatories, colonies, or refuges). In some of the so-called agrarian colonies only, a block or cottage system was implemented, which more or less mimicked a family. Foster families, although they would have been a logical outgrowth of the idea of wet-nursing schemes for foundlings in former centuries, were not used for criminal children on a wide scale. However, children in urban reformatories were sometimes put out to artisans, or adopted by a benefactor as a substitute parent upon leaving the institution.

According to Abram de Swaan "humanitarian sensitivity" has been gradually replaced since the middle of the nineteenth century by "social awareness": a notion of interdependency and a feeling of responsibility for all kinds of social phenomena, from health care to education, coupled with the conviction that these are a concern for the state.[10] In my view, these phenomena include the correction of delinquent children. This rise of the state and of state intervention in public life may have been especially obvious in the development of compulsory schooling, but it has also been highly important in the penitentiary field. Professionalization of the experts involved and funding by central governments have indeed resulted in state-sponsored public care for dangerous and endangered children since the end of the nineteenth century.[11]

The Penitentiary Congresses

European integration and communication are not just recent phenomena in a globalizing world. One can be quite astonished to note the busy traffic and long absences from home involved in the many travels members of the bourgeois classes made to visit friends and acquaintances all over the Continent and abroad. Gradually, mutual visits were expanded into common gatherings. In the fields of prison reform, penal law, juvenile care, and questions of welfare in general, several truly international gatherings, conferences, and congresses took place from 1846 onward in the major European cities.[12] These congresses acted as nodes in a network of philanthropists, prison directors and inspectors, lawyers, government officials and delegates, architects, and other "moral entrepreneurs" from European and even American states.[13] It is noteworthy that the congresses' initial focus sometimes was very broad, not to say blurred. One of their prime features is the growth of scientific specialization in the course of the century.[14] The Frankfurt Welfare Congress of 1857, for instance, had a special section on penitentiary issues and was attended by much the same category of visitors as the preceding Brussels Penitentiary Congress of 1847 and the *Congrès international de Bienfaisance* of 1856, both organized by E. Ducpétiaux in his dual function as general inspector of Belgian prisons and welfare institutions.[15]

Penitentiary congresses developed from casual, nonobligatory debating conventions in the 1850s into large-scale, trend-setting congresses after formal organization in the 1870s. Because of this evolution, their proceedings—on which I base this research—varied considerably in the course of the nineteenth century. They gained both in substance and in length, but there were also certain characteristics that remained constant: in many cases a day order or agenda for the congress was given, followed by a transcript or literary account of the discussions during the congress. Usually conclusions, resolutions, or answers to the questions stated in the day order followed the discussions. Often, it was mentioned whether resolutions had been passed by majority or unanimous votes.[16]

The way in which the agendas were put together was subject to change over time as well. The day orders in the 1850s were usually concocted by the congress's organizer (e.g., Johann Georg Varrentrapp at the first gathering in Frankfurt am Main and Édouard Ducpétiaux at the second Brussels session) more or less in concordance with the prospective visitors. In the 1870s the agenda was formally put together by a special committee, officially set up by a congressional board, after consultation with several experts in certain penitentiary fields.[17] Moreover, congresses sometimes decided to put an unresolved topic on the next congress's

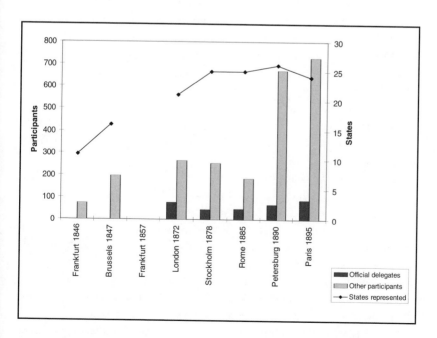

Figure 1 Participants and States at the Penitentiary Congresses, 1846–1895

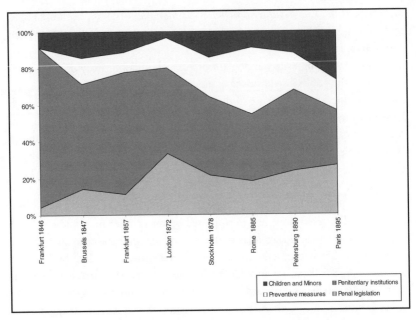

Figure 2 Questions Posed at the Penitentiary Congresses, 1846–1895

agenda. Deliberations of the congresses took resolutions or answers to questions as a result. These, together with deliberations, were printed and published. These proceedings must have been circulated on a rather wide scale.[18] This was an important feature, especially of the first congresses, because they had no official status. Their only means of "spreading the news" was by publishing proceedings and reports in national organizations, giving lectures, writing in newspapers, and so forth. This is a major reason why from the very beginning official government representatives were explicitly invited to the congresses: This would prove to be a direct, more efficient way to put the ideas forward before decisions to implement them were to be made.[19] As can be seen in figure 1, this could not be effectuated until the London congress of 1872.

The scope of the congresses shifted considerably over time. Until the Paris convention of 1895, all topics were summarized in three sections, namely, Penal Legislation, Penitentiary Institutions, and Preventive Measures; thereafter a fourth section on Children and Minors was formed. This in itself is an indicator of the growing importance of the childhood debate, resulting in many measures for children taken all over Europe by the end of the century. As can be seen in figure 2, the relative importance of questions on penal legislation and penitentiary institutions diminished over time, while the subjects of preventive measures and children and minors gained in relative weight, especially after the London congress of 1872.[20] Matters concerning juveniles and minors came to the fore in almost every discussion about crime and crime prevention and were listed on the agendas of all conference sessions, with a steady gain in the course of the century and a sudden, steep rise at the Paris congress of 1895.

As a next step I will trace these discussions for two periods in the course of the nineteenth century: in the mid-1840s (i.e., the 1846 and 1847 congresses in Frankfurt and Brussels) and after 1870 (notably the 1872 congress of London, and the Paris congress of 1895), thus giving an idea of long term developments.

Discourses on Children at the Congresses

At Frankfurt and Brussels, in 1846 and 1847, solitary confinement generally was seen as the best type of confinement for all adult prisoners.[21] Although communications on aftercare societies and asylums for young delinquents had been put on the official agenda of the seventy-four delegates in Frankfurt, discussions on how solitary confinement had to be implemented in general had taken up all the time allotted at the congress.[22] As can be derived from the transcript of the discussions, the chairman of the Dutch Prison Society, W. H. Suringar, played an all-important role as opinion leader at this gathering. After a remarkable change of mind a few years before, he had become a zealous advocate of the system of solitary confinement, a "cellomaniac" in the words of his Dutch opponents.[23]

At the 1847 convention in Brussels, patronage or aftercare was once again proposed as an indispensable completion of penitentiary reform, and the total or partial application of solitary confinement for young delinquents was explicitly discussed as well. It was decided in the congress's list of resolutions that for young delinquents special houses of correctional education had to be erected in which a combined regime of solitary confinement and outplacement in agrarian colonies or apprenticeships with farmers, artisans, or industrialists had to be maintained. From this resolution one could conclude that solitary confinement was but one of several means to ameliorate juveniles, but on closer inspection of the proceedings an almost nasty battle took place between cellomaniacs, under severe command by W. H. Suringar, and "agrarian colonists," led not by Fréderic-August Demetz, famous director of the Mettray colony, as one would expect, but by a relative outsider, Louis Wolowski, who consequently referred to the solitary cell as a "chemise de pierre."[24]

It was Marie Matthieu Von Baumhauer, a recent Dutch admirer of Suringar, who had been able to rescue the cause of the solitary confinement of young delinquents by persuading the congress participants to restrict their deliberations to the group of juvenile delinquents who were above the age of legal responsibility. The younger group, the "innocent" children, for which perhaps other measures had to be taken, would have to be on the agenda of another session.[25] It seems that all arguments were allowed to forward one's case. One of the most questionable ways of gaining votes for the cause of solitary confinement was Suringar's confidential remark to the plenum of the congress that Elizabeth Fry had entrusted him that she in the end truly believed in solitary confinement, even for women. Thereupon, Lord Pearson declared that he had read a letter from Fry to Alphonse M. M. T. Bérenger, written some moments before she died, in which she—to the contrary—rejected solitary confinement. This comedy was concluded by the Dutchman Jean Etienne Mollet who "confessed" that he and Fry had spent a whole day together, some six weeks before her death *when she was still in good health,* talking about prison systems. Having explained to her that solitary confinement would not mean total solitude, but—quite to the contrary—a regular communication with the prisoner, she supposedly had approved with all her heart.[26]

At these early penitentiary congresses, "patronage" or aftercare was usually discussed as an annex to the general program. During the 1846 conference in Frankfurt—although explicitly on the agenda[27]—discussions on aftercare were postponed to the Brussels meeting of 1847, because visitors were absorbed by discussions on solitary confinement in the second penitentiary institutions section. Nevertheless, in between one-liners on solitary confinement, one can come across the statement that "the foundation of care for released prisoners is a necessary completion of penitentiary Reform."[28] But even in Brussels only a few official remarks on aftercare were made, because most of the time was taken by discussions to secure solitary confinement for some of the criminal juveniles. Nevertheless, aftercare—institutional or otherwise—was in the air, as can be concluded from the many accounts of aftercare, patronage societies, and other experiments that were submitted to the congress's organizing committee, of which agrarian colonies and *maisons de refuge,* as the institutional parts of patronage, were perhaps the most popular for the time being. At the Brussels congress considerable pressure was felt from advocates of these prison extensions. They included the famous Elisabeth Fry (posthumously), and the Frenchmen Louis Wolowski, Léon Faucher, and Frédéric Auguste Demetz, the latter cofounder of the *Société de Patronage des jeunes détenus et des jeunes libérés de la Seine,* whose fame had reached the congress. Experiments with *maisons de refuge* for released women, by De Barolière in Lyon and Alphonse De Lamartine in Paris were known at the time.[29]

Twenty-five years later, at the London congress in 1872, the need for reformatory treatment still seemed to be so pressing it was even reflected in the congress's official name: International Congress on the Prevention and Repression of Crime, Including Penal and *Reformatory Treatment.*[30] The London convention, however, did not reflect a need for critical inspection of what had been done in the field of juvenile delinquency. Instead, it can best be seen as a new start of the prison reform movement in general. It was carefully prepared and organized by Enoch Cobb Wines, Commissioner of the United States to International Prison Congress, to be of a more official nature, with government representation and formalized proceedings.[31] Presumably, this was thought to be one way of getting rid of the exhausting and sometimes circular discussions on solitary confinement.[32] Moreover, there was an unmistakable influence from American organizations, like the American Prison Association, with different, not to say opposite, ideas on prison reform.[33] With nine visitors, the Dutch delegation was bigger than that of France or Prussia.[34]

Because of this new start, the agenda in London gave room for a lot of contemplation. In the children and juveniles section, many of the discussants took the opportunity of describing the programs of schools with which they were familiar or which appealed to their fancy. Thus, such places as Mettray, the institution of Demetz, the Ohio Industrial School at Lancaster, the Wisconsin reform school, and the Feltham school in Britain were discussed. The question of "what is the treatment likely to be most effective for the reformation of juvenile offenders" led to a prolonged statement by Mary Carpenter, "English Reformatories and Certified Industrial Schools," and the reading of a paper by Charles Loring Brace from New York, "The Prevention of Juvenile Crime in Large Cities." Even after the section had been adjourned and met again on the last day of the Congress in a second sectional meeting, no other useful decision was made or resolution taken than the quite superficial agreement "that large congregate schools were to be deplored and that schools on the cottage or family plan were highly desirable." According to N. K. Teeters, this subject exhausted a great deal of time of the full Congress, apparently without much of a result.[35] Nevertheless, we can conclude that a noticeable shift had taken place in the juvenile question since the midcentury congresses: no more discussions on solitary confinement for minors, but a range of views on the many possible ways of applying some sort of reeducational, reformatory system.

After the London formalities, at the gatherings in Stockholm four years later, in Rome in 1885, and St. Petersburg in the 1890s, these new views were brought to the fore in a more substantial and effective way. For instance, the third "preventive" section of the Stockholm congress took up the question that had been neglected since the Brussels convention, how children below the age of legal responsibility were to be cared for institutionally, in addition to measures to be taken for young vagabonds, abandoned children, and so forth. It is quite important to see that for all these children it was officially declared in the conference resolutions "that it is not a question of executing a penalty or chastisement, but of giving an education, whose aim is to place the children in a condition where they can gain an honest living and be useful to society instead of injuring it."[36] Of course in many European countries, a shift to reeducational treatment of children had already been made in earlier years, but Stockholm pinpoints the overall shift from punishment to reeducation. At the Stockholm deliberations, the idea of institutions imitating the family was propagated: Establishments ought to be small, with a mutual responsibility in the different units, with correspondence "to the conditions in which the working classes live. Hence, a scholastic instruction on a level with that of elementary schools; the greatest simplicity in the food, clothing and lodging of the children; and above all, labor."[37]

This obsessive, but often ambiguous clinging to the family resounded in one of the outstanding resolutions on children made at the congresses, in the session in Rome in 1885. There the problem of parental, namely fatherly, powers and responsibilities for one's children was discussed at length. In the discourse on children who had committed illegal acts, more and more emphasis was laid on their actual innocence, whereas their parents were more and more held to be responsible for these acts. However, to not honor or even to doubt the laws that existed in various countries regarding parental rights would be considered quite unique, even in 1885. Nevertheless, a resolution was taken clearly stating that "one of the methods to be recommended is to authorize the courts to declare, for a determined period, whole or part of the parental rights forfeited when there is sufficient evidence of a responsibility on the part of the parents."[38]

The Petersburg congress of 1890 followed up on Rome, by once again emphasizing the need for a court's authority to forfeit parental rights in certain cases but added the possibility for the court to fix the term of tutelary education in correctional establishments or in public or private aid institutions until the age of majority.[39] This in practice could mean a definitive forfeiture of parental rights.

In economic terms the Paris congress of 1895, copresided over by the Dutch professor of law Meinard S. Pols, was the moment of enlarging market share and product diversification in the realm of juvenile care. As pointed out, the children question had matured, leading to a new fourth section of the congress. In its first appearance, the agenda of the section on children and minors was overloaded. Eight questions were put to the fore ranging from "legal age of penal minority," via "guardianship of the state," "schools" and "houses of correction for minors," "physical training," "duration of correctional detention," and "supervision of children placed with families," to the prevention and repression of "prostitution of young girls."[40] According to Samuel June Barrows, reporter of the U.S. Senate, "it proved to be one of the most popular sections. . . . The fourth section was more general in membership, having a good representation of the bar, the clergy, and of prison experts; also directors of educational and correctional institutions for the young, Protestant ministers, Roman Catholic priests, Jewish rabbis, and a large delegation of women."[41] This may have been so, judging from the huge six-volume congress proceedings in which at least one hundred pages are taken up by the discussions in this fourth section as well as the general discussions in plenum on the answers to questions that had been delegated to this fourth section.

The official proceedings witnessed stormy discussions in the first plenary session, where the answers on questions six and seven, formulated in the children and minors section, were to be ratified. The answer to the sixth question regarding a fixed duration of stay in correctional institutions for minors, for instance, had been elaborated by Felix Voisin, counselor at the French *Cour de Cassation* and member of the consultative committee for the congress. It was adopted by the plenum without any further discussion or alteration, deciding that this was solely up to the state to decide. Then senator Jules LeJeune, Belgian minister of state and vice president of the congress bureau, stepped down from the stage to report on the seventh question, regarding the issue of how and by whom oversight should be maintained of individual outplacement in families of children coming from penitentiary colonies: by aftercare societies (*sociétés de patronage*) themselves or by a governmental administration? Referring to his own experience in Belgium as head of the justice department, LeJeune clearly pointed to the private aftercare societies as the body to be in charge and argued to not disturb them in their activities by asking for reports and paperwork: "their zeal would greatly diminish, if you require them to write reports and do other paper work." He concluded his deliberations by exclaiming: "while in office as Minister of Justice I did not inspect them at all, because I had more confidence in them than in myself," upon which the audience reacted with "très bien, très bien!"[42] However, not all were convinced. Especially some French members argued that circumstances in France were different from those in Belgium and that the proposition would not be applicable all over Europe, which should be the case. Nevertheless, the majority of the audience definitely was on LeJeune's side, interrupting with applause and "let us vote." In the end, LeJeune's answer was adopted. During the next days several other statements were adopted by the plenum.[43]

To sum up the most prominent features regarding criminal children at the penitentiary congresses, it is important to stress that special care and educational measures for criminal juveniles were on the agenda of the congresses at an early stage, in fact from the second congress in 1847 in Brussels onward, but gradually gained in momentum with a culminating point at the Paris congress in 1895. In general, the tendency was toward greater differentiation between convicted juvenile delinquents and children who had acted without the ability to tell right from wrong. This meant more wishes and possibilities of diversification according to age and crime, longer stay, more reeducation, and institutional diversification. Although solitary confinement for children was widely discussed, the focus of attention soon shifted toward reeducation in colonies and other childlike institutions. In the realm of aftercare, especially for children and minors, independent, private aftercare societies were held to be the best guarantee for a good surveillance of those released from penal institutions. The congresses themselves formalized aftercare after 1872, giving room for rivalry between private and public or governmental organizations. Dutch representatives, both governmental and private, played an active role at the various congresses, notably William Hendrk Suringar, Marie MatthieuVon Baumhauer, Johan Domela Nieuwenhuis, and Meinard

S. Pols. This brings us to the question of how they interacted between this European level and their national fields of action.

The National Level: The Dutch Connection

In the course of the nineteenth century, the Dutch established special prisons and reformatories for juvenile offenders.[44] Representatives of the bourgeois classes, united in a privately organized prison society, initially brought about these new institutions. This *Nederlands Genootschap tot Zedelijke Verbetering der Gevangenen* (Dutch Society for the Moral Improvement of Prisoners, hereafter Dutch Prison Society) turned out to be the main source of ideas on the moral treatment of criminals in general and especially juveniles between 1823 and about 1850. In the realm of law, prison, and criminality, the Dutch Prison Society's activities mainly consisted of a spread of bourgeois values by way of personal contact in visiting criminals, giving lectures, lending books, and especially taking care of primary and vocational education in the institutions. But quite a few of the members had a much wider view and took interest in other matters of social and societal policy, from public education to pawnbrokers' shops and from visiting the poor to building public bath houses.[45] Many of them were inspired by their Protestant faith, but they generally had a liberal outlook on the world. Members of the Prison Society, like some of their American counterparts, were actively involved in and inspired by minority religions such as the Quakers and the Remonstrant Church. They had no great expectations of results with adult criminals, but they did have high hopes for children because they were supposed to be more receptive and could of course be redirected for a much longer time than adults.

During the first half of the nineteenth century, the ideas and practices of the Prison Society focused almost exclusively on the care of criminal children. Whereas the newly formed Dutch state and its rudimentary governmental institutions were hardly able to lead and maintain a proper prison organization, the Prison Society had ample opportunities to develop a penitentiary youth care facility in accordance with its own views. As a result of its efforts, in 1833—quite early in comparison with other European countries—a first youth prison was opened in the city of Rotterdam: a dark, damp building in the center of town, initially used for boys and girls without distinction, at the same time. In this institution, the Prison Society developed a special care for the juvenile inmates, focusing on their moral education. The government took responsibility only for the maintenance of the prison building and the guards. The regime of these early youth prisons was not solitary confinement as in the *Petite Roquette* prison in Paris, but a rather hybrid mix of a classification system and an Auburn system of silence.[46] In practice it was a hierarchy of three classes with increasing privileges, recognizable by clothes, place at table, and speech. In the lowest of the three classes, all speech was forbidden, except during stay—not play—on the building's small courtyard. Moreover, children in these classes were forced to eat separately from the others and with their faces directed to the dining room's walls. Boys in the highest class were allowed to speak, except during meals, and could receive their parents or relatives every fortnight.[47] As with all these institutions, effectiveness could not be guaranteed in a reliable way. Only the number of recidivists is available as an indicator, although disputable. To be frank, this number was not in favor of the Rotterdam prison. Between 1863 and 1865 recidivists in the total number of inhabitants increased from 5 percent to a soaring 35 percent in the 1860s.

Meanwhile, ideas circulating at the European congresses were considered locally as well. Suringar, as the main source of information, now and then tried to apply solitary confinement to children and minors, but after his visits to French Mettray, in the company of Von Baumhauer, he seemed quite satisfied to push for the general application of the solitary confinement system to adults alone, while diverse reeducational and reformative systems could be used for criminal children. Following ideas developed at the congresses on making more precise distinctions between children above and below the age of legal responsibility, these moral entrepreneurs in the Dutch Prison Society saw new opportunities for more effectiveness in the reeducational field. This was because normally convicted children were sentenced for perhaps a few months as a general rule, whereas the younger children, sent to an institution for reeducation, usually were to remain there until eighteen years of age. This led Suringar especially to advocate the establishment of a special institution for these children, which after his French experiences and discussions in Brussels and Frankfurt, he loved to call "Dutch Mettray," thereby stating that it should be a rural institution, a colony with a small-scale, family-structured base, where "the soil would be made better by the children and the children by the soil."[48] The 1850s were a crucial period in the Netherlands: At the same time two new, intertwined branches on the reformatory tree developed. On the one hand, special reeducational institutions for the "innocent" juveniles were established, although not as a logical follow-up on the private initiatives by the Dutch Prison Society in Rotterdam and Amsterdam. On the other hand, a Dutch Mettray was indeed realized, but not for young delinquents.

When Suringar launched the idea of a Dutch rural colony like Mettray in France, he imagined this to be an institution for delinquent boys, especially the youngest ones. This group would probably give a better guarantee for successful reeducation than the recidivist lot in the youth prisons. However, the main financial resource, a Protestant benefactor from Amsterdam, insisted that no boys would be allowed who had been in contact with the police or the judiciary. For Suringar and some of his fellow philanthropists, this really was not a problem: Dutch Mettray was simply redirected toward the residential treatment of so-called endangered children, with which the punishment of criminal children shared common ground. In this field of Dutch residential, nonpenitentiary reeducation, one sees a rapid rise in the number of privately organized institutions after the model of Dutch Mettray in the 1850s. Residential reeducation soon outnumbered even the penitentiary system with room for some 12,500 children after the turn of the nineteenth century.[49]

Meanwhile, a second change took place. As an early supporter of the views of the international penitentiary community, the Dutch government took responsibility and action in this field. This was more or less forced by ongoing parliamentary battles focusing first on the preferred prison system, after that on the vigor with which solitary confinement should be enforced, and finally, in the early 1860s, on alternative systems.[50] But the Dutch government's actions should also be viewed as a logical outcome of state building and expanding governance in the second half of the nineteenth century,[51] as well as a result of appeals made to members of parliament, brochures, letters to editors, and speeches of the Dutch Prison Society urging changes in penal policies in reference to the insights of the international community of penal specialists at the international congresses. With the newly appointed general prison inspector, Alstorphius Grevelink, as its booster, the Dutch government itself established new institutions for juveniles who had committed a crime while below the age of legal responsibility. In addition to sincere convictions on the proper way of treating juveniles, this governmental penetration of an until then privately driven market was also meant to curb the unbridled claims of the Dutch Prison Society, which at the time proceeded even in the field of institutional aftercare for released male delinquents.

Such a governmental reformatory was maintained in the city of Alkmaar from 1857 onward. In this reformatory new educational ideas were added to the moral treatment developed in the youth prison. The children entering the reformatory were of a somewhat different nature than the population of the Rotterdam prison. In court, but inside the reformatory as well, more emphasis was placed on their mental, physical, and intellectual shortcomings, and their social background of neglect. Besides, they were usually quite young and supposed to stay at Alkmaar for a long time, until eighteen years of age. In the reformatory they were not treated as criminals, but primarily as children. The governmental care reflected the older ideas on moral treatment but added some new ones, of which the notion of strengthening the pupil's will was most prominent. This treatment proved successful and became the general form of treatment of criminal children in the youth prisons as well. These developments were formally recorded in the new Dutch penal code of 1886. Afterward, this treatment of criminal children in general was to become primarily educational and in fact a carbon copy of the treatment of endangered children in the reeducational institutions outside the penitentiary field of action. However, by comparison, this institutional treatment of juvenile criminals was much smaller in number. Its capacity grew from a mere one hundred beds in 1833 to about twelve hundred in 1915, taking care of about twelve thousand children, of which after 1850 those below the age of legal responsibility became a majority.[52]

To summarize these developments in the Netherlands: A threefold shift in ideas and practices from punishment of juvenile criminals to reeducating criminal and dangerous children to preventive education of endangered children took place at an early stage. Leadership in these matters shifted from private initiative to government responsibility (to public–private partnership, not to say a return of private initiative in daily practice, at the end of the nineteenth century). This was accompanied with a lot of dispute and rivalry. Discourses on the responsibility of the criminal child shifted from guilt to innocence, whereas their parents' responsibility and guilt became increasingly common. This was not just a moral conviction but once again also a pretext to intervene in an even more thorough and permanent way.

The Dutch case seems a good example of international developments in penitentiary ideas and practices in the realm of children and childhood between 1830 and the end of the nineteenth century. In fact, it can be summarized in two residential models or ideal types: on the one hand the youth prison, on the other hand the reeducational institution. Both ideal types have had an existence in real life, but of course not in their pure form.

From the beginning, the Dutch youth prison had been changed by reformatory ideas, at first because of the sheer coexistence of children above and below the age of legal responsibility, but from the beginning of 1833 also because of a greater than average effort to supply basic schooling and vocational training. Finally, new reformatory ideas were implemented, like a progressive carrot-and-stick system, to promote good behavior on the spot and moral reform in the long run. It is important to note that the Rotterdam boys' prison and its Amsterdam female counterpart largely were privately funded and organized institutions.

The Dutch state—only recently resurrected from French domination, and just starting to recover from the Belgian liberation—was neither able nor willing to provide funds for anything exceeding basic detention. This fits in nicely with Cunningham's periodization and alternation of private and public involvement in matters of childhood in the course of the nineteenth century. Not before the middle of the century can one notice a cautious comeback of governmental agencies urging the start of a proper reeducational institution in the city of Alkmaar. It is noteworthy that romantic, religious, or even mercantilist ideas were not put into practice for all criminal children without any distinction but were at first introduced and canalized through the category that could be more easily excluded from the generally discrediting and disqualifying discourses on juvenile criminals: Children who, according to the penal code, had acted without the ability to tell right from wrong were more childish, in fact innocent, and because of that deserved to be educated instead of imprisoned. On the wave of growing interest in children and childhood in Dutch society, this new discourse of childishness and innocence gradually expanded to almost all criminal children from the 1880s onward—precisely in the period where Cunningham observes the start of greater involvement by the state in juvenile matters.

Comparing Care for Criminal Children in Europe

For a tentative comparison with other European countries, I will consider here two issues. First, the debate on childhood—attitudes and conceptions of childhood—must be reviewed for discussions concerning the nature of children in general and criminal children as a special category. Questions to be considered are: Was there a common shift in classification from guilt to innocence, and were criminal children seen as a category apart from criminals in general? Second, public–private cooperation, controversies, and other communications must be reviewed—the organizational setting of childcare. Who took the initiative in caring for criminal children? Was there a gradual evolution from penitentiary to pedagogic initiatives, or were they—along these very lines—divided between state and private organizations? I will compare the Dutch case with the French and British, basing my comparison on secondary evidence.

In various European countries experiments involving special, usually residential, care for juveniles had been made a few years before the first congress of Frankfurt in 1846. In Britain, separate youth prisons had been erected in Millbank in 1823 and Parkhurst in 1838.[53] In France a cellular prison for children, La Petite Roquette, had been started in Paris in 1836.[54] In Belgium Saint Hubert, also a prison for juveniles, was opened in the Ardennes in 1840.[55] For German states I have not been able to determine if separate youth prisons existed at all, except for some facilities annexed to general prisons in the major cities.[56] In due time these children's prisons were followed or joined by special institutions explicitly aimed at a resocialization of the young by special education and intensive, prolonged care. In this category the Raue Haus near Hamburg, Germany, started in 1833 by Johann Hinrich Wichern, has been seen as *the* model for several initiatives of this kind elsewhere in Europe, like the famous agrarian colony Mettray near Tours in France by Fréderic-August Demetz in 1840, Red Hill in Surrey, Britain by S. Turner in 1841, and the Belgian Ruisselede and Beernem in 1849–1852 by Ducpétiaux.[57]

In the second half of the nineteenth century, few real innovations had taken place for juveniles since the introduction of the famous models of youth prisons, reformatories, and colonies in the first part of the century. Nevertheless, an enormous leap had indeed been made in terms of sheer numbers. Before 1860 some eighteen new agrarian colonies had been set up in France, and new naval and industrial colonies and *ouvroirs* for girls had been established after the seventies.

In Britain, under the Youthful Offenders Act, children could be sent to a reformatory school after a short stay in prison. In the Netherlands, separate reformatories for delinquent boys and girls were opened in 1857 and 1859.[58] What were the ideas that gave rise to these institutions and by which public–private agencies were they put into practice?

In France during the first half of the century, according to Rachel Fuchs, criminal juveniles were viewed as fundamentally evil and immoral: they supposedly had criminal tendencies within themselves. Especially after the French revolts of 1830, 1848, and 1871, all measures were taken to rid the streets of potentially dangerous urban youths. They were many. In Paris the number of vagrant and abandoned children was greater than before the Revolution, and according to Berlanstein they met widespread public concern.[59] The bourgeoisie defined and redefined juvenile delinquency and accordingly designed and redesigned policies dealing with the youth problem of crime. By the last decades of the century, a transformation in attitudes arose when reformers and legislators began to concern themselves with preserving the lives of children and then protecting and educating them.[60] Three broad categories of social policies dealing with children can be ascertained: paternal correction, still *en vogue* during the Restoration period through the Second Republic and even later; acquittal according to article 66 of the *Code Pénal* and remand to the parents or a reformatory; and conviction and sentencing to youth prison proper. The institutions were not developed on this threefold basis. All categories of children, without any distinction, were detained in youth prisons—of which the Madelonettes and La Petite Roquette in Paris were the most well known but exceptional cases—and in agrarian colonies, with of course Mettray as its hallmark. During the Second Republic the idea of aftercare or patronage societies for discharged minors was introduced, as a first nonresidential policy.[61] During the Third Republic (1871–1940), other institutions were added like industrial colonies and *ouvriers*.

In Britain, ideas on childhood were primarily founded on the problem of working children and only secondarily on the problem of street and criminal children. Because of that, developments in ideas on childhood date back long before the nineteenth century. Cunningham questions the general rule that poor children had to be inured to work from an early age in the 1780s, referring to the works of Jonas Hanway (e.g., his *Sentimental History of Chimney Sweepers* from 1785, in which climbing boys were depicted as children earning "mercy and tenderest kindness").[62] Peter King is quite confident in stating that before the nineteenth century "contemporary commentators rarely regarded young *offenders* as a separate, distinct problem." They were tried before the same courts as their adult counterparts, were put into the same prisons, and were subjected to the same range of sentences. Radical transformation took place during the nineteenth century, when "juvenile delinquency was established as a major social problem and a focus of great anxiety amongst the propertied."[63] Also, Susan Magarey states that in the 1820–1850 period the English became aware of a growing problem of juvenile delinquency, but in fact this was exaggerated because new forms of behavior were criminalized and benevolent measures were turned into additional punishments.[64] Around the middle of the century, Shaftbury estimated that thirty thousand children behaved like "tribes of lawless freebooters" in London alone and rendered "the state of society more perilous than in any former day."[65] This midcentury "moral panic" was characterized by firm views and ideas and associated with the growth of the major towns and industrial conurbations. Juvenile delinquents were seen as a race of their own; the "life and business" of that race was "to follow up a determined warfare against the constituted authorities by living on idleness and plunder."[66] Margaret May's view that state recognition of reformatory and industrial schools in 1854 and 1857 in fact marked the "invention of juvenile delinquency" in Britain is seriously criticized and refuted by King's research into the Old Bailey's court records on juveniles, from which a steep rise in the number of juvenile offenders as early as the 1820s can be ascertained.[67]

Turning to the issue of public versus private initiatives, let us first consider France again. In that country, parental care and authority constituted the preferred supervision of children, authorized by the penal code. According to O'Brien, 96 percent of all children in French correctional institutions had been placed there based on the penal code.[68] Most of these institutions were privately managed or a kind of public–private cooperation, like La Petite Roquette, started by Gabriel Delessert, a Paris police prefect, or Les Madelonnettes, founded by Louis Mathurin Moreau-Christophe, inspector-general of prisons in the Seine department. In both cases, maintenance was done by the public authorities, whereas private societies took care of visiting the young inmates, supplying books, and so on. French champions of the agricultural colonies were Charles Lucas and Frédéric-August Demetz, who cofounded the *Société Paternelle* in Paris in 1839. Under the direction of this Society, the colony at Mettray was founded.[69]

Navigating on King's and David J.Bosley's directions, British institutions for delinquent children originally were governmental initiatives, notably the unsuccessful Millbank Prison and the Parkhurst Prison of 1838.[70] But even before this, in the 1780s and 1790s, private initiatives by the Philanthropic Society had led to a school, factory, and house of reform for criminal and abandoned boys and girls at Hackney and Southwark. In 1849 new fuel was given to this refuge by Sydney Turner, the new director of the Philanthropic Society, changing it into an agricultural reformatory in Redhill, a copy of French Mettray, which he visited twice. Also, the thrust behind the Youthful Offenders Act of 1854, leading to reformatory and industrial schools, seems to have been by private individuals, among others Sydney Turner, Mary Carpenter, and Mathew Davenport Hill.[71]

Thus, the developments in Britain, France, and the Netherlands were characterized by differences and similarities. It is important to note that today's legalistic distinctions between criminal and not-yet-criminal children were not made in nineteenth-century ideas and practices. As in Suringar's implementation of Dutch Mettray, the reformatory model was in its nature rather imperialistic: The earlier a child could be taken into some sort of custody, the better a chance for reform this would give. On the other side of the intervention, this could be made even more effective by keeping children under some sort of guidance as long as possible: The Dutch Prison Society's experiment with residential aftercare in Leiden was started for that purpose. It is along these lines that the directions of care for children in the countries under study can be brought together. In all three countries discussed here—and probably in most European countries—the tendency was to extend the juvenile age group, prolong the period of stay, and to intervene forcibly in a child's life. The first two elements of this tendency were reflected in the general idea of employing arguments related to legal responsibility, setting aside common legal sanctions, implementing unspecified measures up to a child's maturity, and extending care to nonconvicted children in danger. The third element was integrated in the British Youthful Offenders Act from the very beginning: more or less organized systems of aftercare and parole. In France and the Netherlands—with the Leiden refuge as an exception to the rule—this genuinely belonged to a next stage in the debate on childhood that was not to come before the end of the nineteenth century and the beginning of the twentieth, with new child acts, specialized juvenile courts, dedicated aftercare, and parole organizations.

And what about the differences? The exceptional application of solitary confinement in the French youth prisons did not turn out to be successful for the young children and was dropped in the 1860s. Nevertheless, even in 1886 for Dutch children above sixteen, solitary confinement was made the rule, because they were tried as adults. A rather distinct feature of English penal policy was that corporal punishment of juveniles, like whipping those under fourteen years of age instead of sending them to prison, played such an important role in the second part of the nineteenth century up to 1948 when this was abolished.[72] Paternal correction—another French specialty—generally changed into its opposite because in the course of the century the responsibility for the child's mischief was more and more shifted toward its parents. The British custom of requesting financial participation of the parents in the reeducation of their children in a reformatory can be seen as a forerunner of this change, soon to be followed by the general idea that responsibility or guilt was not to be sought in the child but in its parents in the first place.

Conclusion

Over the period of a half century, in most parts of Europe, there was a considerable change in the way criminal children were conceptualized, treated, and looked at. In public discourse they often evolved from pernicious, punishable wrong-doers into helpless, vulnerable beings, needing love and care. I seriously doubt, though, whether this has led to a greater "enjoyment of childhood" for the children involved, as Cunningham argues. However, it was not just the concept of these children that changed. With it the whole penitentiary and reformatory system, all "forces of organized virtue" included, changed as well: It became an all encompassing system of care for all dangerous and endangered, *priceless* juveniles, maintained by governmental and private organizations. This widening scope, these mutual influences, can be ascertained at the pan-European level—namely, at the penitentiary congresses—as well as at the various national levels.

In view of the steady and prominent involvement of Dutch experts and delegates in the penitentiary congresses, one would perhaps have expected innovative, pioneering penitentiary practices in the Netherlands. This was not the case. Instead the Dutch did play a role at the international level in the development and pushing of ideas and setting into practice of ideas elsewhere in Europe. The question of why practices in the Netherlands were not innovative is difficult to answer and needs further research. One hypothesis might be that the typically Dutch public–private controversy led to alienation between the Dutch Prison Society and governmental representatives, to a conservative mummification of private enterprise in the Prison Society, and to a shift of innovative elements to the nonpenitentiary field of care for endangered children.

Do the international penitentiary congresses add up to social control on an international, European level? Taking into account the working definition of social control adopted in the introduction to this contribution, I am inclined to say yes, at least to the idea that there has been a quest for social control. Besides the boost in quantity and opportunity for straightforward sharing and exchanging of penitentiary ideas on an abstract, theoretical level that the congresses brought about, there was a change of quality and impact as well. Reading the proceedings of the congresses, one can sometimes catch a sense of the thrill that occasionally took hold of their visitors: The idea that so many people shared a concern for certain social policies, the conviction that on such a large, international scale all lofty ideas could be effectively brought into practice without tedious negotiations and compromises that were so common at the national level, that with their common effort and patience, in the end, crime could be overcome, criminals could be rehabilitated, and juveniles could be reeducated, that indeed a better world was in the offing.

This all-encompassing, surveying view on the world can be illustrated with a small insight in congress culture at the Paris meeting. On Sunday, July 7, 1895, members of the congress visited the penitentiary colony of Douaires. There, in a big tent, was going to be a supper, *artistiquement aménagée* by the colony's children. All members of the congress sat down with a good appetite, because of the walk they had just had. "During the meal, . . . all conversations were about the future reserved for these young colonists. How would one be able to fight the hereditary influences? How could one find a place for these youngsters when they would leave home?"[73]

Although no complete or constant correlation in timing and agendas between the penitentiary congresses and the national level of decision making in the field of juvenile care has been demonstrated, there is nevertheless much evidence in support of the idea that the European international penitentiary congresses on the whole played an important role in transnational social policy making during the nineteenth century.

Notes

1. Suringar, quoted in Leonards, *De ontdekking,* 165. Translation is mine.

2. verLoren van Themaat, *Zorg,* 320.

3. Ducpétiaux, ed., *Débats;* Moreau Christophe, ed., *Débats;* Suringar, "Adviezen"; Varrentrapp, ed., *Verhandlungen;* Von Baumhauer, "Verslag."

4. Cohen, *Visions,* 1–2.

5. Mayer, "Notes towards a Working Definition," 26–27.

6. Dupont-Bouchat, "Du tourisme pénitentiaire."

7. Leonards, *De ontdekking,* passim.

8. Lasch, *Haven in a Heartless World,* 167–89.

9. Cunningham, *Children and Childhood,* 134.

10. De Swaan, *In Care of the State.*

11. Although some reservation has to be made for the Dutch case, where pillarization produced a public–private partnership in many fields of social action, residential care for juveniles being one of them. (Pillarization is the structuring of society into organizational complexes that promote social functions and activities on a religious or ideological basis.)

12. Besides penitentiary congresses there was a growing number of other congresses (e.g., with a focus on medicine, poor relief, statistics, philology, law, feminism, peace, etc.). See Gregory, ed., *International Congresses.* Elsewhere, I hope to discuss congress culture in the nineteenth century from a sociocultural perspective.

13. "Moral entrepreneurs" in my view closely resemble Christopher Lasch's "forces of organized virtue" (Lasch, *Haven in a Heartless World,* 169).

14. Rasmussen, "Jalons pour une histoire," 115–33.

15. The Frankfurt congress had three sections: Welfare, Education, and Penitentiary Reform. See *Congrès international de Bienfaisance,* 4–5.

16. Moreover, all proceedings contain a list of members, adherents, or visitors to the congress in a specific year. Usually the country of origin and the trade or profession of the person are mentioned as well and, though quite different in nature and

expansion, reports, advices, preparatory investigations, speeches, addresses, and so forth are provided in several appendixes or even separate volumes in the course of time. Also, account is given of special trips, visits, expositions, demonstrations, concerts, banquets, parties, soirées, and so on. This primary source can be supported, strengthened, and completed with circumstantial evidence (e.g., personal accounts of visitors, official reports to national governments, commentaries, newspaper clippings, and articles in journals).

17. This Commission Pénitentiaire Internationale was formed in 1874 after the London congress. Its first chairman was E. C. Wines (verLoren van Themaat, *Zorg*, 381). The coming development of associations and committees in the course of the congresses' lifespans can be viewed as part of their formalization (Rasmussen, "Jalons pour une histoire," 121).

18. So far, I have not been able to study the actual diffusion of the proceedings, the number of copies being unknown, but all instances in which copies of these proceedings can be found in libraries of prison-related institutions, government libraries, and so forth make it likely that the circulation was indeed large of scale.

19. The statistics used in this essay are based on disparate sources, notably: *Actes du Congrès Pénitentiaire International de Paris; Actes du Congrès Pénitentiaire International de Rome;* Ducpétiaux, ed., *Débats;* Guillaume, ed., *Actes du Congrès Pénitentiaire International de Saint-Petersbourg;* Guillaume, ed., *Le Congrès Pénitentiaire International de Stockholm;* Guillaume and Didion, eds., *Actes du Congrès Pénitentiaire International de Bruxelles;* Moreau Christophe, ed., *Débats;* Pears, ed., *Prisons and Reformatories;* Ruggles-Brise, *Prison Reform;* Suringar and Jolles, *Oordeel;* Suringar, "Adviezen"; Suringar, "Discours Prononcés"; Teeters, *Deliberations;* verLoren van Themaat, *Zorg;* Von Baumhauer, "Verslag."

20. A list of questions and answers, and resolutions and opinions, on matters regarding children and juveniles between 1846 and 1895 can be found at www.unimaas.nl/gandi/leonards/QandA.html.

21. Ducpétiaux, ed., *Débats;* Moreau Christophe, ed., *Débats.*

22. Von Baumhauer, "Verslag."

23. See, on his change of mind, Suringar, *Gedachten,* 3–4.

24. A "stone shirt," like a "chemise de bois," which in French is a coffin.

25. Ducpétiaux, ed., *Débats.* Just two years earlier Von Baumhauer and Suringar had visited French Mettray and reported very enthusiastically about the colony. The former even offered his book on that visit to the secretary of the Brussels congress, Ducpétiaux (Von Baumhauer, *De landbouwkolonie te Mettray*).

26. Ducpétiaux, ed., *Débats,* 89–90 (italics in Mollet's citation are mine). As a devil's advocate Suringar consistently called solitary confinement the system of good company ("bonne compagnie").

27. "Communications et discussion sur l'organisation du patronage en faveur des détenus libérés" (Moreau Christophe, ed., *Débats,* 5).

28. "Die Gründung einer Obsorge für die entlassenen Sträflinge ist eine nothwendige

Ergänzung der Penitentiar Reform" (Varrentrapp, ed., *Verhandlungen der ersten Versammlung*).

29. Ducpétiaux, ed., *Débats,* passim. Dupont-Bouchat characterizes this era of the genesis of patronage up to 1878 as "the prehistory of patronage." Following eighteenth-century and early-nineteenth-century initiatives, she ascertains a second wave of "the public model," consisting of governmental aftercare institutions between 1830 and 1878, and she finally distinguishes a new era of "privatization of patronage" after 1880 (Dupont-Bouchat, "La Belgique capitale internationale," 286–97).

30. Domela Nieuwenhuis and Mackay, "Verslag aan het hoofdbestuur"; Pears, ed., *Prisons and Reformatories.* Italics in title are mine.

31. verLoren van Themaat, *Zorg,* 334.

32. Although all preceding congresses had adopted solitary confinement as the only good, effective, and preferable system, it had not been implemented on a wide scale. Instead, since the 1850s a growing number of voices could be heard arguing against the exclusive idea of the cell, propagating intermediate or progressive systems like the Irish system (ibid., 337–38).

33. At the London congress eighty-two persons from different American states were present.

34. The Dutch delegation included D. I. Mackay and J. Domela Nieuwenhuis on behalf of the Dutch Prison Society. W. H. Suringar was unable to attend and died in September 1872, two months after the congress. B. J. Ploos van Amstel and M. S. Pols officially represented the Dutch government.

35. Teeters, *Deliberations.*

36. Guillaume, ed., *Le Congrès Pénitentiaire International de Stockholm;* Ruggles-Brise, *Prison Reform.*

37. Teeters, *Deliberations.*

38. Ibid.

39. Guillaume, ed., *Actes du Congrès Pénitentiaire International de Saint-Petersbourg.*

40. Teeters, *Deliberations,* 97–102.

41. Barrows, "Report of the Delegates," 57.

42. *Actes du Congrès Pénitentiaire International de Paris,* vol. 1, 54–55. Translation is mine.

43. Ibid.; Teeters, *Deliberations.*

44. Leonards, *De ontdekking,* 113–65, 199–253.

45. Helsloot, "Een geschiedenis"; Kruithof, "De deugdzame natie"; Mijnhardt and Wichers, eds., *Om het algemeen volksgeluk;* Van der Velde, "De maatschappij."

46. Until the 1840s the Dutch parliament favored the Auburn system (Franke, *The Emancipation of Prisoners*), whereas the majority of the Prison Society still clung to a classification system, until 1843, when its leader, Suringar, chose solitary confinement as the better system (Suringar, *Gedachten,* 5–8).

47. Leonards, *De ontdekking,* 141–42.

48. See Dekker, *Straffen, Redden en Opvoeden*, 48–53.

49. Ibid.; Groenveld et al., eds., *Wezen en Boefjes,* chap. 2, passim; Leonards, *De Ontdekking,* 56–66.

50. Franke, *The Emancipation of Prisoners.*

51. De Swaan, *In Care of the State.*

52. Leonards, *De ontdekking,* 57–59.

53. Bosley, "The Problem"; King and Noel, "The Origins."

54. Perrot, "Les Enfants de la Petite-Roquette."

55. Christiaens, *De geboorte van de jeugddelinquent;* Dupont-Bouchat, *De la prison à l'ecole.*

56. Oberwittler, "Changing Penal Responses."

57. Bosley, "The Problem of the Young Offender"; Christiaens, *De geboorte van de jeugddelinquent;* Dupont-Bouchat, *De la prison a l'ecole;* Gaillac, *Les maisons de correction;* King and Noel, "The Origins"; Leonards, *De ontdekking.* The Raue Haus, though, was meant for all sorts of wayward children, rather than criminal children alone.

58. Bosley, "The Problem"; Fuchs, "Juvenile Delinquency"; Gaillac, *Les maisons de correction;* Leonards, *De ontdekking;* May, "Innocence and Experience"; Meuwissen and Delaet-van Gasse, "Quelques aspects."

59. Berlanstein, "Vagrants, Beggars and Thieves."

60. Fuchs, "Juvenile Delinquency," 266. Her classification seems to derive from Chevalier, *Classes laborieuses et classes dangereuses.*

61. Bosley, "The Problem," 293.

62. Cunningham, *Children and Childhood,* 139.

63. King and Noel, "The Origins," 17. Italics are mine.

64. Magarey, "The Invention of Juvenile Delinquency," 325.

65. Quoted in Cunningham, *Children and Childhood,* 145.

66. Magarey, "The Invention of Juvenile Delinquency," 327.

67. King and Noel, "The Origins"; May, "Innocence and Experience."

68. O'Brien, *The Promise of Punishment,* 120.

69. Gaillac, *Les maisons de correction.*

70. King and Noel, "The Origins," 18.

71. Bosley, "The Problem," 298.

72. Oberwittler, "Changing Penal Responses," 17.

73. *Actes du Congrès Pénitentiaire International de Paris,* vol. 1, 322.

CHAPTER 6

Caring or Controlling?
The East End of London in the
1880s and 1890s

ROSEMARY O'DAY

Britain had a mixed economy of welfare during the nineteenth and twentieth centuries—state, voluntary sector, family, and market were all involved. The fabric of society was made up of a "great ramshackle mass of private, pluralistic and voluntary institutions" as well as central and local government.[1] The old view, in which the history of the welfare state was seen as a movement from individualism to collectivism with increasing benevolent state intervention, was too simplistic.[2] One might add that state and voluntary intervention were not inevitably antagonistic to one another. They sometimes worked together and even more often acted in a complementary way with agreed upon boundaries between their roles: for example, the Charity Organisation (usually referred to as the COS) would help the helpable but leave assisting the destitute to the Poor Law authorities. The state sometimes used private institutions as think tanks to investigate and debate pertinent issues. The Royal Statistical Society was used in such a way: It fed ideas into the Office of the Registrar about the census and its role; it sponsored investigations into public health, housing, and labor; it disseminated through its meetings, its publications, and its membership up-to-date information and ideas.[3] The importance of the agencies of welfare (state, voluntary, family, and market) varied considerably from time to time and place to place.

As historians we must beware of placing overmuch reliance upon the declared opinions of representatives of these agencies and insufficient emphasis upon a reading of what actually happened. For instance, the COS declared itself opposed to the extension of state involvement in social welfare provision. Yet, when we as historians view provision in the late-nineteenth and early-twentieth centuries, we see both state and voluntary sectors operating and, frequently, the same individuals involved in both. Members of the COS saw welfare provision both as a sphere for charitable endeavor and as an opportunity for close coop-eration with the state poor law.[4] There were many differing approaches to the poor, which can be summed up quite baldly as: repression; regulation; reform; observation; management; negotiation; exclusion; education; and conversion. But these approaches sometimes coexisted as it were in the same bosom. Equally, they sometimes conveniently represent the characteristic approaches of different social actors. Helen Dendy Bosanquet and Octavia Hill emphasized working *with* the poor, changing their values and their lives; Charles Booth, having analyzed the nature of poverty, wanted to remove his classes A and B from society, con-tributing to the important contemporary debate about exclusion and the cre-ation of internal colonies for the residuum; Samuel and Henrietta Barnett, while sharing many of the aims of Bosanquet and Hill, wanted to convert and accul-turate the poor; the work of the young Beatrice Potter and her colleague Ella Pycroft was founded upon the premise that through a process of management and negotiation the values and lives of the semiemployed poor could be trans-formed.

Philanthropic endeavor and public welfare provision have been seen by his-torians as fertile ground for social control.[5] There are many possible approaches to studying relationships between the middle classes and the working classes through the economy of welfare and thus identifying the place of social control within them.[6] A case study approach is adopted here for several reasons: First, it makes manageable within a relatively short space a topic with boundless possibilities; second, it enables us to explore the concept of social control in some detail and to convey a nuanced picture of its implementation; third, it extends our knowl-edge of the subject area—much of the data has not been studied previously. In this paper there will be some examination of the work of the voluntary sector in the inner ring of the East End of London in manipulating the poor working classes through their physical environment; of attempts by the voluntary sector to shape the family life of inhabitants through philanthropic visiting on the Octavian (for Octavia Hill) model; of the attitudes of members of the voluntary sector to this work; of the ways in which the community of model dwelling buildings, at fam-ily and other levels, operated.[7]

For this purpose a detailed case study of Katharine Buildings, Cartwright Street, has been selected. While it remains a case study and as such is highly specific, it has been selected because it involves some of the key figures in late-nineteenth-century social reform and philanthropy—Octavia Hill, Samuel Barnett, Charles Booth, Kate Courtney, and Beatrice Potter (Webb)—and reveals a good deal about their motivations in seeking to shape the lives of the poor. To reduce everything to power relations, however, is highly inadvisable. Using one case study can certainly demonstrate that social control had many facets, but there were other influences at work, and there are other very important questions to ask. For instance, social work offered middle-class women acceptable forms of occupation, and a woman such as Beatrice Potter (later Webb) was motivated perhaps as much by this as by any desire to control others. We should also ask whether social reform rather than social control or social discipline was the issue. Sincere religious belief and genuine compassion for the poor should also be taken seriously as motivations for action. Social control was perhaps on occasion a side effect of the relationships developed between reformers, philanthropists, and workers on the one hand and the poor on the other hand, rather than a motivating factor.

Samuel Barnett and the East End Dwellings Company

On November 1, 1882, Samuel Augustus Barnett, Vicar of St. Jude's Whitechapel, chaired a meeting at his vicarage to form a company to provide housing for the poor in that part of London. In February 1884 the East End Dwellings Company was finally established, and in the following December its first model dwellings development, Katharine Buildings, was standing. It is tempting to see this initiative (and later building development of the same kind) simply as part of the history of housing—a direct response to the perceived need to level the slums of inner London and to rehouse their former inhabitants. An archaeology of the Katharine Buildings project reveals that its foundations were deeper and its origins more convoluted than any such analysis would suggest.

Certainly the legislative framework was provided by the Artisans' and Labourers' Dwellings Improvement Act of 1875. This made detailed provision for the clearance of slums and the sale of the land upon which they had stood to private companies to build suitable housing for the inhabitants according to plans approved by the local authorities. It was laid down that as many people must be rehoused on the land as had previously lived there; even after the relaxation of this clause in 1879, high densities were both assumed and accepted. But the act itself was a product of revived middle-class interest in the problems of poverty and the need to alleviate the physical conditions in which the poor lived, and the private companies that were set up to execute its provisions were frequently semiphilanthropic in their structure and intent. Moreover, the philanthropic wellspring drew upon many tributaries. These included traditional Christian charity; the institutions of the Anglican parish; the work of the Charity Organisation Society; and the personal chemistry between several individuals.

It will be as well to ask to what extent this philanthropy was motivated by fears of social disorder. Historians have long subscribed to the view that mid-Victorian social reform was rooted in "a universe of discourse which reflected a profound sense of fear and disgust, coupled with muffled . . . intimations of social catastrophe." The social crisis of the 1880s followed hard on the heels of these mid-Victorian terrors.[8] Widespread fear of an imminent social earthquake and of the poor as a volcano about to erupt had to some extent subsided by the final decade of the century. While events such as the Trafalgar Square riots and the Ripper or Whitechapel murders made middle-class Londoners quake in their beds and certainly formed part of the backdrop, Charles Booth's inquiry in the 1880s and 1890s had comforted them that the poor were not, in general, to be feared. (This wealthy and quirky individual financed and organized an enormous investigation into the *Life and Labour of the People in London,* and it became a major contribution to contemporary discourse about the nature of poverty and how to approach the social problems it engendered.) Philanthropic endeavor did not diminish in proportion to the diminution of fear.[9] The sight of so many in abject poverty stirred other emotions, upon which many middle-class men and women acted. Five percent philanthropy, also, was intended to appeal to the profit motive among members of the middle classes, who wished to reap dividends from their charity. It was assumed that some people would not give unless they also got.[10]

The Katharine Buildings initiative grew directly out of Samuel Barnett's long history of involvement with the COS. In the 1870s Samuel and Henrietta Barnett were close to Octavia Hill and her workers, both in their Christianity and in their approach to the problem of poverty. It was in the 1880s that they drew apart. A commitment to self-giving and, through it, to social action motivated them all in the 1870s. Octavia Hill equated herself with the Martha of the Gospels: "My pity and sympathy were always with Martha, and I have felt it hard to believe that hers was not the better part, if she had learned to worship while she worked."

In about 1870 Hill wrote to Mary Harris of a "glorious talk" with Barnett and lauded his teaching. "He spoke of the mistake of those who left men with the idea of entering into nearer communion with God; that only as we lived among them could we learn the true beauties of their various natures, and that slowly, year by year, as we gathered these fragments of glory, the old notion of corrupt humanity would vanish, and we should see gradually that these fragments made up the mighty humanity which was Christ himself."[11] Hill was committed to bringing about a transformation of the social order in line with Christian ideals and to enlisting the poor themselves in this process:

> I want the tenants to feel, above all things, that, as I hope to help them,
> I am perfectly conscious that the only way to do this is through awaken-
> ing in them a deeper sense of their own duties, as in us a deeper sense of
> ours. Such worn, haggard, careworn women cringing down to me, who
> have never suffered and struggled as they have without teaching or help,
> deadened to all sense of order or cleanliness and self-respect. "My
> friends," I feel inclined to say to them, "don't treat me with such respect.
> In spirit I bow down to you, feeling that you deserve reverence, in that
> you have preserved any atom of God's image in you, degraded and bat-
> tered as you are by the world's pressure. But God is mightier than that

world, my friends, and He, Who has kept in you whatever grace remains in you, has put it into our hearts to come among you, to help you struggle with the pressure of these enemies of yours and ours. Take us in as part of your nation; take us in as fellow-workers on God's earth. Let us try if together we cannot make it a little fairer place for His children's dwelling."[12]

In the anxiety of modern historians to emphasize the contribution made by late-nineteenth-century activists to a tradition of social policy and social work, the motivations for these men and women have been taken out of their context and their distinctiveness has been diluted. While we may recoil from the sentiments expressed by Hill or Barnett, to see them as primarily rooted in a desire for social control "by hook or by crook" would be mistaken. The wellspring of Hill's and Barnett's work was their Christianity. It was expressed in the community.

Octavia Hill's work has been described as a system. But her work grew out of the ancient organization of the parish and the commitment of the Church of England to parish visiting, no matter her heartfelt criticism of the practical application of or neglect of this commitment. In Marylebone she achieved through personal endeavor the cooperation between the COS, the Clergy, and the Poor Law authorities that she thought should prevail everywhere. Because she sat on the various committees, there was no chasm between hard men on the committees and wet women visiting the homes of the poor. Here at Marylebone individual work among the poor was given attention commensurate with that accorded the prevention of mendacity.

Samuel Barnett came directly under the influence of Octavia Hill when he was curate at St. Mary's Bryanstone Square, Marylebone, in 1870. In that year nineteen-year-old Henrietta Rowland (in 1872 to become Mrs. Barnett) was working in Hill's "pioneer" scheme. With the rector's support Hill had started a workroom for women and created an odd-job department for the houses she managed. Schools and night schools were begun, and Rowland devoted three nights a week to the night schools in Barrett's Court. Each of the relief districts of the parish was placed under the care of a visitor, and all applicants therefrom were offered work as a test of their needs and capabilities. Rowland became one of these visitors (working the Circus Street district) and, as such, worked alongside Barnett who acquired a detailed knowledge of his parishioners and their needs. His early letters to Rowland are full of references to individual cases of hardship and sickness within the parish.[13]

Hill secured the vicarage of St. Jude's Whitechapel, the worst parish in the London diocese, for the Barnetts, who coveted the challenge. The couple took it over in March 1873. The vicarage, however, was still occupied, and for a while they stayed in Eldon Street, Finsbury, in a mouse-infested lodging behind the Great Eastern railway. By day they "traversed the terrible courts lying between the parish and our rooms" to return exhausted by the work and the degradation of the people. On Sundays the ill-lit, cold, and smelly church attracted only six or seven old women, expecting doles as payment for attendance.[14] The church schools drew no children. There was no functioning parochial organization. Apart from the inhabitants of a notorious common lodging house, the parish included forty shopkeepers and their families who lived and worked along Whitechapel High Street; the lessees of warehouses on both sides of Commercial Street; the almost entirely Jewish population of two or three narrow streets; and the inhabitants of a congeries of unpaved courts and alleys. It was fertile ground for a Christian philanthropic work over. Some of the houses crammed together in these courts were three stories high with sanitary accommodation in pits in the cellars. In other courts the houses were wooden, low structures serviced only by a standpipe at the end of the court. Families lived one to a room—sometimes they owned their own furniture but more often were renting furnished rooms at 8d a night. Broken windows were repaired by paper and rags. Wallpaper hung from the walls in shreds, the home of countless vermin. To improve this situation significantly, it was adjudged that ownership had to be wrested from the landlords. In 1874 Hill set about trying to purchase one such court—inappropriately named Angel Alley—which was in a very dilapidated condition.

But neither Hill nor the Barnetts were modern social reformers or social workers. Barnett was impatient of those who wrote of the East End as "pressed down by poverty" and sought primarily to alleviate suffering. To Barnett the enemy was sin "in its widest sense," sin that meant missing the best, sin that would not allow mankind to come to God, sin that "mars the grandeur of human life." Culture, knowledge, and religion were the influences to which the inhabitants of St. Jude's must be exposed. (This was the impulse behind his involvement in the foundation of Toynbee Hall.) "That all such power may be brought to bear on our people, the organisation of the parish has been started," he wrote in 1877. Their first instinct was to mingle with the people and get to know them. Barnett dressed like a layman when they went out together on such jaunts—he was not infrequently mistaken for an insurance agent or, fearfully, the rent collector or landlord. He had a genuine compassion for the people, unmotivated by a conscious desire for social control. This did not translate itself into a willingness to give financial aid. He avoided confusion between relief and religion, heeding the warning of one man who, when he discovered that his visitor was the vicar, exclaimed: "Crikey, there's bust me old gel's chance of getting grub out of the church!"[15] Instead, Barnett would interview personally each applicant for relief and send him to the Charity Organization Society. When the COS had investigated the case and made a recommendation, Barnett would summon the man to appear before the Parish Committee on Friday night. In some cases a gift of money or a loan would be made; in others relief would be refused but self-help counseled and aided; work was frequently offered.[16]

Charity was also accorded the elderly but respectable. A few were eventually rehoused in Katharine Buildings. Others became recipients of pensions made by the new pensions committee that Barnett formed. Such thorough help was rare. Hundreds of "less worthy" candidates were refused the doles they begged for and the doles that before 1873 they would have received. This aroused great anger among some of the parishioners (many of them transients) who believed that doles were their right.

As a result of a growing feeling of impotence in such a parish, the Barnetts seriously contemplated giving up the vicarage and moving into one of the slums, Crown Court, nearer the people and their problems. Henrietta was very serious in her intent. Staring in the face the possibility of crowding into a one-room dwelling with no copper (boiler), no sink, no water tap, no lavatory, no cupboards, no coal cellar, no bath, vermin and bed-bugs, drunken neighbors, noisy children, a common staircase, a boltless front entrance, windows that would not open, doors that would not shut, and flimsy partitions made the couple draw back but made them aware as never before of the living conditions of their parishioners and the need for change. Theirs would not have been "slumming" but true "slum-dwelling."[17]

The Barnetts certainly breathed fresh life into the normal parochial institutions—mothers' meetings (where talks were offered on matters of practical interest such as "Bodies and babies," family ethics, and public morals), children's worship, choirs, oratorios, maternity clubs, night schools, communicants' societies.[18] The work was undertaken by a number of middle-class women—jocularly referred to as "the Canon's Ladies"—Mrs. Thurston Holland, Mrs. Godwin, Miss Murray Smith, Miss Gardiner, Miss Paterson, Miss Townsend, and Miss Potter.[19] One scholar has shrewdly observed that the emphasis on "moral and physical cleansing of the nation's homes" grew as more and more strong-minded middle-class women became involved in philanthropy.[20] Existing traditions of work with families, servants, and schoolchildren were, therefore, reinforced.

Kate Potter, daughter of the businessman Richard, hated the social scene available to the wellborn young woman and in 1875 determined to leave home and go to Octavia Hill to "be trained for her work in London." She was immediately sent to St. Jude's, and worked there for eight years. She not only excelled as a rent collector visitor who offered wise counsel and friendship to the tenants but also brought with her additional helpers in the form of her two sisters Theresa and Beatrice Potter and their friends.

The work that these young women did, under the Barnetts' watchful supervision, took many forms. Marion Paterson and Yetta Barnett had the dubious privilege of delousing the young slum girls, dressing them, and teaching them before matching them with families for an apprenticeship in "service." Soon the organization was formalized as the Whitechapel branch of the Metropolitan Association for Befriending Young Servants (MABYS) and took some responsibility for children raised in the workhouse schools as well. After a year, Pauline Douglas Townsend joined them. In 1877, 192 girls were found places and, in 1889, 512. Kate Withers, one of the most neglected girls, was taken in by a "good woman."

> Is it possible to forget that mistress's visit and her description of Kate's seizing the baby by its long clothes and swinging it round her head to throw at its mother?
> "Why did you do it?" said I to the dismissed Kate.
> "She jest riled me, and the baby was 'andy," was to her an adequate reason. . . . Thus did standards differ.[21]

The girls placed each year were made the responsibility of a few ladies who maintained contact, befriended them, and held parties, meetings, outings, and so on. Mothers, mistresses, and maids were brought together. Beatrice Potter noted in her diary the occasion on which she brought girls from MABYS to her father's grand London home. Side by side with MABYS worked "the parish machinery to influence them aright." The parish supported a girls' club, an evening home for girls, a Band of White and Gold, a Guild of Hope and Pity, the St. Jude's Guild for older girls, the Daisy Guild for working girls and servants, the gymnasium in Bucks Row.[22] The girls' club was opened "on a democratic principle in an aesthetic room under scientific guidance" by Mrs. Barnett in 1884.[23]

The physical conditions in which the inhabitants of St. Jude's parish lived preoccupied the Barnetts. In the mid-1870s it was estimated that 80 percent of the paupers of Whitechapel lived in houses that had been condemned by the Artisans' Dwellings Act. Approximately one thousand families were the beneficiaries of small-scale projects in the area such as those in Angel Alley and in Wentworth Street. Some of the housing was too appalling either to renovate or to manage in the way that Octavia Hill had contemplated, however. A piece of land near the Toynbee Tennis Courts was bought by A. G. Crowder, and on it was constructed a block of fifty model dwellings at a weekly rent of 2s 6d a room.[24] The Barnetts had the rooms in their gift, and they decided on the following rules for admission: "At least we decided that if we were to admit any applicants from our parish, all we could demand was that the new tenants should not earn their living by vice. Those occasionally vicious, drunken or lawless we had to accept, and only draw the line when sin was their stock-in-trade."

Katharine Buildings, Cartwright Street, East Smithfield

The Barnetts and their friends and coworkers, however, were well aware that they were just scratching the surface of the problem. While they deplored the values of many of the poor, they also felt deep compassion. "My hope of one day having a parish with houses fit for decent people has grown very faint" bemoaned the canon lugubriously in 1881. The records of the East End Dwellings Company tell of the frustration of the Barnetts, Crowder, Edward Bond, and Maurice Paul at the reluctance of the Metropolitan Board to proceed quickly to clear and distribute land for rehousing the slum dwellers, and of their consequent determination to go it alone and their decision to raise the necessary money by offering a financial incentive to investors. The model that they chose was that of five percent philanthropy, pioneered by Peabody and Waterlow (providers of charitable housing) in the 1860s.[25]

Katharine Buildings was intended, unlike Peabody Buildings, to provide accommodation for unskilled laborers, day workers at the docks, and men and women living by casual employment. From the very start it was designed to be rented in single rooms and to be managed on the Octavian system. The COS helped to circulate copies of the prospectus. The full set of minutes of the company indicates that the directors' philanthropic concern was very much to the fore. The flats, sadly lacking in amenities when compared with the accommodation of middle-class families in the late-twentieth century, offered good basic housing with cooking facilities and access to proper sanitation when compared with contemporary East End housing.

The directors also looked to influence the family life of tenants in ways other than their physical environment. Lady visitors cum rent collectors would work with the tenants on the Octavian model, encouraging thrift, good housekeeping and cooking, and responsible parenthood. Kate Potter Courtney took on the task of organizing this work within the buildings from October 1884. She also influenced the fitting out of the rooms themselves, making improvements to the amenities. In December 1884 the five-story Katharine Buildings (named—after Royal Mint Buildings was thought objectionable by the Master of the Royal Mint!—for Katharine Courtney) was standing. By March 1885 the first tenants had moved in, although the building was not fully ready until June 1885.

The rules drawn up to determine life in the buildings, although they were undoubtedly honored more in the breach than in the observation, are nonetheless indicative of the predispositions of the directors and the manager. They do, of course, suggest that the management had very definite ideas about the way in which tenants should live. Victorian middle-class values and assumptions abound. Cleanliness was next to godliness. Wives should stay at home and housekeep and child nurture. A lady visitor, Margaret Wynne Nevinson, commented on the inadequate homemaking skills of the tenants, which were, in her opinion, not just owing to poverty. She compared, for example, the lack of culinary and dietary knowledge with that of working people she had met in France and Germany. In Whitechapel tenants despised cereal foods as "work'us stuff," and the staple diet was stewed tea, bread and butter, and fried steak, liver, or "lights" (a form of offal).

Most of the mothers had worked in pickle or jam factories and knew nothing of housekeeping. Their ill-nourished husbands pardonably took to drink, and the unfortunate babies, brought up on strong tea, sips of beer and gin, stuffed with adulterated sweets, tempted with whelks and winkles, died quickly. . . . a few men, who had the foresight to marry domestic servants, had their food properly cooked and their homes kept clean.[26]

The rooms were intended as homes and not as workshops, reflecting the belief of Barnett and his circle that the home was the principal agency of social transformation. Any attempt by the tenants to use the rooms or the facilities as a base for paid work was to be quashed. Tenants were to be allowed to use the eight coppers in each of the washhouses in the yard only for their own clothes and not for a laundry business. No fowls or rabbits or other animals were to be kept in the rooms. This was not because of a hatred of pets or a sensitivity to the needs of poor defenseless animals but a declaration in advance that small-holdings in the living room were not to be tolerated. Neither could tenants engage in subletting to eke out a living. The lady manager wished to keep close control over the tenants and their behavior—subletting and the taking in of lodgers were therefore anathema. Health problems, noise problems, problems of overcrowding were no doubt at the root of some of these rules, and on one level they were sensible enough. There is every suggestion that the rules were rigorously enforced. For instance, when Michael Roberts, a clerk in the Tower of London, moved with his two children into two rooms in the buildings in October 1888, all seemed well. Then his wife returned from Ireland "and came back bringing fowls—bantams, which she allowed to run about the room till I remonstrated." Mrs. Roberts assured Ella Pycroft that she would remove the poultry to the Tower, but instead "she sent them to the back room, & made a cage for them of the shelf of a wash-hand stand, till I found them out again!"[27]

Right from the start the management involved itself in providing facilities within the buildings for the amusement and occupation of the inhabitants. The club room was signed over for the use of the lady collectors and provided with a lockup cupboard as early as January 1885. The caretaker, Mr. Durell, was to clean the room in exchange for a supply of gas to his living room. By May 4 the Directors had agreed to furnish the room and rent it to either Mrs. Courtney, the paid lady manager, or Miss Pycroft, the paid lady collector, at a weekly rent designed to cover the depreciation of the furniture and the expense of gas. This rent was later fixed at 2s 6d a week. The room was to be used for social meetings, entertainments, a lending library, and so on. Twelve chairs, two tables, fenders and fire irons, blinds, and a bookcase were ordered. The lower parts of the windows were provided with curtains to prevent "persons in the street looking in."

The question of the stoves and cooking ranges installed in the rooms exercised both the directors and Kate Courtney and her assistants. By January these ladies included both Beatrice Potter and Ella Pycroft, a doctor's daughter from Devon, who was prominently involved in the management of the buildings and the implementation of the Octavian system of visiting within them. In January Beatrice was looking at models of stoves with Mr. Edward Bond and trying to remedy the problem they were having with excessive smoke from them in the rooms, especially on the top floor. Also Ella Pycroft, a new acquaintance, came to stay, and they discussed the organization of rent collecting and visiting. In March Beatrice was traipsing around Whitechapel chasing down potential tenants' references. Kate Courtney was still in charge as far as the directors were concerned: for example, in March Courtney was given authority to order small repairs. Yet the impression is that in reality Beatrice and Ella were in charge of day-to-day affairs at Katharine Buildings and, increasingly, just Ella. For, by March 1885, Beatrice was already declaring her intention to concentrate on observation of the tenants and to do less of the management. In her case the practical work of the philanthropic visitor investigating case histories slid easily into that of the observer and social investigator. By the second half of the eighties, she had outgrown her early beliefs that individual case work could effect a transformation of the lives of the poor and was using Octavia Hill's system as the basis of social research.

The rent collector/visitor system operated at Katharine Buildings was one in which an army of middle-class volunteers, mainly but not exclusively female, was responsible for collecting rents and for working with individual families to ensure that they found it possible to pay that rent through careful and responsible housekeeping. The educative and informing function of the visiting was undeniable. Yet, the visitors were also required to be the friends of the families they visited (and especially of the women and children with whom they came into most contact), and this friendship was to be heartfelt and of inspirational value to the visited: They were to be "to the poor a 'vision of delight' every week, like primroses in spring to us."[28] Efficiency was not sufficient of itself. Meanwhile, the manager and the caretaker of the buildings were responsible for providing an ordered environment as a backdrop for this reforming activity.

The records indicate that, at least with respect to the tenants housed in the 1880s and 1890s, the concern for their well-being as individuals and families was genuine. Potter, Pycroft, Maurice Paul, and Margaret Wynne Nevinson no less than the Barnetts wrestled with the problems that this friendship with and compassion for the people they knew created, when they had to make hard decisions about the nature of the help they offered. These men and women were profoundly aware that the need was not simply for the housing of the poor to be of sound and sanitary structure but for it to allow the same poor to live family lives that were responsible and not vicious, for them to live according to given mores without recourse to vice.

Equally, however, they were supremely confident that these mores were those that prevailed in English middle-class society and never entertained any idea that there might be independent virtues in the working-class way of life and the values contained within it. Charles Booth was among the very few who admired aspects of working-class culture and life. To the modern scholar it is the superior and often self-righteous stance of these "friends" of the tenants (softened a little by their evident concern and compassion) that jars. Friendship was, it is clear, an unequal affair, conducted entirely on the terms dictated by the middle-class partner. It was not friendship in the modern sense of that word but in the early modern—the friend was a quasi-patron and one who acted in the interests of an individual rather than a confidante and congenial companion. Tenants were viewed as "children," unable to live independently and in need of the same disciplining and civilizing forces as were accorded to the very young. Hill's paternalist comment about the behavior of her own tenants on a steamer excursion in 1870—"the delight of watching kept them quite amused and good the whole time" —finds its counterpart in Ella Pycroft's disagreements with the Katharine Buildings' Tenants in the 1880s and 1890s, when she finds their assertions of independence and self-control unpalatable.[29] Both Pycroft and Potter saw the tenants as in need of civilizing: Potter famously identified the people as "aborigines of the East End" while Pycroft's efforts to expose them to culture were undertaken from a position of authority.

> They [the men] sang songs I very much disapproved of, & Mr Aarons brought forward a friend to sing & dance though Mr Paul & I had distinctly said we would not have it. My black looks stopped the men. . . . then Elliott came forward to sing (to help me out of my difficulty I thought) but he made a speech most insolently finding fault with my conduct & I had to answer him & assert my authority; and then Aarons appealed to the people to know if he hadn't succeeded in amusing them, & all the low set applauded him. It was horrid. I talked to the two men after the concert was over & said we were not going to quarrel but such a thing must never happen again & that I should talk to them about it another time & then went away with my friend . . . & got hissed by the rough set as we went out.[30]
>
> [Later] I made them . . . acknowledge that it was possible to laugh without having vulgar jokes or worse, & that we ought to try and raise the tone of the people & so on; & made them clearly understand that the Club room was let to me & I'd have no disputing my authority in it & we parted with smiles all round.[31]

Until this point Beatrice Potter had been in favor of setting up a tenants' committee to assist in managing the buildings and to help toward self-dependence, but Pycroft's comment that "they must never have a loose rein again, it has all been my fault for trusting them too much" cast doubt upon the wisdom of such a policy.[32] Until the tenants were imbued with the same values as the managers and visitors, they could not be trusted to make decisions. They were like the children of St. Jude's parish crossing "the bridge which divides the period of obedience from the period of responsibility."[33] Civilization and transformation had to precede independence. Such friendship was seen as a means of civilizing the working classes, using philanthropic control of decent housing and facilities and traditions of deference as leverage to persuade the poor to cooperate. This leverage was frequently unsuccessful: After Pycroft's set-to with the tenants, the concerts were poorly attended, tickets had to be given away, and Margaret Nevinson observed that those who did frequent the entertainments were bored to tears with being "compulsorily uplifted."[34] This said, Pycroft as manager of Katharine Buildings did continue to consult tenant opinion on practical issues such as the desirability of placing the women's and men's lavatories on separate floors to ensure privacy and "decency."[35]

The records of the East End Dwellings Company shed some light on the manner in which the relationship between the company and its employees (the manager, collector, and caretaker/superintendent) on the one hand and the tenants on the other hand evolved. Not only did the company listen to its employees and recognize the validity of many of their complaints about the suitability of the rooms for the tenants, they used their expertise to guide them when building a model dwelling on Thrawl Street (later named Lolesworth Buildings). The arrangement of the lavatories, for example, was seen as crucial to the program of reforming the morals and behavior of the tenants. "Miss Pycroft and Miss Potter attended and explained their experience of the working of Katharine Buildings as bearing on the plans for building on this site. On the motion of Mr Foster it was resolved that the latrines be not placed on the stairs as at Katharine Buildings."[36] The lady visitors attempted to influence the lives of the poor tenants through diligent and regular visitation. The following example drawn from the Katharine Buildings ledger (and other cases like it) shows the high level of involvement and the subtle and not so subtle ways in which the lady manager sought to manipulate the behavior of the tenants.[37] Mrs. Nagle, her husband, and disabled son lived in room 188 from March 1885 until late August 1886. John Nagle was a plasterer with "seldom any work"; his wife was an old (second-hand) clothes dealer and the sister of Mrs. Lyons, who lived in 183; their son John had been injured in an accident and helped either parent as occasion demanded. Amongst the first intake of tenants, they were regarded favorably and optimistically: "Regular in payment. Clean, respectable, hardworking." In May 1886, to the visitor's dismay, mother and son quarreled with the father and moved to room 129. Eventually, the quarrel was resolved, and the Nagles decided to take a large and a small room together. But then Ella Pycroft found that "Mrs N. had quarrelled with her son because of his courting Mr Debond's daughter" and said she must leave altogether. John Nagle Jr. had told the Debond girl that he could earn £2 a week. Miss Pycroft stepped in and "tried to make Mrs Debond see the madness of letting her girl marry such a cripple but she couldn't." The summer came, the Debonds went off "hopping" (picking hops in Kent), and by the time they returned the romance was over. The Nagles then moved to number 133 on August 30, 1886 and rented in addition room 131 in September 1887. In the winter of 1887 John Nagle Jr. was taken extremely ill with rheumatism; John Nagle Sr. "was seized with one of his maniacal fits of jealousy of his wife. He was almost, if not quite, dangerous." The rooms were rented in the son's name so Ella Pycroft made him give notice for room 133 "as he & his mother were in 131" (remember that the rooms were not connected in any way). "Then I told the old man he was either a trespasser or a tenant, as the latter I gave him notice— He went to the workhouse—returning his wife threw water over him; so he left again." The advice of Edward Bond of the East End Dwellings Company was sought. In the end Nagle came back to his wife. "I said if he stayed they must leave—However, finally I agreed to let them stay. Nagle got work in the summer & behaved well." In May 1888 they moved to room 274, then to room 134. Unfortunately, in the summer of 1888 Mrs. Nagle had a bad leg, which prevented her working. "I paid her rent for two weeks on condition she stayed in bed," recorded Pycroft and "later on helped her in same way with Lord Airlie's money [a philanthropic bequest]."

Yes, the middle-class directors and managers of Katharine Buildings did seek to order the lives of the inhabitants and to impose their own values upon them. But this presents an unnuanced and an unforgiving picture of the relationship struck between the middle classes and the poor in London's East End. Contemporaries were aware of the consequences of allowing poverty to go unchecked— in terms of social unrest and threats to life, property, and health, as well as the denial of Christian responsibility to love one's neighbor—but the poor certainly did not enjoy poverty and also wanted to share in some of the advantages possessed by middle-class Londoners. The Katharine Buildings initiative could not succeed without the voluntary cooperation of laboring people. The tenants of the buildings chose to apply for rooms, and they entered them on a contractual basis—if they failed to keep the rules they could be evicted, but if they kept the rules they received in return a habitable single-family accommodation with what were much improved facilities (compared to most housing for the semiemployed in London) and an ordered environment. The choice was limited, but it was a choice nonetheless. Study of the Katharine Buildings ledger reveals just how difficult many tenants found it to adjust to the imposed values of the COS. When they found it too difficult, they voted with their feet or were evicted.[38] Equally, however, the ledger demonstrates that many tenants found the relationship with the lady manager and her team of visitors of benefit to them, at least temporarily, and were willing to cooperate.[39]

The managers tried to avoid eviction: Above all they wanted families with whom they could work and they tried all manner of types of persuasion to render families compliant. Potter and Pycroft were painfully aware of the problems faced by the tenants in making adjustments, and they bent over backward to assist them in so doing. Concern and compassion were as much the keys to their approach as overt control. Indeed they were aware that they could not compel. When a given family simply refused to keep its side of the contract, however, the working relationship broke down, the tenancy was ended, and the efforts of the system to reform had failed.

Sometimes the two discovered that the families and individuals they had taken on as tenants were beyond the kind of help that the lady managers were prepared to give even if the tenants as individuals were cooperative. These young and inexperienced women gradually came to realize that enabling the poor to live an independent life was not a simple matter of providing a clean dwelling and "friendship." In July 1886 Ella Pycroft told Beatrice: "I am trying to bolster up a woman in Kath. Buildings now who has been half-starved, & she will come back from a Convalescent home to which she is going pretty strong & then it will begin all over again—& I know, (or think that I do that if I had left her to die, it would have been one less to struggle for food here."[40] The case of the crippled John Shermann was to make Potter, Pycroft, and Paul question both the philosophy of the COS that only the deserving should be given money doles and the philosophy of the Social Darwinists that those who could not be self-supporting should not be artificially supported by money doles but sent to the wall.[41]

Conclusion

The concept of social control is too crude to be helpful in accurately describing the ideals and work of middle-class "social workers" in Victorian Britain. The desire to win over others to conform to the same values, standards of behavior, beliefs, philosophies, and ways of communicating is common throughout human societies, and while it is especially pronounced in hierarchical systems, it is by no means peculiar to them. All social work is a type of social control.[42] This statement does not take us very far. Infinitely more interesting are the motivating forces impelling the social workers and the ways in which they strove to realize their aims and interacted with that portion of society that they sought to control. Two generations of social reformers in Victorian London subscribed to a philosophy of transformation. While the poor might be as children, in need of guidance, discipline, and control, they were working in cooperation with their middle-class "friends" toward a different social order in which the poor were to be independent and participating members of the community. Ella Pycroft, for instance, admired the socialist Ferdinand Lassalle's "arguments about the people raising themselves from serfdom and becoming active citizens."[43] The "class" dimension of such caring relationships cannot and should not be denied but neither should the genuineness of the caring. H. D. Rawnsley, in his sonnet to Octavia Hill, expressed well her ideal:

> . . . ever strove
> To help with clear-eyed wisdom, strenuous love,
> The poor to feel that better far than dole
> was self-respect, self-help, and self-control.[44]

The Barnetts and their fellow workers in St. Jude's parish, in the East End Dwellings' Improvement Company, and at Toynbee Hall shared this goal, if not, in all cases, the means advocated for achieving it. Some, like Beatrice Potter, began to focus on the need to tackle the structural basis of poverty once her apprenticeship in Katharine Buildings had taught her the painful way that individual case work could not reform the working poor. Ultimately this experience had been a depressing one for all concerned in working with the tenants:

> The respectable tenants keep rigidly to themselves. The meeting places, there is something grotesquely coarse in this, are the water-closets. Boys and girls crowd in these landings. . . . The lady collectors are an altogether superficial thing. Undoubtedly their gentleness and kindness bring light into many homes—but what are they in face of this collected brutality?[45]

Notes

1. Harris, "Society and the State," 63.

2. Lewis, *The Voluntary Sector*, 3.

3. Englander and O'Day, *Retrieved Riches*, 10–11, 23–25.

4. See Fido, "Charity Organisation Society," 207–30 (and especially 208), for a useful summary.

5. Jones, *Outcast London*, passim (a position modified in his later writings, especially "Class Expression versus Social Control?" 162–70); Morris, "Voluntary Societies," 95–118; Donajgrodski, ed., *Social Control*.

6. Prochaska, *Women and Philanthropy*; Prochaska, "Body and Soul," 336–48; and Prochaska, "Philanthropy," 357–93.

7. For further detail see O'Day, *Family and Family Relationships*; O'Day, "How Families Lived Then"; O'Day, forthcoming, *Katharine Buildings*.

8. See Storch, "Problem of Working-Class Leisure," 138–62.

9. Prochaska, "Philanthropy," 371, makes this point with regard to postrevolutionary periods.

10. Tarn, *Five Per Cent Philanthropy*. (The term *five percent philanthropy* describes the practice of setting up companies for philanthropic endeavor—such as housing for the poor—in which investors would make a profit on their money.)

11. Undated letter from Octavia Hill to Mary Harris, c.1870, printed in Maurice, *Octavia Hill*, 108–9. See also her letters to Mary Harris about her sense of Christian duty toward the poor tenants of Paradise Place, 189–95.

12. Undated letter of Octavia Hill to Mary Harris, c.1864, printed in Maurice, *Octavia Hill*, 190.

13. Barnett, *Canon Barnett*.

14. Barnett, *Canon Barnett*, 74.

15. Barnett, *Canon Barnett*, 82.

16. Letter of Canon Barnett, 1874, quoted at length in Barnett, *Canon Barnett*, 83–84.

17. Barnett, *Canon Barnett*, 89–90.

18. Barnett, *Canon Barnett*, 99–103; see Prochaska, "A Mother's Country"; and O'Day, "Women in Victorian Religion," 339–63.

19. Barnett, *Canon Barnett*, 104–7.

20. Prochaska, "Philanthropy," 384–86.

21. Barnett, *Canon Barnett*, 116–17.

22. Leaflet used to advertise a sale in aid of the clubs cited in Barnett, *Canon Barnett*, 122.

23. Letter from Canon Barnett to Frank Barnett, quoted in Barnett, *Canon Barnett*, 122–23.

24. Barnett, *Canon Barnett*, 132.

25. Registers of the East End Dwellings Company; Tarn, *Five Per Cent Philanthropy*; Tarn, *Working Class Housing*, 72, figure 34, for photograph of rear of Katharine Buildings.

26. Nevinson, *Life's Fitful Fever*, 94.

27. Passfield, Holograph Diary of Beatrice Potter Webb; Ledger of the Inhabitants of Katharine Buildings, Rooms 115, 118, 114.

28. Letter of Oscar Tottie, quoted in Barnett, *Canon Barnett*, 133.

29. Letter of Octavia Hill to Mary Harris, 17 July 1870, printed in Maurice, *Octavia Hill*, 109–10.

30. Passfield, 9 February 1886, Ella Pycroft to Beatrice Potter.

31. Passfield, 11 February 1886, Pycroft to Potter.

32. Ibid.

33. Letter from Canon Barnett in 1888, quoted in Barnett, *Canon Barnett*, 122, and describing the work of St. Jude's with the girls of East London.

34. Nevinson, *Life's Fitful Fever*, 97ff.

35. Passfield, 26 February 1886, Pycroft to Potter.

36. Registers of the East End Dwellings Company, 1887.

37. Ledger of the Inhabitants of Katharine Buildings, 1885–1890, under rooms 188, 183, 129, 133, 131, 274, 134.

38. See, for example, Nevinson, *Life's Fitful Fever,* 91.

39. White, *Rothschild's Buildings,* based on later recollections by tenants of another model dwelling buildings, reinforces this point and suggests that it has a more general application.

40. Passfield, 15 July 1886, Pycroft to Potter.

41. Passfield, 21 August 1886 and 4 September 1886. See a more detailed discussion in O'Day, "How Families Lived Then," 155; Lewis, *Women and Social Action,* 99–103, makes some shrewd comments about this questioning of the COS philosophy and of social Darwinist theories.

42. Sutherland, "Education," 129, makes a similar point with respect to education.

43. Passfield, 4 March 1886, Pycroft to Potter.

44. Rawnsley, *Octavia Hill,* 13 August 1912.

45. Passfield, Holograph Diary of Beatrice Potter Webb, 7 November 1886.

CHAPTER 7

Community and Social Control: An Enquiry into the Dutch Experience

Vincent Sleebe

Although the study of social control has been rather popular within the field of social science, this subject has been examined with a somewhat one-sided approach. Since the interest of social scientists and historians has been drawn mainly toward the state apparatus as an agent of social control, relatively little attention has been given to the field of informal social control and community.

Recently, more informal forms of social control, which are exercised by church bodies, philanthropists' societies, or welfare institutions, have been the topic of social historical investigations. And during the last decade or so, we have witnessed a rediscovery of the neighborhood, not only in the present but also in the past. In that regard, social historians are investigating all aspects of everyday life in the neighborhood: social control among neighbors, fighting in the street, fraternities, and the way in which neighbors took care of one another.

However, these investigations have focused mostly on premodern societies. Although the myth of the modern, anonymous city with a lack of social control among neighbors has long since faded away, informal social control still seems to have its base in the traditional life of small rural communities that have not yet been transformed by the economic and political changes of the last century or two.[1]

There is also an ideological side to this. Until very recently, informal social control, at least in Western society, was considered to be a relict of a remote past, conflicting with both the exigencies of modern industrialized society and the ideal of personal freedom. Recently, however, there has been a shift in the appraisal of local communities. Perhaps this newly won popularity of the neighborhood has to be understood against the background of political discourse. After a long period in which neighborhoods were associated with old ladies watching everything and everyone, governments are now trying to restore lost values that, in their opinion, used to keep society together. One of these values might, corresponding to good citizenship, be labeled "good neighborship." People should show more interest in their neighbors and help them if necessary. Social control among neighbors is no longer considered to be an idea of past times. Instead, for politicians of all backgrounds it constitutes a perfect means to fight criminality at relatively low cost. In the same way, neighbors taking care of one another during illness and old age might reduce the overwhelming costs for professional caretaking.[2]

Thus far, two very closely connected themes, "community" and "informal social control," have come to attention. But before we can discuss the relationship between these two any further, some issues have to be clarified. First, there is the question of what constitutes formal social control and informal social control. Most obvious is the form in which social control is exercised. For example, there might be laws that are vigorously imposed upon the population, sermons and other ecclesiastical methods of influencing people's behavior, or unwritten norms and values that are held by certain if not all groups of the population. In the informal sphere, attention should be drawn to gossip, accusations of sorcery, violence, mockery, carnival, rough music, or even folk tales as a means of performing social control within and between communities.[3]

Formal and informal social control cannot be understood without looking at its agents: the state, the church, the community, the family. These agents not only represent certain norms and values, but they also determine the way in which these norms and values are promoted within society. In this respect, it is of extreme importance to acknowledge the role of individual persons or officials and their relationships toward the people they are supposed to "control." Of course "the state" is not the same in 2000 as it was in 1800, not to mention local and regional authorities. An early-nineteenth-century county constable is quite different from the late-twentieth-century city police, both in their places in society as in their means of power.

Second, it may not altogether be clear where the borderline between formal and informal social control is to be drawn. In most literature state control is labeled formal, whereas social control within communities and families is called informal. The main criterion would then be whether social control is exercised by institutions and authorities or by people "among themselves."[4] However, I think that this borderline is rather vague and that a strict dichotomy should be avoided. For example, it seems clear that social control as exercised by the state constitutes formal social control. But what if this control is exercised on the local level by officials who are supposed to represent their neighbors and who need a large amount of informal support to persuade their neighbors to obey the state's laws? Or what if these strict written laws remain unobserved due to lack of adequate enforcement? In contrast, unwritten "common law" may sometimes be enforced quite strictly, even without anyone knowing its precise contents. And should written agreements concerning neighbors' social duties be considered formal or informal social control? A complexity is also represented by the church, which promulgates quite strict behavioral rules (although this may be a matter of debate) without (at least in modern times) having the formal means to enforce them upon their flock.

I would argue that the position of the "social controller" alone is not the only criterion for distinguishing between formal and informal social control. The second criterion should concern the question by which means this control is exercised. In that case, standardized and documented regulations and procedures point to a more formal social control, whereas common values that are maintained by means of unofficial procedures and mechanisms are more informal. Furthermore, I think types of formal and informal social control should be conceived as a continuum, ranging from the most formal level (the judicial system of the state) to the most informal level (the upkeep of norms and values within a neighborhood). In between both extremes on this scale, one finds all different kinds of social control.

This brings us to the third issue, the society in which social control is exercised. The way in which social control is exercised and its success is highly dependent upon the form of society. We have seen many attempts—both inside and outside Europe—to impose formal law as a form of state control upon rural peasant societies where informal law was until then dominant. In many cases these attempts did not succeed without a great deal of struggle. However, societies may be in a state of transition—economic, social, or political—that makes a shift of social control inevitable or even desirable. It is not always against the interests of an entire population that the state has tried to strengthen its own position by enforcing formal social control. Nor is an informal type of social control necessarily in the interest of the whole community. Within this community there might exist severe conflicts of opinion and interest.

Like social control, "community" constitutes an equally vague concept. As one of the most important agents of informal social control, "the" community plays of course an important role. But what constitutes a community? Since Tönnies' thesis on *Gemeinschaft* and *Gesellschaft,* this question has been under constant debate. The conclusion seems to be that there is not one kind of community. As Garrioch points out, a community is more characterized by interaction between individuals than by a certain geographically or socially defined group of people. The more and stronger a community's members' bonds are concentrated within a community, the more cohesive that community is. This leads Garrioch to distinguish two criteria for defining an urban community: First, there must be social bonds between members of a community, such as kinship, neighborhood, or occupation. Second, these bonds must lead to a high incidence of social interaction. From this it follows that communities are not stable when people develop bonds that lay outside their neighborhood or social class; for example, they can become less inclined to rely exclusively on their own community.

In the field of social control, Garrioch emphasizes the importance of a set of common values and unwritten rules. These standards are used to evaluate others' behavior. It is primarily insiders who are corrected by means of social control whenever their behavior does not meet the common standard. When outsiders are involved, the community will not undertake action as easily, because it does not feel entitled to do so.[5]

Although Garrioch's analysis is meant to pertain to premodern urban neighborhoods, it could easily be transported to either premodern rural communities or modern communities. In the first instance, villages might be labeled communities even more than their urban counterparts. As people living in a village or hamlet were often connected by kinship, occupation, and geographical closeness, this kind of community should have been relatively strong. In the second instance, inhabitants of urban neighborhoods in modern society are less exclusively—or even hardly at all—oriented toward their neighbors. Most of their kin live outside their own neighborhood (even if many do live close by), and their work place may also be in another part of town. In Garrioch's view, there might be a smaller base for community than in the past.

The concept of community is especially important in the practice of social control. For example, gossip is, according to Garrioch, based on familiarity. In eighteenth-century Paris it was the members of the neighborhood who were talked about and who cared what their peers thought and said about them. The desire to uphold one's reputation, which could be threatened by any accusation or scolding, made it important for people to counter these insults, either by answering them with violence or by complaining to the authorities. By keeping up one's honor one was able to maintain or even advance one's position in the local community. As outsiders had no position to maintain, they were less vulnerable to gossip.[6]

One objection, however, can be made against Garrioch's analysis. In order to set the moral and behavioral standards for a community and to uphold them, it is often useful to have a mirror. As Elias and Scotson have shown, gossiping within a neighborhood not only concerns individuals in the same community, as a means to prevent them from stepping out of line. It is also directed against some sort of "other," which is shown as a bad example. Outsiders, then, are useful for reestablishing the integrity of one's own group, the insiders.[7] In this respect, a community might be reinforced when it is confronted with outsiders.

What is argued about gossip can be extrapolated to other forms of social control, such as charivari. Even more than gossip, charivari as a means of showing disapproval and eventually correcting individuals presupposes a certain amount of community spirit. The actors must share a set of values, not only between themselves but also with the victim. The victim must at least recognize these values in order to break them and to be shown how to behave properly. Just like gossip, being the object of charivari means a heavy loss of honor and reputation.

It was not out of the blue that in the southern part of the Netherlands one of the most common forms of charivari was to force someone to plow his own farmyard. A farmyard that was heavily trodden meant that its owner was an important person within the community, as many people came to visit. Plowing a yard and keeping it plowed meant social isolation, at least for some time. It was a sign that the inhabitants of that house were not considered members of the community.[8]

In contrast, however, charivari could just as easily be directed against outsiders, like foreign tax collectors or judges who were accused of infringing upon the community's rights. These outsiders should be taught a lesson in how to behave toward the community. So, their behavior was not only considered a bad example (as in the case of gossip) but also seen as hostile and dangerous to the community.

In conclusion one might say that social control within a neighborhood or other kind of local community is primarily directed at keeping every member in line. In this sense, it primarily concerns insiders of the community. In order to maintain their place within this community, people have to combat any attack on their integrity that is made through accusations and insults. Social control can also involve outsiders. In that case these outsiders are considered examples of how one should not behave. They form a negative reference group.

One point still needs clarification. Using a concept like community easily leads to a rather harmonious and romantic view of the past. This view is of course false. A true *Gemeinschaft* is an idealization that has never existed. As Garrioch stresses, there is an apparent paradox in that people are anxious to fit into a community, whereas there is a constant competition for honor and positions, which sometimes may have a destructive effect.[9] Beside this more or less constant internal strife, there are economic, social, political, and cultural changes that have their impact on community life. Often these changes are presented as disruptive or even devastating factors. However, it might be more fruitful to see how communities tend to change under the impact of these societal trends.

That is the aim of this contribution. I want to explore how communities, both urban and rural, have developed in the Netherlands since the end of the ancien régime, especially in relationship to social control. I will do this by describing three subsequent major developments in the last two centuries: the process of state formation in the nineteenth century, socioeconomic change during the nineteenth and twentieth centuries, and the so-called cleavage movement (also known as pillarization), which started in the last decades of the nineteenth century and lasted well into the twentieth. Although it should be borne in mind that these processes were not isolated phenomena and were in many respects even intertwined, for the sake of argument I will deal with them separately.

State Formation, 1800–1850

In 1795, the invasion of the Dutch republic by French revolutionary troops and the setting up of a new government brought about the breakdown of the, until then, persistent structure of seven independent states, which only worked together in foreign affairs and defense. For the other fields of policy, these states had maintained their own administrations. This was not all of it, as the numerous cities and jurisdictions within the Republic each had had their own judicial systems to which they adhered quite steadfastly.

Earlier attempts to gain a more centralized structure had failed, and it was only after considerable political struggle that the Dutch formed a more centralized state. Soon this state was to be taken over by its sponsors, the French, first as a kingdom under Napoleon's brother Louis and after 1810 as part of the Bonaparte Empire. Under French rule, the centralization process was rapidly carried further. The numerous jurisdictions lost their autonomy and were enclosed in the strictly hierarchic system of local, regional, and provincial courts, with the supreme court far away in Paris. Correspondingly, local administrations were compelled to submit to the higher officials, again with the top of the hierarchy in Paris.[10] When, after Napoleon's defeat, the family of Orange, the former stadholders, returned to the Netherlands, there was no way back to the former Republican structure. On the contrary, king William I eagerly took over the absolutist position prepared by his French predecessors. His ambitions were even advanced, when the Congress of Vienna joined the Northern Netherlands and Belgium into one state.

So, for the first time and relatively late, the Netherlands were turned into a centralist state. For the common people, this centralization process was noticeable by the introduction of new taxes. Although the new taxes partly replaced the former local and provincial taxes, they meant an aggravation of the tax burden and discontent increased. Especially the introduction of a land tax in the 1830s met with resistance in some parts of the country, where people refused to pay, and military police were brought in to protect the tax collectors. This was particularly the case in the northernmost provinces.[11]

When the Belgians started to revolt against Dutch supremacy and declared themselves independent, taxes were raised once again. Moreover, people felt the burden of another French novelty: the forced conscription into the army, which every young man had to undergo. For the first (and until 1940 last) time, this new national army was to march and go fighting, albeit for only ten days. The military conscription also led to discontent and disturbances.

The Belgian secession also had another impact. The Belgians were predominantly Catholic. As a larger part of the Dutch population was Protestant, and the state government was dominated by Protestants as well, the authorities tended to distrust the Catholic minority, which was largely centered in the southern part of the Netherlands. Since the establishment of the Dutch republic in the seventeenth century, this part had formed a remote and oppressed province, where communities had to put up with the burdens caused by the "foreigners." Hence, for the authorities it was not altogether certain that the southern population would not join the rebelling Belgians. As a consequence they started to tighten their grip upon the peasant population living in the southern parts (e.g., by stationing military police).[12]

It was not only the Catholics who challenged the unity of the state. Within the leading Protestant church, there was an orthodox minority that was horrified by the growing influence of the enlightened tradition among clergymen and administrators. Moreover, in spite of the formal segregation of church and state, the state had a strong influence in church affairs, which was also a grievance for the adherents of "true Calvinism." The orthodox resistance led to a so-called secession from the Dutch Reformed Church, which was directed against the modernist leaders as well as against the authorities. The movement had its base in the north, but soon spread over the entire country.

In the field of community and social control, these orthodox Protestants held views that strongly coincided with folk beliefs. Also, the means of maintaining these views closely resembled those existing within the community. The Calvinist churches restored the old practice of discipline that once had characterized the Protestant church. Gossip and rumors were important sources for these practices. People accused of having committed a sin were forced to defend themselves before the church consistory, and if they could not prove these allegations false, they had to do penance in public.[13] Apart from a theological goal, this form of public social control also served a social cause. It kept the religious community together and cleansed it from internal tensions and disputes. It might not be coincidental that the secession movement was most successful in regions where the old communities were in a state of social transition (which I will discuss later). On the other hand, the secession reinforced this transition by breaking up whole villages into two camps.[14]

There is still debate about the base of the orthodox movement. Traditionally, it was called a movement of "small people" who had successfully emancipated themselves and gradually won political and social power. However, it is a matter of debate how small these small people actually were. Research at a micro level has shown that local orthodox leaders have to be looked for in the strata of farmers, craftsmen, and shopkeepers, rather than among laborers and servants. Especially the poor were often too much dependent upon church poor relief to be able to leave the leading church.[15]

Although the state's power had a large impact on informal social control, its influence should not be exaggerated. Especially in regions and communities where the state officials remained outsiders, informal social control might even have been reinforced. In the province of Brabant, adjacent to the southern border, the local inhabitants adhered to the idea of settling disputes among themselves and keeping the constable or mayor out of it. Whenever a fight in an inn was reported to the authorities, possible witnesses would claim that they had seen nothing, because it was too dark. However, when the offender was an outsider or the act also violated local standards, neighbors would not hesitate to call in the authorities. This was, for example, the case with infanticide, which in many instances was committed by maids coming in from other villages. People did know how to find help from the authorities when they needed it.[16]

Introducing a centralist political and judicial system and expanding the state police force were not the only means for the Dutch central state to widen its grip over society. It also tried to spread a centralist ideology. One of the means to do this was an active involvement in education. Although compulsory education was not introduced until 1901, the authorities made serious efforts to improve the state of education. In order to achieve this, the state took over control from the churches. After that, it erected new and better buildings and forced the teachers to comply with higher standards, both professional and moral. Teachers had to teach the one official pronunciation and spelling of Dutch and drop any accent. They could not indulge in an immoral way of life such as excessive drinking. In order to control them, a nationwide inspection system was introduced. School inspectors would cross their district to visit even the remotest schools and rebuke the teachers for any imperfection.[17]

It is hard to say whether this new school system had a large impact on local communities and informal social control. It certainly did not as yet have the impact attributed to it by both contemporaries and later scholars.[18] True, literacy rates went up slowly and pupils acquired more understanding of their country, but as most of the pupils started working at about twelve years of age, if not earlier, and were never in their lives to read again, the direct impact might have been relatively small. Only the higher social classes were able to develop a kind of national identity.

Orthodox Calvinists and Roman Catholics resented not only the state's power in the field of education but also the religious tolerance it claimed to promote. In the long run, these religious minorities were to establish their own schools, thus starting a fierce political struggle for state-subsidized, yet private "denominational" education. In this sense, improving education, originally undertaken to form a national identity, contributed to developing a sense of religious community identity.[19]

In 1848, in reaction to the events taking place in Paris and in some German states, the Dutch king Willem II decided to yield to liberal pressure for state reform, and parliamentary democracy was introduced. For local communities also this reform was very important as local councils attained more power to manage their own affairs, such as the maintenance of public order. However, most local councils were dominated by the local rich. Especially in the period of classical liberalism, these local elites were inclined to improve conditions for economic growth.

Socioeconomic Developments: Towns and Cities

In spite of the political and judicial changes since the end of the ancien régime, community life might not have changed much at first. As industrialization and mass migration to the cities were not to begin before the last decades of the nineteenth century, labor relations did not undergo radical change. Small workshops and close daily contact between masters and employees still characterized urban social life. This made it difficult for either party to break unwritten rules dealing with working hours, wages, and mutual obligations. There was, however, one difference: since 1798 the craft guilds had been abolished. In the ancien régime, these corporations had formed a semiofficial agent of social control, not only in the field of working conditions but also as societies for mutual help in times of illness and death. The guild members would, for example, arrange for the funeral of deceased fellow members and support their widows and orphans. It is not certain whether during the nineteenth century these help systems still existed, but they were no longer the written rule.[20]

In the second half of the nineteenth century, there was a slow but constant worsening of working and living conditions for workers. One of the factors that contributed to this might have been the weakening of mutual social control between employers and workers. The liberals were eager to remove all impediments to a truly free market. So, maximum prices for bread and other essentials were abolished to let the market do its work. In most cities, the last remnants of professional corporatism were removed.

This gradual breaking down of traditional labor systems could easily go against the interests of the lower social classes. For example, in various cities, such as Dordrecht, there were still regulations in force stipulating a fair trade for dockers. Tradesmen and shipowners were not to employ other workers than those listed as members of the dockers' corporations.[21] When trade in this city collapsed in the middle of the nineteenth century, these corporations tried to close themselves off from newcomers. In this policy they were supported by the traditional elite of old merchants' families to which they were tied by a system of clientelism. When this elite had to yield power to new liberal merchants and manufacturers, the corporations lost their last resort. Gradually, they were deprived of their privileged position. They had to compete with a growing number of workers who came in from other crafts (where labor demand was decreasing) and immigrants coming in from the countryside.

The same treatment that the guilds had experienced was given to the neighborhood corporations. During the Dutch Republic, in most towns there had been formal neighborhood societies. The inhabitants of neighborhoods had united by signing so-called *buurtbrieven* (neighborhood contracts). In these contracts they promised to uphold friendship, to help one another in times of difficulty, and to defend fellow neighbors against the outside world.[22]

Roughly speaking, neighbors' assistance was centered on *rites de passage* (birth, marriage, and death) and illness. When a woman was in labor, the nearest—usually four—neighboring women had to assist at the birth. When a member of the family died, the neighbors would come in, take care of the body, ring the church bells, sometimes make the coffin, and carry the body to the churchyard. The exact number of assisting households would depend on the age and sometimes on the sex of the deceased. To express their sense of community, the neighbors would organize annual banquets in which every household participated. Every inhabitant was a member of a neighborhood, and every immigrant was supposed to pay an entrance fee in order to be admitted into the neighborhood association.[23]

As early as the seventeenth and early-eighteenth centuries, in many towns, these associations already tended to disintegrate. One of the most important factors leading to this disintegration was a steady social polarization. A merging class of rich merchants, the so-called *burghers,* who gained political control over the newly established state, developed a luxurious lifestyle, which made them less inclined to associate socially with their less wealthy neighbors. By the beginning of the nineteenth century, formal neighborhood associations had vanished altogether. Their tasks were taken over by new burial societies. In the same way, shortly after the middle of the nineteenth century, small-scale sick-funds emerged. They attracted mainly craftsmen and skilled workers. These funds were, however, intended to compensate for loss of income rather than for attending to the sick. In this respect, they were successors to the former guilds rather than to the neighborhood societies.

Nonetheless, the disappearance of formal neighborhood societies did not mean that mechanisms of mutual help no longer existed. Nineteenth-century municipalities kept on calling in citizens to perform community tasks such as maintaining the neighborhood watch, putting out fires, and cleaning the streets. These tasks only gradually disappeared with the professionalization of the police force, fire squads, and other public services. In the meantime, the poor had created a form of mutual help of their own, which more likely expanded than diminished during the nineteenth century. Among the poor, mutual help became (if not already formed) one of several survival strategies. People would donate food, when their neighbors were short of cash to buy food, or shelter, when their neighbors were thrown out of their houses.[24]

In this form of informal mutual assistance among neighbors, reciprocity was a strong motive. One helped one's neighbor expecting to receive help in the future. In this respect, there was little difference with the more formalized forms of mutual help. Of course this expectation could only be fulfilled when the other party was able to help. When everybody was struck by misfortune, for example during an economic crisis, this system would come under severe pressure. Another impediment to receiving help from the neighborhood was one's place within the local community. People who were less popular were not in a position to hope for much help. In its informal shape, this neighborship did not pass social boundaries. It was primarily common among the lower social classes. The middle classes and elites would rather turn to relatives or friends when they needed help. This had to do also with a growing concern for privacy and class consciousness. "Don't let the neighbors find out," became a basic rule of life.

Relatively little is known about informal social control in nineteenth-century cities. It might not have been very different from that in the seventeenth and eighteenth centuries, such as described for Amsterdam by Roodenburg and for Paris by Garrioch.[25] In the first decades of the nineteenth century, honor and reputation still played important roles in everyday street life. People went easily to the authorities to complain when they were insulted. Just like in the ancien régime, honesty and integrity were grounds upon which most men were criticized, while women had to deal with accusations and allegations involving their sexual behavior.[26]

However, there are signs that the classical means of social control, such as gossip, violence, or charivari, had lost much of their impact. Gossip was still quite common in most groups, but the gossip circles had become more confined and, probably, smaller than before. Heavy social sanctions, such as the use of charivari, were mainly applied within the lower social classes, if applied at all. It was the lower classes that stuck to these old forms of social control, whereas the rich welcomed the formal social control system of the authorities in order to protect themselves against the workers' protest actions. As a consequence, the old forms of social control lost their impact.

This was of course not a process that had just started. We have already seen that the formal neighborhood had begun to disintegrate as early as the seventeenth century. This process was now only being completed. Perhaps one could say that with the growing social one-sidedness of the neighborhood, the sense of community within the lower social echelons increased. According to Garrioch's line of reasoning, the inhabitants of these neighborhoods had more in common, especially their poverty.[27] It was at this time that the romantic view of labor-class quarters as havens of neighborliness started to rise.

Socioeconomic Developments: The Countryside

In the countryside the situation remained more stable than in the cities. However, in order to understand neighborhood tendencies in the Dutch countryside during the past two centuries, it is necessary to draw attention to the differences between the northern and the western coastal area on the one hand and the eastern and southern interior on the other hand. Since the seventeenth century, especially in the west, agriculture had already become very market-oriented, mainly by producing dairy and horticultural products for the expanding urban market. During the eighteenth and early-nineteenth centuries, the north of the country had gradually changed into the country's corn belt. In the eastern and southern provinces, subsistence agriculture survived well into the nineteenth century. Mixed farms mainly produced for household needs and for fiscal payments. In order to expand their cash revenues, most farms were engaged in cottage industries, such as spinning and weaving.

These macroeconomic differences also had an impact on society and culture. In the market-oriented areas, a class of rich farmers existed side-by-side with an ever growing labor force, which possessed hardly any land.[28] As early as the eighteenth century, social relations in these areas had become rather polarized, and during the nineteenth century northern society became the battlefield of intense class struggle. As the farmers grew richer and richer, they tended to detach themselves from village life and the moral standards that obtained there. As a consequence, informal social control was marginalized. Some of its elements, such as organized mutual help and informal poor relief, vanished altogether. Other social mechanisms lost influence because their impact became more and more confined to the lower social classes within society, without any effect on the population at large, just as had happened in the cities.

Especially in the north, neighborhood was weakening fast. How the system of mutual assistance changed can be examined by looking closely at everyday practices, as I have done for the northeastern province of Groningen. In the beginning of the nineteenth century, it was fairly common for all villagers to be engaged in mutual assistance at peaks in the agricultural cycle, at births, and at deaths. As was described by contemporaries, sometimes the whole village assisted with harvesting grain or threshing rapeseed (the oil of which was used for lighting). Although every farm had a number of workers and servants, it could not survive without the help of neighbors and others during these peaks.

These labor-intensive activities, that usually took place in the hot summer months, were concluded by large-scale festivities, in which the participants were treated with abundant eating and drinking. In this way, the farmer showed his gratitude for the voluntary help he had received from his fellow villagers. However, as one contemporary witness put it, by this time the farmers had become so rich and powerful, that local artisans and shopkeepers did not dare to refuse helping out in the summer, for they feared losing rich customers. So, in spite of its nominally reciprocal nature, the custom had changed in favor of the farmers.[29]

As the number of workers in this area grew steadily beyond the point of maximum employment, farmers no longer needed the goodwill of their neighbors.

They could simply hire a bunch of unemployed workers, who were glad to earn some money. The farmer could save the money he had to spend on the meals and drinks for the people helping him out. Instead, he only had to pay minimal wages and could dispense with meals and drinks. By the end of the nineteenth century, the big festivities following the harvest had disappeared altogether.

Not only within the agricultural context but also in that of neighborly duties, things changed in nineteenth-century Groningen. Up until the early-nineteenth century, neighborhoods and villages had a strong sense of community. Whenever people were in need, their neighbors would rush to give assistance, just as they were used to doing in the interior parts of the country. However, as the economic gap between social classes grew wider, they were less inclined to attend each other's births, marriages, and funerals. Rich people and poor people were leading separate lives. The rich were no longer interested in spending time with their laborers and servants, whom they came to consider uncivilized and undisciplined. In contrast, the rich farmers themselves were developing a more sophisticated way of life. In this new, more private style of life, women who had just given birth received fewer visitors, while meals after funerals, with their abundant eating and drinking, were no longer thought appropriate.

But there was more to it. As differences in wealth grew steadily, the amount of money individual households could spend on these visits and meals became highly variable. Whereas farmers' households developed a kind of conspicuous consumption to show off their newly acquired wealth, workers' families could not afford any of that. Thus, the idea of reciprocity, lying at the base of neighborhood, vanished.

Local authorities showed a somewhat ambiguous reaction to these developments. On the one hand, they tried to make funerals, marriages, and baptisms more sober by prohibiting too many guests from being invited or too much money spent on consumption. In this way, they took away the "fun part" of neighbors' assistance. On the other hand, they tried to keep the system from breaking down by imposing legal standards. As they saw the great advantages of the system in terms of the costs and efforts they themselves would not have to make, they tried to benefit as much as possible. Thus, not only were caring for new mothers, the sick, and the dead to be carried out by neighbors but also numerous tasks in repairing roads, fire control, and police vigilance were imposed upon the local inhabitants. People who neglected their duties toward their neighbors or community could be brought to trial and fined. These efforts were in vain. By the end of the nineteenth century, semiformal neighborhood had vanished.

The dissolution of the neighborhood as an organized assistance body did not serve the interests of the poor. As they lacked the means to take part in burial societies or to hire professionals, they remained strongly dependent upon their neighbors' help. But they could no longer enforce this help. Only by means of informal social control, could neighborhood be effected. In this respect, neighborhood became a marginalized phenomenon, both socially and economically.

In the sandy interior of the country, agriculture remained rather backward until the second half of the nineteenth century. This meant that local communities remained mostly isolated and village life mostly autonomous, as it was in large parts of the Continent. Although the nobility played some part, most farms were relatively small. Landless laborers were far from nonexistent, but there was a large class of cottagers and crofters. The more or less egalitarian social structure of the interior was reflected in the existence of numerous arrangements that controlled agriculture and were meant to secure the population's subsistence. Agricultural tasks such as harvesting and threshing were performed by mutual arrangement. After the harvest everyone's fields were opened up for the common herds of sheep or cows. In the case of illness, birth, and death, people would help their neighbors, as they were morally obliged to do so. As in other parts of the country, they attended births, looked after the sick and old, made the necessary preparations for burials, and attended funerals. Traditionally, mutual help was given in agricultural activities that could not be performed by a household alone, such as harvesting, threshing, or the building of a house.[30]

Neighbor assistance had both an economic and a social character. Among poor peasants it was crucial for their subsistence. Therefore, reciprocity was essential. People helped others because they could expect to be helped when they themselves were in need of assistance. For the village as a whole, these arrangements contributed to safeguarding the peasants' way of life. On a cultural level, mutual assistance helped to build coherence between the villagers. This coherence was symbolized by celebrations and festivities at the end of difficult tasks (e.g., harvest feasts). On the individual level, support from neighbors was rewarded by giving them plenty of food and drink. As mutual assistance was provided without payments, the treat might be (and often was) considered a payment in kind. Hence, people who were considered to be stingy ran the risk of being subjected to rough music or social exclusion.

There has up until now been little investigation into the social aspects of this system of mutual assistance. Despite a strong egalitarian ideology, there were certainly differences in wealth. These differences could have influenced systems of mutual assistance, by which richer farmers might have been able to profit more from collective arrangements than poorer households. In comparison, in the north of Portugal, where collective arrangements and forms of cooperation among peasants survived until very recently, larger farmers were able to draw more benefit from mutual assistance and communal resources (such as commons, water supplies, and threshing fields) than their poorer neighbors.[31] Whether this was the case in the Netherlands as well remains an unanswered question. Some cases indicate otherwise. In some parts, there were regulations to the advantage of smallholders over larger farms. They were, for example, permitted to harvest on Sunday, which was formally an obligatory day of rest.[32] However, this permission might have been given in order to ensure that they had plenty of time to help the larger farms during the week.

In contrast with the coastal areas of the Netherlands, in the sandy interior, with its socially more egalitarian structure, the process of marginalization of neighborhood went much slower and only took place in the course of the twentieth century. Even today, in farmers' communities neighborship has continued to play an enormously important role. Nevertheless, neighborhood in these areas has some striking features. At least since the end of the nineteenth century, a more exclusive use of *neighborship* seems to have developed. The neighborhood no longer comprised all households living in a certain area, but the word was used to designate a fixed group of households that called themselves each other's neighbors. But these households would not necessarily lie next door to each other. People who lived nearer to one another might still be excluded from this neighborhood and form part of another neighborhood.[33]

It is not certain whether this more or less voluntary neighborhood was in fact different from earlier periods, when territorial neighborhood and social neighborhood had coincided. The available material suggests it was. Perhaps one of the factors that contributed to the formation of different neighborhoods within one former neighborhood was the settlement of households in newly built cottages in between the older farms. These new farms might not have been admitted to the existing neighborhood. As these new farms were often very small compared to the existing ones, it can be suggested that neighborhood, even in so-called egalitarian communities, became more socially differentiated than is usually supposed. But, because of a lack of evidence, this suggestion remains very tentative.

Just like community and neighborship, informal social control remained fairly strong in the sandy areas. It was in these regions that informal social control like charivari lived well into the twentieth century. It is, however, noteworthy that some orthodox Calvinist communities retained a high standard of informal social control and folk justice as well. In the long run these so-called traditional regions became more and more scarce, as large parts of the countryside became industrialized or opened up to peat digging.

The Cleavage Movement: From Geographical to Socioreligious Community, 1870–1950

Roughly between 1870 and 1914, industrialization and urbanization changed Dutch city life. Some cities, such as Amsterdam and Rotterdam, underwent an enormous population growth. Other, smaller towns started to change into large industrial centers. Thousands of people streamed in from the countryside, driven by the agrarian depression of the 1880s and lured by the new industries and trade that developed in the cities. At the same time social relations started to change. As large enterprises developed and the labor movement came into existence, labor relations became less patriarchal and more modern. Paternalism and personal bonds of patronage between rich and poor diminished, as traditional poor relief changed into a modern social security system.

In the last decades of the nineteenth century, new groups were putting the liberal dominance to question, both politically and economically. The first movement to challenge the existing order was that of the religious (confessional) parties, both orthodox Calvinist and Roman Catholic. As we have seen earlier, the orthodox Calvinist movement had started in the 1830s as secession within the partly state-based Reformed Church. In the 1880s it was followed by a new exodus of orthodox Calvinists from the central Church. The result of the various schisms was a whole range of Calvinist churches that in spite of their internal divisions had one object in common: turning the country into an almost theocratic state. In spite of their organizational fragmentation, they slowly gained more political power. One of the most important mechanisms for this was the struggle for denominational schools, to be subsidized by the state. The harder the liberal governments adhered to the concept of one neutral state school and tried to prevent educational diversification, the harder they were attacked by the confessional parties.

The Calvinist parties had an ally in the Catholic minority. Although in a religious context Calvinists and Catholics were poles apart, politically their objectives were quite similar. Just like the Calvinist parties, the Catholics were interested in building a system of schools and organizations for their own population groups. In order to achieve this, they were willing to work together to fight the liberal hegemony. In the long run they succeeded, as the confessional parties were to take part in political power and to become a significant political factor.

They were not the only ones, as the socialist movement also pushed to get the political power it claimed. The labor movement had followed the same recipe as the religious parties to unite its supporters and strengthen its organization: by erecting a whole body of political, social, and cultural clubs. With the introduction of universal suffrage in 1917, the political system was modernized and political parties took over the leading position of the old elites. The socialists then became one of the leading political powers, especially within local government.

So, this social and political struggle has given birth to what used to be called "pillarization" (*verzuiling*) but has nowadays become known as the cleavage movement. While in this cleavage movement, the "common people" were encouraged to isolate themselves in religious or sociopolitical "pillars," and political leaders at the top of society had to "accommodate" and work together to form governments and rule the country, thus preserving social order and preventing internal turmoil. This cleavage movement permeated Dutch society until at least the 1960s and was characterized by extreme divisions in political, social, and cultural life. Even sporting clubs were organized along religious and political lines.

There has been a lot of debate as to how to explain the rise and perseverance of this social system. Early scholars sought the answer at the top, claiming that the maintenance of social order, and especially the prevention of class struggle, was the main goal of the cleavage movement. Others have maintained that the cleavage movement was an outcome of the emancipation process of social and religious groups that had until then played a very submissive role in society. Recent research on a local level seems to support the second vision. It has drawn attention to the fact that the first signs of cleavage were visible long before the labor movement came into being. It was not so much the working classes as the lower-middle classes (craftsmen, petty shopkeepers) that adhered to the new religious movements.[34]

In terms of social control, the cleavage movement had an enormous impact upon everyday life, as the new groups in power were eager to reform society according to their own principles. Thus, they started a range of policies that have often been described as "disciplinary offensives" or "civilizing offensives." Although there had been such offensives in the seventeenth and early-nineteenth centuries as well, especially the one conducted in the late-nineteenth and early-twentieth centuries was extremely successful. This led, for example, to the criminalization of alcohol abuse, the ban on prostitution and other deviant forms of sexuality, and to the abolition of fairs and other public feasts. Many aspects of daily life, such as premarital conception, excessive drinking, and popular culture, were repressed and replaced by more "decent" forms of behavior. The stress on family values and middle-class standards has greatly influenced public and private life throughout the twentieth century.

Moreover, the cleavage movement might have led to a shift in community life as well. As people were increasingly involved in activities that did not surpass religious boundaries, interactions with people from other denominations were more limited. There are numerous examples of people who refused to frequent shops whose owners did not go to the same church. On Sundays, in the village of Ottoland (not far from Rotterdam), adherents of the Dutch Reformed Church would walk on one side of the canal that ran across the village, while their orthodox "opponents" would take the opposite side. Even today, older people tell of the fights that used to take place between pupils of state, Catholic, and Calvinist schools. Religiously mixed marriage met with huge disapproval, not only from church leaders but from family and neighbors as well. This rivalry was of course stronger in towns and religiously divided villages than in socially and religiously more homogeneous communities.

Another impact of the cleavage movement was centered on class relations. This was especially the case in the large cities. With the building of new residential districts in the first decades of the twentieth century, social classes were separated geographically. In the 1920s and 1930s, the concept of the garden city found massive application. Gradually the better-off skilled laborers left the old working-class quarters in the town centers for social housing projects in the outskirts of the cities. As prosperity rose, they were more able to meet the social standards of the middle class than before. They developed a lifestyle in which order, decency, and respect played an important part. No more excessive drinking, not even at birthdays or holidays. No more sitting in the street chatting and doing nothing useful. Architects deliberately designed apartment buildings with small windows in order to prevent housewives from hanging out of the windows and gossiping all day.[35]

This process of "respectabilization" was reinforced by existing socioreligious boundaries, which as we have seen, tended to be accentuated. As most house building societies were either socialist, Calvinist, or Catholic oriented, it was common policy to build separate quarters for these groups. In this respect, the better-off labor class became one of the "pillars" of the civilizing offensives that flourished in the cleavage period.

But even where quarters had a mixed population, people would center their social lives on those belonging to their own circle. Although they knew the others by face or even by name, they maintained a great distance. In fact, the other groups were met with distrust and hostility. In her analysis of the changes in a Rotterdam working-class neighborhood between the First World War and today, Blokland-Potters shows the strong distinctions that used to exist between Catholics and Protestants, between socialists and nonsocialists, between skilled and unskilled workers. All these categories primarily focused on their own social circles, whether religious organizations, peer groups, or colleagues from work. Thus, they were inclined to maintain a strong "we and they" concept in assessing one's behavior, which was based upon stereotypes. But, as is argued by Blokland-Potters, this was not to say that people did not know each other. These categorizations could only be made thanks to the geographical closeness. As people constantly met in the streets, even if they did not mix socially, they knew enough to fit "the other" in one or another category.[36]

Of course, not all working-class families made the step toward an improved standard of living and more respectability. The slums, in as far as they were not pulled down and replaced with better houses, came to be associated with so-called antisocial population groups. The unskilled, semi-unemployed workers and their families living in these quarters were increasingly the subject of attempts from local authorities to improve their moral and behavioral standards. In several cities, the worst cases of misconduct were sent to remote camps in order to undergo intensive training for a better way of life. Like almost all public activities in these days, this policy also had a political background. Especially socialist municipalities were eager to fight this battle against drunkenness, bad upbringing, and lack of order and cleanliness. They saw it as a means to achieve a better world for everyone, including the lowest social classes. Forcing people to alter their public and moral behavior was meant to be for their own good.[37]

However, this new civilizing offensive, although now fiercer and more directed at individual households than ever, did not have the effect that its agents hoped for. Especially during the Great Depression, with its huge unemployment and steeply falling standard of living, many could not live up to the requirements of respectability. It is even suggested that this economic crisis gave birth to new poverty and thus to another wave of antisocial classes, the traces of which were still to be found in the 1960s and 1970s.[38] It was in these quarters that the old way of living remained vivid. Systems of reciprocal assistance, petty criminality, and a harsh mutual social control were characteristic for these quarters. These microsocieties have been the subject of enormous romanticism. Especially the assumed solidarity and the so-called coziness are often idealized. One of the best-known examples of this is that of the Jordaan, a very crowded and poor quarter in Amsterdam that turned into a center of Dutch popular music.

In the countryside, the already existing differences between the northwestern and southeastern parts of the Netherlands remained in force. Whereas the north and west modernized quickly, within the religiously homogeneous communities in the eastern and southern countryside, community identification remained strong throughout the twentieth century. It was in these parts that informal social control in its classical form remained strong. Instances of charivari are reported from the eastern as well as the southern provinces up until this very day. One could even say that in areas where orthodoxy was predominant, charivari was still quite accepted as a means of social control. This might have to do with the communities in these areas being very close and restricted to outsiders.[39]

In the course of the twentieth century, however, neighborship in the countryside, even if it did not vanish altogether, became of a more sober nature. This process can be attributed to two factors. First, there were the developments in agriculture. With mechanization and commercialization since the beginning of the twentieth century, traditions of cooperation and mutual assistance were no longer vital for the continuity of the farm. Neighbors did continue to help out whenever it was necessary, but this help was of a more incidental and voluntary nature.[40]

The same impact came from the professionalization of health care and burials. These societies took over major tasks. The foundation of these burial societies, which usually had a local base, was sometimes opposed by the lower classes. As membership of these societies had to be paid for, they were more inclined to adhere to the older forms of assistance from the neighborhood. In contrast, middle-class and richer farms tended to support the idea of the burial society.[41] This conflict also had a cultural side. Traditionally, funerals had been massive events, attended by a large number of people, who were treated with elaborate meals and plenty of drink. These feasts met with much disapproval. Since not only the upper classes but, more important, the middle classes and skilled workers developed other, more civilized standards of behavior, old customs tended to disappear or to be transformed into more appropriate practices. One of the customs affected by this civilization process was the holding of elaborate funerals in the east and south of the Netherlands. Meals were replaced by sandwiches or cake, beer and liquor by coffee and tea. And above all, the number of people attending the funerals decreased.[42]

Informal Social Control after World War II

The societal changes that have taken place since the Second World War have had an enormous impact on mechanisms of informal social control. The so-called depillarization that has happened largely since the 1960s made people less dependent upon the approval of the church authorities in making personal choices and choosing a lifestyle. Also, as the former religious bonds weakened, the strongly religious communities tended to fall apart. The same applied to the socialist pillar. With economic and social changes, such as the growing chances for upward mobility and the shrinking importance of industrial labor, the old blue-collar communities became increasingly mixed up with other social groups. As labor politics became more and more a force in the center, the old movement as it were died out.

The traditional role of the labor movement was taken over by a number of welfare institutions, which had for a large part originated within the pillars, but had gradually detached themselves from their roots to form large and usually state-subsidized institutions. The rise of the welfare state made people less vulnerable socially and caused them to rely less upon their families and neighbors for material support. As a consequence, they became less inclined to keep on good terms with their neighbors. An important factor influencing the degree of neighbors' assistance in the Dutch countryside was the change in agricultural life, as we have seen. As the process of mechanization continued and even accelerated, farms became isolated family farms with little cooperation between themselves.

The result of these changes was that neighborhood in the post–World War II period became less institutionalized. The social function of neighborhood dominated the economic function. In fact, one can speak of a process of informalization of neighborhood. Only in the post–World War II period, when other forms of social security became predominant and welfare spread more evenly among the population, neighborhood became of less importance as a necessary means of existence than it had been before. That does not mean that neighborhood vanished. Especially, in working-class areas it remained an important, often romanticized, feature of everyday life. But with the expansion of public health services, pension schemes, and unemployment benefits, even the lower classes were no longer dependent upon their neighbors. Thus, as welfare increased, neighborship became less of a necessary strategy to survive and more based upon personal choice. Furthermore, as the bonds of churches and work lost their overwhelming impact, people began to develop more personal orientations.

During the last decades, these trends have intensified. As a consequence of mass immigration from foreign countries, suburbanization and reconstruction of old city quarters, the old means of social control that had characterized these quarters, have weakened. Many of the old inhabitants moved away. Their places were taken over by either newcomers with a different cultural background or groups operating at the margins of society (e.g., drug dealers and prostitutes). The local communities have become more anonymous.

Among certain class or ethnic groups, for example Mediterranean communities in the cities, neighborhood is still a very strong force, although it is probably organized differently from that of the local population. For example, among Mediterranean groups, people do not lend sugar or coffee, one of the most common features of neighborship. [43] Among Turkish population groups the notion of family honor leads to a strict informal social control that reminds one of the ancien régime in Europe.[44] Also, the large gap between the Dutch "permissive society" and severe methods of upbringing within the family is often seen as one of the contributing factors to high criminality rates among Moroccan youngsters. Even in cases where relationships between ethnic groups seem to be working very well, such as in an Utrecht neighborhood that is nicknamed "the *kasbah*," these groups turn out to live quite separate lives and hardly mix socially.[45] In this respect, the situation resembles that of the distance between socioreligious groups before 1940.

In short, neighborhood has become a marginalized phenomenon, important more as lubricating oil for good relations within a local community than as means of survival. Relationships within a community have tended to become more personal. As Blokland-Potters puts it, friendship ties have taken over the role of neighborship. However, the interdependence between neighbors has not diminished in every respect. On the contrary, as anonymity has increased, it has become more difficult to deal with people who cause a nuisance. Those staying behind sometimes respond to this trend by creating an *imagined community:* based upon their collective memories of the prewar period, they glorify this past, when the neighborhood was supposed to be united, and attribute a process of disintegration to the newcomers.[46]

These are the circumstances that cause many problems in contemporary urban neighborhoods and have led sociologists and politicians to draw much attention to community life in modern cities. Almost invariably, this attention has resulted in attempts to restore and enhance a community spirit in which the old social control should become more important. For example, the inhabitants of a particular street in Rotterdam have installed a big clock outside to indicate the time when all children should be indoors and not roaming the streets. Also, there are numerous examples of inhabitants collectively cleaning the street, called *opzoomeren* after another Rotterdam street, which has aroused enormous enthusiasm from local authorities.

Conclusion

In my contribution, I have tried to provide an overview of the trends that have developed within the field of informal social control in the Netherlands during the last two hundred years. I have placed special emphasis on the impact of various social factors that, in my opinion, over these years have influenced community life, both in the city and in the countryside. As informal social control is closely tied to this community, changes in community life may have an important impact upon the form and range of informal social control.

The last decade has seen almost desperate attempts from local and national authorities to revive the community spirit that once prevailed. Restoring informal social control "as it used to be" is seen as one of the major contributions to the "war against criminality." But when was this "as it used to be"? In 1950? In 1900? In 1800? Or still earlier? Complaints about the loss of community spirit have been raised throughout history. This leads Blokland-Potters to criticize contemporary policies aimed at "restoring community spirit." In her view, such a community spirit hardly ever existed, if at all, and the authorities are chasing a ghost. Although, in my opinion, she rightly criticizes the romantic view of working-class neighborhoods in the past, this view is not altogether without its problems. People in these ancient neighborhoods at least felt some kind of responsibility for one another and made themselves heard whenever something was wrong. As Blokland-Potters herself states, in the early-twentieth century, inhabitants of a neighborhood might have been locked up in their own pillarized organizations and daily routine, but at least they knew the members of other pillars by face, which is nowadays seldom the case. Nevertheless, informal social control will probably never be like it was in those days and any attempts to restore it are bound to fail.

Notes

1. Spierenburg, *De verbroken betovering,* chap. 3.
2. For the discussion in the Netherlands, cf. Blokland-Potters, *Wat stadsbewoners bindt,* 1–5.

3. Elias and Scotson, *The Established;* Bergmann, *Klatsch,* 198–213; Garrioch, *Neighbourhood,* 33–55. This raises the question whether social control should be considered to represent only sanctions of disapproved behavior or whether it also consists of preventive mechanisms. Are, for example, education and rebellion forms of social control? And is raising children within the family? If this wider definition of the field of social control is followed, the concept might lose its force. Social control would then mean practically all social interaction. For the purpose of this paper, it seems wise to concentrate fully upon sanctions, which might be both negative (punishments) and positive (rewards).

4. Cf. Cachet, *Politie,* 51–52.

5. Garrioch, *Neighbourhood,* 3–5.

6. Garrioch, *Neighbourhood,* 33ff. Cf. Keunen and Roodenburg, *Schimpen,* Introduction, 289–94; and Roodenburg, "De notaris."

7. Elias and Scotson, *The Established.*

8. Rooijakkers, *Rituele repertoires,* 425–29.

9. Garrioch, *Neighbourhood,* 41.

10. Sleebe, *In termen,* 153–56.

11. Nijman, "Spanningen."

12. How oppressed this province really was, is a matter of debate. Recently, the relative autonomy of these communities has been emphasized. Rooijakkers, *Religieuze repertoires,* 53–58.

13. Within the Calvinist churches, this had been the practice since the sixteenth century; cf. Roodenburg, *Onder censuur.* By the beginning of the nineteenth century, it had largely disappeared within the leading Dutch Reformed Church.

14. Sleebe, *In termen,* 119–31.

15. Mulder, *Revolte der fijnen;* Verrips, *En boven de polder.*

16. Rombach, "Verbalen," states that there were only few cases of infanticide and that because of its atrocious character it was reported immediately.

17. Verhoeven, *Ter vorming;* Boekholt, *Onderwijs.*

18. Cf. for France: Weber, *Peasants.*

19. Verhoeven, *Ter vorming.*

20. This view of the guilds might, however, be too romantic, as many guilds were already in decay long before they were officially abolished.

21. Municipal archives of the city of Dordrecht (1813–1851), nr. 12, Town Council Resolutions 1819.

22. Roodenburg, "Naar een etnografie."

23. Ibid., 239.

24. E.g., for the city of Leiden: Pot, *Arm Leiden,* 225–26; for Amsterdam: Van Leeuwen, *Bijstand,* 278.

25. Roodenburg, "De notaris," 367–87; Garrioch, *Neighbourhood.*

26. Keunen, "Ongaarne bericht," 415–31.

27. On this discussion cf. Garrioch, *Neighbourhood,* 205–56.

28. In these regions large landowners such as those existing in England or Germany were rather scarce.

29. Sleebe, *In termen*, 372–75.

30. Gras, *Op de grens*, 147–50.

31. Bennema, *Traditions;* Pina Cabral, *Sons of Adam;* O'Neill, *Social Inequality.*

32. Gras, *Op de grens*, 150.

33. Heuvel, *Oud-Achterhoeks Boerenleven.*

34. E.g., Lijphart, *Verzuiling;* Stuurman, *Verzuiling,* Van der Laarse, *Bevoogding;* Van Miert, *Wars van clubgeest.*

35. De Regt, *Arbeidersgezinnen.*

36. Blokland-Potters, *Wat stadsbewoners bindt,* English summary, 381–91.

37. De Regt, *Arbeidersgezinnen.*

38. Knotter, *Rondom de Stokstraat.*

39. Van den Bergh, ed., *Staphorst.*

40. Hobbelink, *Je trouwt niet alleen.*

41. Boer, *Dorp in Drente.*

42. Sleebe, "Burenhulp."

43. Blokland-Potters, *Wat stadsbewoners bindt,* 287ff.

44. De Vries, *Roddel;* Yesilgöz, "Namus."

45. Dibbits and Meder, "Kasbah."

46. Blokland-Potters, *Wat stadsbewoners bindt,* 256.

Part Two

POLICING AND THE STATE:
LIBERAL VS. TOTALITARIAN REGIMES

Control and Legitimacy: The Police in Comparative Perspective since circa 1800

Clive Emsley

W hen E. A. Ross coined the term "social control" at the beginning of the twentieth century, he argued that social order was not simply the product of law but involved the workings of much more complex phenomena. These phenomena could be moral and ethical, shaped from sentiment rather than utility, and enforced through, among other things, public opinion and personal discipline. They might also be more specifically the tools of policy, such as the law and education, designed or developed by a few to control and shape the many. The concept of social control was particularly in vogue among academics, and greatly expanded by them, in the aftermath of World War II; it was used by sociologists of the conservative, functionalist school as well as by radicals and Marxists. It was, and at times still is, deployed by historians, often as if it was clearly agreed what the concept meant and as if it was quite unproblematic.[1] This essay focuses on the agency that, more than any other, can be and has been perceived as a controller and supervisor within modern society—professional, bureaucratic police. Yet it is important to remember that discipline and supervisory strategies were employed within different communities long before the introduction of professional police. Many of these have virtually disappeared, but others have persisted and evolved.

Twenty years ago Keith Wrightson published an important essay stressing that there were commonly two views of order in the early modern English village: that of the community itself and that of the jurist. The latter sought "a coherent structure of social relationships and moral values" while the local communities' aspirations were rather more intimate, seeking little more than the absence of disruptive conflict locally and conformity to "a fairly malleable local custom which was considerably more flexible than statute law."[2] While Wrightson's focus was specifically England, his argument had far wider resonances.

It might be argued that one of the key aims of the European state since the early modern period has been to impose on its territories the concept of order envisaged by its jurists and legislators. Since the early modern period the European state, jealous of its own authority, has systematically worn away that of its rivals notably the Church, the nobility and gentry, and the municipalities. Moreover, it has stressed to its subjects, and subsequently its citizens, that matters such as ensuring public conformity, enforcing good public behavior, preventing and punishing public transgressions should be left primarily to its agencies.

A variety of measures have been available within local communities for enforcing social norms. At the most basic and dramatic level was the vigilantism by which a community made a violent attack on those who transgressed. Such behavior can explode in modern, liberal democratic societies as was revealed by the outcry and attacks on the homes of suspected pedophiles in England in the summer of 2000.[3] The folkloric practices of charivari—*Katzenmusik,* rough music, *scampanate*—appear increasingly to have declined in the industrializing and urbanizing world of the nineteenth and twentieth centuries, though vestiges continued even in urban areas and in political protests.[4] Community gossip, usually dominated by women, remained a means of marking out norms and stigmatizing those who transgressed.[5] Both thefts and assaults—ranging from fights to rape—could be resolved by infrajudicial means, in other words by the meeting of interested parties before an independent, respected member of the community such as a priest, a notary, the mayor, his deputy, even a seigneurial agent, who would then seek some form of resolution in the form of a monetary payment, the return of disputed goods, or perhaps, in the case of rape or sexual assault, a marriage. There remain questions about both the scale of such behavior and its apparent decline.[6] It appears to continue today, even in the most modern European societies, among marginal groups.[7] Moreover, in communities where the state is weak or intensely disliked and distrusted, it is possible for infrajudicial activities to evolve into alternative structures. Mafia in Sicily is one such example where families and communities have preferred to preserve their affairs in their own hands through a system of clientage and reciprocity, rather than involve any external authority, particularly the representatives of an unpopular state. The unofficial "courts" and punishments administered by paramilitaries within the embattled communities of Northern Ireland provide another.

The concept of police, in the sense of the internal management of a state or a specific territory, has been around for centuries, but the nineteenth century witnessed the development of bureaucratic police organizations across the states of Europe and their empires, and across the United States. The state, Max Weber famously suggested, may be defined as that collectivity of institutions enjoying a monopoly of violence within a continuously bounded territory; and within the modern state the bureaucratic police officer is the only individual legally empowered to use force in his day-to-day dealings with the citizens. Popularly, these dealings are perceived as the prevention of crime and the detection and pursuit of offenders, but more generally they concern the maintenance of order which can range from ensuring that the public highways are open to free access and movement, to the suppression of brawling and violent disorder. Of course, modern society would not collapse without such police control and supervision, but it *could* be more chaotic and more dangerous. The intention in what follows is to explore the extent to which the police have exercised control and supervision over society, and also to assess the extent to which such control and supervision may have changed and developed through time, the limitations upon it, and what alternative arrangements have been available for achieving such control objectives as the police may have had.

Origins of Police

Reading between the lines of the sources and contemplating hidden agendas is the stock-in trade of the modern social historian. Traditional historians of the police in Britain, in contrast, tended to take their sources at face value. As far as historians like Charles Reith and David Ascoli were concerned, if Sir Robert Peel, the Home Secretary, told the House of Commons in 1829 that he was introducing legislation to establish a centralized police organization for London because of an increase in crime in the city, and if other police reformers argued similarly about increasing crime and disorder, then that was the reason why the police were created.[8] Allan Silver's influential essay on the demand for order in civil society, comparing concerns about crime and rioting and the resulting police developments in Britain and the United States, suggested a rather different perspective.[9] Subsequently two seminal articles by Robert D. Storch, based on extensive archival research, took this perspective a stage further.[10] Storch's work suggested that the police in England were established essentially as domestic missionaries designed for imposing a new kind of order on the emergent working class. The issue, of course, was not resolved by Storch's work though, arguably, a new broad consensus is emerging that recognizes the significance of both concerns about crime and the demand for a new threshold of public order.

The recent debates about the origins of the modern bureaucratic police have focused largely on the British experience and that of the United States; the major exception here is Hsi-Huey Liang's assessment of the development of police in continental Europe from the end of the Napoleonic wars to the end of the Second World War, which, while ignoring developments in Britain, is still infused with traditional Whig teleology.[11] Moreover, omitting the British or English model in discussing continental Europe is dangerous, since this model, which was really a picture of the Metropolitan Police of London often refracted through rose-tinted spectacles, was popular with Liberals, and others, in nineteenth-century Europe, as well as with municipal reformers in the United States. Of course, there were other models of police available with different pedigrees, but their development has not been subjected to the same degree of detailed historical analysis and debate.[12]

Police reform was not something that began during the nineteenth century in continental Europe. Eighteenth-century France was generally regarded as the best-policed state in Europe and some of its policing organizations were seen as models by princes and their ministers elsewhere on the Continent. In Paris there were some three thousand men working under the *lieutenant général de police;* deterrent patrols of uniformed, armed men circulated the streets and manned police posts, while other agents, in civilian clothes, carried out a plethora of tasks ranging from the investigation of crimes to the regulation of markets and the supervision of wet nurses. Moreover, as the century progressed, the *lieutenant général's* agents began to take over some of the welfare role of the Church, notably some aspects of poor relief, and certain of its pastoral roles concerning the admonition of libertine husbands and wayward children, and receiving complaints about prostitutes and the lax sexual morals of neighbors.[13]

In rural France the *Maréchaussée* was established in small brigades that patrolled the main roads, supervised markets and feast days, and were available for dealing with emergencies such as the appearance of a group of brigands, an outbreak of *taxation populaire,* or other instances of disorder. The oligarchies that ran the cities and towns in France were generally jealous of their rights and privileges; they sought to use the *Maréchaussée* to their own ends, or to limit its appearance within their jurisdiction. They financed and recruited their own police; but the size and effectiveness of these organizations depended upon the will of the municipal authorities to find money and to establish such.[14]

The French *Maréchaussée* was unique; elsewhere in rural Europe where such tasks were performed at all they were usually left to soldiers, and the facility generally disappeared when there were other demands on the military, most obviously a war. In Italy much policing, which was seen as a task without honor, was left in the hands of the hated *sbirri,* often little better than the brigands they were charged with pursuing. Princes and their ministers in continental Europe, as well as municipal authorities, aspired to the "well-ordered police state" and consequently published ordinances and new laws rooted in reason and involving the state ever more closely with its citizens, both developing the economy and supervising the population. These actors did not always find the money or the will to establish the institutions necessary for enforcement of the ordinances, though as the eighteenth century progressed there were significant developments.[15] Economic upheaval pushed more and more people on to the roads and into towns and cities looking for work; the fears generated by vagabonds and wanderers on the roads and by the unemployed or underemployed in the cities and towns prompted some institutional police developments. Debates about crime and how best to deal with offenders, which were given a particularly sharp focus with the publication of Cesare Beccaria's *Dei delitti e delle pene* in 1764, fostered discussions that could not help but touch on policing arrangements. At the same time the aims of Enlightened princes and ministers to reduce the powers of intermediary bodies such as nobles, gentry, Church, and cities, involved undermining the legal and policing responsibilities of these bodies, and this, in turn, necessitated their replacement with effective institutions of the state.

The French Revolution and the Napoleonic imperium provided new fears, as well as incentives, opportunities, and models for developments in policing. The fear of popular upheaval such as that which had helped to bring down the old regime in France, and the contiguous concerns about Jacobin ideology, encouraged governments to improve their organs of political surveillance. The expansion of some states, particularly in Germany, brought them new populations of uncertain loyalty. The fears about vagabonds on the roads were exacerbated by twenty years of war with the accompanying menace of straggling or disbanded soldiers, draft dodgers, and deserters. But, at the same time, the reorganization of states under Napoleonic impetus often put state finances on a better foundation and provided new opportunities for limiting the power of the intermediary bodies. Moreover, the French police, both civilian *commissaires* and military gendarmes—the descendants of the old *Maréchaussée*—provided the models that appeared effective in pursuing and apprehending offenders, suppressing minor disorder, and bringing in conscripts and even taxes. In the aftermath of Napoleon's fall there may have been attempts to gloss over the French imperial origins of gendarmeries—in Piedmont they became *carabinieri,* in Württemberg the *Landjägerkorps*—but the model remained essentially intact though adapted to different national contexts.[16]

Yet, however different the pedigrees of the police organizations in continental Europe and in Britain, in the early-nineteenth century three distinct types of police can be perceived as common to most states. There were state civilian police, like London's Metropolitan Police and the organization responsible to the Prefect of Police in Paris created by Napoleon; these were institutions that answered directly to the central government. Municipalities still had the power to recruit and employ their own police, at their own expense, but as the century wore on these powers were increasingly constrained by state regulations, and sometimes a superior, supervisory officer was appointed by the central state. This municipal model remained predominant throughout the United States, and here it developed without any interference from the federal government. Rural areas in continental Europe, and in European colonies, were commonly patrolled by gendarmeries—military policemen directly responsible to the central government. England was a notable exception here with rural policing based largely on a municipal model and directed by the county magistracies until 1888, when elected county councilors were also given some involvement; but Ireland, and particularly rural parts of the British Empire, was patrolled by police institutions similar to the gendarmerie model.[17]

The Nineteenth-Century Police: Social Controllers?

Modern, bureaucratic policemen, whatever their type and whatever their origins, are by definition agents of the state—recognizing, of course, that the state can be local, or municipal, as well as national. As such, it was, and remains, the task of policemen to enforce particular policies established by the state. Leaving aside whether such enforcement has to be equated with social control, the exploration of police policy and practice, and the relations between police and the communities in which they operate, still constitute an important area for research.

The English police were instructed that their prime task was "the prevention of crime." This emphasis first appeared in the initial instructions issued to the Metropolitan Police in 1829 and was taken up by many, perhaps most, other British forces as they were established.[18] The idea of preventing crime was to be found in continental Europe, though it never appears to have become the mantra that it did in Britain.[19] But it is one thing to identify a task; it can be quite another to achieve it. Moreover, when individuals announce that it is their intention to prevent crime, then it has to be assumed that they have a clear perception of what they mean by crime and who they believe to be responsible for committing it. In declaring his intention to introduce legislation for creating the Metropolitan Police, Peel deployed statistics to demonstrate rising theft in London. A few years later Colonel Charles Rowan, one of the two men appointed by Peel to command the new police, told a parliamentary inquiry that they saw it as their task to protect St. James, a district populated by the wealthy and respectable, by watching St. Giles, a notorious slum area, "and bad places in general." [20]

During the first two-thirds of the nineteenth century, British police reformers and senior policemen, while not using the term "dangerous classes" until the 1840s and "criminal classes" rarely before the 1860s, appear to have considered crime as something committed by a section of the plebeian order dwelling particularly in the least salubrious areas of the big cities. Theorizing crime and criminals in this way made it logical to develop police policy toward the supervision and management of those groups, not because the newly emerging society required a pliant workforce for its factory system, but because these were the people perceived as the criminals. Police reformers, who are now increasingly seen as overlapping with moral entrepreneurs in general, also had clear perceptions of what made people criminal, and often this was the very habits frowned upon by those entrepreneurs: drink, idleness, love of "luxury," irreligion.[21] It was logical, therefore, that the new thresholds of order enforced by the police should include the supervision of public houses and the suppression of rough plebeian sports and pastimes—especially those enjoyed in public space. Moreover, since the able-bodied pauper was stigmatized as a potential criminal—for many moral entrepreneurs, such an individual was only a pauper because of a reluctance to do an honest day's work for an honest day's pay—there were those who wanted the new police to be linked with the New Poor Law. Indeed, in many Victorian police forces in England, individual policemen acted as poor law relieving officers (welfare functionaries) and as inspectors of lodging houses.

Moral entrepreneurs and police bureaucrats in continental Europe shared these beliefs. It was, after all, a French government bureaucrat with close links to the police, Honoré Frégier, who coined the term *les classes dangereuses;* and a leading detective from the Prefecture, Louis Canler, claimed to be writing his memoirs, at least in part, so as to warn the respectable about the tricks of malefactors.[22] The French may have been suspicious of copying the English Poor Law during the nineteenth century,[23] but both police and gendarmes regularly apprehended beggars, vagrants, and *gens sans aveu,* while their supervision of inns and lodging houses went back to the old regime. The *Carabinieri Reali* were given similar directives when established in Restoration Piedmont;[24] and there was similar supervision in Germany, where from the eighteenth century police bureaucrats had circulated books of wanted offenders across state frontiers. From the early-nineteenth century these books suggest an increasing professionalism among the police, and also that the police, like other moral entrepreneurs, increasingly saw criminals as rooted in the plebeian order and not simply drawn from Gypsies, Jews, and general social outcasts.[25] Police focus on drunks, prostitutes, vagrants, and on idle working-class men who were commonly suspected as thieves, was something that appealed to even the most liberal bourgeois in nineteenth-century Europe. It meant that in Germany, and in Prussia in particular, where the police had wide powers of arrest and imprisonment (*Polizeihaft*), the respectable bourgeois commonly turned a blind eye to the police use of these powers and paid the price in as much as their use contributed to the militarization of everyday life.[26] In Italy, fear of the southern brigand and the red revolutionary contributed to governmental reluctance in curbing, and tacit bourgeois approval of, carabinieri and P.S. (*Pubblica Sicurezza*) agents whose first resort when confronting popular disorder at the turn of the century was often to use their guns.[27]

Supervision and control of the dangerous or criminal classes was, of course, not the only task of the nineteenth-century police. In Restoration Piedmont, where the French-created ministry of police was rechristened *Buon Governo,* there was an earnest desire shared by Victor Emanuel and his advisors to maintain devotion to the Catholic Church and to enforce moral values in the face of what they perceived as increasing, widespread licentiousness and a callousness toward the weak and innocent.[28] In the Netherlands policing remained primarily in the hands of local authorities, but the state military police, the *Koninklijke Marechaussee,* first established to supervise the Catholic south of the country, was moved into the northern provinces during the 1830s and 1840s to enforce tax demands.[29] The Catholic faith of the people of the southern provinces of the Netherlands made them politically suspect in the immediate aftermath of the Napoleonic wars, and across nineteenth-century Europe police institutions were expected to maintain a surveillance of political subversives. This was something that had a much more central role among the police of continental Europe than in Britain, and it could sometimes overlap with surveillance of the working class, as with, for example, the special unit of the Hamburg Police that, during the *Kaiserreich,* spent its time sitting in beer houses listening to the conversations of workers and then writing lengthy reports on what they had heard.[30]

But policemen also ensured the free flow of traffic both pedestrian and horse drawn; and if a horse bolted, or a terrified animal escaped from an abattoir and ran amok in the streets, it was usually a policeman who tried to capture it, calm it, or put the unfortunate creature down. Policemen also fought fires and brought assistance in times of disaster. Edwin Chadwick, perhaps the most celebrated moral entrepreneur of Victorian England, hoped that these "collateral, beneficent services" would contribute to the general acceptance of the police by the public, "relieve the monotony of mere sentinel work" for the policeman himself, and become a more central part of the police role as time went on and "the preventive service against crime prevails."[31] If Chadwick was rather too sanguine about the potential for preventive policing, probably he was right in suggesting that the welfare and assistance provided by policemen brought them closer to the public. Moral entrepreneurs may have hoped that the police would control the plebeian classes. Some social scientists and police historians may have concluded that this was the reason for the creation of the police and that this was essentially the role that the police performed. But the relationship between police and different sections of the public appears to have been considerably more complex. Recent work on the control of public space in the Victorian town, for example, has shown the police receiving strong support from the anonymous gaze of citizens who, from a variety of perspectives—class, gender, temperance—used the correspondence columns of the local press to advise and exhort the police and others concerned with the supervision of urban space. The police themselves were not spared by this "gaze of civilization," and they were commonly admonished from these same perspectives for any shortcomings.[32]

There were never enough policemen to ensure absolute control over those sections of society feared by the respectable classes. The state, both central and local, gets its revenue from different forms of taxation, and during the nineteenth century even the absolutist empires of central and eastern Europe saw a limit to how much they could demand from their peoples. Limitations on finances, together with the demands from elsewhere within the state, meant that there were limits on the number of policemen who could be recruited and deployed. The problem is seen, perhaps, at its clearest with the Habsburg Gendarmerie, which, established in 1849, reached a peak in numbers in 1857 with just under nineteen thousand men and then, as a result of the parlous condition of the imperial finances, was progressively reorganized and reduced in number until in 1876 there were just fifty-seven hundred gendarmes to patrol an empire with a population of around thirty-six million.[33] At the turn of the century in Italy, successive disorders prompted demands to the government from some worried prefects for more *Carabinieri* or *Pubblica Sicurezza* police. At the same time prefects in more tranquil regions made counterdemands that the police in their jurisdiction not be reduced to deal with problems elsewhere as this would encourage local criminals and subversives. The government testily suggested that the danger was being overestimated, and then went on to emphasize that the numbers of P.S. police and Carabinieri were finite.[34]

But however many police there were, and even in the most rigorously regimented states, it remained possible for even the strictest police controls to be circumvented and for police officials to be deceived into issuing genuine journeymen's passes and travel papers for the wrong reasons.[35] The police themselves were commonly aware of their limitations and, at times, preferred to allow rough areas to supervise themselves as long as the rough lifestyle, and any forms of criminal behavior, did not spill too obviously beyond designated boundaries. The police watched and contained but interfered only when absolutely necessary. Senior police officers were never simply the tools of moral entrepreneurs. They recognized the limitations of their men's numbers and of what they could do; they also recognized that workers had the right to some forms of recreation and relaxation. Herman Hirsch, the director of the Royal Police in Eberfeld in the mid 1850s, was determined to eliminate unauthorized drinking establishments, yet he vigorously defended a legitimate, popular beer hall against accusations of impropriety originating from an ardent Protestant group.[36] The Metropolitan Police of London resisted pressure for more rigorous action over brothels and drink, and for the abolition of the city's fairs.[37] And Jennifer Davis has shown how the same force was prepared to let the inhabitants of the tough tenements of Jennings Buildings police themselves, provided that their behavior did not disturb the peace of respectable Kensington.[38] Such pragmatism was probably even more pronounced among some individual policemen patrolling alone on the streets, and among some small squads of gendarmes in isolated barracks far from the supervision of senior officers.

At the same time for all classes, but especially for the lower social groups in the countryside, the police were filling gaps left by the disappearance of the old intermediary bodies and by the decline of opportunities for the infrajudicial resolution of complaints and injuries. Most nineteenth-century states promised equality before the law and spoke of the police as providing security and welfare. On occasion this provision of security could mean policemen stepping in to assist or to protect an individual who had been stigmatized by, or who was under threat from, a local community. This area warrants more detailed research, but there are examples of this sort involving female victims of sexual assault, stigmatized in their community for a past of sexual activity, and both men and women who had transgressed community norms of cohabitation or sexual mores.[39] Even for those individuals who had little time for the police and who had little concept of the state as anything other than a distant entity making demands in the sense of money for taxes and young men for the military, the state's promise of equality and of a life free from crime and disorder was an attractive one. The rhetoric of the state encouraged even these individuals to perceive of the police as agents who would make such abstract promises a reality. Prostitutes in nineteenth-century Paris were commonly abused by the police and were subjected to the rigorous supervision of the *brigade des moeurs,* yet these same prostitutes resorted to policemen as informal judges in disputes on the streets and, in times of trouble, sought assistance and refuge at police posts or commissariats.[40] In Berlin in the period 1900 to 1914, roughly 40 percent of street disorder, usually involving young men on warm summer nights, was directed against the police; but as much as 13 percent was directed against different kinds of offenders and in support, or in the absence, of police action.[41]

Twentieth-Century Police: Controllers, or the Public in Uniform?

During the twentieth century perceptions of the gap between the police of liberal democratic societies and those of the so-called totalitarian states probably became much wider than any similar differences perceived during the nineteenth century. Yet there has been remarkably little historical analysis of the extent of control aspired to, and exercised by, the liberal democratic police, while some of the recent research on the police of totalitarian regimes has yielded rather unexpected results.

In the first half of the century apologists for the British police, including their historians, held them up as the model for liberal democratic societies. They were "the best police in the world," and foreigners were popularly quoted to this effect.[42] Notions were presented of British policing being based on the consent of the policed. The police officer was no more than a civilian in uniform entrusted by the community with its protection. He[43] took his authority from the Crown. He was nonpolitical, standing above both local and national party politics; his actions were governed only by the law, and he was answerable only to the law. The idea of "control" had no place in such rhetoric, except in so far as it was the policeman's task to bring "criminals" under control. In effect, little had changed on the streets. The British bobby still "pounded his beat" at the regulation pace of two and a half miles an hour, checking doors and windows after dark. He could still be felt as a pressure in working-class districts, but there continued to be negotiation and public service, as well as supervision. Harry Daley, who joined the Metropolitan Police in 1925, left a glowing portrait of the busy station to which he was first posted, Hammersmith Broadway, in West London:

> the public seemed to spend most of the time popping in and out for help and advice, as chummy as you like and often on Christian name terms. Last night's drunk popped in to see if we had his hat; women pushing kids in prams with squeaky wheels would cock a hopeful eye at the copper on the door and pop in to have them oiled; costers popped in to complain of being moved on with their barrows, and women to complain of their neighbours; old ladies feeling faint popped in for a glass of water and a sit down; and dotty people in great numbers, unwelcome in their homes till bedtime and knowing the vicar was too busy organising his money-making schemes to bother with them, popped in to unwind their endless rigmaroles, knowing they would be heard with sympathetic kindness.
> But then there were the genteel snobs, who "wouldn't be seen dead in the police station for anything," and "the wild inhabitants" from "the shocking" Rayleigh Road who seem to have been responsible for much of the petty theft in the district and who seem only to have entered the station when under arrest.[44]

Daley's picture of Hammersmith Broadway police station fits with the comfortable, traditional image of the best police in the world. It is clearly not a picture of control being exercised over the community as a whole—Rayleigh Road was different and hardly under police control—but rather of a general acceptance of the police presence and a relaxed interplay between policemen and public. Yet Daley himself does not conform to a typical policeman's image. Proud of his working-class origins, he expressed surprise that a working man could ever vote for the Conservative Party. But what really set him apart from the typical image was his homosexual orientation, something that provoked, from some of his colleagues, "malicious remarks, disguised as jokes . . . the sort of triviality that spoils lives and can cause as much unhappiness as a permanent prison sentence or illness." [45] Such behavior in itself may be seen as a form of social control designed to enforce a kind of self-conscious masculine conformity amongst men engaged in a tough, masculine, working-class occupation. It might have compelled some, perhaps most, to conform or quit; though it seems to have had little effect on Daley who never conformed to heterosexual "norms," yet served in the police for twenty-five years, retiring as a sergeant and with a certificate of "exemplary" conduct.[46]

Daley's description of the police is echoed elsewhere, but there is comment, from other policemen, that they expected respect on their beats and, when posted to a new beat, a man might consider it necessary initially to exert his authority forcefully so that his new community knew what he expected. Poor working-class districts could still be rough in the interwar period, and policemen relied on their personal toughness as well as the law to maintain their authority. Sometimes they might interpret the law to suit their purposes in what they jokingly referred to as "the Ways and Means Act." Sometimes their personal toughness and pre-paredness to acknowledge and accept communities and their mores as they found them led to individual policemen becoming honorary members of the roughest communities.

Take, for example, Ginger ("Mister" to his face) Mullins, "of great physique and as strong as an ox," who would put his helmet and belt on his neatly folded jacket before interfering in a street fight "with fist and boot." Remarkably, "no one would ever think of stealing [his uniform] whilst he was restoring law and order."[47]

Moreover, even if the police were unpopular and generally unwelcome in some of the poorest working-class districts, they could still be called upon to protect wives and children from violent husbands and fathers and to help in times of emergency and tragedy. But poor, rough working-class districts were not the only areas that the police patrolled. The interwar years witnessed a massive expansion of the suburbs; in 1937, for example, the commissioner of the Metropolitan Police reported that, in the preceding seven years, the street mileage in just one of his divisions had increased by 226 miles, and the number of houses by 53,000.[48] But police budgets, and in consequence police numbers, did not keep pace. Moreover there were other demands on police time.

Public disorder can be seen as the most striking instance of the failure of police control. Britain during the interwar years had a sprinkling of such disorder both economic and political, but the idea of special riot squads was decried as un-British, and the casualties overall were far less serious than in similar confrontations in continental Europe or in the United States. At the same time, the police found themselves having to confront major new traffic problems with the development of the motor car and, for the first time in Britain, this brought about direct, and frequent, confrontation between the police and the middle class.[49] All of this leaves a rather fuzzy image of what the police in Britain were there to do, particularly of the extent to which control in its many manifestations was a central remit. In theory the situation should have been rather clearer in the repressive, totali-tarian regimes of the interwar period.

In Weimar Germany there were attempts to liberalize the police, to make them less military and less obviously agents for enforcing petty regulations. This occurred partly as a result of allied pressure. The *Sicherheitspolizei,* or *Sipo,* established in the summer of 1919 was viewed by the allied victors as an attempt to get round the restrictions on German military strength; it was disbanded in October 1920. But probably more significant were the ideas of men like Dr. Wilhelm Abegg, *Ministerialdirektor* and head of the Police Section of the Prussian Interior Ministry, and later *Staatssekretär*. Abegg wanted to create what he considered to be a modern police department, an organization different from the militarized institutions of the Kaiserreich. He saw the police as defenders of the state, but also as protectors and helpers of the public. He emphasized the need for the police to be professional, to be nonpartisan politically, and to embrace the opportunities provided by modern technology. It has, however, been forcefully and cogently argued that it was this supposedly nonpolitical, nonmilitary Weimar police, with its stress on professionalism and technical competence, which helped smooth the political transition of 1933. Moreover, this same organization was easily transformed into an agency of the so-called police state of the Nazis.[50]

The number of police that would be required rigidly to control every aspect of life in a society is probably far beyond the financial abilities of any state. This does not mean that a climate of fear cannot be created to help suppress dissent; nor does it mean that such police as exist do not play a significant role by warning and arresting different kinds of dissenters. The Nazi state created fear and authorized its police to take action against dissidents and deviants. Indeed, the development of *Polizeijustiz* enabled both the detective police, the *Kripo,* and the secret police, the *Gestapo,* virtual free reign over who should be dealt with by the judicial system. The police could employ preventive detention and ignore or even overrule court decisions if they considered it necessary. This freedom of action for the police contributed to the climate of fear within Nazi Germany, and it was accompanied by the dismantling of most of the liberal democratic institutions that the Weimar state had established. But, climate of fear notwithstanding, the police in Nazi Germany also relied heavily on denunciations from the general public.[51]

There should be no surprise at this; in many respects much within Nazi ideology was largely a logical, if particularly unpleasant, working through of the eugenicist theories that had emerged across Europe during the nineteenth century as a means of explaining, and hence controlling, deviants, dissidents, and those who were simply "different." And a logical progression might also be found from the general acceptance among "respectable" social groups of police controls over the "dangerous classes" during the nineteenth century. No one wanted his property to fall prey to petty thieves, or to suffer threats from bullies, especially from bullying neighbors. It was but a small step from here to agree to, and to assist, the police in controlling the disrespectful young people of the *Eidelweiß Piraten* or those simply interested in "Swing." Another small step led to the denunciation of those with a different sexual orientation, and thence to those who were from an alien "race." Not everyone needed to take each of the small steps; silence meant tacit acceptance, but opposition might mean being labeled as dissident or deviant. To the extent that the *Kripo* and, to a much lesser extent, the *Gestapo* used *Polizeijustiz* to control those perceived as petty criminals, thugs, and bullies, they were pursuing what might be called a policy of authoritarian populism. Policing in Nazi Germany may have been more clearly concerned with control than policing in interwar Britain, yet to see it purely in these terms is to ignore the complexities and the extent of popular support for the police and what they were doing.

There is also the problem of comparison between what are commonly labeled totalitarian police states. Nazi Germany contained relatively few secret, political policemen in comparison with its contemporary the Soviet Union; popular denunciations and other methods of what might be termed self-policing were generally helpful to the Nazi authorities. The authorities in the Soviet Union and, after 1945, also in the German Democratic Republic benefited from denunciations, yet in these states the secret police and the networks of informers were ever expanding and the element of self-policing and self-regulation within the community seems much less pronounced.[52] In Mussolini's Italy, as in Nazi Germany, much of the liberal democratic state was demolished for policing benefits. In Italy, however, while denunciation to the police may have been underestimated by historians, it does not appear to have been quite as common as in Nazi Germany. Tim Mason drew attention to this a decade ago, suggesting that this may have been one reason why the repressive power of the Italian dictatorship was not as great as that of Germany and urging that much more comparative research was needed into German and Italian cultural and social history during the period. He considered that the Italians thought denunciation more dishonorable.[53] If Mason was right then clearly some explanation is needed. No doubt much here depended on differing attitudes to the state itself rather than on differing attitudes to policemen, but the work remains to be done.

Conclusion

Nineteenth-century police reformers, and senior officers of the early bureaucratic police organizations, may have considered the police role to be, at least in part, controlling problem groups within the plebeian order. Yet, given the increasing complexity of society together with the size of the police forces, something that has always been at least partly related to the other demands on state finances, it is both simplistic and naive to see the police as controllers, easily and successfully implementing the desires and decisions of government, even in absolutist or totalitarian societies. The state context within which the police have functioned—absolutist, liberal, totalitarian, democratic—has created the climate and environment for police action and specified the scale of regulation for that action. Police numbers, and the desire for a degree of legitimacy, have always prompted some degree of negotiation between police and people and of pragmatism on the part of the police. These are variables that require further research and comparative assessment; and detailed comparative assessment of this sort remains a challenge for social historians to accept.

Notes

1. Ross, *Social Control.* A useful, sympathetic introduction to the term and arguing its potential for social historians is to be found in the introduction to Donajgrodzki, ed., *Social Control in Nineteenth-Century Britain.* An important essay collection surveying the development of the concept and its continuing validity is Bergalli and Sumner, eds., *Social Control and Political Order.*

2. Wrightson, "Two Concepts of Order," 22, 24.

3. The disorders were well covered in the British press. The best publicized outbreak went on for several days in the first two weeks of August in the Paulsgrove district of Portsmouth.

4. The best introduction to this phenomenon is the collection of comparative essays, Le Goff and Schmitt, eds., *Le Charivari.*

5. Tebbutt, *Women's Talk.*

6. Garnot, "Justice, infrajustice, parajustice et extrajustice."

7. I have a close relative who works as a solicitor in England, generally representing petty offenders in magistrates' courts. Having acquired the trust of two Roma families by acting for members in this way, he was asked by the heads of these families to adjudicate in a conflict between them. He drew up an agreement, explained it to the parties, who were both illiterate, and keeps the agreement in the safe of his office. It has never been broken.

8. Reith, *The Police Idea;* idem, *British Police and the Democratic Ideal;* Ascoli, *The Queen's Peace.*

9. Silver, "The Demand for Order in Civil Society."

10. Storch, "The Plague of Blue Locusts"; idem, "The Policeman As Domestic Missionary."

11. Liang, *The Rise of Modern Police;* and see the critical reviews by Clive Emsley in *European History Quarterly* 24 (1994): 472–74; and by Mark Mazower in *Criminal Justice History,* 14 (1993): 208–10.

12. For a discussion of the different models of police during the nineteenth century, see Emsley, "A Typology."

13. Garrioch, *Neighbourhood and Community;* and see in general, Williams, *The Police of Paris.*

14. For an important comparison on the very significant developments in policing in five major towns on the Franco-Belgian border during the eighteenth century, see Denys, *Police et sécurité au XVIIIe siècle.*

15. Raeff, *The Well-Ordered Police State;* Axtmann, "'Police' and the Formation of the Modern State."

16. Emsley, *Gendarmes and the State.*

17. Emsley, "A Typology."

18. Emsley, *Crime and Society in England,* 233.

19. It is also worth noting that what appears to be the same word can have very different meanings in different national contexts. While preventive policing in England tended to mean a police officer patrolling his beat and preventing crime by his presence and alertness, in Italy *polizia preventiva* meant the surveillance of particular groups and individuals. The kind of patrolling that the English police considered to be preventive was, in Italy, *polizia repressiva,* and the last thing that any British government could sanction for its English national territory during the nineteenth and twentieth centuries was any form of policing that was called "repressive."

20. *Parliamentary Papers,* 1834 (600) XVI, *Select Committee on the Police of the Metropolis,* q. 166.

21. An important, recent study of one of the less well-known of the English moral entrepreneurs is Philips, *William Augustus Miles.*

22. Frégier, *Des Classes dangereuses;* Canler, *Mémoirs de Canler,* 18.

23. Smith, "The Ideology of Charity."

24. See, for example, *Regie Patenti,* 17 November 1821, *Capitolo Nono, Attribuzioni de' Carabinieri Reali,* especially paragraphs 13 and 21.

25. Lucassen, "'Harmful Tramps,'" 33–35.

26. Evans, "Polizei, Politik und Gesellschaft in Deutschland," 619–20. Evans is here drawing significantly on Funk, *Polizei und Rechtsstaat.*

27. Collin, "The Italian Police and Internal Security," chap. 1.

28. Broers, "Sexual Politics and Political Ideology."

29. Sleebe, *In termen van fatsoen.*

30. Evans, *Kneipengespräche im Kaiserreich.* For a brief comparative survey of nineteenth-century political police see Emsley, "Political Police and the European Nation-State in the Nineteenth Century."

31. Chadwick, "On the Consolidation of Police Force," 16, 17.

32. Croll, "Street Disorder, Surveillance and Shame."

33. Kepler, *Die Gendarmerie in Österreich,* 87, 89.

34. Dunnage, *The Italian Police and the Rise of Fascism,* 29.

35. Evans, *Tales from the German Underworld,* 154–55.

36. Spencer, *Police and the Social Order in German Cities,* 69.

37. Petrow, *Policing Morals;* Cunningham, "The Metropolitan Fairs."

38. Davis, "From 'Rookeries' to 'Communities.'"

39. Le Clercq, "Violences sexuelles, scandale et ordre public."

40. Harsin, *Policing Prostitution,* 200–2.

41. Lindenberger, *Straßenpolitik,* 121–49.

42. See, for example, *On and Off Duty,* June 1926, 88–89, for praise from "an American" and a "Polish lady."

43. I use the male personal pronoun advisedly since there were no women police officers in Britain until World War I, while their authority, responsibilities, and numbers were greatly restricted until after World War II.

44. Daley, *This Small Cloud,* 92–93.

45. Ibid., 112–13.

46. My thanks to the staff of the Metropolitan Police Museum and Archive for information on Daley's police record, which like other police personnel files remains closed to public scrutiny.

47. White, *The Worst Street in North London,* 115; Brogden, *On the Mersey Beat,* chap. 4; Weinberger, *The Best Police in the World,* 32–33.

48. *Annual Report of the Commissioner of the Police of the Metropolis,* 1937, 7.

49. Emsley, "'Mother, What *Did* Policemen Do When There Weren't Any Motors?'"

50. Bessel, "Policing, Professionalisation and Politics in Weimar Germany."

51. Gellatelly, "L'émergence de la 'Polizeijustiz.'"; idem, *The Gestapo and German Society;* idem, *Backing Hitler,* especially chap. 2.

52. See *Practices of Denunciation in Modern European History, 1789–1989,* a special edition of the *Journal of Modern History,* 68, vol. 4 (1996). Johnson, *The Nazi Terror,* qualifies the role of denunciation and the complicity of the German population in Nazi crimes by reemphasizing the culpability and capability, in certain key respects, of organizations like the Gestapo.

53. Mason, "Whatever Happened to 'Fascism'?" 259. See also Dunnage in this volume.

CHAPTER 9

Policing the Poor in England and France, 1850–1900

PAUL LAWRENCE

Introduction

The concept of social control has provoked a prolonged debate among sociologists and historians of all genres. First delineated by E. A. Ross in his 1901 work *Social Control,* its fundamental premise is that a multiplicity of agencies exist via which powerful elites attempt to shape society to their benefit and satisfaction. These agencies can range from the obvious "official" instruments of state control, such as education and the law,[1] to the "popular" moral and ethical sentiments inherent within the public sphere.[2] Of course, not every agent of social control functions in a self-aware fashion—Anthony Donajgrodzki notes that "many social control mechanisms operate independently of any conscious manipulative process"[3]—but it has now been posited by many historians that organizations as diverse as law courts, schools, social security agencies, and the police have all functioned to organize society in ways considered ethically and morally acceptable by power elites. Even those theoreticians advancing a more limited view of social control, such as the sociologist Talcott Parsons, have still maintained that control mechanisms exist that counteract deviancy at points where socialization has failed and hence act to produce an equilibrium conducive to the continuation of existing socioeconomic relationships.

Perhaps more than any other single institution, it is the police who have been popularly perceived as obvious agents of social control, enforcing a hegemonic ideology in a one-directional manner. Robert Storch, among others, has claimed for the early police the role of "domestic missionaries." He asserts that the repressive, class-based legislation implemented by the "New Police" in relation to urban discipline meant that the advent of modern policing could be likened to "the installation of the eyes and ears of ruling élites at the very centres of working class daily life."[4] Stefan Petrow also notes that of all the nineteenth-century administrative agencies, it was the police who were "central to the state's attempt to impose a certain social discipline on the poorer classes."[5] However, such assertions are clearly far from unproblematic. Historians such as F. M. L. Thompson have since produced convincing counterarguments concerning the efficacy of many of the supposed agents of social control, arguing that it is overly simplistic to view the police as simple agents of control from above and that "it is, indeed, unwarrantably condescending to the humble and anonymous masses to suppose that they were incapable of cultural development except as a result of . . . coercion from outside."[6] Stephen Inwood and Jennifer Davis have also highlighted the extent to which popular street culture was far more resistant to police control than anticipated and claim that early police forces had neither the desire nor the practical capability to alter decisively working-class behavior.[7]

However, many of the analyses arguing for and against the efficacy of the police as agents of social control have so far focused exclusively on their relationship with the mass of the working class. Issues such as street order, the control of fairs, and the enforcement of licensing legislation have been comprehensively investigated, but so far much less research has concerned the social control implications of the policing of the poor and the destitute.[8] Thus, it is the interaction between the police and the very poor (more specifically, those rarely or never working) in England and France, during the latter half of the nineteenth century, that will be considered here. In assessing these complex relationships, an attempt will be made to ascertain not just how the police treated the poor but also their perceptions of the poorer classes. The conclusion will attempt to assess whether the treatment of the poor by the police can be justly referred to as a form of "social control," or whether in fact a more complex and subtle process was involved.

Poverty and Crime

An important preliminary point to note is that within both French and English societies, even at the turn of the century, perceptions of crime and patterns of policing were still undoubtedly determined by issues of class. Poverty was not necessarily regarded as the cause of crime, but it was certainly seen as "the hallmark of most criminals."[9] Most commentators would have agreed with Honoré Frégier that "the poorer classes have always been and always will be the most productive nursery of all types of criminals."[10] Moreover, it was common to view the causes of both poverty and crime as intrinsic to the individual rather than collective and inherent within society. Poverty itself was routinely viewed as the end result of lax personal morality, laziness, and drunkenness. Thus, even if the resultant destitution necessitated crime, this was still the fault of reasoning individuals who could be held responsible for their own actions. Certainly, as the conclusions of the Royal Commission on a Constabulary Force in 1839 demonstrate, it was believed that "the notion that any considerable proportion of the crimes against property are caused by blameless poverty or destitution we find disproved at every step."[11] Thus, the policing of the poor was seen by many middle-class contemporaries as the necessary regulation of social deviancy. The poor were often perceived as unwilling to contribute to the smooth "progress" of society and hence required practical and moral guidance from above.

Toward the end of the century, such attitudes were in a state of flux. Moralistic explanations of the links between poverty and crime were ceding ground to new theories of degeneration and urban decay, as attempts were now made to define the criminal not just socially but also physiologically. Closely associated with the work of the Italian criminologist Cesare Lombroso, there was a growing interest in the corrupting influences of urban life on the poor and the relationship of this to their perceived criminality. Many texts reveal a shift toward a more collective view of both poverty and crime, linking the two via the determining factor of urban degeneration and decay. For example, the chief constable of the Metropolitan Police, writing about Whitechapel (a poor area in East London), noted in 1875 that "children born in such places are generally puny and delicate, many of them growing up unfit for manual labour, and are driven therefore either to crime or begging for a livelihood."[12] There was a shift in emphasis from personal to impersonal forces in perceptions of poverty and crime. However, this medicalization of crime, which was closely linked to the growing authority of the scientific professions within society in general, did not fundamentally alter the prevalent conception of the lower ranks of the poor as socially deficient and in need of regulation and control. The "control" of the poor, which had at the beginning of the century been exercised primarily in the context of personal relationships, gradually became increasingly formal and institutionalized. It was assumed at the time that the police should be at the forefront of those forces arrayed against the threat of the so-called residuum.[13]

At first glance, police statistics seem to bear out the assumption that much of their work was directed toward the control and containment of the poor. It is clear that what are today perceived to be the core activities of the police—the management and investigation of serious, violent crime—formed only a small part of police duties, even at the turn of the century. Offenses traditionally associated with the lower classes, such as drunkenness and petty theft, took up large amounts of police time in both countries. Most important, however, police involvement with offenses relating primarily to the very poor, such as vagrancy and begging, still formed a very significant part of police duties. This focus on such seemingly victimless offenses is perhaps particularly indicative of a desire for class-based regulation and control. For example, over a third of all arrests in Paris during the 1880s were for vagrancy offenses.[14] Certainly then, "the hand of the law . . . fell most heavily on the poor and the ragged."[15] Thompson makes the point that it was not really until the advent of mass motoring and its concomitant offenses that the middle-classes ever came into regular contact with the police.[16] There were, of course, peaks and troughs of both arrest figures and police activity, but this general picture remained stable until the very last years of the nineteenth century, when judicial leniency meant that vagrancy and begging statistics first began their permanent decline.

However, "the relationship between ideology, control and crime is . . . a complex one,"[17] and such statistics cannot be used in a simplistic fashion as evidence of the social control functions of the nineteenth-century police. This class-based focus was at least partly due to a lack of resources, which meant that forces tended to concentrate their activities around limited geographical and investigative areas perceived as particularly troublesome. This in turn presumably meant that crime statistics reflecting the perceived criminality of the poor became somewhat self-fulfilling. Also, a lack of manpower would certainly have necessitated a degree of tact and public support, both inconsistent with a simplistic view of the police as enforcers of middle-class morality. A closer look at policing practices reveals a complex picture of enforcement and restraint. Where the issue of vagrancy is considered, police actions were often harsh, in keeping with popular conceptions of *défense sociale*,[18] whereas in other areas police treatment of the poor was in many cases lenient and tinged with sympathy. First, the issue of vagrancy will be considered.

The Policing of Vagrants and Beggars

For much of the latter half of the nineteenth century, police attitudes toward vagrants were rigid and harsh, in many ways reflecting contemporary social anxieties in both countries. To be without a home, employment, and adequate resources was still an offense in France and England at the start of the twentieth century, and the fears inspired by itinerants were such that even commonplace acts like possessing a pocketknife (merely routine for French laborers) carried severe penalties for vagrants. There is no doubt that vagrants were the most unpopular element of the poorer classes. As David Jones notes, "most social investigators viewed vagrants from a distance, as a separate and inferior class, and even sympathetic observers were highly critical of their values and behavior."[19] Tramps and itinerants have, of course, always been perceived as outsiders and targets of suspicion. Robert Schwartz has noted how the eighteenth-century vagrant "was characterized as exhibiting to the worst degree the preference of the poor for leisure over labor,"[20] but as the industrial economies of England and France solidified, a migratory lifestyle became less and less acceptable. Vagrancy became identified as synonymous with deviance and criminality, with vagrants themselves perceived as separate from the increasingly static working classes.

In 1840 Frégier had claimed that "the vagabond is the personification of all kinds of criminals," and attitudes had changed little by the end of the century.[21] Writing in 1891 the commentator Henri Joly still thought that "vagrancy is only a façade, criminality is the real core."[22] If anything, the suspicions of the middle classes had been heightened by the passage of time. Scandals such as the trial of the vagrant Joseph Vacher, convicted in August 1897 of a series of brutal murders, confirmed for many anxieties that had been widespread since the start of the 1880s. There is still some controversy concerning the extent to which these fears were justified,[23] but the important point to note is that many within the upper classes were terrified of the rootlessness and anonymity that vagrants represented and wanted the police to enforce rigorous control. There were numerous calls for police action in the press, and not a year went by without the publication of another tract advocating tougher measures. The 1899 publication *Les Plaies Sociales: Vagabondage et Mendicité,* written by Fernand Chanteau, was typical of many in claiming that vagrancy was a type of "social disease," describing vagrants as "these gnawing ulcers which spread daily."[24] Louis Rivière, writing in 1902, agreed that vagrants must be sought out and arrested, as they were "in a state of permanent rebellion against the social order" and could at any moment lapse into criminality.[25]

Attitudes were much the same in England at the time. Continual distaste was punctuated by periods of heightened concern, particularly during the economic downturns of the 1880s. A reporter from *The Standard* noted in 1887 that "for several days I have been keeping observation of St James's Park, where I find that some 200 tramps, male and female, spend the day lounging on the grass. They are well-fed, depraved and lazy-looking, yawning evidently being a fatiguing exertion to many of them."[26] A focus on habitual vagrants as willful criminals served to deflect inquiries into the inadequacies of the capitalist system. A tract from 1872 noted that "many of those who travel for the sake of begging do not hesitate to rob when the opportunity presents itself," but there was little real investigation into why this should be the case.[27] Again, as in France, and despite the presence of the workhouse system of casual wards, there was increasing pressure for vagrancy to be made more of a police issue.[28] Those not actually arrested would still be dealt with by the police in their role as Poor Law Relieving Officers, in an attempt to make casual relief less attractive to "undeserving" vagrants. There was a strong sense that leniency and personal charity were "sources of demoralisation" for the poorer classes and that what was required were tougher penalties and decisive police action.[29] How then did the police in both countries respond to this pressure? Were they happy to act as the mere agents of those in authority or did they perhaps have their own agenda?

Certainly in England, police attitudes reflected fairly accurately the middle-class perceptions outlined above and were typified by suspicion, intolerance, and distaste. Although Inwood claims that "the Metropolitan Police regarded the policing . . . of vagrancy as one of their more delicate and difficult tasks," evidence from other sources suggests that the English police by no means relished contact with itinerants.[30] Cheshire Chief Constable William Chadwick had no doubts as to the criminal nature of most vagrants, referring to them as "this social blot on our civilisation" and "the scum which floats on the surface of our social system."[31] Indeed, Jones claims that by the late 1860s "police cynicism on this point had reached a stage where they were willing to treat all wayfarers as scroungers and potential criminals."[32] In a report compiled by the Metropolitan Police in 1870, 90 percent of those applying for relief were believed by the police "to have never worked." and to lead "an idle and dissolute life." The investigating officer also added his own personal opinion that "without some measures . . . to make labour compulsory and inevitable they will never work."[33]

Not only did the English police share the distaste of the middle classes for "tramps and suspicious looking characters," they were also more than willing to act against them. Richard Jervis, a superintendent from the north of England, noted that "I made . . . a special feature of stopping and searching tramps . . . on the road, and the results justified the means—a great many did I pick up with stolen property in their possession."[34] A general order of October 27, 1880, required superintendents to issue special instructions for "the detection and prevention as far as possible of vagrancy" and even advocated the use of plainclothes constables (often looked upon with suspicion in England) to facilitate matters.[35] Such methods were used in many counties, and other forces went as far as producing posters warning vagrants to keep clear, advising the public against indiscriminate almsgiving, and requesting information or "tip-offs." Indeed, such was the zeal with which some officers set about this task that magistrates in Cheshire, Gloucestershire, and Staffordshire had occasion to reprimand policemen for extracting false confessions and bringing forward unreliable witnesses.[36] The English police even viewed those wayfarers respectable enough to obtain casual relief in workhouses with suspicion. To obtain a night's lodging in the casual wards of the workhouse, respectable tramps had to apply to the local police for a ticket. The commissioner of the Metropolitan Police noted in 1869 that "the casuals are a nuisance and an annoyance to the police" and that "the contact of the Police with the casuals as Relieving Officers is . . . very distasteful to the Police."[37] Thus, in essence, the police in England shared the desire of the upper classes to watch and control the movements of tramps and vagrants. They were viewed with suspicion as potential, if not actual, criminals who could only be controlled by the strictest possible measures. In most regards the situation was exactly the same across the Channel, if not even more pronounced.

Gustave Macé, one-time head of the Paris *Sûreté*, expressed the opinions of many *policiers* when he claimed that "every vagabond has the makings of a criminal, and will become one sooner or later."[38] Pierre Boué, a former *commissaire,* claimed in his memoirs that "in a region infected by vagabonds . . . it was our duty to protect the inhabitants of towns against the misdeeds of these unscrupulous individuals."[39] His choice of the word *infectée,* with its implications of sickness and external menace, is instructive, and numerous other police memoirs contain similar phraseology.

In France the welfare infrastructure for dealing with itinerant poverty was even more underdeveloped than in England. Whereas in England casual wards at workhouses were provided for tramps, in France only a very limited number of hospitals and *Dépôts de Mendicité* offered such sanctuary. Smith notes that "the remarkable backwardness, inadequacy and inaccessibility of French hospitals as well as the general lack of public assistance institutions served to exacerbate the problems of begging and vagrancy,"[40] and this deficiency certainly placed the police at the front line of efforts to deal with the problem. They responded accordingly, and in large cities police arrest figures were often startling. In Paris, for example, despite the fact that the police force was roughly half the size of that in London, they managed to arrest more than double the number of vagrants for most of the 1880s and 1890s.[41] They were also more than willing to seek out and arrest specific individuals in response to public complaints.[42] Like their English counterparts, the French police did, however, show some awareness of genuine cases of homelessness. The prefect of the Paris police noted in 1885 that many of those arrested were "workers whom unemployment and poverty had reduced to begging, and in some cases to vagrancy."[43] In such cases offenders were often merely cautioned and released. In general, however, the police shared the prejudices of the middle classes and were willing to enforce draconian attempts to restrict the problem of vagrancy. As late as 1908 *Le Matin* reported that the Paris prefect of police, Lépine, had issued instructions to his force "*de pourchasser sans pitié*" all vagrants and beggars.[44]

The prejudices of the French police are even more apparent when the related issue of gypsies is considered. Where most vagrants were concerned there was at least the possibility that they were in actuality honest laborers down on their luck, but the caravans and clothing of gypsies immediately identified them as wanderers by choice, and the police seem to have assumed, mostly without question, their innate criminality. Again, such perceptions readily translated into action. From 1895, attempts were periodically made to photograph and classify gypsy families, and in keeping with contemporary theories of degeneration the police often made associations between gypsy caravans and outbreaks of typhoid (such as those in Lille, Amiens, and Paris in 1893). Police circulars from as late as 1907 instructed officers that "concerning the groups of nomads designated under the generic term *romanys,* I remind you that they are all too often composed of criminals."[45] There is also evidence of numerous local antigypsy campaigns by police, often acting on their own initiative and not in response to complaints or orders from above.[46] In 1907 and 1908 stand-offs occurred on both the Belgian and Swiss borders as French gendarmes tried to eject *bohemien* caravans, and their counterparts on the other side of the border tried to do the same. In 1911 new, even stricter, measures were introduced whereby all *romanichels* were required by the police to carry a *carnet anthropométrique*—a detailed identity card.[47]

It is likely that in this desire to control vagrants and to exercise what Dominique Kalifa refers to as a "*prophylaxie sociale,*" the police were again merely reflecting current societal trends.[48] The ongoing development of modern, urban society with its relatively durable economic interrelationships was increasingly leading to a fear of mobility and the problems it could cause, and a concomitant desire for identification and stability.[49] Repressive police attitudes toward vagrants must thus be viewed alongside other initiatives with similar aims, including the Bertillon system of bodily measurement (for identifying recidivists), and the creation of the *brigades mobiles* to track offenders across the country.

Thus, in both France and England, police attitudes toward (and hence treatment of) vagrants were remarkably congruent with those of the middle and upper classes and seem to reflect a desire for social control—that is, restrictions on the activities of one social group principally for the benefit of another. However, in other aspects of their work, the actions of the police seem to contradict this portrayal. In the policing of prostitution and gambling many officers appear tolerant and on occasion sympathetic toward the poor, even those guilty of offenses.

The Policing of Prostitution, Gambling Clubs, and Street Traders

In a number of areas of their work, police attitudes and policies appear to have run counter to the intolerance and distaste for the poor outlined above. This was certainly the case in the policing of prostitution. The practice was viewed with extreme disdain (at least publicly) by the "respectable" classes. Not only was prostitution held to propagate contagion and attendant crime; it was also viewed by many as a "demoralizing force," a trade that encouraged a life of dissolution and depravity and that could have only the worst consequences for society as a whole. Without doubt it was a problem primarily associated with the poor. Petrow notes that "analysis of the background of prostitutes rescued by the Salvation Army in late-Victorian London confirms that poverty was the mainspring of prostitution."[50] In England, police files and complaint books contain numerous letters, petitions, and calls for action against the trade.[51] Some of these originated from private individuals aggrieved at being solicited, but many were from parish vestries, ratepayers associations, and other official bodies such as the Society for the Suppression of Vice and the National Vigilance Association.

However, contrary to what might be expected in the light of their actions against vagrants, the police were often unwilling to proceed in response to such complaints.

In the face of repeated, specific grievances they would take limited action but in general were disinclined to involve themselves. Inwood notes of Whitechapel that "the vast majority of the almost seven thousand prostitutes 'known to the police' were left to do their nightly work in peace."[52] Police Orders from 1887, at perhaps the height of public concern over the "problem of the poor," noted that "the commissioner directs that in future Police Officers should not be employed in specially watching Brothels for the Parish Authorities."[53] In the same year the commissioner of the Metropolitan Police wrote to the under secretary of state formally protesting the involvement of the police in the regulation of brothels: "The whole subject . . . is one which will require legislation but as long as there is a demand for prostitutes on the part of the public there is no doubt they will exist in spite of the Vestries and Vigilance Societies, and the more they are driven out of their brothels into the back slums, the worse it will become for law and order."[54] Although it should be noted that, for a variety of reasons, the police in London may have been more lenient than elsewhere—Judith Walkowitz notes that some prostitutes moved to London as a "haven from police harassment"[55]—such an attitude is surely far removed from the social control functions that might be expected of them. Many police officers realized that prostitutes were forced to their trade by dire poverty rather than choice and were happy to tolerate it as long as it was not taking place on street corners or public places.

The situation was somewhat more complex in France. The legislation governing the policing of prostitution was extremely vague—Berlière describes it as "*une grande confusion.*"[56] A system of *inscription* existed by which prostitutes were required to register with the police and to agree to submit to regular medical examinations. The *police des moeurs* enforcing these regulations were often criticized by the public, and there were continual complaints that such an authoritarian system had no basis in legislation and ran counter to the libertarian ideals of the Third Republic. Jill Harsin notes that "all the vague fears, tensions, anxieties, and the misogyny of the nineteenth century got tangled up in the control of prostitution, as normally stalwart officials found themselves unable to contemplate the idea of extending to prostitutes the rights granted to ordinary criminals."[57] A series of widely publicized cases of mistreatment and wrongful arrest in the 1870s and 1880s further served to strengthen the abolitionists' cause.[58] However, beneath the undoubtedly tougher approach to prostitution pursued by the French police, some basic similarities to the English case can be discerned. As across the Channel, tolerance was perhaps the key defining term. The police in France never attempted, or wished to attempt, the eradication of the trade. Paris Prefect of Police Lépine noted, "I am not a teacher of morality . . . I only regulate prostitution from the point of view of public health and good order in the streets."[59] Rather than bow to pressure to attempt to eradicate prostitution, the police instead aimed to confine the practice to specific *maisons de tolérance,* where it could be more easily regulated and controlled. This semiofficial system led to what Harsin has termed a "cliental relationship" between the police and many prostitutes, and she further notes that "this special relationship led the prefecture, on occasion, to mix compassion with repression, allowing prostitutes to use the various prisons as refuges."[60]

Although there was still undoubtedly, as Berlière notes, an "*inégalité de traitement selon la classe,*" it is still possible to find expressions of empathy among the French police. For example, Louis Hamon (a Paris *commissaire*) noted that "what is particularly striking about prostitutes is the way in which their ignoble trade is often combined with real honesty and a respect for propriety,"[61] and certainly the real antipathy of the police was customarily reserved for pimps, who were seen as hardened criminals preying on poor young women and their customers alike. At least as far as prostitution is concerned, the French police appear to have been both unwilling to enforce the social control functions requested of them from above and keen to retain their wide discretionary powers. Their agenda revolved around the maintenance of public order, and they sustained a more pragmatic and sympathetic view of prostitutes than most of the middle classes, although this was allied with a desire to maintain an acceptable level of public order and a willingness to act accordingly. In other areas of police activity, too, similar trends can be discerned.

Gambling was another vice supposedly associated with both poverty and criminality, which many reformers felt should be eradicated from among the lower classes. The police were certainly willing to admit that gaming dens were a problem among the poor but again were often unwilling to intervene decisively in the fashion required. Instead they pursued their own autonomous aims. An 1889 Metropolitan Police report stated that "police records offer abundant proof that much poverty and crime are caused by gaming houses among certain sections of the poorer classes in London."[62] Yet the same report outlined that "on grounds of policy it seemed desirable to begin by suppressing houses frequented by persons of the wealthier classes in the West End." Indeed a police raid on the Field Club in St. James' in the same year demonstrates the willingness of the police to act against those higher up the social scale. A baccarat game was taking place before the raid, and £5,000 in stake money was confiscated. Those arrested included three lords and an earl.[63] This was hardly social control from above. The police again had their own independent agenda, which revolved around the maintenance of a minimum standard of public order.

Similar leniency can be discerned on the part of the French police on other issues. For example, in order to set up stalls selling petty wares on the streets, *marchands ambulants* had to apply to the prefecture for a permit that supposedly allowed the police to regulate the system. The Paris police understood extremely well the extent to which permission to sell small items, particularly food, in this way kept many from destitution. Police circulars often instructed officers to consider the problems that the confiscation of goods might cause before acting against infringements.[64] According to research by Jean-Michel Baruch-Gourden, their knowledge of the hardships of life in the poorer quarters often inspired in the police "*une étonnante permissivité*" in such matters, especially during harsh winters.[65] Again, evidence such as this appears to run counter to an image of the nineteenth-century police as the authoritarian enforcers of social control. The daily contact of the police with the poor engendered a pragmatic approach to many of their duties and even seems to have inspired a degree of sympathy that prompted some officers to offer practical assistance.

Individuals such as Superintendent James Bent, an officer in the north of England, routinely displayed a genuine humanitarianism. During the severe winter of 1878, he set up a soup kitchen in the drill hall at Old Trafford Police Station. He initially intended to feed around twenty destitute children whom he had befriended on his beat. However, on the second day 180 children presented themselves, and on the third this figure had risen to 580. Such charitable work continued into his retirement. A report in the *Manchester Courier* over a decade later noted that between 1,500 and 2,000 meals were still being provided daily and described his work as "of very substantial advantage to a genuinely necessitous and usually deserving class."[66] Bent was not unique. Other officers also ran soup kitchens and made charitable collections. Richard Jervis arranged for new clothes to be distributed to the homeless on many occasions, and on Christmas Days the Ormskirk police distributed over one hundred Christmas meals with blankets. Indeed, Clive Emsley notes that "police charities supplying boots and clothing to the poor continued until well into the twentieth century."[67] Nor were such social welfare initiatives always confined to the lower ranks. The prefect of the Paris police, Louis Andrieux, went to considerable efforts during the 1880s to secure an annual budget of sixty thousand francs reserved solely to provide assistance to those among the poor behind with their rent and in danger of eviction. He explained that "there is no sadder spectacle than when one sees these unfortunates, with their children . . . in the midst of their old rags and mattresses thrown out on the pavement."[68]

Care must be taken, however, not to overemphasize such compassion. Police action undoubtedly weighed most heavily on the shoulders of the poorer classes, and the police were often resented for it, as statistics for attacks on officers show.[69] Moreover, violence on the part of the police and a bias against the poorer classes were still very much in evidence at the end of the century. Yves Guyot, for example, in his study of the French police in the 1880s, alleged that many police *commissaires* did not respect the poor and that they "had a constant tendency to believe a well-off, sober individual, over one who is badly turned out."[70] However, it does seem likely that social repression and control functions of the police were tinged with pragmatism and even sympathy more than might initially be expected. How then can these two divergent pictures of nineteenth-century policing—the harsh repression of vagrants and the leniency extended to other sections of the poorer classes—be reconciled?

Conclusions

As Donajgrodzki noted in the 1970s, it is certainly true that, during the latter half of the nineteenth century, "the ruling classes often saw the control of the poor as a problem."[71] The ongoing development of modern, European societies, characterized by increasingly fixed socioeconomic relationships, meant that the very poor were progressively perceived as divergent from the working classes, who were gradually coopted into "respectable" society. By the 1880s the personal dimension previously associated with the regulation of the poor had all but disappeared. At the same time, harsh economic conditions (often the result of structural shifts in patterns of production), coupled with increasing urbanization, meant that the poorer districts of towns and cities were increasingly viewed as a *terra incognita* by the middle classes and appeared to represent a real danger to social stability.[72] The advent of social Darwinism, coupled with Victorian ideals of progress, produced a real reforming zeal on the part of many social commentators and added to a perception of the poor as a residuum, socially unproductive and dissolute. Certainly then, many expected the newly established police to be at the forefront of efforts to control and reform the dangerous poorer classes.

The police had wide ranging powers at their disposal. Moreover, Thompson notes that much of the legislation they enforced (for example, the 1824 Vagrancy Act in Britain) was "vague and generic," allowing in practice "considerable discretion" in its interpretation.[73] The police could very often decide for themselves what did or did not constitute an offense in particular circumstances, yet it seems that they did not always enforce the existing legislation as its originators intended. As Petrow states, "discretion enabled the police to strike an operational balance between the demands of the law, their superiors, and moral reformers and the often different attitudes of residents in the local areas they policed, and their own views and backgrounds."[74] Certainly the police were unwilling to act as mere tools of moral reformers, as the commissioner of the Metropolitan Police made clear in 1869, stating that "at best the Police can only make clean the outside of the platter; the improvement of the morals and manners of the people must be left to higher agencies."[75]

Rather than attempt to enforce the law rigorously in response to middle-class pressure, the police instead attempted to manufacture a minimum standard of public order. Thus, they were willing to act against vagrants because they perceived them to be possible, if not actual, criminals. They were less willing to proceed against prostitution and certain other offenses because they considered them to be less of a public-order issue. In attempting to mediate between two conflicting social realities—that of the upper-class elite and that of the intended subjects of their legislation—it is clear that, as Inwood notes, "[the aim of the police] in general was to establish minimum standards of public order, but not to provoke social conflict by aspiring to unattainable ideals."[76] There are three possible reasons why this should have been the case.

First, a lack of adequate resources undoubtedly hampered the police in both England and France. Given that a lack of manpower prevented the full implementation of legislation designed to restrict the freedoms of the poorer classes, a type of informal negotiated order necessarily developed. The police required a certain degree of tacit consent among the lower classes to act effectively and thus could not realistically attempt to accomplish everything demanded of them.

Second, the social background of police recruits must also be considered. Certainly in England police recruits were often more than familiar with the plight of the poor, being but little removed from them socially in many cases. When Sir Robert Peel formed the Metropolitan Police in 1829, he specified that constables were to be drawn from the working class and could subsequently move into the senior ranks. Clive Emsley and Mark Clapson confirm that police forces nationwide "drew heavily on the unskilled and semi-skilled working class."[77] In France, too, although the military laws of 1872, 1889, and 1905 meant that a large proportion of police posts were reserved for former soldiers, policing was by no means considered a prestigious career. Berlière notes that it was not until Lépine's reforms of 1894, which increased the wages of the Paris Police by 50 percent and introduced clothing and housing allowances, that levels of resignation began to fall.[78] It is thus likely that in France, too, those enrolling in the police were initially drawn from the lower end of the social spectrum. Given this, it is perhaps understandable that the police in both countries adopted a more "down to earth" view of criminality among the poor than certain other social commentators. Petrow notes that many constables were unwilling to enforce antigambling legislation because they "shared the general working-class view that betting was not sinful or harmful."[79] Yet, such considerations may also go some way toward explaining police hostility toward vagrants, as such attitudes were becoming increasingly common among the working class at the time.

Last, it is probable that the French and English police were privy to a more pragmatic, street-level view of the poor than the middle-class theorists and undercover newspaper reporters who formed their blanket impressions over the course of a few days and then left again. It seems hard to doubt that the continual exposure of the police to the hardships experienced daily by the poorer classes can have been wholly without effect. The understanding and practical assistance shown by some officers may well have been inspired as much by a common-sense attempt to remain on friendly terms with the frequent object of police investigations as by altruism, yet it seems likely that the control functions of the police were tempered more often than might at first be expected by the dictates of practicality and empathy.

While the actions of the police during the nineteenth century were framed within the intentions of elite groups—as expressed via legislation—it is unconvincing to depict the police as merely a dependent agency of social control. In certain instances the police agreed with and enforced elite attempts to regulate the behavior of the poor, but in others they used their discretionary power to impose their own agenda. Caught between two very different worlds, it was pragmatism combined with a limited operational autonomy that was the crucial components of police strategy at this time.

Notes

1. See, for example, Storch, "The Policeman As Domestic Missionary," 481–508.
2. See, for example, Croll, "Street Disorder, Surveillance and Shame," 250–68.
3. Donajgrodzki, ed., *Social Control,* 11.
4. Storch, "The Policeman As Domestic Missionary," 496.
5. Petrow, *Policing Morals,* 32.
6. Thompson, "Social Control in Victorian Britain," 196.
7. Inwood, "Policing London's Morals," 129–46. Also, Davis, "Law Breaking and Law Enforcement," 183–85.
8. Some notable recent exceptions include Lucassen, "'Harmful Tramps,'" 29–50. Also, Wagniart, *Le Vagabond.*
9. Emsley, *Crime and Society,* 56.
10. Frégier, *Des Classes Dangereuses,* 11.
11. "Royal Commission on a Constabulary Force," *Parliamentary Papers* (PP), 73, Paragraph 65.
12. "Report of the Commissioner of Police of the Metropolis, 1875," (PP).
13. For a comprehensive analysis of the concept of the residuum in Victorian society, see Harris, "Between Civic Virtue and Social Darwinism," 67–87.
14. Smith, "Assistance and Repression," 824.
15. Inwood, "Policing London's Morals," 142.
16. Thompson, "Social Control in Victorian Britain," 199.
17. Jones, *Crime, Protest, Community and Police,* 23.
18. For a fuller exposition of this concept, see Kalifa, "Concepts de Défense Sociale," 233–40.
19. Jones, *Crime, Protest, Community and Police,* 180.

20. Schwartz, *Policing the Poor*, 26.

21. Frégier, *Des Classes Dangereuses*, 133.

22. Joly, *Le Combat contre le Crime*, 344.

23. Wright, *Between the Guillotine and Liberty*, chap. 7, argues that popular belief outran facts. Smith, "Assistance and Repression," 821–46, claims that in fact there is no doubt that vagrancy was on the increase during the 1880s.

24. Chanteau, *Les Plaies Sociales*, 8.

25. Rivière, *Mendiantes et Vagabonds*, 227.

26. *The Standard,* Public Record Office (PRO), 31 August 1887.

27. Mansel-Pleydell, *The Milborne Reformatory,* 6.

28. The New Poor Law of 1834 had specified that workhouses (which many members of the poorer classes were compelled to enter to receive state relief) had to contain a "casual" ward, where tramps could shelter for the night, in return for a day's labor.

29. Peek, *Social Wreckage,* iv.

30. Inwood, "Policing London's Morals," 141.

31. Chadwick, *Reminiscences of a Chief Constable,* 128–32. Jones, *Crime, Protest, Community and Police,* 190.

33. "Report of the Commissioner of Police of the Metropolis, 1869, appendix D," (PP). Although the report on the casual poor did recognize some cases of genuine need among former soldiers, it was in the main overwhelmingly negative.

34. Jervis, *Lancashire's Crime and Criminals,* 14.

35. "Methods of Dealing with Vagrancy," PRO.

36. See Jones, *Crime, Protest, Community and Police,* p.196.

37. "Report of the Commissioner of the Police of the Metropolis, 1869," (PP).

38. Macé, *La Service de la Sûreté,* 271.

39. Boué, *Vagabondage et Mendicité,* 8.

40. Smith, "Assistance and Repression," 827.

41. For statistical data for London and Paris see, for example, the annual "Report of the Commissioner of Police of the Metropolis," (PP); ; and "Crimes et Délits," Archives de la Préfecture de la Police (APP).

42. See, for example, "Case of M. Broughan," (APP).

43. "Rapport sur la crise économique 1885," (APP).

44. *Le Matin,* 17 September 1908.

45. "Circulaire Ministerielle, Direction de la Sûreté Générale to Commissaires," (APP), 200.

46. Berlière, "L'Institution Policière," 360.

47. Ibid.

48. Kalifa, "Concept de Défense Sociale," 235. Nor were the French and English police alone in their attitudes. See Lucassen, "Harmful Tramps."

49. For further information on the marginalization of the vagrant within modern French society, see Wagniart, *Le Vagabond.*

50. Petrow, *Policing Morals*, 119.

51. See, for example, "Complaints Concerning Prostitution," (PRO).

52. Inwood, "Policing London's Morals," 140.

53. "Police Observation of Brothels and Disorderly Houses" and "Police Orders dated Wednesday July 20ᵗʰ 1887," P.R.O.

54. Ibid., Letter, Commissioner to Under Secretary of State, 31 October 1887.

55. Walkowitz, *Prostitution and Victorian Society*, 22.

56. Berlière, "L'Institution Policière," 243.

57. Harsin, *Policing Prostitution*, xx.

58. For details see Berlière, "L'Institution Policière," 255ff.

59. Cited in Berlière, "L'Institution Policière," 286.

60. Harsin, *Policing Prostitution*, 236.

61. Hamon, *Police et Criminalité*, 296.

62. "Report of the Commission of Police of the Metropolis, 1889," *Parliamentary Papers, 1890–1891*, XLII.355.

63. "Police Raids on Gambling Clubs," P.R.O.

64. See, for example, "Professions Ambulants," (APP).

65. Baruch-Gourden, "La police et le commerce ambulant," 259.

66. *Manchester Courier*, 23 March 1888.

67. Emsley, *The English Police*, 155.

68. Andrieux, *Souvenirs d'un Préfet de Police*, 331.

69. See, for example, Storch, "The Policeman As Domestic Missionary," statistical appendix.

70. Guyot, *La Police*, 96–98.

71. Donajgrodzki, *Social Control*, 19.

72. This phrase was coined by Stedman-Jones, *Outcast London*.

73. Thompson, "Social Control," 197.

74. Petrow, *Policing Morals*, 43.

75. "Report of the Commissioner of Police of the Metropolis, 1869," (PP).

76. Inwood, "Policing London's Morals," 144.

77. Emsley and Clapson, "Recruiting the English Policeman," 283. See also the work of Klein, "Invisible Working Class Men."

78. Berlière, *Le Monde des Polices*.

79. Petrow, *Policing Morals*, 240.

CHAPTER 10

The Police, Gender, and Social Control: German Servants in Dutch Towns, 1918–1940

LEO LUCASSEN

In April 1936 the head of the Leiden aliens police received a letter from Mrs. De Wilde, who accused her German servant of having an affair with her husband and who asked the police to expel her. Thereupon, the police interviewed all parties involved, starting with the husband. He declared that the nineteen-year-old servant, Trautchen Netzlaff, was hired in January 1935, when the childless couple was still living in The Hague. He further admitted that their marriage was unhappy and he had indeed slept with Netzlaff, who, he said, would do anything to get a Dutch husband. His wife partly backed up his story by pointing at the German servant as the one who had taken the initiative and thereby threatened their marriage, which until her appearance had been a solid one. Netzlaff denied everything and told the police that De Wilde had harassed her and moreover had paid her poorly, so that she had decided to leave them and work for another employer.

The head of the Leiden police, reviewing all statements, suspected that notwithstanding the declaration of Netzlaff she had had a sexual relationship with De Wilde. Moreover, when she was summoned to come to the police station to be questioned, she was drunk, and when she left she was picked up by two young men.[1] It may be clear that her behavior strengthened the already negative impression the Leiden police had of her. Surprisingly enough, however, no measures were taken to expel Netzlaff from the Netherlands. The main reason was that the police, as well as the attorney general in The Hague—who had the final responsibility for expulsions—did not trust the statements of Mr. and Mrs. De Wilde. Instead, the police informed the girl's parents, warning them that if their daughter did not change her conduct, she ran the risk of being sent home.[2]

The attitude of the Leiden police in the Netzlaff case, which as we will see was not an isolated example, is quite remarkable when we confront it with the dominant image in the literature on German servants during the interwar period. It has been suggested that the police in Dutch towns did not have much consideration for these women. As soon as suspicion arose that their conduct was "immoral," or when they lost their jobs, they were expelled without hesitation. German servants were virtually without any rights and fully dependent on the whims of the employers and the police. In conflicts between employers and servants, the police almost always chose the side of the first party. Especially the aliens police in The Hague, which Barbara Henkes argues were one of the principal targets for complaints made by German maids, had quite a reputation in this regard.[3] Henkes's conclusions, however, are not founded on systematic file research and thus mainly rely on impressionistic accounts from the cities of Groningen, The Hague, and Amsterdam, as well as on interviews with former servants. It therefore remains an open question how representative—both for the cities Henkes mentions and for the Netherlands as a whole—her evidence is.

Information from the files of the Leiden aliens police provides reasons to doubt that the Dutch police in general were particularly severe in their treatment of German servants. When we review this material, a much more nuanced picture emerges. As in the case of Trautchen Netzlaff, the police checked the accusations, and in several instances not the servant but the employer was blamed. Moreover, expulsions from Leiden were quite rare.

I will first underpin this thesis and show what this tells us about the social control exercised by the Leiden police. Although many scholars have discredited this concept from the 1980s onward,[4] it may be useful when we want to get a better insight into the attitude of the Dutch aliens police toward female servants. As social control has been defined in many ways, it is important to explain the approach chosen in this paper. In this case study on the Leiden aliens police, I will concentrate on formal control mechanisms and the state.[5] Within this restricted domain, however, the classical focus on the repression of deviance alone is insufficient.[6] The main reason is that the actions of the Leiden aliens police were not restricted to punishment; more than that, the bulk of the time police officers devoted to aliens had to do with registration and arbitration. This last aspect has been stressed by many students of social control. In his model of social control as a dependent variable, Donald Black for instance places arbitration in the middle of the spectrum running from friendly participation to repressive pacification.[7]

To better understand the functioning of social control, we have to take into account the emergence of a specialized aliens police and the categorization of foreigners. Both were stimulated during and immediately after World War I through an interplay of growing state intervention in the national economy, the creation of (albeit modest) state-financed welfare schemes, especially unemployment benefits, and the process of democratization. These factors forced governments for the first time to consider the position of native workers in times of economic difficulties and—at least in a symbolic sense—give them preferential treatment to aliens.[8] On top of this cascade of structural changes in western European societies, came the fear of alien revolutionaries and the millions of refugees that the Great War produced. As these temporal upheavals faded away, the structural changes created a new migration regime,[9] characterized by a fundamental distinction between citizens and aliens, which made the latter much more vulnerable than before. It was the time that, in the words of the American sociologist Everett Hughes, aliens obtained a "master status."[10]

This development fits in the more general process of state formation as analyzed by scholars such as Charles Tilly, who in this respect stresses the monitoring function of the state. Another idea that is useful in the study of the aliens police is Anthony Giddens concept of administrative power: "By administrative power I do not mean primarily, as Foucault does, in speaking of 'disciplinary power.' . . . Rather, I mean something else which brooks quite large in Foucault's analyses, control over the timing and spacing of human activities."[11] In modern states, Giddens argues, this administrative power expands through "documentary" activities of the state, involving an upsurge in the collection and collation of information devoted to administrative purposes.[12] These definitions, albeit broad, put the activities of the aliens police into a new light, which makes it possible to apply insights in the field of social control in a fruitful way to the history of migration control and the control of migrants. The analytical tools of both Tilly and Giddens help us to pave a way through the now vast literature on the historical development of the police in western Europe. Doing so, it becomes clear that relatively little attention has been paid to the documentary activities of the police and the administrative power that follows from it.[13]

This essay focuses on the consequences of the specialization of the aliens police for the exertion of social control, of which four dimensions can be distinguished: the enforcement of acts and regulations; the enforcement of unwritten norms; arbitration; and administrative control through registration. More specifically, I will build up my argument using the midsized Dutch town of Leiden (70,000 inhabitants in 1930), situated between The Hague and Amsterdam in the western part of the country, and focusing specifically on alien female domestic servants. The choice for Leiden has to do with the availability of a well-kept archive (both the registration and files on aliens). The concentration on female servants was almost forced upon me, because they constituted the single most important group of migrants in the urban labor market. Moreover, because of the gendered nature of this category and the fear, prevailing at the time, that these young women were in great risk of losing their respectability through immoral behavior, a great deal of the time and energy of the aliens police was devoted to these women. A problem with the Leiden case, however, is that this town is one of the very few where files on aliens were systematically kept during the interwar period, and we therefore do not know whether the attitude of the Leiden police was an exception or the rule. In the final paragraph I therefore will try to put the results into perspective by analyzing expulsion data at the national level.

The Migration of Female Servants

Female servants from abroad are not a modern phenomenon in the Netherlands. Already in the early modern period, servants from neighboring countries as well as Norway came to the then prosperous Dutch republic.[14] In the nineteenth century the immigration waned, and during World War I it came to an absolute standstill. After the war, however, the influx of alien servants, predominantly from Germany, but also some from Austria, Hungary, Czechoslovakia, and Poland, increased suddenly and massively. Especially in the big cities in the western part of the country, ten of thousands of female servants found jobs and soon composed a considerable part of the total immigrant population. In Leiden, alien servants, 90 percent of whom came from Germany, formed almost 25 percent of all aliens in the interwar period, and recent calculations estimate that some 175,000 alien servants worked in the Netherlands in this time span.

The immigration of these maids can be explained both in push and pull terms. The dramatic economic situation in Germany during the years following the armistice led to towering inflation and huge unemployment. Many young women, who were desperately in search of jobs, mainly to contribute to the family income, therefore headed for the rich "guilder country." In the Netherlands the war had not devastated the economy, and since the turn of the century the Netherlands had been confronted with a shortage of female domestic servants. Most young Dutch women preferred jobs in factories or shops to the long hours and low pay that characterized domestic service.[15] The sudden availability of a large supply of cheap foreign servants, a status symbol that now came within the reach of the middle class, caused many Dutch families in the western part of the country to hire these women. Recruitment took place both through intermediaries and by placing advertisements in German newspapers, especially in the Ruhr area, where most of the women came from.

The massive immigration of servants coincided with the introduction of unprecedented measures to register and supervise aliens in the Netherlands in 1918.[16] As in most western European countries, directly after World War I, acts were issued that made it obligatory for aliens (and Dutch citizens who housed them) to report themselves to the local police. As a result the police were ordered to keep records of these aliens in a much more systematic way than ever before.[17]

Initially, the aim of this legislation was to keep track of dangerous revolution-aries, but soon the protection of the Dutch housing and labor markets started to prevail. The aim of the 1918 act, and the ensuing regulations, was twofold: to monitor aliens through registration and the exchange of information between various Dutch local police forces (and with the Central Aliens Office in The Hague);[18] and, furthermore, to see to it that aliens did not break the law. The first function consisted of building up large and impressive registration lists of all aliens who came to a certain municipality for either shorter or longer peri-ods. This information was retained after an alien left, because many returned after a while (servants who went back home each year for one or more holidays, for example). The second function mainly concerned regulations with regard to the labor market and good (moral) conduct. Depending on the economic situ-ation, aliens had to obtain visas on their passports, which could only be obtained when there were no Dutch citizens unemployed in a certain sector. Although German female servants were exempted from this rule because of the already men-tioned shortage,[19] the police had to make sure that these women complied with their contracts and did not shift to jobs for which a visa was obligatory. Furthermore, their moral behavior was a point of concern. Although the law was not very specific on this point, sexual relations with married men could be a cause for expulsion, whereas conduct that was labeled frivolous or "immoral," for exam-ple going out with different young men and coming home late, could have the same consequence.

For this paper, I consulted the collection of about five thousand files on aliens from the Leiden police. The approach used to sift through this massive pile of documentation, I admit, is somewhat subjective. I selected only files on female servants that contained substantive and contextual information.[20] To counter-balance this selectivity, I furthermore selected all files on female servants in 1922 and 1930, both peak years in the immigration of female servants to Leiden (and the Netherlands as a whole).[21] The result was some fifty detailed files covering the period 1920–1936. Most of the complaints concerned "immoral behavior" (60 percent). Another 25 percent had to do with a breach of contract or lack-ing means of subsistence. Only a few files mentioned criminal acts (theft) or sex-ual harassment. When we evaluate the material, we must be aware that the complaints about maids concern a tiny minority of all the women who came to Leiden: only 3 percent of them gave cause for the police to create a file.[22] Most of the women simply registered, worked for some time, and then left the country (or married a Dutchman).[23]

In order to test the idea that the Dutch police in general took a very harsh stance toward non-Dutch servants, we will now look more systematically at the files kept by the Leiden police concerning female servants. For a nuanced eval-uation of the attitudes of the Leiden police, their motives for interference are broken down into different categories: economic, moral, and criminal.

Breach of Contract and Unemployment

Female servants who agreed to work for a Dutch family placed themselves under the Dutch labor law, which implied that they could not just leave their jobs without notice. Whereas the ultimate penalty for Dutch servants was dismissal, alien servants could be expelled from the country. Among the seven cases that involved such a complaint, only two resulted in an expulsion order, but for different reasons both were not implemented. The Hungarian Vilma Kovacs was not accepted by the Dutch border commissioner, probably because he was afraid that his German colleague would refuse to accept her.[24] Leopoldine Mikulitsch (born in Vienna in 1903) in 1926 successfully appealed to the Austrian legation, arguing that she had left her employer because he had harassed her sexually.[25] The police did not believe her but were blocked by the Austrian legation, who argued that the punishment of expulsion was much too severe and refused to cooperate. The Leiden police thereupon advised the central passport bureau in The Hague to give Mikulitsch a new visa, arguing that it appeared she could not be blamed entirely, because she had not understood that leaving her employer could have such grave consequences. In the other five cases, the police did not even consider expulsion, nor any other measure, because the officer concerned was not convinced of the sincerity of the employer.[26] It is striking that accusations of employers were not accepted at face value, and in many cases an inquest followed in which not only the employer but also the servant and sometimes others involved were heard. The result was that accusations often proved false or partly false, so that no further action was taken.

Domestic servants who changed to other kind of jobs could come into trouble once the police found out. Servants did not need to obtain permission from the local labor office to change jobs, because of the lack of domestic servants in the Netherlands. The moment that they decided to quit and take up another kind of job (mostly as a shop assistant or a waitress), a declaration to that effect—for Germans until late 1926—was obligatory. Anna Röpti, for example, who came to Leiden in 1924 and soon took up a job as waitress in a milk bar, was warned that if her employer did not get a work permit her visa would be annulled and she would have to leave the country.[27] In the same year, Frieda Staperfeld decided to leave her job as domestic servant and was offered a position in a barbershop.[28] The police found out, and the employer was unable to get a work permit for a shop servant. As expulsion loomed, the Dutch owner offered her a job as a ladies' barber, an occupation for which no permit was needed. The aliens police suspected that this move was only a formal one and tried to gather as much information as possible to prove that Frieda in reality worked as a shop servant. The central aliens office in the Hague, however, refused to annul her visa, because the evidence offered by the Leiden police was too scanty.

Both cases show that the police took it very seriously when an alien woman left domestic service for another job without obtaining proper permission to do so. Interestingly enough, however, they could not just act on their own and needed the consent of the central aliens authorities in The Hague, who were not satisfied with mere accusations and suspicions. In neither case was the servant involved at the mercy of the discretion of the local police but could rely on the formal regulations.

Less successful were domestic servants who for various reasons lost their jobs and were unable to find other ones. For them the 1918 Aliens Act was clear and strict. Already the first Aliens Act of 1849 stipulated that aliens without means of existence could be expelled without further ado, and this clause (as well as the act itself) was still in effect in the interwar period.[29] When the police found out that a domestic servant was without a job and had no means to support herself, her chances of being sent home were considerable. For most foreign servants it was no problem to get another job, and only a small minority found themselves in this position.[30]

Domestic servants who committed criminal offenses are rarely found in the archives of the Leiden police, and when it occurred it concerned small amounts of money, clothes, or valuables from the household they served. When it could be proved, the sanction was nearly always expulsion.[31]

Immorality

In contrast to the economic domain, complaints about moral conduct were less easy to judge. The judicial foundation was that aliens should not act contrary to public decency.[32] How this clause was interpreted depended much on the opinions of the police officers concerned. In some cases their judgment was quickly formed, as with twenty-one-year-old Gerda Schoppmeijer who on a Wednesday in July 1921 asked her employer for permission to spend the afternoon in a nearby sea resort (Katwijk). Contrary to their agreement she stayed overnight and returned the next evening at five o'clock, declaring she had fallen off her bike and was taken in by a sympathetic family kind enough to let her stay the night. Her mistress found this very suspicious and called the police. The officer in charge took Gerda Schoppmeijer to Katwijk, but she failed to point out the house where she had allegedly stayed. Soon her story broke down: In fact she had met a man and spent the night with him in a Leiden hotel, pretending to be husband and wife. Thereupon, the police advised the central aliens authority in The Hague to expel her, and eight days after the fatal night two policemen took her by train to the German border.[33]

This example is not surprising and fits the general image put forward by Henkes that even the slightest accusation of immoral behavior easily led to expulsion.[34] Evaluating the twenty-six cases on moral conduct, however, this statement is too sweeping, at least for the situation in Leiden. First, in most cases about alleged immoral behavior, the police were cautious and did not take such drastic measures.[35] On the contrary, confronted with complaints about alleged immoral conduct of alien maids (coming home late, going out with young men, or even having affairs with married men), the police saw it as their task to find out whether the employers themselves, or others, were to blame. More than once all persons involved were interviewed, and the conclusion was reached that the accusation was false or exaggerated.

An interesting case in this respect is the complaint of Johanna Verhoeff (age thirty-two). She told the police that her father, who was a widower and lived alone with his two youngest sons (twelve and seventeen), had an intimate relationship with his seventeen-year-old Czechoslovakian maid Maria Zabel. She depicted her as a girl of very low standards who would often walk almost naked through the house in the presence of her father and younger brothers. Although she also blamed her father, she urged the police to expel Zabel, especially in the interest of her brothers. The detective in charge decided first to question the maid and the father, who both denied the accusations. Apparently, these statements did not fully corroborate the declaration made by Johanna Verhoeff, as an excerpt from the twenty-page report of the detective shows: "To me it seems that what is said of the girl's conduct is exaggerated, although it cannot be denied that the relation between Verhoeff senior and Zabel is not such as one would wish between a male employer and a maid. In my opinion it would be better if Maria Zabel looked for another family, also because the older sons of Verhoeff have a rather dubious reputation."[36] The striking thing about this report is that while the girl's behavior was regarded as improper, the police focused on the part played by the employer and his sons. It is certainly not so straightforward that accusations about immorality voiced by Dutch citizens about aliens were uncritically accepted.

Tolerance and understanding, instead of prejudice and ruthlessness, were also encountered in cases involving maids who had started affairs with married men, but who had been unaware of the men's civil status. Anna Wieser, for example, became engaged to Willem Martens. Only after his wife complained to the police did Anna find out that he was married. She immediately ended the relationship and was left alone. Had she not done this, she probably would have been expelled.[37] From the thirteen servants who willingly continued having a relationship with married men, five were expelled for this reason.

Also in these cases this decision was not made overnight, as is illustrated by the affair in 1923 between Amalia Badzionc (born 1893) and a German man named Hubert Müller (born 1875).[38] The police became involved after receiving a letter from Müller's wife, who still lived in Germany. Both persons were questioned, and Amalia declared that Müller had concealed that he was married. She admitted that he had asked her several times to have sexual intercourse but that she had refused: "Although he had persuaded her once to commit acts not to be circumscribed any further, which she regretted when she heard that Müller was married."[39] A week later the head of the aliens police saw them walking together near the railway station. From this he deduced that Badzionc had not given up the relationship. He further noticed that Müller often changed addresses in order to evade police supervision. He therefore advised the central aliens authority (the inspector of the Royal Military Police, IKM) to expel both of them from the kingdom with the argument that "Although Müller fulfills his financial obligations to his family, his immoral behavior toward his daily environment remains. When others see that such an indecent relationship is silently tolerated in this country, this will surely have a demoralizing influence."[40] The IKM instructed the Leiden police to expel only Müller, because on the basis of the evidence presented he was not convinced that Badzionc had really continued her intimate affair after she had discovered that he was married. The Leiden police, however, did not give up and three days later reported to the IKM that when Müller was summoned to pack his things Badzionc had been present: "from the way they said goodbye, it was obvious that they had not broken off their relationship, whereas Müller said that he would never let her go."[41] Nevertheless, the IKM found these statements still insufficient to go along with the expulsion of Amalia Badzionc.

Whereas in this case the local police wanted to send Amalia back to Germany, they sometimes showed remarkable sympathy toward maids who got themselves into trouble because of an affair. The best example of this that I came across was an affair between Mathilda Spindler and her mistress.[42] The first time the police was informed about this relationship was in 1929, when the mistress had accused Mathilda of slander, after she had publicly divulged their alleged lesbian affair. The police took this matter very seriously and held a series of extensive interviews, mainly with the two women. Although the employer kept denying the affair, the detailed testimony provided by Mathilda was considered to be more or less the truth. It appeared that she took up service with her mistress in 1917, when she was sixteen years old. Her widowed employer lived at the time with her two children in a village close to Leiden. After only three weeks had passed, she seduced her domestic servant, and according to Mathilda, until 1929 they frequently slept with each other and had sex. When her employer found Mathilda's passion lacking, she fired her. Probably she regretted this decision, as she took her in again soon thereafter. As a result, Mathilda began suffering from severe strain and started her public accusations.

From the information in the elaborate file it is clear that the police were convinced that Spindler had told the truth, and they therefore decided to hold the Dutch employer responsible for what had happened. Nevertheless, they asked the attorney general in The Hague, who after 1926 replaced the IKM as the highest authority where expulsions were concerned, to send her back to Germany, because Spindler was too much under the spell of her mistress. The attorney general, however, was not convinced, because Spindler had means of subsistence and the acts committed did not violate *public* decency. Only when she lost her job a few years later and became without means, was Mathilde Spindler finally sent back to Germany.

Liberties

Finally, I will write a few words about servants who complained about sexual harassment by male employers or their sons. The frequency of these liberties is almost by definition unknown. Many women were afraid or too embarrassed to complain, and only a few of them went to the police for this reason. Nevertheless, I found four files that contain accusations of this sort.[43] The first case is situated in 1923 when a Leiden citizen had gone to the police because a former servant, Lily Stapelfeld (born 1904), had accused him in public of sexual harassment, involving not only herself but also other German maids who had worked for him. He demanded that the police take action and send the servant back to Germany. For the police these were difficult cases, as it was almost invariably one person's word against another. Nevertheless, the complaint was taken seriously, and apart from the parties directly involved, other informants were heard as well. Although the police were unable to ascertain what had really happened, the employer obviously had made a bad impression, whereas the story of the servant was considered trustworthy, so no action was taken.[44] This is not to say that it could not have consequences for the man or family concerned. Their reputation was noted and, if necessary, would be used in the future to warn prospective domestic servants, their parents, or foreign colleagues who inquired about the reliability of such a family.

In the other three cases sexual harassment was given as the motive for breaking the contract. On two occasions the police were not convinced and interpreted the accusations as fictitious. Especially the fact that the families concerned held good reputations played an important role. As with the example of Lily Stapelfeld, information provided by neighbors or others could lead to the opposite viewpoint, even when the family concerned belonged to the town elite. This is shown by the investigation into the complaint by Frida Katschmann (born 1902) who in 1924 explained her sudden departure from a wealthy family by saying that she no longer wanted to be confronted with the filthy talk of the son: In the morning "the son is always the first to come downstairs, and I am asked by his mother to have the breakfast table ready; a few days before I quit my service he put his arms around me, after which I fended him off. He then said to me that it was a pity that I was not as hot as the coffee."[45] The detective in charge was not satisfied with the statements of the son, his mother (the father had died), and the servant and also talked with Frida's former employers, a couple who directed the Jewish orphanage in Leiden. Their opinion was very favorable toward Frida (they described her as correct, honest, and hard working), but negative about the family she now worked for. They had even warned her, because the deceased husband of the widow had a reputation of harassing women when he was superior of the orphanage. This last statement was considered as convincing, and no action was taken.

Putting Leiden in a National Perspective

Since we do not have similar systematic collections of alien files in other Dutch towns with substantial numbers of German servants, it is difficult to ascertain how representative the attitudes of the Leiden police were. I therefore analyzed the expulsion data published by the General Police Journal (*Algemeen Politieblad*). In this Journal, founded in 1852, all aliens who were expelled from the Netherlands are mentioned with name, age, occupation, and the local police force responsible for the expulsion. To find out how many servants were sent home and from which towns, I first looked at the share of women among the entire expelled population (table 1). Because women during the interwar period constituted almost 50 percent of all immigrants, the low percentages show that they were less likely to be expelled than men, notwithstanding the fact that women were more vulnerable because of their young age (on average) and they ran a higher risk of being seduced, getting pregnant, and lapsing into what at the time was regarded as immoral behavior.

Subsequently, we can establish the relative differences in local policies toward servants by differentiating between Dutch cities. The conclusion from table 2 is that the yearly number of expelled female servants was not very high. When we realize that in 1930 some 40,000 servants worked in the Netherlands, some shorter

Table 1   Expulsions of aliens from the Netherlands and the share of women, 1920–1935

	1920	1923	1925	1930	1935
Total number of expulsions	3498	6681	1874	5535	2906
Percentage women	19%	20%	30%	15%	26%

Source: Lucassen, "Administrative into Social Control," p. 337

Table 2   Expulsions of German female servants from Dutch municipalities, 1920–1935

	1920	1923	1925	1930	1935
The Hague	26	37	45	42	45
Amsterdam	26	22	27	28	24
Rotterdam	13	10	13	13	11
Haarlem	0	4	3	8	5
Utrecht	3	2	1	2	2
Groningen	3	1	0	1	0
Venlo	0	0	0	1	0
Heerlen	15	15	4	0	0
Enschede	1	0	0	0	0
Amersfoort	1	0	0	0	0
Leiden	0	1	0	0	1
Bussum	0	0	1	0	0
Maastricht	0	0	0	0	2
Hilversum	0	0	0	0	0
Rest	12	8	6	6	10
Total	100	100	100	100	100
$N =$	68	425	253	401	369

Source: Lucassen, "Administrative into Social Control," p. 338.

term, some longer term, the 401 expelled servants in that year represents only 1 percent. More interesting, however, are the differences between Dutch cities and the relationship between the percentage of expelled German servants and the percentage of German servants in these municipalities. Table 3 shows a considerable difference between big and small towns. Especially in the five major cities (varying between 120,000 and 750,000 inhabitants), the expulsion rates were above the national average, whereas in smaller towns like Leiden (70,000), Hilversum (57,000), or Bussum (25,000), servants ran a much lower risk of being expelled. Second, there are significant differences among the big cities, which is evident when we look at The Hague and Amsterdam. Due to the lack of empirical data from other cities, explanations for these diverging patterns can only be provisional. Having said that, we can differentiate between two sorts of compatible explanations.

Let us first consider the structural explanations. Since the police of small towns seem to have acted with more leniency and understanding, the conjecture is not too far fetched that there must be a structural relationship between the attitude

Table 3 Relation between the percentage of German servants and the
number of expulsions of these women in Dutch cities, 1920–1935

		Expulsions			
	% German Servants	1920	1923	1925	1930
Amsterdam	18	1.4	1.2	1.5	1.5
The Hague	13	2	2.8	3.4	3.2
Rotterdam	6	2.2	1.7	2.2	2.2
Haarlem	2	0	2	1.5	4
Utrecht	1	3	2	1	2
Hilversum	1	0	0	0	0
Bussum	1	0	1	1	0.2
Leiden	0.5	0	2	0.8	0.5
Rest	56.5	0.2	0.2	0.2	0.1
Netherlands	100	1	1	1	1

Source: Lucassen, "Administrative into Social Control," p. 338.

Note: The numbers are calculated by dividing the percentage of expelled German servants in table 2 by the percentage of German servants in each city ("% German Servants," column 2 in this table). When the number is greater than 1, it indicates that more servants were expelled than the average (2 means twice as many expulsions as the average, etc.).

of the aliens police and the size of the city. The image that arises from the files of the Leiden police may well have been, therefore, representative of other smaller cities with a relatively large (or even larger) number of German servants. The explanation for this size effect brings us back to the social control issue. In this case it would imply that the nature of social control exercised by the police depended on the degree of anonymity, which increased with the number of inhabitants. Moreover, the aliens police in Amsterdam and Rotterdam had to deal with much larger numbers of aliens than, for example, in Leiden and Bussum, so that the chances of personal contact, and thus more understanding, between the police and aliens decreased accordingly. Although in these relatively small places we cannot really speak of face-to-face communities, the police not only knew more about "their" aliens but also about the Dutch inhabitants. This was clear in a number of Leiden files, which showed that the reason not to believe accusations against German servants had to do with knowledge about the reputation of the employers.

A second structural explanation may be found in the extent of professionalization and bureaucratization of the aliens police, which was much more advanced in big cities. The more developed the bureaucracy, the greater the chance that rules and procedures take over from individually based decisions. So even when policemen in, say, Amsterdam had more personal knowledge about aliens and thus more compassion, they probably had to follow procedures set by their senior officers.

Let me now turn to individual explanations, regarding not only the structure of the police force but also the personal influence of leading officers. When combined with general features, this can be a valuable addition to structural explanations. Guus Meershoek, who studied the attitude of the Amsterdam police toward the German occupation forces during World War II, for example, has stressed that in order to understand the active involvement of the Amsterdam police in rounding up the Jewish population, the role of the charismatic chief commissioner Tulp is crucial.[46]

It is conceivable, however, that more repressively inclined officers had greater chances of being recruited by large police forces than by small ones. If that is the case, the head of the aliens police in The Hague (Lucas) would not be an exception. Table 3, however, makes clear that this hypothesis does not hold, because the chances of being expelled in The Hague were much higher than in the other two big cities Amsterdam and Rotterdam. To explain the exceptional position of The Hague, personal factors can therefore not be dismissed.

Compared with other cities, the policy in The Hague seems to have been the exception rather than the rule. This is corroborated by correspondence between the chief commissioner of The Hague and his superior, the attorney general in that city. In one of his letters, in the fall of 1928, he complains about the much too tolerant attitude of the police toward pregnant foreign women (most of them servants) in other cities. His colleague in Rotterdam, confronted with this accusation, however, acknowledged that his stance was much less severe and stressed that it was unfair to punish only these women, because in many cases it was the Dutch men who were to blame.

Conclusion

This article has made clear that the social control the Leiden aliens police was able to exert from 1918 onward, both on aliens and Dutch citizens, was enabled by a combination of an increase in monitoring as well as the administrative power that went with it. More concretely, it was a logical consequence of the revolution in the migration regime that took place throughout the Western world around World War I.[47] The enforcement and implementation of a passport regime to control migration, and to protect national labor markets, brought about a system of registration and social control over aliens. This development, embodied in the 1918 Aliens Act, consisted of three separate, but intertwined steps: (1)

the creation of aliens as a dominant category in the sense of Hughes's "master status"; (2) the specialization of local aliens police sections (at least in the big cities) and the setting up of a systematic registration at the local level; (3) the establishment of a national and coordinating aliens authority (the IKM and later the attorneys general). This new regime soon led to a greater symbolic visibility of aliens. The line between aliens and citizens was drawn much clearer, both in terms of rights and obligations as well as in a symbolic sense.

The consequences for daily police work after World War I were notable, especially for the newly created alien police branches. It would be unjustified and misleading to label it as social control, because the bulk of the police involvement in this domain was concerned with registration, and thus more with administrative than with social control. Only occasionally, when confronted with "deviant" behavior, did administrative control lead to social control. The cases I analyzed in this article, therefore, may be crucial for a better understanding of the dealing of the police with female aliens. But it is equally important to keep in mind that this kind of action, and the social control that often was part of it, touched only a tiny minority of all female aliens who lived in Leiden.

As a rule the attitude of the Leiden police can be typified as reactive. They took action only after they received complaints. Cases in which the police took the initiative are scarce. When confronted with a complaint, however, the police did not hesitate to investigate the matter and then relied on the proactive nature of the alien's registration and, in some cases, earlier files on the person in question. At a glance the registration card of an alien could teach the police a lot: when did she come to Leiden? With whom did she live? Who were her employers? Were there problems before? In evaluating these Leiden cases, it is striking that social control was not so much exerted through punishment, as in the case of homosexuals who in this period were mainly confronted with repressive policy, but by arbitration.[48]

Although in most cases control remained dormant and restricted to the recurring reporting of foreigners with the aliens police, the consequences of the new regime for aliens could be far reaching. Their right to work was limited, and the breaking of rules could lead to expulsion. Apart from that, this expression of administrative power through documentary activities, as Giddens called it, could be combined with extensive investigations into the personal life of both aliens and Dutch citizens. In these cases it becomes evident that the police tried to uphold and reproduce the basic moral norms of the time.

Finally, this case study enabled me to test the quite bleak picture of the attitude of the aliens police toward foreign female servants. First, my data make clear that servants were not playthings in the hands of the local police, at least not in Leiden and cities with a similar or smaller size. Although their legal as well as discretionary power was considerable, two factors restrained an arbitrary and restrictive policy. One is the consent they needed from the central aliens authorities

(IKM and the respective attorney general), before they could expel a certain alien. These central agencies proved more cautious, and especially in the moral domain, they were not satisfied with suspicions alone. The main reason might have been that they did not want conflicts with the diplomatic representatives of the countries concerned. Especially the Austrian legation in The Hague was successful in obstructing expulsions when there was insufficient proof. Furthermore it was not so easy to expel aliens from eastern European countries, because German authorities were not obliged to let them pass through their country on their way back home.

The other factor that explains the at times lenient and understanding attitude of the Leiden police is that the detectives and constables involved were not necessarily prejudiced against aliens and that they also considered the role played by Leiden citizens. Moreover, in many instances they took great pains to verify complaints, and they thus demonstrated a certain amount of tolerance and compassion. In this sense they fit the bottom-up approach of the American political scientist Michael Lipsky, who in his study *Street-Level Bureaucracy* stressed the relative autonomy of (among others) civil servants whose work consists of daily contacts with clients (in our case aliens).[49]

We have to be careful, however, about generalizing on the basis of this specific group, because young female domestic servants may not be representative for aliens in general. The combination of age, gender, and social position made them a special category in the eyes of the police. Because they were young and female, the police regarded them on the one hand as vulnerable—the classic image (not always unjustified) of the girl who is easily misled and misused.[50] When this image dominated, policemen showed paternalistic behavior and sometimes acted as surrogate parents. Their attitude is well captured by the concepts of "bureaucratic paternalism"[51] and "caring power," although in this case not exercised by professional women (as in social case work) but by men.[52] On the other hand, domestic servants could also be considered as a moral threat. Most of them having come from working-class backgrounds, they easily fitted the image of women of loose moral standing who could endanger the public morale of the Netherlands. This ambivalent image of foreign domestic servants explains the corresponding variation in the treatment of the complaints.

Notes

This article was published in a different version in *Social History* 27 (2002): 327–42.

1. These appeared to be the sons of her new employer, who celebrated his anniversary that day.

2. *Municipal Archive Leiden* (MAL), Police, inv. nr. E1718/1936/76.

3. Henkes, *Heimat in Holland,* 121–23.

4. See, for example, Gattrel, "The Decline of Theft and Violence"; Mayer, "Notes towards a Working Definition," 17–38; Cohen, "Introduction," in Sebba, ed., *Social Control and Justice: Inside and Outside the Law?;* Black, "Social Control As a Dependent Variable," 1–36; and Horwitz, *The Logic of Social Control.*

5. Ibid., 1.

6. Mayer, "Notes towards a Working Definition," 25.

7. Black, "Social Control As a Dependent Variable," 21.

8. Lucassen, "The Great War."

9. Moch, *Moving Europeans,* chap. 5; Lucassen, "The Great War."

10. Hughes, "Dilemmas."

11. Giddens, *Violence and the Nation State,* 47.

12. Ibid., 173. This links up with Weber's ideas of bureaucratic administration as a means to exert authority through knowledge (Torstendahl, *Bureaucratization,* 12). See also Scott, *Seeing like a State.*

13. In the German police historiography (Reinke, ". . . *nur für die Sicherheit da . . .*"; Nitschke, *Die Deutsche Polizei*). Alf Lüdtke is one of the few who systematically pays attention to registration (e.g., Lüdtke, "Willkürgewalt des Staates," 35–55). The best study on the relationship between aliens police and registration is Noiriel, *La Tyrannie du National* (on France). See also Torpey, *The Invention of the Passport;* Lucassen, "A Many-Headed Monster"; and idem, "Revolutionaries into Beggars."

14. Lucassen and Penninx, *Newcomers.*

15. For the general background, I rely on Henkes, *Heimat in Holland.*

16. This paragraph is based on Lucassen, "The Great War"; idem, "Bringing Structure Back In"; and van der Harst and Lucassen, *Nieuw in Leiden,* 9–12.

17. The first Dutch Aliens Act of 1849 also induced the police to register aliens, but not in a way as systematic and encompassing as the Aliens Act of 1918.

18. The *Rijkspaspoortenkantoor* (abolished in October 1926) and after that the administration of Border Control and Aliens Supervision (AGVD).

19. In the autumn of 1931 more severe regulations toward alien domestic servants under eighteen years of age were issued. By that time the visa requirement had already vanished, but now these women had to have a declaration from their employer stating that they had hired this servant and containing a stamp of the local police as proof that this family was trustworthy. Without such a declaration girls under eighteen could be sent back (Henkes, *Heimat in Holland,* 120).

20. Many files contained only one or two letters or notes, which was not enough to reconstruct the context.

21. Lucassen, "Bringing Structure Back In."

22. Our systematic sample of the aliens registration in Leiden showed that during the interwar period some 4,000 female servants worked in this town, some shorter term, some longer term (van der Harst and Lucassen, *Nieuw in Leiden,* 70). In 1922 (400)

and 1930 (360) servants came to Leiden, whereas in these years only twenty-five of them gave employers or others cause to put in a complaint.

23. As with all registrations underregistration occurred. Our impression from the files, however, is that in general aliens or the persons housing them did register.

24. Vilma came back to Leiden, but the police kept her passport and tried to persuade the Hungarian legation to agree to her expulsion. What came of this is unknown, because Vilma moved to The Hague, and the Leiden police thereby lost track: Municipal Archive Leiden, Police, E1690/1926/156).

25. MAL, Police, E1691/1926/8.

26. MAL, Police, E1691/1926/61; E 1702/1930/85; E1705/1931/123; E1707 /1932/199; E1715/1935/4.

27. MAL, Police, E1759/1924/147.

28. MAL, Police, E1759/1924/187.

29. The new Aliens Act of 1918 did not replace the 1849 Act but must be considered as a supplement and specification.

30. Moreover, Dutch authorities could not prevent such a servant from reentering the country when she secured a new job and visa. In 1930 a special commission was installed that had to look into this matter and asked local police forces to what extent expelled aliens had returned (MAL, Police, E1703/1930/102).

31. MAL, Police, E1709/1933/50; E1691/1926/28; and E1702/1930/88. It is possible that instances of theft and other criminal acts were recorded separately (not in the aliens files), so that at this point we cannot make final statements about the frequency of these acts among servants.

32. As formulated by the attorney general of The Hague in his letter to the Leiden police, dated 12 November 1930 no. 3270 (MAL, Police, E1703/1930/133).

33. MAL, Police, E1751/1921/87.

34. Henkes, *Heimat in Holland,* 123.

35. Of twenty-six cases regarding alleged immoral behavior, only nine led to expulsion. A more common reaction was giving a warning.

36. Report dated 2 June 1933 (MAL, Police, E1709/1933/85).

37. MAL, Police, E1698/1928/103.

38. MAL, Police, E1755/1923/40.

39. MAL, letter from the Leiden police to the Inspector of the Royal Military Police (IKM stands for Inspecteur van de Koninklijke Marechaussee, who was the central authority of the Dutch aliens policy), dated 1 May 1923.

40. Letter to the IKM, dated 29 May 1923.

41. Letter from the Leiden police to the IKM, dated 4 June 1923.

42. MAL, Police, E1701/1929/116.

43. Two of them were mixed with "breach of contract" and were listed under this heading in table 1.

44. MAL, Police, E1756/1923/170.

45. MAL, Police, E1759/1924/101: report dated 28 March 1924.

46. Meershoek, *Dienaren van het gezag*. See also his contribution to this volume.

47. That is to say at least western Europe and the United States. This is not to suggest that before World War I comparable systems of social control were nonexistent. In the nineteenth century people who were considered political radicals and revolutionaries were, especially in France and Germany, closely watched by the police. Furthermore, in Germany gypsies were already confronted with registration and surveillance from the end of the nineteenth century onward (Lucassen, "Harmful Tramps").

48. On the policy toward homosexuals: Koenders, *Tussen christelijk réveil en seksuele revolutie*.

49. Lipsky, *Street-Level Bureaucracy*, cited in Böcker and Clermonts, *Poortwachters*, 9.

50. Compare Henkes, *Heimat in Holland*.

51. I borrow this from Haia Shpayer-Makov's contribution to this volume.

52. See Van Drenth and De Haan, *The Rise of Caring Power*.

Some Thoughts on Social Control in "Totalitarian" Society: The Case of Nazi Germany

Eric A. Johnson

T his essay and several that follow consider what many would believe to be the ultimate examples of social control in modern history, namely the allegedly totalitarian societies of the twentieth century under Nazi, Fascist, or Communist rule. Whereas one cannot contest that the leaders of these societies did most certainly develop organs of surveillance and enforcement to deter their enemies, promote their ideological aims, and solidify their bases of power that were often extremely powerful, ruthless, and effective, new research on Nazi Germany, Soviet Russia, and other European dictatorships is now calling into question some of the fundamental notions that both scholars and laymen have held about them for over half a century, and, in particular, about the control they exerted over their citizenries. Thus, using the classic formulation of totalitarian society put forward by Hannah Arendt in her seminal study *The Origins of Totalitarianism* as a kind of jumping-off point, this essay on social control in Nazi Germany and the essays following it on social control in Fascist Italy and Spain, Vichy France, the Netherlands under occupation, and postwar Hungary will concentrate on the following questions: In the area of social control, how much of a radical break did these societies really make with the past? To what extent, as Arendt alleges, did a climate of "mutual suspicion" and "ubiquitous spying, where everybody may be a police agent and each individual feels himself under constant surveillance" really develop in these societies? How intrusive were the secret police and the other agents of law enforcement, and how successfully did they penetrate into the private spheres of individual citizens in these societies? Did coercion completely replace cooperation, consensus, and negotiation in the quest for social control? Indeed, how "total" was "totalitarian" social control?

To address the issue of social control in Nazi Germany, I will do two things. First, I will review briefly the main institutions that exercised formal social control functions in the Third Reich. Here, I will assume that most readers are already relatively well aware of these institutions, so only a cursory treatment is required. After this foundation has been laid, however, I will then proceed at somewhat greater length to answer the specific questions raised above by providing, in particular, a preliminary analysis of a unique body of survey evidence dealing with the experiences of thousands of ordinary German citizens, both Jewish and non-Jewish, who experienced social control in the Third Reich at first hand.

Institutions Exercising Formal Social Control in Nazi Germany

The main institutions that exercised formal social control in Nazi Germany are familiar to many: the police, the courts, the Nazi Party, and, one might argue, the Church (although the Church might also be considered an institution exercising semiformal or informal social control, and some have argued that a large part of it, like the Catholic and the Confessing churches, did more to sponsor social and political opposition than conformity and social order). The police in Nazi Germany or in any other modern society are probably rightly seen as the leading organs of formal social control. What separated the Nazi police from the German police force in the past and the police forces of other countries, however, was presumably, above all, the Nazi secret state police, or Gestapo, and its ruthlessness, inhumanity, power, and alleged omnipresence. Certainly Hannah Arendt believed this to be true as she referred to the German Gestapo and to the secret police forces in other totalitarian countries as "the power nucleus of the country" and assumed them to be "super-efficient and super competent." Whereas the normal uniformed police force in the Third Reich, known as the Schutzpolizei or Schupo, and the detective force, known as the Kriminalpolizei or Kripo, retained the names they had used in the past and carried out the same basic functions in the Third Reich, as they always had done, of fighting crime and safeguarding order in the streets (although these traditional police forces also were given wide powers and latitude to fight newly defined political crimes and political enemies in Hitler's Germany), the notorious and feared Gestapo was a new institution set up in April 1933 to combat all real and potential political and ideological enemies of the state. Invested with wide powers of surveillance, allowed to carry out house searches, dragnets, and forceful interrogations according to its whim, and, not constrained by concerns for habeas corpus or due process, having the ability to hold people for long periods in "protective custody" or send them to concentration camps without judicial review, and with supposedly an enormous network of spies and agents, this institution above all others allegedly made the Nazi state truly Orwellian in its dictatorial powers.

In addition to these policing organizations, one can also name several other paramilitary, strong-arm, and intelligence bodies such as the SA brown shirts, SS and SD black shirts, and the military's Abwehr that also played important social control and policing functions, especially in regard to enforcing political and ideological conformity. When these fearsome organizations are added to the Gestapo and the normal police agencies, it seems incontestable that the Nazi state truly deserved its reputation of being a police state that had the means and power to penetrate into the most private aspects of people's lives.

The law courts of Nazi Germany have perhaps stirred fewer passions in the popular mind than the Nazi policing, paramilitary, and surveillance organizations, as on the surface at least, they seem to have been less significant and less novel. Some, on the one hand, might imagine them to have been largely superfluous, given the punishment powers enjoyed by the Gestapo and the other policing organizations. Others, who have seen footage from Nazi newsreels with the notorious hanging judge Roland Freisler, of the people's court in Berlin, excoriating those unfortunate personages before him in the dock before passing his preferred sentence, might, on the other hand, assume that all of them were staffed with Nazi zealots who paid absolutely no respect even to Nazi law, something that sounds like a fiendish oxymoron in itself, nearly as barbarous as the Gestapo. In fairness, it should be noted that in recent years considerable scholarly attention has been placed on the role of the law courts and their personnel in Nazi Germany, and a much more nuanced picture has emerged of their activities.[1]

While this picture is by no means a pleasant one, we now know that most of the judges and prosecutors in Nazi Germany were highly trained individuals who often had remained in the same positions they had held in the democratic Weimar Republic and not infrequently did their best to pass judgments based on the time-honored German practice of legal positivism. Although Jews and the few leftists who had plied the legal profession were removed from the benches, many judges and attorneys were not members of the Nazi Party or were not enthusiastic Nazis, even if they did join the Nazi Party. The law codes that they used were largely the same as had been in existence since the late-nineteenth century, although they had been expanded by many exceptional laws added in an ad hoc fashion during the Third Reich, especially in the area of political criminality. As with the police, the "normal" courts that considered primarily "normal" criminal offenses like murders, rapes, and robberies retained their old names and jurisdictions at the local and provincial levels. But, also like the police, new court institutions were established to combat political offenses and to ensure conformity and social order. Most significant among these new court institutions were the so-called Special Courts at the provincial level and the People's Court at the national level. These new Nazi legal institutions and their personnel speedily dispensed political justice to the state's enemies that the Gestapo had not decided to punish by itself.

Sometimes the verdicts they rendered were extremely harsh and capricious, as in the case of a middle-aged Cologne seamstress who was put to death on June 3, 1942, three days after she had returned to her bombed-out apartment building to retrieve her belongings and had pilfered from the smoking remains some curtains, a few pairs of men's underwear, a dress, and three cans of coffee.[2] Most of the time, however, the pressure was not on the courts to make such foreboding examples of the accused, and the courts often showed surprising leniency and dismissed large numbers of cases even before they came to trial. One example of this that also comes from the Cologne Special Court case files involves a cranky sixty-two-year-old grandmother from the village of Quadrath outside of Cologne. In 1937 charges made against her for libeling Hitler and the Nazi Party were dismissed by the Cologne prosecuting attorney even though the wife of a local Nazi official had testified to the police that the grandmother had told her that "Hitler is [nothing] but an *Arschficker*" and had said to her husband, the local *Blockleiter* himself, that "the [Nazi] Party can lick my ass."[3]

The social control functions of the Nazi Party may even have outstripped that of the police and the courts. Within six months after Hitler took power on January 30, 1933, the Nazi Party became the only legal political party in the country. Organized in a uniform and hierarchical fashion across the country and with military-type ranks, it indeed penetrated into nearly every neighborhood and even into nearly every residential dwelling in the country. Not officially invested with policing powers per se, it nonetheless had important surveillance functions. The Gestapo and the police frequently counted on it to provide information on the reputation and activities of individual citizens. Furthermore, it received large numbers of denunciations from people who reported willingly on the activities and views of their fellow citizens, and it often passed these on to the Gestapo, which used them in turn to initiate its investigations against the politically unreliable or unwanted.[4]

The Nazi Party never opened its doors to the majority of the population, and in particular women were for the most part excluded. It had, however, auxiliary wings for almost every aspect of human endeavor. One of its organizations, the German Labor Front (DAF), for example, replaced all previous labor organizations and eventually included almost every worker in the country. The Nazi Party's youth organizations, Hitler Youth (HJ) for boys and German Girls' League (BDM) for girls, replaced all other youth organizations by the mid-1930s and eventually became compulsory. Its women's, business, welfare, housing, and various trade organizations also replaced most other organizations from these parts of German society and, like the other organizations named above, enforced ideological conformity and helped maintain the prescribed social order.

Perhaps more than any other institution in Nazi Germany, the Nazi Party penetrated into the private spheres of individual Germans and regulated their lives. With a *Hauswart* in every major residential dwelling and a *Blockwart* (or

Blockleiter) in every neighborhood—who ensured that people paid for their subscriptions to the Nazi newspaper, went regularly to cast their votes for Nazi Party candidates, gave contributions to the Nazi welfare organizations, observed the lights out during bombing attacks, and were watched in their comings and goings— and with the necessity of having to go to the Nazi Party's district offices to get a marriage certificate, a new apartment, or almost anything else, the Nazi Party seemed to maintain social order with a vengeance.

The Church was perhaps the most significant institution in Nazi Germany that played an important role in maintaining social order that never came fully under Nazi control. Actually one should probably say "the churches," as there were several of them. The majority of Germans, about two-thirds of them, were members of the main Protestant group, the Evangelical Lutheran Church, when Hitler came to power in 1933. The Catholic Church was the church of preference for most of the rest of the population, but there also were a number of small denominations or "sects" like the Jehovah's Witnesses, Seventh Day Adventists, and Baptists whom the Nazis treated with a great deal of suspicion and disdain. Jews represented about 1 percent of the population. Although most of the established churches adhered to a line of obedience to the state and advocated social conformity, the Nazis were wary of their influence and somewhat unsure as to what to do with them. The Lutheran Evangelical Church divided into two different camps not long after Hitler took power. The larger wing, known as the German Christians, strongly identified with the Nazi state and even called themselves "stormtroopers of Jesus Christ." They hoisted the Nazi flag as their church flag, sang the Nazi anthem, the "*Horst Wessel Lied*," during church services, and pushed a religious struggle of Christianity against Jews, Communists, and pacifists. The somewhat smaller wing of the Evangelical Church, known as the Confessing Church, boasted famous resistance figures like Martin Niemoeller and Dietrich Bonhoeffer among their members. They were less supportive of Nazi ideals than the German Christians, sometimes criticized the Nazi's policies, especially in defense of their religious freedom, and had many clergymen whom the Nazis cracked down upon and sometimes punished severely. On the whole, however, they were loyal Germans and also fostered obedience, social order, and conformity.

In the postwar period a myth developed about the supposed resistance of the Catholic Church and, to a lesser extent, about the Confessing Church. Thousands of Catholic priests were indeed subjected to searches, surveillance, and interrogations, especially in the mid-1930s when the Nazis carried out a large propaganda campaign against the supposed evil influence of the Catholic Church and the wayward morality of many of its clergy. Some priests and ministers gave the Nazis real grounds to worry, like the brave Archbishop von Galen of Münster who protested the Nazis' euthanasia policy in a famous sermon on August 3, 1941, that played a significant role in causing the Nazis to discontinue their policy of murdering the mentally retarded and the physically ill (upward of seventy thousand people had been killed between 1939 and 1941 in this pre-cursor to the Holocaust).[5] On the whole, however, most Catholic priests, like most Protestant ministers, supported the Nazi state and admonished their fol-lowers to do the same. Although the Church was well informed about the con-centration camps and the murder of the Jews, it did not protest. As Archbishop von Galen's famous sermon proved, the Church could have had a powerful effect had it spoken out. Hence, the social control functions of the established churches remain a question mark. My feeling, however, is that they largely pro-moted the Nazi social order and reinforced it with a religious blessing.

How Penetrating and Total Was Nazi Social Control?

The standard interpretation of Nazi Germany as a totalitarian police state that almost totally destroyed the private sphere while maintaining social order through fear and intimidation held sway in the postwar period for several decades. Because of the social control organizations mentioned above and, especially, because of the mind-numbing fear supposedly inspired by an allegedly all powerful, all knowing, and omnipresent Gestapo, it was believed that only truly insane indi-viduals would have undertaken criminal, political, or nonconformist acts against the Nazi regime after it had destroyed its main internal opposition within Hitler's first few years in power. By the 1970s, however, this viewpoint had come under heavy attack, and soon a new paradigm emerged that asserted that the Nazi state was less efficiently organized and far more disorderly than had been previously assumed. The Munich historian Martin Broszat was probably the father of this new interpretation. In a pioneering study published first in German in 1969 and later in English under the title *The Hitler State,* Broszat argued that Nazi Germany should not be seen as a streamlined monolithic structure, for it was full of overlapping jurisdictions, ragtag bureaucratic structures, and politi-cal rivalries and infighting that only Hitler himself could have kept glued together. A decade or so after this book appeared, Broszat presided over an equally sem-inal study, this time in the form of a huge, multivolume, edited work entitled *Bayern in der NS-Zeit,* which concentrated on minor acts of resistance in the south-ern German state of Bavaria in an attempt to prove that the German populace itself had been just as disorderly as the Nazi state.

After publication of this work, a spate of studies of resistance and opposition soon appeared that treated nearly every city, town, and corner of Nazi German society. What one looks for one finds if one has a sufficiently wide definition of what is desired. Some of these works have been summarized in a volume pub-lished in English translation in 1987 by Detlev Peukert, who was one of the most prolific practitioners of the new "everyday life approach" to modern German history that developed in the 1970s and 1980s. Entitled *Inside Nazi Germany: Conformity, Opposition and Racism in Everyday Life,* Peukert's book documents how many German youths refused to go along with their flag-waving Hitler contemporaries. They organized their own organizations like Swing Youth, for the middle classes, and Edelweiss Pirates, for the lower classes, that scorned Nazi ideology, celebrated nonconformity, and sometimes even took up active, armed resistance against the regime. Peukert's book also demonstrates that a relatively large number of Germans frequently told anti-Nazi jokes, spread anti-Nazi criticism, and personally harbored anti-Nazi beliefs.

In the 1990s the everyday life approach and its emphasis on nonconformity and noncompliance led several scholars to take a fresh look at the day-to-day workings of the main organs of Nazi terror and social control like the Gestapo. Using for evidence an analysis of Gestapo case files and court records in various localities, scholars like the Canadian historian Robert Gellately and the German historians Gerhard Paul and Klaus-Michael Mallmann, among others, soon started arguing that the fundamental appraisal of the Gestapo's power and influence needed to be changed.[6] The Gestapo, they explain, did not in fact preside over a huge army of spies and agents. Rather it was only a relatively small force, made up primarily of old policemen from the political police section of the old Weimar criminal police force, which should be understood more as a reactive than as a proactive organization. With only one agent per ten thousand people in German cities, and usually no agents at all in countryside villages and towns, the Gestapo had to rely primarily on denunciations from the civilian population for its information.

These scholars have indeed demonstrated that the Gestapo and other Nazi organizations like the regular police and the Party received large numbers of denunciations and that the Gestapo's investigations of several types of German citizens as well as non-Germans living in the Reich as foreign laborers were more often initiated by denunciations than by information the Gestapo received through other channels, whether through its own forced interrogations, its limited spy network, or other means of information gathering. Placing enormous weight on the importance of these denunciations, these scholars are now to the point of arguing that the German people largely controlled themselves, and they even question whether Nazi Germany should be considered to have been a police state. Hence, according to this line of argument, many of the most important social control functions were performed rather informally by average citizens, not by police and other bodies who would have had next to no information had the people not willingly supplied it to them.

This interpretation could also be turned on its head and used to argue that the Nazi state was so successful in penetrating the private sphere that the majority of its citizens were happy to do its bidding without its having to ask them to do so. But I think that would be a false interpretation. I also think that this newest conception of Nazi society that places so much stress on civilian denunciations and so little stress on the Gestapo's and the other police organizations' own efforts has other problems as well. Although voluntary denunciations were most certainly important sources of information for the Gestapo and the police, they were much more important in some kinds of cases than in others. Quite often they had their genesis in insignificant neighborly quarrels and involved only trivial indiscretions on the part of the accused that the Gestapo knew it did not have to worry about. Furthermore, even if no one ever denounced anyone in the Third Reich, many of the major crimes against humanity that the Nazis perpetrated, like the mass murder of the Jews and the mentally retarded and physically handicapped, would still have occurred.

Notwithstanding the criticisms that can be leveled against this newest paradigm, there can be no doubt that it has merit, for "ordinary Germans" most certainly played major roles in the maintenance of social order and political conformity in the Third Reich. And they usually did this voluntarily. As Christopher Browning in his celebrated book *Ordinary Men* and Daniel Goldhagen in his controversial bestseller *Hitler's Willing Executioners* have both uncovered in recent years, ordinary Germans also voluntarily played vital roles in the carrying out of the Holocaust. Still, even if large numbers of ordinary Germans willingly denounced and willingly murdered, this does not mean that the Gestapo and the other Nazi terror and social control organizations were ineffective, weak, or merely reactive, or that Nazi society was not a police state.

In my own examinations of the issues of terror and control in Nazi Germany, I have tried to provide a balanced explanation of Nazi terror and social control that charts perhaps something of a middle course among the "totalitarian," "everyday life," and "ordinary German" or "ordinary men" perspectives. By arguing that the Nazi authorities applied a kind of selective terror that concentrated on targeted enemies of the regime and did not waste its limited resources on minor acts of nonconformity, I have, I think, been able to show that the Gestapo was indeed competent, effective, and highly active when it needed to be, in rooting out and destroying the Nazi regime's enemies. At the same time, however, it wisely provided considerable space to the mainly loyal but sometimes grumbling German civilian population to air grievances and, on occasion, to act in a disorderly fashion, while at the same time capitalizing on the voluntary assistance offered by many ordinary Germans. Thus for the stated enemies of the Nazi leadership, like Jews and Communists and a few other targeted minorities, Nazi Germany was indeed a powerful police state. But, for the majority of the German population, the Nazi police seldom intruded upon their lives and did not even try to penetrate their private sphere because this was unnecessary and could have turned petty deviance into meaningful opposition.

To this point, I have primarily employed archival evidence to support this argument. In a book published in 2000, *Nazi Terror: The Gestapo, Jews, and Ordinary*

Germans, I analyzed in minute detail a huge random sample of over one thousand individual Gestapo and Special Court case files in three German cities of different sizes—the large city of Cologne, the medium-sized city of Krefeld, and the small city of Bergheim—and their surrounding rural communities. Also, I followed the careers of the Gestapo and police officers who had worked in these cities from cradle to grave and tried to assess their mentality and culpability. To do this I read and compared their applications for joining the Gestapo or police or SS during the Nazi period and their denazification proceedings and their crimes against humanity trials in the postwar years.

What I found in all of these documents might be summarized briefly as follows. A large percentage of all cases brought before the police (there were no Gestapo officers stationed in the small community of Bergheim or in the rural towns and villages outside of Cologne and Krefeld) and the Gestapo did indeed begin with an accusation made voluntarily by an ordinary German citizen. But most of these "denunciations" were made in rather trivial cases, like listening to BBC (which probably a majority of the German population listened to even though it was illegal during the war years) or telling rather harmless anti-Nazi jokes, and in the end the Gestapo or the police typically dismissed the charges against the accused after a brief investigation and no other action was taken. Only occasionally in such cases was the case sent on to the courts, and almost never was the accused in such cases taken into protective custody or sent to a concentration camp. If a case of this nature was passed on to the courts, the state attorney's office usually conducted its own brief investigation and then dismissed the case before going to trial.

Cases involving targeted enemies of the regime, however, had a quite different trajectory. In the early years of the Third Reich, most of these concerned Communist activists and either clergymen or members of recalcitrant religious groups like the Jehovah's Witnesses. Few of these cases of a more serious nature originated with denunciations. Often the Gestapo and police proceeded against these people with utmost severity, including torture-induced confessions that led to a snowballing of arrests, and placement in protective custody and concentration camps without any legal recourse on the part of the accused. Many of these cases might also be passed on to the Special Courts. And, when they were, they usually ended in jail and prison sentences. Both before and during the war, Jews made up a disproportionate number of the Gestapo's and the police's caseloads. Usually the cases against them involved charges of minor infractions not unlike those of the nontargeted majority. Also, like those of the ordinary German population, they frequently began with voluntary denunciations from neighbors and other acquaintances. In the 1930s the Gestapo or the police investigators usually dismissed their cases as well, for Nazi policy at the time aimed at harassing the Jews and forcing them to emigrate, and a mere investigation and interrogation often produced the desired result. In the war years, a Gestapo or police case against a Jew, however it originated, most often resulted in a trip to a concentration camp that was tantamount to a death sentence.

Finally, the archival evidence shows that the Gestapo officers in cities like Cologne and Krefeld and the policemen who were assigned cases of a political nature in small communities like Bergheim were men of modest intelligence, solid training, and usually pronounced ideological commitment, although not all were members of the SS and some never even joined the Nazi Party until the late 1930s. As scholars like Paul, Mallmann, and Gellately have noted, these officers were rather few in number (the Krefeld Gestapo employed only about twenty officers in a city of almost 200,000 inhabitants and the Cologne Gestapo had only ninety-nine officers before the war and sixty-nine during the war in a city of nearly one million people). Also, as these scholars have argued about the Gestapo generally, the Cologne and Krefeld Gestapo and the Bergheim police force had limited support staffs (often they had to type their own interrogation transcripts and case summaries), limited technical means (torture, for instance, was applied most often by threatening to arrest the accused person's family members, or holding a gun to their heads, or beating them with the fist or with a leg of a chair), and limited numbers of paid informants (but enough to provide them often with crucial information in cases involving targeted opponents). Despite their limited capabilities, these Gestapo and police officers acted efficiently, especially by distinguishing between important and nonimportant cases. Among the targeted enemies of the regime, they were rightly feared; among the majority of the German population, they held much respect, and especially so by many leading figures of the society. After the war most Gestapo officers could count on their fellow citizens to provide them with letters and other testimonies of support when they were trying to regain their government pensions or avoid being prosecuted for their inhumane acts during the Third Reich. As I demonstrated in *Nazi Terror,* leading members of both the Catholic and Lutheran Evangelical churches in Cologne and Krefeld, heads of business and commerce, remaining top police officers, and other important figures in these communities helped them to wash their dirty records clean. To many of the pillars of society and to many less distinguished Germans as well, both during the Nazi period and after it, these Gestapo officers were apparently kindred spirits.[7]

In the remainder of this essay, I would like to introduce another kind of evidence to provide further support for my selective terror argument. This is evidence of a less traditional type for historians as it does not come from archives and libraries that most historians favor but from surveys and interviews that many historians tend to distrust. Without belaboring the point, I might note that all types of evidence have problems, and this is true of archival evidence as well as survey and interview evidence. With archival evidence, one can never be sure if the scholar is missing vital information that has been either lost or somehow overlooked. With survey and interview evidence, one cannot be sure how much one can trust the recollections of the survey or interview participants. But, if only because the archival evidence of the type we are discussing here was prepared by the perpetrators and the survey and interview evidence comes from the victims and bystanders, it would seem fair and wise not to distrust the latter any more than the former.[8]

Over the past decade, I have worked together with Karl-Heinz Reuband, a German sociologist and expert in opinion research who is currently a professor of sociology at the University of Düsseldorf, on a sizable study of the attitudes and experiences of German Jews and non-Jews who lived in the Third Reich, which we will soon publish in book form.[9] For our study we sent out written questionnaires to random samples of thousands of non-Jews who were born in 1928 or earlier (the median birth year is 1921) and who were living in the cities of Cologne, Krefeld, Berlin, or Dresden at the time we conducted our surveys between 1993 and 2000. We also, with the help of the United States Holocaust Museum in Washington, D.C., sent out questionnaires to nearly one thousand Jews who had lived in Nazi Germany (their median birth year is also 1921), but who now reside in countries around the world. From both groups we received the favorable response rate of approximately 50 percent, depending on whether one wants to include people who could not complete the surveys because they were either dead, ill, or could not be reached. In addition to these surveys, we have conducted nearly two hundred face-to-face interviews with selected respondents to help us be sure that our questionnaire results can be trusted and to provide us with additional in-depth information.

Filling out the more than one hundred questions on the questionnaire took the average respondent about one hour to complete. The interviews ranged from one hour to several days, and all were recorded on audio tape. The questions we asked focused on the everyday life experiences of the participants, on their experiences with harassment and discrimination, on their involvement in activities considered illegal in the Third Reich, and on their treatment by the Nazi authorities. Although we are still in the process of analyzing the data generated by our surveys and interviews and some figures might be modified slightly before we publish our main findings in our forthcoming book, a few of our results pertinent to the issue of social control and the argument about selective terror can be offered in this essay. The most salient of these are found in tables 1 and 2. Both contain only simple percentages that are readily understandable.

Table 1 reports on a question we asked about people's perceptions; table 2 reports on a series of questions we asked about people's actual experiences. In both tables the responses of Jewish survivors of the Third Reich are compared with the responses of non-Jews. The figures in table 1 summarize the answers we received to the following question that was asked in German to the non-Jews and in English to the Jews: "In the city in which you lived in Germany [during the Third Reich] did you personally have fear of being arrested by the Gestapo

Table 1   Percentage of Jews and non-Jews experiencing fear of arrest by the Gestapo

	Jews		Non-Jews			
	All Jews	Jews in Germany	Cologne	Krefeld	Dresden	Berlin
Constant fear	48	65	5	7	5	3
Occasional fear	31	24	19	17	20	13
Other	7	4	1	1	5	4
No fear	34	30	37	36	40	43
Number of cases	420	74	938	404	678	923

Table 2   Percentage of Jews and non-Jews who committed illegal activities

	Jews		Non-Jews			
	All Jews	Jews in Germany	Cologne	Krefeld	Dresden	Berlin
Member of illegal youth group	21	22	6	7	1	4
Listened to foreign radio broadcasts	31	42	46	47	36	53
Told anti-Nazi jokes	15	20	33	35	22	32
Criticized Hitler in discussions	20	27	15	15	13	11
Criticized Nazis in discussions	23	32	21	21	15	16
Distributed anti-Nazi fliers	2	4	3	3	2	2
Helped people threatened by the Nazis	8	15	12	14	10	11
Member of an active resistance organization	2	3	1	1	1	1
Other	7	4	1	1	5	4
Did none of the above	34	30	37	36	40	43
Number of cases	420	74	938	404	678	923

or did you have no fear of this happening to you?" As one notes in table 1, we provide the responses given by all of the 420 Jews in the survey born in 1928 or earlier and by a smaller group of 74 Jews, who were born in the same years but, unlike most German Jews, had not emigrated sometime in the 1930s and were still in Germany after the war had broken out in the fall of 1939. Only a few of those in the latter group managed to leave the country while it was still possible after this date, and almost all the rest were eventually sent to concentration camps after the Holocaust began in earnest around the time of the Russian invasion in the summer of 1941. Also presented in the table are the responses from random samples of 2,943 Germans born before 1929 who lived at the time the survey was conducted in either Cologne, Krefeld, Dresden, or Berlin (during the Nazi period about half of the people in the survey had lived in other cities and towns of the Third Reich).

The responses demonstrate readily that there is an enormous difference between German Jews and non-Jews in their perceptions about the danger that the Gestapo had posed to them. Among the German survey participants residing in Cologne, Krefeld, Dresden, and Berlin (cities of quite different natures: Cologne and Krefeld situated in the western parts of Germany along the Rhine, near the borders with Holland and Belgium, and predominantly Catholic; Dresden and Berlin lying near Germany's eastern borders with Poland and the Czech Republic and mostly Protestant), only a small minority answered that they had constantly feared arrest in Nazi Germany (ranging from 7 percent in Krefeld and to 3 percent in Berlin). To this minority can be added another modest minority of the participants who answered that they had occasionally feared arrest at the time. But for the overwhelming majority, upward of three-quarters in fact, the people from these cities answered that they had absolutely no fear at any time of being arrested for any reason by the Gestapo during the Third Reich.

Among the Jews who had lived in Germany during the Third Reich, these percentages were reversed. Of those Jews who were still in Germany after the war broke out, only 11 percent reported that they had not feared being arrested by the Gestapo while nearly two-thirds of them had held constant fear that this would have happened to them. Among all of the Jews in the survey, even though most had left Germany in the 1930s when they were only in their teenage years and Nazi policy at the time did not yet call for Jewish extermination, less than one-quarter reported that they had not feared Gestapo arrest while a near majority had constantly lived in fear that the Gestapo would come to arrest them.

The perceptions of these Jews and non-Jews were based on sound calculations. Not reported in either of the two tables are the answers to a question we asked about whether the survey participants had ever been interrogated by either the Gestapo or the police in a case involving alleged illegal activity on their part. While 15 percent of all of the Jews in the survey and 21 percent of the Jews still remaining in Germany after 1939 had suffered such interrogations, fewer than 2 percent of the Germans from the cities of Cologne, Krefeld, Dresden, or Berlin had ever been interrogated by the Gestapo or police at any time during the Third Reich (3 percent in Cologne, and 1 percent in each of the other three cities). This means, of course, that the likelihood of being investigated for any kind of illegal activity in the Third Reich was approximately ten times higher for Jews than for non-Jews. Since we also know from the archival data found in Gestapo case files that non-Jews typically had their cases dismissed after brief investigations but that Jews were very often punished severely for even minor and not necessarily proven infractions, we can easily understand why Jews say they had much more fear of arrest than non-Jews.

When we asked both Jews and non-Jews about their actual involvement in illegal activity, however, there was less of a difference between them. Table 2 reports the results of a series of questions we asked about possible illegal activities that the survey participants had been involved in during the Third Reich. At the bottom of the table, we see that only about one-third of both Jews and non-Jews say that they had not committed an illegal act in Nazi Germany. The most common illegal activity was listening to outlawed radio broadcasts like those of the BBC. Among the non-Jews, around one-half of the respondents answered that they had done this, and this number rises considerably if we select out only the older respondents in the survey as many of the younger ones were either fighting at the front when this activity was deemed illegal or were too young at the time to be very interested in such broadcasts. Among the Jews, whose radio sets were taken from them and for whom the consequences of undertaking this kind of illegal activity could have been extremely serious if they were caught (although ostensibly a death sentence could have resulted for even a non-Jew for this, but this almost never happened), a somewhat lower, but still significantly high, percentage say that they had done this. Other than listening to illegal foreign radio broadcasts, most Jews and non-Jews alike had also committed at least one other kind of illegal activity for which the Gestapo or the police might have arrested them. While very few people in either group had distributed anti-Nazi fliers or been actual members of resistance organizations, which were very serious manifestations of disobedience, more had either told anti-Nazi jokes, criticized Hitler and other Nazis in discussions with friends, family, and acquaintances, belonged to an illegal youth group (although here the numbers are much higher for the Jews than for the non-Jews), or committed some other offense.

This survey evidence, therefore, reinforces the evidence found in Gestapo and Special Court case files and demonstrates anew that the terror and social control efforts of the Nazi authorities selectively targeted the Jewish minority population while turning a blind eye to the indiscretions and illegal activities of the non-Jewish majority population. When one considers that some of the non-Jewish respondents had come from Communist backgrounds while others had been homosexuals or members of targeted religious minorities who all had real reason to fear arrest like the Jews, but that, even with them included, only a tiny number of non-Jews had ever been arrested or even had feared arrest despite the fact that almost everyone had committed an illegal act from time to time, one has to conclude that the Gestapo and the other Nazi policing bodies had little interest in and did not even try to penetrate into the private lives of most German citizens in Nazi Germany. Social control in Nazi Germany was, therefore, far from total.

In the following essays on policing and social control in Europe under Nazi, Fascist, and Communist leadership, similar arguments will be made. In all of these societies there was something of a break with the past in the area of social control, but this break should not be overestimated as scholars of the totalitarian school once did. There were indeed powerful control organizations operating in all of these societies, and they usually had greater invasive powers than in the past. But even so-called totalitarian societies had to rely on compromise and consensus on the part of the civilian population, and they had to be respectful of popular opinion and willing to negotiate. That they did these things helps to account for their popularity.

Notes

1. See, for example, Angermund, *Deutscher Richterschaft, 1919–1945;* Gruchmann, *Justiz im Dritten Reich;* Koch, *In the Name of the Volk;* and Müller, *Hitler's Justice.*

2. Wüllenweber, *Sondergerichte im Dritten Reich,* 17.

3. Nordrhein-Westfälisches Hauptstaatsarchiv Düsseldorf-Kaiserswerth, Schloss Kalkum, Rep. 112/10739 and 112/15295. For a longer discussion of this case in English, see Johnson, *Nazi Terror,* 297–98.

4. See, for example, Diewald-Kerkmann, *Politische Denunziation im NS-Regime.*

5. Burleigh and Wippermann, *The Racial State,* 152–53. For a broader treatment of the euthanasia program, see Friedlander, *The Origins of Nazi Genocide.*

6. Gellately, *The Gestapo and German Society;* Gellately, *Backing Hitler;* Mallmann and Paul, *Herrschaft und Alltag;* Paul and Mallmann, eds., *Die Gestapo;* and Mann, *Protest und Kontrolle im Dritten Reich.*

7. Johnson, *Nazi Terror,* 463–81.

8. On the importance of survivor testimony, see, for example, Hass, *The Aftermath.*

9. The working title of our book is *What We Knew: Terror, Mass Murder, and Everyday Life in the Third Reich.* To this point, the only published material from our survey efforts is found in a modest article based on a pilot study of our German survey that we conducted in Cologne in 1993. See Johnson and Reuband, "Die populäre Einschätzung der Gestapo," 417–36. Funding to support our research has been generously provided by the National Endowment for the Humanities, the National Science

Foundation, and the Alexander von Humboldt Stiftung. Between 1992 and 1995, when we began our project and conducted the pilot study in Cologne and the main surveys with the Cologne and Krefeld populations, our project was housed at the Center for Historical Social Research of the Central Archive for Empirical Social Research of the University of Cologne.

CHAPTER 12

Social Control in Fascist Italy: The Role of the Police

Jonathan Dunnage

This essay examines the evolution of the Italian police during the Fascist dictatorship. It aims to answer two closely related questions: To what extent did the policing of Fascist Italy represent a break in continuity with that of the liberal period? With how much success was the Mussolinian model of totalitarian social control implemented? Though it is recognized by most historians that Italian fascism fell short of a proper totalitarian system, the Fascists used the term "totalitarian" in heralding the start of a process through which all aspects of life would be fascistized, to be undertaken by an all-powerful state, to which every individual was subordinated. This echoed the description of fascism by the Hegelian philosopher and pedagogue Giovanni Gentile as a "total conception of life," and Mussolini's formulation of the idea of "everything within the state, nothing outside the state, nothing against the state" as a definition of a totalitarian system in which all boundaries between society and state disappeared.[1]

This model of totalitarianism, characterized by the subordinate position of the Fascist Party with regard to the state, clearly does not fit that of Hannah Arendt.[2] From 1926 onward, as part of Mussolini's concept of a statist totalitarian system, the powers of the Italian police were intensified in order to enforce and defend Fascist policies, and the areas of life in which they could intervene were widened. While this saw the creation of a formidable system of social control for the purpose of preventing and repressing activities against the regime and allowing a state monopoly on the dissemination of information, in fulfillment of the idea that the Fascist state should "look after the minds as well as the bodies of citizens,"[3] it was far from Arendt's concept of a totalitarian system of terror based on the elimination of objective enemies.[4]

More recent historical analysis, taking a view of what constitutes totalitarianism that is not as extreme as Arendt's, has argued that Italian fascism showed several important totalitarian characteristics and that—using modern techniques of mass communication, a prominent party network (though subordinate to the will of the state), and a highly repressive police apparatus—there was, particularly from the midthirties onward, a move in the direction of the creation of a totalitarian society.[5] This was only partially successful, however, because of long-term compromises rooted in the founding of the dictatorship. In order to consolidate the regime, Mussolini relied above all on the collaboration of "uncommitted sympathizers," many of whom, including the police, had been servants of the liberal state, as well as the support of such institutions as the Catholic Church and the monarchy. This precluded the possibility of setting up a proper system of terror, made fascism more authoritarian and conservative than revolutionary, and limited the extent to which Fascist ideology could dominate society unchallenged.[6]

The Transition from the Liberal to the Fascist Police

Analysis of legislation at the root of the dramatic increase in policing powers that fascism brought illustrates how Mussolini's model of totalitarianism was founded on the exploitation rather than the destruction of the existing state police. Most historians agree that liberal police legislation formed the basis of the Fascist police code (*Testo Unico delle Leggi di Pubblica Sicurezza*) of 1926 (revised in 1931 with only minor alterations), though opinions as to the extent of continuity between the two vary. This has in turn depended on historians' concepts of the nature of liberal policing. Some have claimed that levels of "prevention" of crime before the need for its repression, typical of an authoritarian regime, were extremely high during the liberal period, with the consequent violation of all civil and political rights enshrined in the 1848 constitution (*Statuto Albertino*). In particular, the use of emergency preventive legislation in the 1890s suggests similarities with the Fascist period. Romano Canosa argues that the liberal state maximized prevention over repression with the result that the police had little concern for human rights. Moreover, they ignored any legislative guarantees against abuse of power, and the judiciary tolerated this. Consequently, Canosa does not give too much importance to the rise of Fascism or the new police code.[7]

Certainly, both regimes gave priority to the policing of political activities rather than common crime, denoting a strong anti-Marxist political continuity. Recent research by Richard Jensen on policing in the second half of the nineteenth century has, however, argued that there was a greater balance between the use of prevention and repression by the liberal state, such that comparison with the later Mussolinian regime is inappropriate.[8] Other historians argue that under the formal democracy of the liberal state, citizens had some safeguards against arbitrary police powers, which were used to make life as difficult as possible for the political opposition but not systematically. By contrast, Fascist legislation allowed a significant amplification of police powers in line with Mussolini's desire to create a totalitarian society. Giuliano Amato notes that the new police code endowed the forces of law and order with greater powers and limited judicial control over them, turning them into a more effective instrument of political persecution.[9] Similarly, Paola Carucci argues that the 1926 legislation amplified police powers to the point that citizens had no legal protection against the powers, since police were allowed the violation of human rights without citizens' being permitted accusations of arbitrary behavior on the part of police.[10]

Effectively, many of the articles of the Fascist code increased police powers and established severer punishments for crimes committed. One of the most innovative was Article 2 (1931), which allowed the prefect to take those measures that he deemed necessary to maintain order at all costs—even if this meant violating other laws. In liberal Italy it had been recognized that such measures of policing could only be authorized through the passing of special legislation.[11] Although the institutions of *domicilio coatto* (internal exile) and *ammonizione* (imposing restrictions on the activities and movements of individuals) were strongly characteristic of the liberal state, the new legislation took responsibility for their application out of the hands of the judiciary and put them in the hands of mixed committees of police, administrative, and Fascist Party representatives. The rights of appeal of those sentenced were reduced considerably.[12]

As Amato points out, the Fascist code reversed the effects of the 1889 law, which had given citizens greater guarantees against police abuse of power regarding ammonizione and domicilio coatto. According to the 1889 legislation, idlers, vagabonds, and individuals repeatedly sentenced for crimes or twice acquitted for lack of evidence (*diffamati*) were liable to be assigned to ammonizione. Although the liberal legislation allowed ammonizione to be used as a political instrument, the Fascist police code made it easier to persecute antifascists by specifically including crimes against the state among those for which ammonizione was prescribed. Only one instance of acquittal for lack of evidence was required. The new legislation also allowed individuals merely *suspected* (i.e., not even brought before a court of law) of being socially or politically dangerous to be assigned to ammonizione. Under fascism internal exile was no longer a consequence of repeated violation of the terms of ammonizione by those assigned to it, as under the liberal state. The harsher punishment of internal exile (under the new name of *confino*) could be prescribed instead of ammonizione.[13] It should be noted that when the special tribunals (*Tribunali speciali per la difesa dello Stato*) set up in 1926 to deal specifically with crimes against the state—another example of the regime's desire to reduce the influence of the magistracy[14]—acquitted defendants, the police were able to have them sentenced to confino purely on the basis of the threat they allegedly posed to national security.[15]

Other articles of the Fascist police code illustrate how police powers were amplified. Whereas the 1889 legislation stated that the police had the right to arrest individuals outside their place of residence for suspicious behavior on "reasonable" grounds, the word "reasonable" was removed from the Fascist code, since it was seen as compromising the efficiency of police activities. The categories of those liable to be arrested were extended to include individuals considered dangerous to public order, security, or morality, according to Article 158 (1926). This article was frequently used by the Fascist police to temporarily arrest antifascists on special occasions, such as May Day or visits by Mussolini, regardless of whether they were outside their place of residence.[16] For the first time all associations had to be registered with the police, providing a copy of their statute and regulations and a list of their activities and members (Article 214, 1926).[17] Police powers of censorship were widened, too. Press organizations were now required to apply for a license from the police, a more effective means of guaranteeing their political conformity (Article 111, 1926). Giuseppe Cuomo also notes a change in police control over theatrical performances, from surveillance and formal respect of the principle of liberty under the liberal legislation, to more active interference by the police in fulfillment of Fascist Party requirements.[18]

The effects of the Fascist police code must be considered within the overall context of the demolition of many of the institutions of the liberal state (the neutralizing of parliament, the abolition of elections, and the disbanding of political parties, associations, and trade unions opposed to the Fascist government). Moreover, the Fascist criminal code of 1930 supported limitations on citizens' rights before the law by asserting the principle of state authority before legality (not vice versa as under the liberal state). Individual rights were sacrificed to collective ones as all crimes, whether political or common, took on an antinational character. Punishments became harsher, and the rights of legal defense were reduced to fit in with the Fascist concept of the infallibility of the state.[19]

Independently of the question of levels of continuity between liberal and Fascist legislation, a clear distinction between the two regimes lies in the aims behind the use of measures of prevention. Recent work in this area by Jensen argues quite convincingly, for example, that liberal government preventive policies of the 1890s were not the result of premeditated political designs. They represented a panic reaction in the face of widespread political dissent, by a political class that was aware of how weak its police forces were but that for the most part still saw the promotion of principles of liberty as constituting the ideal manner in which to govern.[20] Clearly, the Fascist preventive police system aimed at the destruction of principles of personal and political freedom and was not in any way conditioned by a sense of vulnerability in the face of political dissent.

As a result of the above legislative modifications, therefore, the scope of police repression was dramatically widened and their powers increased. Besides the repression of all political activities considered against "national" interests, the police aimed to prevent practices carrying social implications of an equally antinational character. Abortion, homosexuality, and usury, for example, like political subversion, were punishable by confino.[21] The police played a far more active role in the censorship of films, theatrical productions, radio broadcasts, and foreign material. The monitoring of religious activities was intensified. In spite of the autonomy granted to the Catholic Church, activities in this domain were carefully checked, as was the movement of foreigners and, from the autumn of 1938, that of Italian and foreign Jews.[22] The Fascist period saw the extension of the political register of subversives (*Casellario Politico Centrale*), founded during the 1890s under the rule of Francesco Crispi, in order to deal with a widened range of police activities and allow more efficient and rapid prevention and repression of plots against the regime. This included the creation of new registers for all political suspects, ethnic minorities, those suspected of spying, foreigners staying in Italian territory (originally set up in 1915 but suppressed in 1918), and even priests.[23] Hotel porters and landlords had to register anyone staying in their property and faced police sanctions if they failed to do so.[24] Another practice of liberal origin but used far more widely during Fascism was mail censorship and phone tapping.[25] The traditional role of the Italian police in providing bureaucratic services, such as the issuing of licenses and passports, became an indirect means of policing antifascist activities, since the willingness of the police to oblige depended on the political color of the individual requesting their services.[26]

One of the hallmarks of Fascist policing was the use—as part of the intensification of preventive strategies—of secret police organizations employing informers. Mussolini's personal conception of the police was, indeed, of a monstrous tentacled organization constantly watching over and controlling the Italians and able to immobilize them at the slightest hint of a false move.[27] Though police intelligence organs had existed before fascism, and the liberal police system was characterized by the use of informers and "agents provocateurs," from 1923 such tendencies were institutionalized and amplified by a number of laws that allowed the recruitment of unqualified, noncareer personnel for special jobs.[28] The police were also able to take advantage of the control they exercised over certain professions for spying purposes. Article 62 of the 1931 police code, for example, gave them the authority to determine the suitability of individuals as porters or caretakers in public buildings and apartment blocks. In this way such individuals, who had to be registered with the police, could easily be encouraged to act as informers.[29]

The founding in 1927 of the Political Police Division (*Divisione Polizia Politica*) concentrated control over a myriad of political organizations in the hands of the Interior Ministry police, headed by Arturo Bocchini, a former career prefect, who was accountable only to Mussolini himself.[30] At the provincial level there were three political police organizations: the *Servizio Politico di Investigazione,* directed by a police official under the control of the prefect[31]; the *Uffici Politici Investigativi* of the Fascist Party Militia (also answerable to the prefect); and the *Opera Vigilanza e Repressione dell'Anti-fascismo* (OVRA) with its zone representatives, who were not answerable to the provincial police or prefect and were probably responsible to Bocchini alone.[32] OVRA was used for the surveillance of dissident Fascists as well as antifascists.[33] Many of its informers were members of the underground political movements it was fighting and were usually recruited following their arrest.[34] There was also a special organization for controlling Slav antifascism in the border region of Venezia-Giulia.

The activities of the above organizations need to be placed within a broader scenario that saw cooperation with the police by members of the Fascist Party, the militia, the Fascist youth organizations, unions, and leisure organizations, as well as ordinary members of the public, in the supply of information concerning antifascist activities and suspicious behavior.[35] However, the extent to which private citizens, apart from the several hundred paid informers to the secret police,[36] voluntarily denounced individuals to the police is questionable. Tim Mason suggests they did so less frequently than in Nazi Germany and argues that explanations for this might be found in social and cultural factors, such as the strong tradition of *omertà* in Italy.[37] More recent research on this subject suggests, however, that the involvement of Italians in denouncing fellow citizens has been underestimated.[38]

There is no doubt, however, that a system of social control characterized by fear and repression existed. This was concerned not only with repressing organized antifascism but also controlling those sectors of the population most sensitive to antifascist propaganda in view of the economic hardships they suffered, namely the working classes. As a consequence of this, the police punished acts of existential antifascism, such as publicly criticizing or offending Mussolini or the regime, with ammonizione, or for repeat offenders, confino. Examination of the files for 1930 to 1931 concerning this offense shows that the majority of those charged were not politically active and usually in a state of drunkenness at the moment of committing the offense. Police measures were sometimes limited to a warning (*diffida*).[39]

In terms of the extent of terror that the Fascist police organs were able to exert, it is widely accepted that levels characteristic of the Nazi and Soviet regimes were never reached. Examination of figures of those sent to confino or *ammoniti* during the Fascist period demonstrates that a far lower number of individuals were persecuted under Mussolini's regime than in Nazi Germany. Nevertheless, the figures are much higher than those for the liberal period. Between 1926 and 1943, 5,620 antifascists were tried by the special tribunals. Around 17,000 citizens were sentenced to confino and 160,000 to ammonizione or placed under special surveillance. While 110,000 individuals were placed in the register of subversives (*Casellario Politico Centrale*) between 1926 and 1943, only 40,000 had been registered between 1896 and 1926.[40] During the 1890s the total number of individuals sentenced each year to ammonizione and domicilio coatto amounted to a few thousand at most.[41]

In dealing with such illegal economic manifestations as strikes and demonstrations by the unemployed, the police were zealous only if they believed that the organizers were attempting to benefit politically from such activities. In the case of a demonstration by the unemployed in San Giovanni in Persiceto (Bologna) in May 1931, for example, the *Carabinieri* broke up the assembly but only arrested one of the demonstrators, a communist, who they felt had no serious economic difficulties, who was put forward for ammonizione. A similar demonstration in Sant'Agata Bolognese was not seen as having been provoked by communist or antifascist elements, since there was a high level of unemployment in the area concerned.[42] Moreover, it appears that on occasion the Bolognese authorities preferred to resort to liberal tactics of social prevention such as public works programs, in order to prevent economic hardship from turning into protest.[43] In the area of industrial disputes, the police were concerned to root out troublemakers and political agitators but also tried to prevent work stoppages through negotiation. Those strikers not seen as politically benefiting from their actions usually faced more lenient treatment, such as warnings from the police, or if prosecuted for illegal strike action could benefit from amnesty.[44]

In distinguishing Fascist Italy from the "terror" systems associated with totalitarian regimes, it needs to be pointed out that those individuals who were not considered more than potentially dangerous on account of their apolitical status were often able to benefit from amnesties, the personal clemency of Mussolini, and the possibility of transferring from the harshest penal environments for health reasons, while their families on occasions received state subsidies.[45] Often individuals accused of minor political offenses were able to get away with a warning from the police, as the above examples have demonstrated. Moreover, it appears that militant antifascists were left alone if the police were sure that they were no longer involved in political activities.[46] Such practices were partly a result of the regime's realization that since a full process of fascistization of society was not immediately possible, those sections of society unsympathetic toward fascism could only be brought around to some form of acceptance through concessions.[47] They were also a result of the fact that policing decisions were to some extent conditioned by clientelistic considerations, as discussed below.

In contrast, while a system of police terror typical of Nazi Germany or the Soviet Union was not operated, there is evidence to suggest brutal treatment of those subjected to police repression during the Fascist period. Ernesto Rossi, one of the most prominent antifascist figures, responded to claims during the postwar period by the former OVRA director Guido Leto that the Fascist police had not used excessively violent methods, by arguing that because of the removal of any guarantees against arbitrary behavior, antifascists were at the total mercy of the police and the Fascist militia, the latter being given a prominent role in the policing of islands to which individuals sentenced to confino were sent. He claims that both the regular police and OVRA tortured their prisoners, several of whom died as a result.[48] OVRA officials were particularly unscrupulous in their methods, as evidenced by their capacity to enroll informers from among arrested antifascists, and several of their own reports on interrogations of antifascists suggest that heavy-handed methods might have been used to extract information.[49] With particular regard to OVRA, however, Italo Savella suggests that while its officials made use of threats and blackmail to achieve their ends, physical torture was not employed. Bocchini had no intention of creating martyrs for the antifascist cause, and any ill-treatment was far more likely to have been administered by the regular police—who usually carried out arrests on the instructions of OVRA—and prison wardens.[50] There is no doubt, however, that the police leadership was involved in political murders in defense of the regime. Annibale Paloscia notes the involvement, for example, of Carabinieri counterespionage agents in the murder of the leaders of the *Giustizia e Libertà* antifascist organization, Carlo and Nello Rosselli, on Bocchini's orders.[51]

Finally, while the anti-Jewish laws of 1938 did not lead directly to the terrors of the concentration camp system, and while there is little doubt that some policemen showed restraint in enforcing these laws, the resulting discrimination measures, in which the police as an institution played a key role, marked an acceleration of the process of fascistization of Italian society characterized by the creation of an "objective" enemy and prepared the terrain for Nazi deportations after 1943. Police reports reveal a variety of attitudes toward the "Jewish question." Many provincial police chiefs, while enforcing the Race Laws, made it clear that they did not see the Jews living in their territory as a threat to law and order, at least until the outbreak of the Second World War, when some suggested that foreign Jews should be put in prison camps or ghettoized. Some urged the intensification of discrimination procedures, though as a means of appeasing the more radical Fascists, who had begun to assault individual Jews and vandalize their property. Others, clearly animated by anti-Semitic feelings, showed in their reports a particularly intransigent attitude, which cannot be interpreted as mere lip service to the regime.[52]

We may conclude so far that, within the broader context of compromises upon which the dictatorship was founded, a policing system of social control was set up that, though far from the terror-based concept of totalitarianism of Arendt, was at least potentially highly repressive and "terroristic" in its persecution of those opposed to the regime and in its overall surveillance of society by way of a myriad of secret police organizations and networks of informers. In this sense Carl Friedrich and Zbigniew Brzezinski argue that the Italian police and Fascist Party shared in the manipulation of fear typical of totalitarian regimes, "though on the whole the system was less total, less frightful, and hence less 'mature' than in Germany and the Soviet Union, and in China and the satellites."[53]

An Assessment of the Performance of the Fascist Police

The potential of the system of social control described above was undoubtedly offset by factors concerning the internal organization of the police. First, we should consider the effects of the creation of a multiplicity of policing hierarchies under fascism. Although the creation of a police system based on the coexistence of several organizations formed part of the Fascist leadership's divide and rule strategy, it is clear that this often limited the capacity of the police to maintain order and repress political opposition. In the liberal state, conflict between military and civilian circles was reflected in the coexistence of the military police (Carabinieri) and the Interior Ministry police. The abolition of the Interior Ministry police corps (*Guardie Regie*) at the end of 1922, shortly after the rise to power of Mussolini, marked the Fascist leader's initial preference for the Carabinieri.[54] However, the reconstitution of the corps (under the name of *Guardie di Pubblica Sicurezza*) in 1925 illustrated Mussolini's realization of the foremost loyalty of the Carabinieri to the crown.[55]

During the Fascist period, problems of rivalry between the Interior Ministry police and the Carabinieri persisted. There were often cases of obstinacy on the part of Carabinieri commanders over the use of their forces by the Interior Ministry,[56] and the former often neglected to inform the latter about their police operations. In March 1929, for example, the Carabinieri of Fidenza carried out a series of mass arrests of alleged antifascists using an outdated list, with consequent embarrassment for the police, especially since many of those arrested had since become supportive of the regime. The incident would have been avoided if the Carabinieri had informed the Interior Ministry police prior to carrying out the operation.[57]

The founding of the Fascist Party Militia (*Milizia Volontaria per la Sicurezza Nazionale*) in 1923 to work alongside the traditional police forces also resulted in tensions and unnecessary duplication of tasks. Mussolini's decision in 1925 to rely mainly on the state police (the Carabinieri for the maintenance of law and order and the Interior Ministry police for political policing) lay in his overall strategy for the creation of a state-based rather than party-based regime and the lack of technical expertise and generally undisciplined nature of the militia. Indeed, between the March on Rome and the establishment of the dictatorship, the militia proved to be a mere fig leaf for continued squad violence. Their relegation to a secondary position after 1924 was part of a process of normalization in which the use of political violence outside the state—also characterized by the brutal activities of Mussolini's personal secret police (Ceka) culminating in the murder of the Socialist deputy, Giacomo Matteotti, in June 1924,[58]—was abandoned. Even though the militia remained in existence throughout the Fascist period, albeit under the close supervision of the army, apart from the greater margin of security that they offered to Mussolini, their only other raison d'être lay in the need to demonstrate by their presence that a "Fascist revolution" had taken place.[59]

The founding of a myriad of overlapping secret police organizations only added to the hierarchical confusion and functional inefficiency of a police state in which everyone was spying on and being spied on by everyone else.[60] Carucci notes, for example, that at the provincial level OVRA inspectors worked sometimes in cooperation with, sometimes in opposition to, and sometimes unknown to the Interior Ministry provincial police authorities. Under the leadership of Bocchini, many policing functions were taken away from the prefect, in spite of his being declared supreme head of the province, and concentrated in the Interior Ministry police. Provincial police chiefs were also given more autonomy from the prefect in political investigations.[61]

Examination of police documents suggests that at the provincial level the police faced difficulties because of inadequate resources. During the early thirties the provincial authorities considered that forces available to maintain public order on the occasion of official visits by government or royal family members were insufficient. In particular, the overall number of Carabinieri was reduced from seventy-five thousand to fifty thousand, with the result that where reinforcements were needed, they had to be taken from regular forces elsewhere. Prefects and provincial police chiefs claimed that they were unable to prevent organized crime in areas such as Sardinia. Although it is clear that secret political missions reduced the availability of policemen for other activities, on occasions they complained that there was not enough personnel for the prevention and repression of subversive political activities.[62]

Angelo D'Orsi argues that as a result of the intensification of prevention strategies under fascism the police were able to penetrate the lives of individual Italians as never before, such that forms of repression characteristic of the liberal state involving violent confrontation during strikes and demonstrations more or less disappeared.[63] Yet, at least until the midthirties, policing often resembled that of the liberal period, given a surprising number of illegal strikes and demonstrations against unemployment. On occasions the police and Carabinieri used firearms to restore order, killing or injuring demonstrators, and this was sometimes a result of policemen or Carabinieri being outnumbered and overpowered.[64] It is also generally argued that the type of sporadic illegal violence, involving criminal and political groups and sometimes relied upon by the liberal state, of which Fascist *squadrismo* was the culmination, was removed or institutionalized during the dictatorship. Yet, on occasion during illegal strikes and demonstrations, squads of Fascists still came into action for punitive purposes.[65] Whether this was encouraged by the local police as the only possible means of restoring order in view of their own lack of resources remains to be verified.

Inspections of the provinces during the Fascist period revealed outdated policing facilities. Many police headquarters and sleeping quarters were housed in old buildings in which levels of hygiene were low and heating and lighting inadequate. Telegraphic and telephone services were often insufficient.[66] Giorgio Fabre notes that even officials belonging to such an important organization as OVRA usually sent messages to the central government by post and were forced to work without motorized means of transport.[67] Despite the implementation of legislation to improve the quality of policemen and to remove those who were considered too old or incapable, inspections continually revealed problems in this area.[68] Many policemen showed limited dedication to the job, failed to cooperate with their colleagues, lacked discipline, and left much to be desired from a moral point of view. In many cases the mentality of older policemen created difficulties in adapting to changes brought by fascism.[69]

In spite of blows suffered by the antifascist movements during the early thirties, the inspections suggest that the underground movements may have benefited from police negligence. Registers of subversives, which had been reorganized as a means of allowing more efficient prevention and repression of antifascist activities, were constantly reported as not being kept up-to-date, if not in total disorder. In particular the system by which all hoteliers and landlords had to immediately inform the police of the arrival and departure of their guests was neglected. It often occurred that individuals sought after by the police were able to spend a night in hotels or rented accommodation and leave before the notification of their arrival had reached the police.[70] While most inspections emphasized the faults of individual policemen, it is more than plausible, as occasionally admitted in the inspection reports themselves, that lack of government spending on policing, coupled with a higher workload in view of the widened range of policing activities under fascism, were partly to blame for such poor quality. Moreover, the investigations of police headquarters were carried out by Interior Ministry police inspectors, who represented some of the most dedicated policemen, who were also entrusted with the organization of OVRA operations. This may have reinforced in their minds an image of less efficient and more slowly moving provincial forces when they carried out the inspections.

The effectiveness of Fascist repression could be offset by corrupt administrative practices that had their roots in the liberal period. Inspections of police headquarters and investigations of individual policemen during the late twenties revealed cases of individuals avoiding punishment for political crimes through bribery and family connections in the police. The police chief of Taranto, for example, enjoyed the professional services of an artisan who had been sentenced to ammonizione. This was later revoked on account of the exceptionally low cost of such services. His successor had contacts with prominent antifascists, which led to the revocation of ammonizione of a local communist.[71] Inspections of other provinces revealed cases of the issuing of licenses and passports and the granting of concessions to political prisoners or individuals subject to ammonizione in return for cash payments and even sexual favors.[72] It is not unlikely that police corruption was heightened as a result of an increase in their powers, which effectively allowed them to blackmail their victims in return for personal benefits. An investigation report of 1929 claimed, for example, that the police chief of Taranto had threatened an individual with confino to dissuade him from taking legal action against him over an unpaid debt.[73] In Novara the fate of an arrested antifascist teacher depended on the willingness of his daughter to "give herself" to the commissioner dealing with the case.[74]

It is likely that as a result of inspections and investigations, and on the basis of new legislation making it easier to sack policemen, some progress was made in controlling the worst manifestations of corruption within the police.[75] However, this problem needs to be considered within a broader scenario in which clientelistic practices characterizing all walks of life and the resulting corruption were inherited from the liberal period and stood in the way of the fascistization of Italian society. Several historians have referred to Bocchini's organization of the police into his personal fiefdom, in which in the absence of legal protection, corruption was the only means of guaranteeing oneself against persecution.[76] With regard to police repression itself, Ernesto Rossi, militant of *Giustizia e Libertà* and victim of police repression, claimed that while the most brutal forms of treatment were applied against lower-class political prisoners, those belonging to the middle classes were spared them because policemen were afraid that they might have powerful relatives.[77]

To What Extent Were the Italian Police "Fascistized"?

As we have seen, Mussolini's reliance on the state police rather than the militia lay in his preference for properly trained professionals that could also be used as a counterpart to the Fascist Party.[78] Only in the case of prefects were some appointments given to Fascists.[79] Police loyalties to the regime were to be guaranteed through the implementation of measures placing them in very much tighter career positions. New legislation made it easier, at least theoretically, to sack policemen who were professionally incompetent or who could not guarantee to fulfill the government's political directives.[80] The task was made easier by the fact that the police were servants of the Fascist state not the party. By being loyal to the regime the police were able to maintain certain privileges and thereby fend off attempts by party exponents to remove what they considered to be the excessive power and influence of the state.

While it is true that from 1932 membership of the Fascist Party (or youth organizations) was required for new recruits to the police, this rule regarded employment throughout the state and was of no serious ideological significance beyond the need to create an image of the state being ideologically at one with the governing party, as was the wearing of black shirts for ceremonies by police officials and the introduction of an obligatory Roman salute within the police. [81] In recruiting policemen a limited priority was given to applicants who had taken part in the March on Rome or had been long standing members of the Fascist Party, alongside those who had been injured in war. There is, however, little to suggest from entrance examinations and training courses that aspiring policemen and trainees were expected to show a grasp of Fascist ideology beyond knowledge of the working of new Fascist laws and institutions and recent national history.[82]

According to Franco Fucci, career personnel of both the Interior Ministry police and the Carabinieri were "fascistized," in the sense that they served the regime loyally. But they were not Fascist, in that they remained politically indifferent to the regime, which did not go unnoticed by the most fanatical party chiefs.[83] While there is little evidence to suggest that policemen were convinced Fascists, Fucci's definition is somewhat ambiguous in the face of evidence that police loyalty to the regime, particularly within the upper echelons, was partly motivated by professional benefits that fascism brought and political identification with some aspects of Fascist ideology. Fascism brought back strength to the police after the turbulent period of the *biennio rosso,* during which they had lost their ability to control the status quo in the face of widespread socialist strikes and land and factory occupations. Moreover, unlike the liberal period, those individuals selected for the most politically sensitive policing jobs by the regime had made police careers as commissioners, police chiefs, and inspectors, rather than administrative careers in the ministries, with the result, Giovanna Tosatti argues, that the *ventennio* was the only period in which the police enjoyed true autonomy and decisional power.[84] Fascism's law and order policies, which increased police powers and widened their areas of social control, were in synchrony with a police tradition based on suspicion of the social and political activities of citizens, particularly on the Left.

Alongside the above professional and political considerations, it is also likely that the clientelistic nature of the administration of the liberal state constituted another factor accounting for the relatively smooth adaptation of the police to fascism. Policemen were used to working within a system in which administrative norms and legal considerations were often ignored in the face of state political imperatives. Yet, such practices, which as we have seen continued to condition the maintenance of law and order during the Fascist period, allowed policemen, like all civil servants, to create margins of personal power and autonomy that would stand in the way of the regime's ability both to maintain total control over them and, in broader terms, to fully implement the fascistization of society.

It is plausible that, particularly after the antifascist movements had suffered serious defeats during the early thirties and an apparent consensus for fascism was registered from the midthirties onward, in line with a more general attitude within the Fascist state bureaucracy of "keeping heads down," some police officials became increasingly lax. They merely paid lip service to the regime and told their superiors what they wanted to be told, namely that law and order were being maintained. This is clearly evident from the midthirties onward in reports from the Interior Ministry police General and Confidential Affairs division in Rome to the government, in which almost identical and highly rhetorical sentences, if not whole paragraphs, emphasizing the successes of the regime and stressing the merits of the police, were repeated fairly frequently.[85]

Once it was clear that the regime's days were numbered, many policemen dissociated themselves from it. Rather than representing an ideologically motivated stance, such moves reflected their desire to interpret more carefully the general moods of society and act in synchrony with growing public dissatisfaction with the regime and the movements of the monarchy in the face of Italy's humiliating military defeats and economic crisis during the Second World War. Indeed, as Paloscia notes, even Bocchini and his successor, Carmine Senise, along with a number of prefects and high ranking police officials, who had initially been zealous in their enforcement of the anti-Jewish laws, began to distance themselves from fascism in anticipation of its political defeat.[86]

Conclusion

Examination of the working of the Fascist police demonstrates that a proper totalitarian system of social control was never implemented on account of Mussolini's particular conception of totalitarianism and compromises at the root of the consolidation of his dictatorship. However, there clearly was a break in continuity from liberal methods of social control under fascism. Although the liberal state was potentially authoritarian and although most of the police instruments used by the Fascist regime had their roots therein, the creation of the dictatorship saw a widening of areas of police social intervention, a significant increase in police powers, and their greater immunity from accountability for their actions, such that a regime of fear and repression was created. Yet, Italian fascism by its conservative nature allowed for a certain amount of discretion to be exercised in dealing with crimes against the regime, as illustrated by use of amnesty and clemency.

It is likely, however, that the efficiency of the Fascist police apparatus in repressing dissent was affected by serious professional deficiencies and practices of corruption. In this sense, there was a fundamental contradiction in the employment in the state administration of career personnel who were prepared to formally serve the regime, playing ideological lip service to it, in return for job security and favorable salary conditions, but who were not always able or willing to adapt to its requirements. The extent to which the above factors jeopardized the effectiveness of the Fascist police apparatus in defending the regime remains to be established more clearly. There is little doubt that as a result of police repression contacts between antifascist party officials and the larger number of less politically organized opponents of fascism became very difficult, particularly from the early thirties onward.[87] However, a recent case study of Sesto San Giovanni (Lombardy) argues that even where antifascist parties were driven underground, new groups were formed by younger individuals with no past political record and therefore unknown to the police. It was also possible to escape repression by forming networks outside areas, such as the factories, where there was a large presence of police informers.[88]

While there is no doubt that the atmosphere of fear and repression characterized by the presence of spies affected the functioning of normal social relations, recent social historical research suggests that the police apparatus had difficulty penetrating the Italians' private spheres. From the moment that the fascistization of large sections of the adult population was limited to the creation of little more than public approval of the regime, it was on the whole possible for individuals and their families, relations, and friends to maintain a subversive culture in the privacy of their own homes. De Luna argues, for example, that the family, previously abandoned by its members as they engaged in political activities, often became the basis of antifascist activities.[89]

Given the limited capacity of the police to penetrate private spheres, coupled with the inability of citizens to express their feelings and opinions publicly, the efficiency of the consensus-building machine, which relied on police information, is also questionable. Moreover, police reports to the regime on shifts of public mood were often conditioned by their particular mentality and, most significantly, by their career needs. Even the most dedicated policemen were conditioned in this way. They hoped to be rewarded for their ability to suppress underground antifascist movements and consequently desired to demonstrate the difficulties that suppressing such movements presented, so as to appear all the more deserving of praise. But by doing so they risked being reprimanded for having allowed underground antifascism to grow to such strengths before suppressing it. This created a potentially contradictory situation that led to practices of self-censorship.[90]

Notes

1. Morgan, *Italian Fascism*, 79–81.
2. Arendt, *The Origins of Totalitarianism*, 256–59, describes the Fascist regime as

"an ordinary nationalist dictatorship" until 1938.

3. These words were pronounced by the justice minister, Alfredo Rocco, in his speech to the Italian parliament in May 1925, part of which is reproduced in Aquarone, *L'organizzazione dello stato totalitario,* 69–70.

4. Arendt, *The Origins of Totalitarianism,* 421–23.

5. For a recent analysis of Italian fascism that strongly supports the theory that there was a significant move in the direction of the creation of a totalitarian society, see Gentile, *La via italiana al totalitarismo.*

6. De Felice, *Mussolini il duce: II,* 10; Thompson, *State Control in Fascist Italy,* 63–66.

7. Canosa, "Polizie," 693–97. See also Canosa, *La polizia in Italia,* chap. 1.

8. Jensen, *Liberty and Order,* esp. 178–82.

9. Amato, "La libertà personale," 153.

10. Carucci, "Arturo Bocchini," 72.

11. Corso, *L'ordine pubblico,* 242.

12. Articles 168 and 176 of the 1926 police code stated that sentences of ammonizione were pronounced by a provincial commission consisting of the prefect, the public prosecutor, the *questore* (provincial police chief), the Carabinieri commander, and a high-ranking militia officer. Article 186 stated that decisions on domicilio coatto (renamed confino) were pronounced by the same commission. During the liberal period domicilio coatto sentences had been pronounced by a mixed commission of judicial and police officials.

13. Amato, "La libertà personale," 154–56; Corso, *L'ordine pubblico,* 281–82. The emergency legislation of 1894 also gave the police greater powers to persecute individuals only suspected of crimes, though the use of such powers was abandoned from the beginning of the century.

14. This is demonstrated by the strongly political composition of the special tribunals. According to Schwarzenberg, *Diritto e giustizia,* 87, the president of the tribunal was an army or militia general and the judges were Fascist consuls and *squadristi.*

15. Ambrosio, *Nel novero dei sovversivi,* 5.

16. Galizia, "La libertà di circolazione," 533–34. Corso, *L'ordine pubblico,* 147–48.

17. Cheli, "Libertà di associazione," 296.

18. Cuomo, "La libertà di manifestazione del pensiero," 229–30, 235.

19. Schwarzenberg, *Diritto e giustizia,* 184–93. Schwarzenberg notes (188) that the right of individuals not to be prosecuted for offensive or violent behavior toward public officials when public officials had exceeded the limits of their authority, as stipulated by articles 192 and 199 of the 1889 criminal code, was removed from the 1930 code.

20. Jensen, *Liberty and Order,* esp. 180–82. See also Davis, *Conflict and Control,* 232–41. My own case study of policing in Bologna during the late 1890s largely supports Jensen's argument (Dunnage, *The Italian Police,* 23–33).

21. Tosatti, "La repressione del dissenso politico," 254.

22. Such policing activities are discussed in annual reports of the Divisione Affari

Generali e Riservati of the Interior Ministry police (Archivio Centrale dello Stato, Ministero dell'Interno, Direzione Generale di Pubblica Sicurezza, Divisione Affari Generali e Riservati [henceforth ACS.DAGR], *Massime*, b. 24 and 25) and the reports of the provincial police chiefs (*questori*) to the chief of the Interior Ministry police between 1937 and 1943 (in ACS.DAGR *1941, 1942, 1943*). See also Tosatti, "La repressione del dissenso politico," 239.

23. Tosatti, "L'anagrafe dei sovversivi italiani," 140–43; Tosatti, "La repressione del dissenso politico," 251.

24. ACS.DAGR, *Atti diversi (1898–1943)*, b. 6, f. 31 "Circolari," Interior Ministry circular to prefects and police chief of Rome, 1 March 1937. Tosatti notes ("La repressione del dissenso politico," 251) that this system was originally set up under Crispi.

25. Ibid., 243–44.

26. Ibid., 239.

27. D'Orsi, *La polizia*, 36.

28. Carucci, "Arturo Bocchini," 67–69, 84–85; Fucci, *Le polizie di Mussolini*, 49–55, 125.

29. Barile, "Relazione generale," 32.

30. Discussed in detail in Carucci, "L'organizzazione dei servizi di polizia," 100–103; and "Arturo Bocchini," 84–94.

31. For documents concerning the employment of secret agents and informers by the prefects, see Archivio Centrale dello Stato, Ministero dell'Interno, Direzione Generale di Pubblica Sicurezza, Divisione Polizia Politica *(materia)*, b. 193 and 194.

32. The question of the hierarchical dependency of OVRA is discussed in Fabre, "Le polizie del fascismo," 144–45.

33. Aquarone, *L'organizzazione dello stato totalitario*, 108.

34. For government instructions on the recruitment of OVRA informers among members of the Communist Party, for example, see ACS.DAGR, *Atti diversi (1898–1943)*, b. 6, f. 31 "Circolari," Interior Ministry circular (441/3592 - K.R) to prefects and police chief of Rome, 24 September 1930.

35. Tosatti, "La repressione del dissenso politico," 242–43. See also ACS.DAGR, *Atti diversi (1898–1943)*, b. 6, f. 31 "Circolari," chief of Interior Ministry police to prefects and police chief of Rome, 31 July 1936.

36. Tosatti, "La repressione del dissenso politico," 242, n. 99.

37. Mason, "Whatever Happened to 'Fascism'?" 259; "Massenwiderstand," 35.

38. See, for example, Franzinelli, *Delatori*.

39. See, for example, ACS.DAGR *(1930–1931)*, b. 341 and 342, f. "Offese a S.E. il Primo Ministro."

40. Morgan, *Italian Fascism*, 123; De Luna, *Donne in oggetto*, 17, 19.

41. Jensen, *Liberty and Order*, 302–3. In 1894—the year of the application of the *leggi eccezionali*, often seen as demonstrating the dictatorial nature of the Liberal regime—2,738 individuals were assigned to ammonizione. In 1894–1895, 2,170 were sentenced to domicilio coatto. At the turn of the century, the total number of ammoniti

amounted to 8,233 and those in exile to 3,379.

42. ACS.DAGR, *1930–1931,* b. 312, Bologna, f. "disoccupazione," prefect of Bologna to chief of Interior Ministry police, 5 May 1930, and prefect of Bologna to Divisione Affari Generali e Riservati of Interior Ministry police, 19 May 1931.

43. Casali, "'Per il pane,'" 325.

44. ACS.DAGR, *1930–1931,* b. 317, Genoa f. "Agitazioni operaie."

45. Carucci, "L'organizzazione dei servizi di polizia," 87. This also emerges in the annual reports of the Divisione Affari Generali e Riservati of the Interior Ministry police, in ACS.DAGR, *Massime,* b. 24.

46. ACS.DAGR, *1941,* b. 49, police chief of Bergamo to chief of Interior Ministry police, 31 May 1938.

47. Given the lack of political consciousness of broad sections of the adult population, coupled with a realization that large numbers of Italians were hostile or unsympathetic, initially propaganda initiatives toward the adult masses were limited to a combination of welfare and organized recreational activities, embodying a watered-down ideological approach, while a proper program of fascistization was limited to the education of the youngest (Thompson, *State Control in Fascist Italy,* chaps. 3 and 4).

48. Rossi, *La pupilla del duce,* chaps. 1 and 2. See also Leto, *OVRA.* Friedrich and Brzezinski in their analysis of totalitarian dictatorships (*Totalitarian Dictatorship and Autocracy,* 178–79) argue that the Italian penal islands took the place of Hitler's concentration camps, adding that: "Though conditions were not as serious, they were surrounded by the same air of terrifying mystery and, when combined with the common practice of beating up individuals at random, sufficed to create the characteristic atmosphere of totalitarian terror."

49. For the recruitment of OVRA informers, see note 34. For examples of accounts of OVRA interrogations, see ACS.DAGR, *Movimento comunista,* 1936, b.28, inspector general of police to chief of Interior Ministry police, 26 November 1936 and 12 December 1936.

50. Savella, *Mussolini's "Fouché,"* esp. 286–95.

51. Paloscia, *I segreti del Viminale,* 65–66.

52. For police reports on the Jewish community and the enforcement of the Race Laws, see ACS.DAGR, *1941* (including reports from 1937 to 1941), *1942* and *1943.* See also Collotti and Klinkhammer, *Il fascismo e l'Italia in guerra,* 38–39; Paloscia, *I segreti del Viminale,* 70–76.

53. Friedrich and Brzezinski, *Totalitarian Dictatorship,* 179.

54. Donati, "La Guardia Regia," 472–78, 485.

55. Collin, "Police and Internal Security," 430.

56. See letter from police chief of Reggio Emilia to prefect, 11 May 1930, concerning the Carabinieri (ACS.DAGR, *1930–1931,* b. 302).

57. Archivio Centrale dello Stato, Ministero dell'Interno, Direzione Generale di Pubblica Sicurezza, Divisione Personale, Fascicoli personali di Pubblica Sicurezza [henceforth ACS.DP], *Versamento 1963–1965,* b. 170, f. "Fidenza," inspector general of police to

chief of Interior Ministry police, 21 May 1929.

58. Tosatti, "La repressione del dissenso politico," 239.

59. Aquarone, *L'organizzazione dello stato totalitario,* 247–55. See also Lyttelton, *The Seizure of Power,* 244–50. For details of militia violence, see Dunnage, *The Italian Police,* chap. 7.

60. Aquarone, *L'organizzazione dello stato totalitario,* 108–9.

61. Carucci, "Arturo Bocchini," 84–85, 88–91.

62. Such difficulties in maintaining law and order are evident in reports and communications contained in ACS.DAGR, *1930–1931,* b. 302 and 304.

63. D'Orsi, *La polizia,* 27.

64. For details of the repression of strikes and demonstrations during the Fascist period, see Viola, *Polizia,* 62–78. According to Viola, there were fifty-six cases of strikes and protest demonstrations (against unemployment, for example) in 1933 alone. In several southern localities demonstrators were killed by the police (67–69). See also, Tarantini, *La maniera forte,* 282–83.

65. Ibid., 283.

66. Reports of inspections of police headquarters during the Fascist period are contained in ACS.DP, *Versamento 1963–1965.*

67. Fabre, "Le polizie del fascismo," 169–70.

68. Legislation included decree law 9 January 1927, which allowed the removal of policemen who were too old or lacking in ability and their replacement by younger men through rigorous selection procedures, and which created eight hundred extra office jobs in order to relieve ordinary policemen of bureaucratic tasks. Decree law 1595 of 17 November 1932 tightened the academic qualifications and practical experience required for the recruitment and promotion of police officials. Italian laws passed after unification may be consulted in the periodical, *Gazzetta ufficiale.*

69. See reports on inspections of police headquarters during the Fascist period contained in ACS.DP, *Versamento 1963–1965.*

70. ACS.DAGR, *Atti diversi (1898–1943),* b. 6, f. 32, chief of Interior Ministry police to prefects and police chief of Rome, 16 November 1929, chief of Interior Ministry police to high commissioner of Naples, prefects, police chief of Rome, special commissioner for the Pontine Marshes, regional and general inspectors of police, 30 November 1934; ACS.DAGR, *Atti diversi (1898–1943),* b. 7, f. 34 "Circolari," Divisione Affari Generali e Riservati of Interior Ministry police to prefects, police chief of Rome, regional and general inspectors of police, 10 January 1935.

71. ACS.DP, *Versamento 1963–1965,* b. 170, general inspector of police to chief of Interior Ministry police, 30 June 1929, 5 October 1929.

72. See, for example, ACS.DP, *Versamento 1963–1965,* b. 170, report on police chief of Reggio Calabria (9 October 1929) and b. 178 for report on police headquarters of Milan (26 July 1928).

73. ACS.DP, *Versamento 1963–1965,* b. 170, general inspector of police to chief of Interior Ministry police, 30 June 1929.

74. ACS.DP, *Versamento 1963–1965*, b. 170, general inspector of police to chief of Interior Ministry police, 6 June 1929.

75. It is noticeable that those inspections of police headquarters of the thirties (in ACS.DP, *Versamento 1963*–1965, various boxes) that I have been able to examine do not reveal levels of corruption evident in reports of 1928 and 1929.

76. Carucci, "Arturo Bocchini," 80–81. For specific cases of acceptance of bribes by Bocchini, see Alexander Stille, *Benevolence and Betrayal*, 133–34.

77. Rossi, *La pupilla del duce*, chaps. 1 and 2. See also Leto, *OVRA*.

78. D'Orsi, *La polizia*, 38.

79. Fried, *The Italian Prefects*, 183–84. Fried notes that by the midthirties half the prefects serving in the provinces were from outside the administrative profession. This pacified Fascist elements who resented the supremacy (albeit nominal) of the prefect, and it enabled prefects to exercise their authority and control over Fascists without the risk of accusations of antifascism.

80. See decree law 2960 of 30 December 1923; decree law 57 of 6 January 1927; decree law 33 of 9 January 1927. See also ACS.DP, *Versamento 1961*, b. 16, f. "Attività svolta dall'avvento del Fascismo al 1934 per la riorganizzazione del Personale di P.S."

81. For the question of party membership for state employees, see Aquarone, *L'organizzazione dello stato totalitario*, 257–60. In 1932 party membership became obligatory for admittance to employment in state administration. Only in 1940, however, did membership become obligatory for career advancement for those employed before 1932. For examples of the use of black shirts by the police, see ACS.DAGR, *1933. Sezione 2*, b.43, head secretary of chief of Interior Ministry police to all Interior Ministry police division chiefs, 13 October 1933. For norms concerning the use of Roman salutes among the police, moreover, which appear to have been widely ignored, see ACS.DP, *Versamento 1961*, b. 16, f. "obbligo del saluto."

82. Details of requirements for entry to the police can be found in announcements of competitions published in the *Gazzetta ufficiale*.

83. Fucci, *Le polizie di Mussolini*, 68.

84. Tosatti, "La repressione del dissenso politico," 247–48, 255.

85. ACS.DAGR, *Massime*, b. 25.

86. Paloscia, *I segreti del Viminale*, 70–76. It is likely that earlier instances of policemen avoiding enforcement of the Race Laws were also a result of the limited enthusiasm that the laws met within society as a whole.

87. De Luna, *Donne in oggetto*, 70–79. See also ACS.DAGR, *Massime*, b. 24, Interior Ministry police report to Fascist Grand Council, September 1931. The report claimed that as a result of police infiltration of the underground communist movement in Liguria, such an atmosphere of suspicion and mistrust was created that the party decided to concentrate its energies in other regions.

88. Bell, *Sesto San Giovanni*, 187–90.

89. De Luna, *Donne in oggetto*, 181.

90. This is discussed in Preti, "Spirito pubblico," 44–45.

CHAPTER 13

Violence, Surveillance, and Denunciation: Social Cleavage in the Spanish Civil War and Francoism, 1936–1950

Angela Cenarro

The aim of this essay is to offer an overview of how social control was exercised in Franco's Spain. Some intellectual traditions, both Spanish and European, have tended to see Spain as a "different country," set apart from the general currents of economic, social, and political developments in Europe. Thus, Franco's regime is not analyzed here as a completely different and unique regime but placed in a comparative framework that helps to explain its similarities and differences with other contemporary European experiences. A historical comparative perspective becomes crucial in order to understand the social, political, and economic processes that led to the breakdown of democratic regimes in interwar Europe. It is also necessary for explaining the establishment and consolidation of fascist dictatorships, as well as its meaning and significance in social terms.[1]

The Franco regime and the Spanish Civil War (1936–1939) cannot be analyzed separately. In fact, the true nature of the Franco regime lies in its violent origins. The military coup d'état in July 1936 that led to the Civil War was conceived as a violent solution to the Spanish crisis of the 1930s. Although military intervention in politics had been a regular feature in Spain since the nineteenth century, the 1936 coup d'état was different because of its bloody character. It was the first military coup followed by bloodshed in Spanish history. Precisely, this is one of the most striking peculiarities of the Spanish solution to the interwar crisis. The army had been the oligarchy's traditional instrument for maintaining or restoring public order in periods of crisis since the beginning of the twentieth century, such as in 1909, 1917, and 1921–1923. In 1936 when the crisis was exacerbated after five years of democracy and social unrest, the army was the institution in charge of putting an end to the Republican regime (1931–1936).

And it was carried out through highly violent means. There is no doubt that violence—conceived in the broad sense of the word, but especially physical violence—was far more intense in Spain than in the Fascist regime of Mussolini, and it could even be said that the Spanish dictatorship was no less bloody than the Nazi regime in Germany in the period prior to World War II and the subsequent radicalization leading to the Holocaust.

Partly, this is due to the fact that the origins of the Francoist dictatorship lie in a bloody civil war. But if we compare the aftermath of the Spanish conflict with the outcomes of other civil wars, the conclusion is that nowhere else was violence the main ingredient of the postwar reconstruction. At least 81,000 Spaniards were exterminated from 1936 to the mid-40s. Therefore, even if we cannot talk about the Francoist dictatorship as a totalitarian regime in the sense defined by Hannah Arendt, we should take into account that the violence unleashed during and after the Civil War marked a radical break in the Spanish trajectory to the point that there has been no true reconciliation in Spanish society since the introduction of democracy in 1975. Nevertheless, this leads us to issues that are not the object of this paper.[2]

All these questions will be analyzed in the following pages. Beforehand, it would be useful to point out that in order to define the essence of the Francoist dictatorship, we should be aware that the main objective of the military coup and the subsequent repression was to reestablish the traditional social order that had been questioned during the Second Republic (1931–1936). Therefore, it is the meaning and the transcendence of the Republican regime that has to be explained in order to understand the nature of the reaction in 1936.

The Spanish Background: The Second Republic (1931–1936)

Since the final decades of the nineteenth century, political, social, and economic power had gone together in Spain, as well as in Germany and Italy. Despite the importance of industrialization, it was land ownership that allowed people to enjoy a privileged political and social position within the state and local communities. This prominent position had crystallized in the imposition of socialization habits led by the Catholic Church, because the Church as an institution, as well as its representatives in every parish, had sided with the landed oligarchy in order to have its interests defended in the context of the emergence and consolidation of the liberal state. At the same time, landowners' and industrialists' political interests were effectively preserved by means of a clientelist network and electoral manipulation that guaranteed the exclusion from the political arena of the interests of the middle class, workers, and peasants. To sum up, from 1875 onward the Spanish state emerged as a highly ineffective and nondemocratic state.

The first democratic experience in Spain put an end to this situation. The Second Republic was born in April 1931 as an ambitious reformist project. Its main objective was to create an inclusive state where the traditionally marginalized social sectors could defend their interests by political means—that is, free elections were allowed and Republican and left-wing parties could have their representatives in parliament. In order to do so, the traditional elite, comprised of industrialists and landowners, was removed from political power. When Republican and Socialist representatives were elected in the free local elections of April 1931, "caciques" and "dynastic" politicians had to leave key political posts.

Some of the most radical measures approved by the new Republican-Socialist government tried to solve long-term problems. The most important reforms focused on the two most conflictive issues related to the configuration of the state. On the one hand, laicizing legislation was a threat to the rule of the Catholic Church and its traditional ally, the oligarchy. It was also perceived as a threat by Catholic and conservative peasants, urban middle classes, and middle classes of provincial towns, who traditionally had identified social hierarchy, public order, and private morality with Catholic faith and practice. Obviously, in the context of the 1930s economic crisis, preservation of old values that inspired a sense of security became crucial for wide social sectors. On the other hand, the Agrarian Reform Bill (1932) was implemented to expropriate large estates in the south of Spain. The objective was not fully achieved—in the end the number of peasants who benefited with a piece of land (110,000) was less than expected—but landowners considered that it was a threat to their economic power as well as their traditional social preeminence. So did smallholders from northern areas, who thought their land would be expropriated as well. Other issues that aroused great opposition were the decentralization measures—Catalonia and the Basque country were allowed to have a Statute of Autonomy and women were emancipated, with the subsequent alteration of traditional gender relations. As a result, some social sectors expressed their displeasure with Republican reforms and could be easily mobilized against the Second Republic.

If Republican political reforms questioned the traditional social order, the left-wing—basically socialist and anarcho-syndicalist—mobilization experienced a marked increase as a result of democracy and challenged it thoroughly. Nevertheless, despite Republican ambitions, the traditional elite was able to use its enormous and untouched economic and social power to block and dismantle the Republican political reforms. First, the elite tried to recover political power by electoral means—the right-wing Catholic party, CEDA (*Confederación Española de Derechas Autónomas*), was created in order to defend old interests in the new democratic context—and it managed to do so in the 1933 elections thanks to the successful mobilization and electoral campaign carried out by the Church itself and different Catholic organizations such as agrarian unions, Catholic Action, and CEDA. When the victory of the Popular Front coalition in the February 1936 elections showed that democratic means had become useless for halting reforms, the elite decided to overthrow the Republican regime by violent means.

Therefore, to put an end to the Republican regime was the essential precondition for recovering political power and to reinforce or reestablish the old social hierarchy. In so far as this was the objective of the fascist seizure of power in other European countries, the military uprising of July 1936 can be identified as the Fascist solution to the Spanish crisis. The uprising was followed by bloodshed and by the defeat of the Republican army three years later. Thus, the reconstruction of the state in the 1940s was carried out on the basis of violence and the maintenance of a divided society. Obviously, social control was employed to reach these objectives.

An Outburst of Violence: The Spanish Civil War (1936–1939)

Physical repression was carefully planned by the rebel officers as the rebellion against the Second Republic (1931–1936) was taking shape. The so-called *Alzamiento* on July 18, 1936, succeeded in places such as Seville, Zaragoza, Oviedo, and Castillian rural areas but failed in the most important cities of Madrid, Barcelona, and Bilbao. In the latter places, working-class resistance was reinforced by broad sectors of the army deciding not to back the uprising or by security forces such as the police, the *Guardia Civil* (hereafter Civil Guard), and the Republican *Guardia de Asalto*. In fact, military and security corps action was crucial and contributed actively in defining every town's fate. In places where police, Civil Guard, and *Guardia de Asalto* did not join the rebellion, the military coup d'état did not manage to succeed. Conversely, where these forces were involved in the uprising, rebel officers were able to suppress working-class resistance. The violence carried out by the rebels throughout the summer of 1936 was not spontaneous and fortuitous at all, although neither can it be considered as the necessary consequence of the war context. In fact, it started immediately after the military coup, when the state of war was declared by rebel officers on July 28, and military justice prevailed over ordinary justice. The conflict was conceived by the rebel officers as a "war of annihilation": Extermination of the enemy was the priority; it was even more important than achieving a coherent military strategy. The bulk of the rebel officers had been forged in the Moroccan colonial wars, and their colonial mentality and brutal methods used against native populations were applied to Spaniards during the Civil War. Terror was also efficiently used to paralyze the enemy and to neutralize its resistance.[3]

An important question arises here. As it has been said before, military interventionism in politics had been a peculiarity of Spanish history since the beginning of the nineteenth century.[4] The Spanish army had always been in charge of maintaining public order, and consequently military justice was preeminent in enforcing it. Therefore, we can talk of the existence of the so-called *militarismo,* that is, the predominance of the army as an institution not only in the government and the administration but also in the organization of security. This means that the police and the Civil Guard, the Spanish security corps, were organized as a military body, subjected to the military justice code, and commanded by military officers. In a few words, the security corps was completely militarized. In addition, several laws were implemented to confirm the military control of public order, such as the *Ley de Jurisdicciones* of 1906 and the *Ley de Orden público* of 1933, whereby the army was allowed to declare a state of war in moments of crisis. What happened in July 1936 was a new example of an old tradition. When on July 28 the *Junta de Defensa Nacional*—formed by several military officers who had rebelled against the Republican government ten days before— launched the *Bando declaratorio del Estado de guerra,* they were acting according to well-known rules, because modern Spanish history had been marked by several states of war since 1812.

Although rebel officers implemented and controlled the repressive machinery from the very beginning, and as a consequence the army had absolute control of what happened in the nationalist rearguard, they were not the only perpetrators. Conservative and right-wing politicians, Fascist militants (members of the *Falange Española y de las JONS*), and thousands of right-wing volunteers who quickly joined the militias or paramilitary forces were equally involved in the detention, incarceration, and execution of Spaniards. Spanish society had reached high levels of mobilization since 1917 and throughout the Second Republic, following European trends in the interwar period. During the Republican regime, the upper and middle classes—smallholders and Catholics and provincial and urban middle classes—threatened by the reformist legislation, especially the Law of Agrarian Reform and anticlerical measures, mobilized in order to fight back against the left-wing mobilization and to attack the Republic itself.

These mobilized sectors constituted a social base ready to back any attempt to overthrow the Republic. This explains how the 1936 military uprising was followed by an unprecedented right-wing mobilization that was channeled through militias such as the Fascist Falange, the traditionalist or Carlist *Requeté,* and others such as *Acción Ciudadana* (an urban militia in various cities). The right-wing mobilization carried out during the Republic crystallized and increased with the coup d'état and the context of war. Thousands of volunteers who wanted to fight on the rebel side joined these militias after the coup, which provided the necessary cadres to play an important role in the battlefield or in the rearguard—especially fulfilling repressive and assistance tasks. Although these militias mainly welcomed petit bourgeois members, prominent conservative local politicians and local caciques also had a place. This was the case in the Aragonese province of Teruel, where the so-called *Milicia Aguado* was controlled by Luis Julián, brother of one of the most important right-wing local deputies. In the southern areas of Andalucia, these columns were commanded by rich landowners whose first military operations were directed at the recovery of their estates that had been taken by rural workers (*jornaleros*) during the Republican period. In some rural provinces of the north, such as Navarra and Vitoria, the Carlist leaders ordered and organized the right-wing mobilization. Besides, they encouraged people to adhere to and support the military coup by informal means, such as pressure, persuasion, and threats. Social nets of kinship, friendship, patronage, and neighborhood were efficiently instrumentalized to fulfill this task.[5] Since mobilization was closely linked to the war effort, the militias were submitted to military control from the beginning—when the military justice code prevailed in July 1936—although more clearly from December 1936 onward, when they were militarized by decree. As a result, all the bodies in charge of implementing social control in Francoist Spain—police, Civil Guard, and militias—were subordinate to the army.

Physical violence was implemented as follows. From July 1936 the detention of "red" elements and subsequent killing or incarceration was authorized by the rebel army carried out by militias. A high percentage of the victims were assassinated in the period between July and December 1936. They were urban and rural workers who had joined socialist and anarchist unions, but also left-wing and Republican politicians and some liberal and anticlerical middle-class members. Although repression was basically class-oriented, since the Spanish Civil War was fundamentally the materialization of a long-term class conflict, violence did not only go across class lines. It was also used to solve other conflicts such as clericalism and anticlericalism or centralism and regional nationalism. As I have explained before, both issues were closely related to the configuration of the Spanish state and had acquired a special predominance during the Second Republic. During the summer of 1936, when most of the assassinations happened, there was no kind of judicial process for the victims. This method was applied only to the military officers who had not joined the rebellion. In fact, military officers and left-wing or Republican politicians—those that had been democratically elected and had removed old politicians from key power posts—were the main targets in the first days after the coup d'état. It was only some days later that the bulk of the rank and file of left-wing parties was affected by the bloody wave. Their names and addresses had been taken from the workers' union files, after they were sacked by the Falangist and Carlist militiamen, and they provided valuable information for a thorough organization of the bloodshed in the following months.

In rural areas, the Civil Guard and the Falangist militias were the main agents of the task of repression. But they were not alien institutions to the small communities. The Civil Guard had a long tradition of collaboration with the local caciques and the most influential people in every village, and the militias increased their membership by integrating the most right-wing inhabitants and volunteers. Nevertheless, occasionally these militias also absorbed working-class members looking for protection. This was the case, for example, in Seville, where these new members, the so-called *camisas nuevas,* were forced by the Falange leaders to denounce and arrest people from their working enviroment.[6] In places where people knew each other and neighborhood ties and friendship had been forged for generations, denunciation and revenge flourished easily. The context of war created by the military uprising offered the chance to solve long-term local conflicts. This was the case in the Aragonese village of Calamocha, where during the Republican period the new legal framework allowed several tenants to benefit when the local judge sentenced in favor of them and against the landlord. In the summer of 1936, the landlord, José Jaime, had the chance to gain revenge and denounced the judge to the military authority. He was executed a few days later. This case is an example of the dynamics of violence in local communities. Personal rivalries and enmities were mixed with social conflicts around questions mainly related to land structure. The military coup d'état created suitable conditions "from above" to settle them. Although the background had been forged for years or decades and violence only worked by means of denunciation and society involvement from below, it was the state of war declared by the rebel officers that made this kind of solution to underlying conflicts possible.

Methods of violence changed throughout the Civil War. In the first stage (mainly July–December 1936, but not exclusively) many people were assassinated in the streets, or denounced and imprisoned. After a while, prisoners were taken out of the prison in groups and executed near the cemeteries at dawn. This method was called *saca.* During these months most of the victims did not enjoy any kind of judicial protection, and many deaths were not officially registered. Many were buried in a common grave and were registered as "man" or "woman." It was only after several months, especially from 1937 onward, that violence was regularized and executions after a military trial—the so-called *consejos de guerra* carried out by the military authorities—became the usual way of exercising physical violence. The intensity of repression declined as well. In fact, about 80 to 90 percent of the assassinations took place in the first six months of the conflict. Therefore, the centralization of violence paralleled the decrease in figures. Nevertheless, this process was not general because as the Francoist army was advancing, the conditions of the summer of 1936 were recreated. This phenomenon can be analyzed easily in those areas divided by the front, such as Aragon.

This region was divided by a stable war front until March 1938, when the Francoist army carried out a significant advance. As a consequence, the areas that had been loyal to the Republican government were conquered by the rebel cause. Immediately after the entrance of the army, violence had no judicial guarantees and was mainly implemented by militarized militias. The initial phase after March 1938 was characterized by denunciations, imprisonments, torture, and more or less arbitrary executions. Reasons were a bit more complex, since violence carried out by the left-wing committees and the so-called *Tribunales Populares* created by the Republican government had affected the most right-wing neighbors, even if they did not belong to economically or socially prominent sectors, and the priests. These experiences generated an unprecedented desire for revenge and overlapped underlying social conflicts. As a result, the rebel army entrance was followed by repressive measures of an intensity very similar to that of the first stages of the war. It was only after some weeks that violence was centralized and its level of incidence reduced—although it remained quite high in comparison with the repression exercised by the *Tribunales Populares* on the Republican side.

But centralization was a wider process in the Francoist rearguard. As has been explained before, the military uprising was backed by all conservative and right-wing political forces. Unification of these forces was considered an adequate measure to mount the war effort and the future reconstruction of the state. The first step was the election by the officers' junta —although obviously not by democratic means—of Francisco Franco as head of state and the rebel army. Later on, Franco decided to dissolve former conservative and right-wing political forces by decree and to unify them in a single Fascist party in April 1937. Thus, *Falange Española Tradicionalista de las JONS* (FET-JONS) became the organizational umbrella that embraced them. The creation of a unique Francoist party was carried out from above and thus the new single party was subordinate to the state from its inception. Franco himself enjoyed the post of *Jefe Nacional* of the FET-JONS from April 1937. This party, founded on the basis of the Falange and *Comunión Tradicionalista*'s (the Carlist one) previous organizational structures, constituted one of the main pillars of Franco state bureaucracy and offered additional forces to implement social control during and after the Civil War by means of the militia—subordinated to the army since December 1936—and the *Delegación Nacional de Información e Investigación*. Both sections had provincial and local branches that actively contributed to the constant surveillance of local communities.

Franco's victory was beginning to appear likely from the spring of 1938. The uprising had been backed by the Fascist powers Germany and Italy, whose military help was crucial to the outcome of the war. The Second Republic's military defeat was inevitable since the Fascist powers backed Franco, and the Non-Intervention Committee prevented the legally elected Republican government from buying arms on the international market. And since insurgents wanted to carry out a total purge of Spanish society, the rebel victory in April 1939 was not followed by peace but by violence: incarcerations and executions continued throughout the 40s. Republican defeat meant exile for thousands of Spaniards, but also humiliation and silence for those who did not leave the country. Spanish society was divided into victors and vanquished and the Francoist regime kept it divided until the end. There never was any chance for reconciliation.

Military Justice, Social Control, and Denunciation in the Forties: The Basis of the Francoist Reconstruction of the State

The Francoist New State was built upon the Republican defeat. As a result, it took shape as an exclusive and nonintegrative state. The vanquished were segregated from the victors, and there was no place for the vanquished in the New Spain. They were silenced for forty years and their memory erased by Francoist triumphalism. In order to survive, they had to be ready to submit themselves to the victors. We shall now look at the different means by which violence and social control were carried out in postwar Spain.

Justice continued in military hands after the war, because military courts assumed many powers held by ordinary justice before. Political offenses, but also some common crimes, were submitted to military justice.[7] But the army had active and efficient collaborators. Police in the provincial capitals and the Civil Guard in rural areas depended on the Ministry of the Interior (*Gobernación*), but in fact they were militarized institutions in charge of implementing repression and control at the local level by means of detentions, incarcerations, and transference of people from one prison to another. Some Falangist sectors, such as the militia and the Information and Investigation Service, also contributed in carrying out tasks such as espionage and reporting on villages by order of the army or the provincial police. In some rural areas of Andalucia, the falangists were in charge of spying on people in cafes and local pubs, where gatherings against the Franco regime were supposed to take place. They were also ordered by the police to watch fugitives' relatives and to "increase the number of agents and informers to make a net embracing the whole province." In so doing, "it would be very useful to use the returning *excombatientes* [civil people who had fought in Franco's army during the civil war] because they made excellent collaborators whose enthusiasm and adhesion has been proved." Generally, these different institutions in charge of controlling and watching Spanish society were closely linked. For instance, in Barcelona, the Falangist Information and Investigation Service was commanded by a Civil Guard captain, M. Bravo Montero. He created a special brigade, the so-called *Rondín Antimarxista,* that played an important role in detentions and interrogations. He also acted by order of the police chief of the city, the Marquess of Rebalso, a person connected with the former *Somatén* (local armed militia to fight the emergent working movement in the 1920s). Those arrested by him for political reasons were conducted to Bravo Montero who carried out the interrogations.[8]

If military justice prevailed it was not the only type of justice enforced by the Franco regime. On February 9, 1939, the government proclaimed the Law of Political Responsibilities (*Ley de Responsabilidades Políticas*). This law created a special jurisdiction also controlled by the army in order to guarantee the continuation of violence. It also provided the framework for legalizing retroactively the violence exercised since July 1936. As a result, the situation created by arms was consolidated by legal means. In addition, it was also retroactive legislation because it affected anyone who had been involved in politics or had sympathized with left-wing and Republican parties since October 1934 (when a revolutionary uprising took place, although it only succeeded in the mining zone of Asturias). The main targets were those who had enjoyed a political post during the Second Republic, and those who had not shown enough sympathy for the Nationalists or had opposed the so-called *Movimiento Nacional* (the rebels' cause). The law, whose main objective was to implement economic sanctions such as fines and seizures, affected even those who had been previously prosecuted by military justice or were already dead.

Both military justice and the special jurisdictions such as the Law of Political Responsibilities were instruments imposed from above on the dismantled Spanish society of the forties. Nevertheless, unless people collaborated somehow, they could not work properly. As has been pointed out, the social and political tensions of the thirties were radically intensified by the violence—and the subsequent wounds in the social body—unleashed during the Civil War. Thanks to the rebel victory, traditional social order was reinforced or reestablished in every local community, and this consisted basically of the recovery of political power and social prestige by the traditional elite, a phenomenon that was accompanied by revenge—of the caciques, landowners, the Catholic population, and anyone who had sided with Franco—on the defeated. Some testimonies reveal that revenge materialized in public humiliation—insults, threats—and it was made easier by means of the denunciations promoted by the Francoist authorities.

When the war was over, those who had suffered from violence from left-wing militias, or their relatives, could denounce their neighbors involved in the repression. In addition, since the denunciations were the foundation of further accusations and judicial processes, they were an instrument for settling old personal rivalries. So much so that staying in the community or coming back from the "red side" was the precondition for the defeated to purge their "faults." Local authorities forced them to move from their current locality to the former one in order to allow right-wing people to carry out this task successfully by means of denunciation. Obviously, it was a one-direction process: The defeated did not have the chance to denounce those involved in the Francoist repression, which continued throughout the forties with impunity.

The most striking peculiarity of the Spanish case is that the Francoist government formed the so-called *Causa General,* which was supposed to have a merely informative function. But its authority went beyond this. In fact, the *Causa General* was not only the official sanction to the social division of postwar Spain but also a state instrument encouraging denunciation. Comparison with other totalitarian dictatorships reveals that even in Nazi Germany the Gestapo instrumentalized denunciation by the people but, despite the aspirations of some radical national-socialist sectors, there was no legal system of denunciation.[9] The *Causa General Informativa de los hechos delictivos y otros aspectos de la vida en la zona roja desde el 18 de julio de 1936 hasta la liberación* (Informative General Cause for criminal events and other aspects of everyday life on the red side from July 18, 1936 to the liberation) was formed by the decree of April 26, 1940, whereby the *Fiscal del Tribunal Supremo* (Supreme Court prosecutor) was in charge of carrying out the investigation. Although the official aim was to compensate the victims of violence in the loyalist rearguard, in practice it was a legitimizing instrument for the Francoist regime. A public prosecutor was in charge of drawing up several files at the local level (one file for each community or village) in order to have as much information as possible about the repression carried out by the militias on the Republican side during the Civil War. Obviously, the *Causa General* provided the military courts and the Political Responsibilities Court with plenty of supplementary information to complete their task successfully.

The activities of the Political Responsibilities Courts, the military courts (*Auditorías de Guerra*), and the *Causa General* at the local and provincial levels were preceded by public declarations—generally in the press and on the radio—encouraging people to denounce "those that had served or directly or indirectly aided the red-separatist cause." In Barcelona, for instance, the complete addresses of the places where denunciations should be made effective were published in the local newspaper *La Vanguardia.* But this phenomenon took place everywhere in Spain after 1939.[10] Obviously, it was far more intense in areas that were under Republican control for a long time, such as Cataluña or Valencia, or divided by the front line, such as Aragón, because a significant part of their population had been involved in left-wing committees and violent revolutionary activities (assassinations, expropriations, anticlerical attacks, etc.). For instance, the *Causa General* provincial prosecutor of Zaragoza called on the "closest relatives of the people living in the province who were assassinated or had disappeared since the eighteenth of July during the red domination" and "those aware of interesting information on criminal acts" to declare in person or to send a written declaration. Similarly, the Mayor of Teruel, a city that was occupied by the Republican army between December 1937 and February 1938, made the following public declaration in March 1941:

> Seeing as this Corporation is required to compile thoroughly detailed

information for the *Causa General* of Teruel . . . with regard to events leading up to the Glorious National Movement and the way that it arrived in this city, the main activities for and against it, the falling of this city into the hands of the Red army, with the corresponding occurrences and aftermath of crimes perpetrated by the Marxist horde, the people of this city are obliged to provide and facilitate as much data and background as possible for the purposes of justice, and so all citizens of this capital are requested to enable this task to be carried out by appearing at this City Hall within eight days, together with all details and background that they are aware of with regard to the above, thereby fully cooperating with the important task entrusted to this Corporation.[11]

But informants were not always isolated individuals looking for protection or revenge. Official institutions such as the military courts, the Political Responsibilities Court, and local councils were involved in the denunciation dynamic as well. According to conclusions reached by specific research in the Catalan province of Lleida, these institutions—especially the councils—generated the bulk of the denunciations (81 percent) against people affected by the Law of Political Responsibilities.[12] This behavior was due to different reasons. On the one hand, councils were formed by right-wing or new politicians named by the highest provincial authority, the civil governor (*Gobernador Civil*)—who sometimes was a military officer—and had become nondemocratic institutions subjected to the Francoist government. Consequently, these politicians were very well disposed to carrying out the *depuración,* or purging, of the previous left-wing or Republican local politicians and made lists of those in charge during the Republican period or during the Civil War on the Republican side. On the other hand, immediately after the war was over, these local authorities were compelled by the civil governor to create a dossier embracing all the information provided by means of "denunciations and other interesting declarations" about the behavior and activities of those returning to the village or city from the red side.[13] Sometimes, desire for revenge was channeled through more simple ways. It is well known that the Catholic Church as an institution, the Catholic hierarchy, and the clergy sided with the army and backed the uprising. Many priests had to run away in order to avoid being killed in territories under the control of left-wing committees and militias. Once the Francoist army had taken over these areas, the priests returned and called on the population to take revenge against those involved in Republican rearguard activities. This was the case in the Aragonese village of Alcorisa, where the priest, Domingo Buj, publicly declared, "Don't worry about them. They'll fall soon enough—half of them in the cemetery." [14]

The enforcement of the Political Responsibilities Law, or military justice, required that denunciations were followed by the judge's decision to start proceedings. In order to do so, he made inquiries and asked for information from different institutions. The most common were the mayor, the municipal judge, the local head of the Falange, the local Civil Guard post, and the priest. Although there was no single source of information but several, this phenomenon in postwar Spain was far from a real pluralism because all the people and institutions who were actively involved in repression and surveillance belonged to the victors' sector. And as it has been said, all of them had traditionally shown their desire to maintain or restore the traditional social order and had sided with or were closely related to the most prominent people in every village or community. The reports' content was about political activities during the Second Republic, the degree and type of involvement of anyone on the Republican side during the Civil War (resistance to military uprising, crimes, denunciations, property destructions, a post on any committee, guards), ideology, political affiliation, profession, social position, connections (friends, marriages, lovers), and sexual behavior, especially in the case of women. This particular aspect reveals the regime's vocation to invade the private sphere. But reports were only a part of the whole control system established by the victors. A positive reference (the so-called *aval*) written and signed by any recognized Franco supporter was necessary to release somebody from a prison or concentration camp. So women had to make an effort to obtain them at any price. Generally, they asked for the reference from their employers—especially if they worked in domestic service—or any other socially relevant people, such as the cacique or the priest. In the event that they could not get the reference, they asked for it in shops and businesses of the neighborhood or village. Consequently, the victor's sector of Spanish society had the chance to decide the destiny of the vanquished, and the way to implement marginalization, revenge, or humiliation—or conversely protection in some cases—was open.[15]

Paradoxically, the official encouragement to denunciations paralleled a different phenomenon. Francoist authorities also summoned the population to calm down and not to take the law into their own hands. In the Aragonese provinces, for instance, the civil governor's instructions were directed at "protecting" those returning to their locality from the red side. Of course, they had to be submitted to control and reports, and in most cases to detention, imprisonment, and to the disposal of the military judicial authority, but at the same time neighbors had to trust "Spain's justice" and not to "harass those coming back and their families" and "to avoid any aggression individually or collectively." In April 1939 the Civil Guard of Bronchales (Teruel) asked the civil governor for information about how to deal with the "reds" returning to the village since right-wing people whose relatives had been assassinated were very agitated. The civil governor answered that all of them should be admitted into the community and only in the event that they had committed crimes should they be arrested. The rest of them would be kept under observation and right-wing people had to remain calm and to be aware that "the Caudillo's justice has to be merciful because he has ordered that no revenge be taken on the defeated."[16]

Similarly, Falangists who committed excesses in the first days after the arrival of the Francoist army were prosecuted by the military authorities. This was the case in the village of Calanda, where the repression was extremely intense in March 1938 and was carried out by local Falangists raping women and torturing people to death. Following the military court's instruction, the Falangist local leaders started a full investigation of the actions two years later. A similar case took place in Valencia, where some Falangists used brutal methods against the vanquished. The local leader of the Falange criticized them strongly, and later they were submitted to military justice and executed.[17] Both episodes lead us to analyze several questions. On the one hand, it was the most obvious example of how efficient the centralization and control of violence reached by military authority was. As I have said before, rebel violence was never uncontrolled, but at the beginning some license was allowed by the army. The army doubtless profited from it, and once this apparently uncontrolled—or less controlled—violence had crystallized, carried out by Falangists or individuals, it was submitted to strict control from above and its perpetrators were judged and sentenced. On the other hand, the centralization process was the most effective way of showing Franco's authority and the regime's identification with "peace" and bourgeois social order and the subsequent elimination of excesses. Thus, violence control was instrumentalized to create consensus around the New State by means of offering a united and cohesive image of the regime.

Together with the control of violence, denunciation was considered one of the most effective instruments for involving the population in the emergent dictatorial regime and for creating a consensus around the New State. But civil society involvement went beyond this practice. Police and Civil Guard forces were insufficient to carry out all the tasks of repression and control, and the whole of society was required to cooperate somehow. A military officer complained about the shortage of Civil Guard troops to enforce successfully the army's orders. When the war was over, imprisoned population figures were extremely high, and municipal and provincial prisons were full. It was necessary to set up new establishments in order to absorb all the people returning from the former Republican army or the red side. In some cases, the Catholic Church provided some of their sites, such as the seminary basements, and armed neighbors took part as guards. Similarly, in the Pyrenees borderland it was necessary to place special forces to fight against the *maquis* crossing the frontier in the midforties. Nevertheless, in practice, frontier surveillance was basically carried out by armed neighbors reinforced by army and Civil Guard troops. Civil elements constituted the bulk of the forces in the province of Huesca, since there were 120 armed citizens living in the nearby villages and only fifty-six Civil Guards in charge of watching the frontier under military control.[18]

Furthermore, involvement in these tasks of repression and control had a proselytizing dimension, because all Spaniards were urged to be "good patriots" and were compelled to cooperate with justice in order to build a *Patria* or national community. The significance of this message lies in the broader discourse about the *Patria,* whose intellectual framework was provided by National Catholicism. Although the origins of the most reactionary version of Catholicism date back to the mid-nineteenth century, a more consistent synthesis emerged after the intense national crisis following the Disaster of 1898. It appeared as one of the various ideological currents attempting to overcome the crisis and to "regenerate" Spain by looking for a more prominent place in the international context. It could be considered a variant of the social-Darwinist discourse of degeneration in Europe. Since national unity and imperial nostalgia were some of its key concepts, Catholicism became the Spanish version of other radical right-wing ideologies in the context of the interwar European crisis and paralleled the pre-fascist tradition in Italy and the *völkisch* nationalism in Germany.[19] As the necessary first step toward the recreation of the Spanish Empire, the *Patria* was supposed to reinforce the Spanish nation and overcome the fractures that allegedly had spoiled and disintegrated Spain since the nineteenth century and especially since 1931: class divisions, regional nationalism, laicization and anticlericalism, and to a lesser extent female emancipation. These were the fractures that the Francoist state sought to suppress by means of violence and to dissolve in a strong and powerful unified national community. Therefore, the New State could only be forged by those "good Spaniards," or patriots, willing to submit to the Caudillo's orders, whereas "bad Spaniards," constituting the "Anti-Spain," had to be expelled after a purifying process.[20]

The main effects of this situation were the creation of a permanent state of terror that ruined private lives, transformed everyday life, and destroyed families and social networks. The banishment from the usual place of residence of the vanquished was also a widespread strategy to reestablish the victors' domination. The limitation of freedom of residence was one of the penalties laid down in the Law of Political Responsibilities. Sometimes the prosecuted were confined to the Spanish possessions in North Africa or, if they were under the system of conditional liberty, they could not live in their previous place of residence. But also expulsion from the village could be forced by the cacique or could be voluntarily decided by the vanquished. Leaving their community to start a new life somewhere else resulted from the breaking of the traditional social ties by violence, denunciation, or humiliation. Isolation was the consequence for those who decided to remain in the village or returned after several years in prison. This exemplifies how repression could be more than torture and execution: The destruction of the old neighborhood and friendship relationships, the dismantling of traditional association networks, were a precondition of the "safe" reconstruction of the social order in the forties.[21]

Family, Catholicism, and Public Decency:
Old Ingredients for a New State

As the alternative ways to establish relationships were hindered, the traditional family strengthened. As has been analyzed, most migrations after the war were directed toward places where other relatives lived. This was so because in the context of revenge, denunciation, and threats, the nuclear family appeared to be the only safe institution. Similarly, there is information about the emergence of elementary solidarity networks formed by women, mainly through family ties—although not exclusively. Since most of them were widows or their husbands were imprisoned, they helped each other to survive economically or to care for children. This more or less spontaneous bottom-up phenomenon derived from the hostile conditions of life established in every community for the vanquished. But it was completed with decisions taken by the Francoist government from above. It was not by chance that the reconstruction of the state had been conceived as being built upon a normalized society according to the traditional bourgeois order, whose backbone was the family. Thus the family was considered to be a microcosm of the state, and it was supposed to reproduce the old social order or hierarchy. This also explains why the Francoist regime implemented measures to protect the family—that is, the Law of Family Subsidies in 1938 and the *Plus de Cargas Familiares* (Child Benefit) in 1945—and to promote probirth policies in order to compensate for the losses produced by the Civil War.[22]

The protection of the family resulted in the subordination of women, who were supposed to be the pillars of the family and subsequently the main regenerators of society. The Second Republic had not altered their traditional role of wives and mothers, but there is no doubt that the foundations of change had been laid— female suffrage, divorce, the right to hold office, and so forth. The mechanisms of Francoist violence against women were different: apart from being imprisoned and executed, women were purged with castor oil and their heads shaved. These special mechanisms of violence had a "purifying" significance, because women were destined to play a crucial role in the New Spain.[23] The purpose was to confine women in the home, a decision that not only contributed to consolidating a patriarchal structure of society but also to exercising particular measures of social control over women. Women were relegated from the public sphere in order to keep them apart from the labor market to relieve unemployment and in order to reinforce the role of women as wives and mothers. Sometimes, reports show that this role made them responsible for their closest male relative's behavior—especially husbands—before and during the Civil War. Women were also considered to be reproductive bodies and subjected to special control: the greatest assistance organized by the regime was directed toward the promotion of childbirth and the care of children. In so doing, the women mobilized by the female section of the Falange organized home visits and delivered courses on hygiene, acting as state representatives invading the private sphere. Women were mobilized and indoctrinated in order to control themselves, other women, and society as a whole.

Women were also the main target of the regime's obsession with public decency. To start with, sexual behavior was especially taken into account in reports ordered by the military authority. Left-wing women were singled out for showing inappropriate female behavior because they "had cohabited with local red leaders" or because they "were in favor of free love." In some reports, "free love" was generally associated with Communism. Francoist moralization followed the Catholic pattern that sought to keep them away from "vice" (prostitution), despite the paradoxical fact that prostitution was allowed by the regime until it was prohibited in 1956. In order to do so, the *Patronato de Protección a la Mujer,* which had been abolished by the Republic, was reestablished by a decree of the Ministry of Justice on November 6, 1941, and controlled by the Catholic hierarchy and the *Sección Femenina.* In addition, special training courses—sewing, cooking, and so forth—were given in the evening by Catholic Action for working women. Sexual offenses were probably the most worrisome because they were linked to the idea of female purity according to the Catholic pattern, and to the control of sexuality within the boundaries of marriage as the basis of the family.[24]

If women were particularly affected by moralization, society in general was submitted to it as well. Tramps were subjected to control and arrest by the police and the Civil Guard because of the underlying fear that they might be *maquis* or simply "vanquished." Hooliganism (*gamberrismo*) was also prosecuted because it was considered an attempt on the idea of decency, a widespread value among provincial and rural middle classes. The accusations of immorality served as an excuse to close down public places where resistance against the regime might take place. In some cities the *Bloque Social contra la Inmoralidad Pública* was created by the female Catholic Action in 1941 to put into practice campaigns against blasphemy and in favor of good manners, which sought to involve society as a whole to carry out this task. If the "purification" of society had been achieved by repression and purges, the following step was social regeneration, which was defined as the restoration of those elements that had traditionally structured society but had been questioned or challenged during Second Republic and the Civil War (on the Republican side). To sum up, a regenerated society would lay the foundations of the New State.

Conclusions

The Franco regime cannot be considered a totalitarian regime in the sense defined by Hannah Arendt and other theorists of totalitarianism. As we have seen through-out this paper, the army was the predominant institution, and there was not a powerful Fascist party in power, although it existed since 1937 and constituted one of the main pillars of Francoist bureaucracy. As in the dictatorial regimes of Fascist Italy and Nazi Germany, it was subordinated to the state. The Catholic Church's involvement went further than in the case of Italy, since it backed Franco in July 1936 and actively contributed to the indoctrination and mobilization of society. Party, army, and Church, altogether with Catholic and conservative elites and middle classes, were actively involved in the rebellion leading to the Civil War (1936–1939) and the subsequent reconstruction of the state in the forties. In fact, the presence of the Catholic Church and the army had been the most striking peculiarities of the Spanish state since the nineteenth century, and they continued to be under Franco's dictatorship. Nevertheless, the prominent role of these institutions should not lead to the conclusion that the Spanish dicta-torship was softer than the Italian or German ones, nor that continuity prevailed at a higher level than in these regimes. On the contrary, the Civil War repre-sented a radical break in the Spanish trajectory, because the intense violence unleashed after the military coup of 1936 lasted for a decade and marked society and com-munities deeply.

The magnitude of the break can be perceived in a bottom-up analysis. As we have seen in this essay, a wide sector of Spanish society (the future victors) was involved in repression by different means against those they considered the Anti-Spain. Many of them were volunteers in July 1936, and others denounced or, if they had a post in a local institution, they were in charge of writing reports against the vanquished. But none of this could have taken place unless the army had rebelled against the legitimate government of the Republic, declared a state of war (until 1948), and enforced the military code over Spain. It was only the military coup that allowed underlying social conflicts to be resolved by means of violence and the crystallization of social cleavages in the forties. There was a complex relationship between society and the state, since denunciation and threats flourished from below as the consequence of long-term social conflicts and wounds related to the war but were fostered, channeled, and instrumentalized by the state. Furthermore, daily life under Franco was organized according to traditional bour-geois models in which Catholic practices, family, and public decency were key elements. Together with terror, tradition was a useful instrument of the regime to exhibit its victory and to promote an active acceptance of the new regime by the population. Far from being an obstacle for state action, the Catholic Church and traditions in general contributed actively in trying to achieve a consensus during the Franco regime, as well as reinforcing the domination of the traditional elite upon a divided society.

Notes

1. Some works have made interesting contributions to the comparative analysis, such as Preston, *The Politics of Revenge;* Luebbert, *Liberalism, Fascism or Social Democracy;* Blinkhorn, ed., *Fascists and Conservatives;* Casanova, "La sombra del franquismo: ignorar la historia y huir del pasado"; Casali, ed., *Annale;* Collotti, *Fascismo, fascismi.*

2. The figure of eighty-one thousand deaths is the toll calculated by Juliá, ed., *Víctimas de la guerra civil.* This is a useful and interesting synthesis of the local and regional research on twenty-four provinces studied completely and five provinces partially, out of the fifty-two Spanish provinces. A useful comparison between different civil wars in Europe and their aftermaths has been made by Casanova, "Civil Wars, Revolutions and Counterrevolutions"; and also by Kekkonen, "Judicial Repression." Both agree that the Spanish Civil War and postwar period were the most violent and unrepresentative in Europe.

3. In the last decade, many local, provincial, and regional studies about the Francoist repression have been carried out. For a recent synthesis of the main conclusions reached by these different pieces, see Cenarro, "Muerte y subordinación."

4. On militarism see Christiansen, *The Origins of Military Power;* Payne, *Politics and the Military in Modern Spain;* Ballbé, *Orden público y militarismo.*

5. Cenarro, *El fin de la esperanza,* 63. The case of Andalusia has been related by Lazo, *Retrato de fascismo rural,* 12–13; and the northern provinces have been analyzed by Ugarte, *La nueva Covadonga insurgente.*

6. Ortiz Villalba, *Sevilla 1936,* 63. See also Lazo, *Retrato de Fascismo rural,* 32–47 about Falange affiliations in 1936.

7. See Lanero Táboas, *Una milicia de la justicia,* 318–28.

8. Lazo, *Retrato de fascismo rural,* 55–59; Fabre, "La delació," 30–39. The security forces militarization in López Garrido, *El aparato policial,* 64–65. See also López Garrido, *La Guardia Civil.*

9. This particular point has been noted by De Toro Muñoz, "Policía, denuncia y control social," who provides a useful synthesis of the main contributions on this subject with regard to the German and Austrian cases.

10. For references to the Catalan case, see Solé i Sabaté and Villarroya "La ocupación total de Cataluña," 239. See also Fabre, "La delació."

11. Both declarations were published in the local press: *Heraldo de Aragón,* 20 October 1940; and *Amanecer,* 6 March 1941, respectively.

12. Mir et al., *Repressió Econòmica i Franquisme,* 177–81.

13. *Heraldo de Aragón,* 19 April 1939.

14. Rújula, *Alcorisa,* 322.

15. Vilanova, *Las mayorías invisibles,* 52–53.

16. *Heraldo de Aragón,* 19 April 1939, y AHP de Teruel, Gobierno Civil, Sección Orden Público, 1101/60.

17. The case of Calanda in Cenarro, "El triunfo de la reacción: fascistas y conservadores en Teruel," 187; and the case of Valencia in Gabarda, *Els afusellaments,* 38.

18. Letter from the "General Jefe del Estado Mayor Central" to the "Capitán General de la 5ª Región Militar," 8 July 1944. The Civil Guard forces shortage letter from "General Subsecretario del Ministerio del Ejército" to "Capitán General de la 5ª Región Militar," 22 November 1945. The civil elements involvement by guards in the letter from the Military Governor of Teruel to the "General Jefe del Cuerpo de Ejército de Aragón," 17 April 1940. Archivo de Capitanía Militar de Zaragoza, file 55, "Vigilancia de fronteras," file 43 and file 38-A "Prisioneros," respectively. The provision of sites for prisons by the Church in Archivo Provincial de Teruel, Fondo Gobierno Civil, Sección Orden Público, file 1101/78.

19. This is one of the hypotheses of Blinkhorn, "Conservatism, Traditionalism and Fascism in Spain, 1898–1937," 118–137. See also Botti, *Cielo y dinero.*

20. The discourse about the "Patria" has been analyzed by Morodo, *Los orígenes ideológicos del franquismo;* and Blinkhorn, "Spain: The 'Spanish Problem' and the Imperial Myth."

21. This has been confirmed in the memoirs of the son of the assassinated mayor of Sobradiel (Zaragoza). Ezquerra, *Un ayer que es todavía.* He also relates that his father and several friends used to meet after dinner every day to have a chat related to political issues or anything else (the so-called "tertulia"). The Civil War put an end to these meetings. See also Fraser, *Mijas,* where all interviewed left the village forever or returned after several years. Harding, *Remaking Ibieca,* especially chap. 2 where she describes how many people had to leave the village or to live in isolation. I have analyzed the population movements after the war in Cenarro, "Muerte, control y ruptura social."

22. The family was considered an efficient instrument to prevent and contain deviation. Cohen, *Visiones de control social,* 124–25. The topic of female resistance in Vilanova, *Las mayorías invisibles,* 50–51.

23. Ripa, "La tonte purificatrice."

24. The reports' content on women has been analyzed by Barrado, "Mujer y derrota." See also Graham, "Gender and the State: Women in the 1940s."

CHAPTER 14

Vichy France: Police Forces and Policemen, 1940–1944

Jean-Marc Berlière

F rance was the only vanquished country to sign an armistice with Germany. It was also the only one to preserve an "independent" government on its territory during the Nazi occupation. This new situation, the new and unexpected players on the national stage, placed the French administration—especially its police—in an ambiguous position.[1] The new regime and the men who directed it were keen to exert full power and anxious to affirm the sovereignty of the French state. They were also possessed of an ideology—*la Révolution nationale*—that partly overlapped with that of the occupying forces, particularly with reference to anticommunism and anti-Semitism.

A dependable, numerous, modern, effective police force constituted an essential tool for building the new order and enforcing the repressive policy of exclusion that it implied. The police that the Vichy government inherited could hardly have satisfied it or inspired confidence. How could this government employ an institution that its members had denounced before the war as "a sinister Cheka in the service of freemasons"? How could it possibly put up with a police force faithful to the Republic, or with police officers who had previously pursued its supporters with determination and effectiveness when they were trying to overthrow a republic they call *la gueuse* (a girl who is easy to get)?

The Vichy State and the Police Force: Specific Needs

Democratic or authoritarian, for internal affairs the majority of regimes have recourse to the double arm of police and secret funds. Constans and Clemenceau did not shirk from using the police on a large scale—the necessity of a well-armed and well-equipped police force has never been contested by anyone.[2] In reality, and in contrast to what the former chief of the civil cabinet of Marshal Pétain wrote, Vichy needed the police more than any other political regime.

The police institution constitutes a traditional and invaluable tool in the paraphernalia of power. In 1940 it was seen as essential for the new state to assert its authority. This was especially the case for the men of the right who, since the Dreyfus affair,[3] in their radical opposition to the Republic had lived with an obsessive fear of police crime and secret capacities.[4] It was "the active and murderous element of masonry" that they accused of having killed Syveton, Almereyda, Philippe Daudet, Stavisky, and Prince. The police were the Praetorian guards who had saved the Republic on February 6, 1934, in the Place de la Concorde. It was the police that had exposed and ruined the plot of the OSAR (the secret organization of revolutionary action) known as the *Cagoule*. It was officers of the *Sûreté nationale* who had arrested or harassed a number of characters who now, if they did not occupy high ranking functions of Vichy bureaucracy, haunted the corridors and anterooms hoping for positions.[5]

As the carrier of an ideological project founded on order and exclusion, the authoritarian and repressive Vichy state had to give the police an importance comparable with that of other strong states. Not only was the police essential for the maintenance of order, for limiting freedom, and enforcing the policy of exclusion, it was also seen by the new rulers as the privileged instrument of national restoration.[6] Furthermore, the police was an executive arm of the government's sovereignty, and thus in no small measure, of its reality. As the government of a country of which three-fifths was under occupation, and that was deprived of a credible and autonomous army and diplomatic staff, Vichy was always in search of legitimacy and recognition. It was avid for independence and autonomy, and above all for opportunities to assert its sovereignty. The Vichy state constantly sought to exert all of its prerogatives in the areas of policing and justice. It remained permanently anxious to assert its full sovereignty over the whole of France and to avoid the humiliation of seeing the occupier give orders, or worse, replace French administration. Vichy always claimed responsibility for exerting repression, thus running the risk of serving the interests of the occupier. At the same time, the government sought to show that France deserved a central place in the new Europe, which it believed would remain dominated by Germany.

The important role that the new government intended for the police has to be set against the total and absolute mistrust that the men who had come to power following the defeat felt for an institution that they considered to be not only rotten and corrupt but also badly organized and essentially in the hands of the municipalities. Worse still, they felt that they could not trust a Republican police force that appeared penetrated by freemasonry, radicalism, even socialism, a prey to the trade union "evil," and in the hands of creatures of the Popular

Front. A note written in the spring of 1941 provides just one example of the opinion that the new men in power had of the police:

> Given the importance of police to the state, the action of this organization has been a considerable evil.
>
> Regarding the police in the streets:
>
> For several years, and up until the arrival of the present government, the municipal police of Paris was in the hands of the Trade Union of the Gardiens de la Paix. This was the true master of the destiny of the Prefecture of Police. The union was consulted over the nominations of senior officers, over the recruitment of personnel, even over police activity. As a consequence the most important posts were put into the hands of left-wing militants who rapidly brought about the ruin of hierarchy and discipline.
>
> Regarding politics:
>
> The Special Branch was in the hands of the Jew Simon, a creature of Blum who never ceased to serve his master even during the ministries of Daladier and Reynaud. From the perspective of internal politics this service is of capital importance since the information that it collects frequently dictates government decisions. Under Simon it has become the model of a corrupt service.[7]

Even greater than the mistrust directed toward the Paris police, was the mistrust—nourished by both fear and resentment—that was directed toward those who belonged to *la Sûreté nationale* and who were labeled by *Action Française* as the "bloody men" of a "criminal conspiracy." The rest of the police bequeathed by the Third Republic worried them less, though they were not reassured by their apparent weakness. The law of 1884 had confirmed that policing powers in France were, with a few exceptions, municipal. The men of Vichy, whatever their origins and their careers, had only scorn for these "electoral police forces," without bonds uniting them, in the hands of the mayors, and generally too few in number. They doubted that an instrument that was outside the control of the state and whose fragmented organization seemed prejudicial to effectiveness could ever discharge essential, innovating missions on behalf of the state. In addition they characterized police personnel as incompetent, often senile, and lacking in activity and temperament. They had no intention of preserving such a tool and such personnel. Confronted with constraining technical and political requirements, confronted with their logics, their priorities, their desires, and the requirements and interests of the Germans, the men in power devised a series of policies that were as significant for their paradoxes and contradictions, as for their extreme consequences.

The Need and the Urgency, July 1940–Spring 1941

Whatever their anxieties, the new men in power were conscious that, at least initially, they needed the professional competence of the existing police officers. Consequently, they had to compromise and put up with these men "who were opponents in the past" and "committed mistakes" but with whom they were prepared "to let bygones be bygones: today we have need of men of your character."[8] But this compromise could be only temporary. While the Vichy state waited for the installation of a police force in conformity with its ideas, its policy toward the existing police can be summed up in four words: threats, promises, competition, reform: "Policemen of the Third Republic, you have much need of forgiveness. Don't forget that new times are coming, and a new order is about to be born. You owe it duty and obedience. I will be pitiless to those among you who are wrongheaded. Be aware that I am watching you!"[9]

The threat could not have been more serious or made more clear. Beginning with the first days of its existence, the Law of July 17 gave the regime the ability to remove, without formality, any civil servant who did not give satisfaction. The first set of removals began in September. Their relative moderation is explained by the new state's need of professionals.[10] In spite of this moderation, and the subsequent rehabilitations that were forced by need, during the following winter *juilletisation* constituted a real threat. The threat, however, was accompanied by promises of reforms that were sufficient to mollify part of the police world. The promised reforms were nationalization, which police officers had been demanding since the beginning of the century and which would relieve them of the burden of municipal supervision, modernization, and substantial improvements in means, wages, and career prospects. Promises and threats alternated with the ceaseless reference to the legitimacy of the government, the explicit calls for obedience, and appeals to the professional culture of the police world, the duty, the discipline, and the necessary respect for a law that sometimes dated from the preceding government. Many of their appeals contributed, with the continuity of missions against the same old adversaries such as the Communists, to providing an illusion of continuity that misled a great many police officers, some of them until the end of the occupation.[11]

Meanwhile, concerned that it could trust neither police officers nor the overall apparatus that it had to preserve for want of anything better, the new government outlined the premises of two longer-term policies. Peyrouton, the minister of the interior, outlined these in a letter to Marshal Pétain on December 17, 1940: "I have organized a national police because I have noted the deficiencies in the electoral police throughout France; more than a month ago I sent a proposal for the nationalization of the police to the occupying authorities."[12] Moreover, since the existing police inspired only relative trust, why not double it with a "parallel" police recruited from men who would mitigate their lack of professionalism by an unstinting fidelity to the new regime? As early as September 1940, a semi-official, partisan organization was created. The *Centre d'information et d'enquête* (CIE) of Colonel Groussard was backed with secret funds and included an information collecting service, the *Service de renseignement* (SR), and an executive arm, the *Groupes de protection* (GP), entrusted to two notorious *cagoulards,* Dr. Martin and Méténier. This organization constituted a semiofficial politcal police in the service of the government. It was charged with collecting information on the population, informing, and surveillance, none of which, it was felt, could be entrusted to the official police force. Collusion with the government was total, and this only served to spread disorder and confusion among professional police officers. Colonel Groussard was appointed *Inspecteur général of the Sûreté nationale,* while a circular of October 16 from the Ministry of the Interior to the prefects outlined the missions of this first parapolice of Vichy: "to inform on activities of any nature that by secretive or open means were likely to impede the activities of government" and "to participate in the maintenance of order and the repression of any trouble that might arise."[13]

The CIE, described by an officer of *Sûreté nationale* as a "band of adventurers," and a "group of spies and cagoulards,"[14] foreshadowed the *polices d'occasion* that became typical of the Vichy government. Entirely in the hands of cagoulards (Groussard, Méténier, Martin, Degans, Darnand) and members of the PPF (Detmar), the CIE included sections specialized in the conflict against "the Anti-France": communists, freemasons, and Jews. These sections were directed by specialists who were always to be found in such conflicts (Detmar, Lécussan, Labat). However, both the CIE and the GP were short-lived. Both were dissolved at the request of the Germans, the former in February 1941, and the latter even earlier, in the preceding December.

Vichy's main intention with regard to the police remained the construction of a modern, numerous police institution, adapted to the government's new missions and comprised of "young men . . . healthy, upright, and without political ties." Circulars from the Ministry of the Interior urged the prefects to direct such young men toward this corps d'élite, in order to "bring an active contribution to national regeneration." The cornerstone of this ambitious reform, entrusted to Peyrouton, was the nationalization of the municipal police that he disparagingly called *polices électorales.*[15] According to its designers, this nationalization (or rather "prefectoralization," a more appropriate term) had four advantages: It would provide a more rational organization by means of unification and centralization, and this would be accompanied by a modernization of means and a substantial increase in the numbers of policemen that would lead to greater effectiveness; the state would now have direct control of the police; police officers themselves would be satisfied, and thus more likely to be loyal and honest; and finally, the organization of the new *Polices régionales d'état* and a massive increase in police numbers would enable the elimination or dispersal of Republican and otherwise doubtful or disobedient officers.

The Construction of an Adapted Instrument and the Time of the "Auxiliary Police Forces," Spring 1941–Spring 1942

The Vichy plan for the reorganization of the police was actually inspired by a project drawn up by the trade union of police *commissaires* during the 1930s. It was drafted by Marquet, the first, transitory minister of the interior of Vichy, and Chavin, the director of the *Sûreté nationale,* completed by Peyrouton, and ready by autumn 1940. But its implementation was delayed since the German occupiers were reluctant to accept it, and the arrest of Laval on December 13 resulted in a change of government personnel, in particular, the departure of Peyrouton. In addition, the rivalry between the prefectoral body and high ranking police officials over the direction of the new police held the project up until well into 1941.[16]

The Third Republic had been unable to nationalize the municipal police forces primarily for ideological and financial reasons. Nationalization constituted the most spectacular step in Vichy's reform. The law of April 23, 1941, that reorganized the police had been recommended and expected by many police officers. It affected all towns with ten thousand or more inhabitants, removing their police from control by the mayor. The regional prefects, established by the law of April 19 and the decree of May 13, 1941, together with the *Intendants* of police who were to assist them, were charged with setting up the police in the twenty new regional districts. Other legislation provided for the creation of the *Ecole nationale supérieure de police* for the training of *commissaires,* of regional schools for members of the new regionally based state police, and of a new civil force for the maintenance of law and order set up by a decree of July 7—*les Groupes Mobiles de Réserve* (GMR). The decree of June 1, 1941, established the *Direction générale de la police nationale.* This replaced the *Direction de la Sûreté nationale* but was a body of much greater significance since it directed the new regional structure. Under the authority of the secretary general for police, three departments shared the three main categories of policing duties: *la Police judiciaire* (Criminal Investigation Department), which became *la Police de sûreté* in October 1942; the *Renseignements généraux* (special branch); and the *Sécurité publique,* which was responsible for police stations, the members of the nationalized municipal police forces, and until they received their own management in 1943, the *Groupes Mobiles de Réserve.*

This reorganization, in particular the nationalization of the municipal police forces, required a massive increase in both policemen and finance. It was also accompanied by material advantages for policemen in the shape of improved wages, allowances and various bonuses, the renovation of police buildings, and so forth, all aimed at attracting recruits of quality and at restoring the prestige of a police organization that the Vichy state intended to turn into a vanguard for the cleansing and renovating tasks that were its main goals for France. But while waiting for these reforms to bear fruit and give rise to the new corps d'élite that Vichy wished, and in order not to leave the monopoly of repression to the Germans, the idea was adopted of doubling the police force by means of deploying special agencies.

The Vichy government was particularly sensitive about the discreet installation of specialized services by the occupying Germans. These services were often composed of French police officers who, on request, had been placed at the Germans' disposal by the French administration. A determination to demonstrate its sovereignty compelled the government to react. The example of the antimasonic police offers a good example of the mechanisms and competitions at work.

On April 1, 1941, following the request of Lieutenant Stüber, the *Service spécial des associations dissoutes* was created by the Prefecture of Police. Occupying the buildings of the old Theosophic Society, in Rapp Square, it functioned first with twenty, then forty police officers detached by the prefecture. They were placed, as specified in a German report dated February 25, 1942, addressed to Von Stulpnagel, under German responsibility and control.[17] This was an unacceptable situation for the French authorities who had created their own antimasonic police in Vichy in May 1941.[18] Installed at 11, rue Hubert Colombier, this organization was directly financed by the civil cabinet of Pétain and initially directed by a *contrôleur général* of *Sûreté nationale*. In August, "on account of the general absence of results," it was entrusted to Lieutenant Commander Robert Labat, a former member of the CIE. The *Service des sociétés secrètes* (SSS), as this organization was known, was responsible for enforcing antimasonic legislation. It was mentioned by Pétain in his short broadcast speech of August 12, 1941: "I have created a special police whose task is to break the resistance that abuse of legal regulations, bureaucracy, or the activities of secret societies can mount to our national regeneration." An attempt to extend the SSS to the whole of France revealed the high stakes and the competition that embroiled the Vichy government, the extremists of collaboration, French police officers, and the German forces of occupation in the field of policing. At the end of November 1941, German agreement was obtained to subordinate to the Ministry of the Interior those French police officers working under German control.[19] Vichy tried to exploit this with the decree of December 15 creating a branch of the SSS in the Occupied Zone.[20] The direction of this branch, to reassure the Germans, was entrusted to a notorious collaborator, Jean Marquès-Rivière. But the Germans were not to be deceived by the maneuver. They very clearly, and on several occasions, refused to recognize the existence of the SSS in the Occupied Zone. They considered it superfluous because of the existence of the organization in Rapp Square.[21]

There was a similar competition with reference to the treatment of the Jews. After the adoption of the second *Statut des juifs* on June 2, 1941, the S.S. Chief Dannecker had secured the creation of a service made up of a dozen police officers detached from the Paris prefecture, directed by *Commissaire* Schweblin, a fanatical anti-Semite from Alsace. This French police agency worked in close collaboration with Service IV J installed at Avenue Foch and was completely independent of the *Commissariat général aux questions juives* (CGQJ) created by Vichy in March 1941. Xavier Vallat, the head of the CGQJ, tried constantly to get his own anti-Jewish police made responsible for researching infringements of the June statute. His efforts finally achieved success with a decree, which was not published in *The Official Journal,* of October 19, 1941; but because the article was not published and thus the Germans didn't know about the existence of the law, it only served to generate permanent friction with German agencies and the official French police.

Pucheu, who was appointed minister of the interior in the autumn of 1941, was obsessed with not yielding any prerogative regarding the repression of the "common enemies"—Jews, communists, and freemasons. He was very close to the PPF and the *Comité des forges,* and he completely mistrusted former police personnel.[22] The doctrine that he solemnly recalled in Paris at the beginning of 1942—at the height of the conflict with the Germans over the question of the extension into the northern zone of the antimasonic police of Labat—was clear: "the maintenance of public order, indispensable to national life, must be assured by French hands, French arms, and French heads."[23] But the ability to dispute systematically with the occupiers over the exercise of repression foundered on both the absence of autonomous French instruments adapted to this policy and the Germans' skepticism.[24]

It was to make up for the incapacity of the official police[25] to fulfill the special missions demanded by government[26] that Vichy proceeded to the installation of a triptych of *polices auxiliaires* specialized in the fight against the Anti-France: the *Service de police anticommuniste* (SPAC), the *Service de police des sociétés secrètes* (SSS), and the *Police aux questions juives* (PQJ). Established in parallel with the new National Police, structured around a few dozen officers from the *Sûreté nationale* or the Prefecture of Police and primarily recruited from among the senior officers of the CIE, these auxiliary police differed from the official police by their determination in hunting for the "perpetual enemies."[27] But the creation of these special police was disliked and opposed by official police officers. As Colonel Groussard, the creator of the CIE, noted: "The traditional police don't look kindly on the structure of the new organization and have even insisted that the GP should be put at the disposition of the police authorities."[28] The paramount preoccupation of an institution jealous of its prerogatives was to seek to eliminate competitors. As soon as the PQJ was created in October

1941, problems arose over its relationship with official police services. To meet with the concerns of the administration but also to seek to establish some control over this auxiliary service, Rivalland, the *secrétaire général à la police,* dispatched multiple circulars to the regional prefects and the *intendants* of police. In these circulars he took care to specify that the role of the agents of this auxiliary police, recruited directly by and responsible to the CGQJ, was limited to the investigation of infringements of the statute of June 2 and communicating such to the official police services. Similar circulars were issued with reference to the SSS and the SPAC. But attempts to bring the auxiliary police under the control of the Ministry of the Interior and the general secretariat of the police were successful only with the restoration of Laval to power.

The Policy of Administrative and National Reconquest and Its Consequences, May 1942–December 1943

In spring 1942 the situation changed dramatically with the return of Laval to power. His culture and his past as a statesman had left him prepared to use systems that he knew and appreciated. Furthermore, his temperament drove him to be wary of the partisan initiatives of his predecessors.[29] He replaced "fanatical" admirals and amateurs and appointed in their places reliable civil servants. Bussière, the former director of the *Sûreté nationale* under Marx Dormoy, took over the Prefecture of Police, and René Bousquet who, in spite of his youth, had important administrative experience, took over as the General Secretariat of Police. Bousquet was as prepared as Pucheu to argue with the Germans about the exercise of repression, but equipped as he was with a different culture and with experience of the *Sûreté nationale,*[30] he sought a double reconquest in the field of repression: a national reconquest, at the expense of the Germans, especially in the Occupied Zone where it was important to affirm the sovereignty of Vichy, and an administrative reconquest, reconsolidating the diffusion of power established with the parallel police structure set up in 1941. This policy, which was in keeping with his personal ambitions, was facilitated first by the fact that the reforms of April 1941 were finally beginning to bear fruit, and second by a change in tactics on the part of the Germans.[31] The substitution of the *Wehrmacht* by the *Sipo-Sd* in the spring of 1942 for the exercise of policing powers in occupied France resulted in a change of policy. As SS General Oberg said at his trial: "it was in our interest that the French police should be united in one hand." Under the joint pressure of the needs of the war in Russia and the "final solution," Heydrich and his subordinates, Oberg and Knochen, decided to play the card of collaboration between police.[32] This suited perfectly with French interests, while the Germans considered that they gained more than they lost.

From the German point of view, entrusting more autonomy and responsibility to the French police was not much of a risk, and it offered considerable advantages, such as the possibility of concealing themselves behind police teams more respectable than agencies like a French Gestapo. This collaboration had two significant outcomes: It compromised French police officers by requiring a more positive engagement from them, and it meant a considerable saving in German manpower with a corresponding increased effectiveness. On May 15, 1942, shortly after his conversations with Heydrich, Bousquet explained to the regional prefects of the Occupied Zone "that it is necessary to show that the French police is not failing and perhaps, in the future, the police will acquire more power." There were serious consequences; under the pretext of French sovereignty, the French police were now required to serve German interests. In order to win the trust of the occupier and to reduce the profile of the auxiliary police, it was necessary to give pledges concerning the effectiveness and goodwill of French police officers and official departments. It meant that the official French police acquired the responsibility for the repressive tasks hitherto undertaken by the auxiliary police and the Germans. As Bousquet wrote Oberg on June 18, 1942: "You know the French police force well. It undoubtedly has its defects, but also its qualities. I am persuaded that once reorganized on new bases, and vigorously directed, it will prove extremely useful. Already in many cases, you have noted the effectiveness of its action. I am certain that it can do still better."[33]

The national and administrative reconquest desired by Bousquet and Laval was carried out at the cost of the proliferation in the number of specialized police services like that of the Jewish Affairs created at the direction of the *Police judiciare* within the Prefecture of Police, or the *Sections des affaires politiques* of the *Sûreté nationale* created in the autumn of 1942.[34] These were services in which material advantages and fast promotions fostered "effectiveness." Suffering from a clear case of "Bridge on the River Kwai syndrome," the secretary general of the police explained to the departmental prefects the necessity for the French police to achieve results.

> It will not have escaped you that even if the note from General Oberg has given the French police the means of action that it did not have before (as much on the moral as the material plane), it is important that the police demonstrate their real worth, by even greater activity and the results they will achieve. It is up to you to give the vigorous impetus that, like me, you feel is essential in the present circumstances.

As Robert Paxton has noted, this policy of unceasing administrative presence fostered an anti-Jewish activism.[35] The test of commitment was the arrest by French police officers and gendarmes, acting on their own, of several thousand foreign-born or stateless Jews in the occupied and nonoccupied zones during July and

August 1942. General Oberg's good report of this operation was accompanied by gestures of goodwill such as the extension, in October 1942, of the reform of 1941 into the Occupied Zone.[36] The Germans, for their part, found clear advantages: "If in France we could have fewer police [than in Belgium and Holland], it is because there was an established government and an official police force instead of an auxiliary police force as in the other countries."[37]

However, if this collaboration produced tangible results, it also fostered resistance, inertia, passivity, and sabotage by those French police officers less and less enthusiastic about the nature of their new missions and well aware of the military evolution of the war. Some continued to pursue those whom Buffet, their former colleague appointed director of *Police de Sûreté*, referred to in June 1944 as "criminals [who] attached a political or patriotic label to themselves, to mask their misdeeds." But the police success looked increasingly poor measured against the zeal and the activism of the *Milice* with its ideological soundness. The upshot was that Bousquet was replaced by Darnand, not so much because the former had been a disappointment but because the latter was considered to be able to do still better.

Final Toughening, January–Summer 1944

The extremists of collaboration were largely in agreement with the report on the attitude of the police drawn up on All Saints' Day 1943 by Admiral Charles Platon, chief of the SSS:

> The forces of order are unreliable, impotent, mired in an incapacity to act by regulations made for happier times when it was enough to show force in order not to have to use it . . . the consequence is that the only notable security operations in France that have been effective up to now were carried out either by French irregular forces unknown to, or not recognized by, the French government, or by the German authorities.[38]

The conclusion was clear: It was necessary to replace the French police, who "too often did nothing with information other than use it to let culprits flee," with a reliable force that was devoted to the marshal and the national revolution and that would not be troubled by legal niceties.

The *Milice française* was created in January 1943. On April 29 Pétain affirmed that the *Milice* "must constitute the essential force for conducting the fight against hidden powers [and] be invested with the missions of a vanguard, in particular, those relating to the achievement of law and order . . . [and] to the fight against Communism." The *Milice* seemed able to achieve the repressive tasks that the police appeared more and more openly reluctant to undertake. It was directed by the former cagoulard Joseph Darnand, now, perhaps, the most faithful and committed of all to the Vichy regime. It competed more and more openly with the police; friction and clashes between the two institutions became numerous.[39] At the end of 1943, Darnand was given responsibility for the maintenance of law and order, and thus it was that the *Milice* inherited the direction of all the forces of repression. Vichy's choice well suited the Nazis.

As early as May 1943, in spite of the strong impression that the secretary general of police had made on Himmler,[40] Oberg planned to replace Bousquet and to entrust repression to "a movement showing major affinities with the SS and able to give a new impulse to the French police." Bousquet continued to demonstrate honesty[41] and loyalty to the regime,[42] but, nevertheless, during the summer he declared that "any militiaman who devotes himself to a police operation or an operation of provocation must be immediately stopped." In December Darnand replaced Bousquet and took over as head of what became the *Secrétariat général au maintien de l'ordre.* The decree of January 10, 1944, specified that "by delegation of the chief of the government, the Minister of the Interior, Joseph Darnand, *Secrétaire général au maintien de l'ordre,* has authority over the whole of the police, personnel, and services, responsible for the public safety and the interior safety of the state." This nomination was to be the final misfortune for the policing policies of a French state that was now no more than a facade behind which the most extremist currents of collaboration clashed.

The legal barriers that Pétain and Platon had denounced in August 1942 and November 1943 respectively and that constituted obstacles to repression were now removed. Changes of methods and changes of men characterized the last months of the occupation. The *Milice* condemned the weakness and the formal legalism of the police as barriers to repressive action. It denounced the passivity, the two-timing, the wait-and-see policies, the sabotage, even treason of police officers. Now it took repression in hand; there would be no more two-timing, no more caution, complicity, or "legality." Henceforth, all means available were to be permitted in the struggle against bad Frenchmen, terrorists, and traitors. New teams and new men, most of them coming from the *Milice,* but also from formations like the PPF, and with a sprinkling of a few police officers zealous, compromised, or blinded, took over the direction of new departments such as the *Délégations régionales des Renseignements Généraux* (the famous Poinsot brigades). This body was created in the spring of 1944 and, like the two *Brigades Spéciales* of the *Direction des Renseignements Généraux* of the Prefecture of Police, it launched repressive missions based on the information accumulated in the RG files.

The determination of the *Secrétaire général au maintien de l'ordre* to limit the capacities of traditional administration—the creation of an *Inspection générale au maintien de l'ordre,* the reorganization of the central administration of the RG under *Milice* direction, the transformation of the *Intendants de police* into *Intendants du maintien de l'ordre,* the appointment of men from the *Milice* as *intendants*—demonstrated that the whole machinery of policing was directed to waging a pitiless war hand in hand with the German occupiers. Many police officers, rightly or wrongly suspected of double-dealing or resistance, were arrested, tortured, or sent to concentration camps. "Adapted" legislation, in particular a decree of April 1, 1944, authorized the creation of special courts to try treacherous police officers, while the dismissals of the unreliable elements or the partisans of a wait-and-see policy increased. At the same time, a special decision of the *Secrétariat général au maintien de l'ordre* meant that ordinary police officers who had demonstrated zeal and activity against terrorists and criminal, antinational elements were rewarded with exceptional promotion, while militiamen and the more effective elements of the parallel and auxiliary police organizations (the SEC, which succeeded the PQJ, and the SRMAN, which succeeded the SPAC) were integrated with the National Police. The takeover of the police and the occupation of strategic positions by fanatics and extremists of the collaboration and the proliferation of special departments (special brigades of the *Milice,* the Poinsot brigades) resulted in missions and practices drifting apart. In an atmosphere of civil war, nothing impeded these new police officers, and in certain regions, the *Milice* dream of a police state turned into a nightmare for others.

The *Milice* state that Vichy became at the last, and the crimes committed by auxiliary police in the service of the Gestapo, made it possible for members of the official police to assert after the war that the official police institution had never compromised with the requirements and the missions of the new political order. It also provided the opportunity for people in charge, such as Bousquet, to present themselves as successful impediments to an extremist drift until the changes of 1944. These arguments did not carry the same weight for all those who were asked for explanations.[43]

Nevertheless, whatever the interpretation given to the attitude of the police during the occupation, the period of Vichy did constitute a break in the history of the French police. The durable legislation of the spring of 1941 brought significant changes in organization, professional culture, and manpower, with a profound renewal that resulted from massive recruitment rather than purges. The drifting apart of missions and practices, the shipwreck of Republican principles, the recognition of the price of the zeal and the risks produced by professional values of policemen were all to have lasting effects as the Fourth Republic was to discover to its cost. Moreover, in terms of image, the police forces of Pétain contributed in no small measure to the unflattering perception that the French public still has of the French police.

Notes

1. On these problems, see Berlière, *Le monde des Polices,* 163 et seq.

2. Du Moulin de la Barthète, *Le temps des illusions,* 295.

3. Berlière, "La généalogie d'une double tradition policière."

4. "Ces gens-là sont sérieux," Charles Maurras allegedly said, shortly after Syveton's death. Action Française always regarded this as a police and Masonic crime. For this obsession, see the work of Léon Daudet, in particular *La police politique,* and compare with the book of one of those responsible for this "caverne de voleurs et d'assassins"—Louis Ducloux, *Du chantage à la trahison.*

5. Among these men were Raphaël Alibert, minister of justice; Gabriel Jeantet, *inspecteur général à la propagande;* Xavier Vallat, future *Commissaire aux questions juives;* Colonel Groussard, appointed *Inspecteur général de la Sûreté nationale* in September 1940; François Méténier, future chief of the *Groupes de protection du Centre d'information et d'enquête* (CIE); Captain Labat, in charge of the *Service des sociétés secrètes;* Doctor Martin, chief of the SR of the CIE; and Joseph Darnand, in charge of this same CIE in Nice before becoming the chief of the *Milice* and *Secrétaire général au maintien de l'ordre.* This does not include the cagoulards or the individuals linked with the *Cagoule* within the sphere of power from the first days of Vichy. In addition, a number of these men owed their release from prison to the defeat and collapse of the Republic.

6. "C'est à la police que l'Etat, ébranlé dans ses assises sociale et politique, aux deux tiers occupé, devra son redressement national" (note probably dating from the summer of 1940, Archives Nationales (AN), 2AG 520 CC 104 A).

7. Quoted by Sabah, *Une police politique,* 233.

8. Remarks made during the evening of July 10, 1940 in front of the Hotel du Parc by Doriot and Méténier with Jules Belin—one of the "aces" of the Sûreté who had pursued the men of the *Cagoule* and contributed to the arrest of the assassins of the Rosselli brothers (Belin, *Trente ans de Sûreté Nationale,* 322).

9. Speech of Colonel Groussard on taking up his functions as Inspecteur général de la Sûreté nationale, quoted by Belin, *Trente ans,* 317.

10. The removals primarily involved old police officers and concerned those accused of incompetence and professional misconduct rather than trade union or political affiliations. On police purges and the renewal of the personnel under the occupation, see Berlière, "IIIᵉ République, Vichy, Occupation, Libération."

11. Communists were pursued under the Daladier decree issued shortly after the Nazi-Soviet Pact on September 26, 1939.

12. AN 3W 310.

13. *Journal officiel,* 5 October 1940.

14. Quotations in Belin, 316.

15. The expression is in the letter of Peyrouton to Pétain, 17 December 1940, AN 3W 310.

16. Baruch, *Servir l'Etat français,* 378 et seq.

17. Quoted by Sabah, 436.

18. "Aussi regrettable que soit cette constatation, il est de fait que la création du SSS est due à une pression des autorités allemandes qui seules jusque là avaient opéré contre la franc-maçonnerie" (report of Labat, chief of the SSS, summer of 1941, quoted by Sabah, 370 et seq.).

19. The talks were carried out with Dr. Best.

20. This decree was not published in the *Journal Officiel* but supplemented by a circular on December 19, 1941.

21. German report of 25 December 1941 quoted by Sabah, 434; and in Marquès-Rivière to Bousquet, May 1942 (AN F7 15345).

22. He endeavored to secure them by various measures such as an oath imposed on all the police officers and especially by a second wave of revocations, much more severe than that of the autumn of 1940, and aimed particularly at the police officers who were freemasons from the summer of 1941. Conversely, an attempt to reform the Prefecture de Police, and to bring it under more direct control, failed.

23. A short speech made at the time of the oath of service taken by the Parisian police officers, January 20, 1942, at the Palais de Chaillot (*Bulletin hebdomadaire du ministère de l'Intérieur,* no. 74, 27 January 1942).

24. "L'expérience qu'on a eue jusqu'ici avec la police juive française, montre amplement avec quelle indolence les milieux responsables français soutiennent la lutte contre les adversaires de toujours" (report quoted earlier concerning the antimasonic police, 25, December 1941). Similar reservations were expressed by Dannecker, for example that the French police "did not understand anything regarding the Jewish question."

25. This was aggravated by a succession of difficulties and delays in implementing the reforms of the spring of 1941, not least because of persistent difficulties over recruitment and German reluctance: Nationalization and the reforms of spring 1941 were applied in the northern zone starting from the decree of October 27, 1942 only. For local examples of the difficulty of implementing the law of April 23, 1941, see Berlière and Peschanski, eds., *La police,* passim.

26. "La Sûreté nationale a montré depuis la loi du 13 août 1940 portant dissolution des sociétés secrètes qu'elle n'était pas en mesure, eu égard à l'état d'esprit général du personnel, de poursuivre l'application de cette loi dans le sens nettement précisé par le Maréchal" (from the Labat report quoted earlier, note 18). This problem is generally explained by the number of police officers belonging to the Freemasons: "pour qu'une action soit réellement efficace, il faut procéder à l'examen des dossiers en commençant par la police (quoted by Sabah, 479). One finds the same analysis from the pen of Moritz who directed the service in Rapp Square: "the various services of the police force in charge of the Masonic questions were for the most part made up of freemasons" (quoted by Sabah, 79, n. 133).

27. Moritz who "ne [s']oppose pas à l'emploi de fonctionnaires français appartenant à l'ancien GP du capitaine Méténier (sic) a pu constater à plusieurs reprises que les anciens GP étaient les seuls éléments anti-maçonniques parmi les fonctionnaires français" (Ibid.).

28. Groussard, *Services secrets.*

29. "Est-ce ma faute si les gouvernants novices ou réactionnaires qui se sont succédé en France depuis que l'on m'a chassé, le 13 décembre 1940, ont pris quelque peu modèle sur les institutions totalitaires?" (quoted by Clermont, *L'homme qu'il fallait tuer,* 91).

30. Bousquet, linked with radicals and freemasons in the southwest, had held a number of administrative posts during the 1930s. He was the head of the *grand fichier central* of the Sûreté in 1936, during the ministries of Albert Sarraut and Roger Salengro.

31. Bousquet was thirty-four years old in 1943 and, in addition to the police, he was in charge of the *Gendarmerie nationale,* prison administration, the economic control service, and the protection of communication routes. He concentrated greater power in his hands than Fouché could have hoped for.

32. However, even at the best moments of police collaboration, this did not prevent mistrust, expressed in particular by the control exerted over all the sensitive nominations and promotions to the senior positions in the police hierarchy, the reluctance to arm heavily the GMR, and the persistent use of auxiliaries drawn from collaborationist movements and the criminal underworld in services completely escaping the French authority, such as the "French Gestapo," in the rue Lauriston.

33. AN WIII-89, quoted in Klarsfeld, *Vichy-Auschwitz,* 211.

34. On these special services and on the drift of the old "Brigades mobiles de police judiciaire," the model for a Republican police according to Clemenceau, see Berlière, "La seule police," 311–23.

35. Paxton, "La spécificité," 605–19. During the preparation for his trial in the High Court in August 1948, Bousquet presented this policy as "un acte de sauvegarde et de défense des intérêts français."

36. Oberg wrote on to Bousquet on July 23: "Je vous confirme bien volontiers que la police française a réalisé jusqu'ici une tâche digne d'éloge" (quoted in Klarsfeld, *Le calendrier,* 259).

37. Deposition of Knochen, September 1948 (file of the Bousquet case, quoted by Froment, *Rene Bousquet,* 221). In the autumn of 1941, the relevant German personnel in Occupied France numbered only twenty-nine hundred, fewer than in the Netherlands (Paxton, *Annales,* 615, n. 25).

38. Report to Marshall Pétain (AN 2AG 616, no. 570, quoted by Sabah, 221).

39. *Commissaire* David, head of the *Brigade spéciale anticommuniste* of the Prefecture of Police, declared at his trial, without being contradicted, that he had told his men "d'abattre comme un chien tout milicien français qui gênerait leur action" ("to shoot down like a dog any French militia who would hamper their activities/investigations").

40. "The *Reichsführer* was impressed by the personality of Bousquet. He manifestly shares the opinions expressed by Oberg: Namely that Bousquet is an invaluable collaborator for police work and that he would be a dangerous adversary if he were pushed into another camp" (AN, W III 89, quoted by Klarsfeld, *Vichy-Auschwitz,* 54).

41. At a meeting in Vichy in April 1943, he ordered the *intendants* of police "to

eliminate without pity all incompetents and to intern those who lacked honesty." Furthermore he outlined "the rules to apply . . . get rid of the incapable immediately, laziness can be dealt with in the long term, but the filth must be punished."

42. In the autumn of 1943, while protesting the lack of autonomy and armament entrusted to the French police by the Germans, he informed Oberg of the creation of the *secrétariat général au maintien de l'ordre* and the installation of courts-martial and special courts to accelerate and deregulate the repression of the common enemies—Communists, terrorists, and saboteurs. Oberg responded in similar vein: "in the new Europe, the criminal and political criminal will not be able to disturb the work of regenerating the people."

43. On this subject see Berlière, *Les policiers français sous l'Occupation.*

CHAPTER 15

Political Justice in the Netherlands: The Instrumentalization of the Judicial System during the German Occupation, 1940–1945

GERALDIEN VON FRIJTAG DRABBE KÜNZEL

Introduction

Before the German attack on the Netherlands on May 10, 1940, the judicial system in the Netherlands had been a perfect example of how a system should be within a modern, democratic, liberal constitution: Montesquieu's notion of the separation of powers, *trias politica,* had been evident. The Dutch judiciary performed the duty of a controller of the executive. The other organs of this judicial system—police and public prosecutor—were supervised by the minister of justice.

There had not been much judicial repression in the prewar Netherlands. Strict rules applied to investigation and prosecution: The use of coercion or physical violence during interrogation, for instance, was strictly forbidden. Legal assistance was provided for all and at all stages of the legal procedure. Also, the death penalty had been banned from the Dutch penal code. As social tensions were almost absent and severe social disturbances were quite uncommon, the social climate could be defined as mild.

Hitler's *Machtübernahme* in Germany, in January 1933, did not affect the Dutch situation. Only a few Dutch lawyers sympathized with the ideology of the new German regime and the way its policy changed the German legal profession.[1] The outbreak of the war in Europe in September 1939 caused a rise in the number of convictions in the Netherlands, but this had been due largely to the growing number of violations of new legislation on the matter of rationing. As a result of limited trade since September, some foods, like sugar, had become scarce in the Netherlands. Therefore, the Dutch state had started a policy of rationing. A growing number of foods could be bought and sold only as rationed. Buying and selling without coupons had become penal offenses. The scarcity that emerged, however, also had given rise to breaches of these new regulations. The perpetrators were sentenced by the Dutch courts.[2]

Thus, with the exception of black market–related offenses, the crime rate remained low. Serious criminal acts, disturbances of the public order, and political revolts seldom occurred. Clashes between political groups, as there had been in Germany in the beginning of the 1930s, did not take place. A special apparatus for oppressing and punishing political opposition—such as the German *Geheime Staatspolizei* (Gestapo) or special German courts like the *Volksgerichtshof* and the *Sondergerichte*—did not exist in the prewar Netherlands. Although both the public prosecutor and the police were controlled and to some extent directed by the government (via the minister of justice), the Dutch judicial system as a whole remained politically neutral.

How did this situation change after the German attack? How did the German occupation affect the Dutch judicial system, and how did this system change? Was there a radical break in comparison with the prewar years?

In this article I intend to show that the Dutch judicial system was transformed profoundly during the years of occupation. On the one hand, the existing Dutch system lost much of its sovereignty vis-à-vis the German regime. On the other hand, a new German judicial system, set up by this same regime, started to work alongside the existing Dutch system. This German system became a most effective tool of repression. How this situation came into existence and how it evolved during the occupation are the two main questions to be answered in this article.

The First Nine Months: The Introduction of New Rules and New Courts

In the nine months that followed the German attack on the Netherlands, the Dutch were confronted by some minor, yet telling, changes in the area of justice. First, the Dutch got acquainted with new German agencies and authorities. The Gestapo, for example, started to arrest Dutch citizens almost immediately. During the summer of 1940, dozens of men and women who had allegedly displayed anti-German behavior prior to May 10, 1940 were arrested and transported across the border. Once in Germany, some of them were tried before German courts.[3]

At the same time, as had happened in other occupied parts of Europe,[4] the highest German military command issued an order whereby a German penal code and German military courts (*Feldgerichte*) were introduced.[5] The jurisdiction of these *Feldgerichte* was wide as a variety of acts became punishable from

May 10, 1940 onward, ranging from insulting a German soldier and listening to foreign radio broadcasts to espionage, high treason, and other acts in support of the enemy. These military courts could punish suspects severely. The death penalty was reintroduced.

In fact, already during the summer and early autumn of 1940, some hundreds of Dutch citizens had been sentenced by a *Feldgericht.*[6] Some were convicted because they had tried to flee to England. Others were sentenced for having cut telephone lines and electricity cables that were used by German agencies. Most of the suspects, though, were punished because they had insulted a German. Penalties were harsh, sometimes totally out of proportion by Dutch standards. Thus, for example, a young man who had used an elastic band to shoot a small needle in the direction of a German soldier was sentenced to prison for two months.[7]

More would change after the appointment of Arthur Seyss-Inquart as *Reichskommissar* for the occupied Netherlands.[8] Seyss-Inquart was a lawyer and Nazi Party dignitary who had played a prominent role in the Austrian *Anschluss* in 1938, in particular by providing a semilegal basis for the Anschluss. He also had experience with governing in occupied territory as he had worked with Hans Frank in the occupied zone of Poland called the *Generalgouvernement.* As soon as he arrived in the Netherlands it became clear that Seyss-Inquart had a special interest in justice: In contrast to his colleagues abroad like Reichskommissar Josef Terboven in Norway,[9] he rearranged things in this field at once. His aims were evident: on the one hand, a continuation of the Dutch administration of justice on the condition that this administration be supervised by German authorities; on the other hand, the creation of a German apparatus that would protect the German supremacy in the Netherlands by hunting down and punishing those who opposed the occupation.

To that end, first, restraints were put on the "old" Dutch judicial system. Seyss-Inquart's first order (May 29, 1940) made clear that he expected Dutch judges to follow his legislation to the letter. He also prohibited the administration of justice "in the name of the Queen." Henceforth, justice had to be rendered "in the name of the law."[10] In the fall Jews were banned from the legal profession. At the same time three non-Jewish attorneys general, the highest authorities of the Dutch Department of Prosecution, were replaced by members of the Dutch Nazi Party.[11] Furthermore, Seyss-Inquart stated that Dutch judgments in certain cases would need to be confirmed by him before they could be executed. And finally, he restricted the scope of the jurisdiction of Dutch courts: Offenses committed by or directed against a German citizen could no longer be investigated by Dutch policemen or tried by Dutch judges.[12]

These cases had to be handed over to the Gestapo. New German nonmilitary courts were set up to try these cases: *Landesgerichte* and *Obergerichte,* two courts that also had jurisdiction over Dutch citizens who acted against the Greater German Reich (*Großdeutsches Reich*), the German people, the Nazi Party, or German citizens. The same applied to those accused of crimes that were considered a "threat to the common good" (*gemeingefährlich*) by which was also meant deeds that had a negative effect on the Dutch economy.

It was to be expected that these two German courts in particular were to become instruments of political oppression. Until the public revolt of February 1941, however, their work was marginal. The first cases were tried in August 1940.[13] One of the suspects was a Dutch drunkard who had insulted the *Wehrmacht* by suggesting that the attack on the Netherlands was a criminal act. The *Landesgericht* sentenced him to prison for two and a half years. In the remaining months of 1940, the Landesgericht issued judgments in approximately one hundred cases; the *Obergericht* in not more than seven cases.

The Strike in Amsterdam and Its Aftermath: The Birth of Political Justice, 1941–1943

Even though the number of cases tried by these two German courts was still small, the judicial system in the Netherlands had started to change within a few months after the attack. The Dutch judiciary lost its independence, or at least some of it. At the same time, political opposition was criminalized, and to investigate and punish these new crimes, German organs of police and justice were introduced.

This process of alteration was accelerated by two extremely violent days in early 1941, when popular discontent with the new situation was shown in both a clear and violent way. The German police and military used a heavy hand to end the revolt.[14] After that short period of unrest the German coercion grew. Two specific groups of the Dutch population became the main targets of German aggression during the next two years: Jews and, since the German attack on the Soviet Union in June 1941, Dutch Communists.

In these two years the Dutch judicial system had to put up with new German interferences. For example, a new type of Dutch court was set up by the German regime: the so-called courts of peace. A Dutch citizen accused of having insulted or attacked a Dutch Nazi could be brought before this new type of Dutch court. Although the Dutch legal profession protested, it could not prevent the arrival of these new courts.[15]

During the same period the two already mentioned German courts came into their own. Cases against Dutch civilians increased rapidly. In 1942, for example, the *Landesgericht* tried more than 2,800 cases; the *Obergericht* about 250.[16] The procedure in these cases could differ. Asked about their impression of the German courts, some Dutch people stated after the war that their treatment had been quite normal, as it would have been in cases tried by a Dutch court. Others, though, said they had never seen a lawyer and had been maltreated during their interrogation and during their time in prison.[17]

The sentences varied too. The Landesgericht tried the most cases, but these cases were also less serious. This is reflected in the sentences. Most suspects in Landesgericht cases were sentenced to prison.[18] The Obergericht dealt with the more serious cases. This court also sentenced convicts to death.[19] As a part of German policy, these more severe cases and sentences were often published. The Dutch press received strict orders from the German authorities on which cases should be reported and which sentences should be made publicly known. Clearly the intention was to deter other Dutch citizens from criminal and political acts.

Hundreds of verdicts of the Obergericht have been preserved. An analysis of the motivation of this court's verdicts demonstrates how the judges, or at least the Nazified ones, thought. Predominant is the idea of society (*Volksgemeinschaft*) prevailing over individuals. In short, those among the accused whom the court regarded as threatening to the political regime and the Volksgemeinschaft were to be eliminated (*ausgemerzt*). In one case, for example, three burglars were condemned to death. The German court supported its decision by pointing out that these three were antisocial citizens (*asoziale Elemente)* who had never been of any use to the Volksgemeinschaft. Such people, the court concluded, had no right to exist (*keine Existenzberechtigung).*[20]

It is remarkable that these courts hardly played a role in the German racial policy. Cases against Jews or those married to Jews were rare. The persecution of Jews in the Netherlands seems to have been an exclusive matter of the German police.[21]

Nevertheless, the role of these two German courts in fighting political opposition was in some ways limited. The severe cases against members of the resistance were outnumbered by cases dealing with more modest crimes like stealing from a German soldier or insulting a German citizen. Moreover, these two courts did not have a monopoly in punishing opponents of the regime. Political cases were also brought before the German military courts (the already mentioned Feldgerichte) since these courts were entitled to sentence acts "in favor of the enemy" (*Feindbegünstigung*), which could be interpreted as almost anything.

Even more important is that the Gestapo also had quasi-judicial powers. The Gestapo could simply refuse to bring a suspect before a court. In that case, the suspect stayed in the hands of the Gestapo and received what could be called quasi-judicial punishment. In practice, this often meant that he was sent off "until further notice" (*bis auf Weiteres*) to concentration camps under protective custody (*Schutzhaft*).

The Gestapo gained more and more power after the spring of 1941, and its predominance in the field of repression grew stronger. As was already stated, the persecution of Jews in the Netherlands was directed and executed by the Gestapo. The same could be said about the tracking down of Dutch Communists and other "enemies" of the political regime. The methods of the Gestapo (the use of coercion, violence, and spies) were to become notorious. However, it should be stressed that, at least during the first part of the German occupation, the Gestapo could count on some assistance from Dutch authorities and individuals. Based on the files of about two hundred cases that were brought before the *Obergericht*, it can be stated that in most of the more severe political cases, in particular cases against Communists, denunciation and spying by Dutch citizens had led to the tracking down of suspects and the breaking up of resistance groups. Some of these Dutch "assistants" were professionals (*Vertrauensmänner*) and were employed by the Gestapo. Others were motivated by various reasons. Some saw it as their duty as good citizens or good servants to inform the police. Others hoped to profit financially: Denunciation could be attractive as the Gestapo frequently rewarded the denouncers.[22]

Personal resentment and frustration could also play a part. In one case, for instance, a father wanted to teach his obstinate son a lesson by telling the German police of his son's political activities. He had hoped a week or so in a German jail would discipline his disobedient son. But things got totally out of his control once the Gestapo started the investigation. Repeatedly, the father tried to get his son set free; without success, however. On top of the months in custody, the son was sentenced by the German *Obergericht* to prison for two years.[23]

Of great importance too was the willingness, especially initially, of the Dutch administration to cooperate. This is particularly the case with regard to the Secretary-General. As the stand-in for the minister, his task was to direct and to supervise the Dutch police and the Public Department of Prosecution. During the first nine months after the German attack, this position was held by J. C. Tenkink. Although not sympathizing with the Nazi ideology, Tenkink accepted German rule and instructed his civil servants accordingly because he feared that, if the Dutch did not cooperate but instead fought German rule, the influence of the Dutch authorities would only diminish in favor of German power and even more would change. In the spring of 1941, however, Tenkink could no longer cope with German policies and resigned. J. J. Schrieke, a prominent Dutch Nazi, was appointed by Seyss-Inquart. From then on the German regime had a very compliant authority as its Dutch counterpart.[24]

Radicalizing the System: The Rise of the Gestapo, 1943–1944

During the two years that followed the revolt in February 1941, the German regime strengthened its grip on the Dutch judicial system. At the same time, a German judicial system, which had already been set up in 1940, showed its political might in these two years, by implementing the German policy of oppression and by fighting and punishing those who opposed the new order. Although the leading role was played by German organs (Gestapo and German courts), there was some assistance by Dutch authorities, agencies, and citizens.

The relatively compliant attitude of the Dutch diminished, however, as German coercion grew. This became evident in 1943. Faced with enormous losses on the eastern front and shortages of manpower in German industry, Berlin decided to bring in foreign workers on a much larger scale. In this year the regime in the Netherlands, being instructed accordingly, started to force Dutch men to work in Germany (*Arbeitseinsatz*). The Arbeitseinsatz in the Netherlands was not restricted to specific groups as had been the case with the persecution of Jews and Communists. Quite the contrary, the Arbeitseinsatz affected almost every Dutch family. Ordinary citizens began to suffer from the German coercion. As a result of this, the willingness to cooperate also decreased drastically.[25]

One event in the beginning of May 1943 illustrated this development. A German order to all members of the disbanded Dutch army to report for internment as prisoners of war was linked by the Dutch population with the policy of Arbeitseinsatz. Thousands laid down their work in protest at this measure.[26] The strikes were isolated and therefore relatively easy to fight. Again, the judicial system was adapted to the new situation. Seyss-Inquart introduced a new kind of court: the *Polizeistandgericht* (Summary Police Court). In May 1943 this German court tried offenses that breached summary law. In theory, anyone who breached the public order was to face the death penalty. The justice administered by this Summary Police Court was, in part, the justice of laymen, for the tribunal consisted of a presiding SS judge and two accompanying SS officers. A great many people were brought before this new type of court, and the death sentence was passed on a little over one hundred Dutch people as a result. Nearly all the death sentences were carried out immediately.

Within two weeks, the strikes had been broken. The number of victims who fell in this short period was high: Dozens of people had been shot down in the streets, hundreds had been arrested, and nearly all the people who had been sentenced to death by a Summary Police Court had been shot by firing squad.

Tranquility did not, however, return after this bloody episode—quite the contrary. Increasingly, Dutch citizens failed to comply with German orders and commands. Numerous people began to help the "disobedients" (especially young men who refused to work in Germany). The provision of organized help to those who chose to go into hiding got well under way in the months that followed the strikes of May 1943. Also, the resistance began to use violence more often. Raids on banks, stores, prisons, and buildings of the Dutch administration became part of the everyday reality of the occupation over the course of time. Assassination attempts on those who supported or worked for the German occupiers also took place more frequently.

This change of scene, again, had consequences for the judicial system. As to the Dutch system, German pressure increased. From May 1943 onward the Gestapo operated even more harshly and started to intervene with the Dutch administration of law. Complete groups of suspects, like those charged with having violated the rationing laws, were now removed from the jurisdiction of the Dutch courts. The Gestapo and the German courts took over these cases. In general this meant that these suspects were sentenced to severe sentences. At the same time, Dutch judges whose light sentences had come to the attention of the German authorities ran the risk of being dismissed. Sentences already handed down that the German authorities deemed too lenient were simply "supplemented" by the Gestapo. Several Dutch men, who had served out their sentences imposed by a Dutch court, were arrested again and imprisoned by the Gestapo.

There were also changes in the German judicial system after the strikes of May 1943. First, the Feldgerichte were freed of work: From 1943, cases of minor significance were more frequently handed over to other German courts, like the Landesgericht. As a consequence, the importance of the latter court was marginalized, as from May onward this court dealt merely with petty crimes, like theft from Germans, the possession of pigeons, and some trivial acts of political disobedience, such as the possession of a radio. The Landesgericht was overloaded by these cases. Until the early summer of 1944, the Landesgericht dealt with an average of more than two hundred cases monthly.

Compared to the Landesgericht, the *Obergericht* never had a busy schedule. This remained the same from May 1943 until September 1944. Just a few hundred cases were brought before this court. The performance of other organizations could be considered an important explanation for the relatively low number of cases brought before the *Obergericht*. The Gestapo and its quasi-judicial powers have been mentioned before. But in September 1943, Seyss-Inquart also decided that the Summary Police Court could administer justice in "normal" times (i.e., without a state of summary police law being declared first). From that point onward, political opponents were often brought before this court.[27] The Summary Police Court tried its first case in the third week of September 1943; the last one followed in July 1944. In the intervening period the Summary Police Court is estimated to have sentenced to death more than two hundred members of the Dutch resistance. The accuseds' positions before this court were weak, and the proceedings themselves were exceptionally short in duration. In a great many cases, judgment and sentence would be handed down within a few hours of the case having begun, and the sentence carried out within a few hours.

Thus, this new court took over some of the work of the Obergericht. Of importance too had been the growth, both in severity and number, of punishments without recourse to the courts. Burning down houses, hostage taking, executing citizens who had not been condemned to death by a judge became new ways in which the German authorities responded to Dutch acts of resistance. These extrajudicial measures were not always directed against suspects. An example of this was "operation spruce" (*Silbertanne-Aktion,* after the metaphor of chopping trees as killing innocent people, used by the head of the Gestapo), initiated in the fall of 1943: Attacks on people who worked for, or sympathized with, the German regime were avenged by reprisals on innocent civilians.[28]

This operation spruce signified that the German regime was shifting from the policy of punishing the culprits to one of taking revenge on innocents for anti-German activities. The Gestapo was the main executor of this and other similar measures. Courts, Dutch and German alike, did not participate in this policy.

Months of Terror: The Judicial System during the Last Phase of the German Occupation

From the late summer of 1944, citizens who allegedly acted against the German regime were only rarely brought before a court. The Landesgericht was the first to stop trying cases. It seems as if the German regime, having looked at the reality of the occupation, gradually began to have their doubts about the relevance of trying these less severe cases.[29] In the course of 1944, the number of minor cases that were tried dropped sharply. With regard to the other German courts, the general trend was the same: Only occasionally did a court take on cases in this final period of the occupation.

The Gestapo, during that time, gained an almost untouchable position. On the one hand, this organ used such extrajudicial methods as were mentioned above. On the other hand, the Gestapo achieved just about a monopoly in terms of tracking down, persecuting, and punishing suspects. Since September 1944, the fate of the arrested suspects was in the hands of the Gestapo. Those who were involved in serious political cases feared for their lives. In the occupied Netherlands it became the custom to delay execution until an act of resistance was committed in the vicinity, so that the execution by firing squad could serve as an act of reprisal. For purposes of general intimidation, this would be communicated to the Dutch public at large. Hundreds of Dutch civilians fell victim to these executions.[30]

Some Conclusions

It is precisely this last period of the occupation that determines the postwar view on the judicial system during the occupation. In this view there is no place for normalcy or continuity. The break with the prewar years was complete and radical.

As has been demonstrated, this is in fact true: During the German occupation the judicial system changed drastically. The politically independent system was transformed into a political system, an instrument of the German regime. On the one hand, the existing Dutch system lost its political neutrality and autonomy as it became subjected to German supervision (and, eventually, intervention). On the other hand, the organs of the new German system—police, public prosecutor, and judiciary—acquired political tasks as they started to chase, persecute, and punish those citizens who were regarded as enemies of this regime.

However, it should be emphasized that, first, the break did not occur at once, but bit by bit, crack by crack. The transformation into a political apparatus was a gradual process that should be seen in a much broader context: Developments inside, and outside, Dutch society influenced the judicial system constantly. One could consider this instrumentalization of the judicial system a reflection of the worsening relationship between occupier and suppressed population. This relationship became especially critical at three specific moments: February 1941, when street fights in Amsterdam resulted in a general strike; May 1943, when Dutch citizens went on strike as a reaction to the German policy of forcing Dutch men to work in Germany; September 1944, when allied troops invaded the Netherlands and liberated parts of it. These three episodes also marked drastic changes in the judicial system.

Second, one should keep in mind that the Gestapo, although powerful from the start, was not always the only organ of this system. There was some cooperation by Dutch citizens and authorities alike. Until late summer 1944 various courts were set up to try those accused of opposing German rule. More then twelve thousand cases were brought before the *Landesgericht* and *Obergericht*, for example.[31] Besides these German courts, the Dutch courts continued the administration of law, although under the supervision of German authorities.

As German coercion became less selective and more people suffered from this, the initial cooperation of the Dutch diminished rapidly. From then on, the German regime relied more and more on the Gestapo as its organ of repression. The German supervision of Dutch courts changed into intervention. Fewer cases were brought before the German courts. Other, extrajudicial methods were tried to fight resistance and social disobedience. Gradually, terror became a part of daily life in the Netherlands. By then the break with the prewar years was complete.

Notes

1. Ruller and Faber, *Afdoening van Strafzaken*, 23; Rutgers, *Strafrecht en Rechtsstaat*, 48; Langemeijer, "'Crisis' en Verscherpte Straffen," 69–77.
2. Centraal Bureau voor de Statistiek, ed., *Crimineele Statistiek*.

3. Netherlands Institute of War Documentation (NIOD), arch.215, ds.15, 1 J 217/40, 9 J 292/41g; ds.16, 2 J 318/40g; ds.18, 2 J 333/40g, 1 J 129/40g, 1 J 192/40g; ds.19B, 1 J 185/40g, 10 J 239/40; ds.20B, 9 J 237/40, 1 J 128/40g; arch.206, ds.7, doc.1361–1–1500 (2 J 333/40g); ds.8, doc.1361–1-5425 (1 J 252/40g); ds.8, doc.1361–1-6320 (2 J 319/40g).

4. Moritz, *Gerichtsbarkeit;* Umbreit, "Auf dem Weg zur Kontinentalherrschaft."

5. *Verordnung des Oberbefehlshabers der Heeresgruppe B über die Einführung deutschen Strafrechts in den von deutschen Truppen besetzten Gebieten der Niederlande und Belgiens vom 10. Mai 1940.* In Nestler, *Dokumentedition Europa unterm Hakenkreuz 4,* 93–94.

6. Frijtag, *Het Recht van de Sterkste,* 67–68.

7. *De Telegraaf* (3 September 1940).

8. *Erlaß des Führers über Ausübung der Regierungsbefugnisse in den Niederlanden vom 18. Mai 1940. Verordeningenblad voor het bezette Nederlandse gebied (Vobl.)* 1940, 2.

9. Frijtag, "Rechtspolitik im Reichskommissariat," 461–90.

10. *Verordening (vo) 3/40* (29 May 1940). Vobl. 1940, 8.

11. De Rijke, Dubois en Van Genechten. Vergadering van het College van Secretarissen-Generaal (10 September 1940). NIOD, arch. 216, ds. 1, mp. 2a.

12. Vo 52/40 (17 July 1940). Vobl. 1940, 181.

13. For an overall view of the number of cases that were dealt with by *Landesgericht* and *Obergericht,* see the annual registers of the German courts (L-Register, O-Register, Ns-Register) and the German public prosecutor (StA-Register, VR-Register). These registers are at the NIOD. The statements on the German administration of law are based on data derived from the archives of the NIOD, especially arch. 34–37 and coll. 214.

14. About the strike, see Meershoek, *Dienaren van het Gezag;* Pelt, *Vrede door Revolutie;* Reuter, *De Communistische Partij van Nederland;* Roest, *Oorlog in de Stad;* Sijes, *De Februaristaking.*

15. For more information on these courts of peace, see Geus, "Vrederechtspraak," 48–86.

16. Frijtag, *Het Recht van de Sterkste,* 322–23.

17. Interviews with J. E. (14 October 1996), P. de J. (10 September 1996), S. M. (24 September 1996), J. G. T. (15 October 1996), J. V. (18 October 1996), J. W. (18 September 1996), S. H. W. (9 October 1996).

18. Frijtag, *Het Recht van de Sterkste,* 331.

19. Ibid., 332–33. These numbers are related to the period of occupation as a whole (that is, from May 1940 to May 1945).

20. SG 34/42. NIOD, arch.35, ds.21.

21. For further information on the persecution of Jews, see Presser, *Ondergang;* Romijn, "De oorlog," 313–50; Moore, *Victim and Survivors.* On the role of the Dutch police: Meershoek, *Dienaren van het Gezag.*

22. Frijtag, *Het Recht van de Sterkste,* 153–55.

23. SG 43/42. NIOD, arch.35, ds.22.

24. Frijtag, *Het Recht van de Sterkste,* passim, in particular 54–57, 68–76. On Secretary-General Schrieke: Knegtmans et al, *Collaborateurs op niveau.*

25. In this respect, from 1943 the situation in the Netherlands started to differ drastically from that in Germany, as outlined by the American historian Eric Johnson in his book *Nazi Terror.* As more people suffered from coercion in the Netherlands since the forced labor policy started, one could say that, contrary to the German situation, the Nazi terror in the Netherlands had become less selective and exclusive.

26. For further information about this strike in 1943, see Bouman, *De April-Meistakingen.*

27. The *Reichskommissar* later extended its jurisdiction to encompass people who had allegedly been involved in burglary raids on government institutions and agencies.

28. See Cohen, "Schuldig Slachtoffer," 192–210.

29. The instructions given to German police officers about passing only serious cases on to the courts in future should be seen in the context of these doubts. Telex Deppner to all Außenstellen (7 June 1944). Bundesarchiv Berlin, R 70 NL/16.

30. Telex Schöngarth to *Posten, Stellen, Kommandos* (11 September 1944). NIOD, arch. 77–85, mp. 193Cd. Also, Cohen, "Een onbekende tijdgenoot," 170–91.

31. Frijtag, *Het Recht van de Sterkste,* 322–23.

CHAPTER 16

Policing Amsterdam during the German Occupation: How Radical Was the Break?

Guus Meershoek

During the last two decades, research on National Socialism has become a transnational enterprise. Historiographical debates on the topic are no longer restricted to national communities of historians. At the same time, major new areas of research have opened up. Research on the Holocaust has extended from the top to the lower levels of the administration of destruction. The opening of the archives of the former Communist countries has resulted in profound studies of the German army's invasion of the Soviet Union and on the rule of the Nazi-occupied areas in eastern Europe. Repressive institutions have received much attention.[1]

Confronted with the many new findings, a reflection on their significance is necessary for our understanding of the Nazi regime. In their new collection of essays on the Gestapo, the German historians Gerhard Paul and Klaus-Michael Mallmann indicate how the new research has refined our perception of the political police in Nazi Germany. The Gestapo was less powerful than its public image and its position at the top of the political system suggested, while denunciations and the ability of society to police itself were more important than generally assumed. It is made clear that the role of the Gestapo in the occupied eastern countries differed much from its role in western Europe. More has become known of the professional and ideological convictions that led the policemen involved to their acts of violence and destruction. Their findings have led Paul and Mallmann also to reassess Hannah Arendt's *The Origins of Totalitarianism*, a book (originally published in 1951) that historians had already given up decades ago for lack of empirical foundations and conceptual clarity.[2]

In this article, I will reflect on policing in Amsterdam during the Second World War. I will draw on the results of my own historical research on this subject and put them into a broader context.[3] More specifically, I will use Arendt's idea of totalitarianism to assess how radical policing changed in Amsterdam in these years. Arendt's concept presumed to indicate the main features of a radically new kind of political system that she supposed had appeared in Nazi Germany and the Soviet Union. Her analysis has been much debated.[4] I will not prolong this debate but simply use the concept to assess changes in policing. Considering that Arendt's concept of totalitarianism characterizes a full-grown regime, how much did policing in Amsterdam meet the standard? At first, I will shortly introduce the prewar Amsterdam police, the main events during the occupation, and Arendt's theory of totalitarianism. Then I will extract from her theory three theses that allegedly account for totalitarianism's effectiveness and see if they fit the Amsterdam situation.

Police and Social Control in Prewar Amsterdam[5]

Before the war, The Netherlands was a stable democracy with a modern, liberal constitution and a decentralized polity with oligarchic features. The government had not been confronted with violent disturbances such as war or revolution for more than a century. Popular revolts in Amsterdam never really threatened the position of the ruling elites. Modern policing had appeared rather late. The national government left policing to the mayors and maintained a small gendarmerie only for intervention in case of disorder, in addition to the army. It was not until 1878 that the Amsterdam night watch was abolished, and a modern police force was created. Cities like Rotterdam and The Hague did not follow this example until the end of the century.

After the First World War, the Amsterdam police force grew in size, adopted new technologies, and started to play an active role in society. New departments were created: a traffic police, a vice squad, and a political intelligence unit. In 1940, the Amsterdam police force employed some twenty-four hundred persons and was led by a chief constable who was immediately answerable to the mayor. Seven police stations, each led by a superintendent, were responsible for police action in their own part of the city. Somewhat prior to 1940, the force had become more militarized, and the influence of central authorities like the attorney general had strengthened.

In the Netherlands, policing was regulated by a national system of quite liberal laws and local Police Acts that were promulgated by the municipal councils and that consequently differed according to the local situation. After an uprising in 1934, the Amsterdam Police Act was renewed. Police powers to regulate behavior in public were strengthened, and the freedom to demonstrate or distribute newspapers and leaflets in the street was restricted. These measures, especially directed against radical right-wing and left-wing political parties, proved to be effective.

Day-to-day policing was organized in Amsterdam according to the London system of surveillance that provided for a permanent, close observation of the population. In the twenties, patrolmen got more freedom of movement but became at the same time centrally directed and closely supervised by their headquarters. They were urged to police offenders more stringently. Convinced of the central importance of keeping a strong presence on the street, patrolmen kept on primarily using a wide range of informal disciplinary methods. A patrolman of the police station Warmoesstraat in the city center told what happened with a barrow that was left on the road:

> Patrolmen knew exactly what to do. That barrow was driven into the Damrak [canal]. The owner was not ticketed because that caused paperwork. Next day, the owner came to complain. The patrolman present said: "If you leave your property on the road, anything can happen." The owner instantly realized what had happened and never left his barrow on the road again.[6]

With their daily presence on the street, their intimate knowledge of the neighborhood (most of them stayed their whole career at the same station), the use of force against "troublemakers," and their professional solidarity, patrolmen were able to prevail.

The Amsterdam Police and the German Occupation: The Main Events[7]

After the defeat of the Dutch army in May 1940, the government fled to London. Hitler sent a *Reichskommissar* to the Netherlands, the Austrian National Socialist lawyer Arthur Seyss-Inquart. The Dutch police was supervised by *Höhere SS- und Polizeiführer* Hanns Albin Rauter, who also directed some German police forces. At first, Seyss-Inquart respected the Dutch administrative hierarchy, making his wishes known to the secretaries-general who represented the executive departments. In January 1941 his Amsterdam representative, who supervised the local government, abruptly put an end to this cooperation by requiring the municipality to make preparations for the creation of a ghetto and by inciting Dutch National Socialists to acts of violence against Jews. The outrage provoked a public revolt: the February strike, that was suppressed by German and Amsterdam police. The mayor and the chief constable were replaced by Dutch National Socialists.

The new chief constable, Sybren Tulp, a Dutch military man from the colonies turned National Socialist, did not transform the organization of the police force but only added over time new units that operated independently under his personal authority: a political investigation department, a barracks unit, and a bureau of Jewish affairs. He proved to be a charismatic leader and quickly enhanced his authority over the force. After a few months he was very popular with his personnel. One inspector stated characteristically to a colleague at the time: "When the war is over, he [Tulp] must be executed, but with a golden bullet."[8]

When Rauter in September 1941 unilaterally prohibited Jews from public places, Tulp did not wait for the usual instructions from the Department of Justice but ordered his personnel to implement the decree to the letter. Upon his own authority, he allotted the Jews one cafe and one theater and prohibited them from entering others. At first, the patrolmen did not heed his instructions. When some weeks later other governmental bodies also started to do the same, Tulp took special disciplinary measures to force his personnel to implement the orders. Although these proved to be effective, a few weeks later the patrolmen fell back into the old pattern and refrained from arresting violators.

In July 1942, the *Reichskommissariat* started to deport Jews, pretending to send them to Germany for forced labor. When the number of Jews that registered decreased, the Amsterdam police was given the order to take Jews from their homes and put them on the train. Although aversion to the measures was strong, Tulp did not have to force the personnel to comply with the measures against the Jews. Potential resisters among the police gave in to the pressure of colleagues and resistance was nipped in the bud. When Tulp fell ill and died in October 1942, the regular force was relieved of the task of enforcing the anti-Jewish measures, and a special barracks unit took over the job.

In the spring of 1943, those among the leadership of the police who wanted to shirk German orders became dominant. Without engaging in open confrontation with Rauter, they succeeded in removing the force from rounding up Jews for deportation and young men for forced labor in Germany. The political investigation department was dismantled. From the summer of 1943 onward, nothing was left to the Amsterdam police but to maintain order and to fight criminality, for the most part, economic criminality.

Arendt's Concept of Totalitarianism

Hannah Arendt (1906–1975) was not an historian and did not pretend to be one. She studied philosophy and considered herself to be a political theorist. Her analysis of politics and society grew out of her experience in the thirties and forties.[9] She witnessed the Nazi takeover in Berlin and escaped first to France, where she became engaged in the relief of German refugees, and later fled to the United States. By 1943, while in the United States, she became aware that the European Jews were being systematically destroyed. She was shocked and puzzled, as she explained in an interview many years later:

> At first we didn't believe it—although my husband and I always said that we expected anything from that bunch. We didn't believe this because militarily it was unnecessary and uncalled for. . . . And then a half-year later we believed it after all, because we had the proof. That was the real shock. Before that we said: Well, one has enemies. That is entirely natural. Why shouldn't a people have enemies? But this was different. It was really as if an abyss had opened.[10]

The shock impelled her to start researching into the backgrounds of the Nazi regime. This research would result in her first and best-known book *The Origins of Totalitarianism* (1951). It consists of three parts, entitled Anti-Semitism, Imperialism, and Totalitarianism, and is a historical narrative only at first appearance. By analyzing such various cases as the Dreyfus Affair in France and the Boer War in South Africa, Arendt wants to show how European societies got out of joint and how the resulting disorder, the resulting moral vacuum, was the perfect environment for a radically new political phenomenon: totalitarianism.

The foundation of Arendt's analysis is Montesquieu's reading of Aristotle's well-known threefold division of polities in republics, monarchies, and tyrannies. According to the French political theorist, each of these regimes is based on a particular principle that directs the actions of its representatives. The guiding principle of republics is virtue, in the sense of "love for the laws and one's homeland." In a republic citizens strive for a good reputation by devoting themselves to the public cause and by excelling in public action. The nobility, that constitutes the governing elite in monarchies, does not want to be virtuous and avoids risk in public. In monarchies, "the state continues to exist independently of love of the homeland, desire for true glory, self-renunciation, the sacrifice of one's dearest interests, and all those heroic virtues we find in the ancients and know only by hearsay."[11] The nobility accedes to the wishes of the ruler and his environment, caring about honor first of all. Fear is the guiding principle of despotic regimes. It puts the tyrant up to permanent vigilance against threats to his position, and it deters the rest of society from independent actions. Most polities are combinations of the three kinds of regimes. Only tyrannies are plainly evil.

Arendt is convinced that Nazi Germany and Stalin's Soviet Russia do not fit with Montesquieu's threefold classification.[12] They negate central features of all three regimes. In monarchies and republics, the rule of law creates stability. Although stability is absent in tyrannies, their internal affairs are dominated by power politics, which gives their citizens something to hang on to. In the new totalitarian regimes, even this minimal certainty is nonexistent. They have, according to Arendt, "exploded the very alternative on which all definitions of the essence of governments have been based in political philosophy, that is the alternative between lawful and lawless government, between arbitrary and legitimate power."[13] Totalitarianism is radically new.

The political movements that established totalitarian regimes set themselves the task of fulfilling the law of nature (National Socialism) or the law of history (Communism). This mission impossible does have serious consequences for the polity concerned: "The term 'law' itself changed its meaning: from expressing the framework of stability within which human actions and motions take place, it became the expression of the motion itself."[14] In totalitarian societies, human beings are forced to make permanent adaptations to this fiction, to be permanently on the move. Nobody knows for sure what is expected:

> It is the monstrous, yet seemingly unanswerable claim of totalitarian rule that, far from being lawless, it goes to the sources of authority from which positive laws received their ultimate legitimation, that far from being arbitrary it is more obedient to these suprahuman forces than any government ever was before, and that far from wielding its power in the interest of one man, it is quite prepared to sacrifice everybody's vital immediate interests to the execution of what it assumes to be the law of History or the law of Nature.[15]

By constantly chasing a fiction and forcing subordinates to do so as well, totalitarian regimes are not able to stabilize their form of government. Their institutions are in constant flux.

In the melee of institutions that characterizes totalitarian political systems, the political police inevitably ends up in the central position. It starts by tracing and arresting opponents of the regime, firmly controlled by the political leadership. As soon as it has fulfilled this task, the hunt for "objective enemies" begins: "[The 'objective enemy'] is defined by the policy of the government and not by his own desire to overthrow it. He is never an individual whose dangerous thoughts must be provoked or whose past justifies suspicion, but a 'carrier of tendencies' like the carrier of a disease."[16] In the hunt for "objective enemies," traditional police practices lose their value, and the political police acts more on its own instead of following directions from higher political authorities.

Totalitarianism negates the principles that according to Montesquieu are directing actions in politics: honor, virtue, and fear. Forced to pursue fictitious ends, rulers and subjects are permanently afraid not to live up to what is expected, to stand in the way of progress, to be considered an "objective enemy." They are no longer guided by principles, but by ideology and terror. These substitutes generate loneliness, the total absence of ordinary social relations, which stands out from fear, the basic experience in tyrannies, because it disables men from action: "Totalitarian domination as a form of government is new in that it is not content with this isolation [that is produced by tyrannies] and destroys private life as well. It bases itself on loneliness, on the experience of not belonging to the world at all, which is the most radical and desperate experience of man."[17] While the totalitarian regimes are permanently changing, never reliable, their subjects are forced to a standstill, to refrain from expressing themselves in action.

In the next paragraphs, I will assess whether Arendt's concept of totalitarianism fits the changes in policing in Amsterdam during the German occupation. Three aspects will be looked at specifically: the political system and the role of ideology; social control and the behavior of the population; and terror. In each of these three cases, my inquiry is guided by specific questions.

The clear-cut division at the start between the Dutch government and the police that continued to rule along traditional lines as much as possible, and a small occupational administration that only intervened when its objectives were at stake, disappeared after some time. What were the driving forces behind this change? How was the local police integrated into the occupational administration? Were Dutch and German institutions amalgamating?

The Netherlands were occupied by a foreign power that considered the population to belong to the Germanic race and tried to win its support. How did the inhabitants of Amsterdam react to the traditional and new techniques of policing? Did these cause not only fear but loneliness too? Did the population refrain from expressing itself in action?

The *Reichskommissariat* had a political police at its disposal, the *Sicherheitspolizei* (SD), and created inside the Amsterdam police a separate political investigation department that played a key role in tracing and arresting political opponents. How important were traditional investigating practices in their work? Did terror intensify when the opposition was destroyed?

The Political System and the Role of Ideology[18]

Until the summer of 1941, the *Reichskommissariat* generally acted as a supervisor, refraining from imposing its ideology. Although he had dissolved parliament and usurped the right to give instructions to the Dutch administration, Seyss-Inquart declared that he respected the Dutch laws. He came out with some harsh measures against the Jews but did not overrule the secretaries-general: he pressed these measures upon them. Most new regulatory measures like the distribution of scarce goods, the introduction of identity cards, and the creation of a national criminal investigation department were initiated by the Dutch executive. Many of these reforms had been prepared before the war, but soon measures were being taken that anticipated German wishes. For fear of German retaliation, the administration tried "to remain one step ahead of the occupier."[19] The Dutch administration was not prompted by ideology but by a technocratic attitude.

The National Socialist chief constable Tulp played a key role in inserting the Amsterdam police force into the German repressive apparatus, but he remained an exception in the Dutch police. Moreover, he did not exert himself to disseminate the National Socialist ideology in the police. Only some 5 percent of its members joined National Socialist organizations. Considered totally reliable, they were placed in special units like the political investigation department and the Bureau of Jewish Affairs. Although they were prepared to assist the German police in fighting economic crime, most members of the force kept a reticent attitude in the execution of so-called political tasks. In general, the *Reichskommissariat* was satisfied with this.

Only occasionally was more expected. At these moments, the assistance of the Amsterdam police force did not result from a technocratic attitude or ideological affinity but from confrontations with the *Reichskommissariat.* Rauter had difficulty in instructing the Dutch executive properly; his interventions did not always bear the desired result, and he remained heavily dependent on supporters inside the administration to transmit his intentions to the actual enforcers. When they were confronted with radical German demands, chief constable Tulp and the new units prompted the other members of the force to execute the loathed tasks. In each case German instructions became more concise. A telephone call was sufficient to start the round up of Jews in September 1942. The lack of elaborate instructions from the German authorities was compensated for by the Dutch policemen's acquired ability to recognize the moments that they had to obey unconditionally.

After the death of Tulp and the defeat of the German army in Stalingrad, the Amsterdam police force opposed further cooperation. In April 1943, the German *Ordnungspolizei* put down a public protest. Because the Dutch police refused to assist in this, the *Reichskommissariat* lost its interest in the force. Evidently, for the Germans, ideological considerations were no longer very important.

Social Control and the Behavior of the Population[20]

In the summer of 1940, the German occupiers pressed the Dutch authorities to lift the police acts that constrained the radical (right-wing) parties. Although they were confronted by gradually more aggressive Dutch National Socialists and German soldiers, the patrolmen informally stuck to the old policy until after some weeks they were explicitly instructed to redirect their actions: not against National Socialists anymore but against their opponents. "According to official directives the public has to become used to the wearing of uniforms in public and to be disciplined in this respect."[21] At first, patrolmen still found a way out. According to one of them:

> For some time, it was a game for the patrolmen to arrest the [Dutch] girls [that visited cafes with German soldiers during curfew] because they were not allowed to be on the street. One could get into serious trouble [by doing that], even being shot. It was extremely chancy, but it was a game. . . . Such a girl had to stay at the police station until four o'clock. But at a certain moment, headquarters instructed us explicitly to keep our hands off of these girls.[22]

Step by step the patrolmen lost the opportunity of relying upon informal means of control. Order could only be kept by pressing the public to remain calm against the provocations of the National Socialists. The Amsterdam population was prohibited from expressing itself. This policy was predestined to fail, as happened in February 1941 when the population revolted against the maltreatment of Jews.

The new chief constable Tulp relied on deterrence to maintain order. According to him, the police force had to first regain its self-confidence in order to be able to impress the public. He instructed the patrolmen to no longer tolerate any aggression by National Socialists and took care to be often on the beat himself. Plainclothes policemen had to look for persons who distributed leaflets or painted slogans on the walls and had to reprimand citizens who discussed politics in public. The new political investigation department started to assess the mood of the population and to report about it monthly. Evidently, the new approach was more an authoritarian than a totalitarian way of policing.

Maybe as a result of the intensified surveillance, transgressions and disorders decreased in the second half of 1941. Attendance at the cinemas slowly increased, although the prewar level was not reached. At the end of 1941, a split was observed between a large majority of the population that acquiesced to the German occupation and a small group that hardened in its rejection of it. In 1942 public acts of disorder were absent. New anti-Jewish measures stimulated clandestine calls for protest in May, but these did not find a response among the population. The round up of the Jews, partly carried out by the familiar Amsterdam police, had a strong impact on Jews as well as on non-Jews in September 1942. For the Jews resistance seemed futile. Non-Jews turned their attention away from the events. Attendance at theaters and cinemas returned to prewar levels. The political investigation department reported: "The measures against the Jews still arouse some unrest, especially pity, among the population, but do not generate action."[23]

The German military defeats at Stalingrad and in Africa stimulated the creation of resistance networks in Dutch society. The public was interested in the developments at the front but hardly reacted to important events. The political investigation department reported large-scale war weariness, interrupted only by some moments of excitement. When Italy capitulated in September 1943, there was "a festive air about the city. Most cafes were overcrowded and everyone was in high spirits. At some places young people let off fireworks."[24] Most of the time, however, the population was preoccupied with mundane matters like getting enough food to eat. Street life fully disappeared. In the spring of 1944 the police reported that "nobody talked about the front anymore. Discussions in public mainly concerned the troubles in the distribution of food. . . . Many do still make jokes about it, but as far as could be observed opposition or rebellious discontent at the malfunctioning system of distribution are fully absent."[25] Attendance at theaters, cinemas, and football matches remained at high prewar levels. Although the Dutch populace was successfully restrained from taking public action, Dutch citizens were not fully cut off from society. They were not lonely as Arendt considers members of a totalitarian community to be.

Terror[26]

During the occupation, Dutch citizens who harmed German institutions, persons, or the so-called common welfare (*Gemeinwohl*) were punishable by the German judiciary. The German *Sipo* (SD) was charged with the task of uncovering Dutch violators. Because German detectives had much trouble in finding their way in Dutch society, local Dutch police forces were pushed to create special criminal investigation units to assist them. In Amsterdam the forty-nine-year-old inspector Douwe Bakker was charged with this task in the spring of 1941. Bakker was a fanatic. In May 1940, he had written in his diary: "The Gestapo has arrived: justice will be done. . . . The final judgment will be passed over the damned plutocrats. Lies and deceit, Jewry and Capitalism will get what they deserve. The genius Adolf Hitler will destroy them."[27]

At first, Bakker received assignments from the local *Sipo* (SD) and brought arrested suspects there after interrogation. Soon, he started to initiate investigations himself. This irritated the *Sipo* (SD), who feared losing control. After a few months Bakker was summoned to the *Sipo* (SD) headquarters on suspicion of falsifying a warrant, interrogated, and incarcerated for some days. In the end he was released for lack of evidence and was allowed to resume his work. Not discouraged by this setback, Bakker and his fifty detectives became very active in investigating resistance networks from the summer of 1941 onward.

An example of their proceedings is the investigation of a twenty-four-year-old clerk named Adri Addicks, who distributed a clandestine Social-Democratic newsletter. As usual, the investigation started with the receipt of an anonymous accusatory letter in August 1941. When two detectives tried to arrest him, Addicks managed to escape. Subsequently, his personal description was distributed among the Dutch police, and some of his friends were arrested. When a second anonymous letter was received, Bakker's detectives laid an ambush. Addicks, however, was on the alert and defended himself with his pistol and succeeded in escaping again. One and a half weeks later, the unit was informed that a stranger was hiding on the roof of a building in the city center. It proved to be Addicks. This time, the local chief of the *Sipo* (SD) personally directed the action. He instructed the German police to fence off the neighborhood and entered the apartment with Bakker and his detectives. Afterward Bakker reported in his diary:

> Addicks was caught indeed: stirred up, he was standing there, very thin and nervous, wounded. It was a German officer who saw him first. During the pursuit Addicks jumped from the second to the first floor of a flat. [The Dutch detective] S. jumped on him without hesitation, while the German [detective] was ready to shoot him with his machine-gun if necessary. . . . That was the end of Addicks. For sure, he is a dead man.[28]

Addicks was indeed sentenced to death by a German court and executed. In going after opponents of the German occupation, Bakker and his detectives did not have to care about traditional procedures. But even though they profited much from traditional police informers, they still needed their own expertise in criminal investigations.

Between the summer of 1941 and that of 1942, Bakker's unit tracked down the majority of the arrested members of resistance networks in Amsterdam. Dismayed by Bakker's leading role in the repression of the opposition, which threatened his own position in the German apparatus, the local chief of the *Sipo* (SD) unsuccessfully tried to dismantle the Dutch criminal investigation unit in the spring of 1942. When the deportation of the Jews started, he tried again and succeeded. As soon as the opposition was broken in Amsterdam, the persecution of potential resisters was mitigated while the hunt for the Jews was intensified.

How Radical Was the Break?

Amsterdam policing during the German occupation did not meet the standard of totalitarianism as described by Arendt, although elements of totalitarianism were clearly present. The new chief constable used his charisma and his military style of leadership to insert the police force into the German repressive apparatus, but he hardly propagated National Socialism. His success was partly based on the disciplinary and self-disciplinary processes that are inherent in all bureaucratic organizations. Lacking ideological zeal, the Amsterdam police force did not adapt smoothly to the German goals but more unevenly, by a succession of shocks. The members of the Dutch police force were not convinced supporters of National Socialist goals and measures but learned by experience when to obey unconditionally. Apart from the February Strike, the Amsterdam population was restrained from mounting protest and disorder, at first by traditional forms of social control, later by deterrence. In this case, ideology did not play an important role. The population was not fully cut off from society, as Arendt said was the case in totalitarian regimes, but participated in sports and cultural activities on the same scale as before the war. After the summer of 1943, lethargy became dominant. Terror played a key role in Amsterdam policing, but when the resistance was broken, it was not intensified but redirected against the Jews. The political investigation department did become more important, but its strivings were regularly curtailed by the *Sipo* (SD).

Notes

1. An overview of research about the German political police can be found in Paul and Mallmann, eds., *Die Gestapo: Mythos und Realität;* and Paul and Mallmann, eds., *Die Gestapo im Zweiten Weltkrieg.* On research about the destruction of the Jews, see Browning, *Nazi Policy.*

2. Paul and Mallmann, eds., *Gestapo im Zweiten Weltkrieg,* 599–650. For an assessment of the concept of totalitarianism: Luykx, "Een concept ondermijnd," 500–529.

3. Meershoek, *Dienaren van het Gezag.*

4. An overview: Luykx, "Een concept ondermijnd."

5. Meershoek, *Dienaren van het Gezag.*

6. Interview of C. Verbiest, 20 March 1990, collection of the author.

7. Meershoek, *Dienaren van het Gezag.*

8. Interview of G. Duisterwinkel, 2 December 1990, collection of the author.

9. Young-Bruehl, *Hannah Arendt.*

10. "What Remains? The Language Remains," in Arendt, *Essays in Understanding,* 13–14.

11. Montesquieu, *The Spirit of the Laws,* 25.

12. "Understanding and Politics" and "On the Nature of Totalitarianism," in Arendt, *Essays in Understanding,* 307–27, 328–60.

13. Arendt, *The Origins of Totalitarianism,* 461.

14. Ibid., 464.

15. Ibid., 461–62.

16. Ibid., 243–44.

17. Ibid., 475.

18. Meershoek, *Dienaren van het Gezag,* 112–16, 147–59, 240–50.

19. Meershoek, "Zonder de wolven te prikkelen," 95–116.

20. Meershoek, *Dienaren van het Gezag,* 105–9, 119–22, 159–63, 254–57.

21. Notitie Versteeg, 21 June 1940, in 5225-BHC-D6–1940–1, Archives of the Amsterdam municipality (GAA).

22. Interview of C. Verbiest, 30 March 1990, collection of the author.

23. Maandverslag, 15 August 1942–15 September 1942, in 5225-BHC-V22 I-25, GAA.

24. Maandverslag, 15 August 1943–15 September 1943, in 5225-BHC-V22 I-25, GAA.

25. Maandverslag, 15 March 1944–15 April 1944, in 5225-BHC-V22 I-25, GAA.

26. Meershoek, *Dienaren van het Gezag,* 190–210.

27. Diary of D. Bakker, 21 May 1940, 244, Netherlands Institute of War Documentation (NIOD).

28. Diary of D. Bakker, 27 September 1941, 244, NIOD.

CHAPTER 17

Control and Consent in Eastern Europe's Workers' States, 1945–1989: Some Reflections on Totalitarianism, Social Organization, and Social Control

MARK PITTAWAY

I n concluding remarks to an article on the impact of the introduction of Soviet-style economic planning on shop floor relations in early socialist Hungary, I wrote that the analysis presented "points to the way in which approaches which stress the dominance of the state in socialist society have misread reality."[1] This paper clarifies and develops the point made in that article. As such it is as much an examination of historical treatments of the role of the state in East-Central European society between 1945 and 1989 as it is a presentation of the findings of new empirical research. The argument to be presented here sheds much light on the concept of "social control," its advantages as well as its real limitations when examining the reality of state–society relations in postwar East-Central Europe.

If concepts of "social control" accurately identify the dynamic relationship between the state and social groups anywhere and at any time, then according to much informed opinion, they do so for East-Central Europe between 1945 and 1989. During the 1950s and 1960s, Western political scientists described the socialist dictatorships as "totalitarian states." A party-dominated state with a rigid, dogmatic ideology subordinated society, eliminating not only political opposition but any kind of independent social organization ruthlessly atomizing society in the process.[2] The classical "totalitarian" model has been much criticized over the past thirty years and has been replaced with a number of more nuanced descriptions of the extent and role of state intervention. Many political scientists have come to describe the region's socialist regimes as Leninist, arguing that the authoritarianism of socialist regimes was located in the ideology of their founding fathers and not in the novel techniques of twentieth-century dictatorship.[3] Left-wing dissidents in East-Central Europe developed concepts such as that of "the dictatorship over needs" to analyze the political system under which they lived.[4] Since 1989 social historians have argued that the former German Democratic Republic was "a thoroughly dominated society"—an analysis that has implications for other East-Central European societies.[5]

Models of state dominance have been adapted to describe the role of the state in social relations in those socialist states, such as Hungary and Yugoslavia, where political liberalization occurred and market elements were introduced into the economy.[6] The trajectory of Hungarian socialism in particular has been described in terms of an initial decade when the state ruthlessly subordinated society to its goals and then gradually liberalized. The "second society," "embryonic civil society," and "second economy" that are held to have emerged from this process of liberalization are said to have prepared the ground for Hungary's transformation during the 1990s.[7] Despite their recognition that state–society relations changed over time, such interpretations regard the essence of socialism as pervasive state control. Furthermore, society is still seen as being fundamentally passive in the face of dictatorship, only occupying autonomous spaces vacated by the state as part of its liberalization drive.

What all of these arguments have in common is that they suggest that the socialist states managed to so thoroughly dominate Eastern European societies that they managed to emasculate them. There are several elements that have to be addressed if such arguments are to be critically interrogated. The first element is the question of how far a repressive state was able to suppress popular opposition. The second is the question of the effectiveness of the opposition that was able to manifest itself. The third element is the degree to which the socialist dictatorships were able to remold society in their own image. The answers to these questions are by no means as simple as those who point to the pervasiveness of state action would suggest.

Repression and Protest

There can be no doubt that during the first decade of socialist rule across the region the dictatorships sought to ruthlessly transform the societies they governed. In peasant societies, collectivization drives were initiated that sought to destroy the way of life of many of those who worked the land and that aimed to fundamentally transform rural society.[8] In industry work relations were transformed while labor mobilization policies forced millions of East Europeans to take jobs in industry.[9] Private business was almost eliminated as early as the later 1940s in Hungary, though not until the early 1970s in the German Democratic

Republic.[10] As a result society in East-Central European states became more homogeneous than ever before as previously diverse social groups began to share a common culture as the "working people" of their respective states.[11]

Furthermore, from the late 1940s onward the institutions of single-party socialist dictatorships were built in all the East-Central European states, albeit with some national variation.[12] With the institutionalization of socialist-party states, came the creation of a huge apparatus of political control. Agitation and propaganda departments within the ruling parties as well as social organizations were transformed into transmission belts designed to mobilize the populace behind the goals of radical social transformation.[13] Alongside the institutions of mobilization, those of outright coercion were created. Policing was transformed across Soviet-occupied Eastern Europe on the morrow of Nazi defeat in 1945.[14] Secret police forces were initially formed in the political departments of the regular police. In most Eastern European states in 1948 and 1949, the secret police forces were merged with the border guards, separated institutionally from regular police forces, radically expanded, and placed under the dual control of the Ministry of the Interior and the party.[15]

The creation of large secret police forces occurred in tandem with the intensification of the first Cold War and the tension in the socialist block that followed Yugoslavia's departure from the Soviet orbit. New domestic police forces operating under extensive Soviet guidance began a wave of purges that spread from Hungary across East-Central Europe, severely hitting functionaries in the ruling parties and the intelligentsia.[16] The dawn of Stalinism in Eastern Europe has been often cited to support the notion that the new socialist dictatorships were authentically totalitarian states. Yet, if one moves away from a focus on the effect of Stalinization on the party bureaucracy and the intelligentsia, how justified is this view? How effective was the apparatus of mobilization and repression introduced by the new ruling parties in securing at least the outward obedience of society?

On paper—in the factories, on the collective farms, and in local communities across the region—a seamless apparatus of control existed. The party employed propagandists—"peoples' educators"—in all walks of life. Their function was to support the political campaigns initiated by the party leadership. In Hungary, for example, throughout the 1950s the Stalinist leadership attempted to partly finance its industrialization program through so-called peace loans. The population would "voluntarily" pledge to "lend" 10 percent of their annual income to the state. It was ultimately the job of the peoples' educators to solicit these contributions from ordinary Hungarians. These "loans" were far from popular. The peoples' educators were confronted with the complaints of the population, their dissatisfaction with state policies, and sometimes their outright opposition. Such information would be used in two ways. First and most important, it was used to identify "enemy behavior" among the population—the identities of such "oppositional elements" would be passed on to the secret police. Second, it was used to compile "reports on the climate of opinion" that provided a distorted view of the state of public opinion across the country.[17]

Alongside this the secret police themselves operated at the very local level. As one Hungarian miner remembered after escaping to the West in 1954, "the secret police officers from time to time would appear at the mine and would go in and out of the party offices. They were also accustomed to come down the mine, but not in uniform, always in miners' work clothes. We only knew that they were secret policemen because they were strangers, and we could tell from their expressions that they were always watching us."[18] The secret police forces employed a vast army of informers recruited through methods that often included blackmail and outright coercion. This has been best documented in the case of the former GDR though it occurred across the region.[19] A dairy worker from the Hungarian town of Moson Magyaróvár remembered that in the early 1950s "at the dairy there was an ÁVO (secret police) department, which tried to make me an informer. They reasoned that I was declassed (of former middle-class origin), that I had to work in a menial capacity, and as a result was dissatisfied with my environment and therefore would gladly inform on my fellow workers. This sort of thing was very difficult to refuse. They tried to blackmail people to become informers in the factory and other places."[20]

In much of Eastern Europe between 1948 and 1953, this apparently seamless apparatus of coercion was relatively successful in preventing open collective protest. It must also be stated that it was a period of unprecedented state-directed social change. Collectivization campaigns of varying strength were implemented across the region, and programs of forced industrialization were put into practice. Living standards fell across the region though the degree of that fall was relatively modest in Czechoslovakia and at its greatest in Hungary.[21] Popular protest was extremely sporadic. In Hungary from 1949 up to the outbreak of Revolution in October 1956, no strike lasted more than three hours,[22] and there was only occasional open peasant resistance to the collectivization drives.[23] In the GDR there was isolated industrial unrest prior to 1953,[24] and in Yugoslavia there was one major peasant uprising against Tito's collectivization drives in Biha? in northern Bosnia in 1951.[25] Although there were many other similar incidents, these occurred on a small scale. If this is the whole picture, then the picture of "thoroughly dominated societies" looks like an accurate one. If one digs deeper, however, the picture is substantially modified.

The first and most obvious problem with this view is that if one scans the history of open popular protest in socialist Eastern Europe the picture is one of several years of silence, punctuated by loud and dramatic explosions of discontent that began in one state and resonated across the region.[26] Region-wide explosions of discontent were particularly characteristic of the transition from Stalinism in the region during the mid-1950s. The year 1953 is associated with the dramatic June events in the GDR, yet it was not the only country that witnessed mass discontent during late spring and early summer. In May tobacco workers at Plovdiv in Bulgaria rioted, while in the same month violent protest against regime attempts to wipe out workers' savings paralyzed the industrial city of Plzeň.[27] In the following month came the dramatic events in the GDR that had repercussions in other East European states. The notion that a population could express its discontent openly in a socialist state began, albeit slowly, to lift the lid on a well of discontent. Industrial workers in Budapest openly stated that "the Hungarian party can learn from the German party that it is not correct to apply pressure all the time through the work norms."[28] The second wave of pan-regional popular protest came in 1956 with riots in Poznan in Poland and then, most dramatically, with the outright collapse of the socialist regime, popular revolution, and Soviet intervention in Hungary in the autumn.[29] As in 1953 the shock waves of the Polish and Hungarian events in 1956 hit other states in a less spectacular fashion—we know something of their repercussions in both Romania, Czechoslovakia, and the GDR.[30]

While the upheavals of 1956 did not represent the last wave of significant popular protest prior to 1989, they did contribute to the radical remaking of socialism across the region in a way in which those of 1968 did not. The questions of 1968 and of the Polish events of 1980–1981 are ones that will not be directly addressed by this paper—at this point it is important to develop the point that the state dominance paradigm has some problems in explaining the tumultuous events of the mid-1950s. For the Polish case Padraic Kenney has argued effectively that the Stalinist state in Poland was simply unable to suppress pre-socialist traditions of industrial protest. He implies that workers were able to draw on these traditions of protest during the course of upheavals against the socialist state after the Stalinization of the country.[31] The various advocates of a state dominance paradigm when analyzing Hungarian Stalinism have much the same problem studying the causes and social roots of 1956. There is a general consensus that society was either atomized or demobilized by the Stalinist state among such scholars. This atomization was brought to an end by the outbreak of popular revolution in 1956 when society, having been banished from the play up until then, staged a sudden entrance. Many defined the events of 1956 as an "antitotalitarian" revolution or, stressing Soviet domination, celebrate it as a national revolution against Communism. What remains unexplained is that if Hungarian society was as effectively atomized by the Stalinist experience as advocates of the state dominance paradigm claim, how was it able to assert an alternative set of social and political values during the events of 1956?[32]

The question of popular protest against Stalinism in the period before 1953, and by implication between 1953 and 1956, needs a second look. An examination of the archival documents generated by the official apparatus does not suggest that either an atomized or terrorized society existed during the early 1950s.

They suggest that while socialist citizens were aware of the very real limits that police control placed on popular protest, when one concentrates on either individual or small-scale acts one can detect the existence of a culture of social protest across the region. In Hungary workers resorted at times to sabotage, endemic theft, the use of graffiti, rumor mongering, the disruption of systems of supervision in the workplace, and small scale work stoppages.[33] The agricultural population, faced with high taxation, the compulsory delivery of agricultural produce, and collectivization, adopted similar strategies. Tax avoidance, the intimidation of local officials, and powerful solidarity among villagers against the state were deployed to destroy the agricultural policies of the Hungarian regime, disrupting food distribution and thus creating discontent in the towns.[34] According to Katherine McCarthy, who has studied peasant action in central Croatia during this period, similar patterns of resistance were used by peasants that shook Yugoslavia's collectivization drive to its foundations.[35] For the early years of the GDR, Andrew Port has documented the widespread use by industrial workers of individual forms of protest similar to those identified in Stalinist Hungary, as has Peter Heumos for the industrial districts of early socialist Czechoslovakia.[36]

That a shift of focus from collective action to what anthropologist James Scott has conceptualized as "infrapolitical resistance" creates a picture of a conflict-ridden society should be no surprise.[37] One should, however, treat the whole question of individual or infrapolitical resistance with some care for two reasons. The first is that in the absence of any consideration of motivation almost every act can be conceptualized as resistance. Despite the problems in identifying motivation, Andrew Port correctly cautions us about the need to distinguish between acts of self-conscious political resistance and public apathy, for example.[38] A second related qualification comes from the Hungarian experience—namely that an individual act may be both an act of protest and have another motivation as well. Recognizing that an act is motivated by protest does not necessarily mean that it can be straightforwardly reduced to protest.

Workplace theft and the motivations surrounding it provide a useful illustration of this problem. In Hungary during the early 1950s, workplace theft became endemic—a party inspector at one construction site remarked that during this period "from the director down everyone stole."[39] Low wages and persistent good shortages forced most workers to supplement their wages with another illegal income by participating in the black economy. One skilled worker who worked in the railway carriage workshop in Györ in western Hungary described the forms of secondary economic activity: "About half of my friends together with me worked part-time at odd jobs; this was all on the sly, for this was illegal. This . . . work brought in good money if one had special skills. Some went out in the fields to hoe for smallholders, getting thirty forints for half a day's work. Others, like myself, specialized in repair jobs from motorcycles to watches and everything else. Some painted houses, some took fuel down to the basement. I mainly fixed motor-cycles, putting in new parts. I could not do major repair work. . . . This was due to the fact that mechanical goods were very difficult to obtain."[40] Scarce goods necessary for such activities had to be either stolen from the workplace directly or bought from those who were able to steal them.[41] Therefore, work-place theft in Stalinist Hungary was very much about survival—something that an exclusive concentration on individual protest would ignore. Yet, it was legit-imized by popular discontent with the state. As one worker put it, "smaller thefts increased because people were forced to commit them due to the bad economic situation. When somebody stole from his factory or enterprise, it was not con-sidered immoral, but resourceful. To cause damage to the state did not hurt any one."[42] Another worker put it a little more strongly: "psychologically the situ-ation was . . . that they [the workers] were happy if they could harm the Communist system."[43]

The example of workplace theft in the early 1950s suggests a number of things when attempting to conceptualize state control, popular protest, and resistance in a socialist society. First, the absence of large-scale collective action and the existence of considerable repression should not be taken to mean that no pop-ular discontent existed nor that it had no means of expression. Second, the expres-sions of popular discontent were not straightforwardly acts of resistance in the political sense. Third, strategies designed to ameliorate certain conditions could also be seen as acts of protest against those perceived to have created those con-ditions. Fourth, protest and resistance were determined by the conditions in which prospective protesters found themselves—repression closed off the option of col-lective mass protest, while the forms of protest that did arise were conditioned by the climate of shortages and low wages. Last, the history of popular protest cannot be divorced from the more general social history of the region.

Even though the strategies described by István Rév, Katherine McCarthy, Andrew Port, and me cannot be unambiguously characterized as acts of resistance, they undoubtedly undermined state authority. The cumulative effect of peasant action during the early 1950s was to derail collectivization campaigns. The food supply situation in Yugoslavia led to the permanent abandonment of agricultural collectivization in 1953, and in Hungary its temporary abandonment in the same year. In Poland the politics of food supply led to the permanent abandonment of the collectivization drive in 1956. In Hungary, though private farming would be eliminated in 1961, compulsory deliveries permanently disappeared in 1956.[44] Although the majority of private businesses were formally nationalized in much of the region, legal private business destabilized the state sector, while a large illegal sector assumed a major role in society.[45] In industry the state lacked authority over labor—this manifested itself in discipline problems within the work-place, labor mobility, plan underfulfillment, the failure of the state to control wage rates, and the low quality of goods produced.[46]

In other words the state attempted to transform society using its apparatus of mobilization and repression during the first ten years of socialist rule. Agricultural cooperatives were created, and peasants were subjected to extraordinary taxation, coercion, and police supervision. Private industry was decimated in most of the region, and large numbers of people were forced into state industrial jobs. In short, large numbers of people were forced by the state to change their way of life on an unprecedented scale. This picture, however, is one-sided. Collectivization and compulsory deliveries were abandoned across the region. Many private businesses were liquidated, but nonstate economic activity did not disappear—large black markets fueled by the failure of the state sector and endemic corruption undermined the functioning of the state sector. Informal wage bargaining, labor mobility, and behavior termed "labor indiscipline" essentially meant that the state lacked authority over those forced into state industrial jobs.

The Nature of State Socialism

To many familiar with the literature of East European Stalinism, and indeed that which analyzes the socialist dictatorships more generally, this will seem a provocative conclusion. On the basis of the evidence presented, one might conclude that although state control was far from complete, it was still—in any comparative perspective—extremely pervasive. Some social historians indeed adopt this perspective. Andrew Port in his work on industrial protest in the GDR refers to the totalitarian project of the socialist dictatorship making a distinction between state intention and social outcome.[47] John Connelly, in an impressive comparative study of higher education in the early socialist GDR, Czechoslovakia, and Poland, makes a similar distinction.[48] An equivalent distinction is implicit in the work of those social historians of the GDR who explore "the limits of dictatorship."[49]

What is wrong therefore with this perspective? So far as it goes, it is empirically correct—the states of the region employed a security apparatus that aimed to control the population to an unprecedented extent. Furthermore, there can be little doubt of the wide ranging and radical changes to daily life that the state sought to direct. The fundamental problem of the approach is that it reduces the goals of the socialist dictatorships to the institutional means—namely state control and authority—that the dictatorships employed to realize their social program. This leads to fundamental misunderstandings of the nature of state intervention in society under the dictatorships. Before discussing that social program, it is worthwhile to pause and develop the point about the misunderstandings that can result.

All the analyses that fit into the state dominance paradigm identify the nature of state socialism in its institutional arrangements and the pervasiveness of its control over society. According to advocates of the "totalitarian" paradigm, dictatorial socialism's essence was captured by an ideological party state employing terror and the techniques of mass mobilization to secure consent. The economy was almost entirely nationalized and subject to control through comprehensive economic planning. Highly collectivist solutions to social problems led to state intrusion into the private sphere. Though the advocates of "totalitarianism" identified socialism as having a distinct ideology, there was always some lack of clarity as to whether ideology was a motivating force for the dictators, or merely a tool to justify a relentless drive for total power.[50] Though few theoretical analysts of the trajectory of state socialism would now use the term "totalitarianism" to describe the dictatorships, its essential foundations have been preserved in newer, more nuanced arguments. Arguments that describe socialism as "dictatorship over needs" identify socialism's uniqueness in terms of the degree of state control over economic behavior.[51] Elemér Hankiss and Iván Szelényi—two Hungarian sociologists writing influential accounts of state socialism's historical trajectory—see the essence of early socialism in the fact that it dissolved civil society and almost completely abolished private property.[52] It was therefore the negation of political liberalism. Reformist socialism lay in between the two, where the socialist state coexisted uneasily with a "second society" and "socialist entrepreneurs."[53]

The equation of socialism with statism obscures rather than illuminates the whole question of intention. Elemér Hankiss's account—drawing primarily on Hungarian examples—describes a seventeen-year period from 1948 to 1965 that he characterizes as "the paralyzed society." He describes the destruction of multiparty democracy and of independent social organizations. He discusses the party's monopolization of public life in post-1948 Hungary, and various interventions in society interpreted in terms of the dictatorship's attempt to "demobilize" society. Hankiss does not discuss the motivations and beliefs of the party elite. As a result the reader is left with no understanding of the motivations that led many Communists to believe in "forced" industrialization, collectivization, and comprehensive economic planning.[54] One might argue that Communists were ever really interested only in power, and few believed their own ideology. A full and definitive answer to this objection must await the outcome of detailed empirical research into the dictators, their followers, and policy-making processes. Yet, there is considerable evidence that many Communists—including the dictators themselves—believed in what they were doing. Hungary's former Stalinist prime minister turned dissident, András Hegedüs, remembered in 1989 of the country's ranking authority in Stalinist economic policy Ernö Gerö that "he was a convinced propagandist of a very definite ideology."[55] What is left though in Hankiss's account is that complete control is assumed to be the intention of the dictators.

In the state-centered paradigm, socialism is reduced to statism, while the intentions of its leaders are reduced to a drive for absolute power in and of itself. These assumptions result in some misunderstandings that seriously distort our understanding of the socialist dictatorships. First, all state action is reduced to a drive for political control. As Annette Timm has pointed out, if the logic of "the thoroughly governed society" argument were applied to the creation of a state health service in the GDR, it would be seen simply as an agent of state domination and control. The social policy motivations that informed its creation would be lost from the analysis.[56] Second, the use of these frameworks has led many analysts to confuse intention and outcome. In an analysis of the impact of shortages in everyday life on ordinary Romanians during the 1980s, the anthropologist Katherine Verdery describes food and goods shortages as "seizures of time" that "were basic to producing subjects who would not see themselves as independent agents."[57] This at least is plausible and is supported by evidence from other contexts. Verdery then shifts focus to discuss causation. Although she does not deny the complex nature of phenomena such as shortage, she strongly suggests that this was deliberate strategy of the state: "time in Ceauşescu's Romania, by contrast, stood still, the medium for producing not profits but subjection, for immobilizing persons in the Party's grip."[58]

The implication is that food queues and regular work stoppages were not just symptoms of the malfunctioning of the economy but were themselves instruments of social control. Perhaps the Romanian state intended food shortages to subject the population, though Verdery presents no actual evidence that this was party policy. Furthermore, it flies in the face of what we know about the politics of food shortages elsewhere in the region, albeit in an earlier period of socialist rule. In Hungary the regime was extremely nervous about the political impact of such shortages and the open discontent they could lead to. For Poland Padraic Kenney has argued that protests around consumption were just as corrosive of state authority as were protests at the point of production.[59] What is more, among those who have examined state intentions across the region in the sphere of consumption, there is a consensus that the socialist states aimed, though failed, to ensure a general abundance of cheap food and consumer goods for the population.[60] What appears more likely is that a notion of the all-pervasive nature of the socialist state has led to the confusion of social outcomes and state intentions. The impression of a monolithic, all-pervasive state is reinforced by arguments that draw on the use of theories, not empirical investigations, of intention that are applied to the observation of social outcome. For those who explicitly study society rather than politics, this is a real pitfall to be avoided.

The third point—related to the first two—is that theories of state dominance often lead analysts to misunderstand the nature of state intervention in the social realm. By way of example it is worth examining the criminalization of job quitting and absenteeism in Hungary in 1952. The state made leaving one's job and getting another without permission, or even taking the day off, a criminal offense— a draconian measure by any means. This has been widely interpreted as part of a determined drive for control by the Stalinist state over society. Along with labor recruitment campaigns, the subordination of unions to the state, and central- ized wage regulations, it has been regarded as part of the state's "nationalization of labor."[61] In other words—according to this view—it formed part of the state's drive to subordinate a part of society to its social program. The archives suggest something quite different—that it was a generally ineffective panic measure that revealed the state's lack of control over labor, one that was very unevenly imple- mented, and then widely ignored by managers. It was introduced in response to statistics that showed almost two-thirds of all new recruits to industry left their jobs and more than the total recruited sought to change jobs in the construc- tion sector in 1951. Some enterprises found it impossible to crack down because of the pervasiveness of job quitting and absenteeism, workers furthermore became adept at modifying their behavior to avoid prosecution, and enterprises themselves refused to prosecute offenders—much to the consternation and despite the protests of policy makers in Budapest.[62] The general point to be made is that an excessive focus on state domination can lead writers to see all state actions as being part of a ceaseless and ultimately successful drive for state domination. The motivations behind such actions, however, are likely to have been more spe- cific and complex. Draconian acts, furthermore, were as likely to be reactions to a perceived lack of control by the dictatorship as they were signs of preten- sions of "total" control. Moreover, the state and its institutions were less unified than many have believed. Indeed, it might be argued that socialist states were like others, a collection of social institutions bound together "in the face of struc- tural tensions and internal political struggles."[63]

There are two implications for the writing of the history of Eastern Europe's socialist dictatorships that flow from such arguments. The first is that all notions of "totalitarianism," "total dictatorship," or "thoroughly dominated soci- eties" are likely to obscure as much as they reveal about social outcomes and state intentions. As such they should either be abandoned completely, or thoroughly interrogated and qualified before they are used in historical analysis. The sec- ond is that concepts such as state intention, state dominance, and state control need unpacking. In short if we assume automatically that the intention of the state was to gain absolute control or dominance of all social processes, we will see the fingerprints of the state over all social behavior—and the likelihood is that we will misread reality.

There is, however, one key respect in which proponents of the state domi- nance paradigm describe state socialism accurately—its suppression and super- vision of all political or associational activity. Former dissident János Kenédi has collected Hungarian police documents from the relatively liberal, later years of Hungarian socialism that demonstrate the lengths to which police forces went in seeking to control even those who organized small-scale demonstrations, cir-culated leaflets, or left anti-Communist graffiti in Budapest underpasses.[64] Historian and journalist Timothy Garton-Ash has shown the resources the GDR's secret police force were prepared to devote to the surveillance of foreign nation-als and indeed of the tiny minority of intellectuals termed dissidents.[65] Linguist and historian Dennis Deletant has recently documented the institutionalized para-noia that shaped the day-to-day behavior of Romania's Securitate under Ceausescu.[66] In addition to the published material, there is much anecdotal evi-dence of the degree to which the state was suspicious of nonpolitical associa-tions such as unofficial residents' groups, or for that matter intolerant of independent political action within legally permitted organizations.[67]

The socialist states effectively abolished "civil society"—the sphere of inde-pendent institutions between the state and the realm of daily life that form the infrastructure on which organized political activity is built in liberal democra-tic states.[68] The socialist-party states enjoyed a monopoly on legitimate political activity, broken perhaps during the early 1980s in Poland, for a few months in 1968 in Czechoslovakia, to a highly limited extent by the Protestant Church in the GDR, and then as socialism decomposed from 1987 onward in Poland and Hungary. The apparatus of mobilization and coercion was therefore effective in a much more limited sense than has often been understood. It prevented the devel-opment of effective political alternatives and indeed open communication about political issues unless permitted by the relevant branch of the state. To use historian Jan Gross's expression, the socialist states were "spoiler" states that prevented other social actors taking important initiatives in society.[69] While the abolition of civil society meant that state control over association was consider-able, it did not mean that state control over society was complete.

The abolition of civil society and the pervasiveness of state supervision that prevented the growth of one from below were undoubtedly important social phe-nomena in their own right. They also had consequences for the state. Though the state sought to gauge public opinion through the collection of information, the channels of communication between state institutions and social groups were clogged. Because of the risks that the expression of political views entailed, few were prepared to state their views before representatives of the state. Furthermore, public discontent had few outlets. This undoubtedly contributed to the violence of much antiregime protest in postwar Eastern Europe as well as its suddenness. In Hungary in 1956 the lack of a real public discourse about the discontent with the socialist system meant that both the state apparatus and the party intellectuals who initiated the first waves of demonstrations were genuinely taken aback by the extent and degree of the popular anger with the socialist state.[70] Yet, outside the periods—like in Hungary in 1956—when state authority col-lapsed, the dictatorships were able to prevent discontent assuming a formal or public nature. Much discontent was to take infrapolitical forms, and much social activity occurred partially hidden from the public realm.

Yet, the elimination of civil society and the development of the spoiler state were not the only defining characteristics of Eastern European state socialism. What all of the variants of the state dominance paradigm have in common is that they concentrate on the realm of political institutions. When this concern is projected onto society, all social phenomena are reduced to politics. When examining state socialism from the point of view of society, it is important to ask what state intentions looked like when viewed from the perspective of social history. The elimination of civil society ceases to be the major element in the equation. The state in this account was not focused on a drive for total control *per se;* it was more interested on implementing the program of Marxism-Leninism. What in concrete terms did this entail?

Above all it meant the creation of a socialist society. Membership of such a society was to be dependent upon one's status as a "worker." Private ownership of the means of production was eliminated through nationalization and collectivization. This entailed not merely a radical change in the definition of citizenship, but a decisive shift in the social role of labor. To become a full member of socialist society, one had ideologically to be considered a part of the "working people." To join this group an individual had to work either in a sector of the economy that was already socialized, or one that was approved by regime policy. Membership of the "working people" was to be extended to previously marginalized groups, such as women, the Roma, and the unemployed, in order to "integrate" them fully into the new society.[71] In return for socialist labor an individual gained rights to a wide range of benefits—indeed social rights were to be largely exercised through the workplace.[72]

Ákos Róna-Tas has argued in developing his "institutional" model of state socialism that "universal state employment" in the sense that I described above was the central instrument of social control in postwar Eastern Europe.[73] It was, however, much more than this—the reduction of citizenship to socialist labor, and the conflation of politics with work, informed the development of all social institutions in early socialist Eastern Europe. At the level of institutional design and of ideology, the Eastern European dictatorships saw themselves very much as "workers' states." Hungary's 1949 constitution stated that "the basis of the social order of the Hungarian People's Republic is work." The basis of citizenship was to perform labor and thus to contribute to the generation of the social product. As the state was to direct "the construction of socialism," labor was to be performed in the socialist sector.[74] Production became the arena in which worker-citizens could make their political contribution, at least according to the ideology of the country's new rulers.

This could be seen, for example, in the way in which most party members by the early 1950s were members of their workplace cells rather than members of the party organization where they lived. Of the recorded members and candidates for membership of the party in Hungary's Fejér county in 1952, the over-whelming majority were members of workplace-based organizations.[75] Performance in production was promoted as a measure of social worth and of the support of the worker for the new state, as citizens were mobilized behind the goal of building a "new" socialist society. The various labor competition campaigns became rituals designed to demonstrate worker support for the goals, policies, and often the leaders of the Stalinist state. In December 1949 the spread of individual forms of labor competition culminated in the Stalin shift, in which the workers of Hungary were to celebrate the seventieth birthday of Stalin through the achievement of ever higher production targets. The labor competition campaign that followed the revision of the norms in August 1950 was named the Korea Week and presented ideologically as an opportunity for Hungarian workers to show their unity with the Communist North. In 1951 the second congress of the Hungarian Workers' Party coincided with a major labor competition campaign across the country, in which workers were to celebrate the congress through achieving record production levels. In March 1952 workers were requested to increase production as part of the official celebration of the sixtieth birthday of Mátyás Rákosi—Hungary's Stalinist-era dictator.[76]

As Alf Lüdtke has shown for the GDR, and Padraic Kenney for Poland, these notions were replicated across Eastern Europe and shaped the design of the new states across the region.[77] Although some of the policies provoked massive resistance—the nationalization of industry and the collectivization of agriculture—this resistance could be dismissed as the actions of a "class enemy" opposed to the "building of socialism." An examination of the internal documents and speeches of policy makers reveals that they believed that as property relations were changed by state intervention, social attitudes to work and the state would follow. For those trained in the doctrines of Marxism-Leninism, the belief that attitudes stemmed from social classes was second nature. There is no need to think that Stalinist-era policy makers did nothing other than believe a doctrine that suggested a "dictatorship of the proletariat" could remake property relations from above and create "new" socialist men and women. Indeed, it could be said that many of the problems of Stalinism stemmed from the blindness with which many followed these beliefs. The traces of this kind of thinking can be seen throughout the Hungarian archives. One party investigator visited the Danube Shoe Factory in the northern Budapest suburb of Újpest during 1950 and stated in his report that "political backwardness, that is closely connected with skill-based backwardness, can be felt in the factory. A large proportion of the workforce was artisans whose relationship to their work has not yet developed."[78] The implication was clear: "political backwardness" was related to their "class" origin and this would disappear when their relationship to their work improved. This in turn would come when they became accustomed to their new identity as socialist worker-citizens.

The Ideology of Socialist Citizens As Workers

Yet, the East European dictatorships were not able to turn their populations into model socialist citizens, nor were they able to lay the economic foundations for socialism by guaranteeing economic success. Economic plans dictated by the demands of the Soviet military at the height of the Cold War led to unrealistic demands on sources of energy and on natural resources. Shortages resulted in disorganized production so that the "command economy" ever really existed only on paper.[79] These shortages were fueled by the consequences of the state's failure to secure consent from the social groups—the "working peasantry" and the working class—that its rule was built on. This was the key paradox of Eastern European Stalinism. Though it could deploy the strength of a repressive state to suppress protest, it was dependent on securing the consent and active participation of the workforce and the peasantry to lay the foundations of socialism. To meet the goals of the plan they had to produce more and better, while instead as we saw at the beginning of this article, considerable discontent existed with the state.[80]

The architects of this productivist socialism believed that by using the state to reshape property relations from above they could transform individuals' relations to their work and create new socialist men and women. The state furthermore sought to mobilize workers behind the goals of building socialism. Wages were individualized as far as possible and closely related to the goals laid down in economic plans. Rewards between workers were to be sharply differentiated as a stimulus to improved production performance.[81] The state did not rely on merely monetary incentives but also on moral, or ideological, ones. It projected an ideology of national reconstruction across the region, of a new society based on productive labor; "the country is yours, build it for yourselves" was perhaps the central slogan of early socialism in Hungary. In parallel with this it adapted to its own goals an earlier rhetoric of the "honor of labor". Stakhanovism, very much part of the speed up of production, was also part of the public celebration of exceptional achievement in production. In tandem with this the state sought to draw a distinction between those who lived from work and those who did not; "he who does not work, should not eat!"[82]

This ideology should have found resonance among the workers and poor peasants of the region. Anthropologists, social observers, and folklorists have pointed to the prevalence of a work ethic that stressed the moral and social worth of productive labor across the region.[83] Ideology could have become a powerful agent of social control establishing a cultural interface between state and society, and to some extent, during the later years of the dictatorships, in some countries, it did. This did not happen, however, during the early years of socialism for reasons that are crucial to understanding the development of social relations until

1989. The first reason was that the institutions of labor that socialism attempted to impose on the population had little popular support from the working populations of the states. Collectivization was bitterly opposed by even poor peasants for whom the private ownership of land was both a sign of independence and social status and was tightly linked to their sense of self. The implementation of the planned economy at shop floor level entailed the Taylorization of factory relations that directly opposed existing work, skill-based, and class cultures. Just as the state claimed rhetorically that it celebrated productive labor, it attacked the material bases of the identities of many East Europeans who might have bought into its ideology.[84] The second reason was that regime economic policies squeezed living standards that were only beginning to recover from the effects of World War Two, the collectivization drives drove the agricultural population close to starvation, and consequent food shortages in the cities fueled the problem. In short, early socialism was experienced as a system in which people had to work harder for no material reward—an exploitative system managed by a "bloodsucking government" as one Hungarian worker put it in 1953 within hearing of a party propagandist.[85] Third, those who expressed their discontent or failed to work to the targets of the plan could easily find themselves described as a "class enemy" and subject to the apparatus of repression. One Hungarian engineer complained to a party committee in 1953 that he "feared arrest and feared the internment camps, because production did not proceed as it should have done."[86]

Ideology and experience during the early 1950s across the region flatly contradicted each other. Far from mobilizing workers behind the goals of the plan, the reconceptualization of work as a political act contributed to the destruction of state authority. One example from Hungary illustrates this. In 1951 the state introduced a movement for the saving of raw materials in order to facilitate their more efficient use. One worker's response points to how politicized rhetoric led workers to frustrate even this measure: "the 'Gazda' movement was started in the interests of saving raw materials. In any case it would be a good thing to do because the workers today really waste raw materials . . . they are happy if they can harm the Communist system."[87]

The early socialist state was weak precisely because of its role in broader social relations. This does not mean that the state was not repressive or that it was incapable of initiating major social change. What it means is that it was incapable either through repression or mobilization of enforcing its authority to the degree needed to fulfill its program of social transformation. This furthermore meant that it was unable to maintain its political authority or even to guarantee its stability, except by recognizing at least implicitly the limits to its power.

This brings me to the last point I want to make about the state dominance paradigm. So far, the discussion has concentrated on the early socialist period. This has been necessary as it was during the first years of socialist rule that the constraints on the socialist dictatorships emerged. These very real constraints reveal much about the trajectories of Eastern European socialism until 1989. The states remained weak, but state–society relations were reshaped in later periods. The social history of the region in the 1950s is undeveloped enough, yet that of the 1960s, 1970s, and 1980s is largely virgin territory. Despite this, it is worth rethinking the way changes to state–society relations have been conceptualized, however sketchy this process of rethinking may be.

The advocates of the state dominance paradigm have developed a model of state–society relations in which the early socialist, or Stalinist, state is conceptualized as monolithic, presiding over an effectively subordinated society. Reform and popular protest forced the state to gradually cede power to society, allowing the gradual emergence of a quasi-formal private sector and an embryonic civil society. This process of state withdrawal is said to have culminated in the velvet revolutions of 1989, when the upheavals of that year replaced the project of reform with the twin projects of marketization and democratization.[88] There are several obvious initial criticisms to be made of this framework before dealing with more substantial ones. The most important one is that it fits only three countries—Hungary, Poland, and Yugoslavia—very well. It fails to take into account the Czechoslovak case where reform and liberalization were thrown into sudden reverse after the Soviet intervention to end the Prague Spring of 1968.[89] It also cannot account for the Romanian case where Nicolae Ceausescu, despite coopting nationalist intellectuals, during the 1980s attacked the living standards of the population with a ferocity reminiscent of the 1950s.[90]

Yet, once it is argued that the early socialist state was a weak state as I have argued here, the periodization advanced collapses. We are then faced with the question of how to situate the early socialist state in the history of the East European dictatorships, and by extension how the role of the state in East European society changed between 1945 and 1989. In contrast to the arguments of those like Elemér Hankiss, during the Stalinist years the socialist state was highly unstable, while by the mid-1960s it had managed to consolidate its authority across the region. Andrew Port has argued of the 1950s that "the early years of the GDR were a highly volatile period, connected in large part to the introduction of key aspects of the Soviet political and economic system."[91] Melinda Kálmár has argued that the degree to which socialism collapsed in 1956 in Hungary meant that the government installed by Soviet troops had no system left to restore. Instead, János Kádár and his allies were forced to "reconstruct" socialism from scratch.[92] The instability of the Stalinist state can be seen in both the extent of violent protest in Eastern Europe during the mid-1950s, as well as the change in emphasis in state policy across the region during the same period.

The instability of early socialism can be located in the attempt to implement the political program of Marxism-Leninism too completely while attempting radical industrialization, as I have suggested in the account of early socialism presented above. From the mid-1950s onward regimes across the region began to de-emphasize the building of socialism and to place more weight on political consolidation as a goal. This shift in gears had a great deal to do with factors that were both internal and external to the dictatorships themselves. By the mid-1950s the rival blocks in Europe were much more clearly drawn than they had been in 1949. The Austrian *Staatsvertrag,* German rearmament, and the signature of the Warsaw Pact in 1955, as well as the Soviets' violent response to Hungary's attempts to leave the Soviet orbit in 1956, clarified the postwar division of Europe. Since the death of Stalin the Soviet Union had expressed mounting concern about political instability in the East European states and pressured parties in the GDR and Hungary to initiate New Course policies.[93]

This shift in emphasis was to produce a series of different settlements in the countries of the region that await more systematic comparative investigation. Yugoslavia's Republic of Producers—outside the Soviet block—emerged out of the turmoil of the early 1950s.[94] Hungary tied the reconstruction of socialism domestically to the explicit promotion of consumerism from 1957 onward.[95] The GDR, Poland, and Czechoslovakia adopted less radical settlements that nevertheless differed from the practice of early socialism—higher living standards and the greater provision of consumer goods were emphasized, but they adapted the socialist social model less radically than some of their neighbors.[96] Bulgaria, despite outward conformity to the Soviet model, experimented with the reform of the institutions of socialism at the local level.[97] In Romania the regime attempted to appropriate the agenda of nationalist intellectuals, creating a form of socialism in which independence from Moscow was aggressively asserted, while internally the regime sought to subordinate its population to its goals.[98]

As historians begin to explore the virgin land that is the history of socialism from the mid-1950s onward, they would do well to examine the history of later socialism in the light of the experience of early socialism. For Yugoslavia Susan Woodward has described shifts in economic policy that were not plucked out of thin air but emerged over the course of the early socialist period.[99] Zsuzsanna Varga argues that post-1957 policies toward agriculture in Hungary were as much the result of the engagement of party experts with the failures of policy during the early socialist years as they were the outcome of the 1956 Revolution.[100] Historians might examine how local practices that were semi-legal in the early period were absorbed into the reforms of later socialist states. Varga has strongly argued this for the development of agricultural producer cooperatives during the 1960s in Hungary.[101] This process was identified in Bulgaria by anthropologist Gerald Creed, who describes it as forming the key element in what he terms "the domestication of socialism."[102] Of course historians might focus on the social constraints under which socialist states worked that were derived from their early socialist histories, which constrained their freedom of action and ultimately proved their undoing. Jeffrey Kopstein has argued that the SED regime in the GDR was trapped by the need to secure the consent of the country's industrial workforce. Unable to undertake reform to boost productivity for fear of inciting worker protest, and forced to increase living standards and expand the social wage for the same reason, it was forced into ever greater indebtedness throughout the 1970s and 1980s.[103] The case of Poland, where state-directed rising prices provoked protests in 1970 and Eastern Europe's first independent trade union was founded in 1980, forms the most graphic example of the severe social constraints under which late socialist regimes operated.[104] György Földes has argued that the problems of *gulyás* socialism in Hungary likewise stemmed from the need to maintain "the national compromise" vital to political stability in the post-1956 period that ruled out the kinds of economic measures necessary to prevent rising indebtedness.[105]

Conclusion

The argument presented here has been that theories of state socialism that focus on state dominance over society have very little to contribute to our understanding of Eastern European socialism between 1945 and 1989. This article has been a plea for a real social history of the dictatorships that discards tired state-centered models of the socialist experience. The major implication of the argument of this essay for those seeking to embark on writing the histories of the workers' states is that they should start to reconstruct the dictatorships from the bottom up, skeptically examining the existing orthodoxies and subjecting them to critical scrutiny. A different conceptualization of state–society relations under East European socialism has been presented here—one that gives scope for the examination of the motives of the state without reducing them to a ceaseless drive for political power. It is also a framework that places the concerns of social history—so much neglected in writing about this region—at the center of the stage. One nostalgic collection of photographs of everyday life in Hungary during the years of *gulyás* socialism reminds us that the years of the workers' states were those in which millions of Eastern Europeans gained electricity, running water, a refrigerator, a television, and a car for the first time.[106] It serves as a useful counterpoint to an alternative image of Eastern European socialism—of brave dissidents sitting behind typewriters producing pages of *samizdat* pursued by armies of secret policemen and their networks of informers.[107] Yet, useful counterpoint or not both of these pictures are stereotypes forged by memory. Socialist consumerism and political police forces were both elements of a functioning political system and of a distinctive kind of society that deserves to be understood in full. No one would argue that the history of East European socialism could be written without reference to the state, but far too many are prepared to maintain that society was merely and simply at the mercy of politics.

What does the experience of postwar Eastern Europe suggest about the usefulness of the concept of social control as an analytical tool for historians? It certainly should not be dismissed—state institutions such as the police, state welfare services, schools, and a variety of others all played their role in maintaining the social order. Yet, such institutions were not only designed to maintain social order. This and the discussion above suggest that concepts of control should be applied with considerable care. The danger of misusing the concept is that of overdetermining the motivations behind the actions of such institutions. Ideology might also be used as an instrument of control, but such arguments should always be considered carefully. For an explanation based on ideological control assumes that its exponents deploy it merely as an instrument of control—without believing it themselves. This, I would maintain, is very rarely the case. Furthermore, some care needs to be taken to examine the circumstances in which it can become an agent of control. In other words, people have to be able to believe the ideology and to buy into its key tenets. The ultimate implication of this is, of course, that social control as a concept might be useful in a restricted sense. It might explain the exercise of power over society in restricted contexts and in highly limited ways. The notion of totally controlled societies needs to be dismissed. Even political and social processes in modern dictatorships—with all the techniques of surveillance and control open to them—were based on the complex interplay between the state and social actors.

Notes

1. Pittaway, "The Social Limits of State Control," 292.

2. For a history of "totalitarianism" as a concept see Gleason, *Totalitarianism;* for a classic analysis of East-Central European developments written from a "totalitarian" perspective, see Brzezinski, *The Soviet Bloc: Unity and Conflict.*

3. Many follow the lead of Ken Jowitt. See his *New World Disorder.*

4. Fehér et al., *Dictatorship over Needs.*

5. Kocka, "Eine durchherrschte Gesellschaft."

6. For the best survey of how the Hungarian model differed from the rest of the socialist dictatorships, see Swain, *Hungary;* for Yugoslavia see Woodward, *Socialist Unemployment.*

7. See Hankiss, *East European Alternatives;* Szelényi, *Socialist Entrepreneurs;* Ákos Róna-Tas, *The Great Surprise of the Small Transformation.*

8. For the former GDR see Bauerkämper, "Von der Bodenreform zur Kollektivierung"; for Hungary see Rév, "The Advantages of Being Atomized"; for Yugoslavia see Bokovoy, *Peasants and Communists.;* for Romania see Kideckel, "The Socialist

Trans-formation of Agriculture in a Romanian Commune"; for Bulgaria see Creed, *Domesticating Revolution*, 53–69; Jarosz, "Polish Peasants versus Stalinism."

9. For the transformation of work relations in the former GDR, see Hübner, *Konsens, Konflikt und Kompromiß*, 16–57; and Lüdtke, "Helden der Arbeit"; for Hungary see Pittaway, "The Social Limits of State Control"; for Poland see Kenney, *Rebuilding Poland*. For Czechoslovakia see Heumos, "Aspekte des sozialen Milieus der Industriearbeiterschaft." On the proletarianization of nonindustrial labor in Hungary, see Pittaway, "Industrial Workers, Socialist Industrialisation and the State."

10. For Hungary see Róna-Tas, *The Great Surprise of the Small Transformation*, 33–72; for the former GDR see Kopstein, *The Politics of Economic Decline in East Germany;* and Wolle, *Die heile Welt der Diktatur,* 195–97.

11. For a discussion of this process in the former GDR, see Merkel, "Arbeiter und Konsum im real exitierenden Sozialismus"; for Hungary see my discussion in Pittaway, "Stalinism, Working Class Housing and Individual Autonomy."

12. The most significant national variation was in Yugoslavia with its federal structure. See Irvine, "Introduction"; for the GDR see Naimark, *The Russians in Germany.;* for Hungary see Standeisky et al., eds., *A fordulat évei, 1947–1949;* for Poland see Kenney, *Rebuilding Poland;* for Romania see Deletant, *Communist Terror in Romania.*

13. Surprisingly very little work has been done on the role of propaganda and mass mobilization—an exception to this is the unique Yugoslav case: see Lilly, *Power and Persuasion.*

14. The history of policing and criminal justice in postwar East-Central Europe is an underdeveloped area; however, work has been done only on the GDR and Hungary as far as the author is aware. For the GDR see Bessel, "Grenzen des Polizeistaates"; for Hungary see Gyarmati et al., *Magyar Hétköznapok,* 80–85.

15. On Romania see Deletant, *Communist Terror in Romania,* 114–45; on Hungary see Ormos et al., *Törvénytelen Szocializmus,* 64–68; Berki, *Az Államvédelmi Hatóság,* 71–82; on the former GDR see Childs and Popplewell, *The Stasi.*

16. By far the best account of Eastern Europe's postwar show trials is Hodos, *Show Trials.*

17. This seems to have been true across Eastern Europe. For my views on the "reports on the climate of opinion" as historical sources, see Pittaway, "Industrial Workers, Socialist Industrialisation and the State," preface.

18. Open Society Archives (hereafter OSA) Radio Free Europe (RFE) Magyar Gy.6/Item No. 8083/54, p. 4.

19. Müller-Enbergs, ed., *Inoffizielle Mitarbeiter des Ministeriums fur Staatssicherheit.*

20. Columbia University Libraries Rare Book and Manuscript Library (hereafter CUL RB&ML), Bakhmeteff Archive (hereafter BAR), Hungarian Refugees Project (hereafter CURPH), Box 10, Interview No. 203, p. 28.

21. According to András Hegedüs, a Hungarian central party committee functionary for much of the period and then Prime Minister between 1955 and 1956, official sta-

tistics available to the party elite at the time showed that in Czechoslovakia real wages in 1952 were 8 percent lower than in 1948, in Poland the standard of living in 1953 was only 87 percent of its 1949 level, and real wages in Hungary in 1952 were only 82 percent of their 1949 level; see Heged?s, *A Történelem és a Hatalom Igézetében*, 198–99.

22. See Pittaway, "Retreat from Collective Protest," 199–200.

23. Pünkösti, *Rákosi a Csúcson*, 260.

24. Port, "When Workers Rumbled."

25. Bokovoy, *Peasants and Communists*, 134–40.

26. Ekiert, *The State against Society.*

27. Crampton, *A Short History of Modern Bulgaria*, 176; Ulc, "Pilsen: The Unknown Revolt."

28. Magyar Országos Levéltár (Hungarian National Archive, hereafter MOL) M-Bp.-95f.2/215ö.e., pp. 54–55.

29. For both crises see Zinner., ed., *National Communism and Popular Revolt* (incredibly, still in print). For Poland see Syrop, *Spring in October.* For Hungary the best English-language account is more recent: see Litván, ed., *The Hungarian Revolution of 1956.*

30. For Romania see Deletant, *Communist Terror in Romania*, 257–71; and Retegan, "A román kommunizmus." For the GDR see Fulbrook, *Anatomy of a Dictatorship.*

31. See both the introduction and conclusion to Kenney, *Rebuilding Poland.*

32. For treatments of de-Stalinization that follow this scheme, see Brzezinski, *The Soviet Bloc*, chap. 10. For an account of the 1956 Revolution that subscribes to a left-wing version of the antitotalitarian thesis, see Lefort, "La permiére révolution antito-talitaire"; for the classic view of the events of 1956 as a national, anti-Communist uprising, see Váli, *Rift and Revolt in Hungary;* for a further standard account, see Zinner, *Revolution in Hungary.*

33. Pittaway "The Social Limits of State Control," 288–89; Pittaway "Retreat from Collective Protest," 9–26; Pittaway, "The Reproduction of Hierarchy."

34. Rév, "The Advantages of Being Atomized"; Pittaway, "Industrial Workers, Socialist Industrialisation and the State," 198–206.

35. McCarthy, "Peasant Revolutionaries and Partisan Power."

36. Port, "The 'Grumble Gesellschaft.'" Heumos, "Aspekte des sozialen Milieus."

37. Scott, *Domination and the Arts of Resistance: Hidden Transcripts.*

38. Port, "The 'Grumble Gesellschaft,'", 806–7.

39. MOL M-KS-276f.94/827ö.e., p. 251.

40. CUL RB&ML BAR CURPH, Box 11, Interview No. 221, p. 24.

41. CUL RB&ML BAR CURPH, Box 4, Interview No. 82-M, p. X/29.

42. CUL RB&ML BAR CURPH, Box 3, Interview No. 31-M, p. VI/15.

43. OSA RFE Magyar Gy.6/ Item No. 08794/53, p. 1.

44. On Yugoslavia see Bokovoy, *Peasants and Communists*, 126–52; for Poland see Jarosz, "Peasants versus Stalinism"; for Hungary in 1953 see Rév, "The Advantages of

Being Atomized"; and for the post-1956 period, see Varga, *Politika, Paraszti Érdekérvényesítés és Szövetkezet Magyarországon, 1956–1967.*

45. For the Hungarian case see Pittaway, "Industrial Workers, Socialist Industrialisation and the State," 288–322.

46. For discussion of some of these problems in the GDR, see Kopstein, *The Politics of Economic Decline in East Germany,* chap. 1; and Hübner, *Konsens, Konflikt und Kompromiß.;* for Hungary see Pittaway, "The Social Limits of State Control"; for Czechoslovakia see Heumos, "Aspekte des sozialen Milieus"; for Poland see Lebow, "Public Work, Private Lives."

47. Port, "The 'Grumble Gesellschaft'"; Port, "When Workers Rumbled."

48. Connelly, *Captive University.*

49. Bessel and Jessen, eds., *Die Grenzen der Diktatur.*

50. See note 2 for the totalitarian perspective.

51. Fehér et al., *Dictatorship over Needs.*

52. Hankiss, *East European Alternatives,* 11–49; Szelényi, *Socialist Entrepreneurs,* chap. 3.

53. Ibid.

54. Hankiss, *East European Alternatives,* 11–49.

55. Heged?s, *Élet egy Eszme Árnyékában,* 104.

56. Timm, "Guarding the Health of Worker Families in the GDR.," 466.

57. Verdery, "The 'Etatization' of Time in Ceasescu's Romania, 56.

58. Ibid., 57.

59. For Hungary see Pittaway, "Industrial Workers, Socialist Industrialisation and the State," 291–309; for Poland see Padraic Kenney, "The Gender of Resistance."

60. For the GDR see Merkel, *Utopie und Bedürfnis,* 38–160; and Pence, "Building Socialist Worker-Consumers"; for Poland see Crowley, "Warsaw's Shops in Stalinism and the Thaw"; for Hungary see Pittaway, "Consumption, Political Stabilisation and Social Identity."

61. Róna-Tas, *The Great Surprise of the Small Transformation,* 59.

62. For my discussion of this phenomenon, see Pittaway, "Industrial Workers, Socialist Industrialisation and the State," 221–26.

63. Jessop, *State Theory,* 340.

64. Kenédi, *Kis Állambiztonsági Olvásókönyv.*

65. Garton-Ash, *The File—A Personal History.*

66. Deletant, *Ceausescu and the Securitate.*

67. I am very grateful to the anthropologist László Kürti for his insights.

68. My definition is based most closely on the one advanced in Arato and Cohen, *Civil Society and Political Theory*; it draws also on that advanced in Keane, *Democracy and Civil Society.*

69. Gross, "Social Consequences of War."

70. Pittaway, "Industrial Workers, Socialist Industrialisation and the State," 325–63.

71. This argument comes over very strongly in all of the propaganda during the socialist period. It has also been pointed out by a number of social scientists, particularly but not exclusively anthropologists, who have analyzed social change under state socialism. See Stewart, *The Time of the Gypsies,* for an analysis close to mine in general terms and excellent information on its impact on the Roma. For the importance of proletarianization to the liberation of women and their acquisition of socialist citizenship, see Goven, "The Gendered Foundations of Hungarian Socialism," 66–68; see also Lüdtke, "'Helden der Arbeit.'"

72. This point is very forcefully made by the London-based legal and constitutional historian László Péter in his discussion of the paradoxical role played by the socialist-party state in the development of citizenship rights in Hungary. See Péter, "Volt-e magyar társadalom a XIX. században?," 94; for Hungary see also Szalai, "Társadalmi Válság és Reform-Alternatívák," 58.

73. Róna-Tas, *The Great Surprise of the Small Transformation,* 73–89.

74. *A Dolgozó Nép Alkotmánya,* 37.

75. For these statistics see FML MSZMP FMBA ir. 9f.1/46ö.e.; *Statisztikai Összesz-itö (kerület, járás, város, nagyüzem részére): Fejér megyei összesitö 1952 I. hó.*

76. On the Stalin shift and its connections to the official celebrations of the Soviet leader's seventieth birthday on December 21, 1949, see MOL M-KS-276f.65/76ö.e., pp. 30–31; see also Gyula Hevesi, *Sztahanov Útján.,* 99–104; "Magyar Dolgozók Pártja Központi Vezetöségének Határozata a Szocialista Munkaverseny Eredményeinek Megszilárditásáról és Továbbfejlesztéséröl," reprinted in *A Magyar Dolgozók Pártja,* 87; on the Korea week in factories in southwestern Hungary, see SZKL Zala SZMT/41d./1950; *Nagykanizsa, 1950 augusztus 11;* on the Congress labor competition of 1951, see MOL M-KS-276f.116/38ö.e., pp.1–3; "A Magyar Dolgozók Pártja Központi Vezetöségének válaszlevele a dolgozók kongresszusi munkaverseny-kezdeményezésére (1951 január)," reprinted in *Magyar Dolgozók Pártja,* 124–26; on the competition campaign for the sixtieth birthday of Rákosi in 1952, see Nemes, *Rákosi Mátyás Születésnapja,* 33–36.

77. Lüdtke, "'Helden der Arbeit'"; Kenney, *Rebuilding Poland.*

78. MOL M-Bp–95f.4/147ö.e., p. 74.

79. The best overview of East European economies in this period is Berend, *Central and Eastern Europe, 1944–1993,* 39–93.

80. This point has been made by Rév, "The Advantages of Being Atomized."

81. I make this case in Pittaway, "The Social Limits of State Control."

82. For the GDR see Lüdtke, "'Helden der Arbeit'"; for Hungary see Pittaway, "Industrial Workers, Socialist Industrialisation and the State," 150–66; see also editions of *Szabad Nép,* the party newspaper in Hungary, for some of the slogans of the period.

83. For the developments of the kinds of notions of work in German-speaking Central Europe that could also be found in the rest of the region as well as East of it, see Biernacki, *The Fabrication of Labor;* for attitudes to labor in their more specific East European context, refer to the following: for Hungary see Lampland, *The Object of Labor,* chap.

1; for Romania see Kideckel, *The Solitude of Collectivism,* chap, 1; for Bulgaria see Creed, *Domesticating Revolution.*

84. For these measures see the works cited above in notes 8, 9, and 10.

85. On living standards see note 21 above; for the worker's statement see *Politikatörténeti és Szakszervezeti Levéltár* (Central Archive of the Trade Unions, hereafter PtSzL); *A Volt Szakszervezetek Központi Levéltár anyaga* (Materials of the Former Central Archive of the Trade Unions, hereafter SZKL); *Szakszervezetek Országos Tanácsa* (National Council of Trade Unions, hereafter SZOT); Bér-Munkaügyi osztálya (Wage and Labor Department, hereafter Bérosztály-Munkaügyi) /33d./1953; *Feljegyzés a kormányprogrammal kapcsolatos üzemi tapasztalatokról,* p.1.

86. MOL M-KS-276f.53/145 ö.e.;*Tájékoztató az üzemi dolgozók és az üzemi vezetök által felvetett szociális és kultúrális problémákról,* p. 7.

87. OSA RFE Magyar Gy. 6/ Item No. 08794/53, p. 1.

88. The work that has most influenced this periodization is Hankiss, *East European Alternatives.*

89. The best account of this is still Simecka, *The Restoration of Order.*

90. On Ceausescu's cooption of nationalist intellectuals, see Verdery, *National Ideology under Socialism,* chap. 3; on Romania more generally in this period, see Deletant, *Ceausescu and the Securitate.*

91. Port, "When Workers Rumbled," 146.

92. Kálmár, *Ennivaló és Hozomány,* 15–47.

93. On the Soviet role in the GDR, see Fulbrook, *Anatomy of a Dictatorship,* 181; on their role in Hungary, see Szabó *Új Szakasz az MDP Politikájában,* 7.

94. Woodward, *Socialist Unemployment,* 164–90.

95. Pittaway, "Consumption, Political Stabilisation and Social Identity"; Pittaway, "The Reproduction of Hierarchy," 766–69.

96. For the GDR see Kopstein, *The Politics of Economic Decline;* on Poland see Kenney, "The Gender of Resistance," 408.

97. Creed, *Domesticating Revolution.*

98. On this see Verdery, *National Ideology under Socialism.*

99. Woodward, *Socialist Unemployment,* 164–90.

100. Personal communication, June 1999.

101. Varga, *Politika, Paraszti.*

102. Creed, *Domesticating Revolution.*

103. Kopstein, *The Politics of Economic Decline in East Germany.*

104. Ekiert, "Rebellious Poles."

105. Földes, *Hatalom és mozgalom;* Földes, *Az eladósodás politikatörténete.*

106. Gerö and Petö, eds., *Befejezetlen Szocializmus.*

107. One book that presents such an image of the GDR is Garton-Ash, *The File.*

CHAPTER 18

Deviance, Control, and Democracy: France, 1950–2000

Sebastian Roché

There has been a dramatic surge in crime and delinquency in the Western countries since 1950. Combined with a change in sensitivity to crime, this has led to the emergence of the question of insecurity as a major political problem on the agenda. I intend to offer an explanation of these rising crime rates, by linking them to major alterations not only at an individual level but at the level of society (in the ways people see themselves, use the urban space, express values, etc.).

Social Control, Social Welfare, and Human Constraints

Many theories dating back to the 1970s have portrayed modern societies as societies of control. Marxists presented the school or the judiciary as an "ideological state apparatus." Michel Foucault has spoken of a "disciplinary society" since the seventeenth century, as opposed to the Middle Ages and the Renaissance. He argues that a process of confinement (*le grand renfermement*) has been going on since this period. The model of this society was the general hospital (*Hôpital Général*), opened in 1656, that hosted beggars, vagrants, homosexuals, and madmen. He states that we should not be surprised "if the prison resembles factories, schools, barracks, hospitals, which are all similar to prisons."[1] In his view these institutions had a common mission of taming individuals, making them useful and obedient. Our societies would be driven by trends toward more surveillance and normalization. Foucault equates what he called modern "institutions" with social control: workshops, manufactures, schools, prisons, barracks.

The type of foucaldian general theorization cannot differentiate between social work and the prison, between social sanctions and social integration, or even between totalitarianism and democracy and cannot be supported by empirical facts. Historians have shown that insane people were not well integrated into society before the seventeenth century. No new way of looking at insanity can be observed in that period. There were numerous cases of persecution even during the Middle Ages and the Renaissance, and as Pierre Morel and Claude Quétel have shown, humans have always tried to cure mental disorders. The confinement process never happened during the seventeenth century: "the proportion of madmen locked up per 10,000 inhabitants was 0.7 under the rule of Louis XIV (the period in which Foucault placed the *grand renfermement* of madmen at the General Hospital of Paris), 1.9 at the eve of the Revolution, 3.6 in 1838, 10 at the end of the Second Empire and 20 at the end of the Third Republic."[2] Clearly, if the expression "great confinement" has any meaning it must be applied to the nineteenth century and no other period. A margin of error of two centuries is hardly acceptable.

To situate the process of confinement during the nineteenth century makes a huge difference. The development of asylums and the mass treatment of madness then appear to parallel the rise of the welfare state in European countries. Marcel Gauchet and Gladys Swain (1980) have pinpointed this link between democratization and the treatment of mental disorders. There is no normalization in the sense of pure repression. These two authors have shown how democratization consists of taking care of the weakest and the underprivileged people. The creation of asylums is no exclusion. The moral treatment of mental diseases is a way to attribute to the madman the status of a sick person (who can be cured) and not of an insane person (who has no chance of being cured). The mad person is a human being and not a monster.

Control without Effective Control?

There certainly are many ways to look at social control. Yet, it seems to me a scholar is offered two main directions that might be combined but that are contradictory to each other to a certain extent. There is a difference between social control designed as a series of organizational mechanisms, and social control assessed through its efficiency, that is, the way it affects people's behaviors and even thoughts. My attempt is not to claim that more state is per se more control, but it is to look at the rise in crime and then ask what type of explanation is available.

There cannot be more social control with at the same time more of what is supposed to be controlled. If the prison is a means of social control, it cannot be said that more prisoners equates with more social control if the crime rates are rocketing. How could there be more crime in a more controlled society? To argue that this is possible implies that social control techniques do not necessarily have to be efficient to be seen as social control means. But if social control as such is independent of any real effect on individuals, its definition is lacking any meaning.

Although very commonly used in the social sciences, the notion of social control suffers various weaknesses. I shall argue that it is most convenient to replace it with another notion, human constraints, in line with sociologists like Raymond Boudon or economists such as Douglas North. The concept of social control has many limitations. It is too broad: An addition of formal and informal social controls, it seems to me, it encompasses the range of all human activities (i.e., social, political, economical). For example, there can be positive and negative incitements for action: should we exclude the former? Speaking of social control does not specify the means used in order to achieve control. Therefore, incentives (positive rewards) and disincentives (punishment and other forms), could perhaps both be considered and enter the scope of social control.

Social control is too vague a concept to be useful. We are in need of more precision. Is it a function of who has a look at it, of a standpoint and a position in society? What would a society be without any control? What is a socially controlled society when talking of our current democracies? And how can we prove that there is an effective control? One way of looking at this issue is to narrow the scope of our analysis to a more limited object. It is more feasible to look at the issue of crime as a case in point to examine the idea of a society of control and its possible meanings.

Trends in Crime

To examine crime trends we need empirical sources. A few are available: police data, vital statistics, and the European Crime Victimization Surveys (ECVS). Only the police data are available in the long run for various offenses. The vital statistics portray only homicides. The ECVS were started in 1989. French police statistics give a global overview of two types of crime since 1950: property crime and crime against the person. A more detailed view was rendered possible in 1972 after a reorganization of the crime categories.

Two subperiods must be distinguished: 1950–1985 and 1985–2001. During the first period, there was an upsurge in the number of thefts. It is noteworthy that crime was rising during the golden years (1945–1973) as well as during the post–oil shock period (1973 and after). Crime rates started to increase before the economic crisis occurred. But the crisis did not stop crime rates: The number of thefts climbed until 1985, before going down for a few years.

From 1985 onward, various crimes against the person have increased, along with the number of juveniles as perpetrators. The major increase in assaults did not happen before the mid-1980s, before mass unemployment was a reality in

France. In the end, thefts and assaults have a reversed profile: When the first grow rapidly the second do the same slowly (1950–1985), and conversely during the second period (1985–2001).

Questions are always raised about the validity of police statistics. One way of responding is to be able to confront two sets of data, namely police data and victimization surveys. There have been only few national victimization surveys in France, but they give us precious indications. In 1986, 11,000 people were interviewed regarding their victimization in 1984–1985. In 1996, the National Institute for Statistics and Economical Studies (INSEE) surveyed 6,000 people regarding the years 1994–1995. Therefore, we can look at both sets of data (police and nonpolice) over a ten year period. The authors (Aubusson et al.) concluded that the two sets are coherent, although with some discrepancies.

Assaults, burglaries, vehicle thefts, and other thefts are distinguished. Regarding assaults, victimization data show an increase of 79 percent for reported assaults and 112 percent for all assaults, including nonreported, and police data of 78 percent. Regarding burglaries, victimization data display a decrease of 6 percent for reported burglaries and 13 percent for all burglaries, including nonreported, and police data of 4 percent. For automobile thefts (cars and parts of cars), victimization surveys find an increase of 37 percent for reported thefts and 60 percent for all thefts, including nonreported and police data of 15 percent.[3] Clearly, there are variations between police and victimization data. But, in France as in the rest of the world, the trend is in the same direction: If the surveys find more victimization (assaults, automobile thefts), so do the police statistics. And, if the surveys find less victimization (burglaries), so do the police statistics.

The ECVS started in 1989. Since then, they confirm an increase in violent, nonlethal crimes in France. In most countries, there has been a general long-term trend of decline in the number of homicides.[4] However, since the 1950s, in many countries we have started to count more murders again. The upward trend was dramatic for the United States (as well as the decline during the 1990s) and existed to a lesser extent for France. The vital statistics observed a rate of .6 per 100,000 in 1950, .8 in 1970, 1.2 in 1986, and a stable rate since then. These statistics are computed by the *Institut National de la Santé et la Recherche Médicale* (INSERM) and do not offer a level comparable with the police figures. The police-counted murder rate since 1986 is 2 per 100,000. But observance of both series (INSERM and police) since 1972 unveil similar trends.[5]

Thus, during the last fifty years, France, as most Western countries, has experienced a dramatic surge in crime, mostly thefts, but also assaults and to a lesser extent homicide. One can easily understand why the type of vision developed by theoreticians like Michel Foucault is today in decline (although these theoreticians are still regarded as important because they embody a period of our intellectual history). It does not fit with reality. Many institutions and the agents working for them did not control crime. The past century is deeply marked by state consolidation, and it has witnessed a growing number of intrusions by its servants in numerous areas. It follows that state public policies are at the forefront of social functions, more and more often taking over from shaken social institutions (the family for example), often more local and less based in legal rationality. If one looks at the rate of public expenditures as a proportion of GDP, it rises from 11 percent in 1872 to 48.3 percent in 1980 in France, 6.7 percent to 46.9 percent in Germany, 4.5 to 33.2 percent in the United States.[6] The number of policemen has followed the same trend. Pierre Simula found that there were 126,000 agents (in the police and gendarmerie) in 1960 and 233,000 in 1998.[7] In general, the growth of the state is massive.[8] Of course, it has not been a linear trend: There have been more advances during political or social crises, and also during war.

But, despite a decline, we can find a resurgence of the idea of social control. For example, the criminologist David Garland speaks of a "culture of control" that would characterize the United States and the United Kingdom. I would like to argue that there is no empirical foundation to this idea of more social control in France and probably in Europe as a whole. Based on a careful examination of the available data, I would like to offer a multidimensional explanation of crime trends in France. The second half of the twentieth century is a period of decline in the exercise of mutual constraint among individuals: Individualism, abundance, and economic turmoil are combined in an unprecedented way that has delegitimized social norms as compulsory obligations for individuals. And simultaneously, the penal system is facing a functional crisis and cannot cope with crime.

Poverty and Unemployment As Insufficient Explanations

After the Second World War, France went through various economic stages. The prosperity period gave way to mass unemployment. And, as of 1973, the economic turmoil lasted for more than two decades: It was only in 1997 that unemployment started to decline during several years. It is not possible that long-term hard conditions have not influenced crime. Clearly, the new cities erected in the 1960s and 1970s under an ideal of social blending have turned into social ghettos, gathering the more underprivileged and the ethnic minorities (that actually are a majority in these neighborhoods). This is a social condition that favors delinquency, although it is not a final explanation of crime trends as we will see.

Poverty in France has been measured on a regular basis by INSEE since the 1970s. As we can see in figure 1, there is a correlation between poverty and crime, but this is a negative one. Poverty declined as crime increased, whether property crime or crime against the person. The poverty is defined as less than half the median income of the general population. Poverty continued to decline until the

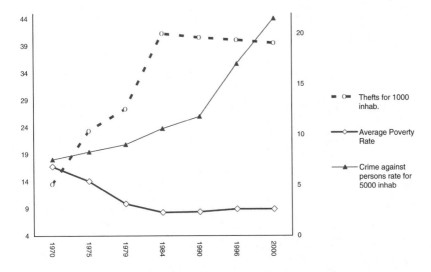

Figure 1 Crime and Poverty, 1970–2000

mid-1980s, along with an increase in both types of crime. And then, while poverty stabilized, thefts did not increase, which is quite a paradox: The number of thefts stopped increasing precisely when poverty stopped declining. Regarding crime against persons, the numbers rocketed during the 1990s, a period in which no increase in poverty was detectable.

Moreover, the INSEE statistics show that poverty is mainly a rural phenomenon, while every survey in crime displays that the latter is an urban problem. Whereas the urban dimension of crime has regularly been noticed by scholars (in Europe, see ECVS), the contradiction between poverty and crime distribution is not so commonly pointed out. In 1970, we find a poverty rate of 33.8 percent in rural settings as opposed to 16.8 percent throughout France, 9.6 percent for cities with a population of 100,000 to two million, and 6.6 percent for Paris. In 1996, the rates were 12.9 percent in rural settings, 8.9 percent throughout France, 7.9 percent in large cities, and 4.7 percent in Paris.[9]

Unemployment is certainly a factor when it comes to delinquency. But it is active only in certain social conditions. If we try to compare the number of crimes and the number of unemployed people across time, we do not find a clear correlation. It must be remembered that in France unemployment is concentrated at the two ends of life: among young people who cannot enter the job market and old people who are in competition with a cheaper and more skilled labor force. Even if we look at the social group that presents the best chances for correlation, the unemployed aged fifteen to twenty-four, the results are very mitigated. As shown in figure 2, unemployment and theft appear to be parallel for almost twenty years (1967–1985) but then diverge significantly. During a period when young people

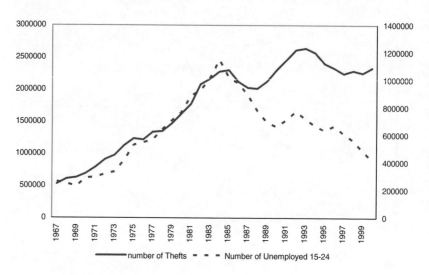

Figure 2   Number of Unemployed Persons under 25 and Number of Thefts
in France, 1967–1999

either went to school for a longer period (the aim of the socialist governments since 1981 was to bring 80 percent of students to A-level), or found jobs because of better economic conditions or public policies targeted at them (the state subsidized the creation of jobs in nonprofit organizations, municipalities, or even state services up to 80 percent in the second half of the 1990s), the statistics of crime went up even more rapidly than before.

The link with assaults is even more unclear. In figure 3 we find the same parallel during the 1967–1985 period, but after that there is a negative correlation: While the number of unemployed young people steadily went down, the number of assaults regularly climbed, to reach slightly over 250,000 cases a year. I do not mean to claim that poor social conditions diminish crime. For example, urban monographs clearly identify poor neighborhoods with high unemployment rates of young people as places with more assaults. I found such results in Marseilles and Hugues Lagrange in Amiens and Montpellier. At a neighborhood level there is a positive relation between poverty among young people and the police rates for assaults.[10] But again, one factor of crime cannot necessarily account for the entire crime trend in a country. Other variables must be added to understand the long-term transformations of the country that allowed for the increase in crime.

Autonomy, Values, and Authority

The perception that each person can and must be the author of the guidelines

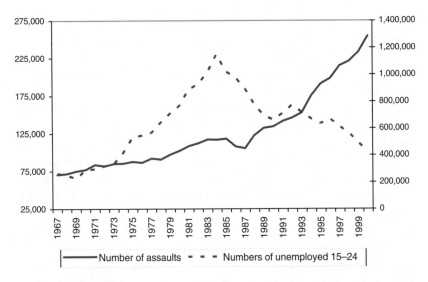

Figure 3 Number of Unemployed Persons under 25 and Number of Assaults
in France, 1967–1999

of his own behavior is spreading within the Western world. This constitutes the fundamental base of an individualization process. This process cannot be termed one of egoistic withdrawal; rather, it constitutes a model for interacting with others. Individualization is a form of liberation vis-à-vis general social norms or interpersonal constraints that has been favored by the economic development of the Western countries after the Second World War.

Since the 1950s, a trend toward individualization has occurred alongside a formidable enrichment of society. The belief system has altered, as Ronald Ingelhart has demonstrated, for many wealthy countries. And the nature of interindividual relations has changed. In his own words: "Prosperity and security are conducive of individual autonomy and diminishing deference to authority."[11] This author calls the broad cultural shift he observes "postmodernization." In Belgium, France, Germany, Great Britain, Italy, and the Netherlands, Ingelhart was able to test his hypothesis. From 1970 to 1988, the Eurobarometers included a version of the postmaterialist index (n = 190,000). As Etienne Schweisguth commented, Ingelhart's results are dramatic: No cohort displays an up or down trend, and aging has no effect on postmaterialist attitudes.[12] But, as one generation replaces the previous, distrust for social norms spills within a society.

Ingelhart explains how basic norms governing politics, work, religion, and the family are transforming. It is very likely that these norms also include subjects like deviance and crime. My point is that the evolution of values regarding autonomy must be taken as a whole. Attitudes toward tolerance and antiauthoritarianism based on the fundamental relativity of human judgments have another side: It is not an easy thing to condemn violence and property crimes. After all, cannot they be interpreted as a form of antiauthoritarianism, of individual freedom versus illegitimate social norms?

While antiauthoritarian attitudes became more frequent along with more toleration for minorities, especially among the younger groups, another aspect of this phenomenon deserves to be noted. The ideas of parents about minor crimes also changed. It is quite difficult to find some empirical foundation for a change in attitudes regarding crime in the 1970s, because crime was not a political issue in Europe then. Therefore, very few questions were asked in the polls with reference to crime. Most of them were focused on husband–wife relations or sexual life (contraception). However, a French political scientist was able to compare two opinion polls dating back to 1975 and 1989. This constitutes a very interesting period because of the continual rise in crime between these two dates. Among various questions, one was posed on theft. It was phrased very carefully, referring to "finding a motorcycle" (and using it), although in real life this is very rare indeed.

In 1975, a national sample of 916 parents and 916 children aged thirteen to eighteen from the same families was interviewed. In 1989, the same survey was performed with 804 children and 804 parents, using the very same questions. As table 1 illustrates, it is very clear that the younger generation is, at any given time, more individualistic than the older: The children choose more often that they do not have to refer to institutions, whether their parents (for contraception), or the state or the church (for their marriage). Their postmodernity is also visible regarding theft: The younger generation regards it as "not shocking" far more often than their parents do. In 1975, 59 percent of the parents found it shocking that one could use somebody else's property without his consent, whereas this was true of only 38 percent of the children.

Commenting on these data, Annick Percheron notes that opinions of parents and children are getting more and more close to one another. She explains this phenomenon with reference to the higher education among parents, their belonging to the post-1968 generation, and the weakening of religious practice. The author insists that the French parents (permissive or rigorist) could better transmit their values to their children in 1989 than in 1975, because in 1975 the children were necessarily far more permissive than their parents were (be they permissive or rigorist). But it could also be argued that the children are transmitting their values to their parents.

It is a fact that the difference in permissiveness between the opinions of parents and children has decreased. If we look at the difference in permissive items, in the case of "as soon as she wants" for taking the pill, it shrinks from fourteen

Table 1 Parents' and children's attitudes in France (1975–1989)

	Parents		Children	
	1975	1989	1975	1989
When should a girl take the pill?				
Never	21	4	14	3
As soon as she wants	28	59	42	55
When attaining her majority	22	23	16	21
When getting married	16	4	12	4
No answer	14	10	16	17
More and more young people live together without being married. Would you say that is:				
Very shocking	23	6	7	3
Quite shocking	30	8	19	6
Not quite shocking	21	21	27	19
Not at all shocking	24	64	42	68
No answer	2	1	5	4
Someone finds a motorcycle and uses it a few days before returning it. Would you say that is:				
Very shocking	59	38	38	32
Quite shocking	32	42	39	43
Not quite shocking	5	13	16	16
Not at all shocking	3	3	6	7
No answer	1	1	1	2

Source: Excerpts from Percheron, 1989, p. 85

to four points, and in the case of "not at all shocking" for living together, from eighteen to four points. And, the same trend is also true for the question regarding theft: The parents who in 1975 were more often very shocked (59 percent vs. 38 percent, i.e., a twenty-one-point difference) were in 1989 only 6 points more likely than their children to disapprove of theft. That was an invisible revolution within the "silent revolution."

This evolution of values regarding minor crimes constitutes an example of a more global issue regarding social norms in an individualistic society. This is a very different situation from the one expressed in the May 1968 slogan "it is forbidden to forbid" (*il est interdit d'interdire*). One could argue that today any reference to the very idea of social regulation has a tendency to vanish, which could be phrased as "I do as I want." The reference to a norm that would be illegitimate has itself disappeared. The social individual is at the center of the production of references for himself.

Hedonism and Autonomy Replace
Asceticism and Submission.

The crisis of authority is deeply intertwined with the emergence of a democratic society based on individuals. Alexis de Tocqueville indicates that individualism translates into a rebellion of individuals against hierarchy in the name of equality and denunciation of traditions in the name of freedom.[13] The trend toward less recognition of authority is clear. If it is to be reversed a few years from now, it might well be because of a perception of insufficient personal safety.

The study of birth cohorts confirms that the renewal of generations is the key to understanding the decline in authoritarian and traditional values. There is more and more acceptance for such behaviors as not getting married, divorce, abortion, and homosexuality. The physical disappearance of the oldest generation gradually favors the long-term rise in new values. The study of attitudes toward discipline is an empirical test of the idea of the crisis of authority. This phenomenon has been recorded with quantitative surveys since 1970 in some European countries and the Unites States. It is currently happening in France, as Schweisguth

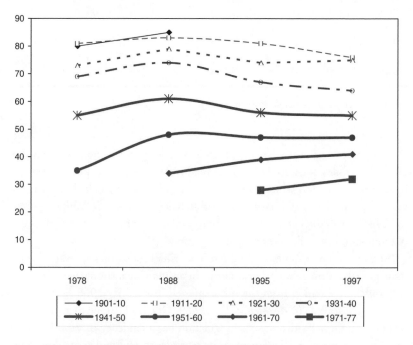

Source: Schweisguth, 1998. Percentages declaring that "school must first of all give a sense of effort and discipline", for age cohorts.

Figure 4 Attitudes toward Effort and Discipline in France, 1978–1997

has shown. As presented in figure 4, it is clear that effort and discipline were traditional values but that they are losing ground. Of the older generations, over 80 percent agreed that "the school must first of all give a sense of effort and discipline"; that proportion has fallen today to 30 percent. This is coherent with the idea that the individual has to learn by himself how to behave and that institutions no longer have the central role of socializing.

Many explanations could be associated with this shift in values. I believe that economic prosperity had an immense impact on the decline in interpersonal constraints. Sociologist Henri Mendras indicates that general enrichment has implied a loosening of constraints that impeded freedom: "The dependence vis-à-vis authority and the parsimonious economy forbade risk taking and autonomous action. The impoverishment between the two world wars had increased these rigidities. Today, food supply and health security are sufficient and that gives the potential freedom of saying no to the 'little boss' in the workshop or in the bureaucracy, . . . to the priest who tells you the truth, the good and the evil, to the old person who invokes his age and experience to make you obey. Bare authority has lost some of its edge."[14] In the words of Cas Wouters, the acceptance of social and moral authority has decreased: "In the relatively long period of peace and rising social and personal security, the arrangements of a caring welfare state were increasingly taken for granted, and this peace in material respects functioned as a breeding ground in which much relational and individual unrest took root."[15]

Social codes were clearly perceived by intellectuals as oppressive, as we have recalled in the first section of this paper. Consequently, the reprobation of crime was seen as a symptom of a reactionary position. There is a trend toward more moral indignation about any demonstration of authority. Of course, hierarchies still are in existence. But those who do not rely on power but on influence based on their past legitimate authority experience a decline.

In a self-reported delinquency survey I note the strength of the negative correlation between the acknowledgement of authority and the propensity to commit crimes. The more delinquent sections of the sample were the more critical of the police and the judiciary (although very few of the respondents actually were caught by the police and only 3 percent were sentenced by a judge), but also of civilian authorities like the mayor. Less respect for the public authorities who uphold legal norms and social codes is a factor in committing an offense, although it is probably not a sufficient explanation of crime in itself.

Education, Relativism, and Rationalization

I see the increase in crime as the result of various factors. Some are well known, such as family structure, impulsive personality, and gender. Here, I want to emphasize some of these factors that have not been given sufficient attention. First, I will look at a change in values in association with a rationalization of behaviors.

One can argue that the normative framework itself is changing. Based on the findings of the European Values Survey, Jean Stoetzel writes that "the moral certainties of Europeans are melting. Only a fourth of Europeans have clear principles to separate good and evil."[16] Individualization is emancipation and therefore implies less certainty vis-à-vis collective codes. Globally, a society perceives more and more frequently that everyone can be the author of his norms. But, what fuels individualism and the norm relativization process? It must be explained why individuals are referring less to institutions as providers of social norms.

The educational factor needs to be taken into consideration. It is generally admitted, along with Norbert Elias, that a higher degree of education in the population favors a decline in interpersonal violence. I believe this must be questioned when looking at recent histories of European countries. In France, since 1950, we have experienced a climbing rate of education. More and more students reach the level of *baccalauréat*. Nonetheless, during the same period, crime was on the rise. That leads us to take into account not only the rise in opportunities and the relaxation in values but also "the changes in the structure of self-controls" among a more educated and calculating population.[17] Norm erosion is in this perspective a correlate to the calculating mind.

The rationalization of individual behavior is a key to understanding a vast array of criminal behavior. If the structure of urban life provides more opportunities and more penal impunity, a rational actor should then commit more crimes. The routine activities theory or the lifestyle theory in criminology have emphasized and developed the role of opportunities provided by contemporary urban life. However, the rationalization process within individuals also deserves attention. Let us have a look at data showing how rationalization and delinquency might have common traits among young people.

Table 2   Acceptability of behaviors for pupils 11–15 years old in France: percentage of pupil respondents who said the described behavior was "Never Acceptable"

Behavior	Third Year	Sixth Year
To lie to avoid being punished	66.2%	28.5%
To cheat during a test	87.4%	44.9%
To refuse to give a job to somebody because of his race or religion	82.5%	91.1%
To say that only whites can be French	77.9%	81.1%

Source: DEP, Ministry of Education, Note of Information 96.34, August 1996, pp. 3–4

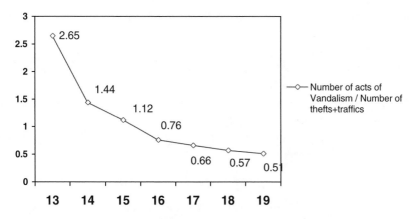

Figure 5   Number of Acts of Vandalism Divided by Those of Theft and Traffic among
Those 13–19 Years Old in France, 1999

It is of interest to look at cross-sectional results among the eleven to fifteen
age group regarding their attitudes toward social constraints, and then their behavior according to a self-reported delinquency survey. Surveys have been carried out
at the request of the French Ministry of Education.[18] The pupils have to say if,
according to them, it is acceptable to lie or cheat in order to avoid being punished. In the first year of senior school, 66.2 percent of them say this is never acceptable. In the fourth year, however, only 28.5 percent of them say so. It is clear how
the rule is questioned in relation to its consequences. The rule does not prevail
per se, but it is assessed through its impact on the individual. The higher the intellectual capabilities, the more frequently the rule is questioned and infringed.

It is very interesting to note that "positive values" are more frequent among
third-year pupils than sixth-year and that, at the same time, the rationalization
of thinking leads them to the conclusion that lying and cheating are not unacceptable (table 2). The same survey was carried out with seventh-year pupils:
they score even higher on tolerance, but lower on the respect of the rules at school.[19]
Data from a self-reported delinquency survey show that it is not only a question
of attitudes but also of behavior. In 1999, a self-reported delinquency survey
(N = 2300) was conducted in two large French cities, St. Etienne and Grenoble
(400,000 inhabitants each). The results display how behaviors are changing in
the young population aged thirteen, sixteen, and nineteen. First, the incidence
of misconduct and crime increases from age thirteen to age sixteen and then sta-
bilizes. Second (figure 5), during the early years, and especially at age thirteen,
their behavior is more disorderly: Very young people mainly vandalize their environment. But, as they grow up and receive more education, they have a tendency
to direct their behavior toward theft. The aim is no longer to destroy things without getting any reward for it but to be less visible and more effective: Stealing,

a profit-oriented activity, becomes the dominant pattern of delinquency.

Instead of asserting, as Talcott Parsons would have it, that socialization through education and interaction provides every member of a society with a common set of references,[20] I would argue rather that education reinforces the analytical capabilities of individuals. Therefore, it does not provide them with norms, but with a propensity to relativize social norms. I believe the rationalization that is observed between ages thirteen and nineteen might well be true for whole generations. If a larger number of people from each generation go to school and stay there for a longer period of time, one should anticipate that this has an impact.

Long-Term Trends in School Attendance

Where is rationalization taught? For the most part, at school. In every European country there has been a long-term trend toward educating more and more children. It might then be interesting to parallel the rise in the proportion of pupils and the crime figures. It is the industrialized countries themselves that have experienced a rise in crime. This is precisely where the effort in providing mass education has been very important. In France, the proportion of a generation reaching the level of *baccalauréat* has been continually growing since the 1950s, and the number of pupils who leave secondary school without a diploma is in constant decline (figure 6). At minimum, there is no reverse correlation between more crime and education in a country. But, could there even be a positive correlation in the sense that more education brings more crime? And why?

As mentioned, Ronald Ingelhart's empirical results show how postmaterialist values are higher when education level is higher. This is consistent with various surveys displaying how liberal, humanist, and permissive values rise with the level in education. However, as Etienne Schweisguth has noted, Ingelhart does not analyze this as an educational factor, but as a sequel of economic development. But it is very likely that the educational level of individuals has a net influence on their value system. It is arguable that more education leads to more permissiveness and tolerance. And therefore, more education leads people to be more reluctant to reject crime. Crime could be taken, wrongly, as a form of social contest (the Robin Hood role model). Street crime could also be depicted as a social construction, which means something relative and arbitrary that did not deserve to be condemned. Even if they did not welcome crime and commit it themselves, people felt reluctant to impose their values on other people. Only the rise in violent street crime started to change attitudes during the 1990s, when the rate of assault in France increased from 2.9 acts per 100 persons in 1989 to 6 in 2000, along with a revival in the perceived need for authority.[21]

However, and this is the second point, it is arguable also that the rise in per-

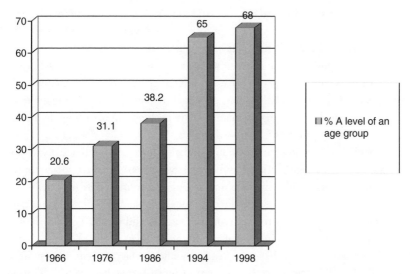

Figure 6   Education in France: Percentage Reaching A-Level, 1966–1998

missiveness combines with the rationalization of individual behavior. Because others do not act in defense of their values, I can anticipate that no reprobation will be directed to me. Therefore, I can act as a rational individual in the sense that I will benefit from the opportunity for crime produced by the structure of society.

Sykes and Matza have pointed out how delinquents must rationalize their behavior: They must find "good reasons" to explain why they committed various crimes. They found five techniques: denial of responsibility, denial of injury, denial of the victim, the condemnation of the condemners, appeal to higher loyalties. According to Sykes and Matza, a person is able to rationalize himself out of the moral bind and justify his delinquent behavior. One needs valid justification for a crime when one knows it is a disapproved form of behavior. I believe that a mass provision of schooling, along with large positive consequences for society, has had unintended side effects: To a large extent, it helps individuals to perceive themselves as free and to use rationalization techniques to allow themselves "good reasons" for breaking the law.

Thanks to reinforced cognitive equipment, the individual manages his own behavior: He can loosen the strength of social rules when he feels they go against his personal interest, or assert the necessity of these rules when they favor his position. Each individual knows how social norms are relative to one social context in which one public is facing him. Because social life in urban settings is made of numerous frames of interaction, no continual social norm can have a hold on an individual. I will come back later to the other factors related to the existence of social groups that are also contributing to this situation.

In an urban situation and a democratic context, the very idea of social norms tends to vanish. The social landscape is value free, not in the sense that individuals have no personal ethics but in the sense that everyone can have his own values and oppose them to every other person. And individuals can claim that every value is legitimate per se because values are perceived as the consequence of a personal choice. And all choices are equal. It is no surprise that many individuals, especially the young population, have problems in orienting themselves at a time when social signs have weakened.

Schooling is an active contribution to individualism. And individualism leads to the search for authenticity and expressiveness as personal social forms. Viewed from that angle, law breaking among the young population reflects a desire to have a social face and to discover one's true identity. The search for oneself is endless in a society that cannot assert values and limits. The blossoming of a "culture of authenticity . . . turns into an apology of the choice for itself: All options are equal for they are taken freely, and the fact of choosing is in itself a high value."[22] What, then, is the realm of social codes that are by definition collective codes? Schooling and individualism also favor the subjectification of social relationships:[23] Society is seen as a succession of interpersonal interactions and not the relation of one individual with a more global entity.

My claim is not that the provision of schooling necessarily implies more crime, and more violent crime at that. It is rather that in Western democracies there has been a rise in crime that must be explained. Although some of the factors, including urbanization and opportunities linked to lifestyle, were common to many Western countries, others were specific, such as racial cleavages, the role of the public sector in leveling inequalities, the urbanism of large cities. Moreover, Continental Europe is not the United States: free high-quality public schools are the rule, social security (social welfare, retirement plans) covers almost every household, racial ghettos are really exceptional, and no large neighborhood is falling apart in the American way. Yet, crime is rising in Europe. France has an overall rate of violent crime—assaults and sexual crimes—that is now comparable with the United States, except for homicide.[24] Again, why is this so? I insist that modern urban life, while it makes crime easier to commit, leaves little room for social values as imperatives that could prevent individuals from engaging in criminal activities. Less group pressure on individuals is one of the keys to understanding French crime and probably European crime.

Informalization: The Spatial Dimension

I would like to argue further that an informalization of daily life occurs in relation to the spatial organization of life. This is a sociological version of the process of informalization, which mirrors the psycho-sociological and historical approach by Cas Wouters referred to earlier. Wouters made the case that today we are facing a "more ego-dominated self-regulation that allows for the reflexive and flexible calculation."[25] The "calculative and flexible self-controls" suggest that inner discipline does exist, for it is necessary to bypass surveillance and social codes. More self-control allows for more crimes. But, this implies an awareness of their emotions by the public. How do people become less inclined to respect social codes and more conscious of their emotions?

A number of transformations in the material world are linked with an informalization process. We need to take a look at the organization of daily life from the perspective of declining interpersonal constraints and, consequently, a decline in the strength of collective rules. I have already made the point that a higher education provides individuals with enhanced analytical means (rather than social norms), and I am now considering the material counterpart of this, the fragmentation of stages where our life is played. Here I use the Goffmanian metaphor of life as a theater. Individuals can be convinced of their autonomy because urban life is actually organized in disjointed settings that have a specialized audience. This favors emancipation of the social agents from collective prescriptions. Precisely, social norms can best exist when defended by a social group that has stabilized in a precise territorial unit. In this conception there can be no room for a transcendent vision of social forms.

The changes in values are related to education, of course, but also to the urbanization of countries. Urban life favors a high relativization, as Rose Laub Coser notes. The individual manages his emotions in relation to social contexts. Melvin Webber and H. W. J. Rittel also note that the volume of information exchanged and technical progress (which provides more mobility to everyone and the opportunity to experience a variety of social frames) favor relativization of the value of rules: It increases the consciousness of personal autonomy, the perception of the freedom of choice.

Despatialization of Society and Social Group Pressure

The general context of our postindustrial societies is one of a less and less territorialized society. Communication, transportation, media, increased urbanization are characteristic of the present era. I feel that this is a new challenge for any source of authority, whether organizational or interpersonal. Another aspect is linked with the process of relativization. Usually, it is admitted that this process benefits democracy because it facilitates the search for compromises and respect for the behavior of minorities. However, if relativization leads to more tolerance vis-à-vis other city dwellers and a greater confidence in them, it also constitutes a factor of "civil inattention," as Erving Goffman puts it. More tolerance equates more civil inattention: This is true for other lifestyles (there are various cultural tastes), but also for crime. More inattention to others translates into less solidarity on the streets. The reason why somebody pays attention to somebody else in the street of an anonymous city is that first he feels he has something in common with the other one.

I want to emphasize the "despatialization of life," to use the expression of Melvin Webber. It encompasses urban mobility that increases with the functionalization of urban settings. This is probably why urbanization is not at all times correlated with more crime,[26] but it is indeed correlated since the 1950s. And today, crime and urbanization are correlated all over Europe.[27] But urbanization is only one aspect of despatialization. Other factors have played a role. For example, communication technologies prolonged the idea of "propinquity without proximity" (the idea selecting friends and relations, as opposed to inheriting them from the immediate environment), and in urban settings we witnessed the multiplication of mass private properties (housing estates, malls, bus, and metro) that had no clear master or ruling authority. During the same period, the agents of these authorities as well as the police were less present in these public places.[28]

Urbanization is associated with the fading of territorialized social groups as sociologists have shown studying the modernization of capital cities like Paris and London.[29] This trend has been called the end of "urban villages" as places where social norms would be coherent and constraining because they were sustained by a community. Instead of people having two lives, a private (home-based) one and a public one, there was a third element: community life in the streets and places of these working-class villages. There was a higher social homogeneity and a local recruitment of friends and even spouses. This not only reflects aspects that we would call positive today but also more mutual surveillance, fewer opportunities to leave the neighborhood, less paid leave (which left the household unsupervised for long periods of time), no cars, and so forth.

The emancipation of the individual from social codes derives from the fact that the place of residence is less and less a place of life. The population tends to sleep in one neighborhood, but it no longer works in the same neighborhood. One can notice this trend as early as in the 1960s in large cities. Henri Coing has described how life has changed in that respect in two quarters of Paris (the 13th and 14th *arrondissements*). In 1954, the population consisted mainly of workers (in the production process, i.e., factories), and 40 percent of them worked and resided in these quarters. In 1961, this was only 33 percent. In addition, a new population was on the rise: the employees (in the service sector, i.e., in offices or on the streets). Of the latter group only 11 percent worked and resided in these neighborhoods. The ascent of this new social group is changing the way everyone uses urban space. And, therefore, the meaning of proximity has altered.

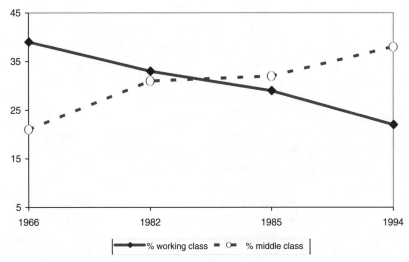

Source: Guy Michelat and Michel Simon, 1997: 175.

Figure 7   Percentage of Social Class Identification with the Working or Middle Class
among Those Who Say They Do Identify with a Social Class,
France, 1966–1994

This does not constitute the only change. The idea of forming a united social group is also fading. With prosperity, a modernization of lifestyles occurred, and the "affluent workers" surfaced. Their group of reference was less and less the working class, but rather the middle class. It is a very heterogeneous population characterized by its lifestyle and access to mass-produced goods. For this reason, the working class started to be less and less perceived as an identification group. Other factors then reinforced the weakening of this social group: immigration from the former colonies, the upward mobility of the sons of peasants and workers, and later the rise of the issue of ethnicity, and also unemployment. This resulted in a numeric decline in the number of workers, their affiliation with trade unions, and their sense of identification with a collective force in combat with the bourgeoisie. The native lower classes see themselves as distinct from the immigrants and envy the lifestyle of the middle class.

Guy Michelat and Michel Simon have traced opinion polls dating back to 1966 that display that the average "feeling of belonging to a social class" has not notably varied since then (61 percent say so). However, if one looks at the feeling of belonging to a specific class, the picture becomes interesting (figure 7). From 1966 to 1994, identification with the working class went down from 39 percent to 22 percent, while that with the middle class went up. Broken down by social status, the results show that identification with the working class went down among workers (minus 22 points, reaching 47 percent), among employees (minus 21 points, reaching 25 percent), and that meanwhile middle-class identification grew among workers (plus 17 points, reaching 30 percent) and employees (plus 15 points to 41 percent).[30] These developments resulted in social groups being less encompassing and less territorialized. This is a new context for crime. The social codes cannot be enforced if no collective actor is ready to defend them through his pressure in a defined location. And, precisely, as collective identity declines as well as local interactions between members of the lower classes, the possibility for social norms to be affirmed is zero. Informal mutual supervision and interpersonal solidarity decline together, hand in hand.

While delinquents find more and more rational reasons to commit crimes, law-abiding citizens see less and less reason to resist crime collectively. For authority can only be based on a collective, continual, and localized social process. The fading of collective authority explains why policies are directed to the use of force and power on the one hand, and persuasion on the other hand.[31]

The Postmodern Paradox: More State Means Fewer Constraints on Crime

An additional element is required to bring the explanation to completion. The state, despite its growing numbers of civil servants, is facing a functional crisis of the penal bureaucracy. More state could mean more social control from an institutional perspective: more means are available (i.e., there are more and more civil servants, an increasing share of GNP in the hands of the state, etc.). But it could also mean less social control when it comes to effectiveness. The data support the second option.

Of course, social control has been a trendy concept in a period when it was exercised by the state, the church, or the family as institutions (i.e., organized bodies that could exert influence and transmit values, in the definition of Mary Douglas). Various theories have been put forward in this respect; let me just recall Michel Foucault and his "biopower" or state interest in the life and death of its citizens through various policies and agents. One could suggest that if you add one civil servant or one organization, the mechanism of social control will become stronger.

This assumption, it seems to me, poses more problems than it actually solves. One central assumption of the foucauldian perspective is that there is a continuum between all institutions (whether schools, social workers, or the police). However, the constant diagnosis of various sociologists and experts since the 1970s—from Peyrefitte to Sueur—is that public services are not coordinated. This explains the success story of catch words like "interagency approach" or "partnership" in

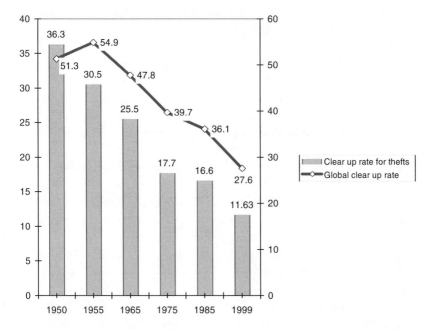

Figure 8   Clear-up Rates in France, 1950–1999

France, and also in the United Kingdom.[32] The incantation of coordinating services could not be understood if the continuum were a reality. Precisely, what the central government cannot achieve is to have different sectors of its bureaucracies work together. Its sectors do not feel they have the same missions to fulfill, and they do not have a common training or appreciate each other. There even exists a high rivalry between them (for example, between the state police and the gendarmerie, or the national police and the municipal forces, or the judiciary and the social workers, and even among the latter between the new "mediators" and traditional street workers).[33] In the end, more public agents does not mean more control, simply because they do not share a common goal or values. It is nowhere natural that all organizations work in a common direction, or that the professionals involved share a definition of what ought to be controlled and how, not to mention their interests as professional groups.

There is no reason to tie together, in a mechanical way, the rise of the state and the rise of social control. A complex society might need far more state than a simpler one to achieve a similar level of control. Per se, the quantity of state in peace time is hardly an indication of its coercive power. More bureaucrats simultaneously trying to control individuals could result in less social control (in the sense of conformity with general norms). For calculating individuals play with their margin for maneuver created by the multiplication of bureaucracies.

From an empirical point of view, I have already noted the steady and blatant increase in crime figures from the Second World War until today. But the productivity of the penal system is also declining along with its grip on society. If we look at clear-up rates in the long run, it appears that they are falling dramatically (figure 8). On average, for both property and personal crimes, the rates have fallen from 51.3 percent to 27.6 percent and for thefts alone from 36 percent to less than 11 percent. This measure is a proxy of the risk taken by the author of a delinquent act to be caught. And the risk is undoubtedly diminishing. For a rational actor, this constitutes a motivational factor.

How is it possible that more policemen and judges do not produce less crime, or at least the same amount of crime? There is in reality a very vague state action against crime, which has fueled the population's feeling of insecurity and its demand for punitive reaction. Even with twice as many policemen in 1999 than in 1950, the clear-up rate has fallen to one-half or one-third.

The reality of state action is by no means more control. Why? Because the state is providing a growing autonomy to individuals (one could also say more self-direction, or an extended superego with reference to Norbert Elias). The first point is that all these public organizations (police, the judiciary) are less and less institutions. That the state has no authority (in the sense of Hanna Arendt again) translates into an overloaded police. Because social norms are not shared, the use of force (legitimate violence) is rendered necessary.

Again, many elements combine to explain the lack of success of state agents against crime. First, the state has not modernized. The police and the judiciary took shape at the end of the nineteenth century and at the beginning of the twentieth century. Since this time, the geographic distribution of the agents has not altered much. That means that the penal agents are located in the rural *départements* with the lowest crime rates. For example, the rural *département* of La Lozère, per 1,000 inhabitants, suffers nine crimes per year, while it has 4.7 policemen. By contrast, the urban *département* of Le Rhône suffers 55 crimes and has 2.3 policemen per 1,000 inhabitants.[34] The distribution of public manpower today does correspond to the reality of the rural France that has disappeared. Could we interpret that as a coherent strategy aiming at social control?

Among the factors of police malfunctioning, the anonymity of contemporary crime has to be pinpointed. France being an urban country, the victim and the perpetrator do not know each other most of the time. They never do for most thefts, they rarely do for street assaults, and it is only for domestic violence that the victim can identify the perpetrator. But it is street crime that is most frequent. This is one of the reasons why the police is so rarely successful in its investigations: If the victim has no idea who committed the crime, he cannot tell the police. It must also be noted that the once successful state polarizes all demands. Because the French state has been so successful in dismantling communities, all citizens' demands tend to reach the public bureaucracy. This translates into a work overload and into a massive number of cases being closed by the judiciary even when the perpetrator of a crime is identified.

Finally, we appear to see the development of a passive citizenship in this democracy. The force of the police is seen as a monopoly, and because members of the public do not see themselves as coherent social groups, people tend to delegate their problems to the professionals who are trained and paid. The paradox is that these bureaucrats are not in a position to take those demands into account and give a response.

Conclusions: Democracy and Control

My perspective in this chapter has been that the form and nature of constraints have substantially changed over the last fifty years and that this explains a large part of the rise in crime. A number of features must be emphasized in relation with human constraints.

a. There has been a shift in values regarding social norms, a social preference for autonomy, and a rationalization of behavior related to the generalization of education.

b. Two factors contributed to an informalization process.: First, a despatialization of human interaction with the consequence of a decline in interpersonal constraints, and second, as a result of the economic crisis and the end of class struggle, a lack of structuring and a loss of collective identity within the working class.

c. A decline in the authority of the state has combined with a crisis of the power to punish in the penal system.

Another feature consists of the changes in the way people interact and the model for these interactions. I have argued that a democratization of the issue of crime is underway. A change in the public debate occurred: Class struggle as a central metaphor was abandoned; the debate is now revolving around the behavior of the middle class. And, therefore, the policing of society is now depicted by the ruling central government as the provision of a service. The lack of police in the deprived neighborhoods (the large outskirts of big cities) is a question of equality facing the public services that should be available to anyone.[35] The police is therefore not a means of social control by the elite over the lower classes, but a reflection of the acute demand for more protection in the most deprived sections of the population and neighborhoods.[36] And it is empirically clear that the lower strata of the urban population are actually more concerned with deviance than the rest of the population. They are more in favor of an increase in police presence.[37] We do not witness a great fear of the bourgeoisie regarding crime and deviance, but we do witness a consistent fear among underprivileged persons, and a desire for more public action. This is not to say that there is no desire for constraints on certain types of disorderly behavior but that an exclusively top-down approach is irrelevant for comprehending it.

This leaves us with a new question of crime: the insecurity issue. It is not a very problematic issue for the rich and famous, but for modest or poor families. We do not diagnose a will of the upper classes to domesticate the underclass. Policing rather has the aim of preventing the middle class from leaving certain quarters of the cities (where they voluntarily came for a living in the 1970s) that might become urban ghettos.

The question of prevention or repression of deviance is closely linked to the democratization of society. The socialist central government was long reluctant to take the direction of more policing. The lower strata have large expectations vis-à-vis the government, and although it is unclear whether the government will fulfill them (and to what extent), the question of security is on the agenda. It includes the reception of victims in police stations, equal access to the police, and equal presence, whatever the level of deprivation of the neighborhood, and politeness of the police toward every inhabitant, including minority groups.

The general context of deviance is that of a pluralist society. Social control can have a simple meaning in a totalitarian social system, but it has a much more complex one in the context of democratic pluralism. It is no longer easy to equate social control with the integration of individuals and communities into something larger. Of course, more police can be viewed as the rule of one community over another and that puts the state in a new position: It could be taking sides rather than promoting a common interest. If the ethnicization of France is strengthening, the state can no longer stand as the traditional referee or third party but appears as a side-taking institution (think of policing the inner cities, for example).

However, the decline in the effectiveness of policing in an individualistic society that also witnesses the resurgence of communities raises as many questions as the potential reinforcement of the penal system. Let us hypothesize that politics is about creating a collective entity. Is there any warden of collective norms? Is it legitimate to defend these codes? And what will happen if this is left to small groups or individuals? One can easily see how the use of the notion of social control is an attempt not to see the complex nature of democratic and individualistic societies, not to understand the balance between tensions, not to observe that the state is no coherent body of organizations and to ignore the links between policing a society and protecting its poorest sections.

Notes

1. Foucault, *Surveiller et punir*, 3.

2. Morel and Quétel, *Les médecines de la folie,* 200.

3. Robert et al., *Les comptes du crime.*

4. Cockburn, *On the History of Violent Crime in Europe and America.*

5. Robert et al., *Les comptes du crime.*

6. André and Delorme, *Matériaux pour une comparaison internationale des dépenses publiques en longue période, le cas de six pays industrialisés.*

7. Simula, *La dynamique des emplois dans la sécurié,* tables 213–15.

8. Rosanvallon, *L'Etat en France.*

9. INSEE, *Revenus et patrimoines des ménages,* 33.

10. Roché, *La délinquance des jeunes, les 13–19 ans racontent leurs délits,* 110–11; Lagrange, *De l'affrontement à l'esquive.*

11. Ingelhart, *La transition culturelle dans les sociétés industrielles avancées,* 296.

12. Schweisguth, *Revue française de science politique.*

13. Renaut, *Faut-il être ce que l'on est ?* 141–42.

14. Mendras, *La seconde révolution française,* 421–22.

15. Wouters, "Changing Patterns," 426.

16. Stoetzel, *Les valeurs du temps présent,* 294.

17. Wouters, "Changing Patterns," 417.

18. By the *Direction de l'évaluation et la Prospective.*

19. Joutard and Théolot, *Réussir l'école: pour une politique éducative,* annex III.6.

20. Ogien, *Sociologie de la déviance,* 168.

21. Data from the ICVS, in Van Kesteren et al., *Criminal Victimisation.*

22. Taylor, *Le malaise de la modernité,* 46.

23. See R. Sennet on Intimacy, or network analysis on preference for private relationships over collective sociability.

24. See Van Kesteren et al., *Criminal Victimisation.*

25. Wouters, "Changing Patterns," 416.

26. In France, see Santucci, *Délinquance et répression au XIXème siècle.*

27. ICVS, 1st wave, see Van Dijk et al, *Experiences of Crime.*

28. Roché, "The Local Governance of Crime and Insecurity in France."

29. Coing, *Rénovation urbaine.*

30. Michelat and Simon, *Changement de société, changement d'opinion,* 177. (The results broken down by social status are not reflected in the figure.)

31. Arendt, *La crise de la culture,* on the definition of authority as opposed to power and persuasion.

32. Crawford, "The Growth of Crime Prevention."

33. On this aspect, see De Maillard, "Les agents locaux"; also, Faget, *La médiation: essai sur la politique pénale.*

34. This is a well-known situation for the central government; see the report *Une meilleure répartition des effectifs de la police et de la gendarmerie pour une meilleure sécurité publique* by MP Roland Carraz and Senator Jacques Hyest, for the Prime Minister.

35. Sueur, *Demain la ville.*

36. Choffel, *Les conditions de vie dans les quartiers prioritaires de la politique de la ville,* 132.

37. Roché, *Tolérance Zéro? Incivilités et Insécurité,* chap. 3.

Bibliography

Primary Sources

A Volt Szakszervezetek Központi Levéltár anyaga (Materials of the Former Central Archive of the Trade Unions). Zala SZMT/41d./1950.

Archives de la Préfecture de la Police. "Case of M. Broughan." D 417.

Archives de la Préfecture de la Police. "Circulaire Ministerielle, Direction de la Sûreté Générale to Commissaires." 27 July 1907. D 200.

Archives de la Préfecture de la Police. "Crimes et Délits." B 1567.

Archives de la Préfecture de la Police. "Professions Ambulants." Circular dated 31 March 1840, D 200.

Archives de la Préfecture de la Police. "Rapport sur la crise économique, 1885." Paris, B 399.

Archives Nationales. 2AG 520 CC 104 A.

Archives Nationales. 3W 310.

Archives Nationales. F7 15345.

Archives of Popular Movements, Luleå, Sweden. Labor union records of the Labor Union of Wood Industry Workers, Section 66. 1904–1907.

Archives of Popular Movements, Luleå, Sweden. Record books for the Workers Association of Båtskärsnäs. 1905–1926.

Archives of the Amsterdam municipality. Maandverslag, 15 August 1942–15 September 1942, in 5225-BHC-V22 I-25.

Archives of the Amsterdam municipality. Maandverslag, 15 August 1943–15 September 1943, in 5225-BHC-V22 I-25.

Archives of the Amsterdam municipality. Maandverslag, 15 March 1944–15 April 1944, in 5225-BHC-V22 I-25.

Archives of the Amsterdam municipality. Notitie Versteeg, 21 June 1940, in 5225-BHC-D6–1940–1.

Archivo de Capitanía Militar de Zaragoza. File 43 and file 38-A, "Prisioneros."

Archivo de Capitanía Militar de Zaragoza. File 55, "Vigilancia de fronteras,"

Archivo Provincial de Teruel, Fondo Gobierno Civil, Sección Orden Público. File 1101/78.

Bér-Munkaügyi osztálya (Wage and Labor Department) /33d./1953 .

Bulletin hebdomadaire du ministère de l'Intérieur, no. 74, 27 January 1942.

Bundesarchiv Berlin. R 70 NL/16.

Columbia University Libraries Rare Book and Manuscript Library, Bakhmeteff Archive, Hungarian Refugees Project. Box 10, Interview No. 203, p. 28.

Columbia University Libraries Rare Book and Manuscript Library, Bakhmeteff Archive, Hungarian Refugees Project. Box 11, Interview No. 221, p. 24.

Columbia University Libraries Rare Book and Manuscript Library, Bakhmeteff Archive, Hungarian Refugees Project. Box 4, Interview No. 82-M, p. X/29.

Columbia University Libraries Rare Book and Manuscript Library, Bakhmeteff Archive, Hungarian Refugees Project. Box 3, Interview No. 31-M, p. VI/15.

FML MSZMP FMBA ir. 9f.1/46ö.e.; *Statisztikai Összesitö (kerület, járás, város, nagyüzem részére): Fejér megyei összesitö 1952 I. hó.*

Magyar Országos Levéltár, Hungarian National Archive. M-Bp.-95f.2/215ö.e., pp. 54–55.

Magyar Országos Levéltár, Hungarian National Archive. M-Bp–95f.4/147ö.e., p. 74.

Magyar Országos Levéltár, Hungarian National Archive. M-KS-276f.116/38ö.e., pp.1–3.

Magyar Országos Levéltár, Hungarian National Archive. M-KS-276f.53/145 ö.e.; *Tájékoztató az üzemi dolgozók és az üzemi vezetök által felvetett szociális és kultúrális problémákról,* p. 7.

Magyar Országos Levéltár, Hungarian National Archive. M-KS-276f.65/76ö.e., pp. 30–31

Magyar Országos Levéltár, Hungarian National Archive. M-KS-276f.94/827ö.e., p. 251.

Municipal Archive Leiden. Police, inv. nr. E 1702/1930/85.

Municipal Archive Leiden. Police, inv. nr. E1690/1926/156.

Municipal Archive Leiden. Police, inv. nr. E1691/1926/28.

Municipal Archive Leiden. Police, inv. nr. E1691/1926/61.

Municipal Archive Leiden. Police, inv. nr. E1691/1926/8.

Municipal Archive Leiden. Police, inv. nr. E1698/1928/103.

Municipal Archive Leiden. Police, inv. nr. E1701/1929/116.

Municipal Archive Leiden. Police, inv. nr. E1702/1930/88.

Municipal Archive Leiden. Police, inv. nr. E1703/1930/102.

Municipal Archive Leiden. Police, inv. nr. E1703/1930/133.

Municipal Archive Leiden. Police, inv. nr. E1705/1931/123.

Municipal Archive Leiden. Police, inv. nr. E1707/1932/199.

Municipal Archive Leiden. Police, inv. nr. E1709/1933/50.

Municipal Archive Leiden. Police, inv. nr. E1709/1933/85.

Municipal Archive Leiden. Police, inv. nr. E1715/1935/4.

Municipal Archive Leiden. Police, inv. nr. E1718/1936/76.

Municipal Archive Leiden. Police, inv. nr. E1751/1921/87.

Municipal Archive Leiden. Police, inv. nr. E1755/1923/40.

Municipal Archive Leiden. Police, inv. nr. E1756/1923/170.

Municipal Archive Leiden. Police, inv. nr. E1759/1924/101.

Municipal Archive Leiden. Police, inv. nr. E1759/1924/147.

Municipal Archive Leiden. Police, inv. nr. E1759/1924/187.

Municipal archives of the city of Dordrecht (1813–1851), nr. 12. Town Council Resolutions 1819.

Netherlands Institute of War Documentation. Annual registers of the German courts (L-Register, O-Register, Ns-Register).

Netherlands Institute of War Documentation. Annual registers of the German public prosecutor (StA-Register, VR-Register).

Netherlands Institute of War Documentation. Arch. 216, ds. 1, mp. 2a.Vergadering van het College van Secretarissen-Generaal (10 September 1940).

Netherlands Institute of War Documentation. Arch. 34–37 and coll. 214.

Netherlands Institute of War Documentation. Arch.206, ds.7, doc.1361–1-1500 (2 J 333/40g).

Netherlands Institute of War Documentation. Arch.206, ds.8, doc.1361–1-5425 (1 J 252/40g).

Netherlands Institute of War Documentation. Arch.206, ds.8, doc.1361–1-6320 (2 J 319/40g).

Netherlands Institute of War Documentation. Arch.215, ds.15, 1 J 217/40.

Netherlands Institute of War Documentation. Arch.215, ds.15, 9 J 292/41g.

Netherlands Institute of War Documentation. Arch.215, ds.16, 2 J 318/40g.

Netherlands Institute of War Documentation. Arch.215, ds.18, 1 J 129/40g.

Netherlands Institute of War Documentation. Arch.215, ds.18, 1 J 192/40g.

Netherlands Institute of War Documentation. Arch.215, ds.18, 2 J 333/40g.

Netherlands Institute of War Documentation. Arch.215, ds.19B, 1 J 185/40g.

Netherlands Institute of War Documentation. Arch.215, ds.19B, 10 J 239/40.

Netherlands Institute of War Documentation. Arch.215, ds.20B, 1 J 128/40g.

Netherlands Institute of War Documentation. Arch.215, ds.20B, 9 J 237/40.

Netherlands Institute of War Documentation. Diary of D. Bakker, 21 May 1940, 244.

Netherlands Institute of War Documentation. Diary of D. Bakker, 27 September 1941, 244.

Netherlands Institute of War Documentation. SG 34/42. Arch.35, ds.21.

Netherlands Institute of War Documentation. SG 43/42. Arch.35, ds.22.

Netherlands Institute of War Documentation. Telex Deppner to all Außenstellen (7 June 1944).

Netherlands Institute of War Documentation. Telex Schöngarth to *Posten, Stellen, Kommandos* (11 September 1944). Arch. 77–85, mp. 193Cd.

Nordrhein-Westfälisches Hauptstaatsarchiv Düsseldorf-Kaiserswerth, Schloss Kalkum. Rep. 112/10739.

Nordrhein-Westfälisches Hauptstaatsarchiv Düsseldorf-Kaiserswerth, Schloss Kalkum. 112/15295.

Open Society Archives, Radio Free Europe. Magyar Gy. 6/ Item No. 08794/53, p. 1.

Open Society Archives, Radio Free Europe. Magyar Gy.6/ Item No. 08794/53, p. 1.

Open Society Archives, Radio Free Europe. Magyar Gy.6/ Item No. 8083/54, p. 4.

Parliamentary Papers. "Accounts Relative to the Metropolitan Police." 1852–1853, vol. LXXVIII.

Parliamentary Papers. "Committee Appointed by the Secretary of State for War to Consider the Terms and Conditions of Service in the Army." 1892, vol. XIX.

Parliamentary Papers. "Departmental Committee of 1889 upon Metropolitan Police Superannuation." 1890, vol. LIX.

Parliamentary Papers. "Report of the Commissioner of Police of the Metropolis, 1869." 1870, XXXVI.461.

Parliamentary Papers. "Report of the Commissioner of Police of the Metropolis, 1875." 1876, XXXIV.315.

Parliamentary Papers. "Report of the Commissioner of Police of the Metropolis, 1889." 1890–1891, XLII.355.

Parliamentary Papers. "Report on the Health of Officers in the Post Office." 1857–1858, vol. XXV.

Parliamentary Papers. "Reports by District and Divisional Superintendents" (in the Annual Report of the Commissioner of the Metropolitan Police to the House of Commons for the Year 1885). 1886, vol. XXXIV.

Parliamentary Papers. "Royal Commission on a Constabulary Force." 1839, House of Commons, XIX, 73, paragraph 65.

Parliamentary Papers. "Royal Commission on Superannuation in the Civil Service." 1903, vol. XXXIV.

Parliamentary Papers. "Select Committee on Police Superannuation Funds." 1875, vol. XIII.

Parliamentary Papers. "Select Committee on Police Superannuation Funds." 1877, vol. XV.

Parliamentary Papers. "Select Committee on the Police Forces (Weekly Rest-Day)." 1908, vol. IX.

Parliamentary Papers. "Select Committee on the Police of the Metropolis." 1834 (600) XVI, q. 166.

Passfield Papers, British Library of Political and Economic Science. London School of Economics. Ledger of the Inhabitants of Katharine Buildings, Rooms 115, 118, 114.

Passfield Papers, British Library of Political and Economic Science. London School of Economics. Beatrice Potter's holograph diary and her correspondence.

Passfield Papers, British Library of Political and Economic Science. London School of Economics, Miscellaneous Collections 43. Ledger of the Inhabitants of Katharine Buildings, Cartwright Street, East Smithfield, 1885–1890.

Public Records Office. "Complaints Concerning Prostitution." MEPO 2/293.

Public Records Office. "Methods of Dealing with Vagrancy." HO 45/9613/A9839.

Public Records Office. "Police Raids on Gambling Clubs." HO 45/9704/A50396.

Public Records Office. The Standard, Kew, England, MEPO 2/181, 31 August 1887.

Research Archives, University of Umeå, Umeå, and the Regional Archives,

Härnösand, Sweden. Parish examination records of the parish of Nederkalix. 1770–1910.

Research Archives, University of Umeå, Umeå, Sweden. Census records of the county of Norrbotten. 1870, 1880, 1890, 1900, 1910, and 1920.

Tower Hamlets Public Library. Registers of the East End Dwellings Company, and Prospectus, 1884.

Books

A Dolgozó Nép Alkotmánya—A Magyar Népköztársaság Alkotmánya. Budapest: Szikra, 1949.

A Magyar Dolgozók Pártja Központi Vezetőségének, Politikai Bizottságának és Szervezö Bizottságának Fontosabb Határozatai. Budapest: Szikra, 1951.

Aubusson, B., N. Lalam, R. Padieu, P. Zanora. "Les statistiques de la délinquante." *France: Portrait Social,* 151–58. Paris: INSEE, 2002.

Actes du Congrès Pénitentiaire International de Paris, 1–9 Juillet 1895. Melun: Imprimerie Administrative, 1897.

Actes du Congrès Pénitentiaire International de Rome Novembre 1885 / Publ. par les soins du Commission Executif. 3474. Rome: Imprimerie des "Mantellate," 1887–1889.

Ågotnes, Hans-Jakob. *Frå handverkar til lønnsarbeidar? Snekkerer og tömmermenn i Bergen, 1801–1912.* Bergen: University of Bergen, 1997.

Agulhon, Maurice, and Pierre Bonte. *Marianne: Les visages de la République.* Paris: Gallimard Découverte, 1992.

Agulhon, Maurice. *Les métamorphoses de Marianne: L'imagerie et la symbolique républicaines, de 1914 à nos jours.* Paris: Flammarion, 2001.

Agulhon, Maurice. *Marianne au combat: L'imagerie et la symbolique républicaines, de 1789 à 1880.* Paris: Flammarion, 1979.

Agulhon, Maurice. *Marianne au pouvoir: L'image et la symbolique républicaines, de 1880 à 1914.* Paris: Flammarion, 1989.

Allwood, Martin S. *Eilert Sundt: A Pioneer in Sociology and Social Anthropology.* Oslo: Norli, 1957.

Almond, Gabriel A. and G. B. Powell, Jr. *Comparative Politics: System, Process and Policy.* New York: Harper Collins, 1993.

Åmark, Klas. *Facklig makt och fackligt medlemsskap: De svenska fackförbundens medlemsutveckling, 1890–1940.* Lund: Arkiv, 1986.

Amato, Giuliano. "La libertà personale." In *La pubblica sicurezza,* edited by Paolo Barile, 51–180. Milan: Neri Pozza, 1967.

Ambjörnsson, Ronny. *Den skötsamme arbetaren: Idéer och ideal i ett norrländskt sågverkssamhälle, 1880–1930.* Stockholm: Carlsson, 1988.

Ambrosio, Piero. *Nel novero dei sovversivi: Vercellesi, biellesi e valsesiani schedati nel Casellario politico centrale (1896–1945)*. Vercelli: Istituto per la Storia della Resistenza e della società contemporanea nelle province di Biella e Vercelli "Cino Moscatelli," 1996.

André, Christian, and Robert Delorme. *Matériaux pour une comparaison internationale des dépenses publiques en longue période, le cas de six pays industrialisés*. Paris: SEEI, ministère de l'économie et des finances, 1983.

Andrieux, Louis. *Souvenirs d'un Préfet de Police*. Paris: Jules Rouff, 1885.

Angermund, Ralph. *Deutsche Richterschaft, 1919–1945: Krisenerfahrung, Illusion, politische Rechtsprechung*. Frankfurt am Main: Fischer Taschenbuch Verlag, 1990.

Anonymous, ed., *L'haleine des faubourgs*. Fontenay-sous-Bois: Recherches, 1977.

Aquarone, Alberto. *L'organizzazione dello stato totalitario*. Turin: Einaudi, 1965.

Arato, Andrew, and Jean Cohen. *Civil Society and Political Theory*. Cambridge: MIT Press, 1994.

Arbetsstatistik E:1. Arbetsinställelser under åren, 1903–1907 jämte öfversikt af arbetsinställelser under åren, 1859–1902 samt den s. k. politiska storstrejken år 1902. Stockholm: Norstedt, 1909.

Arendt, Hanna. *La crise de la culture*. Paris: Gallimard, 1972.

Arendt, Hannah. *Essays in Understanding, 1930–1954*. New York: Harcourt Brace, 1994.

Arendt, Hannah. *The Origins of Totalitarianism*. London: George Leen and Unwin, 1967.

Arendt, Hannah. *The Origins of Totalitarianism*. New York: Harcourt, Brace Jovanovich, 1973.

Arendt, Hannah. *The Origins of Totalitarianism*. San Diego: Harcourt Brace, 1948.

Ariès, Philippe, and Georges Duby, eds. *Histoire de la vie privée*, t.4: *De la Révolution à la Grande guerre*. Paris: Seuil, 1987.

Art, Jan. "Het religieuze leven van de leken, 19de-20ste eeuw." In *Het bisdom Gent (1559–1991): Vier eeuwen geschiedenis*, edited by Michel Cloet, 413–35. Gent: Werkgroep de Geschiedenis van het Bisdom Gent, 1991.

Art, Jan. "Pourquoi la christianisation de la Flandre a-t-elle si bien réussi?" In *La christianisation des campagnes: Actes du colloque du CIHEC (25–27 août 1994)*, edited by J. P. Massaut and M. E. Henneau, vol. 3, 511–20: Rome: Institut Historique Belge de Rome, Bibliothèque, XXXIX, 1994.

Art, Jan. "Religie en secularisering: de voortdurende beeldenstorm." In *Rekenschap, 1650–2000*, edited by D. Fokkema, 95–114. Amsterdam: Staatsuitgeverij, 2001. (Nederlandse cultuur in Europese context, VI).

Art, Jan. "The Historiography of Male Orders and Congregations in Belgium during the 19th and 20th Centuries: A Status Quaestionis." In press.

Art, Jan. *Kerkelijke structuur en pastorale werking in het bisdom Gent tussen, 1830 en 1914*. Heule: UGA, 1977 (Standen en Landen LXXI).

Ascoli, David. *The Queen's Peace: The Origins and Development of the Metropolitan Police, 1829–1979*. London: Hamish Hamilton, 1979.

Axtmann, Roland, "'Police' and the Formation of the Modern State: Legal and Ideological Assumptions on State Capacity in the Austrian Lands of the Habsburg Empire, 1500–1800." *German History* 1, 10 (1992): 39–61.

Ballbé, Manuel. *Orden público y militarismo en la España constitucional (1812–1983)*. Madrid: Alianza, 1983.

Barile, Paolo. "La pubblica sicurezza." In *La pubblica sicurezza,* edited by Paolo Barile, 9–49. Milan: Neri Pozza, 1967.

Barnett, Henrietta. *Canon Barnett: His Life, Work, and Friends.* London: John Murray, 1921.

Barrado, Javier. "Mujer y derrota. La represión de la mujer en el Teruel de la posguerra (1939)." In *Tiempos de silencio. Actas del IV Encuentro de Investigadores del Franquismo.* Valencia: Universitat de Valencia-FEIS, 1999.

Barrows, S. J. "Report of the Delegates of the United States to the Fifth International Congress Held at Paris, France 1895." Washington, D.C.: Senate, Pentagon Office, 1896.

Baruch, Marc-Olivier. *Servir l'Etat français.* Paris: Fayard, 1997.

Baruch-Gourden, Jean-Michel. "La police et le commerce ambulant à Paris au IXᵉsiècle." In *Maintien de l'Ordre et Police en France et Europe au XIXe Siècle,* edited by Alain Faure and Philippe Vigier, 251–67. Paris: Créaphis, 1987.

Bauerkämper, Arnd. "Von der Bodenreform zur Kollektivierung. Zum Wandel der ländlichen Gesellschaft in der Sowjetischen Besatzungszone Deutschlands und DDR, 1945–1952." In *Sozialgeschichte der DDR,* edited by Hartmut Kaelble et al., 119–43. Stuttgart: Klett-Cotta, 1994.

Bayley, David H. "The Police and Political Development in Europe." In *The Formation of National States in Western Europe,* edited by Charles Tilly, 328–79. Princeton: Princeton University Press, 1975.

Beattie, J[ohn] M. *Crime and the Courts in England, 1660–1800.* Oxford: Clarendon Press, 1986.

Beier, A. L. *Masterless Men: The Vagrancy Problem in England, 1560–1640.* London: Methuen, 1985.

Belin, Commissaire. *Trente ans de Sûreté Nationale.* Paris: France soir éditions, 1950.

Bell, C., and H. Newby. "The Sources of Variation in Agricultural Workers' Images of Society." *Sociological Review* 21 (1973): 229–53.

Bell, Donald Howard. *Sesto San Giovanni: Workers, Culture and Politics in an Italian Town, 1880–1922.* New Brunswick: Rutgers University Press, 1986.

Bennassar, Bartolomé et al. *L'Inquisition Espagnole, 15e-19e siècle.* Paris: Hachette, 1979.

Bennema, Jan Willem. *Traditions of Communal Co-Operation.* Amsterdam: Universiteit van Amsterdam, Antropologisch-Sociologisch Centrum, 1978.

Berend, Iván T. *Central and Eastern Europe, 1944–1993: Detour from the Periphery to the Periphery.* Cambridge: Cambridge University Press, 1996.

Bergalli, R., and C. Sumner, eds. *Social Control and Political Order.* London: Sage, 1997.

Bergmann, Jörg R. *Klatsch: Zur Sozialform der diskreten Indiskretion.* Berlin: De Gruyter, 1987.

Bergstedt, Bosse. *Den livsupplysande texten: En läsning av N F S Grundtvigs pedagogiska texter.* Stockholm: Carlsson, 1998.

Berki, Mihály. *Az Államvédelmi Hatóság*. Budapest: privately published, 1994.

Berlanstein, L. "Vagrants, Beggars and Thieves: Delinquent Boys in Mid-Nineteenth Century Paris." *Journal of Social History* 12 (1979): 531–52.

Berlière, Jean-Marc, and Denis Peschanski, eds. *La police française entre permanences et bouleversements, 1930–1960*. Paris: La Documentation Française, 2000.

Berlière, Jean-Marc. "La généalogie d'une double tradition policière." In *La France de l'affaire Dreyfus,* edited by P. Birnbaum, 191–225. Paris: Gallimard, 1994.

Berlière, Jean-Marc. "La seule police qu'une démocratie puisse avouer ? Retour sur un mythe: les brigades du Tigre." In *Servir l'Etat républicain: de Dreyfus à Vichy,* edited by M. O. Baruch and V. Duclert, 311–23. Paris: La Découverte, 2000.

Berlière, Jean-Marc. "IIIᵉ République, Vichy, Occupation, Libération . . . Permanence et renouvellement des policiers: le problème des épurations (1940–1953)." Paper presented to the Police in Transition Conference, Berlin, January 2000. Berlière, Jean-Marc. "L'Institution Policière en France sous la Troisième République, 1875–1914." Ph.D. diss., University of Dijon, 1991.

Berlière, Jean-Marc. *Les policiers français sous l'Occupation*. Paris: Perrin, 2001.

Berlière, Jean-Marc. *Le monde des polices en France, XIXe-XXe siècles*. Brussels: Complexe, 1996.

Bessel, Richard. "Grenzen des Polizeistaates. Polizei und Gesellschaft in der SBZ und frühen DDR, 1945–1953." In *Die Grenzen der Diktatur. Staat und Gesellschaft in der DDR,* edited by Richard Bessel and Ralph Jessen, 224–52. Göttingen: Vandenhoeck & Ruprecht, 1996.

Bessel, Richard. "Policing, Professionalisation and Politics in Weimar Germany." In *Policing Western Europe: Politics, Professionalism and Public Order, 1850–1940,* edited by Clive Emsley and Barbara Weinberger. Westport, Conn.: Greenwood Press, 1991.

Bethencourt, Francisco. *L'Inquisition à l'époque moderne: Espagne, Italie, Portugal, 15e-19e siècle*. Paris: Fayard, 1995.

Biernacki, Richard. *The Fabrication of Labor: Germany and Britain, 1640–1914*. Berkeley: University of California Press, 1995.

Billiet, J., ed. *Tussen bescherming en verovering: Sociologen en historici over zuilvorming*. Leuven: Universitaire Pers, 1988 [with English summary].

Bird, F. B. "How Do Religions Affect Moralities?" *Social Compass* 37, 3 (1990): 291–314.

Black, Donald, ed. *Toward a General Theory of Social Control*. 2 vols. Orlando: Academic Press, 1984.

Blinkhorn, Martin, ed. *Fascists and Conservatives: The Radical Right and the Establishment in Twentieth-Century Europe*. London: Unwin Hyman, 1990.

Blinkhorn, Martin. "Spain: The 'Spanish Problem' and the Imperial Myth." *Journal of Contemporary History* 1, 15 (1980): 5–25.

Bloch Ravn, Thomas. "Oprör, spadseregange og lönstrejker i Köbenhavn för 1870: Traek af arbejderbevaegelsens forhistorie." In *Protest og oprör: Kollektive aktioner i Danmark, 1700–1985,* edited by Flemming Mikkelsen, 47–85. Aarhus: Modtryk, 1986.

Blok, Anton. *De Bokkerijders: Roversbenden en geheime genootschappen in de Landen van Overmaas, 1730–1774*. Amsterdam: Prometheus, 1991.

Blokland-Potters, Talja V. *Wat stadsbewoners bindt: Sociale relaties in een achterstandswijk*. Kampen: Kok Agora, 1998.

Blom, J. C. H., and Emile Lamberts. *History of the Low Countries*. New York: Berghahn Books, 1998.

Böcker, Anita, and Lilian Clermonts. *Poortwachters van de Nederlandse arbeidsmarkt: arbeidsvoorziening en de verlening van tewerkstellingsvergunningen*. Nijmegen: Instituut voor Rechtssociologie, 1995.

Boekholt, P. Th. F. M. "Onderwijs en onderwijzers omstreeks 1828." In *Spiegel van Groningen: Over de Schoolmeesterrapporten van 1828*, edited by P.Th. F. M. Boekholt and J. van der Kooij, 64–82. Assen: Van Gorcum, 1996.

Boer, Jo. *Dorp in Drenthe: Een studie over veranderingen in mens en samenleving in de gemeente Zweeloo gedurende de periode, 1930–1970*. Meppel: Boom, 1975.

Bokovoy, Melissa K. *Peasants and Communists: Politics and Ideology in the Yugoslav Countryside, 1941–1953*. Pittsburgh: University of Pittsburgh Press, 1998.

Bosley, David J. "The Problem of the Young Offender—An Ideal Solution? Agricultural Reformatories in England and France: The Nonage, 1800–1854." In *History of Juvenile Delinquency: A Collection of Essays on Crime Committed by Young Offenders, in History and in Selected Countries*, edited by A. G. Hess and P. F. Clement, 289–325. Aalen: Scientia Verlag, 1990.

Botti, Alfonso. *Cielo y dinero: El nacional-catolicismo en España (1881–1975)*. Madrid: Alianza, 1992.

Boudart, Marina, et al., eds. *Modern Belgium*. Brussels: Modern Belgium Association, 1990

Boudon, Raymond. *La place du désordre*. Paris: PUF, 1984.

Boué, Pierre. *Vagabondage et Mendicité, Moyens de défence*. Paris: Pithiviers, 1906.

Bouman, P. J. *De April-Meistakingen van 1943*. The Haag: Nijhoff, 1950.

Boutry, Philippe. *Prêtres et paroisses au pays du Curé d'Ars*. Paris: Cerf, 1986.

Brennan, Thomas. *Public Drinking and Popular Culture in Eighteenth-Century Paris*. Princeton: Princeton University Press, 1988.

Broers, Michael. "Sexual Politics and Political Ideology under the Savoyard Monarchy, 1814–1821." *English Historical Review* 457, 114 (1999): 607–35.

Brogden, Mike. *On the Mersey Beat: Policing Liverpool between the Wars*. Oxford: Oxford University Press, 1991.

Brooke, Michael Z. *Le Play: Engineer and Social Scientist. The Life and Work of Frédéric Le Play*. London: Longman, 1970.

Broszat, Martin, et. al. *Bayern in der NS-Zeit*. 6 vols. Munich: Oldenbourg, 1977–1983.

Broszat, Martin. *The Hitler State: The Foundation and Development of the Internal Structure of the Third Reich*. Translated by John W. Hiden. London: Longman, 1981.

Browning, Christopher R. *Nazi Policy, Jewish Workers, German Killers*. Cambridge: Cambridge

University Press, 2000.

Browning, Christopher R. *Ordinary Men: Reserve Police Battalion 101 and the Final Solution in Poland.* New York: Harper Collins, 1992.

Brunet, Jean-Paul. *Saint-Denis la ville rouge: 1890–1939.* Paris: Hachette, 1980.

Brzezinski, Zbigniew K. *The Soviet Bloc: Unity and Conflict.* Cambridge: Harvard University Press, 1967.

Burdy, Jean-Paul, et al. "Rôles, travaux et métiers de femmes dans une ville industrielle: Saint-Etienne, 1900–1950." *Le Mouvement Social* 140 (July–September1987): 27–54.

Burdy, Jean-Paul. "Des usages et des images de l'espace à l'identité sociale: pour une lecture d'anthropologie historique de la rue ouvrière, XIXe-XXe s." *Movimento Operaio e Socialista* 1–2 (1989): 93–105.

Burdy, Jean-Paul. "La ville désenchantée? Sécularisation et laïcisation des espaces urbains français (milieu XIXe-milieu XXe s.)." In *Laïcité(s): Actualité et problèmes de la laïcité en France et en Turquie,* edited by J. P. Burdy and Jean Marcou. Paris: AFEMOTI/CERI, 1995.

Burdy, Jean-Paul. *Cahiers d'Etudes sur la Méditerranée orientale et le monde turco-iranien,* edited by Jean-Paul Burdy and Jean Marcou, 129–58. Paris: CEMOTI 19, AFEMOTI/CERI, 1995.

Burdy, Jean-Paul. *Le Soleil noir: Un quartier de Saint-Etienne, 1840–1940.* Lyon: Presses Universitaires de Lyon, 1989.

Burke, Peter. *Popular Culture in Early Modern Europe.* New York: Harper & Row, 1978.

Burleigh, Michael, and Wolfgang Wippermann. *The Racial State: Germany, 1933–1945.* Cambridge: Cambridge University Press, 1991.

Cachet, A. *Politie en sociale controle: Over het effect van politie-optreden: een vergelijkend onderzoek naar verkeersdelicten, gezinsgeweld en drugsgebruik.* Arnhem: Gouda Quint, 1990.

Canler, Louis. *Mémoirs de Canler, Ancien Chef du Service de Sûreté.* New edition, introduced and annotated by Jacques Brenner. Paris: Mercure de France, 1968.

Canosa, Romano. "Polizie." In *Dizionario storico dell'Italia unita,* edited by Nicola Tranfaglia and Bruno Bongiovanni, 693–98. Rome-Bari: Laterza, 1996.

Canosa, Romano. *La polizia in Italia dal 1945 a oggi.* Bologna: Il Mulino, 1976.

Carlsson, Sten. "Befolkningsutvecklingen från 1800-talets mitt." In *Den svenska historien.* Vol. 13, *Emigrationen och det industriella genombrottet,* edited by G. Grenholm, 26–30. Stockholm: Bonnier, 1989.

Carroll, J. *Guilt: The Grey Eminence behind Character, History and Culture.* London: Routledge, 1985.

Carucci, Paola. "Arturo Bocchini." In *Uomini e volti del fascismo,* edited by Ferdinando Cordova, 63–103. Rome: Bulzoni, 1980.

Carucci, Paola. "L'organizzazione dei servizi di polizia dopo l'approvazione del testo unico delle leggi di pubblica sicurezza nel 1926." *Rassegna degli Archivi di Stato* 26 (1976): 82–114.

Casali, Luciano, ed. *Per una definizione della dittadura franchista. Annale* 6 (1990).

Casali, Luciano. "'Per il pane, lavoro, libertà e non guerra': Appunti sulla stampa sindacale clandestina in provincia di Bologna durante il fascismo." In *Il sindacato nel bolognese,* edited by Centro documentazione-Archivio storico della Camera del lavoro territoriale di Bologna, 295–357. Bologna: Ediesse, 1988.

Casanova, Julián, et al. *El pasado oculto: Fascismo y violencia en Aragón (1936–1939).* Madrid: Siglo XXI, 1992.

Casanova, Julián. "Civil Wars, Revolutions and Counterrevolutions in Finland, Spain, and Greece (1918–1949): A Comparative Analysis." Working paper no. 266, The Helen Kellogg Institute for International Studies, University of Notre Dame, March 1999.

Castan, Nicole. *Justice et répression en Languedoc à l'époque des Lumières.* Paris: Flammarion, 1980.

Castan, Yves. *Honnêteté et relations sociales en Languedoc, 1715–1780.* Paris: Plon, 1974.

Cenarro, Ángela. "Muerte y subordinación en la España franquista. El imperio de la violencia como base del 'Nuevo Estado.'" *Historia Social* 30 (1998): 5–22

Cenarro, Ángela. "Muerte, control y ruptura social: la salida de la guerra civil en Teruel, 1939." In *Tiempos de silencio: Actas del IV Encuentro de Investigadores del Franquismo,* 12–15. Valencia: Universitat de Valencia-FEIS, 1999.

Cenarro, Ángela. *El fin de la esperanza: Fascismo y guerra civil en la provincia de Teruel, 1936–1939.* Teruel: Instituto de Estudios Turolenses, 1996.

Cendrars, Blaise, and Robert Doisneau. *La banlieue de Paris (1949).* Paris: Denoël, 1983.

Centraal Bureau voor de Statistiek, ed. *Crimineele Statistiek, Gevangenisstatistiek en Statistiek van de Toepassing der Kinderwetten.* The Haag: Centraal Bureau voor de Statistiek, 1941.

Chadwick, Edwin. "On the Consolidation of Police Force, and the Prevention of Crime." *Fraser's Magazine* 77 (January 1868): 1–18.

Chadwick, William. *Reminiscences of a Chief Constable.* Manchester: J. Heywood, 1900.

Chaloner, W. H. *The Social and Economic Development of Crewe, 1780–1923.* Manchester: Manchester University Press, 1950.

Chanteau, Fernand. *Les Plaies Sociales: Vagabondage et Mendicité.* Paris: A. Pedone, 1899.

Charle, Christophe. *Histoire sociale de la France au XIXe siècle.* Paris: Seuil, 1991.

Cheli, Enzo. "Libertà di associazione e poteri di polizia: Profili storici." In *La pubblica sicurezza,* edited by Paolo Barile, 273–305. Milan: Neri Pozza, 1967.

Chevalier, Louis. *Classes laborieuses et classes dangereuses à Paris pendant la première moité du XIX-ième siècle.* Paris: Hachette, 1984.

Chevandier, Christian. *Cheminots en usine: Les ouvriers des Ateliers d'Oullins au temps de la vapeur.* Lyon: Presses Universitaires de Lyon, 1993.

Child, John. "Quaker Employers and Industrial Relations." *Sociological Review* 3, 12 (1964): 293–315.

Childs, David, and Richard Popplewell. *The Stasi.* Basingstoke: Macmillan, 1996.

Choffel, Philippe. "Les conditions de vie dans les quartiers prioritaires de la politique de la ville." In *Données Urbaines,* edited by Denise Pumain and Francis Godard, 123–33. Paris: Anthropos, 1996.

Christiaens, Jenneke. *De geboorte van de jeugddelinquent (België, 1830–1930).* Vol. 1, *Criminologische Studies.* Brussels: VUBPress, 1999.

Christianisme et monde ouvrier. Exhibition catalog. Paris: Les Editions Ouvrières, 1975.

Christiansen, E. *The Origins of Military Power in Spain, 1800–1854.* Oxford: Oxford University Press, 1967.

Clermont, J. *L'homme qu'il fallait tuer, Pierre Laval.* Paris: Charles de Jonquière, 1949.

Clinton, Alan. *Post Office Workers.* London: George Allen & Unwin, 1984.

Cobb, Richard. *The Police and the People: French Popular Protest, 1789–1820.* Oxford: Oxford University Press, 1970.

Cockburn, J. S. "On the History of Violent Crime in Europe and America." In *Violence in America: Historical and Comparative Perspectives,* edited by Graham Hugh. Davis and Ted Robert Gurr, 353–74. Beverly Hills: Sage, 1979.

Cohen, Elie A. "Een Onbekende Tijdgenoot: De Laatste Befehlshaber der Sicherheitspolizei und des SD in Nederland." In *Studies over Nederland in oorlogstijd,* vol. 1, edited by A. H. (Harry) Paape et al., 170–91. The Haag: Nijhoff, 1972.

Cohen, Elie A. "Schuldig Slachtoffer: De Derde Befehlshaber der Sicherheitspolizei und des SD in Nederland." In *Studies over Nederland in oorlogstijd,* vol. 1, edited by A. H. (Harry) Paape et al., 192–210. The Haag: Nijhoff, 1972.

Cohen, Stanley, and Andrew Scull, eds. *Social Control and the State.* New York: St Martin's Press, 1983.

Cohen, Stanley. "Introduction." In *Social Control and Justice: Inside and Outside the Law?* edited by Leslie Sebba, 9–11. Jerusalem: Magnus Press, 1996.

Cohen, Stanley. *Visiones de control social: Delitos, Castigos y Clasificaciones.* Barcelona: Promociones y Publicaciones Universitarias, 1988.

Cohen, Stanley. *Visions of Social Control: Crime, Punishment and Classification.* Cambridge: Polity Press, 1985.

Coing, H. *Rénovation urbaine et changement social: l'îlot numéro 4, Paris XIIIe.* Paris: Les éditions Ouvrières, 1966.

Collin, Richard Oliver. "The Italian Police and Internal Security from Giolitti to Mussolini." Ph.D. diss., Oxford University, 1983.

Collin, Richard. "Police and Internal Security." In *Historical Dictionary of Fascist Italy,* edited by Philip Cannistraro, 428–32. Westport, Conn.: Greenwood, 1982.

Collins, Patricia Hill. "Shifting the Center: Race, Class, and Feminist Theorizing about Motherhood." In *Mothering: Ideology, Experience, and Agency,* edited by Evelyn Nakano Glenn et al., 45–65. New York: Routledge, 1994.

Collotti, Enzo, and Lutz Klinkhammer. *Il fascismo e l'Italia in Guerra: Una conversazione fra storia e storiografia.* Rome: Ediesse, 1996.

Collotti, Enzo. *Fascismo, fascismi.* Florence: Sansini, 1989.

Colson, Daniel, et al. *Un quartier industriel à Saint-Etienne: Le Marais, entre histoire et planification.* Lyon: LUGD, 1993.

Congrès international de Bienfaisance. London, 1862.

Connelly, John. *Captive University: The Sovietization of East German, Czech and Polish Higher Education, 1945–1956.* Chapel Hill: University of North Carolina Press, 2000.

Cooney, Mark. *Warriors and Peacemakers: How Third Parties Shape Violence.* New York: New York University Press, 1998.

Corbin, Alain. *Les filles de noce: Misère sexuelle et prostitution (XIXe siècle).* Paris: Aubier, 1982.

Cornell, Lasse. *Sundsvallsdistriktets Sågverksarbetare, 1860–1890.* Göteborg: Ekonomisk-historiska institutionen, Göteborgs Universitet, 1982.

Corso, Guido. *L'ordine pubblico.* Bologna: Il Mulino, 1979.

Coser, Rose Laub. "The Complexity of Roles As a Seedbed of Individual Autonomy." In *The Idea of Social Structure: Papers in Honor of Robert K. Merton,* edited by Lewis A. Coser, 237–63. New York: Harcourt Brace Jovanovich, 1975.

Crampton, R. J. *A Short History of Modern Bulgaria.* Cambridge: Cambridge University Press, 1987.

Crawford, Adam. "The Growth of Crime Prevention in France As Contrasted with the English Experience: Some Thoughts on the Politics of Insecurity." In *Crime Prevention and Community Safety: New Directions,* edited by G. Hughes et al., 214–39. London: Sage, 2002.

Creed, Gerald W. *Domesticating Revolution: From Socialist Reform to Ambivalent Transition in a Bulgarian Village.* University Park: The Pennsylvania State University Press, 1998.

Croll, Andy. "Street Disorder, Surveillance and Shame: Regulating Behaviour in the Public Spaces of the Late Victorian British Town." *Social History* 3, 24 (1999): 250–68.

Crowley, David. "Warsaw's Shops in Stalinism and the Thaw." In *Style and Socialism: Modernity and Material Culture in Post-War Eastern Europe,* edited by Susan Emily Reid and David Crowley, 25–47. Oxford: Berg Publishers, 2000.

Cunningham, Hugh. *Children and Childhood in Western Society since 1500.* Edited by J. Morrill and D. Cannadine, *Studies in Modern History.* London: Longman, 1995.

Cuomo, Giuseppe. "La libertà di manifestazione del pensiero (Rassegna di legislazione, 1848–1948)." In *La pubblica sicurezza,* edited by Paolo Barile, 219–38. Milan: Neri Pozza, 1967.

D'Cruze, Shani. *Crimes of Outrage: Sex, Violence and Victorian Working Women.* London: University College of London Press, 1998.

D'Orsi, Angelo. *La polizia: Le forze dell'ordine italiane.* Milan: Feltrinelli, 1972.

Daley, Harry. *This Small Cloud: A Personal Memoir.* London: Weidenfeld and Nicolson, 1986.

Dandeker, Christopher. *Surveillance, Power and Modernity.* Oxford: Polity Press, 1990.

Danker, Uwe. *Räuberbanden im alten Reich um 1700: Ein Beitrag zur Geschichte von*

Herrschaft und Kriminalität in der frühen Neuzeit. 2 vols. Frankfurt am Main: Suhrkamp, 1988.

"Dans la France du Début du XXe siècle." In *Ordre moral et délinquance de l'antiquité au XXe siècle,* edited by Benoit Garnot, 233–40. Dijon: EUD, 1994.

Daudet, Léon. *La police politique: ses moyens, ses crimes.* Paris: Denoël & Steele, 1934.

Daudet, Léon. *Magistrats et policiers.* Paris: Grasset, 1935.

Daumas, Jean-Claude. *L'amour du drap: Blin et Blin Elbeuf.* Besançon: Presses universitaires franc-comtoises, Annales littéraires de l'Université de Franche-Comté, 1999.

Davis, Jennifer. "Law Breaking and Law Enforcement: The Creation of a Criminal Class in Mid-Victorian London." Ph.D. diss., Boston College, 1984.

Davis, Jennifer. "From 'Rookeries' to 'Communities': Race, Poverty and Policing in London, 1850–1985." *History Workshop Journal* 27 (1989): 66–85.

Davis, John A. *Conflict and Control: Law and Order in Nineteenth Century Italy.* London: Macmillan, 1988.

De Felice, Renzo. *Mussolini il duce: II. Lo Stato totalitario, 1936–1940.* Turin: Einaudi, 1981.

De Geus, Machteld. "Vrederechtspraak in Nederland." In *Zesde Jaarboek van het Rijksinstituut voor Oorlogsdocumentatie,* edited by Gerard Aalders et al., 48–86. Zutphen: Walburg Pers, 1995.

De Luna, Giovanni. *Donne in oggetto: L'antifascismo nella società italiana, 1922–1939.* Turin: Bollati Boringhieri, 1995.

De Maeyer, Jan, and Paul Wynants. *De Vincentianen in België, 1842–1992.* Leuven: Universitaire Pers, 1992 (KADOC-Studies 14).

De Maillard , Jacques. "Les agents locaux de médiation sociale: vecteur de recomposition de l'action publique en matière de sécurité intérieure." unpublished article, 2001.

De Pina Cabral, J. *Sons of Adam, Daughters of Eve: The Worldview of the Portuguese Peasant.* Oxford: Clarendon Press, 1986.

De Regt, Ali. *Arbeidersgezinnen en beschavingsarbeid: Ontwikkelingen in Nederland, 1870–1940.* Meppel: Boom, 1985.

De Swaan, Abram. *In Care of the State: Health Care, Education and Welfare in Europe and the USA in the Modern Era, Europe and the International Order.* Cambridge: Polity Press, 1990.

De Toro Muñoz, Francisco Miguel. "Policía, denuncia y control social: Alemania y Austria durante el Tercer Reich." *Historia Social* 34 (1999): 117–34.

De Vries, Marlene. *Roddel nader beschouwd: Turkse meisjes en jonge vrouwen in Nederland: Ogen in je rug.* Leiden: Rijksuniversiteit Leiden, Faculteit der Sociale Wetenschappen, Centrum voor Onderzoek van Maatschappelijke Tegenstellingen, 1990.

Debouzy, Marianne, ed. *Paternalismes d'hier et d'aujourd'hui.* Paris: Les Editions ouvrières, 1988.

Dekker, Jeroen J. H. *Straffen, Redden en Opvoeden: Het ontstaan en de ontwikkeling van de residentiële heropvoeding in West-Europa, 1814–1914, met bijzondere aandacht voor Nederlandsch Mettray.* Assen: Van Gorcum, 1985.

Deletant, Dennis. *Ceausescu and the Securitate: Coercion and Dissent in Romania, 1965–1989.* London: Hurst & Company, 1995.

Deletant, Dennis. *Communist Terror in Romania: Gheorgiu-Dej and the Police State, 1948–1965.* London: Hurst & Company, 1999.

Delumeau, Jean. *L'aveu et le pardon: les difficultés de la confession, XIIIe–XVIIIe siècles.* Paris: Fayard, 1990.

Delumeau, Jean. *La peur en occident, XIVe–XVIIIe siècles: une cité assiégée.* Paris: Pluriel, 1993.

Delumeau, Jean. *Le péché et la peur: la culpabilisation en occident, XIIIe–XVIIIe siècles.* Paris: Fayard, 1983.

Denys, Catherine. *Police et sécurité au VIIIe siècle dans les villes frontière franco-belge.* Paris: L'Harmattan, 2002.

DEP, Ministry of Education, *Note of information* 96.34, August 1996, pp. 3–4.

Devillers, Christian, and Bernard Huet. *Le Creusot: naissance et développement d'une ville industrielle, 1872–1914.* Seyssel: Champ Vallon, 1981.

Dewerpe, Alain. *Le monde du travail en France, 1850–1950.* Paris: 1989.

Dibbits, Hester, and Theo Meder. "Kasbah in de Kanaalstraat: Beeldvorming in en rond een multi-etnische stadswijk: een verkenning." *Volkskundig Bulletin* 25 (1999): 39–70.

Diederiks, Herman. *In een land van justitie: Criminaliteit van vrouwen, soldaten en ambtenaren in de 18e-eeuwse Republiek.* Hilversum: Verloren, 1992.

Diewald-Kerkmann, Gisela. *Politische Denunziation im NS-Regime oder die kleine Macht der "Volksgenossen."* Bonn: Dietz, 1995.

Domela Nieuwenhuis, J., and D. I. Mackay. *Verslag aan het hoofdbestuur van het Nederlandsch Genootschap tot Zedelijke Verbetering der Gevangenen van het internationaal congres over het gevangeniswezen te Londen.* Amsterdam, 1873.

Donajgrodzki, A[nthony] P., ed. *Social Control in Nineteenth-Century Britain.* London: Croom Helm, 1977.

Donati, Lorenzo. "La Guardia Regia." *Storia Contemporanea* 8 (1977): 441–87.

Douglas, Mary. *How Institutions Think.* New York: Syracuse University Press, 1986.

Doyle, Bryan. "The Invention of English." In *Englishness: Politics and Culture, 1880–1920,* edited by Robert Colls and Philip Dodd, 89–115. London: Croom Helm, 1986.

Drenth, Annemieke, and Francisca de Haan. *The Rise of Caring Power: Elizabeth Fry and Josephine Butler in Britain and the Netherlands.* Amsterdam: Amsterdam University Press, 1999.

Droste, Heiko. "Språk och livsform. Patronage i 1600-talets Sverige." *Scandia* 1, 64 (1998): 28–54.

Du Moulin de la Barthète, Henry. *Le temps des illusions: Souvenirs (juillet 1940-avril 1942).* Geneva: Editions du Cheval Ailé, 1946.

Dubesset, Mathilde, and Michelle Zancarini-Fournel. *Parcours de femmes: Réalités et représentations, Saint-Etienne, 1880–1950*. Lyon: Presses Universitaires de Lyon, 1993.

Duby, Georges, ed. *Histoire de la France urbaine*, t.4: *La ville de l'âge industriel*. Paris: Seuil, 1983.

Ducloux, Louis. *Du chantage à la trahison: Crimes de plume et crimes de sang*. Paris: Gallimard, 1955.

Ducpétiaux, E., ed. *Débats du Congrès Pénitentiaire de Bruxelles: Session de 1847, Seances des 20, 21, 22, et 23 Septembre*. Brussels: Deltombe, 1847.

Dunnage, Jonathan. *The Italian Police and the Rise of Fascism: A Case Study of the Province of Bologna, 1897–1925*. Westport, Conn: Praeger, 1997.

Dupont-Bouchat, M. S. *De la prison à l'ecole: Les penitenciers pour enfants en Belgique au XIXe Siècle (1840–1914)*. Edited by A.S.B.L. Section Belge de la Commission Internationale pour l'Histoire des Assemblees d'Etats (Centre National de Recherches, *Anciens Pays Et Assemblees D'etats*). Heule: U.G.A., 1996.

Dupont-Bouchat, Marie-Sylvie. "Du tourisme pénitentiaire à 'l'internationale des philanthropes': La creation d'un réseau à travers les congrès pénitentiaires internationaux (1820–1914)." Paper presented at the Workshop on Doers—Philanthropes and Bureaucrats: Communication, Travelling, and the Building of Expertise, Florence, March 17–18, 2000.

Dupont-Bouchat, M-S. "La Belgique capitale internationale du patronage au XIXe Siècle." In *Justice et Aide Sociale: 100 Ans d'évolution; Reflets et perspectives de politiques criminelle, pénitentiaire et sociale (1894–1994)*, edited by J. Detienne, 281–337. Brussels: Bruylant, 1994.

Durand, Jean-Dominique, ed. *Cent ans de catholicisme social à Lyon et en Rhône-Alpes: la postérité de Rerum Novarum*. Paris: Actes du colloque de Lyon de 1991, 1992.

Dyhouse, Carol. *Feminism and the Family in England, 1880–1939*. Oxford: Basil Blackwell, 1989.

Edwards, Richard. *Contested Terrain*. New York: Basic Books, 1979.

Egmond, Florike. *Underworlds: Organized Crime in the Netherlands, 1650–1800*. Cambridge: Polity Press, 1993.

Ekdahl, Lars. *Arbete mot kapital: Typografer och ny teknik—studier av Stockholms tryckeriindustri under det industriella genombrottet*. Lund: Arkiv, 1983.

Ekiert, Gregorz. *The State against Society: Political Crises and Their Aftermath in East Central Europe*. Princeton: Princeton University Press, 1996.

Ekiert, Gregorz. "Rebellious Poles: Political Crises and Popular Protest under State Socialism, 1945–1989." *East European Politics and Societies* 11, 2 (1997): 299–338.

Elias, Norbert, and John L. Scotson. *The Established and the Outsiders: A Sociological Enquiry into Community Problems*. London: Cass, 1965.

Elias, Norbert. *The History of Manners: The Civilizing Process*. Vol. 1. Oxford: Basil Blackwell, 1978.

Emsley, Clive. *Gendarmes and the State in NineteenthCentury Europe*. Oxford: Oxford University Press, 1999.

Emsley, Clive, and Mark Clapson. "Recruiting the English Policeman, c.1840–1940." *Policing and Society* 3 (1994): 269–86.

Emsley, Clive. *Policing and Its Context, 1750–1870.* London: MacMillan, 1983.

Emsley, Clive. *The English Police: A Political and Social History.* London: Longman, 1991.

Emsley, Clive. "'Mother, What *Did* Policemen Do When There Weren't Any Motors?' The Law, the Police and the Regulation of Motor Traffic in England, 1900–1939." *Historical Journal* 36 (1993): 357–81.

Emsley, Clive. "A Typology of Nineteenth-Century Police." *Crime, Histoire et Sociétés/ Crime, History and Societies* 1, 3 (1999): 29–44.

Emsley, Clive. "Political Police and the European Nation-State in the Nineteenth Century." In *The Policing of Politics in the Twentieth Century,* edited by Mark Mazower, 1–25. Providence, R.I.: Berghahn Books, 1997.

Emsley, Clive. *Crime and Society in England, 1750–1900.* 2nd ed. London: Longman, 1996.

Encrevé, André, and M. Richard. *Les protestants dans les débuts de la IIIe République, Actes du colloque.* Paris: Société de l'histoire du protestantisme français, 1979.

Engberg, Poul. *Grundtvig og det folkelige oprör.* Copenhagen: Samlaren, 1980.

Englander, David, and Rosemary O'Day, eds. *Retrieved Riches: Social Investigation in Britain, 1840–1914.* Aldershot: Scolar Press, 1995.

Erichsen, Björn. *Om arbejderbevaegelsen: En introduktionsbog til dansk arbejderbevaegelses historie.* Copenhagen: Hans Reitzel, 1977.

Estèbe, Jeanine, and Bernard Vogler. "La genèse d'une société protestante: Etude comparée de quelques registres consistoriaux Languedociens et Palatins vers 1600." *Annales ESC* 31 (1976): 362–88.

Evans, Richard J. "Polizei, Politik und Gesellschaft in Deutschland, 1700–1933." *Geschichte und Gesellschaft* 22 (1996): 609–28.

Evans, Richard J. *Kneipengespräche im Kaiserreich: Stimmungsberichte der Hamburger Politischen Polizei, 1892–1914.* Reinbeck bei Hamburg: Rowolt, 1989.

Evans, Richard J. *Rituals of Retribution: Capital Punishment in Germany, 1600–1987.* Oxford: Oxford University Press, 1996.

Evans, Richard J. *Tales from the German Underworld.* New Haven: Yale University Press, 1998.

Ewald, François. *L'Etat-Providence.* Paris: Seuil, 1986.

Eyerman, Ron, and Andrew Jamison. *Social Movements: A Cognitive Approach.* Cambridge: Polity Press, 1991.

Ezquerra, Julián. *Un ayer que es todavía: Estampas de un pueblo republicano.* Zaragoza: Unaluna, 1998.

Faber, Sjoerd. *Strafrechtspleging en criminaliteit te Amsterdam, 1680–1811: De nieuwe menslievendheid.* Arnhem: Gouda Quint, 1983.

Fabre, Giorgio. "Le polizie del fascismo." *Quaderni di storia* 31 (1990): 137–93.

Fabre, Jaume. "La delació dins la repressió franquista de postguerra." *L'Avenç* 75 (1984):

30–39.

Faget, Jacques. *La médiation: essai sur la politique pénale.* Paris: Erès, 1998.

Familistère de Guise ou les équivalents de la richesse. Exhibition catalog. Brussels: Editions des Archives d'Architecture Moderne, 1976.

Familistère Godin à Guise: Habiter l'utopie. Exhibition catalog. Paris: Centre de Création Industrielle, 1982.

Farge, Arlette. *Vivre dans la rue à Paris au XVIIIe siècle.* Paris: Archives Julliard, 1979.

Faure, Alain, ed. *Les premiers banlieusards: aux origines de la banlieue de Paris, 1860–1940.* Paris: Créaphis, 1991.

Faure, Alain. "Classe malpropre, classe dangereuse? Quelques remarques à propos des chiffonniers parisiens au XIXe siècle et de leurs cités." *Recherches* 29 (1977): 79–102.

Faure, Alain. "Comment se logeait le peuple parisien à la Belle Epoque." *Vingtième Siècle: Revue d'Histoire* 64 (October–December1999): 41–51.

Fehér, Ferenc, et al. *Dictatorship over Needs.* Oxford: Basil Blackwell, 1983.

Findlay, George. *The Working and Management of an English Railway.* London: Whittaker, 1889.

Fitzgerald, Robert. *British Labour Management and Industrial Welfare.* London: Croom Helm, 1988.

Flint, John T. *Historical Role Analysis in the Study of Religious Change: Mass Educational Development in Norway, 1740–1891.* Cambridge: Cambridge University Press, 1990.

Földes, György. *Az eladósodás politikatörténete, 1957–1986.* Budapest: Maecenás Könyvkiadó, 1995.

Földes, György. *Hatalom és mozgalom (1956–1989); Társadalmi-politikai eröviszonyok Magyarországon.* Budapest: Reform Könyvkiadó-Kossuth Könyvkiadó, 1989.

Fosdick, R. B. *European Police Systems.* New York: Allen & Unwin, 1915.

Foucault, Michel. *Surveiller et Punir.* Paris: Gallimard, 1975.

Fouilloux, Etienne. *Les Communistes et les Chrétiens: alliance ou dialogue? Madeleine Delbrêl.* 1904, 1933, 1964. Reprint, Paris: Cerf, 1990.

Fourcaut, Annie, ed. *Banlieue rouge, 1920–1960: Années Thorez, années Gabin: arché-type du populaire, banc d'essai des modernités.* Paris: Autrement, 1992.

Fourcaut, Annie, ed. *Un siècle de banlieue parisienne (1859–1964): Guide de recherche.* Paris: L'Harmattan, 1988.

Fourcaut, Annie. *Bobigny, banlieue rouge.* Paris: Editions ouvrières, 1986.

Fox, Alan. *History and Heritage: The Social Origins of the British Industrial Relations System.* London: George Allen, 1985.

Frank, Michael. *Dörfliche Gesellschaft und Kriminalität: Das Fallbeispiel Lippe, 1650–1800.* Paderborn: Ferdinand Schöningh, 1995.

Franke, Herman. *The Emancipation of Prisoners: A Socio-Historical Analysis of the Dutch Prison Experience.* Edinburgh Law and Society Series. Edinburgh: Edinburgh University Press, 1995.

Franzén, Mats. "Egensinne och skötsamhet i svensk arbetarkultur." *Arkiv* 48/49

(1991): 3–20.

Franzinelli, Mimmo. *Delatori: Spie e confidenti anonimi: L'arma segreta del regime fascista.* Milan: Mondadori, 2001.

Fraser, Ronald. *Mijas: República, guerra, franquismo en un pueblo andaluz.* Barcelona: Antoni Bosch, 1985.

Frégier, Honoré A. *Des classes dangereuses de la population dans les grandes villes et des moyens de les rendre meilleures.* 2 vols. Paris: J. B. Ballière, 1840.

Fried, Robert C. *The Italian Prefects: A Study in Administrative Politics.* New Haven: Yale University Press, 1963.

Friedlander, Henry. *The Origins of Nazi Genocide: From Euthanasia to the Final Solution.* Chapel Hill: University of North Carolina Press, 1995.

Friedrich, Carl, and Zbigniew Brzezinski. *Totalitarian Dictatorship and Autocracy.* New York: Praeger, 1965.

Froment, Pascale. *René Bousquet.* Paris: Stock, 1994 (Reissue Fayard, 2001).

Fucci, Franco. *Le polizie di Mussolini.* Milan: Mursia, 1985.

Fuchs, R. G. "Juvenile Delinquency in Nineteenth-Century France." In *History of Juvenile Delinquency: A Collection of Essays on Crime Committed by Young Offenders, in History and in Selected Countries,* edited by A. G. Hess and P. F. Clement, 265–88. Aalen: Scientia Verlag, 1990.

Fulbrook, Mary. *Anatomy of a Dictatorship. Inside the GDR, 1949–1989.* Oxford: Oxford University Press, 1995.

Funk, Albrecht. *Polizei und Rechtsstaat. Die Entwicklung des staatlichen Gewaltmonopols in Preußen, 1848–1918.* Frankfurt am Main: Campus Verlag, 1986.

Furre, Berge. *Vårt hundreår: Norsk historie, 1905–1990.* Oslo: Norske Samlaget, 1991.

Gabarda, Vicente. *Els afusellaments al País Valenciá (1938–1956).* Valencia: Edicions Alfons el Magnànim, 1993.

Gabriels, L. *De Bonden van het Heilig Hart in het Bisdom Gent, 1920–1945.* Aartrijke: Decock, 1991 (Historische Monografieën 5).

Gaillac, Henri. *Les maisons de correction, 1830–1945.* Paris: Editions Cujas, 1971.

Gaillard, Jeanne. *Paris, la Ville (1852–1870).* Paris: Honoré Champion, 1977.

Galizia, Mario. "La libertà di circolazione e soggiorno (dall'Unificazione alla Costituzione repubblicana)." In *La pubblica sicurezza,* edited by Paolo Barile, 482–563. Milan: Neri Pozza, 1967.

Garland, David. *The Culture of Control: Crime and Social Order in Contemporary Society.* Oxford: Oxford University Press, 2001.

Garnot, Benoît. "Justice, infrajustice, parajustice et extrajustice dans la France de l'Ancien Régime." *Crime, Histoire et Sociétés/ Crime, History and Societies.* 1, 4 (2000): 103–20.

Garrioch, David. *Neighbourhood and Community in Paris, 1740–1790.* Cambridge: Cambridge University Press, 1986.

Garton-Ash, Timothy. *The File–A Personal History.* London: Harper Collins, 1997.

Gatrell, V. A. C. "The Decline of Theft and Violence in Victorian and Edwardian England." In *Crime and the Law: The Social History of Crime in Western Europe since 1500,* edited by V. A. C. Gatrell, Bruce Lenman, and Geoffrey Parker, 238–337. London: Europa Publications, 1980.

Gatrell, V. A. C. *The Hanging Tree: Execution and the English People, 1770–1868.* Oxford: Oxford University Press, 1994.

Gauchet, Marcel, and Gladys Swain. *La pratique de l'esprit humain: l'institution asilaire et la Révolution démocratique.* Paris: Gallimard, 1980.

Geijer, Erik Gustaf. *Om vår tids inre samhällsförhållanden: Historiska skrifter i urval och kommentar av Thorsten Nybom.* Stockholm: Tiden, 1980.

Gellately, Robert. *Backing Hitler: Consent and Coercion in Nazi Germany.* Oxford: Oxford University Press, 2001.

Gellately, Robert. *The Gestapo and German Society: Enforcing Racial Policy, 1933–1945.* Oxford: Clarendon Press, 1990.

Gellately, Robert. "L'émergence de la 'Polizeijustiz' dans l'Allemagne nazie." In *Pouvoirs et polices au XXe siècle: Europe, Etats-Unis, Japon,* edited by Jean-Marc Berlière and Denis Peschanski. Brussels: Editions Complexe, 1997.

Gentile, Emilio. *La via italiana al totalitarismo: Il partito e lo Stato nel regime fascista.* Rome: La Nuova Italia Scientifica, 1995.

Geremek, Bronislaw. *Het Kaïnsteken: Het beeld van armen en vagebonden in de Europese literatuur van de 15e tot de 17e eeuw.* Baarn: Anthos, 1992.

Gerö, András, and Iván Petö, eds. *Befejezetlen Szocializmus: Képek a Kádár-Korszakból.* Budapest: Tegnap és Ma Kulturális Alapítvány, 1997.

Giddens, Anthony. *The Nation-State and Violence: Volume II of a Contemporary Critique of Historical Materialism.* Berkeley: University of California Press, 1987.

Gittins, Diana. "Marital Status, Work and Kinship, 1850–1930." In *Labour and Love: Women's Experience of Home and Family, 1850–1940,* edited by Jane Lewis, 249–65. Oxford: Basil Blackwell, 1986.

Gleason, Abbott. *Totalitarianism: The Inner History of the Cold War.* Oxford: Oxford University Press, 1994.

Glete, Jan. *Ägande och industriell omvandling: Ägargrupper, skogsindustri, verkstadsindustri, 1850–1950.* Stockholm: SNS, 1987.

Godin, Jean-Baptiste. *Le Familistère de Guise ou les équivalents de la richesse.* Brussels: Editions des Archives d'Architecture Moderne, 1976.

Godin, Jean-Baptiste. *Le Familistère Godin à Guise. Habiter l'Utopie.* Paris: Centre de Création Industrielle, 1982.

Goldhagen, Daniel. *Hitler's Willing Executioners: Ordinary Germans and the Holocaust.* New York: Knopf, 1996.

Gospel, Howard F. *Markets, Firms, and the Management of Labour in Modern Britain.* Cambridge: Cambridge University Press, 1992.

Goven, Joanna. "The Gendered Foundations of Hungarian Socialism: State, Society and the Anti-Politics of Anti-Feminism, 1948–1990." Ph.D. diss., University of California, Berkeley, 1993.

Gowing, Laura. *Domestic Dangers: Women, Words and Sex in Early Modern London.* Oxford: Clarendon Press, 1996.

Graham, Helen. "Gender and the State: Women in the 1940s." In *Spanish Cultural Studies, An Introduction: The Struggle for Modernity,* edited by Helen Graham and Jo Labanyi, 182–95. Oxford: Oxford University Press, 1995.

Grankvist, Rolf. "Tröndelags-bygderna." In *Thranerösla i norske bygder,* edited by Tore Pryser, 151–74. Oslo: Norske Samlaget, 1977.

Gras, H. *Op de grens van het bestaan: Armen en armenzorg in Drenthe, 1700–1800.* Zuidwolde: Stichting Het Drentse Boek, 1989.

Gregory, Winifred, ed. *International Congresses and Conferences, 1840–1937: A Union List of Their Publications Available in Libraries of the United States and Canada.* Edited by Bibliographical Society of America. New York: Kraus Reprint Corporation, 1938. Reprint, 1967.

Gribaudi, Maurizio. "Identité individuelle et sociabilité de quartier à Turin entre les deux guerres." In *Habiter la ville: XVe-XXe siècle,* edited by Maurice Garden and Yves Lequin, 289–304. Lyon: Presses Universitaires de Lyon, 1985.

Gribaudi, Maurizio. *Itinéraires ouvriers: Espaces et groupes sociaux à Turin au début du XXe siècle.* Paris: Editions de l'EHESS, 1987.

Grint, Keith. *The Sociology of Work.* Cambridge: Polity Press, 1991.

Groenveld, Simon, et al., eds. *Wezen en Boefjes: Zes eeuwen zorg in wees- en kinderhuizen.* Hilversum: Verloren, 1997.

Gross, Jan. "Social Consequences of War: Preliminaries to the Imposition of Communist Regimes in East Central Europe." *East European Politics and Societies* 3, 2 (1989): 198–214.

Groussard, Georges. *Services secrets, 1940–1945.* Paris: La Table Ronde, 1964.

Gruchmann, Lothar. *Justiz im Dritten Reich, 1933–1940: Anpassung und Unterwerfung in der Ära Gürtner.* Munich: Oldenbourg, 1988.

Gueslin, André. "Le paternalisme revisité en Europe occidentale (Seconde moitié XIXe-début XXe s.)." *Genèses* 7 (1992): 201–11.

Guillaume, L., and C. Didion, eds. *Actes du Congrès Pénitentiaire International de Bruxelles: Aout 1900 / publ. sous la dir. de F.-C. De Latour; par le Dr Guillaume et Charles Didion.* 5 vols. Berne: Imprimerie Staempfli, 1901.

Guillaume, L., ed. *Actes du Congrès Pénitentiaire International de Saint-Petersbourg 1890 / Publ. sous la direction de la commission d'organisation par le Dr Guillaume.* 5 vols. Saint-Petersbourg: Bureau de la Commission d'organisation du Congres, 1890–1892.

Guillaume, L., ed. *Le Congrès Pénitentiaire International de Stockholm , 15–26 Aout 1878; Actes du 2me Congrès / Pres. au congrès et publ. sous la dir. de la Commission Pénitentiaire Internationale par le Dr Guillaume.* 2 vols. Stockholm: Bureau de la Commission pénitentiaire internationale, 1879.

Guillaume, Pierre. *La Compagnie des Mines de la Loire (1846–1854): Essai sur l'apparition de la grande industrie capitaliste en France.* Paris: Presses Universitaires de France, 1966.

Guyot, Yves. *La Police–Etudes de Physiologie Sociale.* Paris: G. Charpentier, 1881.

Gyarmati, György, et al. *Magyar Hétköznapok Rákosi Mátyás Két Emigrációja Között, 1945–1956.* Budapest: Minerva, 1988.

Haagdorens, C. "De mobilisatie van de katholieke zuil in de schoolstrijd (mei 1954-juli 1955)." *Belgisch Tijdschrift voor Nieuwste Geschiedenis* 1–2, 15 (1984): 3–70 [with English summary].

Hahn, A., and H. Willems. "Schuld und Bekenntnis in Beichte und Therapie." In *Religion und Kultur,* edited by J. Bergmann et al., 309–30. Opladen: Kölner Zeitschrift für Soziologie und Sozialpsychologie, Sonderhefte, 1993.

Haliczer, Stephen, ed. *Inquisition and Society in Early Modern Europe.* London: Croom Helm, 1987.

Hamon, Louis. *Police et Criminalité–Impressions d'un Vieux Policier.* Paris: Flammarion, 1900.

Hankiss, Elemér. *East European Alternatives.* Oxford: Clarendon Press, 1990.

Harding, Susan. *Remaking Ibieca: Rural Life in Aragon under Franco.* Chapel Hill: University of North Carolina Press, 1984.

Hardy, René. *Controle social et mutation de la culture religieuse au Québec, 1830–1930.* Paris: Seuil, 1999.

Harnesk, Börje. "Patriarkalism och lönearbete: teori och praktik under 1700- och 1800-talen." *Historisk Tidskrift* 3, 106 (1986): 326–55.

Harris, Jose. "Between Civic Virtue and Social Darwinism: The Concept of the Residuum." In *Retrieved Riches: Social Investigation in Britain, 1840–1914,* edited by David Englander and Rosemary O'Day, 67–87. London: Scolar Press, 1995.

Harris, Jose. "Society and the State in Twentieth-Century Britain." In *The Cambridge Social History of Britain, 1750–1950,* edited by F. M. L. Thompson. Vol. 3, *Social Agencies and Institutions,* 63–117. Cambridge: Cambridge University Press, 1990.

Harsin, Jill. *Policing Prostitution in Nineteenth-Century Paris.* Princeton: Princeton University Press, 1985.

Härter, Karl. "Soziale Disziplinierung durch Strafe? Intentionen frühneuzeitlicher Policeyordnungen und staatliche Sanktionspraxis." *Zeitschrift für Historische Forschung* 3, 26 (1999): 365–79.

Hass, Aaron. *The Aftermath: Living with the Holocaust.* Cambridge: Cambridge University Press, 1995.

Hatzfeld, Henri. *Du paupérisme à la sécurité sociale, 1850–1940.* 1971. Reprint, Paris: A.Colin, 1989.

Hau, Michel, et al. "Industrialisation et sociétés de 1880 à la fin des années 60 en Europe occidentale: Bibliographie." *Historiens-Géographes* 358 (1997): 289–344.

Hay, Douglas, et al. *Albion's Fatal Tree: Crime and Society in Eighteenth-Century England.* New York: Pantheon Books, 1975.

Hegedüs, András. *A Történelem és a Hatalom Igézetében: Életrajzi Elemzések.* Budapest: Kossuth Könyvkiadó, 1988.

Hegedüs, András. *Élet egy Eszme Árnyékában.* Budapest: Bethlen Gábor Könyvkiadó, 1989.

Helsloot, P. N. "Een geschiedenis van 200 jaar volksontwikkeling." In *Om het algemeen volksgeluk: Twee eeuwen particulier initiatief: Gedenkboek ter gelegenheid van het tweehonderdjarig bestaan van de Maatschappij tot Nut van 't Algemeen,* edited by W. W. Mijnhardt and A. J. Wichers, 3–187. Edam: Maatschappij tot Nut van 't Algemeen, 1984.

Henkes, Barbara. *Heimat in Holland: Duitse dienstmeisjes, 1920–1950.* Amsterdam: Babylon-De geus, 1995.

Heumos, Peter. "Aspekte des sozialen Milieus der Industriearbeiterschaft in der Tschechoslowakei vom Ende des Zweiten Weltkrieges bis zur Reformbewegung der Sechziger Jahre." *Bohemia* 42, 2 (2001): 323–62.

Heuvel, H. W. *Oud-Achterhoeks Boerenleven in Beeld: Samengesteld.* Edited by Hans van Det and Henk Harmsen. Gaanderen: Gherre, 1991.

Hevesi, Gyula. *Sztahanov Útján: A Magyar Újítómozgalom Fejlödése és Feladatai.* Budapest: Atheneum Könyvkiadó, 1950.

Hirdman, Yvonne. *Vi bygger landet: Den svenska arbetarrörelsens historia från Per Götrek till Olof Palme.* Solna: Pogo press, 1979.

Historisk statistik för Sverige: Del 1. Befolkning, 1720–1967. Stockholm: Statistiska Centralbyrån, 1969.

Hobbelink, Ans. *Je trouwt niet alleen met een boer . . . maar ook met het bedrijf, zijn familie en de hele buurt: Een antropologische studie naar boerinnen in een Nederlandse plattelandsgemeente, 1950–1980.* Nijmegen: Hobbelink, 1982.

Hodos, George H. *Show Trials: Stalinist Purges in Eastern Europe, 1948–1954.* New York: Praeger Publishers, 1987.

Horgby, Björn. *Egensinne och skötsamhet: Arbetarkulturen i Norrköping, 1850–1940.* Stockholm: Carlsson, 1993.

Horwitz, Allan V. *The Logic of Social Control.* New York: Plenum Press, 1990.

Houlbrooke, Ralph. *Church Courts and the People during the English Reformation, 1520–1570.* Oxford: Oxford University Press, 1979.

Huberman, Michael. "Invisible Handshakes in Lancashire: Cotton Spinning in the First Half of the Nineteenth Century." *Journal of Economic History* 4, 46 (1986): 987–98.

Hübner, Peter. *Konsens, Konflikt und Kompromiß: Soziale Arbeiterinteressen und Sozialpolitik in der SBZ/DDR.* Berlin: Akademie Verlag, 1995.

Hufton, Olwen H. *The Poor of Eighteenth-Century France, 1750–1789.* Oxford: Clarendon Press, 1974.

Hughes, Everett C. "Dilemmas and Contradictions of Status." *American Journal of Sociology* 50 (1945): 353–59.

Huussen, A. H., Jr. *Veroordeeld in Friesland: Criminaliteitsbestrijding in de eeuw der Verlichting.* Leeuwarden: Hedeby Publishing, 1994.

Hvamstad, Per. "Rikt foreiningsliv på Hadeland." In *Thranerösla i norske bygder,* edited by Tore Pryser, 69–92. Oslo: Norske Samlaget, 1977.

Ihl, Olivier. *La fête républicaine.* Paris: Gallimard, 1996.

Inglehart, Ronald. *La transition culturelle dans les sociétés industrielles avancées.* Paris: Economica, 1993.

Ingram, Martin. *Church Courts, Sex and Marriage in England, 1570–1640.* Cambridge: Cambridge University Press, 1987.

INSEE. *Revenus et patrimoines des ménages.* Paris: INSEE, collection Synthèse no. 28, édition 1999.

Inwood, Stephen. "Policing London's Morals: The Metropolitan Police and Popular Culture, 1829–1850." *London Journal* 2, 15 (1990): 129–46.

Irvine, Jill A. "Introduction." In *State–Society Relations in Yugoslavia, 1945–1992,* edited by Melissa K. Bokovoy et al., 1–24. New York: St. Martin's Press, 1997.

Jackson, Stevi. "Towards a Historical Sociology of Housework: A Materialist Feminist Analysis." *Women's Studies International Forum* 2, 15 (1992): 153–72.

Jacquemet, Gérard. *Belleville au XIXe siècle: Du faubourg à la ville.* Paris: Editions de l'EHESS, 1984.

Jalla, Daniel. "Le quartier comme territoire et représentation: les barrières ouvrières de Turin au début du XXe siècle." *Le Mouvement social* 118 (January–March 1982): 79–97.

Jarosz, Darius. "Polish Peasants versus Stalinism." In *Stalinism in Poland, 1944–1956,* edited by A. Kemp-Welch, 59–77. Basingstoke: Macmillan, 1999.

Jensen, Richard Bach. *Liberty and Order: The Theory and Practice of Italian Public Security Policy, 1848 to the Crisis of the 1890s.* New York: Garland, 1991.

Jervis, Richard. *Lancashire's Crime and Criminals–with Some Characteristics of the County.* Southport: J. J.Riley, 1908.

Jessop, Bob. *State Theory: Putting the Capitalist State in Its Place.* Cambridge: Polity Press, 1990.

Johansson, Egil. "The History of Literacy in Sweden." In *Literacy and Social Development in the West: A Reader,* edited by Harvey J. Graff, 151–82. Cambridge: Cambridge University Press, 1981.

Johansson, Mats. *Arbetararistokrater och arbetarbyråkrater—om reformistiska och revolutionära tendenser inom den svenska arbetarklassen i början av seklet.* Umeå: Dept. of Sociology, University of Umeå, 1986.

Johnson, Eric A. and Karl-Heinz Reuband. "Die populäre Einschätzung der Gestapo." *Die Gestapo: Mythos and Realität.* Darmstadt: Wissenschaftlicher Buchgesellschaft, 1995: 417–36.

Johnson, Eric A. *Nazi Terror: The Gestapo, Jews and Ordinary Germans.* New York: Basic Books, 1999.

Johnson, Eric A., and Eric H. Monkkonen, eds. *The Civilization of Crime: Violence in Town and Country since the Middle Ages.* Urbana: University of Illinois Press, 1996.

Joly, Henri. *Le Combat contre le Crime.* Paris: L. Cerf, 1891.

Jones, David. *Crime, Protest, Community and Police in Nineteenth Century Britain.* London: Rouledge & Kegan Paul, 1982.

Jones, Gareth Stedman. "Class Expression versus Social Control? A Critique of Recent Trends in the Social History of Leisure." *History Workshop* 4 (1977): 162–70.

Jones, Gareth Stedman. *Outcast London: A Study in the Relationship between Classes in Victorian Society.* Oxford: Clarendon Press,1971.

Jones, Steve. "Cotton Employers and Industrial Welfare between the Wars." In *Employers and Labour in the English Textile Industries, 1850–1939,* edited by J. A. Jowitt and A. J. McIvor, 64–83. London: Routledge, 1988.

Joutard, Philippe, and Claude Thélot. *Réussir l'école: pour une politique éducative.* Paris: Le Seuil, 1999.

Jowitt, Ken. *New World Disorder: The Leninist Extinction.* Berkeley: University of California Press, 1993.

Joyce, Patrick. *Work, Society and Politics: The Culture of the Factory in Later Victorian England.* Brighton: Harvester, 1982.

Kalifa, Dominique. "Concepts de Défense Sociale et Analyses du Fait Délinquant dans la France du début du 20e siècle." In *Ordre Moral et Délinquance de l'Ankigriké au 20e Siècle,* edited by Benoit Garnot, 233–40. Dijon: EUD, 1994.

Kálmár, Melinda. *Ennivaló és Hozomány: A Kora Kádárizmus Ideológiája.* Budapest: Magvetö, 1998.

Keane, John. *Democracy and Civil Society.* London: Verso, 1988.

Kekkonen, Jukka. "Judicial Repression after the Civil Wars in Finland (1918) and Spain (1936–1939): Comments on the Potential of Legal-Historical Comparison." Social Control Conference II, Leuven, July 1998.

Kenédi, János. *Kis Állambiztonsági Olvasókönyv: Október 23–Március 15–Június 16 a Kádár korszakban.* Budapest: Magvetö Könyvkiadó, 1996.

Kenney, Padraic. "The Gender of Resistance in Communist Poland." *American Historical Review* 2, 104 (1999): 399–425.

Kenney, Padraic. *Rebuilding Poland: Workers and Communists, 1945–1950.* Ithaca: Cornell University Press, 1997.

Kent, Joan R. *The English Village Constable, 1580–1642: A Social and Administrative Study.* Oxford: Clarendon Press, 1986.

Kepler, Leopold. *Die Gendarmerie in Österreich, 1849–1974: 125 Jahre Pflichterfüllung.* Graz: Leykham Verlag, 1974.

Keunen, Annemieke, and Herman Roodenburg, eds. *Schimpen en schelden: Eer en beledig-ing in Nederland, c. 1600–c. 1850. Volkskundig Bulletin* 18. Amsterdam: Meertens Instituut, 1992.

Kideckel, David A. "The Socialist Transformation of Agriculture in a Romanian Commune, 1945–1962." *American Ethnologist* 9, 2 (1982): 320–40.

Kideckel, David A. *The Solitude of Collectivism: Romanian Villagers to the Revolution and Beyond.* Ithaca: Cornell University Press, 1993.

King, Peter, and Joan Noel. "The Origins of the 'Problem of Juvenile Delinquency':

The Growth of Juvenile Prosecutions in London in Late Eighteenth and Early Nineteenth Centuries." *Criminal Justice History: An International Journal* 14 (1993): 17–41.

Kingsford, P. W. *Victorian Railwaymen.* London: Frank Cass, 1970.

Kjellberg, Anders. *Facklig organisering i tolv länder.* Lund: Arkiv, 1983.

Klarsfeld, Serge. *Le calendrier de la persécution des juifs en France, 1940–1944.* Paris: FFDJF, 1993.

Klarsfeld, Serge. *Vichy-Auschwitz: Le rôle de Vichy dans la solution finale de la question juive en France, 1942.* Paris: Fayard, 1983.

Klein, Joanne-Marie. "Invisible Working-Class Men: Police Constables in Manchester, Birmingham and Liverpool, 1900–1939." Ph.D. diss., Rice University, 1991.

Knegtmans, Peter Jan, et al. *Collaborateurs op Niveau: Opkomst en Val van de Hoogleraren Schrieke, Snijder en Van Dam.* Amsterdam: Vossiuspers AUP, 1996.

Knotter, Ad. *Rondom de Stokstraat: 'Onmaatschappelijkheid' en 'onderklasse' in de jaren vijftig.* Maastricht: Sociaal Historisch Centrum, Universiteit Maastricht, 1999.

Koch, H. W. *In the Name of the Volk: Political Justice in Hitler's Germany.* London: I. B. Tauris, 1989.

Kocka, Jürgen. "Eine durchherrschte Gesellschaft." In *Sozialgeschichte der DDR,* edited by Hartmut Kaelble et al., 547–53. Stuttgart: Klett-Cotta, 1994.

Koenders, Petrus. *Tussen christelijk réveil en seksuele revolutie: Bestrijding van zedeloosheid in Nederland, met nadruk op de repressie van homoseksualiteit.* Ph.D. diss., University of Leiden, 1996.

Kopstein, Jeffrey. *The Politics of Economic Decline in East Germany, 1945–1989.* Chapel Hill: University of North Carolina Press, 1997.

Kossmann, E. H. *The Low Countries, 1780–1840.* Oxford: Clarendon Press, 1978.

Kruithof, Bernard. "De deugdzame natie: Het burgerlijk beschavingsoffensief van de Maatschappij tot Nut van 't Algemeen tussen, 1784 en 1860." *Symposion, Tijdschrift voor maatschappijwetenschap* 1, 2 (1980): 22–37.

Küther, Carsten. *Menschen auf der Strasse: Vagierende Unterschichten in Bayern, Franken und Schwaben in der zweiten Hälfte des 18. Jahrhunderts.* Göttingen: Vandenhoeck & Ruprecht, 1983.

Laermans, Rudi, et al., eds. *Secularization and Social Integration: Papers in Honor of Karel Dobbelaere.* Leuven: Universitaire Pers, 1998.

Laermans, Rudi. "Roman Catholicism and the 'Methodical Conduct of Life': Catholic Action in Flanders in a Weberian Perspective." *Social Compass* 1, 38 (1991): 87–92.

Lagrange, Hugues. *De l'affrontement à l'esquive.* Paris: Syros, 2001.

Lamberts, Emiel, ed. *De kruistocht tegen het liberalisme.* Leuven: Universitaire Pers, 1984 [with English summaries].

Lamberts, Emiel, ed. *Een kantelend tijdperk, 1890–1910.* Leuven: Universitaire Pers, 1992 (KADOC Studies 13).

Lampland, Martha. *The Object of Labor: Commodification of Labor in Socialist Hungary.* Chicago: University of Chicago Press, 1995.

Lanero Táboas, Mónica. *Una milicia de la justicia: La política judicial del franquismo (1936–1945)*. Madrid: Centro de Estudios Constitucionales, 1996.

Langemeijer, Gerard Eduard. "'Crisis' en Verscherpte Straffen." *Nederlands Juristen Blad* 5, 10 (1935): 69–77.

Larsen, Ejvind. *Det levende ord*. Charlottenlund: Rosinante, 1983.

Lasch, Christopher. *Haven in a Heartless World: The Family Besieged*. New York: Basic Books, 1979.

Lazo, Alfonso. *Retrato de fascismo rural en Sevilla*. Sevilla: Universidad de Sevilla, 1998.

Le Clercq, Geoffroy. "Violences sexuelles, scandale et ordre public: Le regard du législateur, de la justice et d'autres acteurs sociaux au 19ème siècle." *Belgisch Tijdchrift voor Niewste Geschiedenis: Revue Belge d'Histoire Contemporaine* 1–2, 28 (1999): 5–53.

Le Goff, Jacques, and Jean-Claude Schmitt, eds. *Le charivari: Actes de la table ronde organisée à Paris*. Paris: Ecole des Hautes Etudes en Sciences Sociales, 1981.

Le Parisien chez lui au XIXe siècle. Exhibition catalog. Paris: Archives Nationales, 1976.

Lebow, Katherine A. "Public Work, Private Lives: Youth Brigades in Nowa Huta in the 1950s." *Contemporary European History* 2, 10 (2001): 199–219.

Lebrun, François, ed. *Histoire des catholiques en France du XVe siècle à nos jours*. Toulouse: Privat, 1980.

Lefort, Claude. "La permiére révolution antitotalitaire." In *1956 Varsovie-Budapest: La deuxiéme révolution d'Octobre*, edited by Pierre Kende and Krzystof Pomian, 93–99. Paris: Editions du Seuil, 1978.

Leonards, Chris G. T. M. *De ontdekking van het onschuldige criminele kind: Bestraffing en opvoeding van criminele kinderen in jeugdgevangenis en Opvoedingsgesticht, 1833–1886*. Hilversum: Verloren, 1995.

Leonards, Chris G. T. M. *Questions and Resolutions on Matters Regarding Juveniles and Minors, 1846–1895*. http://www.unimaas.nl/gandi/leonards/QandA.html.

Lequin, Yves, ed. *500 Années Lumière de la région Rhône-Alpes*. Paris: Plon, 1991.

Lequin, Yves, ed. *Ouvriers dans la ville*. Paris: Les Editions ouvrières, 1982.

Leto, Guido. *OVRA–fascismo–anti-fascismo*. Bologna: Cappelli, 1951.

Lewis, Jane. "Introduction: Reconstructing Women's Experience of Home and Family." In *Labour and Love: Women's Experiences of Home and Family, 1850–1940*, edited by Jane Lewis, 1–24. Oxford: Basil Blackwell, 1986.

Lewis, Jane. *Women and Social Action in Victorian and Edwardian England*. Aldershot: Edward Elgar, 1991.

Lewis, Jane. *The Voluntary Sector: The State and Social Work in Britain*. Aldershot: Edward Elgar, 1995.

Liang, Hsi-Huey. *The Rise of Modern Police and the European State System from Metternich to the Second World War*. Cambridge: Cambridge University Press, 1992.

Lijphart, A. *Verzuiling, pacificatie en kentering in de Nederlandse politiek*. Amsterdam: De Bussy, 1982.

Lilly, Carol S. *Power and Persuasion: Ideology and Rhetoric in Communist Yugoslavia, 1944–1953*. Boulder: Westview, 2001.

Lindenberger, Thomas. *Straßenpolitik: Zur Sozialgeschichte der öffentlichen Ordnung in Berlin, 1900 bis 1914*. Bonn: Dietz, 1995.

Lindmark, Daniel. *Uppfostran, undervisning, upplysning: Linjer i svensk folkundervisning före folkskolan*. Umeå: Album Regionum Umense, 1995.

Lipsky, M. *Street-Level Bureaucracy: Dilemmas of the Individual in Public Services*. New York: Russell Sage Foundation, 1980.

Litván, György, ed. *The Hungarian Revolution of 1956: Reform, Revolt and Repression, 1953–1963*. London: Longman, 1996.

López Garrido, Diego. *El aparato policial en España: Historia, sociología e ideología*. Barcelona: Ariel, 1987.

López Garrido, Diego. *La Guardia Civil y los orígenes del Estado centralista*. Barcelona: Crítica, 1982.

Lucassen, Jan, and Karel Davids, eds. *A Miracle Mirrored: The Dutch Republic in European Perspective*. Cambridge: Cambridge University Press, 1995.

Lucassen, Jan, and Rinus Penninx. *Newcomers: Immigrants and Their Descendants in the Netherlands, 1550–1995*. Amsterdam: Spinhuis, 1997.

Lucassen, Leo. "'Harmful Tramps': Police Professionalization and Gypsies in Germany, 1700–1945." *Crime, Histoire et Sociétés/Crime, History et Societies* 1, 1 (1997): 27–50.

Lucassen, Leo. "A Many-Headed Monster: The Evolution of the Passport System in the Netherlands and Germany in the Long Nineteenth Century." In *Documenting Individual Identity: The Development of State Practices in the Modern World*, edited by Jane Caplan and John Torpey, 235–55. Princeton: Princeton University Press, 2001.

Lucassen, Leo. "Bringing Structure Back In: Economic and Political Determinants of Immigration in Dutch Cities (1920–1940)." *Social Science History* 26, 3 (fall 2002): 503–29.

Lucassen, Leo. "Revolutionaries into Beggars: Alien Policies in the Netherlands, 1814–1914." In *Migration Control in the North Atlantic World: The Evolution of State Practices in Europe and the United States from the French Revolution to the Inter-War Period*, edited by Andreas Fahrmeir et al., 178–94. New York: Berghahn Books, 2003.

Lucassen, Leo. "The Great War and the End of Free Migration in Western Europe and the United States: Explanations and Refutations." In *Regulation of Migration: International Experiences*, edited by Anita Böcker et al., 45–72. Amsterdam: Spinhuis, 1998.

Lüdtke, Alf. "'Helden der Arbeit'- Mühen beim Arbeiten: Zur mißmütigen Loyalität von Industriearbeitern in der DDR." In *Sozialgeschichte der DDR*, edited by Hartmut Kaelble et al., 188–213. Stuttgart: Klett-Cotta, 1994.

Luebbert, Gregory M. *Liberalism, Fascism or Social Democracy: Social Classes and the Political Origins of Regimes in Interwar Europe*. New York: Oxford University Press, 1991.

Lummis, Trevor. *The Labour Aristocracy, 1851–1914*. Aldershot: Scolar Press, 1994.

Lundgreen-Nielsen, Flemming, ed. *På sporet af dansk identitet*. Copenhagen: Spektrum, 1992.

Lundkvist, Sven. "Folkrörelser och reformer, 1900–1920." In *Från fattigdom till över-flöd*, edited by Steven Koblik, 160–82. Stockholm: Wahlström & Widstrand, 1973.

Luykx, Paul. "Een concept ondermijnd: Nieuwe literatuur over totalitarisme." *Tijdschrift voor Geschiedenis* 110 (1997): 500–29.

Lyttelton, Adrian. *The Seizure of Power: Fascism in Italy, 1919–1929*. London: Weidenfeld and Nicolson, 1973.

Macé, Gustave. *La Service de la Sûreté*. Paris: G. Charpentier, 1885.

Magarey, Susan M. "The Invention of Juvenile Delinquency in Early Nineteenth-Century England." In *History of Juvenile Delinquency: A Collection of Essays on Crime Committed by Young Offenders, in History and in Selected Countries*, edited by A. G. Hess and P. F. Clement, 325–47. Aalen: Scientia Verlag, 1990.

Magri, Susanna, and Christian Topalov, eds. *Villes ouvrières, 1900–1950*. Paris: Belin, 1989.

Magri, Susanna. "Villes, quartiers: proximités et distances sociales dans l'espace urbain." *Genèses* 13 (autumn 1993): 151–65.

Mallmann, Klaus-Michael, and Gerhard Paul. *Herrschaft und Alltag: Ein Industrierevier im Dritten Reich, Widerstand und Verweigerung im Saarland, 1935–1945*. Bonn: Dietz, 1991.

Mann, Reinhard. *Protest und Kontrolle im Dritten Reich: Nationalsozialistische Herrschaft im Alltag einer rheinischen Grosstadt*. Frankfurt am Main: Campus Verlag, 1987.

Mansel-Pleydell, J. C. *The Milborne Reformatory with Remarks upon Recent Legislation and Other Measures for the Suppression of Crime*. Dorchester: H. Spicer, 1872.

Martin, David. "Religion and Public Values: A Catholic-Protestant Contrast ." *Review of Religious Research* 4, 14 (1985): 313–31.

Martin, Jean-Clément. *Blancs et Bleus dans la Vendée déchirée*. Paris: Gallimard, 1986.

Martin, Jean-Clément. *La Vendée de la mémoire*. Paris: Seuil, 1989.

Martling, Carl Henrik. *Fädernas kyrka och folkets: Svenska kyrkan i kyrkovetenskapligt perspektiv*. Stockholm: Verbum, 1992.

Mason, Tim. "Massenwiderstand im NS-Deutschland und im faschistischen Italien." *Journal für Geschichte* 6 (1983): 28–36.

Mason, Tim. "Whatever Happened to 'Fascism'?" In *Reevaluating the Third Reich*, edited by Thomas Childers and Jane Caplan, 253–62. New York: Holmes and Meier, 1993.

Masterman, Charles F. G. "Realities at Home." In *The Heart of the Empire*, 1–50. London: T. Fisher Unwin, 1901.

Masterman, Charles F. G. *The Condition of England*. London: Methuen, 1909.

Maurice, C. Edmund. *Octavia Hill*. London: Macmillan, 1928.

May, Margaret. "Innocence and Experience: The Evolution of the Concept of Juvenile Delinquency in the Mid-Nineteenth Century." *Victorian Studies: A Quarterly Journal of the Humanities, Arts and Sciences* 17 (1973): 7–29.

McCarthy, Katherine. "Peasant Revolutionaries and Partisan Power: Rural Resistance to Communist Agrarian Policies in Croatia, 1941–1953." Ph.D. diss., University of Pittsburgh, 1996.

McKenna, Frank. *The Railway Workers, 1840–1970.* London: Faber and Faber, 1980.

Mcleod, Hugh. *Religion and the People in Western Europe, 1789–1989,* 2nd ed. Oxford: Oxford University Press, 1997.

McMahon, Sean H. *Social Control and Public Intellect: The Legacy of Edward A. Ross.* New Brunswick, N.J.: Transaction Publishers, 1999.

Meershoek, Guus. "Zonder de wolven te prikkelen: Ambtelijke dienstverlening aan de arbeidsinzet en de vervolging van de joden." In *Wat toeval leek te zijn, maar niet was,* edited by Henk Flap and Marnix Croes, 95–116. Amsterdam: Het Spinhuis, 2001.

Meershoek, Guus. *Dienaren van het Gezag: De Amsterdamse Politie tijdens de Bezetting.* Amsterdam: Van Gennep, 1999.

Meier, Robert F. "Perspectives on the Concept of Social Control." *Annual Review of Sociology* 8 (1982): 34–55.

Melling, Joseph. "Industrial Capitalism and the Welfare of the State: The Role of Employers in the Comparative Development of Welfare States: A Review of Recent Research." *Sociology* 25 (May 1991): 219–39.

Melling, Joseph. "Welfare Capitalism and the Origins of Welfare States: British Industry, Workplace Welfare and Social Reform, c. 1870–1914." *Social History* 3, 17 (October 1992): 453–78.

Melucci, Alberto. "Action patronale, pouvoir, organisation: Règlements d'usine et con-trôle de la main-d'oeuvre au XIXe siècle." *Le Mouvement Social* 97 (October–December 1976): 139–59.

Mendras, Henri. *La seconde Révolution française.* Paris: Gallimard, 1988.

Mentzer, Raymond A. *Blood and Belief: Family Survival and Confessional Identity among the Provincial Huguenot Nobility.* West Lafayette, Ind.: Purdue University Press, 1994.

Merkel, Ina. *Utopie und Bedürfnis: Die Geschichte der Konsumkultur in der DDR.* Köln: Böhlau Verlag, 1999.

Merkel, Ina. "Arbeiter und Konsum im real exitierenden Sozialismus." In *Arbeiter in der SBZ/DDR,* edited by Peter Hübner and Klaus Tenfelde, 527–53. Essen: Klartext Verlag, 1999.

Merriman, John. *Limoges la ville rouge: Portrait d'une ville révolutionnaire.* Paris: Seuil, 1990.

Meuwissen, Eric, and Joëlle Delaet-van Gasse. "Quelques aspects du sort réservé aux jeunes délinquants en Belgique au XIXe Siècle." In *History of Juvenile Delinquency: A Collection of Essays on Crime Committed by Young Offenders, in History and in Selected Countries,* edited by A. G. Hess and P. F. Clement, 625–55. Aalen: Scientia Verlag, 1993.

Michelat, Guy, and Simon Michel. "1981–1995: changements de société, changements d'opinion." In *L'Etat de l'Opinion,* edited by Olivier Duhamel et al., 167–86. Paris: Seuil, 1997.

Mijnhardt, W. W., and A. J. Wichers, eds. *Om het algemeen volksgeluk: Twee eeuwen particulier initiatief, 1784–1984: Gedenkboek ter gelegenheid van het tweehonderd-jarig bestaan van de Maatschappij tot Nut van 't Algemeen.* Edam: Maatschappij tot Nut van 't Algemeen, 1984.

Miller, Pavla. *Transformations of Patriarchy in the West, 1500–1900.* Bloomington: Indiana University Press, 1998.

Mir, Conxita, et al., *Repressió Econòmica i Franquisme: L'actuació del Tribunal de Responsabilitats Polítiques a la provincia de Lleida.* Barcelona: Publicacions de l'Abadia de Montserrat, 1997.

Moch, Leslie Page. *Moving Europeans: Migration in Western Europe since 1650.* Bloomington: Indiana University Press, 1992.

Monter, William. *Frontiers of Heresy: The Spanish Inquisition from the Basque Lands to Sicily.* Cambridge: Cambridge University Press, 1990.

Montesquieu, Charles-Louis de Secondat. *The Spirit of the Laws.* Cambridge: Cambridge University Press, 1989.

Montgomery, Arthur. *Industrialismens genombrott i Sverige.* Stockholm: Almqvist & Wiksell, 1970.

Moore, Bob. *Victims and Survivors: The Nazi Persecution of the Jews in the Netherlands, 1940–1945.* London: Arnold, 1997.

Mörch, Sören. *Den ny Danmarkshistorie, 1880–1960.* Copenhagen: Gyldendal, 1983.

Moreau Christophe, M. L., ed. *Débats du Congrès Pénitentiaire de Francfort-Sur Le-Mein, 28, 29 et 30 Septembre 1846.* Paris: E. Marc-Aurel, 1847.

Morel, Pierre, and Claude Quétel. *Les médecines de la folie.* Paris: Hachette, 1985.

Morgan, Philip. *Italian Fascism, 1919–1945.* Basingstoke: Macmillan, 1995.

Moritz, Günther. *Gerichtsbarkeit in den von Deutschland Besetzten Gebieten, 1939–1945.* Tübingen: Institut für Besatzungsfragen, 1955.

Morodo, Raúl. *Los orígenes ideológicos del franquismo: Acción Española.* Madrid: Alianza, 1985.

Morris, Bob, and Jim Smyth. "Paternalism As an Employer Strategy, 1800–1960." In *Employer Strategy and the Labour Market,* edited by Jill Rubery and Frank Wilkinson, 195–225. Oxford: Oxford University Press, 1994.

Morris, R. J. "Voluntary Societies and British Urban Elites, 1780–1850: An Analysis." *Historical Journal* 26 (1983): 95–118.

Moylan, John. *Scotland Yard and the Metropolitan Police.* London: Putnam, 1929.

Muchembled, Robert. *Culture populaire et culture des élites dans la France moderne, 15e-18e siècles.* Paris: Flammarion, 1978.

Mulder, L. H. *Revolte der fijnen: Een studie omtrent de Afscheiding van 1834 als sociaal conflict en sociale beweging met een bronnenonderzoek in een achttal Friese dorpsge-bieden.* Meppel: Boom, 1973.

Müller, Ingo. *Hitler's Justice: The Courts of the Third Reich.* Translated by Deborah Lucas Schneider. Cambridge: Harvard University Press, 1991.

Müller-Enbergs, Helmut, ed. *Inoffizielle Mitarbeiter des Ministeriums für*

Staatssicherheit: Richtlinien und Durchführungsbestimmungen. Berlin: Ch. Links Verlag, 1996.

Münch, Paul. "Kirchenzucht und Nachbarschaft: Zur sozialen Problematik des calvinistischen Seniorats um 1600." In *Kirche und Visitation: Beiträge zur Erforschung des frühneuzeitlichen Visitationswesens in Europa,* edited by Ernst Walter Zeeden and P. Th. Lang, 216–48. Tübingen: Klett-Cotta, 1984.

Murard, Lion, and Patrick Zylberman. *Le petit travailleur infatigable, ou Le prolétaire régénéré.* Fontenay-sous-Bois: Recherches, 1976.

Mykland, Knut, and Per Fuglum, eds. *Norges historie, Bind 12. Norge i stöpeskjeen, 1884–1920.* Oslo: Cappele, 1979.

Mykland, Knut, ed. *Norges historie, Bind 11. To kulturer, En stat, 1851–1884.* Oslo: Cappele, 1978.

Nadeau, Martin. *Léonard, maçon de la Creuse.* 1889. Reprint, Paris: François Maspero, 1976.

Naimark, Norman. *The Russians in Germany: A History of the Soviet Zone of Occupation, 1945–1949.* Cambridge: Harvard University Press–The Belknap Press, 1997.

Navel, Georges. *Passages.* Paris: Gallimard, 1982.

Navel, Georges. *Travaux.* 1945. Reprint, Paris: Gallimard, 1979.

Nemes, János. *Rákosi Mátyás Születésnapja.* Budapest: Láng Kiadó, 1988.

Nestler, Ludwig. *Dokumentedition Europa unterm Hakenkreuz, 4: Die Faschistische Okkupationspolitik in Belgien, Luxemburg und den Niederlanden, 1940–1945.* Berlin: Deutscher Verlag der Wissenschaften, 1990.

Nevinson, Margaret Wynne. *Life's Fitful Fever: A Volume of Memories.* London: A. & C. Black, 1926.

Newby, Howard. "Paternalism and Capitalism." In *Industrial Society: Class, Cleavage and Control,* edited by Richard Scase, 59–73. London: George Allen & Unwin, 1977.

Newby, Howard. "The Deferential Dialect." *Comparative Studies in Society and History* 17 (1975): 139–64.

Niethammer, Lutz, and Franz Bruggemeier. "Urbanisation et expérience ouvrière de l'habitat dans l'Allemagne impériale." *Recherches* 29 (December 1977): 125–30.

Nijman, J. "Spanningen en conflicten tijdens de agrarische crisis in de provincie Groningen: Een onderzoek naar petitiebewegingen in de periode, 1820–1835." Groningen: unpublished thesis, 1988.

Nitschke, Peter, ed. *Die Deutsche Polizei und ihre Geschichte: Beiträge zu einem distanzierten Verhältnis.* Hilden: Verlagsanstalt Deutsche Polizei, 1996.

Noiriel, Gérard. "Du 'patronage' au 'paternalisme': la restructuration des formes de domination de la main-d'oeuvre ouvrière dans l'industrie métallurgique francaise." *Le Mouvement Social* 44 (1988): 17–35.

Noiriel, Gérard. *La tyrannie du national: Le droit d'asile en Europe, 1793–1993.* Paris: Calmann-Lévy, 1991.

Norborg, Lars-Arne, and Lennart Sjöstedt. *Grannländernas historia.* Stockholm: Almqvist & Wiksell, 1996.

Norris, G. M. "Industrial Paternalist Capitalism and Local Labour Markets." *Sociology* 12 (1978): 469–89.

North, Douglas. *Institutions, Economic Change and Economic Performance.* Cambridge: Cambridge University Press, 1990.

O'Brien, Patricia. *The Promise of Punishment: Prisons in 19th Century France.* Princeton: Princeton University Press, 1982.

O'Day, Rosemary, and David Englander. *Mr Charles Booth's Inquiry: Life and Labour of the People in London Reconsidered.* London: Hambledon Press, 1993.

O'Day, Rosemary. "How Families Lived Then: Katharine Buildings, East Smithfield, 1885–1890." In *Studying Family and Community History: Nineteenth and Twentieth Centuries,* edited by Ruth Finnegan and Michael Drake, vol. 1, 129–166. Cambridge: Cambridge University Press, 1994.

O'Day, Rosemary. *Katharine Buildings: The Sweet Trinity of Potter, Pycroft and Paul and the Inhabitants of Model Dwellings, 1885–1914.* Leicester: Leicester University Press: Forthcoming.

O'Day, Rosemary. *The Family and Family Relationships, 1500–1900.* London: Macmillan, 1995.

O'Neill, B. J. *Social Inequality in a Portuguese Hamlet: Land, Late Marriage and Bastardy, 1870–1978.* Cambridge: Cambridge University Press, 1987.

Oberwittler, Dieter. "Changing Penal Responses to Juvenile Delinquency in Late Nineteenth and Early Twentieth Centuries—England and Germany Compared." *Comenius, wetenschappelijk forum voor opvoeding, onderwijs en cultuur* 1, 16 (1994): 7–25.

Ogien, Albert. *Sociologie de la déviance.* Paris: Armand Colin, 1995.

Ormos, Mária, et al. *Törvénytelen Szocializmus: A Tényfeltáró Bizottság Jelentése.* Budapest: Zrinyi Kiadó—Új Magyarország, 1991.

Ortiz Villalba, Juan. *Sevilla 1936: del golpe militar a la guerra civil.* Córdoba: Imprenta Vistalegre, 1998.

Ozouf, Mona. *L'Ecole, l'Eglise et la République, 1871–1914.* Paris: Armand Colin, 1982.

Ozouf, Mona. *La fête révolutionnaire.* Paris: Gallimard, 1976.

Paloscia, Annibale. *I segreti del Viminale.* Rome: Newton Compton, 1989.

Parris, Henry. *Constitutional Bureaucracy.* London: George Allen & Unwin, 1969.

Patrons et ouvriers au XIXe siècle. Exhibition catalog. Paris: La Documentation française, 1973.

Paul, Gerhard, and Klaus-Michael Mallmann, eds. *Die Gestapo im Zweiten Weltkrieg: 'Heimatfront' und besetztes Europa.* Darmstadt: Wissenschaftliche Buchgesellschaft, 2000.

Paul, Gerhard, and Klaus-Michael Mallmann, eds. *Die Gestapo: Mythos und Realität.* Darmstadt: Wisenschaftliche Buchgesellschaft, 1995.

Paxton, Robert. "La spécificité de la persécution des Juifs en France en 1942." *Annales ESC* 3, 48 (1993): 605–19.

Payne, Stanley G. *Politics and the Military in Modern Spain.* Stanford: Stanford University Press, 1967.

Pears, E., ed. *Prisons and Reformatories at Home and Abroad, Being the Transactions of the International Penitentiary Congress Held in London, July 3–13, 1872. Including Official Documents, Discussions, and Papers Presented to the Congress.* London: Longmans & Green, 1872.

Peek, Francis. *Social Wreckage—A Review of the Laws of England As They Affect the Poor.* London: W. Isbister, 1883.

Pelt, Wilhelmus Fredericus Stanislaus. *Vrede door Revolutie: De CPN tijdens het Molotov-Ribbentrop Pact, 1939–1941.* The Haag: SDU, 1990.

Pence, Katherine. "Building Socialist Worker-Consumers: The Paradoxical Construction of the Handelsorganisation–HO, 1948." In *Arbeiter in der SBZ/DDR,* edited by Peter Hübner and Klaus Tenfelde, 497–524. Essen: Klartext Verlag, 1999

Percheron, Annick. "Peut-on encore parler d'héritage politique en 1989?" In *Idéologies, partis politiques et groupes sociaux: Etudes réunies pour Georges Lavau,* edited by Yves Mény, 71–89. Paris: PFNSP, 1989.

Perrot, Michelle, ed. *Métiers de femmes.* Paris: Les Editions Ouvrières, 1987.

Perrot, Michelle, ed. *Travaux de femmes dans la France du XIXe siècle.* Paris: Les Editions ouvrières, 1978.

Perrot, Michelle. "Anthropologie culturelle dans le champ urbain." *Ethnologie française* 2, 12 (April–June 1982): 20–26.

Perrot, Michelle. "Les enfants de la Petite-Roquette." *L'Histoire* 100 (1987): 30–38.

Perrot, Michelle. *Une histoire des femmes est-elle possible?* Paris: Rivages, 1984.

Péter, László. "Volt-e magyar társadalom a XIX. században ? A jogrend és a civil társadalom képzüdése." In *Változás és Állandóság: Tanulmányok a magyar polgári társadalomról,* edited by Endre Karátson and Péter Várdy, 50–99. Utrecht: Hollandiai Mikes Kelemen Kör, 1989.

Petrow, Stefan. *Policing Morals: The Metropolitan Police and the Home Office, 1870–1914.* Oxford: Clarendon Press, 1994.

Peukert, Detlev. *Inside Nazi Germany: Conformity, Opposition, and Racism in Everyday Life.* Translated by Richard Deveson. London: B. T. Batsford, 1987.

Peyrefitte, Alain. *Réponses à la violence.* 2 vols. Paris: Presses Pocket, 1977.

Philips, David. *William Augustus Miles (1796–1851): Crime, Policing and Moral Entrepreneurship in England and Australia.* Melbourne: University of Melbourne Press, 2001.

Pinol, Jean-Luc. *Le monde des villes au XIXe siècle.* Paris: Hachette, 1991.

Pittaway, Mark. "Consumption, Political Stabilisation and Social Identity: The Roots of Socialist Consumerism in Hungary, 1953–1960." Paper presented to the one-day conference Socialist Artefacts, Places and Identities, Victoria and Albert Museum, London, November 11, 1998.

Pittaway, Mark. "Industrial Workers, Socialist Industrialisation and the State in Hungary, 1948–1958." Ph.D. diss.: University of Liverpool, 1998.

Pittaway, Mark. "Retreat from Collective Protest: Household, Gender, Work and Popular Opposition in Stalinist Hungary." In *Rebellious Families: Household Strategies and*

Collective Action in the 19th and 20th Centuries, edited by Jan Kok, 199–229. New York: Berghahn Books, 2002.

Pittaway, Mark. "Stalinism, Working Class Housing and Individual Autonomy: The Encouragement of Private Housebuilding in Hungary's Mining Areas, 1950–1954." In *Style and Socialism: Modernity and Material Culture in Post-War Eastern Europe,* edited by Susan Emily Reid and David Crowley, 49–64. Oxford: Berg Publishers, 2000.

Pittaway, Mark. "The Reproduction of Hierarchy: Skill, Working-Class Culture and the State in Early Socialist Hungary." *Journal of Modern History* 74, 4 (2002): 737–69.

Pittaway, Mark. "The Social Limits of State Control: Time, the Industrial Wage Relation, and Social Identity in Stalinist Hungary, 1948–1953." *Journal of Historical Sociology* 12, 3 (1999): 271–301.

Pleijel, Hilding. "Patriarkalismens samhällsideologi." *Historisk Tidskrift* 2, 107 (1987): 221–34.

Port, Andrew. "The 'Grumble Gesellschaft': Industrial Defiance and Worker Protest in Early East Germany." In *Arbeiter in der SBZ/DDR,* edited by Peter Hübner and Klaus Tenfelde, 787–810. Essen: Klartext Verlag, 1999.

Port, Andrew. "When Workers Rumbled: The Wismut Upheaval of August 1951 in East Germany." *Social History* 22, 2 (1998): 145–73.

Pot, G. P. M. *Arm Leiden: Levenstandaard, bedeling en bedeelden, 1750–1854.* Hilversum: Verloren, 1994.

Poulat, Emile. *Naissance des prêtres-ouvriers.* Tournai: Casterman, 1965.

Poulot, Denis. *Le Sublime, ou le travailleur comme il est en 1870, et ce qu'il peut être.* 1869. Reprint, Paris: François Maspero, 1980.

Practices of Denunciation in Modern European History, 1789–1989, a special edition of the *Journal of Modern History,* 68, vol. 4 (1996).

Presser, Jacques. *Ondergang: De Vervolging en Verdelging van het Nederlandse Jodendom.* The Haag: SDU/Nijhoff, 1965.

Preston, Paul. *The Politics of Revenge: Fascism and the Military in Twentieth-Century Spain.* London: Unwin Hyman, 1990.

Preti, Alberto. "Spirito pubblico, fronte interno e carte di polizia." In *Bologna in guerra, 1940–1945,* edited by Brunella Dalla Casa and Alberto Preti, 41–64. Milan: Franco Angeli, 1995.

Price, Richard. *Labour in British Society.* London: Routledge, 1986.

Price, Richard. *Masters, Union and Men.* Cambridge: Cambridge University Press, 1980.

Prochaska, F. K. "Body and Soul: Bible Nurses and the Poor in Victorian London." *Historical Research* 60 (1987), 336–48.

Prochaska, F. K. "Philanthropy." In *The Cambridge Social History of Britain, 1750–1950,* edited by F. M. L. Thompson. Vol. 3, *Social Agencies and Institutions,* 357–93. Cambridge: Cambridge University Press, 1990.

Prochaska, F. K. *Women and Philanthropy in Nineteenth-Century England.* Oxford: Oxford University Press, 1980.

Prochaska, F. K. "A Mother's Country: Mothers' Meetings and Family Welfare in Britain, 1850–1950." *History* 74 (1989): 379–99.

Pünkösti, Árpád. *Rákosi a Csúcson, 1948–1953.* Budapest: Európa Könyvkiadó, 1996.

Raeff, Marc. *The Well-Ordered Police State: Social and Institutional Change through Law in the Germanies and Russia, 1600–1800.* New Haven: Yale University Press, 1983.

Rasmussen, Anne. "Jalons pour une histoire des congrès internationaux au XIXe Siècle: Régulation scientifique et propagande intellectuelle." *Relations internationales* 62 (summer, 1990): 115–33.

Rawnsley, H. D. *Octavia Hill.* [no place or publisher indicated] 1912.

Redfern, Allan. "Crewe: Leisure in a Railway Town." In *Leisure in Britain, 1780–1939,* edited by John K. Walton and James Walvin, 117–35. Manchester: Manchester University Press, 1983.

Reich, Ebbe Klövedal. *Frederik: En folkebog om Grundtvigs tid og liv.* Copenhagen: Gyldendal, 1986.

Reinke, Herbert, ed. *"?nur für die Sicherheit da?"? Zur Geschichte der Polizei im 19. und 20. Jahrhundert.* Frankfurt am Main: Campus Verlag, 1993.

Reith, Charles. *British Police and the Democratic Ideal.* Oxford: Oxford University Press, 1943.

Reith, Charles. *The Police Idea.* Oxford: Oxford University Press, 1938.

Renaut, Alain. "Faut-il être ce que l'on est?" In *Politesse et sincérité,* edited by Isabelle Albaret and Joel Roman, 135–51. Paris: Esprit, 1994.

Rerup, Lorenz. *Danmarks historie: Bind 6, Tiden, 1864–1914.* Copenhagen: Gyldendal, 1989.

Retegan, Mihai. "A román kommunizmus és az 1956-os magyar és lengyel válság." In *1956-os Intézet Évkönyv V. 1996/1997,* edited by András B. Hegedüs et al., 132–36. Budapest: 1956-os Intézet, 1997.

Reuter, Frits. *De Communistische Partij van Nederland in Oorlogstijd: Herinneringen.* Amsterdam: Van Gennep, 1978.

Rév, István. "The Advantages of Being Atomized: How Hungarian Peasants Coped with Collectivization." *Dissent* (1987): 335–50.

Reynolds, Gerald W., and Anthony Judge. *The Night the Police Went on Strike.* London: Weidenfeld and Nicolson, 1968.

Ribeill, Georges. "Gestion et organisation du travail dans les compagnies de chemin de fer, des origines à 1860." *Annales ESC* 42 (1987): 999–1029.

Ripa, Yannick. "La tonte purificatrice des republicaines pendant la guerre civile espagnole." *Identités féminines et violences politiques (1936–1946): Les cahiers de l'Institut d'Histoire du temps présent* 31 (1995): 39–51.

Rivière, Louis. *Mendiantes et Vagabonds.* Paris: Victor Lecoffre, 1902.

Robert, Philippe, et al. *Les comptes du crime.* Paris: L'Harmattan, 1994.

Roberts, David. *Paternalism in Early Victorian England.* New Brunswick: Rutgers University Press, 1979.

Roché, Sebastian. The Local Governance of Crime and Insecurity in France. In *Crime and Insecurity: The Governance of Safety in Europe*, edited by Adam Crawford, 213–33. London: Willan Publishing, 2002.

Roche, Daniel. *Le peuple de Paris*. Paris: Aubier, 1981.

Roché, Sebastian. *La délinquance des jeunes, les 13–19 ans racontent leurs délits*. Paris: Le Seuil, 2001.

Roché, Sebastian. *Tolérance zéro? Incivilités et Insécurité*. Paris: Odile Jacob, 2002.

Roeck, Bernd. *Als wollt die Welt schier brechen: Eine Stadt im Zeitalter des dreissigjärigen Krieges*. München: Beck, 1991.

Roest, Friso, and J. Scheren. *Oorlog in de Stad: Amsterdam, 1939–1941*. Amsterdam: Van Gennep, 1998.

Rombach, Geurt. "Verbalen, vonnissen en volkscultuur." In *Een pront wijf, een mager paard en een zoon op het seminarie: Aanzetten tot een integrale geschiedenis van oostelijk Noord-Brabant, 1770–1914*, edited by J. van Oudheusden and G. Trienekens, 89–124. 's-Hertogenbosch: Stichting Brabantse Regionale Geschiedbeoefening, 1993.

Romijn, Peter. "De Oorlog." In *Geschiedenis van de Joden in Nederland*, edited by J. C. H. (Hans) Blom et al., 313–50. Amsterdam: Balans, 1995.

Róna-Tas, Ákos. *The Great Surprise of the Small Transformation: The Demise of Communism and the Rise of the Private Sector in Hungary*. Ann Arbor: University of Michigan Press, 1997.

Roodenburg, Herman W. "Naar een etnografie van de vroegmoderne stad: De 'gebuyrten' in Leiden en Den Haag." In *Cultuur en maatschappij in Nederland, 1500–1850: Een historisch-antropologisch perspectief*, edited by Peter te Boekhorst et al., 219–43. Meppel: Boom, 1992.

Roodenburg, Herman. "Freundschaft, Brüderlichkeit und Einigkeit: Städtische Nachbarschaften im Westen der Republik." In *Ausbreitung bürgerlicher Kultur in den Niederlanden und Nordwestdeutschland*, edited by T. Dekker et al., 10–24. Münster: T. Coppenrath Verlag, 1991.

Roodenburg, Herman. *Onder censuur: De kerkelijke tucht in de Gereformeerde gemeente van Amsterdam, 1578–1700*. Hilversum: Verloren, 1990.

Rooijakkers, Gerard, and Tiny Romme, eds. *Charivari in de Nederlanden: Rituele sancties op deviant gedrag*. Amsterdam: P. J. Meertens Instituut, 1989.

Rooijakkers, Gerard. *Rituele repertoires: Volkscultuur in oostelijk Noord-Brabant, 1559–1853*. Nijmegen: SUN, 1994.

Rosanvallon, Pierre. *L'Etat en France*. Paris: Seuil, 1990.

Ross, Edward Alsworth. *Sin and Society: An Analysis of Latter-Day Iniquity: With a Letter from President Roosevelt*. Boston: Houghton Mifflin, 1907.

Ross, Edward Alsworth. *Social Control: A Survey of the Foundations of Order*. 1901. Reprint, London: Macmillan, 1939.

Rossi, Ernesto. *La pupilla del duce: L'O.V.R.A.* Parma: Guanda, 1956.

Roucek, Joseph S. and Associates. *Social Control*. 2nd ed. Westport, Conn.: Greenwood Press, 1970.

Ruggles-Brise, E. *Prison Reform at Home and Abroad: A Short History of the*

International Movement since the London Congress, 1872. London: Macmillan, 1924.

Rújula, Pedro. *Alcorisa: El mundo contemporáneo en el Aragón rural.* Alcorisa: Ayuntamiento de Alcorisa, 1998.

Rutgers, Victor Henri. *Strafrecht en Rechtsstaat: Rede ter Gelegenheid van de 53e Herdenking van de Stichting der Vrije Universiteit op 20 Oktober 1933.* Amsterdam: De Standaard, 1933.

Sabah, Lucien. *Une police politique de Vichy: le service des sociétés secrètes.* Paris: Klincksieck, 1996.

Santos, Juliá, ed. *Víctimas de la guerra civil.* Madrid: Temas de Hoy, 1999.

Santucci, Marie Renée. *Délinquance et répression au XIXème siècle.* Paris: Economica, 1986.

Savella, Italo G. *Mussolini's "Fouché": Arturo Bocchini, the Fascist OVRA, and the Italian Police Tradition.* Ph.D. diss., University of Rochester, New York, 1996.

Schilling, Heinz, ed. *Kirchenzucht und Sozialdisziplinierung im frühneuzeitlichen Europa.* Berlin: Duncker & Humblot, 1994.

Schilling, Heinz. "History of Crime or History of Sin: Some Reflections on the Social History of Early Modern Church Discipline." In *Politics and Society in Reformation Europe: Essays for Sir Geoffrey Elton on His Sixty-Fifth Birthday,* edited by E. I. Kouri and Tom Scott, 289–310. London: MacMillan, 1987.

Schmidt, Heinrich Richard, and Thomas Brodbeck. "Davos zwischen Sünde und Verbrechen: Eine Langzeitstudie über die Tätigkeit der geistlichen und weltlichen Gerichtsbarkeit, 1644–1800." *Jahrbuch der Historischen Gesellschaft von Graubünden* (1997–1998): 143–83.

Schulte, Regina. *Das Dorf im Verhör: Brandstifter, Kindsmörderinnen und Wilderer vor den Schranken des bürgerlichen Gerichts Oberbayern, 1848–1910.* Reinbek bei Hamburg: Rowohlt, 1989.

Schwartz, Olivier. *Le monde privé, des ouvriers: Hommes et femmes du Nord.* Paris: Presses Universitaires de France, 1990.

Schwartz, Robert. *Policing the Poor in Eighteenth-Century France.* Chapel Hill: University of North Carolina Press, 1988.

Schwarzenberg, Claudio. *Diritto e giustizia nell'Italia fascista.* Milan: Mursia, 1977.

Schweisguth, Etienne. "Le post-matérialisme revisité: R. Inglehart persiste et signe." *Revue Française de Science Politique* 5, 47 (1997): 653–58.

Scott, James C. *Domination and the Arts of Resistance: Hidden Transcripts.* New Haven: Yale University Press, 1990.

Scott, James C. *Seeing like a State: How Certain Schemes to Improve the Human Condition Have Failed.* New Haven: Yale University Press, 1998.

Scott, John Paul, and Sarah F. Scott, eds. *Social Control and Social Change.* Chicago: University of Chicago Press, 1971.

Seiler, Daniel-Louis. *Le déclin du cléricalisme.* Brussels: Institut Belge de Science Politique, 1974.

Shpayer-Makov, Haia. "The Appeal of Country Workers: The Case of the Metropolitan Police." *Historical Research* 154, 64 (June 1991): 186–203.

Shpayer-Makov, Haia. "The Making of a Police Labour Force." *Journal of Social History* 24 (fall 1990): 109–34.

Sijes, Ben A. *De Februaristaking, 25–26 Februari 1941.* The Haag: Nijhoff, 1954.

Silver, Allan. "The Demand for Order in Civil Society: A Review of Some Themes in the History of Urban Crime, Police and Riot." In *The Police: Six Sociological Essays,* edited by D. J. Bordua, 1–24. New York: Wiley, 1967.

Simecka, Milan. *The Restoration of Order: The Normalisation of Czechoslovakia.* London: Verso, 1984.

Simula, Pierre. *La dynamique des emplois dans la sécurité.* Paris: IHESI, 1999.

Sleebe, Vincent C. *In termen van fatsoen: Sociale controle in het Groningse kleigebied, 1770–1914.* Assen: Van Gorcum, 1994.

Sleebe, Vincent. "Burenhulp tussen, 1890 en 1950." In *Studies over zekerheidsarrangementen,* edited by Jacques van Gerwen and Marco van Leeuwen, 722–36. Amsterdam: Nederlands Economisch-Historisch Archief, 1998.

Smith, Timothy B. "The Ideology of Charity, the Image of the English Poor Law and the Right to Assistance in France, 1830–1905." *Historical Journal* 40 (1997): 997–1032.

Smith, Timothy. "Assistance and Repression: Rural Exodus, Vagabondage and Social Crisis in France, 1880–1914." *Journal of Social History* 3 (1999): 821–46.

Spencer, Elaine Glovka. *Police and the Social Order in German Cities: The Düsseldorf District, 1848–1914.* De Kalb: Northern Illinois University Press, 1992.

Spierenburg, Pieter, ed. *Men and Violence: Gender, Honor, and Rituals in Modern Europe and America.* Columbus: Ohio State University Press, 1998.

Spierenburg, Pieter. *De verbroken betovering: Mentaliteit en cultuur in preïndustrieel Europa.* Hilversum: Verloren, 1998.

Spierenburg, Pieter. *The Prison Experience: Disciplinary Institutions and Their Inmates in Early Modern Europe.* New Brunswick: Rutgers University Press, 1991.

Spierenburg, Pieter. *The Spectacle of Suffering: Executions and the Evolution of Repression: From a Preindustrial Metropolis to the European Experience.* Cambridge: Cambridge University Press, 1984.

Standeisky, Éva, et al., eds. *A fordulat évei 1947–1949: Politika–Képzömövészet–Építészet.* Budapest: 1956-os Intézet, 1998.

Stedman Jones, Gareth. "Class Expression versus Social Control? A Critique of Recent Trends in the Social History of 'Leisure.'" *History Workshop* 4 (1977): 163–70.

Stedman Jones, Gareth. *Outcast London—A Study in the Relationship between Classes.* Cambridge: Cambridge University Press, 1980.

Steedman, Carolyn. *Policing the Victorian Community.* London: Routledge & Kegan Paul, 1984.

Stewart, Michael. *The Time of the Gypsies.* Boulder: Westview Press, 1997.

Stille, Alexander. *Benevolence and Betrayal: Five Italian Jewish Families under Fascism.* London: Jonathan Cape, 1992.

Stoetzel, J. *Les valeurs du temps présent.* Paris: PUF, 1984.

Storch, Robert D. "The Plague of the Blue Locusts: Police Reform and Popular Resistance in Northern England, 1840–1857." *International Review of Social History* 20 (1975): 61–90.

Storch, Robert D. "The Policeman As Domestic Missionary." *Journal of Social History* 4, 9 (1976): 481–509.

Strikwerda, C. *A House Divided: Catholics, Socialists and Nationalists in Nineteenth-Century Belgium.* Lanham, Md.: Rowman & Littlefield, 1997.

Stuurman, Siep. *Verzuiling, kapitalisme en patriarchaat: Aspecten van de moderne staat in Nederland.* Nijmegen: SUN, 1983.

Sueur, Jean-Pierre. *Demain la ville.* Paris: La Documentation Française, Rapport présenté au ministre de l'Emploi et la Solidarité, 1998.

Suringar, W. H., and J. A. Jolles. *Oordeel van het congres te Frankfort in september 1857 over het stelsel van afzonderlijke opsluiting,* 1857, s.l., n.p. (unpublished piece from the Prison Society's Archive).

Suringar, Willem Hendrik. "Adviezen op het eerste Frankfortse poenitentiair congres in 1846 uitgebragt." *Dagblad van Overijssel* 1847.

Suringar, Willem Hendrik. "Discours prononcés au Congres International de Bienfaisance de Francfort-Sur-Le-Mein, Session de 1857." s.l., 1857 (author's personal offprint of the Compte Rendu).

Suringar, Willem Hendrik. *Gedachten over de eenzame opsluiting der gevangenen.* 2nd ed. Leeuwarden: G. T. N. Suringar, 1843.

Sutherland, Gillian. "Education." In *The Cambridge Social History of Britain, 1750–1950,* edited by F. M. L. Thompson, vol. 3, 119–69. Cambridge: Cambridge University Press, 1990.

Swain, Nigel. *Hungary: The Rise and Fall of Feasible Socialism.* London: Verso, 1992.

Sykes, G., and D. Matza. "Techniques of Neutralization: A Theory of Delinquency." *American Sociological Review* 22 (1957): 664–70.

Syrop, Konrad. *Spring in October: The Polish Revolution of 1956.* London: Weidenfeld & Nicolson, 1957.

Szabó, Bálint. *Új Szakasz az MDP Politikájában, 1953–1954.* Budapest: Kossuth Könyvkiadó, 1984.

Szalai, Júlia. "Társadalmi Válság és Reform-Alternatívák." In *Arat a Magyar: A Szociálpolitikai Értesítö és a Fejlödés-Tanulmányok Sorozat Különszáma,* edited by Júlia Szalai et al., 48–66. Budapest: MTA Szociológiai Kutató Intézete, 1988.

Szelényi, Iván. *Socialist Entrepreneurs: Embourgeoisiement in Rural Hungary.* Oxford: Polity Press, 1988.

Tarantini, Domenico. *La maniera forte: Elogio della polizia: Storia del potere politico in Italia, 1860–1975.* Verona: Bertani Editore, 1975.

Tarn, J. N. *Five Per Cent Philanthropy.* Cambridge: Cambridge University Press, 1974.

Tarn, J. N. *Working Class Housing in Nineteenth-Century Britain.* London: Lund Humphries, 1971.

Taylor, Charles. *Le malaise de la modernité.* Paris: Cerf, 2001.

Tebbutt, Melanie. *Women's Talk: A Social History of Gossip in Working-Class Neighbourhoods, 1880–1960.* Aldershot: Scolar Press, 1995.

Teeters, N. K. *Deliberations of the International Penal and Penitentiary Congresses; Questions and Answers: 1872–1935.* Philadelphia: Temple University Book Store, 1949.

Therborn, Göran. "Hur det hela började: När och varför det moderna Sverige blev vad det blev." In *Sverige—vardag och struktur: Sociologer beskriver det svenska samhället,* edited by Ulf Himmelstrand and Göran Svensson, 23–53. Stockholm: Norstedt, 1988.

Therborn, Göran. "Socialdemokratin träder fram." *Arkiv* 27/28 (1984): 3–71.

Therborn, Göran. *Europa, det moderna.* Stockholm: Carlsson, 1996.

Thompson, Doug. *State Control in Fascist Italy: Culture and Conformity, 1925–1943.* Manchester: Manchester University Press, 1991.

Thompson, Edward P. *The Making of the English Working Class.* London: Pelican, 1963.

Thompson, F. M. L. "Social Control in Victorian Britain." *The Economic History Review* 2, 34 (1981): 188–208.

Thompson, F. M. L., ed. *The Cambridge Social History of Britain, 1750–1950.* Vol. 3, *Social Agencies and Institutions.* Cambridge: Cambridge University Press, 1990.

Tijssens, Jeffrey. *De Schoolkwestie in de jaren vijftig: van conflict naar pacificatie.* Brussels: VUB-Press, 1997.

Tilly, Charles. *Coercion, Capital, and European states, AD 990–1990.* Cambridge, Mass.: Blackwell, 1990.

Timm, Annette F. "Guarding the Health of Worker Families in the GDR: Socialist Health Care, *Bevölkerungspolitik* and Marriage Counselling, 1945–1970." In *Arbeiter in der SBZ/DDR,* edited by Peter Hübner and Klaus Tenfelde. Essen: Klartext Verlag, 1999.

Torstendahl, Rolf. *Bureaucratisation in Northwestern Europe, 1880–1985: Domination and Governance.* London: Taylor & Francis Books, 1991.

Tosatti, Giovanna. "L'anagrafe dei sovversivi italiani: origini e storia del Casellario politico centrale." *Le carte e la storia* 2 (1997):133–50.

Tosatti, Giovanna. "La repressione del dissenso politico tra l'età liberale e il fascismo: L'organizzazione della polizia." *Studi Storici* 1 (1997): 217–55.

Ugarte, Javier. *La nueva Covadonga insurgente: Orígenes sociales y culturales de la sublevación de 1936 en Navarra y el País Vasco.* Madrid: Biblioteca Nueva, 1998.

Ulc, Otto. "Pilsen: The Unknown Revolt." *Problems of Communism* 14, 3 (1965): 46–49.

Umbreit, Hans. "Auf dem Weg zur Kontinentalherrschaft." In *Das Dritte Reich und der Zweite Weltkrieg, Bnd. V/I: Organisation und Mobilisierung des Deutschen Machtbereichs,* edited by Bernhard R. Kroener et al., 3–345. Stuttgart: Deutsche Verlagsanstalt, 1988.

Váli, Ferenc A. *Rift and Revolt in Hungary: Nationalism versus Communism.* Cambridge: Harvard University Press, 1961.

Van den Bergh, C. G. J. J., ed. *Staphorst en zijn gerichten: Verslag van een juridisch-*

antropologisch onderzoek. Meppel, Amsterdam: Boom, 1980.

Van der Harst, Gerard, and Leo Lucassen. *Nieuw in Leiden: Plaats en betekenis van vreemdelingen in een Hollandse stad.* Leiden: Primavera Pers, 1998.

Van der Laarse, R. *Bevoogding en bevinding: Heren en kerkvolk in een Hollandse provinciestad: Woerden, 1780–1930.* Amsterdam: Universiteit van Amsterdam, 1989.

Van der Velde, I. "De Maatschappij tot Nut van 't Algemeen en het volksonderwijs." *Paedagogische Studiën* 36 (1959), 481–97.

Van Deursen, A. Th. *Bavianen en slijkgeuzen: Kerk en kerkvolk ten tijde van Maurits en Oldebarnevelt.* Assen: Van Gorcum, 1974.

Van Dijk, Jan, et al. *Experiences of Crime across the World: Key Findings of the 1989 International Crime Survey.* Deventer: Kluwer, 1991.

Van Doorn, J. "Verzuiling: een eigentijds systeem van sociale controle." *Sociologische Gids* (1956): 41–49.

Van Kesteren, John, et al. *Criminal Victimisation in Seventeen Industrialised Countries: Key Findings from the 2000 International Crime Victims Survey.* The Hague: Onderzoek en Beleid, 2001.

Van Leeuwen, Marco H. D. *Bijstand in Amsterdam, c. 1800–1850: Armenzorg als beheersings- en overlevingsstrategie.* Zwolle: Waanders, 1992.

Van Miert, J. *Wars van clubgeest en partijzucht: Liberalen, natie en verzuiling: Tiel en Winschoten, 1850–1920.* Amsterdam: Amsterdam University Press, 1994.

Van Ruller, Sibo, and S. Faber. *Afdoening van Strafzaken in Nederland sinds 1813: Ontwikkeling in Wetgeving, Beleid en Praktijk.* Amsterdam: Vrije Universiteit, 1995.

Vanoli, Dominique. "Les ouvrières enfermées: les couvents soyeux." *Révoltes Logiques* 2 (1976): 19–39.

Vant, André. *Imagerie et urbanisation: Recherches sur l'exemple stéphanois.* Saint-Etienne: PUSE, 1981.

Varga, Zsuzsanna. *Politika, Paraszti Érdekérvényesítés és Szövetkezet Magyarországon, 1956–1967.* Budapest: Napvílág Kiadó, 2001.

Varrentrapp, J., ed. *Verhandlungen der ersten Versammlung für Gefängnisreform, zusammengetreten im September 1846 in Frankfurt am Main.* Frankfurt am Main: H. J. Kessler, 1847.

Verbeke, H. "De biecht als sociale controle: element van grensbehoud." In *Godsdienst, mentaliteit en dagelijks leven: Religieuze geschiedenis in België sinds 1970,* edited by M. Cloet and F. Daelemans. Brussels: Archief- en bibliotheekwezen in België, extranummer 35, 1988.

Verdery, Katherine. "The 'Etatization' of Time in Ceasescu's Romania." In *What Was Socialism and What Comes Next?* Princeton: Princeton University Press, 1996.

Verdery, Katherine. *National Ideology under Socialism: Identity and Cultural Politics in Ceausescu's Romania.* Berkeley: University of California Press, 1991.

Verhoeven, D. *Ter vorming van verstand en hart: Lager onderwijs in oostelijk Noord-Brabant, c. 1770–1920.* Hilversum: Verloren, 1994.

Verrips, Jojada. *En boven de polder de hemel: Een antropologische studie van een*

Nederlands dorp, 1850–1940. Groningen: Wolters-Noordhoff, 1983.

Viaene, Vincent. *Belgium and the Holy See from Gregory XVI to Pius IX (1831–1859): Catholic Revival, Society and Politics in Nineteenth-Century Europe.* Rome: Institut Historique Belge de Rome, Bibliothèque, L & KADOC -Studies 26, 2001.

Vilanova, Mercedes. *Las mayorías invisibles: Explotación fabril, revolución y represión.* Barcelona: Icaria, 1996.

Vints, C. P. L. *Broekx en de christelijke arbeidersbeweging in Limburg, 1881–1968.* Leuven: Universitaire Pers, 1989 (KADOC-studies 8).

Viola, Gianni. *Polizia, 1860–1977: Cronache e documenti della repressione in Italia.* Verona: Bertani Editore, 1978.

Von Baumhauer, M. M. "Verslag der beraadslagingen op het poenitentiair congres gehouden te Frankfort a/M. 28, 29 en 30 september 1846." s.l.: s.n., 1846.

Von Baumhauer, M. M. *De landbouwkolonie te Mettray (in Frankrijk), een voorbeeld voor Nederland.* Leeuwarden: G. T. N. Suringar, 1847.

Von Bueltzingsloewen, Isabelle, and Denis Pelletier, eds. *La charité en pratique: Chrétiens français et allemands sur le terrain social, XIXe-XXe siècles.* Strasbourg: Presses Universitaires de Strasbourg, 1999.

Von Frijtag Drabbe Künzel, Geraldien. "Rechtspolitik im Reichskommissariat: Zum Einsatz Deutscher Strafrichter in den Niederlanden und in Norwegen, 1940–1944." *Vierteljahrshefte für Zeitgeschichte* 48, 3 (2000): 461–90.

Von Frijtag Drabbe Künzel, Geraldien. *Het Recht van de Sterkste: Duitse Strafrechtspleging in Bezet Nederland.* Amsterdam: Bert Bakker, 1999.

Voyé, Liliane. *Sociologie du geste religieux: De l'analyse de la pratique dominicale en Belgique à une interprétation théorique.* Brussels: Editions Vie Ouvrière, 1973.

VerLoren van Themaat, H. B. *Zorg voor den veroordeelde in het bijzonder na zijne invrijheidsstelling.* 2 vols. Utrecht: P. den Boer, 1910/11.

Wagniart, Jean-François. *Le Vagabond à la fin du XIXe siècle.* Paris: Editions Belin, 1999.

Wåhlin, Vagn. "Opposition og statsmagt." In *Protest og oprör: Kollektive aktioner i Danmark, 1700–1985,* edited by Flemming Mikkelsen, 105–30. Aarhus: Modtryk, 1986.

Walby, Sylvia. "From Private to Public Patriarchy: The Periodisation of British History." *Women's Studies International Forum* 1/2, 13 (1990): 91–104.

Walby, Sylvia. *Patriarchy at Work: Patriarchal and Capitalist Relations in Employment.* Oxford: Polity Press, 1986.

Walkowitz, Judith. *Prostitution and Victorian Society: Women, Class and the State.* London: Routledge & Kegan Paul, 1982.

Webber, Melvin, and H. W. J. Rittel. *Dilemmas in a General Theory of Planning.* Amsterdam: Elzevier, 1973.

Webber, Melvin. "Order and Diversity: Community without Propinquity." In *Cities and Space,* edited by L. Wingo, 25–54. Baltimore: Johns Hopkins University Press, 1963.

Webber, Melvin. "Urbanization and Communications." In *Communication, Technology and Social Policy: Understanding the New Cultural Revolution,* edited by

G. Gerbner et al., 299–318. New York: John Wiley, 1973.

Weber, Eugen. *Peasants into Frenchmen: The Modernization of Rural France, 1870–1914.* Stanford: Stanford University Press, 1976.

Weinberger, Barbara. *The Best Police in the World: An Oral History of English Policing.* Aldershot: Scolar Press, 1995.

White, Jerry. *Rothschild's Buildings: Life in an East End Tenement Block, 1887–1920.* London: Routledge & Kegan Paul, 1980.

White, Jerry. *The Worst Street in North London: Campbell Bunk, Islington, Between the Wars.* London: Routledge & Kegan Paul, 1986.

Wiener, Michael J. "Review of A. P. Donajgrodski (ed.), *Social Control in Nineteenth Century Britain.*" *Journal of Social History* 1, 12 (1978): 314–21.

Williams, Alan. *The Police of Paris.* Baton Rouge: Louisiana State University Press, 1979.

Witte, Els. "The Battle for Monasteries, Cemeteries and Schools: Belgium." In *Culture Wars: Secular-Catholic Conflict in Nineteenth-Century Europe,* edited by Christopher Clark and Wolfram Kaiser, 102–28. New York: Cambridge University Press, 2003.

Witte, Els, et al. *Political History of Belgium from 1830 Onwards.* Brussels: VUB UP, 2000.

Witte, Els, et al. *Politieke geschiedenis van 1830 tot heden.* Brussel: VUB-UP, 1997.

Wolle, Stefan. *Die heile Welt der Diktatur: Alltag und Herrschaft in der DDR, 1971–1989.* Berlin: Ch. Links Verlag, 1998.

Woodward, Susan L. *Socialist Unemployment: The Political Economy of Yugoslavia, 1945–1990.* Princeton: Princeton University Press, 1992.

Wouters, Cas. "Changing Patterns of Social Controls and Self-Controls: On the Rise of Crime since the 1950s and the Sociogenesis of a 'Third Nature.'" *British Journal of Criminology* 3, 39 (1999): 416–31.

Wright, Gordon. *Between the Guillotine and Liberty: Two Centuries of the Crime Problem in France.* Oxford: Oxford University Press, 1983.

Wrightson, Keith. "Two Concepts of Order: Justices, Constables and Jurymen in Seventeenth-Century England." In *An Ungovernable People: The English and Their Law in the Seventeenth and Eighteenth Centuries,* edited by John Brewer and John Styles, 21–46. London: Hutchinson, 1980.

Wüllenweber, Hans. *Sondergerichte im Dritten Reich: Vergessene Verbrechen der Justiz.* Munich: DTV, 1990.

Wynter, A. "The Police and the Thieves." *Quarterly Review* 96 (June 1856): 160–200.

Yeo, Eileen, and Stephen Yeo, eds. *Popular Culture and Class Conflict, 1590–1914.* Brighton: Harvester Press, 1981.

Yesilgöz, Y. "Namus: Eer en eerherstel onder Turken." *Leidschrift* 12 (1996): 111–30.

Young, Peter, and Peter Willmott. *Le village dans la ville.* Paris: Ed. de Beaubourg, 1983.

Young-Bruehl, Elisabeth. *Hannah Arendt: For Love of the World.* New York: Yale University Press, 1982.

Zeldin, Théodore. "Orgueil et intelligence." In *Histoire des passions françaises,* edited by Théodore Zeldin. Vol. 2, *Orgueil et intelligence,* 309–27. Paris: Seuil, 1978.

Zeldin, Théodore. "Religion et anticléricalisme." In *Histoire des passions françaises,* edited by Théodore Zeldin. Vol. 5, *Anxiété et hypocrisie,* 251–316. Paris: Seuil, 1978.

Zinner, Paul. *Revolution in Hungary.* New York: Columbia University Press, 1962.

Zinner, Paul, ed. *National Communism and Popular Revolt in Eastern Europe.* New York: Praeger Publishers, 1956.

Zysberg, André. *Les galériens: Vies et destins de 60,000 forçats sur les galères de France, 1680–1748.* Paris: Sueil, 1987.

Newspapers and Magazines

Amanecer
De Telegraaf
Heraldo de Aragón
Manchester Courier
Police Chronicle
Police Review
Police Service Advertiser
Post
Postman's Gazette
Railway News
Sågverks-och Brädgårdsarbetaren

Index

Agrarian Reform Bill, 283–85
Amsterdam, 327, 330–31, 336, 338–39
anti-fascism, 265–66, 271, 275
anti-fascists, 263–64, 266–69, 271–72, 275, 338
anti-Jewish laws, 268, 274, 308, 310
anti-Semitism, 301, 308
Arendt, Hannah, 18, 245–46, 261, 268, 282, 330–31, 333–34, 340–41, 390
ÁVO (Hungarian Secret Police), 345–46
Barcelona, 284, 291
Barnett, Henrietta, 150, 152, 153, 154, 155, 156, 157, 164
Barnett, Samuel, 150, 151, 152, 153, 154, 155, 156, 157, 164
Baumhauer, Marie Matthieu Von, 131, 135, 137
Beccaria, Cesare, 197
Bergheim, 253, 254
Berlin, 247, 250, 255, 257–58, 325, 333
Bilbao, 284
Blockwart, 248
Bocchini, Arturo, 265, 268, 270, 272
Bologna, 267
Bonaparte, Napoleon, 172, 197
Booth, Charles, 150, 160
Broszat, Martin, 250
brotherhoods, 33–34, 37
Browning, Christopher, 252
Carabinieri, 267–70, 273
Carpenter, Mary, 133, 142
Catholic Action, 284, 297, 298
Catholic Church
   excusing Gestapo members after World War II, 254
   influence of, in Belgium, 112–13
   influence of, in France, 26–28
   organizations of, in France, 30–32

and political parties, in Belgium, 117–18, 120–21
propaganda of, in Belgium, 114–16
propaganda of, in France, 28–30, 61–63
relations with state, in Belgium, 113–14, 119–20
relations with state, in France, 32–33, 35–36
relations with state, in Germany under Nazis, 246, 249–50
relations with state, in Italy, 262, 265
relations with state, in Spain, 282–83, 292, 294, 298
Centre d'Information et d'Enquête (CIE) 305, 307–8
charity, 31–32, 37–39
Charity Organisation Society (COS), England, 149, 151, 152, 153, 154, 155, 157, 162, 163
charivari, 170–71, 177, 185, 195
children
   as criminals, 126–28, 136–43
   social attitudes of, 376–77, 381–82
city life, 57–59, 64–65
cleavage movement, 182–84
Cohen, Stanley, 6–7, 126
Cologne, 248, 253–58
Commissariat Géneral aux Questions Juives (CGQJ), 308–9
communism, 297, 311, 335, 347, 349, 358
communists, 249, 252–53, 258, 262, 271, 304–5, 308, 323–24, 330, 351
concentration camps, 250, 253, 268, 293, 322, 333
Confederación Española de Derechas Autónomas (CEDA), 283–84
Cooney, Mark, 8–10

441

Courtney, Kate, 150, 159
courts. *See also* judicial system
    Dutch, 318–19, 326–27
    German, military, 319–20, 322
    German, regular, 246–48, 253,
        319–22, 324, 326–27, 340
    German, People's, 247–48
    German, Special, 247–48, 253, 258
    Spanish, military, 289, 291–92
crime
    as anti-authoritarianism, 376
    as object of police attention, 262–64
    poverty/unemployment as causes of,
        211–13, 372–74
    trends in, 370–72, 384
    in World War II, 319, 321
Cunningham, Hugh, 127, 140, 141, 144
Czechoslovakia, 257, 347, 350, 360
death penalty, 318–20, 322
Demetz, Fréderic-August, 131, 132, 140,
    142
denunciations, 248, 251–52, 287–95,
    298
deportation, 340
dictatorship, 268–69, 274, 281–82, 294,
    298, 343–44, 350–51, 355, 357, 362
Donajgrodzki, Anthony P., 6
Dresden, 255–58
Ducpétiaux, Édouard, 125, 129, 140
Durkheim, Emile, 2, 126
Dutch National Socialists (NSB), 332,
    337
Dutch Prison Society (Genootschap tot
    Zedelijke Verbetering der
    Gevangenen), 125, 131, 136–44
Dutch government, 336
East End Dwellings Company, 151, 157,
    161, 162, 164
economic growth
    in Denmark, 103–4
    in Norway, 105
    in Sweden, 96
education, 133, 135, 136, 174, 380–82,
    384
Elias, Norbert, 380, 390
European Crime Victimization Surveys
    (ECVS), 370–71, 373
Falange Española y de las JONS (FET-
    JONS), 285, 287–89, 293–94, 297

fascism
    in Germany, 288, 295, 298
    in Italy, movement of, 261–63, 265,
        267, 270–71, 273–74
    in Italy, party of, 261, 264, 266, 268,
        272–73
    in Italy, party militia of, 265, 267,
        269
    in Italy, police code of, 262–65
    in Italy, regime of, 261, 264, 266–67,
        272, 274
    in Spain, 288, 295, 298
fascist period (Italy), 265, 269–70
festivals, 34–35
Foucault, Michel, 36, 42, 228, 368, 369,
    371, 388
Franco, Francisco, 288, 290, 294, 298
Franco's Regime, 281, 286, 290–91, 294,
    296–98
Frégier, Honoré, 197, 199, 211, 214
Freisler, Roland, 247
Fry, Elizabeth, 132
gardens, 52–53
Garland, David, 372
Garrioch, David, 169–70, 173, 177
German attacks, 318–19, 321
German control, 305, 307, 309–11, 313
    (*see also* Nazi occupation)
German Democratic Republic (GDR),
    346–48, 350, 352, 354–56, 360
German Girls' League (BDM), 248
German Labor Front (DAF), 248
German occupation, 319, 323–24, 326,
    327, 330, 332, 336, 340
Germans, 303, 307–9, 320, 322
Germany, 282, 288, 301, 302, 318–19,
    324, 327
Gestapo, 246–48, 250–59, 291, 313,
    319–20, 322–27, 330, 339
Giddens, Anthony, 228
Goldhagen, Daniel, 252
Goussard, Colonel, 305
Groupes Mobiles de Réserve (GMR), 306
Groupes de Protection (GP), 305, 308
Grundtvig, N. F. S., 103, 107
Guardia Civil (Civil Guard, Spain),
    284–87, 289, 293–94, 297
Guardia Asalto, 284
Hauswart, 248

Hill, Octavia, 150, 152–53, 154, 155, 156, 159
Hitler, Adolf, 246, 248, 256, 258, 318, 339
Hitler Youth (HJ), 248
Hungary, 245, 343–49, 351, 352, 354–56, 359–61
Interior Ministry of Police (Italy), 265, 269–71, 273–74
International Penitentiary Congresses, 126, 128–36
interrogation, 253, 257, 268, 318, 322, 339
Jehovah's Witnesses, 249, 253
Jews, 246–47, 249, 252–59, 265, 268, 305, 308, 310, 321, 322, 324, 332–34, 336–41
judicial system
   Dutch, 318–21, 323–26
   German, 319, 323, 325, 339
   Italian, 262, 263
Krefeld, 253–58
Kriminalpolizei (Kripo), 246
labor unions, 97, 99–101, 105–6, 120
labor relations, 71–75, 87–88
Lasalle, Ferdinand, 164
law, 247, 263, 265, 308, 311, 320
liberal Italian state, 261–64, 269–74
lodgers, 47–48
Lombroso, Cesare, 212
Louis XIV of France, 369
Lutheran Church
   excusing Gestapo members after World War II, 254
   influence of, in Sweden, 95–96
   relation to other churches, in Denmark, 103
   relation to other churches, in Sweden, 96–97
   relation to state, in Nazi Germany, 246, 249–50
Madrid, 284
Marxism-Leninism, 356, 359
Metropolitan Association for Befriending Young Servants (MABYS), England, 155–56
Mettray colony (and copies), 131, 133, 137, 140, 141, 142, 143
migration, 44–46

Milice Française, 311–13
Ministry of the Interior (Eastern European countries), 345
Ministry of the Interior (France), 305, 307, 309
Ministry of the Interior (Spain), 289
Moreau-Christophe, Louis-Mathurin, 125, 141
Mussolini, Benito, 261–62, 264–67, 269–70, 272, 274
Mussolini's regime, 282
National Socialism, 335, 337–38, 340–41
Nazi Germany, 245–47, 249–52, 255, 257, 59, 266–68, 282, 291, 298, 330–31, 333–34
Nazi occupation, 301, 313, 333
Nazi party, 246–49, 251, 320
Nazi policy, 249, 251, 253, 257
Nazi regime, 247, 249–51, 330, 334
Nazis, 248–49, 255–56, 258, 301–302, 312, 323, 345
neighborhoods
   characteristics of, 26, 44–46
   life in, 50–53
   relation to city center, 53–57
   and work, 48–50
Nevinson, Margaret Wynne, 159, 161
occupied zone, 307, 309–11
Opera Vigilanza e Repressione dell' Antifascismo (OVRA), 265–68, 270–71
Parsons, Talcott, 210, 382
paternalism, 72–73, 75–76, 84–85
patronage, industrial, 39–41, 100
Peel, Sir Robert, 195, 198, 222
Poland, 257, 347, 349, 352, 359–61
police
   and aliens, 226–41
   and beggars/vagabonds, 199, 213–17
   and criminal/dangerous classes, 198–99, 205
   distribution of, 390
   under fascism in Italy, 261, 262, 264–66, 267, 268, 269, 272, 274–75
   and gambling, 219
   humanitarian/ sympathetic behavior of, 202, 219–20, 233, 234, 237–39
   limitations on, 200–201, 205, 222, 390–91

models of, 197–98
origins of, 195–98
and poor, 212–23
and prostitution, 202, 217–19
and totalitarian societies, in
    Amsterdam, 331–33, 336–37, 340
and totalitarian societies, in Europe,
    205–6
and totalitarian societies, in France,
    301–13
and totalitarian societies, in Germany,
    246–48, 251–54, 257, 321, 323,
    332, 340
and totalitarian societies, in Italy,
    262–75
and totalitarian societies, in the
    Netherlands, 320, 323, 332,
    336–37, 339–41
and totalitarian societies, in Spain,
    284–86, 289, 294
and working class, 200–204, 222
Police aux Questions Juives (PQJ), 308,
    313
policing
    in Germany, 247, 259
    in Italy, 261–62, 265, 268, 270–71
    in the Netherlands, 331–32, 338, 341
policing agencies
    France. See CGQJ, CIE, GMR, GP,
        PQJ, SPAC, SR, SSS
    Germany. See Gestapo, SS, SA, SD
    Italy. See Carabinieri, OVRA, Political
        Police Division, Servizio Politico di
        Investigazione
    Spain. See Guardia Civil, Guardia
        Asalto
political opposition, 262, 264, 267,
    269–70, 275, 283, 284, 286, 289,
    291, 293, 319, 321, 346 (see also resis-
    tance)
Political Responsibility Courts, 291
Political Responsibility Law, 290, 292,
    295
Political Police Division (DPP), 265
Potter, Beatrice, 150, 151, 159–63, 164
Pycroft, Ella, 150, 159–63
religion, 172–74, 182–84
repression, 261–62, 266, 268–72, 275,
    282, 284, 286–87, 289, 291, 293–95,

302, 312, 318–19, 327, 337, 344, 350
resistance, 250–52, 256, 311, 313, 321,
    326–27
Rome 269, 273
Ross, Edward Alsworth
    career of, 1–2
    political views of, 3–5
    Social Control, 2–3, 193, 210
SA, 247
sawmill industry, 97–99
Scandinavia, differences within, 101–2,
    106–7
schools, 33, 116–17
Schutzpolizei (Schupo), 246
SD, 247, 336, 339–41
Second Republic (Spain), 281–88, 293,
    296–98
secret police, 245–46, 265–66, 268–70
SED, 360
Service de Police de Sociétés Secrètes
    (SPAC), 308–9, 313
Service de Renseignement (SR), 305
Service de Sociétés Secrètes (SSS), 307–9,
    311
Servizio Politico di Investigazione, 265
social control
    approaches to, 369–70
    and bureaucratization, 73–74, 82–84
    and conflict settlement, 8–10
    by employers, 41–43
    and gossip, 170, 173, 177
    in historiography, 6
    and the history of church discipline,
        11–12
    and the history of crime, 10–11
    and modern history, 13
    and the history of popular culture,
        12–13
    in industrial environment, 181–86
    in modern/post-modern environment,
        186–88
    by neighbors, 170, 176–77, 179–81,
        185, 193
    origins of the concept, 1–5
    phases in the history of, 14–15
    by police, 194–207, 210–11, 227–28,
        391–92
    in pre-industrial urban environment,
        175–77

in rural environment, 177–81
in sociological textbooks, 5–6, 7
theoretical embeddedness of, 15–16
under totalitarianism, 245–48, 250,
   252, 255, 259, 261, 266, 268–69,
   273–74, 281, 284, 286, 289, 337,
   343, 362
and work, 70–71, 93–94
social disturbance, 318–19
socialism
   in Eastern Europe, 350–52, 355, 359
   in French cities, 60–61
   in Hungary, 344, 353
socialist dictators, 345
socialist regimes, 343, 355, 351
socialists, 283, 286, 348, 356
Soviet Union, 266–68, 330, 334
Spanish Civil War, 281–82, 285–88,
   290–93, 296, 298
Spanish army, 285–86
sports, 35, 83–84
SS, 247, 253, 309, 312, 324
Stalinism, 345–47
state supervision, 350, 354
state control, 352
strikes, 101
subordination of women, 296
suburbs, 59–60
Summary Police Court, 324–25
Sundt, Eilert, 93–94
Suringar, Willem Hendrik, 125, 131,
   132, 135, 137, 143
surveillance, 245–48, 264, 266, 268, 281,
   288, 289, 293, 338, 362
Svanberg, P. A., 98–99

temperance, 96–97
terror, 251–52, 254–55, 266–77, 295,
   327, 339
Third Reich, 246, 253–55, 257
Tilly, Charles, 228
Tönnies, Ferdinand, 2, 169
torture, 253, 268, 288, 294–95
totalitarian regimes, 267–68, 282,
   334–35, 336, 343, 341
totalitarian society, 245, 250, 259,
   261–62
totalitarianism, 261–62, 268, 274, 295,
   331, 333–35, 340, 351
Uffici Politici Investigativi, 265
verzuiling
   in Belgium, 118–20
   in Belgium and The Netherlands com-
      pared, 122
   in The Netherlands. See cleavage
      movement
Vichy state, 302, 304, 307, 312
Vichy, 245, 301–3, 305–9, 313
violence, 282, 286–90, 294–96, 298,
   318
Weber, Max, 2, 194
Weimar Republic, 247
Wesley, John, 115
worker-priests, 63–64
workers
   benefits for, 79–82
   demands from, 86–87
   pensions for, 81–82
   recruitment of, 76–77, 85–86
   supervision of, 77–79
World War II, 268, 274, 282, 330, 358

HISTORY OF CRIME AND CRIMINAL JUSTICE SERIES
David R. Johnson and Jeffrey S. Adler, Series Editors

The series explores the history of crime and criminality, violence, criminal justice, and legal systems without restrictions as to chronological scope, geographical focus, or methodological approach.

Controlling Vice: Regulating Brothel Prostitution in St. Paul, 1865–1883
Joel Best

The Rule of Justice: The People of Chicago vs. Zephyr Davis
Elizabeth Dale

Prostitution and the State in Italy, 1860–1915, Second Edition
Mary Gibson

Murder in America: A History
Roger Lane

*Violent Death in the City: Suicide, Accident, and Murder in Nineteenth-Century
Philadelphia,* Second Edition
Roger Lane

Cops and Bobbies: Police Authority in New York and London, 1830–1870,
Second Edition
Wilbur R. Miller

Crime, Justice, History
Eric Monkkonen

Race, Labor, and Punishment in the New South
Martha A. Myers

*Homicide, North and South: Being a Comparative View of Crime against the Person
in Several Parts of the United States*
H. V. Redfield

Men and Violence: Gender, Honor, and Rituals in Modern Europe and America
Edited by Pieter Spierenburg

Written in Blood: Fatal Attraction in Enlightenment Amsterdam
Pieter Spierenburg

Rethinking Southern Violence: Homicides in Post–Civil War Louisiana, 1866–1884
Gilles Vandal

Five Centuries of Violence in Finland and the Baltic Area
Heikki Ylikangas, Petri Karonen, and Martti Lehti